Statistics for Criminology and Criminal Justice

Statistics for Criminology and Criminal Justice

SECOND EDITION

Ronet Bachman
University of Delaware

Raymond Paternoster
University of Maryland

Boston   Burr Ridge, IL   Dubuque, IA   Madison, WI   New York
San Francisco   St. Louis   Bangkok   Bogotá   Caracas   Kuala Lumpur
Lisbon   London   Madrid   Mexico City   Milan   Montreal   New Delhi
Santiago   Seoul   Singapore   Sydney   Taipei   Toronto

Higher Education

STATISTICS FOR CRIMINOLOGY AND CRIMINAL JUSTICE
Published by McGraw-Hill, a business unit of The McGraw-Hill Companies, Inc., 1221 Avenue of the Americas, New York, NY, 10020. Copyright © 2004, 1997, by The McGraw-Hill Companies, Inc. All rights reserved. No part of this publication may be reproduced or distributed in any form or by any means, or stored in a database of retrieval system, without the prior written consent of The McGraw-Hill Companies, Inc., including, but not limited to, in any network or other electronic storage or transmission, or broadcast for distance learning.
Some ancillaries, including electronic and print components, may not be available to customers outside the United States.

This book is printed on acid-free paper.

2 3 4 5 6 7 8 9 0 FGR/FGR 0 9 8 7 6 5 4 3

ISBN 0-07-251844-8

Publisher: *Phillip A. Butcher*
Sponsoring editor: *Carolyn Henderson Meier*
Senior marketing manager: *Daniel M. Loch*
Media producer: *Shannon Gattens*
Project manager: *Destiny Rynne*
Production supervisor: *Janean A. Utley*
Associate designer: *George Kokkonas*
Supplement associate: *Kathleen Boylan*
Art manager: *Robin Mouat*
Art director: *Jeanne M. Schreiber*
Cover and interior design: *Kay Fulton*
Typeface: *10/12 Palatino*
Compositor: *Carlisle Communications Ltd.*
Printer: *Quebecor World Fairfield Inc.*

Library of Congress Cataloging In-Publication Data

Bachman, Ronet.
  Statistics for criminology and criminal justice / Ronet Bachman, Raymond Paternoster.—
2nd ed.
    p. cm.
  Rev. ed. of: Statistical methods for criminology and criminal justice. ©1997.
  Includes bibliographical references and index.
  ISBN 0-07-251844-8 (alk. paper)
    1. Criminal statistics. I. Paternoster, Raymond. II. Bachman, Ronet. Statistical methods
  for criminology and criminal justice. III. Title.
HV6208.B33 2004
364'.01'519—dc21   2003051231

www.mhhe.com

Brief Contents

Contents

PART 2   Making Inferences in Univariate Analysis: Generalizing from a Sample to a Population

*This book is dedicated to the memory of John B. Paternoster,
and to his namesake, our son, John Bachman-Paternoster.*

Preface

One of the most important aspects of teaching a statistics course is conveying to students the vital role that statistics plays in the study of criminology and criminal justice. After years of teaching statistics courses, we have found that the best avenue for achieving this goal has been to link the teaching of "how to calculate statistics" with contemporary research examples from the field of criminal justice. By combining discussions of the "how to" in statistics with practical research examples from the field, students not only learn how to calculate and understand statistics, they also make the connection between how statistics are used and why they are important.

In *Statistics for Criminology and Criminal Justice* we have tried to present a discussion of basic statistical procedures that is comprehensive in its coverage, yet accessible and readable for students. In view of this general goal, we have chosen to emphasize a practical approach to the use of statistics in research. We have stressed the interpretation and understanding of statistical operations in answering research questions, be they theoretical or policy oriented in nature. Of course, this approach is at the expense of a detailed theoretical or mathematical treatment of statistics. As such, we do not provide the derivations of formulas or present proofs or the underlying statistical theory behind the operations we present in this text.

Given the title, it is clear that we had the student majoring in criminology and criminal justice particularly in mind as a reader of this text. This can easily be seen in the nature of the research examples presented throughout the book. What are the causes of violence? What is the nature of hate crimes in the U.S.? Do different types of police patrolling activities affect rates of crime? Is crime increasing or decreasing? These and many other research questions are examined in examples provided in the book, which we believe not only makes the book more interesting to criminal justice students, but also makes the statistical material easier to understand and apply.

If this book communicates the excitement of research and the importance of careful statistical analysis in research, then our endeavor has succeeded. We hope students enjoy learning how to investigate research questions related to criminal justice and criminology with statistics and perhaps learn how to do some research of their own along the way.

THE SECOND EDITION

Adopters of the First Edition of our text will be happy to know that we continue with our basic approach of describing each statistic's purpose and origins as we go. Similarly, our emphasis on the interpretation and understanding of each statistical operation has not changed. What *has* changed is the level of the text. The majority of the text has been completely rewritten to make the material more accessible for today's student. To this end, we have made the following enhancements:

- All statistical formulas are now accompanied by clear, easy-to-follow step-by-step procedures to make the material easier for students to understand and apply.
- Critical terms and formulas are defined in marginal boxes as students move through each chapter and listed at the close of the chapter for easy reference.
- Coverage throughout has been consistently streamlined and simplified to make it more accessible for the average undergraduate student.
- Finally, each chapter presents case studies of research from the field that bring concepts and statistical techniques to life for students and help them master procedures.

Other important changes to this edition include the following:

- Chapter 1 uses youth violence to underscore the important role statistics play in criminology and criminal justice and includes examples of descriptive research, explanatory research, and evaluation research.
- General Strain Theory is used in Chapter 2 to highlight the difference between independent and dependent variables. Chapter 2 also uses data from the Uniform Crime Reports and National Crime Victimization Survey to highlight various ways of presenting data.
- Chapter 3 examines the many ways to understand data, including easier-to-understand procedures for constructing grouped frequency distributions. Case studies of hate crime data, police response time, and recidivism are used to highlight other graphical techniques. To facilitate continuity and understanding, these same data are used in Chapters 4 and 5 to examine measures of central tendency and dispersion. In addition, we have condensed the discussion of exploratory data analysis—another challenging concept for many students—and integrated it into Chapter 5, "Measures of Dispersion."
- We have streamlined and simplified the discussion of probability theory and the normal distribution into an all-new, easier-to-understand

Chapter 6. In addition, we have used a visceral topic to take students through their first experience with hypothesis testing–evaluating the probability of car theft using a Lo-Jack device versus no such theft protection.

- Chapter 7 opens the world of inferential statistics to students by using examples from newspapers they are bombarded with daily. Case studies from the literature are then presented to highlight the calculation of confidence intervals using the examples of alcohol and drug consumption, the effects of arrest on employment, rape offending patterns, the effects of community policing, and gender differences on attitudes toward crime control.

- Students begin hypothesis testing for population means and proportions in Chapter 8. The steps for hypothesis testing that were introduced in Chapter 6 are spelled out again and again using various case studies including mean rates of crime, mean reading levels from a prison literacy program, attitudes toward gun control and random drug testing of inmates.

- To facilitate the understanding of chi-square, students are first introduced to the one variable goodness of fit Chi-Square test in Chapter 9. They are next taught how to read contingency tables using data on gender and emotions, and attitudes toward school and delinquency. The steps for hypothesis testing are once again spelled out numerous times using various case studies including socio-economic status of neighborhoods and police response time, type of counsel and sentence received by homicide defendants, adolescents' employment and drug and alcohol use, and age of onset for delinquency and future offending.

- Chapter 10 presents hypothesis testing techniques for two population means and proportions using independent samples and matched groups or dependent samples. Although definitional formulas are introduced as learning aids, only computational formulas are used for hypothesis testing. The steps for hypothesis testing are reiterated for each example and include cases studies on state prison expenditures by region, social disorganization theory and crime, boot camps and recidivism, arrest and intimate partner assault, gender and sentencing, problem-oriented policing and crime, siblings and delinquency, and education and recidivism.

- Chapter 11 opens the discussion of Analysis of Variance by reintroducing students to the concept of variance. We next take students through the logic of ANOVA using a case study of police responses to domestic violence. The concepts of total variability, within group variability, and between group variability are highlighted graphically and all procedures necessary for calculation are given in an easy step-by-step manner. The steps for hypothesis testing are reiterated for two other case studies including the relationship between adolescent employment and delinquency and region of the country and rates of homicide.

- In this edition, we start out the discussion of bivariate correlation and regression in Chapter 12 using scatterplots to highlight the relationship between state-level rates of crime and poverty and social disorganization. We have changed the order in which we present the statistical concepts; we now present a discussion of Pearson's correlation coefficient and the coefficient of determination, followed by a discussion of the least squares regression line. The steps for hypothesis testing are reiterated for each case study provided.

- Chapter 13 now begins with a general discussion of the importance of controlling for third variables when making causal interpretations. After the three criteria for making causal statements are highlighted, students are introduced to the concept of statistical control using the visual aid of partial crosstabulation tables. The multivariate OLS regression equation is introduced using the prediction of delinquency as a case study. As we have done throughout the book, the step-by-step procedures for hypothesis testing are reiterated with every example.

- Finally, Chapter 14 highlights the problems with using OLS regression analyses when the dependent variable is a dichotomy with a case study examining the relationship between the age of first delinquent offense and the probability of adult criminality. After students observe the problems that can arise when using OLS procedures to estimate this probability, they are introduced to logistic regression models using one independent variable. Because of the statistical complexity of these equations, the regression equations are not computed by hand and our emphasis is placed on interpretation. Logistic regression models obtained from SPSS are examined and interpreted. The probit regression model is also discussed followed by sections that provide interpretations of multivariate logit and probit regression models. Emphasis is placed on the steps necessary for hypothesis testing using SPSS output for all case studies including examining the interrelationships between the race of the victim, the brutality of a homicide, and likelihood of a prosecutor seeking the death penalty.

ORGANIZATION OF THE BOOK

The book is organized into four basic parts. The first section is titled "Describing Data" and begins with a basic discussion of research and data gathering. Chapters 1 and 2 discuss the research enterprise, sampling techniques, ways of presenting data, and levels of measurement. Chapter 3 provides an overview of interpreting data through the use of such graphical techniques as frequency distributions, pie charts and bar graphs for qualitative data, and histograms, frequency polygons, and time plots for quantitative data. Chapter 4 provides an overview of measures of central tendency and Chapter 5 discusses the various statistical techniques for measuring the dispersion of a variable including the standard deviation as well as the exploratory data analysis techniques of boxplots.

From this discussion of descriptive statistics, we move into the second section, "Making Inferences Using Probability Theory." Chapter 6 outlines the foundation of inferential statistics, probability theory and sampling distributions (the normal distribution). In Chapter 6, you are also introduced to the concept of hypothesis testing using the binomial distribution. The remainder of the book concerns issues related to hypothesis testing and a search for a relationship between one or more independent variables and a dependent variable. Chapter 7 begins the journey into inferential statistics with confidence intervals. The steps to formal hypothesis testing are systematically repeated in each of the subsequent chapters.

The third section focuses on hypothesis testing using one independent variable to predict one dependent variable and is called "Bivariate Hypothesis Testing." Chapter 8 focuses on hypothesis tests for one population mean. Chapter 9 is concerned with hypothesis testing when both independent and dependent variables are categorical using crosstabulation and Chi-Square. In Chapter 10, you will examine hypothesis tests involving two population means or proportions, including tests for independent and matched groups. Chapter 11 involves hypothesis testing involving three or more means using Analysis of Variance techniques. In Chapter 12, you will be introduced to bivariate correlation and Ordinary Least Squares (OLS) regression analysis. This chapter discusses the essential framework of linear regression including the notion of "least squares," the importance of scatterplots, the regression line, and hypothesis tests with slopes and correlation coefficients.

The book concludes by highlighting the importance of controlling for other independent variables through "Multivariate Hypothesis Testing." Chapter 13 extends OLS regression to two independent variables and one dependent variable. Chapter 14 provides a discussion of the essential components of logistic and probit regression models. Although logit and probit models are seldom included in introductory statistics texts, these models have become so prominent in social science research that we felt their omission would have done a great disservice to those wanting some degree of comprehensiveness in their first statistics course.

LEARNING AIDS

Working together, the authors and the editors have developed a format for the text that supports the goal of a readable, user-friendly text. In addition to all of the changes already mentioned, the Second Edition not only includes a host of new tables and figures to amplify text coverage, but also features the following student learning aids:

- Step-by-step lists and marginal key term and key formula boxes are included in every chapter to make mastery of statistical concepts and procedures easier.
- Chapter-opening outlines and chapter-ending summaries are provided to keep students on track.
- *SPSS Practice Problems* are now included at the end of every chapter, and an end-of-book appendix provides a basic introduction to using SPSS to solve statistics problems.
- In addition to SPSS exercises, each chapter also closes with traditional practice problems to give students plenty of hands-on experience with important techniques (solutions to all end-of-chapter problems can be found in an appendix at the end of the book).

SUPPLEMENTS

As a full service publisher of quality educational products, McGraw-Hill does much more than just sell textbooks. We also create and publish supplements for use with those textbooks. Accompanying this text are the following:

- **Instructor's Manual/Testbank**—includes lecture notes, student activities, classroom discussion questions, a complete testbank, and more.
- **Computerized Testbank**—easy-to-use computerized testing program for both Windows and Macintosh computers.
- **SPSS Student Software**—a student version of SPSS can be packaged with the text for use outside the computer lab.
- **Downloadable Data Files**—four real data sets: 1) attitude and perceptual information, including self-reported involvement in delinquency, 2) a state-level data set that includes rates of homicide, burglary, and violent crime along with demographic and social indicators such as poverty, social disorganization, etc., 3) a sample of 1300 homicide defendants whose cases went to trial by jury or judge along with their adjudication outcomes (e.g. sentence and prison terms), 4) a sample of violent victimizations against women from the National Crime Victimization Survey.

ACKNOWLEDGMENTS

We would first like to thank our editor, Carolyn Henderson Meier for all of her support and suggestions throughout the evolution of this edition. We are also indebted to others on the McGraw Hill team, including Pamela Woolf, who marshaled the text through production, and Julie Abodeely, who managed the communication between all parties. Special thanks to Ann Sass, copyeditor, for a job well-done.

We also tip our hats to the external reviewers of this book and the earlier edition:

Dan Powers
University of Texas

Christina DeJong Schwitzer
Michigan State University

Thomas Petee
Auburn University

Jeb A. Booth
Northeastern University

Andre Rosay
University of Alaska

Dr. Ni He
University of Texas-San Antonio

Lenonore Simon
Temple University

Christine Tartaro
The Richard Stockton College of New Jersey

Hannah Scott
University of Memphis

David R. Forde
University of Memphis

William E. Kelly
Auburn University

They are not only dedicated to the classroom but dedicated scholars as well. Their care, attention to detail, and deliberateness with which they reviewed and commented on our work were Herculean.

We thank Paige Gordier of Lake Superior State University for writing a superb appendix on how to use SPSS that helps students build basic SPSS skills without forcing them to purchase yet another text for the course; thanks to Andre Rosay for meticulously writing the instructors manual; and thanks to Nadine Connell, Sarah Bacon, and Rachael Philofsky for their tireless proofreading under pressure.

We continue to be indebted to the many students we have had an opportunity to teach and mentor, at both the undergraduate and graduate levels. In many respects, this book could not have been written without these ongoing reciprocal teaching and learning experiences. You inspire us to become better teachers!

The Purpose of Statistics in the Criminological Sciences

CHAPTER 1

> *You gain strength, courage, and confidence by every experience in which you really stop to look fear in the face.*
> —ELEANOR ROOSEVELT
>
> *The only thing we have to fear is fear itself.*
> —FRANKLIN D. ROOSEVELT

1

INTRODUCTION

Most of you reading this book probably are taking a course in statistics primarily because one is required to graduate. Most of you probably are *not* taking this course because you were seeking a little adventure and thought it would be fun. Nor are you taking the course because there is something missing in your life and, thus, you think the study of statistics is necessary to make you intellectually "well rounded." At least this has been our experience when teaching a statistics course. Perhaps it is universal that every statistics professor must hear the litany of sorrows expressed by his or her students at the beginning of the course. "Oh, I have been putting this off for so long—I dreaded having to take this," or "I have a mental block when it comes to math—I haven't had any math courses since high school."

Except for those fortunate few for whom math comes easy, the rest of us experience apprehension and anxiety when approaching our first statistics course. Psychologists, however, are quick to tell us that what we most often fear is not real—it is merely our mind imagining the worst possible scenario. In fact, an acronym for fear has been developed that describes FEAR as False Expectations Appearing Real. Long ago it was Aristotle who said, "Fear is pain arising from anticipation." But then, this may not comfort you either, because it is not Aristotle who is taking this course—it's you!

Although it is impossible for us to allay all of the fear and apprehension you may be experiencing right now, it may help to know that virtually everyone can and will make it through this course, even those of you who have trouble balancing your checkbooks. This is not, of course, a guarantee, and we are not saying it will be easy. We have found, however, that persistence and tenacity can overcome even the most extreme mathematical handicaps.

Those of you who are particularly rusty with your math, and also those of you who just want a quick confidence builder, should refer to Appendix A, which discusses some basic math lessons in detail. In fact, it reviews the entire math you probably need to know to pass this course. It also includes practice problems and, more important, the answers to those problems. Perhaps by examining this appendix you will be more confident in your statistical and mathematical abilities.

We hope that after this course, you not only will be able to understand and manipulate statistics for yourself, but that you also will be a knowledgeable consumer of the statistical material that you are confronted with daily. Understanding how to manipulate and interpret statistics will be a tremendous asset to you no matter what direction you plan to take in your chosen career. This book is meant to provide you with this understanding. In addition to the mathematical skills required to compute statistics, we also hope to leave you with an understanding of what different statistical tests or operations can and cannot do, and what they do and do not tell us about a given problem.

The foundations for the statistics presented in this book are derived from complicated mathematical theory. You will be glad to know, however, that it is *not* the purpose of this book to provide you with the proofs necessary to substantiate this body of theory. In this book, we provide you with two basic types of knowledge: (1) the basic mathematical foundations of each statistic, including the ability to manipulate and conduct statistical analysis for your own research, and (2) an ability to interpret the results of statistical analysis and to apply these results to the real world.

We want you, then, to have the skills to both calculate and comprehend social statistics. These two purposes are not mutually exclusive but are related. We think the ability to carry out the mathematical manipulations of a formula and come up with a statistical result is almost worthless unless you also can interpret this result and give it meaning. Therefore, information about the mechanics of conducting statistical tests and the tools to interpret the results of those tests will be emphasized equally throughout this text.

Learning about statistics for perhaps the first time does not mean that you will always have to calculate your statistics by hand, with the assistance of only a calculator. Most, if not all, researchers do their statistical analyses with a computer and software programs. Many useful and user-friendly statistical software programs are available, including SPSS, SAS, STATA, and Minitab. Because learning to conduct statistical analyses with a computer is such an essential task to master, we provide a brief discussion of the computer software program SPSS in Appendix B, along with a disk containing five data sets. In Appendix C, we go through examples of data analysis with SPSS procedures that accompany the chapters in this text. In addition, using the data on the disk, we illustrate various statistical operations and provide an interpretation of SPSS statistical output.

You may be wondering why you have to learn statistics and how to calculate them by hand if you can avoid all of this by using a computer. First, we believe it is important for you to understand exactly what the computer is doing when it is calculating statistics. Without this knowledge, you may get results, but you will have no understanding of the logic behind the computer's output; thus, you will have little comprehension as to how those results were obtained. This is not a good way to learn statistics; in fact, it is not really learning statistics at all. Without a firm foundation in the basics of statistics, you will have no real knowledge of what to request of your computer. Despite its talent, the computer is actually fairly stupid; it has no ability to determine if what it is told to do is correct. Neither will the computer make sense out of the results—that will be your responsibility.

SETTING THE STAGE FOR STATISTICAL INQUIRY

Before we become more familiar with statistics in the upcoming chapters, we first want to set the stage for statistical inquiry. The data we utilize in criminology are derived from many different sources, including official government agency data like the Federal Bureau of Investigation's (FBI) Uniform Crime Reports; social surveys conducted by the government (the Bureau of Justice Statistics's National Crime Victimization Survey), ourselves, or other researchers; experiments; direct observation, either as a participant observer or as an unobtrusive observer; or a content analysis of existing images (historical or contemporary), such as newspaper articles or films. As you can see, the research methods we employ are very diverse.

Criminological researchers often conduct secondary data analysis (Reidel, 2000), which, simply put, involves reanalyzing already existing data. Typically, these data are either official data collected by local and federal agencies (e.g., rates of crime reported to police, information on incarcerated offenders from state correctional authorities, adjudication data from the courts) or data collected from surveys sponsored by government agencies or conducted by other researchers. Virtually all of the data collected by government agencies—and a great deal of the survey data collected by independent researchers—are made available to the public through the Inter-University Consortium for Political and Social Research (ICPSR), which is located at the University of Michigan.

ICPSR maintains and provides access to a vast archive of criminological data for research and instruction and offers training in quantitative methods to facilitate effective data use. For example, data available online at ICPSR include Supplementary Homicide Reports (SHR), which are provided by the U.S. Department of Justice and contain information from police reports for each individual homicide, including such things as the relationship between victims and offenders, use of weapons, and other characteristics of victims and offenders; survey data from the National Crime Victimization Survey (NCVS), which interviews a sample of U.S. household residents to determine their experiences with both property and violent crime, regardless of whether the crimes were reported to police or anyone else; survey data from samples of jail and prison inmates; survey data from the National Youth Survey (NYS), a survey conducted from by Delbert Elliot and his colleagues at the University of Colorado to monitor the extent of adolescent delinquency and the factors related to delinquent offending; and survey data from the National Opinion Survey of Crime and Justice, which asks adults for their opinion regarding a wide range of criminal justice issues. These are just a few examples of the immense archive of data made available at the ICPSR (http://www.icpsr.umich.edu).

THE ROLE OF STATISTICAL METHODS IN CRIMINOLOGY AND CRIMINAL JUSTICE

Over the past few decades, statistics and numerical summaries of phenomena including crime rates have increasingly been used to document how "good" or "bad" a society is doing. For example, cities and states are compared as safe or unsafe depending upon their respective levels of violent crime, and age groups frequently are monitored and compared to previous generations to determine their relative levels of deviancy based on criteria such as drug and alcohol use.

Research and statistics are important in the criminology discipline because they allow us to monitor phenomena over time and across geographical locations, and, in addition, they allow us to determine relationships between phenomena. Of course, we make conclusions about the relationships between various phenomena every day, but these conclusions are most often based on biased perceptions and selective personal experiences.

In criminological research, we rely on scientific methods, including statistics, to help us perform these tasks. **Science** relies on logical and systematic methods to answer questions, and it does so in a way that allows others to inspect and evaluate its methods. In the realm of criminological research, these methods are not so unusual. They involve asking questions, observing behavior, and counting people, all of which we often do in our everyday lives. However, criminological researchers develop, refine, apply, and report their understanding of the social world more systematically than Joanna Q. Public.

Let us illustrate the role of research in our field using youth violence as an example. On April 20, 1999, Eric Harris and Dylan Klebold turned Columbine High School, a suburban school in Colorado, into the scene of the deadliest school shooting in American history. After killing 12 students and a teacher, the teens shot and killed themselves. In the end, 15 people died and 28 were injured.

> **Science** relies on logical and systematic methods to answer questions, and it does so in a way that allows others to inspect and evaluate its methods.

After this tragic incident, headlines such as "The School Violence Crisis" and "School Crime Epidemic" were plastered across most media, including newspapers and television. Then President Bill Clinton talked about hate, prejudice, community policing, and conflict resolution as factors related to this so-called epidemic. Charlton Heston, spokesperson for the National Rifle Association (NRA), blamed the absence of armed security guards in schools, even though one was present at Columbine High. Heston also blamed the parents and the school for allowing kids to wear black. Each of you probably had your own ideas about how such a horrible event could have taken place as well.

Despite the use of terms such as "crisis" and "epidemic," criminological data indicated that, even with the rash of other school shootings in 1997 and

1998, the probability of being killed at school was decreasing. In fact, the most recent Bureau of Justice Statistics report on school violence has pointed out that more serious victimizations usually occur away from schools and that even at the time of the Columbine shootings, schools were becoming more, rather than less, safe in terms of victimization statistics. For example, there were 44 school murders in 1992–1993, and only 20 in 1998–1999.[1] Without trying to minimize the pain and tragedy of the school shootings that occurred during 1998 and 1999, the role of criminological research is to determine the statistical reality of phenomena, regardless of media hype.

Descriptive Research Case Study: The Magnitude of Youth Violence

One of the central roles statistics plays in our discipline is that of description. In **descriptive research,** we describe a social phenomenon of interest to determine the answers to such questions as, "How many people are victims of youth violence?" "How many youth are offenders?" "What are the most common crimes committed by youthful offenders?" and "Are youth today more violent compared to youth in the past?"

One methodology that has become instrumental in descriptive research is the survey. Self-report survey studies of both offenders and victims were developed in response to concerns among criminologists that official measures of crime were systematically biased and, as such, provided a distorted image of the magnitude of crime and the factors related to it. Over the past two decades, survey instruments have become increasingly sophisticated at uncovering incidents of both offending and victimization. Prominent surveys in the field designed to measure delinquency and youth violence include the National Youth Survey (NYS), the Monitoring the Future (MTF) survey, the National Household Survey on Drug Abuse (NHSDA), the Cambridge Study in Delinquent Development, and the Rochester Youth Development Study (RYDS).

Another recent study designed to examine the magnitude of youth violence (along with other risk-taking behavior such as taking drugs and smoking) is called the Youth Risk Behavior Survey (YRBS), and it has been conducted every two years in the United States since 1990. Respondents to this survey are a national sample of approximately 16,000 high school students in grades 9 through 12. To determine trends and patterns in violence-related behavior, Nancy Brener, Thomas Simon, Etienne G. Krug, and Richard Lowry examined these data for the years 1991 and 1997 and published their findings in the prestigious *Journal of the American Medical Association* (1999).

To measure the extent of youth violence, students were asked the following questions: "During the past 30 days, on how many days did you carry a weapon such as a gun, knife, or club?" "During the past 12 months, how many times were you in a physical fight?" "During the past 12 months, how many times were you in a physical fight in which you were injured and had to be seen by a doctor or nurse?" "During the past 30 days, how many times did you carry a weapon such as a gun, knife, or club on school property?" "During the past 12 months, how many times were you in a physical fight on school property?" "During the past 12 months, how many times has someone threatened or injured you with a gun, knife, or club on school property?"

Brener and her colleagues (1999) found that the total number of students who carried a weapon within the 30 days preceding the survey actually decreased by 30 percent from 1991 to 1997. Similarly, the number of students who engaged in a physical fight one or more times during the 12 months preceding the survey decreased 14 percent, and the number injured in a physical fight decreased 20 percent. Trends in violence occurring on school property also decreased during this time period. The number of students who carried a gun on school property on one or more of the 30 days preceding the survey decreased 28 percent, and the number of students who engaged in a physical fight on school property one or more times during the 12 months preceding the survey decreased 9 percent. This research is consistent with other studies that have found that official rates of youth violence, and youth homicide in particular, peaked in the early 1990s and have declined thereafter (Cook & Laub, 1998).

Explanatory Research Case Study: The Causes of Youth Violence

Another role statistics plays in our discipline is to help researchers identify explanations for phenomena. **Explanatory research** seeks to identify causes and effects of phenomena, to predict how one phenomenon will change or vary in response to variation in some other phenomenon. Researchers interested in the explanation of youth violence ask such questions as, "What factors are related to the incidence of youth violence?" "Are kids who use alcohol and drugs more likely to engage in violence compared to other youth?" "Are kids from families with higher incomes less likely to engage in violence or are they simply less likely to get caught?" Typically, in explanatory research, a hypothesis that is derived from theory and the existing scientific literature is tested. A **theory** is a logically interrelated set of propositions about empirical reality. Examples of criminological theories include social learning, general strain, social disorganization, and routine activities theory. A **hypothesis** is simply a tentative statement about empirical reality, involving a relationship between two or more phenomena.

Let's go through an example of a study that was designed to determine the factors related to adolescent violence. Researchers Richard Felson, Allen Liska, Scott South, and Thomas McNulty (1994) sought to determine whether individual and group differences in beliefs and attitudes about violence were related to committing acts of delinquency and interpersonal violence. The theoretical argument they were attempting to test is actually termed the

> A **theory** is a logically interrelated set of propositions about empirical reality.

> A **hypothesis** is a tentative statement about empirical reality, involving the relationship between two or more phenomena.

"subculture of violence" thesis (Wolfgang & Ferracuti, 1967). According to this thesis, some groups are more violent than others because they have a distinctive set of values that either support or tolerate violence. The hypothesis, then, would be that individuals whose values and beliefs are more tolerant of the use of violence in resolving conflict will be more likely to engage in violent behavior than individuals who do not endorse the use of violence in resolving conflict.

Felson and his colleagues (1994) used a data set called the Youth in Transition data, which involved a panel study of high school boys. The first interviews were conducted with sophomore boys attending 87 randomly selected public high schools. The second interview was collected 18 months later at the end of the boys' junior year in high school. The researchers measured each boy's adherence to a subculture of violence by asking him about situations in which he would approve of aggression as a legitimate expression of grievances and as an appropriate response to personal attack. For example, each boy was presented a series of personal values and asked whether each was a "good thing for people to do": (1) turning the other cheek and forgiving others when they harm you, (2) replying to anger with gentleness, and (3) being kind to people even if they do things against one's own beliefs. These items each focus on the approval of nonaggressive responses to some type of provocation. Agreement with these statements therefore suggests that respondents disapprove of aggressive responses to personal attacks and wrongdoing. Disagreement with these statements would result in a high score on the subculture-of-violence scale developed by Felson and his colleagues. To measure acts of interpersonal violence, each boy was asked the frequency with which he engaged in eight activities: (1) got into a serious fight with a student in school, (2) obtained something by telling a person something bad would happen to the person if he did not get what he wanted, (3) hurt someone badly enough to need bandages or a doctor, (4) hit a teacher, (5) hit his father, (6) hit his mother, (7) took part in a group brawl in which his friends fought with another group, and (8) used a knife or gun or some other thing to get something from a person. The respondents also were asked about other delinquent acts such as engaging in theft and vandalism.

The students' scores on the subculture-of-violence index were then used to predict scores on the interpersonal violence index, after controlling for the effects of other important variables such as socioeconomic status, race, attitudes toward academic achievement, and family stability. Felson and colleagues (1994) performed analyses using both individual and school-level data and found that in some schools, an aggressive response to a provocation was likely to meet with more peer approval than in other schools. They also found that individuals who approved of aggressive responses to provocation were more likely to commit acts of interpersonal violence. In addition, individuals who went to schools where there was an atmosphere permissive of violence were more likely to act violently, a finding that remained true even after controlling for individual attitudes. Felson and colleagues (1994) attributed this to a social control process and explain, "If boys are expected to re-taliate when provoked, it appears that they are more likely to engage in vio-lence and other delinquent behavior, no matter what their personal values may be." Of course, research also has found that other factors are related to violent offending in young adults, including harsh discipline, urban resi-dence, and residing in a high-crime neighborhood (Farrington, 1998).

Evaluation Research Case Study: School Programs to Prevent Youth Violence

Research and statistics also play a significant role in determining the efficacy of social programs and policies. Such research is called **evaluation research.** Evaluation research considers the implementation and effects of social poli-cies and programs. For example, to combat the fear perceived by parents af-ter the Columbine shooting, literally thousands of school boards across the country have spent millions of dollars on violence prevention training for their students. These programs generally provide cognitive-behavioral and social skills training on various topics using a variety of methods and are commonly referred to as *conflict resolution* and *peer mediation training.* Many of these prevention programs are designed to improve interpersonal prob-lem-solving skills among children and adolescents by training children in cognitive processing, such as identifying the interpersonal problem and gen-erating nonaggressive solutions. Are these programs actually effective in re-ducing violence?

   David Grossman and his colleagues (1997) assessed the efficacy of one such program for children in elementary school called "The Second Step: A Violence Prevention Curriculum." The program involved 30 lessons, each lasting about 35 minutes, taught once or twice a week. Each lesson consisted of a photograph accompanied by a social scenario that formed the basis for discussion, role plays, and conceptual activities. Lessons were arranged in three units: (1) empathy training, in which students identified their own feel-ings and those of others; (2) impulse control, in which students were pre-sented a problem-solving strategy and behavioral skills for effecting solutions (e.g., apologizing or dealing with peer pressure); and (3) anger management, in which students were presented a coping strategy and be-havioral skills for tense situations.

   Twelve elementary schools in King County, Washington, were paired ac-cording to three criteria: the school district, the proportion of students re-ceiving free or reduced-cost lunches, and the proportion of minority enrollment. After pairing, schools in each pair were randomly assigned to re-ceive the Second Step program (experimental groups) or to receive no vio-lence prevention curriculum (control groups). Random assignment was necessary so the researchers could be more confident that any differences observed in aggression and violent behavior between the two groups after the program could be attributed to the program alone and not to some other factor. Violent and aggressive behavior was measured in three ways: teacher ratings of each child's behavior, parent ratings, and direct observation of students by trained observers in the classroom, on the playground, and in the cafeteria. Measures of aggression were taken at three time periods: before the start of the curriculum (baseline), two weeks after the conclusion of the curriculum, and six months after the curriculum.

To determine the effectiveness of the Second Step program, researchers examined the change in aggression between scores measured at baseline and scores from the second and third periods of data collection. Grossman and his colleagues found encouraging results: Observed physically aggressive behavior decreased significantly more among children who engaged in the curriculum than among children in the control group who were not exposed to the Second Step program. Moreover, prosocial behavior increased significantly among children in the Second Step program compared to the control group. The authors of the study concluded, "This violence prevention curriculum appears to lead to modest reductions in levels of aggressive behavior and increases in neutral/prosocial behavior in school among second and third graders" (Grossman et al., 1997). Obviously, more research is needed to determine whether the millions of dollars being spent on such programs are a wise investment.

VALIDITY IN CRIMINOLOGICAL RESEARCH

In criminological research, we seek to develop an accurate understanding of empirical reality by conducting research that leads to valid knowledge about the world. But when is knowledge valid? In general, we have reached the goal of validity when our statements or conclusions about empirical reality are correct. If you look out your window and observe it is raining, this is probably a valid observation. However, if you read in the newspaper that the majority of Americans favor the death penalty for adolescents who commit murder, this conclusion is of questionable validity because it is probably based on an interpretation of a social survey.

Measurement Validity

In general, we can consider **measurement validity** the first concern in establishing the validity of research results, because without having measured what we think we measured, our conclusions may be completely false.[2] To see how important measurement validity is, ask yourself these questions: "How prevalent is youth violence and delinquency in the United States? How many juveniles are involved in delinquency?"

Data on the extent of juvenile delinquency come from two primary sources: official statistics and unofficial surveys. Official statistics are based on the aggregate records of juvenile offenders and offenses processed by agencies of the criminal justice system: police, courts, and corrections. One primary source of official statistics on juvenile delinquency is the Uniform Crime Reports (UCR) produced by the Federal Bureau of Investigation. Unofficial statistics are data produced by people or agencies outside the criminal justice system, such as victimization surveys and self-report studies. The validity of official statistics for measuring the extent of juvenile delinquency is a heated debate among criminologists. While some researchers believe official reports are a valid measure of serious delinquency, others contend that UCR data say more about the behavior of the police than about delinquency. These criminologists think the police are predisposed against certain groups of people or certain types of crimes.

Unquestionably, official reports underestimate the actual amount of delinquency. Obviously, not all acts of delinquency become known to the police. Sometimes delinquent acts are committed and not observed; other times they are observed and not reported. In addition, there is also evidence that UCR data often reflect the political climate and police policies as much as they do criminal activity. Take the United States's "War on Drugs," which heated up in the 1980s. During this time, arrest rates for drug offenses soared, giving the illusion that drug use was increasing at an epidemic pace. However, self-report surveys that asked citizens directly about their drug use behavior during this same time period found that the use of most illicit drugs was actually declining (Regoli & Hewitt, 1994). In your opinion, then, which measure of drug use, the UCR or self-report surveys, was more valid? Before we answer this question, let's continue our delinquency example.

Despite the limitations of official statistics for measuring delinquency, these data were relied on by criminologists and used as a valid measure of the prevalence of delinquency for many decades. As such, delinquency and other violent offending were thought to primarily involve minority populations and/or disadvantaged youth. In 1947, however, Wallerstein and Wyle surveyed a sample of 700 juveniles and found that 91 percent admitted to having committed at least one offense that was punishable by one or more years in prison and 99 percent admitted to at least one offense for which they could have been arrested had they been caught. In 1958, James Short and F. Ivan Nye reported the results from the first large-scale self-report study involving juveniles from a variety of locations. In their research, Short and Nye concluded that delinquency was widespread throughout the adolescent population and that youth from high-income families were just as likely to engage in delinquency as youth from low-income families. Contemporary studies using self-report data from the National Youth Survey (NYS) indicate that the actual amount of delinquency is much greater than that reported by the UCR. Moreover, unlike the official UCR data, in which nonwhites are overrepresented, self-report data indicate that white juveniles commit nearly the identical number of delinquencies as nonwhites, but fewer of them are arrested (Elliott & Ageton, 1980).

This is just one example that highlights the importance of measurement validity, but it should convince you that we must be very careful in designing our measures and in subsequently evaluating how well they have performed. We cannot simply assume that our measurements are valid.

Causal Validity

Causal validity, also known as **internal validity,** is another issue of concern. Causal validity has to do with the truthfulness of an assertion that A causes B. Most research seeks to determine what causes what, so social scientists studying issues in criminology and criminal justice frequently must be concerned with causal validity. Let's go back to the issue of violence prevention programs in schools. Imagine that we are searching for ways to reduce violence in high schools. We start by searching for what seem to be particularly effective violence prevention programs in area schools. We find a program at a local high school, let's call it Nerd Academy, that a lot of people have talked about, and we decide to compare the rates of violence reported to the guidance counselor's office in that school with the rates of violence reported in another school, Cool School, which does not offer a violence prevention program. We find that students in the school with the special program have lower rates of reported violence, and we decide that the program has caused the lower rates. Are you confident about the causal validity of our conclusion? Probably not. Perhaps the school with the special program had lower rates of reported violence even before the special program began.

This is the sort of problem that randomized experiments are designed to resolve. For example, in the Grossman study of the Second Step Violence Prevention Program, by randomly assigning study participants to either receive or not receive the program, the researchers made it very unlikely that youngsters who were more aggressive would be disproportionately represented in either group. In addition, causal conclusions also can prove to be mistaken because of some factor that was not recognized during the planning of a study, even in randomized experiments. Therefore, statistical control of other factors thought to also explain or predict the phenomenon of interest is essential in determining causal validity.

Generalizability

The **generalizability** of a study is the extent to which it can be used to inform us about persons, places, or events that are *not* being studied. Let's say we are interested in the extent to which high school youth are fearful of being attacked or harmed at school or in going to and from their schools. It would be easy to go down to the local high school and hand out a survey asking students to report their levels of fear in these situations. But what if my local high school were located in a remote and rural area of Alaska? Would this sample reflect levels of fear perceived by suburban youth in California or urban youth in New York City? Obviously not. Oftentimes, regardless of the sample utilized, researchers will report "this percentage of high school students is fearful" or "freshman students are more fearful than seniors," as if their study results represent all high school students. Many social researchers and criminologists (and most everyone else, for that matter) are eager to draw conclusions about all individuals they are interested in, not just their samples. Using information obtained from a sample to make inferences about the larger population from which the sample was drawn is termed making *generalizations.* Generalizations make the findings of a research study sound more important. If every high school student were like every other one, generalizations based on observations of one high school student would be valid. But of course, that's not the case.

> Assuming that what you find in a sample will also be true in the larger population from which the sample was drawn is called making **inferences** or **generalizations.**

Generalizability is a key concern in criminological research. We rarely have the resources to study the entire population that is of interest to us, so we have to select cases to study that will allow our findings to be generalized to the population of interest. Because the data we use in criminology are most often obtained from samples, the remainder of this chapter will cover some basic principles of sampling. We provide this discussion because issues of sampling are inextricably linked to the statistical process. We begin with a discussion of samples, populations, and sampling procedures, and we conclude by examining the differences between descriptive and inferential statistics.

POPULATIONS AND SAMPLES

The words "population" and "sample" should already have some meaning to you. When you think of a population, you probably think of the population of some locality, such as the United States, the city or state in which you reside, or the university or college you attend. Although we do not often encounter the concept of a sample in everyday life, you have probably heard of some instance in which samples were taken from a larger whole. News stories related to physical conditions often are accompanied by references to a sample. For example, paint samples in housing developments are used to reveal the paint's lead content, samples of blood are taken to detect rates of HIV infection, urine samples are tested to reveal drug or alcohol use, and samples of people are polled to determine the potential winner of a political election. As with most social science research, samples in criminology most often consist of individuals. Since it is too difficult, too costly, and sometimes impossible to get information on the entire population of interest, we must often solicit the information of interest from samples. **Samples** are simply subsets of a larger **population.**

> A **population** is the larger set of cases or aggregate number of people that a researcher is actually interested in or wishes to know something about. A **sample** is a subset of this population that a researcher must often use to make generalizations about the larger population.

Most official statistics collected by the U.S. government are derived from information obtained from samples, not from the entire population. For example, the National Crime Victimization Survey (NCVS) is a survey used to obtain information on the incidence and characteristics of crime in the U.S. based on a sample of the U.S. population. Every year, the NCVS interviews over 100,000 individuals aged 12 or over to solicit information on their experiences with victimization that were both reported and unreported to the police. Essentially, professional interviewers ask persons who are selected into the sample if they were the victim of a crime in the past six months, regardless of whether this victimization was reported to police. The Uniform Crime Reports, on the other hand, only provide us with the number of crimes that were reported to police. Since over half of all criminal victimizations are never reported to police, the NCVS is obviously a very important tool for ascertaining the extent of victimization in the United States. The purpose of the NCVS is to give us a more "accurate" estimate of the number of people in this country who have experienced an act of violence or theft, particularly victimizations that are less likely to be reported to police such as rape and assault by intimate partners.

You may be thinking right now, "Well, what if I am only interested in a small population? What if I am not interested in the entire U.S. population, but a smaller population like college freshmen?" Good question! Let's say we were interested in all persons convicted of robbery who were incarcerated in state prisons. Although it would be easier to contact every individual in this population than every U.S. citizen, it still would be extremely difficult and costly to obtain information from every person convicted of robbery. In fact, in almost all instances, we have to settle for a sample derived from the population of interest. For this reason, the "population" usually remains an unknown entity whose characteristics we can only estimate.

How do we do this? We make estimates about the characteristics of a population by using information we derive from a sample. As we noted earlier, these estimates are called generalizations. Because the purpose of sampling is to make generalizations, we must be very meticulous when selecting our sample. The primary goal of sampling is to make sure that the sample we select is actually *representative* of the population we are estimating. Think about this for a minute. What is representative? Generally, if the characteristics of a sample (e.g., age, race/ethnicity, gender) are similar to the characteristics of the population, it is said to be representative. For example, if you were interested in estimating the proportion of the population that favors the death penalty, to be representative, your sample should contain about 50 percent men and 50 percent women because that is the makeup of the U.S. population. It also should contain about 85 percent whites and 15 percent nonwhites, because that is the makeup of the U.S. population as well. If your sample included a disproportionately high number of males or nonwhites, it would be unrepresentative. If, on the other hand, your target population was individuals in the U.S. over the age of 65, your sample would have a somewhat different gender distribution. In order to reflect the gender distribution of all individuals in the U.S. over the age of 65, a sample would have to contain approximately 60 percent women and 40 percent men since this is the gender distribution of all individuals over age 65 in the U.S as defined by the Census Bureau (Census counts, although not perfect, are our best estimate).

In sum, the primary question of interest in sample generalizability is: *Can findings from a sample be generalized to the population from which the sample was drawn?* Sample generalizability depends on sample quality, which is determined by the amount of **sampling error** present in a sample. Sampling error generally can be defined as the difference between the characteristics of a sample and the characteristics of the population from which it was selected. The larger the sampling error, the less representative the sample, and as a result, the less generalizable the findings are to the population.

> **Sampling error** is any difference between the characteristics of a sample and the characteristics of the population from which it was taken. The larger the sampling error, the less representative the sample is of the larger population.

With a few special exceptions, a good sample should be representative of the larger population from which it was drawn. A representative sample looks like the population from which it was selected in all respects that are relevant to the study. In an unrepresentative sample, some characteristics are overrepresented and/or some characteristics may be underrepresented. There are various procedures that can be used to obtain a sample; these range from the simple to the complex.

TECHNIQUES OF SAMPLING

From the previous discussion, it should be apparent that accuracy is one of the primary problems we face when generalizing the information obtained from a sample to a population. How accurately does our sample reflect the true population? This question is inherent in any inquiry because with any sample we only represent a part, and sometimes a small part, of the entire population. The goal in obtaining or selecting a sample, then, is to select it in a way that increases the chances of this sample being representative of the entire population.

One of the most important distinctions made about samples is whether they are based on a probability or nonprobability sampling method. Sampling methods that allow us to know in advance how likely it is that any element of a population will be selected for the sample are **probability sampling methods.** Sampling methods that do not let us know the likelihood in advance are **nonprobability sampling methods.** The fundamental element in probability sampling is **random selection.** When a sample is randomly selected from the population, this means every element of the population (e.g., individual, school, city) has a known and independent chance of being selected for the sample. All probability sampling methods rely on a random selection procedure.

> **Random selection** is the fundamental element of **probability samples.** The essential characteristic of random selection is that every element of the population has a **known and independent chance** of being selected for the sample.

Probability sampling techniques not only serve to minimize any potential bias we may have when selecting a sample, they also allow us to gain access to probability theory in our data analysis. This body of mathematical theory allows us to estimate more accurately the degree of error we have when generalizing results obtained from known sample statistics to unknown population parameters. But don't worry about probability theory now. We discuss probability issues in greater detail in Chapter 6. For now, let's examine some of the most common types of probability samples used in research.

Flipping a coin and rolling a set of dice are the typical examples used to characterize random selection. When you flip a coin, you have the same chance of obtaining a head as you do of obtaining a tail: one out of two. Similarly, when rolling a die, you have the same probability of rolling a 2 as you do of rolling a 6: one out of six. In criminology, researchers usually use random numbers tables, such as Table E.1 in Appendix E, or other computer-generated random selection programs to select a sample. Because they are based on random selection, probability sampling methods have no systematic bias; nothing but chance determines which elements are included in the sample. As a result, our sample also is more likely to be representative of the entire population. When the goal is to generalize your findings to a larger population, it is this characteristic that makes probability samples more desirable than nonprobability samples. Using probability sampling techniques serves to restrain any potential bias we may have when selecting a sample ourselves.

PROBABILITY SAMPLING TECHNIQUES

Simple Random Samples

Perhaps the most common type of probability sample to use when we want to generalize information obtained from the sample to a larger population is called a **simple random sample.** Simple random sampling requires a procedure that generates numbers or identifies cases of the population for selection strictly on the basis of chance. The key element in a simple random sample is random selection. As we stated earlier, random selection ensures that every element in the population has a known, and independent chance of being selected for the sample. True simple random sampling is done by replacing a selected element back into the population so that, once again, there is an equal and independent chance of that element being selected. However, if your sample represents a very small percentage of a large population (e.g., under 4 percent), both sampling with and without replacement generally produce equivalent results.

Organizations that conduct large telephone surveys often draw random samples with another automated procedure called *random digit dialing*. In this process, a computer dials random numbers within the phone prefixes corresponding to the area in which the survey is to be conducted. Random digit dialing is particularly useful when a sampling frame is not available. The researcher simply replaces any inappropriate numbers, such as those numbers that are no longer in service or numbers for businesses, with the next randomly generated phone number.

Systematic Random Samples

Simple random sampling is easy to do if your population is organized in a list, such as in a phone book, a registered voters list, a court docket, or a membership list. We can make the process of simple random selection a little less time-consuming, however, by systematically sampling the cases. In **systematic random sampling,** we select the first element into the sample randomly, but instead of continuing with this random selection, we *systematically* choose the rest of the sample. The general rule for systematic random sampling is to begin with the kth element (any number selected randomly) in the population and then proceed to select the sample by choosing every kth element thereafter. The kth element is the only element that is truly selected at random. The starting element can be selected from a random numbers table or by some other random method. Systematic random sampling eliminates the process of deriving a new random number for every element selected, thus saving time.

For systematic sampling procedures to approximate a simple random sample, the population list must be truly random—not ordered. For example, we could not have a list of convicted felons ordered by offense type, age, or some other characteristic. If the list is ordered in any way, this will add bias to the sampling process and the resulting sample will not likely be representative of the population. In virtually all other situations, systematic random sampling yields what is essentially a simple random sample.

Multistage Cluster Samples

There are often times when we do not have the luxury of a population list but still want to collect a random sample. Suppose, for example, we wanted to obtain a sample from the entire United States population. Would there be a list of the entire population available? Well, there are telephone books which list residents of various locales who have telephones, lists of residents who have registered to vote, lists of those who hold driver's licenses, lists of those who pay taxes, and so on. However, all these lists are incomplete (e.g., some people choose not to list their phone number or do not have a telephone, some people do not register to vote, and others do not drive cars). Using these incomplete lists would introduce bias into our sample.

In such cases, the sampling procedures become a little more complex. We usually end up working toward the sample we want through successive approximations: first by extracting a sample from lists of groups or clusters that are available and then sampling the elements of interest from these selected clusters. A *cluster* is a naturally occurring, mixed aggregate of elements of the population, with each element appearing in one and only one cluster. Schools could serve as clusters for sampling students, prisons could serve as clusters for sampling incarcerated offenders, blocks could serve as clusters for sampling city residents, and so on. Sampling procedures of this nature are typically called **multistage cluster samples.**

Drawing a cluster sample is at least a two-stage procedure. First, the researcher draws a random sample of clusters (e.g., blocks, prisons, counties). Next, the researcher draws a random sample of elements within each selected cluster. Because only a fraction of the total clusters from the population are involved, obtaining a list of elements within each of the selected clusters is usually much easier.

Many professionally designed surveys use multistage cluster samples. For example, the U.S. Justice Department's National Crime Victimization Survey (NCVS) is an excellent example of a multistage cluster sample. Because the target population of the NCVS is the entire United States population, the first stage of sampling requires selecting a first-order sample of counties and large metropolitan areas called primary sampling units (PSU). From these PSUs, another stage of sampling involves the selection of geographic districts within each of the PSU's that have been enumerated by the 2000 Census. And finally, a probability sample of residential dwelling units is selected from these geographic districts. These dwelling units, or addresses, represent the final stage of the multistage sampling.

Weighted Samples

In some cases, the types of probability samples described above do not actually serve a study's purposes. Sometimes, we may want to make sure that certain segments of the population of interest are represented within our sample, and we do not want to leave this to chance. Say, for example, that we are interested in incidents of personal larceny involving contact, such as purse snatching or pocket picking. We know from the National Crime Victimization Survey that Americans over the age of 65 are as vulnerable to this type of crime as those who are below the age of 65. We may be interested in whether there are differences in the victimization circumstances (e.g., place or time of occurrence, number of offenders) between two groups of persons: those under the age of 65 and those 65 years of age or older. To investigate this, we want to conduct a sample survey with the entire U.S. population. A simple random sample of the population, however, may not result in a sufficient number of individuals over the age of 65 to use for comparison purposes, because individuals older than 65 make up a relatively small proportion of the entire population (approximately 12 percent).

Imagine a gum ball machine that has 88 percent red gum balls and only 12 percent green gum balls (which represent older Americans). You have 10 pennies to spend and you want to end up with five red and five green gum balls. Given the fact that there are far more red gum balls than green ones, unless you do something to increase the chance of getting a green gum ball, you will not end up with a 50/50 split. There are times, then, when we will want to purposefully "oversample" a particular group. In the purse snatching example, we will want to oversample the age group older than 65 to obtain enough cases for comparison.

One way to achieve this goal would be to weight disproportionately the elements in our population. These samples are referred to as **weighted samples.** Instead of having an equal chance of being selected, as in the case of random samples, individuals would have a known but unequal chance of being selected. That is, some elements would have a greater probability of being selected into the sample than others. This would be necessary in our study of purse snatching because those over the age of 65 represent only about 12 percent of the total U.S. population. Because we want to investigate differences between the victimizations of those younger than and older than 65, we want to have more than this 12 percent proportion represented in our sample. To do this, we would disproportionately weight our sample selection procedures to give persons older than 65 a better chance of being selected. It is important to note that if we were going to make generalizations from a weighted sample to the population, adjustments to our statistics would be necessary to take this sample weighting into account. This is a somewhat complicated procedure that usually is accomplished through the aid of computer technology.[3]

NONPROBABILITY SAMPLING TECHNIQUES

As you can imagine, obtaining a probability sample like those described in the above section, can be a very laborious task. Many researchers do not have the resources, in both time and money, to obtain a probability sample. Instead, many of us rely on samples obtained using *nonprobability sampling procedures.* Unlike the samples we have already discussed, when collecting a sample using nonprobability sampling techniques, elements within the target population *do not* have a known, and independent probability of being selected. Because the chance of one element being selected versus another element remains an unknown, we cannot be certain the selected sample actually represents our target population. Since we are generally interested in making inferences to a larger population, this uncertainty can represent a significant problem.

Why, then, would we want to use nonprobability sampling techniques? Well, they are useful for several purposes, including those situations in which we do not have a population list. Moreover, nonprobability sampling techniques are often the only way to obtain samples from particular populations or for certain types of research questions. Suppose, for example, that we were interested in the crime of shoplifting and we wanted to investigate the various rationales used by shoplifters (e.g., survival, thrills, or to get even). It would be hard to technically define a population here since we don't have a list of shoplifters from which to randomly select. There may be lists of convicted shoplifters, but of course, they only represent those shoplifters who were actually caught. In other cases, we may want to oversample certain subsets of the population. We will discuss three types of nonprobability samples in this section.

Quota Samples

One type of nonprobability sample that would serve our purposes well in a study of the victimization of elderly persons is called a **quota sample.** Quota samples are similar to the weighted samples we discussed in the last section, but they are generally less rigorous and precise in their collection methods. While quota sampling techniques range from the very simple to the very rigorous, all quota samples are still considered nonprobability samples. Very simply, quota sampling involves designating the population into proportions of some group that you would like represented in your sample. In some cases, these proportions may actually represent the true proportions observed in the population. Other times, they may represent predetermined proportions of subsets you want to oversample.

Purposive or Judgment Samples

Another type of nonprobability sample which is often used in the field of criminology is called a **purposive** or **judgment sample.** In general, this type of sample is selected based on the purpose of the researcher's study and his/her judgment of the population. It is often referred to as judgment sampling, because the researcher uses her or his own judgment about whom to select into the sample, rather than drawing sample elements randomly. While this type of sample does not provide the luxury of generalizability, it can provide a wealth of information not otherwise attainable from a typical random sample.

Many classic studies in the field of criminology have been carried out by using a purposive or judgment sample. For example, in the classic book *The Booster and the Snitch: Department Store Shoplifting,* Mary Cameron (1964) tracked a sample of individuals who had been caught shoplifting by department store employees. In following these cases from the initial event of getting caught to the final phase of adjudication in the criminal justice system, she found that only about 11 percent of Caucasians received a formal charge of larceny, compared to 58 percent of apprehended African-Americans. This disparity in sanctioning between the groups may have been somewhat different had Cameron employed other sampling techniques. For example, if she had not traced cases from the initial incident of getting caught, but only taken a sample of shoplifting cases which had been formally processed by police departments, the disparity may not have been revealed.

Another example of purposive/judgment sampling techniques comes from Lawrence Sherman's analysis of the six stages of the "moral career of corrupt policemen." In this study, Sherman (1981) described the process through which a new police officer became a "gafter" (someone who accepts bribes).

Another variation of a purposive sample is called a *snowball sample.* In this case, a researcher obtains information about additional people to sample from every respondent. For example, in their study of residential burglary, *Burglars on the Job,* Wright and Decker (1994) interviewed 105 active burglars operating in St. Louis, Missouri. These burglars were not, of course, randomly selected from some known population of St. Louis burglars. Rather, the sampling process started with an ex-offender working for the two researchers as an informant. In this case, it was not the researchers' judgment that was critical but that of their ex-offender accomplice, who was "in the know" about St. Louis street crime. This ex-offender used his judgment in selecting known burglars in given high-crime areas of St. Louis. These burglars then gave the researchers contact information for other people they knew who had committed burglaries, and so on and so on until the sample grew like a snowball. This process is, of course, enhanced by offering respondents gratuities for referrals! Wright and Decker were able to obtain richly descriptive information about residential burglary in St. Louis. Because this was a purposive/judgment sample, the question remains whether their findings can be generalized to residential burglary committed in other areas. Nonetheless, this study provided a wealth of descriptive information that would not have been attainable by using other sampling techniques.

Availability Samples

The final type of sampling technique we will discuss is one that is perhaps too frequently used and is based solely on the availability of respondents. This type of sample is appropriately termed an **availability sample.** The media often masquerade availability samples as probability samples. Popular magazines and Internet sites periodically survey their readers by asking them to fill out questionnaires; those individuals inclined to respond make up the availability sample for the survey. Follow-up articles then appear in the magazine or on the site, displaying the results under such titles as "What You Think about the Death Penalty for Teenagers." Even if the number of people who responded is large, however, these respondents only make up a tiny fraction of the entire readership and are probably unlike other readers who did not have the interest or time to participate. In sum, these samples are unrepresentative of the total population and even of the total population of a magazine's readers. Because of their nonscientific basis, many Internet and magazine polls now add this disclaimer to their results: "Not a scientific poll; for entertainment only."

We admit that in conducting our own research, we have used this type of sample once or twice. You have probably even been an element in one of these samples. Have you ever been asked to complete a questionnaire in class before? University researchers frequently conduct surveys by passing out questionnaires in their large lecture classes. Usually, the sample obtained from this method consists of those students who voluntarily agree to participate or those who receive course credit for doing so. This voluntary participation adds yet another source of bias into the sample. It is not surprising that this type of sample is so popular; it is one of the easiest and least expensive sampling techniques available. It is also, however, a technique that may produce the least representative and generalizable type of samples. Like most things in life, the price of ease is often precision and accuracy.

We hope that at this point in the text you would be able to outline the disadvantages of these nonprobability sampling techniques if you were asked. A good answer would go something like this:

> As the goal of most research is to learn something about a population and not simply something about a sample from a population, the techniques used to obtain a sample are very important. The use of nonprobability samples, like availability samples, severely limits the ability we have to make inferences from what we observe in the sample to the larger population. Put another way, nonprobability samples limit our ability to generalize sample results to a population.

We believe it is fundamental that you are aware of these issues before beginning a course in statistics. All inferential statistics we will examine in this text assume that the data being examined were taken from some kind of probability sample. What are inferential statistics, you ask? Good question. We will answer this next.

DESCRIPTIVE AND INFERENTIAL STATISTICS

Traditionally, the discipline of statistics has been divided into two parts: descriptive and inferential. In large part, this distinction relies on the extent to which one is interested in (1) simply describing some phenomenon or (2) "inferring" characteristics of some phenomenon from a sample to the entire population. See! An understanding of sampling issues is already necessary.

Descriptive statistics can be used to describe characteristics or some phenomenon from either a sample or a population. The key point here is that you are using the statistics for "description" only. For example, if we wanted to describe the number of parking tickets given out by university police or the amount of revenue these parking tickets generated, we could do this by utilizing various statistics, including simple counts or averages.

If, however, we wanted to generalize this information to university police departments across the country, we would need to move into the realm of **inferential statistics.** Inferential statistics are mathematical tools for estimating how likely it is that a statistical result based on data from a random sample is representative of the population from which the sample has been selected. If our interest is in making inferences, a **sample statistic** is really only an estimate of the population statistic, called a **population parameter,** we want to estimate. Because this sample statistic is only an estimate of the population parameter, there will always be some amount of error present. Inferential statistics are the tools used for calculating the magnitude of this *sampling error.* We will talk about sampling error in greater detail beginning in Chapter 6. As we noted earlier, the larger the sampling error, the less representative our sample will be of the population. Of course, before we are able to utilize inferential statistics, we must be able to assume that our sample is actually representative of the population. And to do this, we must obtain our sample using appropriate probability sampling techniques. The larger picture is, we hope, beginning to emerge!

SUMMARY

Our goal in this introductory chapter is to underscore the importance of statistics in criminology and criminal justice. We have set the stage for us to begin our exploration into the realm of statistics.

We have seen that, unlike the observations we make in everyday life, criminological research relies on scientific methods. Statistical methods play a role in three types of research we conduct in our field: descriptive research, explanatory research, and evaluation research. The goal of all research is validity—when our statements or conclusions about empirical reality are correct. Measurement validity exists when we have actually measured what we think we have measured. Causal or internal validity exists when the assertion that one phenomenon causes another, A causes B, is correct. And external validity, also called generalizability, exists when the findings from our sample are also true for the larger population from which the sample was selected.

Because it is almost never possible to obtain information on every individual or element in the population of interest, our investigations usually rely on data taken from samples of the population. Furthermore, as virtually all of the statistics we will examine in this text are based on assumptions about the origins of our data, we have provided a discussion of the most common types of samples utilized in our field of study. Samples generally fall within two categories: those derived from probability sampling techniques and those derived from nonprobability sampling techniques. The fundamental element in probability sampling is random selection. When a sample is randomly selected from the population, it means that every element (e.g., individual) has a known, equal, and independent chance of being selected for the sample.

We examined four types of probability samples: the simple random sample, the systematic random sample, the multistage cluster sample, and the weighted sample. In addition, we also discussed three types of nonprobability samples: quota samples, purposive or judgment samples, and availability samples. We concluded the chapter with a brief discussion of descriptive and inferential statistics.

KEY TERMS

availability sample
causal validity
descriptive research
descriptive statistics
evaluation research
explanatory research

generalizability
hypothesis
inferential statistics
internal validity
measurement validity
multistage cluster sample

nonprobability sampling
  methods
population
population parameter
probability sampling methods
purposive or judgment sample
quota sample
random selection

sample
sample statistic
sampling error
science
simple random sample
systematic random sampling
  theory
weighted sample

PRACTICE PROBLEMS

1. Obtain a list of students from the statistics or research methods course in which you are currently using this book. Using this list and the random numbers table in Appendix E, select a simple random sample of 15 students. What are the steps you performed in doing this? Comment on the representativeness of this sample to the entire sophomore class. Now conduct a systematic random sample from the same list. Are there any differences?

2. How can you approximate a simple random sample when you do not have a list of the population?

3. Discuss the importance of probability sampling techniques.

4. How does random selection ensure that we are obtaining the most representative sample possible?

5. If we wanted to make sure that certain segments of the population were represented and/or overrepresented within our sample, what are two types of sampling techniques we could use?

6. What is the danger in using nonprobability samples in research?

7. In what types of situations would nonprobability samples be most appropriate?

SPSS PRACTICE PROBLEMS

1. The SPSS exercises at the end of each chapter use the data sets included in the CD-ROM packaged with this book. The data are provided for you to conduct the statistical operations conducted in the text using the popular computer program SPSS. If you are planning on using this program for the course, now would be a good time to become familiar with the operation of the SPSS program. A more detailed guide to getting around in SPSS is provided in Appendix B.

Levels of Measurement and Aggregation

CHAPTER

> *Mathematics, rightly viewed, possesses not only truth, but supreme beauty—a beauty cold and austere, like that of sculpture.*
>
> —BERTRAND RUSSELL

In this chapter, you will learn how to communicate about data sets and variables, which are the primary elements we work with in statistical analysis. You will learn how to identify the two general distinctions made about a variable's level of measurement, quantitative and qualitative, along the four more specific levels called nominal, ordinal, interval, and ratio. You also will learn the difference between an independent and a dependent variable as well as a few of the common forms in which a variable is presented, including raw frequencies, proportions and percents, and rates.

25

INTRODUCTION

In the preceding chapter, we examined various sampling techniques that can be used for selecting a sample from a given population. Once we have selected our sample, we can begin the process of gathering information. The information we gather is usually referred to as "data," and in their entirety these data are called a "data set." In this chapter, we will take a closer look at the types of variables that can make up a data set.

Even though this may be the first time you have been formally exposed to statistics, we are sure each of you has some idea about what a variable is, even though you may not label it as such. A **variable** is any element to which different values can be attributed. Respondents' gender is a variable with two values, male and female. Race/ethnicity is a variable with many values, such as American Indian, African American, Asian, Hispanic, and Caucasian. Age is another variable that can take on different values, such as 2, 16, or 55 years of age.

> A **variable** is a characteristic or property that can vary or take on different values or attributes.

> A **constant** is a characteristic or property that does not vary but takes on only one value.

The entire set of values that a variable takes on is called a **frequency distribution** or an **empirical distribution.** In a given data set, a frequency distribution, or empirical distribution, is a **distribution** (or list) of outcomes or values for a variable. It is referred to as an "empirical" distribution because it is a distribution of empirical (i.e., real and observable) data. Likewise, it is called a "frequency" distribution because it tells us how frequent each value or outcome is in the entire data set. For example, suppose we conduct a survey from a sample of 100 persons in your class at your university. In one of the questions we ask for the respondent's age. Suppose this "age" variable ranges from 18 to 42. There may be 15 people who are 18 years of age, 30 people who are 19 years of age, 17 people who are 20 years of age, only 1 person who is 42 years of age, and so on. An empirical, or frequency, distribution not only tells you what the different ages are, but also how many people of each age are represented in the entire distribution.

In contrast, something that does not vary in a data set is called a **constant.** Unlike a variable, whose values vary or are different, a constant has only one value. For example, if you have a sample of inmates from a male correctional institution, respondents' gender would be considered a constant. Since all elements of the sample would be male, respondents' gender would not vary in that data set. If you selected a sample of 20-year-old students from the sophomore class at a state university, age would be a constant rather than a variable in that sample because the age of each person would be the same (20 years).

Notice that a given characteristic, such as respondents' gender or age, is not always a variable or a constant. Under different conditions, it may be one or the other. For example, in a sample of male prisoners, gender would be a constant, but age would be a variable because the male inmates are likely to be different ages. In the sample of 20-year-old sophomore students from a university, age would be a constant, but respondents' gender would be a variable because some persons in the sample would be male and some would be female.

We can classify variables in many different ways and make several distinctions among them. First, there are differing levels of measurement that can be associated with variables. The first part of this chapter examines these measurement differences, beginning with the classification of variables as either continuous or categorical. We then examine the four measurement classifications within these two broad categories: nominal, ordinal, interval, and ratio. The second section of the chapter addresses the difference between independent and dependent variables and the different ways of presenting variables. In the final section, you will learn how to identify the units of analysis in a research design so you can draw conclusions about the relationships between your variables in the appropriate units.

LEVELS OF MEASUREMENT

Recall that data generally come from one of three places: They are gathered by us personally, gathered by another researcher, or gathered by a government agency. Doing research on a previously collected data set is often referred to as "secondary data analysis" because the data already exist and have been analyzed before. No matter how they were collected, however, data sets are by definition simply a collection of many variables.

For illustrative purposes, imagine that we were interested in the relationship between levels of student drinking and drug use and student demographic characteristics such as gender, age, religion, and year in college (freshman, sophomore, junior, senior). Table 2–1 displays the small data set we may have obtained had we investigated this issue by collecting surveys of 20 college students (a random sample, of course).

To measure the extent to which each student used alcohol and other drugs, let's say we asked them these questions: "How many drinks do you consume in an average month? (By 'drinks' we mean a beer, a mixed drink, or a glass of wine)" "How many times during an average month do you take other drugs, such as ecstasy, marijuana, cocaine, or any other illegal drug?" Each of the other variables in the table relates to other information about each student in the sample. Everything listed in this table, including each respondent's identification number, is a variable. All of these variables combined represent our data set. The first thing you may notice about these variables is that some are represented by categories and some are represented by actual numbers. Gender, for example, is comprised of two categories, female and male. This type of variable often is referred to as a **qualitative** or **categorical** level variable, implying that the values represent qualities or categories only. The values of this variable

> **Qualitative** or **categorical variables**: The values refer to qualities or categories. They tell us what kind, what group, or what type a value is referring to.

> **Quantitative** or **continuous variables**: The values refer to quantities or different measurements. They tell us how much or how many a value has.

have no numeric or quantitative meaning. Other examples in the data set of qualitative variables include college year and religion.

The other variables in our data set, however, have values that do represent numeric values that can be quantified, hence the name **quantitative** variables. Quantitative variables also are referred to as **continuous** variables, denoting the continuous nature of the variable values (not discrete categories). The values of quantitative or continuous variables can be compared in a numerically meaningful way. Respondents' identification number, age, grade point average, and number of drinks and times they used drugs are all quantitative variables. We can compare the values of these variables in a numerically meaningfully way. For example, in Table 2–1 you can see that respondent number 1 has a lower grade point average than respondent 19. You also can see that respondents 1, 7, and 16 have the highest levels of alcohol consumption in the sample.

In Table 2–1, it is relatively easy to identify which variables are qualitative and which are quantitative, simply because the qualitative variables are represented by **alphanumeric data** (the data are represented by words rather

TABLE 2–1

Example of the Format of a Data Set from a Survey of 20 College Students

Number	Gender	Age	College Year	GPA	Average Month		Religion
					# Drinks	# Times Drugs Used	
1	Female	19	Sophomore	2.3	45	22	Catholic
2	Male	22	Senior	3.1	30	10	Other
3	Female	22	Senior	3.8	0	0	Protestant
4	Female	18	Freshman	2.9	35	5	Jewish
5	Male	20	Junior	2.5	20	20	Catholic
6	Female	23	Senior	3.0	10	0	Catholic
7	Male	18	Freshman	1.9	45	25	Not religious
8	Female	19	Sophomore	2.8	28	3	Protestant
9	Male	28	Junior	3.3	9	0	Protestant
10	Female	21	Junior	2.7	0	0	Muslim
11	Female	18	Freshman	3.1	19	2	Jewish
12	Male	19	Sophomore	2.5	25	20	Catholic
13	Female	21	Senior	3.5	2	0	Other
14	Male	21	Junior	1.8	19	33	Protestant
15	Female	42	Sophomore	3.9	10	0	Protestant
16	Female	19	Sophomore	2.3	45	0	Catholic
17	Male	21	Junior	2.8	29	10	Not religious
18	Male	25	Sophomore	3.1	14	0	Other
19	Female	21	Junior	3.5	5	0	Catholic
20	Female	17	Freshman	3.5	28	0	Jewish

than numbers). Data that are represented by numbers are called **numeric data.** A good device for remembering the distinction between these two types of data is to think that *alpha*numeric data consist of letters of the *alpha*bet, whereas *num*eric data consist of *num*bers.

It is certainly possible to include alphanumeric data in a data set, as we have done in Table 2–1, but when stored in a computer, as most data are, alphanumeric data take up a great deal of space. For this reason, these data usually are converted to or represented by numeric data. For example, females may arbitrarily be identified with the number 1 rather than the word "female" and males with the number 2. Assigning numbers to the categorical values of qualitative variables is called "coding" the data. Of course, which numbers get assigned to qualitative variables (for example, 1 for females and 2 for males) is arbitrary because the numerical code (number) assigned has no real quantitative meaning.

Table 2–2 redisplays the data in Table 2–1 numerically, as it would normally be stored in a computer data set. Because values of each variable are

TABLE 2–2

Example of the Data Presented in Table 2–1 as It Would be Stored in a Computer Data File

Number	Gender	Age	College Year	GPA	# Drinks	Average Month # Times Drugs Used	Religion
1	1	19	2	2.3	45	22	1
2	2	22	4	3.1	30	10	6
3	1	22	4	3.8	0	0	2
4	1	18	1	2.9	35	5	3
5	2	20	3	2.5	20	20	1
6	1	23	4	3.0	10	0	1
7	2	18	1	1.9	45	25	5
8	1	19	2	2.8	28	3	2
9	2	28	3	3.3	9	0	2
10	1	21	3	2.7	0	0	4
11	1	18	1	3.1	19	2	3
12	2	19	2	2.5	25	20	1
13	1	21	4	3.5	2	0	6
14	2	21	3	1.8	19	33	2
15	1	42	2	3.9	10	0	2
16	1	19	2	2.3	45	0	1
17	2	21	3	2.8	29	10	5
18	2	25	2	3.1	14	0	6
19	1	21	3	3.5	5	0	1
20	1	17	1	3.5	28	0	3

represented by numbers, it is a little more difficult to distinguish the qualitative variables from the quantitative variables. You have to ask yourself what each of the values really means. For example, for the variable gender, what does the "1" really represent? It represents the code for a female student, and therefore it is not numerically meaningful—it is a random code number given to all female students who filled out the questionnaire. Similarly, the number "1" coded for the religion variable represents those students who said they were Catholic and the code "3" represents those students who said they were Jewish. There is nothing inherently meaningful about the numbers 1 or 3. They simply represent categories for the religion variable. For the variable age, what does the number 19 represent? This is actually a meaningful value—it tells us that this respondent is 19 years of age and it is therefore a quantitative variable.

In addition to distinguishing between qualitative or categorical and quantitative or continuous, we can differentiate variables in terms of what is called their "level of measurement." The four levels of measurement are: (1) nominal, (2) ordinal, (3) interval, and (4) ratio.

Nominal Measurement

Variables measured at the nominal level are exclusively qualitative in nature. The values of **nominal-level variables** convey classification or categorization information only. Therefore, the only thing we can say about two or more nominal-level values of a variable is that they differ. We cannot say that one value reflects more or less of the variable than the other. The most common types of nominal-level variables are gender (male and female), religion (Protestant, Catholic, Jewish, Muslim, etc.), and political party (Democrat, Republican, Independent, etc.). The values of these variables are distinct from one another and can give us only descriptive information about the type or label attached to a value.

Because they represent only distinctions of kind (one is merely different from the other), the categories of a nominal-level variable are not related to one another in any meaningful numeric way. This is true even if the alphanumeric values are converted or coded into numbers. For example, in Table 2–2, the values assigned to the variables gender and religion are given numeric values. Remember, however, that these numbers were simply assigned and have no numerical meaning. The fact that Catholics are assigned the code of 1 and Protestants are assigned the code of 2 does not mean that Protestants have twice as much religion as Catholics or that the Protestant religion is superior to the Catholic religion. The only thing that the codes of 1 and 2 mean is that they refer to different religions. Because we cannot make distinctions of less than or more than with them, then, nominal-level variables do not allow us to rank-order the values of a given variable. In other words, nominal-level measurement does not have the property of order. There is no recognition of less than or more than, just the fact that some values are different from others. Reflecting this, mathematical operations cannot be performed with nominal-level data. With our religion variable, for example, we cannot subtract a 2 (Protestant) from a 3 (Jewish) to get a 1 (Catholic). See how meaningless mathematical operations are with variables measured at the nominal level?

Ordinal Measurement

The values of **ordinal-level variables** are not only categorical in nature, but the categories also have some type of relationship to each other. This relationship is one of order. That is, categories on an ordinal variable can be rank-ordered from high (more of the variable) to low (less of the variable), even though they still cannot be quantified exactly. As a result, while we can know if a value is more or less than another value, we do not know exactly how much more or less. The properties of ordinal-level measurement become clearer with an example.

Let's say that on a survey, we have measured income in such a way that respondents simply checked the income category that best reflected their annual income. The categories provided in the survey are as follows:

1. Less than $20,000
2. $20,001 to $40,000
3. $40,001 to $60,000
4. More than $60,001

Now suppose that one of our respondents checked the first category and that another respondent checked the fourth category. We don't know the exact annual income of each respondent, but we do know that the second respondent makes more than the first. Thus, in addition to knowing that the two respondents have different annual incomes (nominal level), we also know that one income is higher than the other. In reality, the first respondent may make anywhere between no money and $20,000, but because income was measured using ordinal categories, we will never know. Had we measured income in terms of actual dollars earned per year, we would be able to make more precise mathematical distinctions.

Other examples of ordinal-level variables include "Likert-type" response questions, which are designed to solicit an individual's attitudes or perceptions. You are more than likely familiar with this type of survey question. A typical question of this type would say: "Please respond to the following statement by circling the appropriate number: '1' Strongly agree, '2' Agree, '3' Disagree, '4' Strongly disagree." The answers to these questions represent the ordinal level of measurement.

Likert-type response questions were recently used in a criminological study conducted by Alissa Pollitz Worden (1993). Using the Police Services Study, which surveyed police officers in 24 departments in three metropolitan areas (St. Louis, Tampa, and Rochester), Worden examined the gender differences in police officers' attitudes on several issues, including their acceptance of rules and authority, their perceived level of citizen support, and their preparedness for routine encounters. The majority of these attitudes were measured using questions that required the respondent to make one of a limited number of responses. For example, to solicit information on an officer's acceptance of legal restrictions, respondents were asked to give their opinion on the following statements:

1. If police officers in tough neighborhoods had fewer restrictions on their use of force, many of the serious crime problems in those neighborhoods would be greatly reduced.

2. Police officers here would be more effective if they didn't have to worry about "probable cause" requirements for searching citizens.

3. When a police officer is accused of using too much force, only other officers are qualified to judge such a case.

Specifically, respondents were asked to select their level of agreement with each of the statements using the following response choices:

1	2	3	4
Strongly Agree	Agree	Disagree	Strongly Disagree

As we noted above, response categories that rank-order attitudes in this way are often called *Likert* responses (named after Rensis Likert, who is believed to have developed them in the 1930s). The police officers' answers to these questions using the four-point Likert response categories represent the ordinal level of measurement. This type of variable can tell us that one officer disagrees with the question on "probable cause" requirements more or less than another officer, but we do not know the exact magnitude of this disagreement. Even though numbers are attached to each category, these numbers are representative of the categories only. The results of Worden's research revealed very few significant differences in the ways in which male and female police officers define their role or their environment. She concluded, "These findings offer little support for the thesis that female officers define their role, or see their clientele differently than do males, and one must therefore remain skeptical (albeit not disbelieving) about claims that women bring to their beats a distinctive perspective on policing" (Worden, 1993:229).

Interval Measurement

In addition to enabling us to rank-order values, **interval-level variables** allow us to better quantify the numeric relationship among them. To be classified as an interval-level variable, the categories of the variable must have an *equal* and *known* quantity. In other words, we have an interval scale of measurement if the difference between adjacent values along the measurement scale is the same between every two points. In addition to equal values between each value, another characteristic of interval-level measurement is that the zero point is arbitrary. An arbitrary zero means that, although a value of zero is possible, zero does not mean the absence of the phenomenon. A meaningless zero is an arbitrary zero. These characteristics allow scores on an interval scale to be added and subtracted, but meaningful multiplication and division cannot be performed. Sounds a little confusing, doesn't it? An example should help to clarify.

The classic example of interval-level measurement is the measurement of temperature with a Fahrenheit temperature scale. A temperature reading of 73 degrees is higher than a temperature reading of 63 degrees. Thus, Fahrenheit degrees can be rank-ordered in terms of higher or lower, just like an ordinal scale. Unlike an ordinal scale, however, we can say more if we have interval measurement. The temperature difference between 73 degrees and 63 degrees is 10 degrees—this is the same as the difference between 65 degrees and 55 degrees, or between 27 degrees and 17 degrees. In each case, the first temperature is exactly 10 degrees warmer than the second. Similarly, the difference between 80 degrees and 81 degrees is the same as the difference between −20 degrees and −21 degrees, exactly 1 degree. A Fahrenheit temperature scale also has interval-level properties because the zero point is arbitrary. A temperature reading of 0 degrees Fahrenheit does not mean that there is no temperature! It only means that it is colder than a temperature reading of, say, 20 degrees and warmer than a reading of −20 degrees.

Recall that we classified the Likert scale used to measure attitudes and opinions as an ordinal level of measurement. In criminological research, however, some researchers have assumed Likert scales to be measured at the interval level. This assumption is usually made, however, if the researchers are combining several items that have used Likert responses into a scale or index. For example, Stacy De Coster and Karen Heimer (2001) created a "family attachment" variable that added responses to several statements using these response categories: (1) Not at all important, (2) Not important, (3) Somewhat important, (4) Pretty important, and (5) Very important. The questions were: (1) How important is it to you to have a family that does lots of things together? (2) How important is it to you to have parents who comfort you when you are unhappy about something? (3) How important is it to you to have parents who you can talk to about almost everything? The researchers added the responses to these three items together, thereby creating an index that measured the extent to which respondents thought it was important to have parental involvement in their lives. Respondents who thought all three things were very important to them would receive higher scores on the index than those who thought each of the activities was "not at all important." De Coster and Heimer still had to make the assumption, however, that the differences between each of the respondents' scores on this "family attachment" index were equal. For example, that the degree of difference in attachment between those who scored 4 and 6 (2) on the index was the same magnitude of difference as those who scored 12 and 14 (2). If we are not comfortable making this assumption, then we can assume that we have only ordinal-level measurement and therefore we can use the statistics appropriate for that level only.

Ratio Measurement

Ratio-level variables have all the qualities of interval-level variables and, in addition, the numerical difference between values is based on a natural, or true-zero, point. A true-zero point means that a score of zero indicates that the phenomenon is absent. Ratio measurement allows meaningful use of multiplication and division, as well as addition and subtraction. We can, therefore, divide one number by another to form a ratio—hence the name ratio-level of measurement.

Suppose we were conducting a survey of the victimization experiences of residents in rural areas. If one of our survey questions asked them to provide their annual income in dollars, this variable would be an example of the ratio-level of measurement because it has a true-zero point and equal and known distances between adjacent values. For example, a value of no income, "zero bucks," has inherent meaning to all of us, and the difference between $10 and $11 is the same as that between $55,200 and $55,201.

Criminologists' interest in income takes many forms, not merely that of family income. Take the numbers presented in Table 2–3. This table presents a list of U.S. senators according to two variables: (1) their "yes" or "no" vote on the Brady Bill and (2) the contributions each senator received from the National Rifle Association (NRA) from January 1, 1987, to September 30, 1993. To refresh your memory, the Brady Bill requires a five-day waiting period and a background check for potential buyers of handguns. The vote on the Brady Bill variable in this case represents the nominal level of measurement ("yes" or "no"). The contribution variable is clearly measured at the ratio level because it reflects the actual dollar amount contributed by the NRA to each senator. More than 30 senators received no contributions from the NRA. The Senate voted 63 to 36 on November 20, 1993, to approve the Brady Bill. Table 2–3 presents a very interesting picture of the relationship between NRA contributions and a senator's vote. We will leave you to ponder this relationship on your own for now.

Another example of a variable measured at the ratio level is the length of prison sentence received by a convicted offender. Prison sentences usually are measured according to the number of years or months that someone is sentenced to prison. The Bureau of Justice Statistics (BJS) collects data from a nationally representative sample survey of felons convicted in state courts in 344 counties of the U.S. every two years. In 1998, the maximum sentence length (in months) imposed by state courts was as follows:[1]

Primary Offense	Sentence (months)
Murder	258
Rape	125
Robbery	94
Aggravated assault	44
Burglary	39
Drug trafficking	37

TABLE 2–3

U.S. Senators' Votes on the Brady Bill and Previous Contributions ($) Received by Each Senator from the National Rifle Association

Senator	Contributions ($)	Senator	Contributions ($)
Paul Coverdell (R-Ga.)	**95,806**	*Byron L. Dorgan (D-N.D.)*	*4,450*
Alfonse M. D'Amato (R-N.Y.)	**20,486**	**Mitch McConnell (R-Ky.)**	**3,085**
Dan Coats (R-Ind.)	19,800	Mark O. Hatfield (R-Ore.)	3,000
Arlen Specter (R-Pa.)	**18,072**	Bob Packwood (R-Ore.)	2,000
Lauch Faircloth (R-N.C.)	**17,973**	Wendell H. Ford (D-Ky.)	1,568
Jesse Helms (R-N.C.)	**17,957**	**Conrad Burns (R-Mont.)**	**1,000**
Christopher S. Bond (R-Mo.)	14,850	Bob Kerrey (D-Neb.)	1,000
Max Baucus (D-Mont.)	14,639	John. D. Rockefeller IV (D-W.Va.)	1,000
Larry Pressler (R-S.D.)	**14,400**	John W. Warner (R-Va.)	1,000
Kay Bailey Hutchinson (R-Tex.)	11,509	**Hank Brown (R-Colo.)**	**0**
Larry E. Craig (R-Idaho)	**11,286**	**Patrick J. Leahy (D-Vt.)**	**0**
Robert C. Smith (R-N.H.)	**11,000**	**Alan K. Simpson (R-Wyo.)**	**0**
Slade Gorton (R-Wash.)	10,900	Daniel K. Akaka (D-Hawaii)	0
Howell T. Heflin (D-Ala.)	**10,244**	Joseph R. Biden Jr. (D-Del.)	0
Richard C. Shelby (D-Ala.)	**10,226**	David L. Boren (D-Okla.)	0
Ted Stevens (R-Alaska)	**10,197**	Barbara Boxer (D-Calif.)	0
Robert F. Bennett (R-Utah)	**9,900**	Bill Bradley (D-N.J.)	0
John Breaux (D-La.)	**9,900**	Dale Bumpers (D-Ark.)	0
Dirk Kempthorne (R-Idaho)	**9,900**	John H. Chafee (R-R.I.)	0
Phil Gramm (R-Tex.)	**9,900**	Christopher J. Dodd (D-Conn.)	0
Charles E. Grassley (R-Iowa)	**9,900**	Russell Feingold (D-Wis.)	0
Ernest Fl. Hollings (D-S.C.)	**9,900**	Dianne Feinstein (D-Calif.)	0
John McCain (R-Ariz.)	**9,900**	John Glenn (D-Ohio)	0
Frank Murkowski (R-Alaska)	**9,900**	Bob Graham (D-Fla.)	0
Don Nickles (R-Okla.)	**9,900**	Tom Harkin (D-Iowa)	0
James Exon (D-Neb.)	9,900	Daniel K. Inouye (D-Hawaii)	0
Strom Thurmond (R-S.C.)	9,900	James M. Jeffords (R-Vt.)	0
J. Bennett Johnston (D-La.)	**9,508**	Nancy Landon Kassebaum (R-Kan.)	0
Harry M. Reid (D-Nev.)	9,450	Edward M. Kennedy (D-Mass.)	0
Kent Conrad (D-N.D.)	9,450	John F. Kerry (D-Mass.)	0
Malcolm Wallop (R-Wyo.)	**8,764**	Herb Kohl (D-Wis.)	0
Orrin G. Hatch (R-Utah)	**7,950**	Frank R. Lautenberg (D-N.J.)	0
Connie Mack (R-Fla.)	**6,500**	Carl M. Levin (D-Mich.)	0
Trent Lott (R-Miss.)	**6,000**	Joseph I. Lieberman (D-Conn.)	0
Judd Gregg (R-N.H.)	**5,950**	Harlan Mathews (D-Tenn.)	0
Jeff Bingaman (D-N.M.)	5,950	Howard M. Metzenbaum (D-Ohio)	0
Thomas A. Daschle (D-S.D.)	5,950	Barbara A. Mikulski (D-Md.)	0

(Continued)

TABLE 2–3

Continued

Senator	Contributions ($)	Senator	Contributions ($)
Dave Durenberger (R-Minn.)	5,900	George J. Mitchell (D-Maine)	0
Jim Sasser (D-Tenn.)	5,450	Carol Moseley-Brawn (D-Ill.)	0
Richard H. Bryan (D-Nev.)	**4,950**	Daniel Patrick Moynihan (D-N.Y.)	0
Ben Nighthorse Campbell (D-Co.)	**4,950**	Patty Murray (D-Wash.)	0
Thad Cochran (R-Miss.)	**4,950**	Sam Nunn (D-Ga.)	0
Robert J. Dole (R-Kan.)	**4,950**	Claiborne Pell (D-R.I.)	0
Pete V. Domenici (R-N.M.)	**4,950**	David Pryor (D-Ark.)	0
Robert C. Byrd (D-W.Va.)	4,950	Donald W. Riegle Jr. (D-Mich.)	0
Dennis DeConcini (D-Ariz.)	4,950	Charles S. Robb (D-Va.)	0
Richard G. Lugar (R-Ind.)	4,950	Paul S. Sarbanes (D-Md.)	0
William V. Roth Jr. (R-Del.)	4,950	Paul Simon (D-Ill.)	0
William S. Cohen (R-Maine)	4,950	Paul Wellstone (D-Minn.)	0
John C. Danforth (R-Mo.)	4,500	Harris Wofford (D-Pa.)	0

Key: Boldface: Voted against Brady Bill. Lightface: Voted for Brady Bill. Italic: Did not vote.
Source: Adapted from the *Washington Post*, December 8, 1993, p. A21, NRA Money and Handgun Voting.

We can identify two variables in this list: primary offense and sentence length (in months) received by those convicted. You should be able to recognize the first variable, primary offense, as a nominal-level variable. Sentence length is a ratio-level variable. The distance between adjacent values on a ratio scale is presumed to be the same. The difference in sentence length between a sentence of 12 months and one of 18 months (6 months) is the same as that between 24 and 30 months. In addition, there is an absolute zero point—it is possible for some convicted offenders to be sentenced to zero months of incarceration if, for example, they were sentenced to probation or received a fine. With an absolute zero point, division is also meaningful for this variable. We can say, for example, that the ratio of months in prison is over 5 times as great for those convicted of murder than for those convicted of aggravated assault $(258/44 = 5.8)$.

In summary, variables can be classified according to four different levels of measurement: nominal, ordinal, interval, and ratio. In criminology, we work with all four types. Perhaps more importantly, the type of statistical analysis we perform depends, in large part, on the levels of measurement our variables have. This aspect will become more meaningful to you later on. For now, it is important for you to be able to distinguish one level of measurement from another.

Four Types of Measurement

> **Nominal**: Values represent categories or qualities of a case only.

> **Ordinal**: Values not only represent categories, but in addition, values have a logical order.

> **Interval**: In addition to an inherent rank order, a value's relationship to other values is known. There is an equal and constant distance between each value.

> **Ratio**: Not only can distances be determined between values, but these distances are based on a true-zero point.

Qualitative variables always are measured on a nominal scale. Ordinal-level variables fall somewhere in between qualitative and quantitative measurement. They are qualitative in the sense that the difference between the values of an ordinal-level variable cannot be given an absolute numerical value; however, the categories do have a logical rank-order relationship with one another. For the sake of parsimony, we will classify them as quantitative. Interval- and ratio-level variables both are classified as quantitative. You can see from our summary of the four types of measurement that each level of measurement builds upon the previous level(s). Think of it as moving up a quantitative scale; levels of measurement become increasingly quantitative as we move from nominal to ordinal, from ordinal to interval, and from interval to ratio.

Before we leave this section, we would be remiss if we did not tell you that the distinction between interval- and ratio-levels of measurement is at times a very subtle one, particularly in the social sciences. It also is true that the fine distinction between interval- and ratio-level variables has limited practical significance. Most, if not all, of the statistical procedures that can be performed on ratio-level variables also can be confidently performed on variables measured at the interval level. In fact, many statistics books will simply note that a given statistical procedure requires data measured "at least at the interval level," implying that interval- and ratio-level variables are, for all practical purposes, fairly comparable.

INDEPENDENT AND DEPENDENT VARIABLES

In addition to the levels of measurement, researchers frequently distinguish between an **independent variable** and a **dependent variable.** In contrast to the levels of measurement associated with variables, which are governed by distinct numerical properties, defining a variable as independent or dependent relies solely on a researcher's assumptions about the relationship between two or more variables. The designation of a given variable as an independent variable or a dependent variable, therefore, may change according to the nature of the research problem.

> **Independent variables** are the variables thought to affect or in some way contribute to fluctuations or changes in **dependent variables.**

In general, dependent variables in research are those variables that a researcher wishes to explain or predict. Dependent variables are also sometimes referred to as the **outcome variables.** Independent variables are those variables that a researcher assumes will explain or predict the dependent variable(s). Stated another way, a researcher believes that the independent variable will somehow affect change in the dependent variable; the dependent variable, then, *depends* on the independent variable.

For example, think of the crime rate in a given state as a dependent variable. What independent variables could explain this phenomenon? Different people believe that different factors influence the crime rate. Some have argued that poverty is one leading contributor to crime. Higher rates of poverty, they believe, result in a higher rate of crime. In this example, the phenomenon to be explained is the crime rate and the phenomenon doing the explaining is the rate of poverty. Poverty, then, is the independent variable. You also can think of this in cause-and-effect terms. Which factor or condition is thought to be the cause and which is thought to be the effect? In this example, poverty is thought to be at least one of the causes of crime.

Case Study: General Strain Theory and Crime

Let's go through another example from the literature. General strain theory (GST), formulated by Robert Agnew in 1992, contends that delinquency is related to the negative relationships individuals have with others. Agnew postulates three major types of strain (that is, negative relationships) that may occur: others may (1) prevent individuals from achieving their goals (e.g., not getting into college or not getting a desired job); (2) remove or threaten to remove valued stimuli that individuals possess (e.g., the loss of a girl/boyfriend); and (3) present or threaten to present individuals with negatively valued stimuli (e.g., verbal insults or physical assaults).

GST contends that these strains increase the likelihood that individuals will experience a range of negative emotions (e.g., anger) that can, in turn, increase the likelihood of delinquency. In this example, what is the phenomenon we are trying to explain (the dependent variable)? GST is primarily interested in explaining delinquency and other criminal behavior. The independent variable thought to explain or predict delinquency is strain. GST predicts that those individuals with greater levels of strain (independent variable) in their lives will be more likely to engage in delinquency and/or other criminal behavior (dependent variable).

One more example should help solidify in your mind the difference between independent and dependent variables. A very controversial debate today concerns the extent to which there is a relationship between an individual's exposure to media violence (e.g., watching violent movies, playing violent video games) and actual violent behavior. Stated in the form of a research question, "Are individuals who watch violent movies and/or play violent video games more likely to engage in violence themselves compared to individuals who do not witness such violence?" What phenomenon is being explained in this question? This is a bit tricky. In this case, we are interested in predicting or explaining actual violent behavior, so violent behavior is the dependent variable. Violent behavior depicted or portrayed in the media (e.g., movies, video games, television shows) is thought to be the independent variable or the variable that explains or predicts actual violence.

Remember that the distinction between independent and dependent variables is analytic and not static. The designation of a variable as independent or dependent depends completely on the research being conducted and the research questions being addressed. To borrow a cliché, one researcher's independent variable may be another's dependent variable. For example, researchers investigating issues of child abuse sometimes conduct studies to explore those factors that increase the risk of parents abusing their children, such as stress or the loss of a job. In this case, child abuse is the variable being explained; it is the dependent variable. Other researchers, however, may use previous childhood abuse experiences as a predictor of an individual's future abusive behavior as an adult. In this case, the presence of child abuse switches from being the variable we seek to explain (the dependent variable) to being a variable used to explain variation in something else (an independent variable).

WAYS OF PRESENTING VARIABLES

In this section, we examine some of the most commonly used pieces of information you will confront in criminology: counts, rates, ratios, proportions, and percentages. These are simply different ways in which to present, describe, and compare variables.

Counts and Rates

The most elementary way of presenting information is to present the **counts** or **frequencies** of the phenomena you are interested in. A count or frequency is simply the number of times that an event occurs in your data. The number of murder and non-negligent manslaughter victims by age for 1999 are presented below:

Age Group	Number of Victims
Under 14	877
14–17	912
18–24	3,907
25–34	3,889
35–49	3,768
50 and over	1,920

These numbers tell us exactly how many murder victims there were in the U.S. in 1999 within each of the six age groups. For example, we see that there were fewer victims under the age of 14 compared to any other age group. The highest number of murder victims appeared in the young adult category of ages 18–24 (3,907 victims), but a similar number of victims also was reported in the age categories of 25–34 and 35–49. Based on these counts, who is most vulnerable in terms of becoming a murder victim? Do those who are aged 18–24 have a similar risk of becoming the victim of a murder compared to those who are between the ages of 35–49? If we want to make comparisons across different categories, presenting simple counts like this one proves to be problematic because counts and frequencies do not take into account the size of the total at-risk population within each category.

When making comparisons across different categories of a variable (e.g., age group, race/ethnicity group, city, state), the use of counts often will produce misleading results. To accurately make comparisons across units with different population sizes, it is important to control for the size of the populations you are comparing. To do this, it is necessary to calculate the **rate** of an occurrence.

Case Study: The Importance of Rates for Crime Data

Table 2–4 presents the same murder victimization data along with the population counts for each age group. Rates are derived by dividing the observed number of occurrences or phenomena by the total number of occurrences that could, theoretically, have been observed within the population of interest. In addition, rates are usually standardized according to some population base, such as a rate per 1,000 or per 100,000 people:

$$\text{Rate} = \left(\frac{\text{Number in subset}}{\text{Total number}} \right) \times \text{Constant (e.g., 1,000)}$$

For example, to derive the victim rate of murder within age categories, we must first divide the number of actual murder victims observed within an age group by the total number of potential murder victims within that same age group. This latter number would be the entire population for the age group, because, theoretically, everyone in the age group could have become a murder victim. Thus, from the data in Table 2–4, the murder rate for those under the age of 14 would be calculated like this:

$$\frac{\text{Victims under 14}}{\text{Population under 14}} = \frac{877}{54,741,000} = 0.000016 \times 100,000 = 1.6$$

TABLE 2–4

Homicide Victims, Total Population, and Homicide Rates per 100,000 by Age Group, 1999

Age Group	Number of Victims	Total Population	Rate per 100,000
Under 14	877	54,741,000	1.6
14–17	912	15,743,000	5.8
18–24	3,907	26,748,000	14.6
25–34	3,889	37,189,000	10.5
35–49	3,768	64,872,000	5.8
50 and over	1,920	76,768,000	2.5

Source: Homicide data were obtained from Fox & Zawitz, Homicide Trends in the United States, Bureau of Justice Statistics, 2001. Population estimates were obtained for the population in 2000 from the U.S. Census Bureau at http://eire.census.gov/popest/archives/national/nation2/intfile2-1.txt.

Because murder is a relatively rare event compared to other crimes, the FBI usually standardizes murder rates to per 100,000 of the total population. The rate of murder for those under the age of 14 per 100,000 comes to 1.6. When we calculate the murder victimization rates for each age category displayed in Table 2–4, a very different picture of vulnerability to murder emerges. After standardizing for the size of the at-risk population, we see that those between the ages of 18 and 24 have the highest risk of homicide victimization compared to all other age categories. In fact, the risk of victimization for those in this age group is over twice as great as the risk for those who are 35–49 years of age.

Here is another dramatic example that illustrates how a frequency count can mislead you, while a rate will not. In 1999, there were 78,984 serious violent crimes (murder and non-negligent manslaughter, robbery, rape, and aggravated assault) known to police in New York City. In that same year, there were 8,448 serious violent crimes known to police in Washington, DC. You may be thinking, "Well, everyone knows that the 'Big Apple' is a very dangerous place and these numbers prove it!" But before you pack your bags and move to Washington, DC, stop and think about it. Can you compare these raw frequency counts? No. One reason why there are so many more violent crimes in New York City is simply because there are far more people living in this city compared to Washington, DC. In fact, the population of New York City in 2000 was over eight million people (8,008,278), whereas the District of Columbia's population was just over one-half million (572,059).

Now let's take the size of each city's population into account to make our comparisons meaningful. The rate of violent crime per 1,000 people living in New York City would be equal to $(78,984/8,008,278) \times 1,000 = 9.8$. The rate of violent crime for Washington, DC, would be $(8,448/572,059) \times 1,000 = 14.7$. Whoa! It appears that, at least as far as violent crime is concerned, Washington, DC, is a far more dangerous place than New York City. Now where would you feel safer?

A **ratio** is a number that expresses the relationship between two numbers and indicates their relative size. The ratio of x to y is determined by dividing x by y. For example, in our recent example, the violent crime rate for Washington, DC, was 14.7 per 1,000, whereas that for New York City was 9.8 per 1,000. The ratio of violent victimizations in Washington to New York is $14.7/9.8 = 1.5$. This means that for every one violent crime that occurs in New York, there are one and one-half in the District of Columbia. We can state this differently by saying that there were one and one-half times more violent crimes in the District of Columbia than in New York in 1999.

In Table 2–4, the ratio of homicide victimizations committed against youth aged 18–24 to homicide victimizations against those aged 14–17 is $14.6/5.7 = 2.5$. For each murder that occurred against a 14–17 year old in 1999, there were over 2 committed against 18–24 year olds.

Proportions and Percents

Two other common techniques used to present information about variables are **proportions** and **percentages.** These measures are really special kinds of ratios obtained by dividing the number of observations from a subset of your sample by the total number in your sample. In other words, a proportion is obtained by dividing the number of counts for a given event (f) by the total number of events (n). More specifically, proportions are obtained using the following formula:

$$\text{Proportion} = \frac{\text{Number in subset of sample}}{\text{Total number in sample}} = \frac{f}{n}$$

Another name for a proportion is a **relative frequency** because it expresses the number of cases in a given subset (f) relative to the total number of cases (n). In this text, we use the terms proportion and relative frequency interchangeably.

Percentages are obtained simply by multiplying a proportion by 100. This standardizes the numbers to a base of 100, which is generally easier for an audience to interpret.

$$\text{Percent} = \frac{f}{n} \times 100 = \text{Proportion} \times 100$$

Let's go through an example. Using data from the National Crime Victimization Survey (NCVS) for 2000, Table 2–5 presents the number of violent victimizations against males and females by the victim/offender relationship, along with the calculations used to compute proportions and percentages from these numbers. From this table, we can immediately ascertain that female victims of violence are far more likely than male victims to be victimized by known offenders. In fact, only about one out of three violent incidents against females (33 percent) was perpetrated by strangers. Over half of violent victimizations against males (54 percent), however, were perpetrated by strangers. It also can be seen that females are far more likely than males to be victimized by their intimate partners, such as spouses and girl/boyfriends (21 percent versus 3 percent).

UNITS OF ANALYSIS

The final issue we discuss in this chapter is often referred to as the **units of analysis.** The units of analysis are the particular units or objects we have gathered data about and to which we apply our statistical methods. Stated differently, units of analysis refer to what constitutes an observation in our data set. For example, are our observations or data points comprised of persons? Prisons? Court cases? Arrests? States? Nations?

In criminology, we employ many different levels of aggregation for research. Sometimes we use questionnaires or interviews to obtain data from

TABLE 2–5

Victim and Offender Relationship in Violent Crime Victimizations by Gender, NCVS 2000

Relationship with Victim	Number (*f*)	Proportion (*f*/*n*)	Percentage (*f*/*n*) × 100
Male Victims			
Intimate	98,850	.03	3%
Other relative	107,970	.03	3
Friend/acquaintance	1,378,310	.38	38
Stranger	1,945,980	.54	54
Relationship unknown	81,280	.02	2
Total	3,612,390	1.0	100%
Female Victims			
Intimate	556,500	.21	21%
Other relative	231,960	.09	9
Friend/acquaintance	1,002,930	.37	37
Stranger	883,860	.33	33
Relationship unknown	35,090	.01	1
Total	2,710,340	1.0	100%

Source: Rennison, Criminal Victimization 2000, Bureau of Justice Statistics, Table 4. Note: Percentages may not total to 100 percent because of rounding.

individuals. The NCVS, for example, interviews individuals in households from around the United States and asks them about their experiences with criminal victimization. In this research, the units of analysis are the individuals or persons, because the data are obtained from individual respondents.

In other instances, the units of analysis consist of a group or collectivity. Often, these data originally were collected from individuals and then combined or aggregated to form a collectivity. For example, the FBI collects information about the number of crimes reported by individuals to local police departments. However, the FBI aggregates this information, identifying what state the report came from and, in some cases, what city and/or county. Depending on what data you use, then, the units of analysis may be states, counties, or cities.

As an example of data at the city level of analysis, Table 2–6 presents the number of property crime incidents known to police in 1999 for a sample of cities. Each of these relative frequencies (counts) was calculated by using information from local law enforcement agencies in cities (e.g., different precincts within the city) and then aggregating this information to reflect the total number of property crimes within each city. Even though the information is based on smaller levels of aggregation (e.g., at the precinct level), the units of analysis in this case are the cities, not the individual precincts. To

TABLE 2–6

Number of Property Crime Victimizations Known to Police in 1999 for Select Cities with Populations over 25,000

City	Number of Property Crimes
Anchorage, Alaska	11,265
Beverly Hills, California	1,251
Wilmington, Delaware	5,564
Orlando, Florida	21,073
Athens, Georgia	6,351
Chicago, Illinois	173,475
Des Moines, Iowa	10,934
Louisville, Kentucky	13,101
Annapolis, Maryland	2,151
Boston, Massachusetts	27,815
Ann Arbor, Michigan	3,646
Moorhead, Minnesota	817
St. Louis, Missouri	40,100
Omaha, Nebraska	21,632
Las Vegas, Nevada	41,695
Newark, New Jersey	16,282
Albany, New York	6,578
New York City, New York	220,539
Charlotte, North Carolina	45,275
Bowling Green, Ohio	1,058
Tulsa, Oklahoma	23,856
State College, Pennsylvania	1,156
Rapid City, South Dakota	2,998
Houston, Texas	110,257
Virginia Beach, Virginia	15,045
Laramie, Wyoming	747

Source: U.S. Census Bureau, County and City Data Book: 2000, Table C-4.

make sure you have been paying attention, answer this: Is it possible to make meaningful comparisons across these cities to determine which cities have the highest levels of property crime? No. Recall that we must first calculate rates of property crime to reflect the total population at risk within each city before we can make accurate assessments of risk.

SUMMARY

We hope that you now have a better understanding of the differences that exist between the many types of variables and many levels of measurement used in criminological research. It is essential that you understand these concepts so that you can understand their statistical applications.

We have classified the two most general measurement levels of variables as being qualitative or categorical and quantitative or continuous. Henceforth, we will most often refer to these categories as qualitative and quantitative. Be forewarned, however, that we may, at times, interchange them with the terms categorical and continuous. Qualitative variables tell us "what kind" or "what category" a variable's value denotes, and the values of quantitative variables give us numerical information regarding "how much" or the "quantity" a value contains.

Within these two categories, we also have specified the conditions under which a variable can be defined as nominal, ordinal, interval, or ratio level. These levels are hierarchical in nature and can be thought of as a sort of quantitative hierarchy. Values of nominal-level variables tell us the categories or qualities of each case only. Ordinal variables not only represent categories but, in addition, values have a logical order. In addition to an inherent rank order, the distance between categories of an interval-level variable have a known and constant value. And finally, not only can distances be determined between values of a ratio-level variable, but these distances are based on a true-zero point.

We next discussed the difference between what are termed independent and dependent variables. Independent variables are the variables in our research thought to affect some outcome variable; this outcome variable is referred to as the dependent variable.

The remainder of the chapter examined the different ways of presenting, describing, and comparing variables, including simple counts of a phenomenon, referred to as relative frequencies, rates, ratios, proportions, and percentages. Finally, we concluded by providing a discussion of the units of analysis used in research.

KEY TERMS

alphanumeric data
categorical variable
constant
continuous variable
count
dependent variable
distribution
empirical distribution
frequencies
frequency distribution
independent variable
interval-level variable
nominal-level variable

numeric data
ordinal-level variable
outcome variable
percentage
proportion
qualitative variable
quantitative variable
rate
ratio
ratio-level variable
relative frequency
units of analysis
variable

KEY FORMULAS

$$\text{Rate} = \left(\frac{\text{Number in subset}}{\text{Total number}} \right) \times \text{Constant (e.g., } 1{,}000)$$

$$\text{Proportion} = \frac{\text{Number in subset of sample}}{\text{Total number in sample}} = \frac{f}{n}$$

$$\text{Percent} = \frac{f}{n} \times 100 = \text{Proportion} \times 100$$

PRACTICE PROBLEMS

1. For each of the following variables, define the level of measurement as either qualitative or quantitative and, further, as one of the four more distinct measurement levels: nominal, ordinal, interval, or ratio.

    a. A convicted felon's age in years.

    b. A driver's score on the breathalizer exam.

    c. The fine for a parking ticket.

    d. The specific offense code of a felony.

    e. A defendant's gender.

    f. Fines given to industrial companies convicted of violating the Clean Air Act.

2. What distinguishes a variable measured at the ordinal level from a variable measured at the interval level of measurement? What more does the ratio level of measurement add to the ordinal level?

3. In a study examining the effects of arrest on convicted drunk drivers' future drunk-driving behavior, which is the independent and which is the dependent variable?

4. If we are interested in determining the extent to which males and females are more or less afraid to walk outside alone at night, which variable would we designate independent and which variable would be dependent?

5. To compute a rate of violent crime victimizations against 14–18 year olds, what would we use as the numerator and what would we use as the denominator?

6. What are the advantages of rates over frequency counts? Provide an example.

7. From the table below, compute the proportions and percents of the household crime victimizations which were reported to the police by the loss value of the victimization.

	f	Proportion	Percentage
Less than $10	16		
$10–$49	39		
$50–$99	48		
$100–$249	86		
$250–$999	102		
$1,000 or more	251		
	$n = 542$		

8. Jeffrey Benoit and Wallace Kennedy (1992) performed a study of 100 adolescent males incarcerated in a secure residential training school in Florida. They examined the relationship between prior sexual and physical abuse in their childhoods and the type of offense for which they were convicted. What are the units of analysis for this study? What are the independent and dependent variables?

9. To test the existence of a relationship between unemployment and crime, we utilize data from 50 states of the U.S. What are the units of analysis? What would you select to be the independent variable? What would you deem to be the dependent variable?

10. Suppose we are interested in the amount of time police departments take to respond to reports of crime. We track response times for several police departments within large metropolitan areas to see if there are any differences based on the location of the jurisdiction. In this study, what are the units of analysis?

SPSS PRACTICE PROBLEMS

1. Access the file called STATE.XPT. This is a file containing variables measured at the state level. Although we have not yet started to calculate statistics in this book, you can get to know these data by examining each variable's level of measurement. Examine the variable called REGION. Under ANALYZE, ask for DESCRIPTIVE STATISTICS, then FREQUENCIES. After examining the frequency distribution produced by SPSS, describe this variable's level of measurement. What type of information do the values of this variable have?

2. Using the same data set along with the FREQUENCIES command, describe the levels of measurement for the variables MURDER, BURGLARY, POVERTY, and DIVORCE.

3. Access the file called HOMICIDE.XPT. This is a file containing a sample of homicide defendants from a sample of 33 counties, including information on the age of the homicide defendant, the relationship between the homicide defendant and the murder victim, and the outcome of the case (e.g., convicted or not). What are the units of analysis for this data set?

4. Access the file called YOUTH.XPT. This is a file containing a survey of high school youth regarding their attitudes toward delinquency and delinquent behavior. What are the units of analysis for this data set?

5. The variable V77 contains respondent answers to the question, "How wrong do your best friends think it is to steal something worth less than $10?" Under ANALYZE, ask for DESCRIPTIVE STATISTICS, then FREQUENCIES, and then ask for a frequency distribution of this variable. The response categories for this variable are 1—always wrong, 2—usually wrong, 3—sometimes wrong, 4—seldom wrong, 5—never wrong. What level of measurement does this variable have?

6. The variable V1 contains information on the respondent's gender. Under ANALYZE, ask for DESCRIPTIVE STATISTICS, then FREQUENCIES, and then ask for a frequency distribution of this variable. What level of measurement does this variable have?

Understanding Data Distributions
Tabular and Graphical Techniques

The cure for boredom is curiosity. There is no cure for curiosity.

—DOROTHY PARKER

Often the most effective way to describe, explore, and summarize a set of numbers—even a large set—is to look at pictures of those numbers.

—EDWARD TUFTE

One of the first things that you need to do when you are ready to conduct a statistical analysis is to carefully examine your data. One of the best ways to do this is to list all of the values of a variable and present descriptive information for each value, such as its frequency, relative frequency (proportion), and percentages. It is also helpful to graph your variable in order to examine the frequency of each value and the overall shape of the distribution. There are various ways to present this descriptive information about your variable in tabular and graphical form. There are specific descriptive statistics and graphical techniques you can use depending upon the level of measurement of your variable. In addition, data in criminology and criminal justice often are presented over a long period of time. It is a good idea, therefore, to have in your statistical toolbox ways to display data in time plots. This chapter covers many of the most useful ways of displaying your qualitative and quantitative data. You will learn how to construct frequency distributions with other descriptive information for both qualitative and quantitative data. You also will learn ways to graph qualitative data (pie charts and bar charts) and quantitative data (histograms and various line charts). A key objective is to learn the different descriptive statistics and graphs that are appropriate at different levels of measurement. Another objective is to learn that preparing and communicating to others about the characteristics of your data is as much art as it is science. The key question you have to ask when constructing tables and graphs from your data is, "Is this effectively communicating the important characteristics of these variables?"

INTRODUCTION

The first step, and one of the most important, in any statistical analysis is having a clear understanding of the general characteristics or appearance of your data. In statistics, we call this knowing the distribution of your data. One theme that we will be emphasizing throughout this text is that, no matter how simple or complex your statistical analysis is, there is no substitute for first knowing the shape and characteristics of your data—the number of different values each variable has, the frequency or number of cases for each value, whether your observations "bunch up" at a few values of a variable or are more evenly distributed across the different values. All this is valuable information and should be known *before* you do any additional statistical analyses.

The purpose of this chapter is to provide you with some tabular and graphical tools for examining and describing the characteristics and patterns of your data. A tabular display of your data can show you exactly how many values your variable has, how many cases or observations fall into each value (and the percent or proportion of the total that the frequency represents), how extreme your values are, and whether the extent to which the cases "bunch up" or are more evenly spread across the different values. The graphical presentation of the distribution of a variable can show you in a picture form much of the same information, though usually with much less detail. One of the advantages of a graphical display of your data over a tabular presentation, however, is that it immediately and vividly shows you and a reader what your data look like. What a graphical display of your data may lack in precision is made up for in its clarity. In statistics, then, a picture is frequently worth "a thousand words" or, more accurately in this case, a thousand numbers. With almost one glance at a graphical presentation of data, some very important features of your data can be discerned. As you will see, rather than employing only a tabular or a graphical analysis of your data we strongly recommend using both.

Case Study: The Defense of John Gotti

One very vivid "real life" example of the advantage of the graphical display of data can be taken from the trial of Mr. John Gotti. In the 1980s, Mr. Gotti was allegedly the boss or "godfather" of the Gambino family, a very powerful New York mafia crime organization. Mr. Gotti was known as the "Dapper Don" because of his apparent love of expensive clothes, particularly Armani suits. "Don" is the term used for the head of mafia crime families, such as the famous fictional character Don Corrleone portrayed by the actor Marlon Brando in the movie *The Godfather.* For years Mr. Gotti was the subject of intense law enforcement surveillance in an attempt to bring him to trial. The police believed that Mr. Gotti was involved in a wide variety of illegal activities, including murder, drug dealing, prostitution, gambling, and bribery. In 1987, Gotti was finally arrested and tried for criminal racketeering and other charges. At his trial the prosecution used a variety of witnesses against Mr. Gotti, many of whom were themselves in the crime business and members of the Gotti crime family. In other words, the prosecution witnesses, who were being used to testify against John Gotti, were comprised of murderers, thieves, drug sellers, bank robbers, tax evaders, and extortionists.

The defense counsel for Mr. Gotti, Bruce Cutler, wanted to tell the jury that these "witnesses" for the prosecution were not credible and should not be believed. Cutler needed to demonstrate to the members of the jury that these witnesses were so involved in crime themselves that they would not hesitate, and might even find some perverse pleasure, in lying to a jury. How was he to do this? One way would be for him to talk to the jury and tell them directly about the various convictions and arrests of each prosecution witness and let the jurors draw their own conclusions about how extensive and serious the witnesses' criminal histories were. Instead of using his words to make his point, however, Mr. Cutler gave them a simple table. This table, shown for you in Table 3–1, consisted of a grid of two pieces of information. The columns of the table consisted of the names of each of the seven prosecution witnesses against Mr. Gotti. The rows of the table consisted of a list of crimes, 27 in all, ranging from murder to pistol-whipping a priest to reckless endangerment. If a given prosecution witness was convicted of committing one of the 27 crimes, an "X" was placed on the table. What all the words used by defense counsel Cutler could not easily reveal, this graph did. There are "Xs" covering the graph, indicating the many criminal offenses by the prosecution witnesses. Clearly, the jury could not help but get the message that these witnesses were not "choir boys" but had extensive and serious criminal histories of their own and should not be believed.

TABLE 3–1

Crimes Committed by Federal Witnesses in the Trial of John Gotti

Crime	Witness						
	Cardinale	Lofaro	Maloney	Polisi	Senatore	Foronjy	Curro
Murder	X	X					
Attempted murder		X	X				
Heroin possession and sale	X	X		X			X
Cocaine possession and sale	X		X	X			
Marijuana possession and sale							X
Gambling business		X		X		X	
Armed robberies	X		X	X	X		X
Loansharking		X		X			
Kidnapping			X	X			
Extortion			X	X			
Assault	X		X	X			X
Possession of dangerous weapon	X	X	X	X	X		X
Perjury		X				X	
Counterfeiting					X	X	
Bank robbery			X	X			
Armed hijacking				X	X		
Stolen financial documents			X	X	X		
Tax evasion				X		X	
Burglaries	X	X		X	X		
Bribery		X		X			
Theft (auto, money, or other)			X	X	X	X	X
Bail jumping and escape			X	X			
Insurance frauds					X	X	
Forgeries				X	X		
Pistol-whipping a priest	X						
Sexual assault on minor							X
Reckless endangerment							X

Source: Chart supplied by Cunsel, Bruce Cutler, and Susan G. Kellman. Reprinted with permission from Edward Tufte, *Envisioning Information,* Cheshire, CN: Graphics Press

GOTTI IS ACQUITTED BY A FEDERAL JURY IN CONSPIRACY CASE

NEW CHARGES ARE LIKELY

Verdict is the First Setback in Recent Government Drive Against Mafia Leaders

---

By LEONARD BUDER

John Gotti was acquitted of Federal racketeering and conspiracy charges yesterday in the Government's first major setback in its recent assault on organized crime.

Mr. Gotti, who the Government says is the leader of the nation's most powerful Mafia family, and six co-defendants were found not guilty of charges they took part in a criminal enterprise. They were accused of carrying out illegal gambling and loan-sharking operations, armed hijackings and at least two murders over an 18-year period.

Despite yesterday's verdict, Federal investigators said the 46-year-old Mr. Gotti might face indictment on new charges as head of the Gambino crime family. "I can't comment but I won't deny it," said Thomas L. Sheer, head of the Federal Bureau of Investigation in New York, when asked if the F.B.I. was building up another case against Mr. Gotti.

'We'll Be Starting Again'

"They'll be ready to frame us again in two weeks," Mr. Gotti told a reporter before leaving the Brooklyn courthouse in a gray Cadillac that was waiting for him. "In three weeks we'll be starting again, just watch."

Until yesterday, Federal prosecutors in the Southern and Eastern Districts of New York had recorded a string of successes in major organized-crime cases.

Within the last six months, the heads of the city's four other Mafia families have been convicted after trials in Manhattan and Brooklyn. They, like Mr. Gotti and his co-defendants, had been charged under the Federal Racketeer Influenced and Corrupt Organizations Act, or RICO.

Key Witnesses Were Criminals

"Obviously they perceived there was something wrong with the evidence," said Andrew J. Maloney, the United States Attorney in Brooklyn, referring to the jury.

Many of the Government's key witnesses were criminals who testified for the prosecution under grants of immunity or in return for payments and other benefits.

The last piece of evidence requested by the jury for re-examination was a chart introduced by the defense that showed the criminal backgrounds of seven prosecution witnesses. It listed 69 crimes, including murder, drug possession and sales and kidnapping.

Mr. Gotti's lawyer, Bruce Cutler, said the jury showed "courage" because "it's not easy to say no to a Federal prosecutor." He said the jury had not been impressed with the testimony of "paid Government informants who lie, who use drugs, who kill people."

The verdict, which came on the seventh day of jury deliberations after a trial that lasted almost seven months, surprised many in the packed courtroom. Friends of the defendants cheered and applauded; the Government prosecutors, Diane F. Giacalone and John Gleeson, looked glum.

Mr. Gotti, who has been dubbed "Dapper Don" because of his expensive attire and impeccable grooming, and his co-defendants hugged and kissed each other and their lawyers.

Then they stood and applauded as the 12 members of the jury — whose identities had been kept secret to prevent possible tampering — left the room escorted by Federal marshals....

The New York Times

John Gotti

Figure 3–1
Source: The *New York Times*, March 14, 1987, p. 1. Reprinted by permission from Edward R. Tufte, *Envisioning Information*, Cheshire, CN: Graphics Press.

As the *New York Times* article about the case in Figure 3–1 reveals, the graph seems to have made an impression on Gotti's jury. This was the last piece of evidence they asked to re-examine before acquitting him of the charges against him. To make his point about the shady character of the witnesses who were testifying against his client, Mr. Cutler effectively used a very simple picture or graph. One very important lesson to take from the Gotti case is that the presentation of data does not always have to be a lot of numbers and complicated calculations; sometimes a very simple picture or graphical presentation of the data is most effective in communicating the point you wish to make.

There are, then, two reasons for looking at your data with tables and graphs. First, the display of your data either in tabular or graphical form is often a simple yet very effective way to communicate a point you wish to make about those data. Second, as we argued at the beginning of this chapter, tabular and graphical displays are a good way for *you* to understand the characteristics and appearance of your data. In addition to helping others understand your data, then, the creation and examination of tables and graphs will help you recognize and appreciate the important features of your data. In fact, we will argue throughout this text that a careful review of your data, including displays of simple tables, graphs, and charts, should always be done *before* moving on to more complicated statistical analyses. As is true in many other instances in life, the best course of action for the statistical analyst in criminology and criminal justice is to proceed cautiously—"slow and steady wins the race."

In the last chapter we described two major types of data, qualitative and quantitative. We argued there that it was important to know and understand the difference between these two types of data since different types of data call for different statistical techniques. We see this point in operation in this chapter. The kind of numerical operations and graphical presentations you may appropriately use to display a variable depends upon whether the variable is qualitative or quantitative. We will treat nominal-level variables as qualitative, and ordinal and interval/ratio-level variables as quantitative.

THE TABULAR AND GRAPHICAL DISPLAY OF QUALITATIVE DATA

Recall from the previous chapter that qualitative variables, those measured at the nominal level, capture differences in kind among the values only. That is, the values of a nominal-level variable differ in quality and not quantity, which is why they are referred to as qualitative data. Unlike quantitative variables, whose values differ in degree, therefore, nominal variables differ only in kind. The simplest way to first show a nominal-level variable is to report some descriptive information about the variable's values, such as the frequency of each value and the percent or proportion of the total for each value. This is done in a descriptive table of the variable.

An Analysis of Hate Crimes Using Tables

In Table 3–2 we report descriptive information for a nominal-level variable, the types of hate crime incidents reported by law enforcement agencies in the year 2000. Hate crimes are criminal acts that are perpetrated in part or entirely by personal prejudice or animosity against others because of their race, religion, sexual preference, or ethnicity or national background, or because of some real or perceived disability.

In the *Hate Crimes Statistics Act of 1990,* the Congress of the United States required the collection of nationwide information about criminal acts that were motivated by hate or prejudice. To comply with this act, the Federal Bureau of Investigation (FBI) began to compile data about crimes across the United States that were motivated by racial, religious, sexual, ethnic/national origin, or disability hatred. This information is collected in a yearly report, *Hate Crime Statistics.* As part of their reporting to the FBI's Uniform Crime Reporting Program, federal, state, and local law enforcement agencies report crimes they have determined as being motivated by these different forms of hate or bias.

Table 3–2 provides four pieces of information for this nominal-level variable—the different values of the variable "hate crime," the frequency of each value for the variable, the relative frequency or the proportion of the total number of cases for each value, and the percent of the total for each value. Recall from the previous chapter that a frequency (f) is just a count of the number of times each value appears or occurs, the proportion is a relative frequency found by dividing the frequency of each value by the total number of values or observations (Proportion $= f/N$), and the percent is found by multiplying the proportion by 100 (Percent $= f/N \times 100$). This tabular presentation of descriptive data, then, describes a variable by displaying the frequency, proportion, and percent for each of its values.

According to Table 3–2, in the year 2000 there were a total of 8,019 reported incidents of single-bias hate crimes motivated by racial, religious, sexual, or ethnic/national origin bias. A single-bias hate crime is one that is motivated by one source of bias (bias against someone's religion or race, but not both). Table 3–2 breaks these 8,019 incidents down by the specific type or source of the bias (the different values of the variable "hate crime"). The qualitative variable we are interested in is "hate crime," which takes on four different nominal-level values: racial hatred, religious hatred, sexual hatred, and hatred due to the victim's race/national origin. You should be able to determine that this is a nominal or qualitative variable because these values differ only in kind or quality. We can say only that one value of hate crime is simply different from another value, not that one is "more" or "less" of a hate crime than the other. For example, a racially motivated hate crime differs from a sexually motivated hate crime but is not "more" of a hate crime or more hateful than another type of hate crime. The distinction among the different values of hate crimes, then, is simply qualitative.

We can see from this table that of the 8,019 hate crimes that were reported by law enforcement agencies in 2000, 4,337 of them were motivated by racial hatred. In other words, there was a frequency of 4,337 incidents of racially motivated hate crimes. This is the frequency or count of racial hate crimes for

TABLE 3–2

Type of Hate Crime Incident Reported to Police in 2000

Type of Hate	f	Proportion	Percent
Racial	4,337	.5408	54.08%
Religious	1,472	.1836	18.36
Sexual orientation	1,299	.1620	16.20
Ethnicity/national origin	911	.1136	11.36
Total	8,019	1.000	100.00

Source: *Hate Crimes Statistics—2000.* Federal Bureau of Investigation, Uniform Crime Reporting Program.

that year. By dividing this frequency by 8,019 (4,337/8,019), the total number of hate crime incidents, we conclude that racially motivated hate crimes constituted .5408 of the total number of hate crime incidents that year, or just over one-half. Multiplying this by 100 to obtain the percent, we see that racial hate crimes comprised 54.08 percent of the total number of hate crimes in 2000.

Looking at Table 3–2, we can see that 1,472 hate crimes were motivated by religious bias. This is the frequency of religiously motivated hate crimes committed in the year 2000, and they comprised .1836 of the total, or 18.36 percent. A total of 1,299 hate crimes were motivated by hatred against another's sexual preference, and this constituted .1620 of the total number of hate crimes, or 16.20 percent. Finally, the frequency of hate crimes motivated by bias against the victim's ethnicity or national origin was 911, with a proportion of .1136, or 11.36 percent of the total number of hate crimes. In sum, this descriptive table informs us that just over one-half of the reported hate crimes were motivated by racial prejudice, with approximately equal percentages of religious and sexual hate crimes, and about 10 percent motivated by ethnic or national bias. Finally, you should notice that the sum of the frequency column will sum to the total number of observations (8,019 hate crimes), the column of proportions will sum to 1.0 (unless there is some rounding error), and the column of percents will sum to 100.0 (again, unless there is some rounding error).

Pie Charts and Bar Charts

While this tabular presentation of frequency, proportion, and percentage information is helpful in seeing the makeup of the different sources of hate crimes, we would now like to provide a graphical representation of this descriptive data, which may be even more illustrative. When we have qualitative data, such as we have here with "hate crimes," we can graphically present the frequency, proportion, and percentage data using a pie chart or a bar chart. A **pie chart** is exactly what the term implies. It consists of a round "pie" shape divided into parts or "slices"

> The **pie chart** and the **bar chart** are graphical ways to display nominal- or ordinal-level variables. These charts can include frequencies, proportions, or percentages.

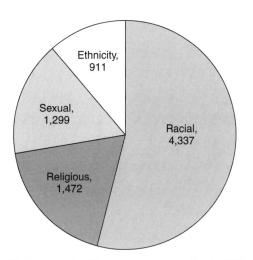

Figure 3–2   Type of hate crime incident reported to police in 2000—frequency data

where each "slice" represents each separate value of the variable. The size of each slice of the pie is proportionate to the frequency (or proportion/percentage of the total) for each value; that is, the greater the contribution that a given value makes to the total number of observations, the larger the slice of the pie for that value. Figure 3–2 shows what a pie chart would look like for the frequency distribution reported in Table 3–2.

This pie chart of the frequency data does a nice job of clearly showing the characteristics of the hate crime data. First, it reports the frequency of each value as did Table 3–2. It shows that there were 4,337 racially motivated hate crimes reported in 2000, 1,472 crimes motivated by religious hatred, 1,299 crimes motivated by sexual bias, and 911 hate crimes committed because of the victim's ethnicity or national origin. In addition, the size of each pie slice vividly shows the relative contribution of each value to the total number of observations. The relative size of the slice for racial crimes clearly indicates that more than one-half of the hate crimes reported by the police in 2000 were racially motivated, about an equal proportion were motivated by either religious or sexual prejudice, and the smallest share of the hate crimes was motivated by ethnicity/national origin bias.

Figure 3–3 provides the same frequency data in the form of a pie chart but adds the percentage for each value along with the frequency count. There was no reason why we could not have reported the proportion rather than the percent in Figure 3–3. It is simply more conventional to report percentages rather than proportions since they make more intuitive sense to most people.

We do, however, think that it is important to report both the frequency for each value in a pie chart and its corresponding percentage (or proportion)

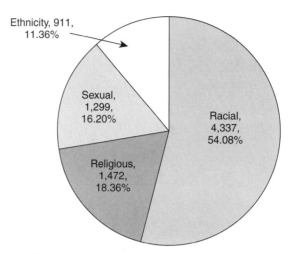

Figure 3–3   Type of hate crime incident reported to police in 2000 (frequency and percentage data)

as we have done in Figure 3–3. It is useful to report the frequencies so that the reader can easily see how many cases there are for a given value; however, comparing percentages or proportions across different values is often more meaningful than comparing raw frequency counts. You should also notice that we reported the percentages with two decimal places, just as we did in Table 3–2.

Let's try another example. You will notice in Table 3–2 that there were 1,299 hate crimes reported in 2000 where the motivation was bias against the victim's sexual orientation. In Table 3–3 we provide another tabular presentation of descriptive data. In this table, we break the 1,299 sexual orientation hate crimes down into five more specific subtypes: antimale homosexual, antifemale homosexual, antihomosexual, antiheterosexual, and antibisexual. As in Table 3–2, we report the raw frequencies, the proportion of each value, and the percent of the total for each value. As you can see, the lion's share of sex-based hate crimes were directed at male homosexuals, 896 of the 1,299, or almost 70 percent. Of the remainder, 179 sexually motivated hate crimes were directed against female homosexuals (about 14 percent), 182 or 14 percent of the total were directed against homosexuals in general (no clear target), 22 (less than 2 percent) of the crimes were directed against heterosexuals, and 20 of the total were directed against bisexuals (less than 2 percent of the total). While almost 7 in 10 sexually motivated hate crimes were directed against male homosexuals, only a little more than 1 in 10 were against female homosexuals. The sum of the frequency column again shows the total number of hate crimes based on bias against the victim's sexual orientation (1,299).

We provide a pie chart of these frequency and percent data in Figure 3–4. You can see quite clearly from the graphical data, and we think more clearly

TABLE 3–3

Hate Crime Incidents Reported to Police in 2000 That Were Motivated by Bias against the Victim's Sexual Orientation

Type of Hate	*f*	Proportion	Percent
Antimale Homosexual	896	.6898	68.98
Antifemale Homosexual	179	.1378	13.78
Antihomosexual	182	.1401	14.01
Antiheterosexual	22	.0169	1.69
Antibisexual	20	.0154	1.54
Total	1,299	1.000	100.00%

Source: *Hate Crimes Statistics—2000.* Federal Bureau of Investigation, Uniform Crime Reporting Program.

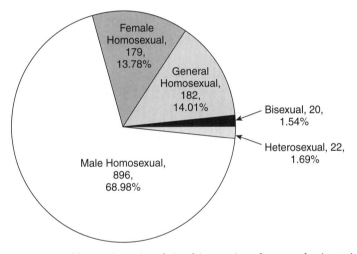

Figure 3–4   Reported hate crimes involving bias against the sexual orientation of the victim—incidents reported to the police in 2000

than from the tabular data alone provided in Table 3–3, that most of the hate crimes committed that involved a sexual orientation motivation were directed against male homosexuals. This is the largest slice of the pie, reflecting how disproportionate this type of sexually motivated hate crime is compared with the others, with smaller and approximately equal shares contributed by antifemale and general antihomosexual hatred, and a very small proportion of antiheterosexual and antibisexual hate crimes.

We will go through one final example of tabular data with a corresponding pie chart. Table 3–2 reports that there were 1,472 hate crime incidents in the year 2000 that were motivated by religious hatred. Table 3–4 focuses on these religiously motivated hate crimes and breaks them down into more

TABLE 3–4

Hate Crime Incidents Reported to Police in 2000 That Were Motivated by Bias against the Victim's Religion

Type of Religious Hate	f	Proportion	Percent
Anti-Jewish	1,109	.7534	75.34%
Anti-Catholic	56	.0380	3.80
Anti-Protestant	59	.0401	4.01
Anti-Islamic	28	.0190	1.90
Anti-other-religions	172	.1168	11.68
Anti-multireligious group	44	.0299	2.99
Anti-agnostic/atheist	4	.0027	.27
Total	1,472	.9999*	99.99%*

*Does not sum to 1.0 or 100 percent due to rounding.
Source: *Hate Crimes Statistics—2000.* Federal Bureau of Investigation, Uniform Crime Reporting Program.

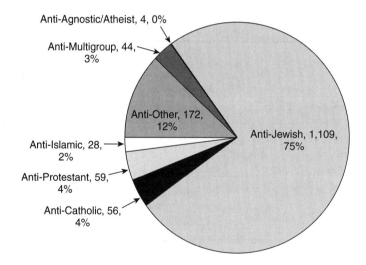

Figure 3–5   Antireligious hate crime incidents reported to the police in 2000—by type of antireligious sentiment

specific subtypes. Table 3–4 presents a tabular presentation of descriptive data for these religiously motivated hate crimes. Most of these incidents of religious hate crimes were directed against victims who were of the Jewish faith (*f* = 1,109, or 75 percent). There was no other faith that was subject to as much hate crime as the Jewish faith. These incidents greatly surpassed that for anti-Catholic (*f* = 56, or 3.80 percent), anti-Protestant (*f* = 59, or 4.01 percent), and anti-Islamic hate crimes (*f* = 28, 1.90 percent). We next take these frequency and percentage data and create a pie chart for graphical illustration, shown in Figure 3–5. Unlike the previous pie charts, this one appears a bit cluttered,

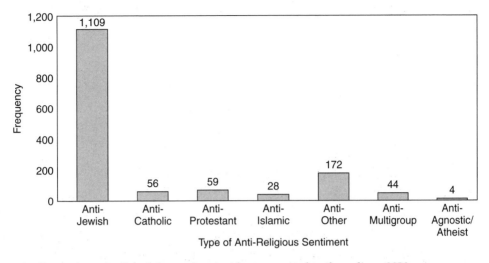

Figure 3–6 Frequency of religious hate crime incidents reported to the police—2000

and while it can easily be seen that the vast majority of religiously motivated hate crimes are anti-Jewish, the other details seem a little lost.

When your pie chart of qualitative data looks a little messy and you think you are losing your ability to communicate the characteristics of your data, a second graphical form for the descriptive data we have been showing (frequency count, proportion, and percent) is the **bar chart.** Like the pie chart, the bar chart is appropriate only for the graphical display of qualitative data. A bar chart represents the frequencies, proportions, or percentages of each value by a vertical or horizontal bar. The width of the bar is equal to 1.0, while the height (or length for a horizontal bar) is equal to the value's frequency, proportion, or percent. By having the width of the bar equal to 1.0 and the height (or length) equal to the value's frequency (or proportion or percent), the total area of a bar in a bar chart corresponds to the area represented by the frequency (or proportion or percent) of that value.

Figure 3–6 shows a bar chart for the frequency data reported in Table 3–4. This is a vertical bar chart because the variable's different values are represented along the x (horizontal) axis while the frequency scale is represented along the y (vertical) axis. Notice that the height of each bar can be followed to the y axis to determine the frequency count, but in this bar chart the frequencies are provided above each bar for easy reading. Notice also that the bars in a bar chart are not connected to each other but are separated along the x axis by a space or gap. This is intentional. It reminds us that the measurement for this variable is not continuous, with one value moving meaningfully along the continuum of measurement to the next, but is discrete and qualitative. Anti-Catholic sentiment in a hate crime is not "more" of a hate crime than anti-Jewish sentiment, it is simply different. We could just as easily and meaningfully have these bars switched in our table with anti-Catholic sentiment coming before anti-Jewish sentiment. The placements of the values of this and other qualitative variables are simply distinctions in quality or kind and their location along the x axis is arbitrary. The gaps between the bars of a bar chart, then, are just another reminder that these values are qualitative and not quantitative distinctions.

The bar chart in Figure 3–6 is far more effective in communicating the distribution of these data than the pie chart because it appears less cluttered. We could just as easily have created a bar chart with the proportion data in Table 3–4 or the percent data. Both pie and bar charts can be used for the graphical display of frequency counts, proportions, or percents (or combinations of the three).

One of the advantages of a bar chart over a pie chart for graphing qualitative data is that you can create overlapping or double bar charts that employ more than one variable. Table 3–5 reports the percent of arrests for violent, property, and total index offenses for both males and females for the year 2000. This is a pretty simple tabular presentation of descriptive data since it reports only percents and not raw frequencies or proportions, but a graph may help illustrate its features. The table shows that in the year 2000 males represented more than 80 percent of the arrests for violent crimes in the United States, 70 percent of the property crimes, and almost three-quarters of the total index arrests.

These data are shown in a vertical bar chart in Figure 3–7. Notice that in this figure we are graphing the percent of the total for each value and not its frequency count. As you can see from this figure, the height of each bar corresponds to the percent for that value. By tracing the height of each bar over to the y axis you can determine the approximate percent. Notice, for example, by following the height of the bar for violent crimes that over 80 percent of the arrests for violent index crimes involved men, and approximately 70 percent of the arrests for both property index crimes and all index crimes were men. Figure 3–8 provides the identical graph in the form of a horizontal bar chart. The only difference between the vertical and the horizontal bar chart is that in the latter the percent for each value is placed on the x (horizontal) axis. Now it is the length of each bar that reflects the relative percentage (or frequency, if it is a frequency bar chart) of each value. You can create either vertical (column) bar charts or horizontal (row) bar charts with your qualitative data; it just depends on what you think looks better.

TABLE 3–5

Percent of Arrests for Violent, Property, and Total Index Crime, by Gender—2000

Crime Type	Male (%)	Female (%)
Violent	82.6%	17.4%
Property	70.1	29.9
Total Index	73.6%	26.4%

Source: *Crime in the United States—2000.* Federal Bureau of Investigation, Uniform Crime Reports, Table 42.

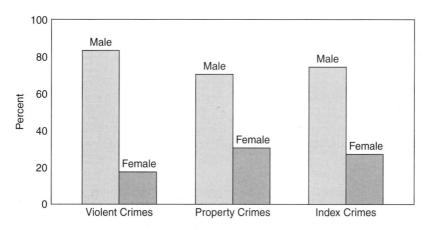

Figure 3–7 Percent of total arrests for violent, property, and index offenses by gender—2000

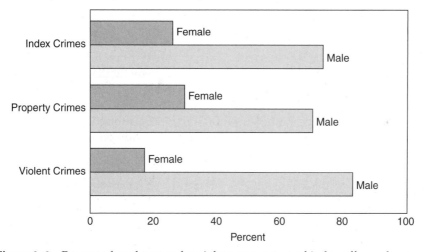

Figure 3–8 Percent of total arrests for violent, property, and index offenses by gender—2000

THE TABULAR AND GRAPHICAL DISPLAY OF QUANTITATIVE DATA

Ungrouped Distributions

Quantitative data are data measured at the ordinal, interval, or ratio level. The values of a quantitative variable express how much of the variable exists. As we learned in the previous chapter, ordinal-level quantitative variables consist of rank-ordered categories, while interval/ and ratio-level variables have values that consist of equidistant intervals that are continuous with either an arbitrary zero (interval scales) or an absolute zero (ratio scales). As with nominal-level data, we can present descriptive information for quantitative data in both tabular and graphic form.

Case Study: Police Response Time   We start with a simple example consisting of ratio-level data. Table 3–6 shows the response times to a sample of fifty 911 (request for police service) calls made to a local police department (rounded to the nearest minute). There is no ordering to these data; they simply appear in the order in which they occurred in the dispatcher's log sheet. As presented in the table, these data do not provide much information about these response times; they are too disorganized and chaotic. This table is simply too hard to read and comprehend. For example, it is difficult to determine the quickest and slowest response times and we cannot easily determine if the data tend to cluster around some typical response time. What we would like to do is to impose some order on these data so our reader (and ourselves) can understand and know exactly what they suggest about police response times. The easiest way to organize these data is to create a table that includes descriptive information, such as the frequency of each value, its proportion, and its percent—just as we did with the qualitative data in the previous section. With quantitative data, however, we can provide even more information.

We begin the process of describing these data by first listing all values in the data in some order, either from lowest to highest (ascending order) or from highest to lowest (descending order). We list all values of the variable in ascending order in the first column of Table 3–7. In the second column we then report the frequency of each value (f), which is a count of the number of times each response time or value occurs in the data. In this case each value represents the time it took the police to respond to a 911 call for police assistance. Table 3–7 is referred to as an **ungrouped frequency distribution.** It is an ungrouped distribution because we have recorded the entire range of scores for the variable in the frequency column—all response times from the lowest of 1 minute to the highest of 11 minutes and all times in between appear in the frequency distribution. An ungrouped

> **>** An **ungrouped frequency distribution** is a distribution that portrays every value or score of a variable and its corresponding frequency.

TABLE 3–6

Hypothetical Response Times of the Police to a 911 Call (in minutes)

7	4	3	1	3	2	6	10	7	2
5	3	5	9	2	4	9	3	1	4
4	4	6	6	5	6	11	5	3	8
3	2	1	4	8	5	6	3	3	2
1	2	6	7	5	3	1	4	4	6

frequency distribution, therefore, lists all of the values of the variable that exist in the data along with how many times each value occurs.

We can see from Table 3–7 that the fastest response time to a 911 call was within 1 minute, and this happened 5 out of 50 times. The slowest police response time was 11 minutes, which happened only once. You will notice from the frequency column that the response times appear to cluster in the 2 to 6 minute range. It seems that most often the police responded to a 911 call somewhere between 2 and 6 minutes. There were only a handful of very quick response times (1 minute or less), and there were only a few that were 7 minutes or longer, with a diminished frequency at the longest response times. Finally, you also can see that the sum of the frequency column equals the number of scores or observations ($\Sigma f = N$). In these data, there were 50 recorded response times to 911 calls. As you can see, the creation of a frequency distribution for these data was a relatively simple task, and yet this presentation provides more useful information, due to its clarity and organization. A simple frequency distribution goes a long way in helping you understand and communicate the important features of a quantitative variable.

In addition to a frequency distribution, Table 3–7 provides in the third column something called a **cumulative frequency distribution** (*cf*). The cumulative frequency distribution indicates how many scores were less (or more) than a given score. You may have noticed that we did not report cumulative frequencies in the table from the previous section of this chapter using qualitative data (Table 3–2). This was because the values of qualitative data only have distinctions of kind and not degree. We cannot, therefore, speak of "more than" or "less than" with qualitative data.

TABLE 3–7

Descriptive Information for 50 Police Response Times

Minutes	*f*	*cf*	*p*	*cp*	%	*c*%
1	5	5	.10	.10	10%	10%
2	6	11	.12	.22	12	22
3	9	20	.18	.40	18	40
4	8	28	.16	.56	16	56
5	6	34	.12	.68	12	68
6	7	41	.14	.82	14	82
7	3	44	.06	.88	6	88
8	2	46	.04	.92	4	92
9	2	48	.04	.96	4	96
10	1	49	.02	.98	2	98
11	1	50	.02	1.00	2	100%
Total	50		1.00		100%	

The column of cumulative frequencies reported in Table 3–7 is created in the following manner. In the first entry of the cumulative frequency column, enter the frequency for the first value. In this example, the first entry is 5, indicating that there were five instances where the police responded to a 911 call within 1 minute. Notice that by subtracting this frequency of 5 from our total number of observations (50) we could also observe that there were 45 instances where the police took more than 1 minute in responding to a call. To continue with the cumulative frequency column, we then add the frequency for the next value (2 minutes) to the first frequency. The cumulative frequency becomes 11 for the second entry in the cumulative frequency column. This tells us that there were 11 times when the police responded to a 911 call in 2 minutes or less (the five times they responded to a call in 1 minute or under and the six times they responded between 1 and 2 minutes). We then proceed to the next value, where there were 9 instances when the police responded between 2 and 3 minutes. We add this to the cumulative frequency accumulated so far, and the entry in the cumulative frequency column is 20 (5 + 6 + 9), indicating that the police responded to a 911 call within 3 minutes 20 times. We continue summing the frequencies for each value in succession. When we get to the last value of 11 minutes, the cumulative frequency is 50, telling us that the police responded to a 911 call in 11 minutes or less all 50 times. This should make intuitive sense since no call was responded to in more than 11 minutes. The final entry in a cumulative frequency column should always equal the total number of observations, or N.

Cumulative frequencies tell us how many observations were at or less than a given value (and by implication, how many observations were more than a given value). For example, Table 3–7 shows that 28 of the 50 calls for police assistance (more than one-half) were responded to in 4 minutes or less. Therefore, slightly less than one-half took more than 4 minutes to respond. We also know that 44 of the 50 calls were responded to in seven minutes or less. This implies that six calls were responded to in more than 7 minutes.

Table 3–7 also reports other descriptive information about the variable "police response time," including the familiar column of proportions and percents. Recall that a proportion is just a relative frequency that indicates the frequency of a given value relative to the total number of cases and is calculated as ($p = f/N$). We can determine from Table 3–7 that .10 of the response times were within 1 minute, .18 of them were responded to within 2 to 3 minutes, and .06 of them took seven minutes to respond to. The column next to the proportion column consists of the **cumulative proportions** (cp). These cumulative proportions are calculated in the same manner as the cumulative frequencies.

Begin with the proportion of the first value, .10, which indicates that .10 (about 1 in 10) of the 911 calls were responded to in 1 minute or less. Since .12 of the calls were responded to within 1 to 2 minutes, we add this to the .10 and note that .22 (the second entry in the cp column) of the calls were responded to in 2 minutes or less. We continue summing the proportions for each successive value until we reach the last value of 11 minutes. Here we see that 1.0 or all of the 911 calls were responded to within 11 minutes. The last entry in a column of cumulative proportions should be 1.0 (or close to that in the presence of rounding error). Cumulative proportions are useful in giving us the proportion of cases at a given value or less. For example, we can quickly see from Table 3–7 that slightly more than one-half (.56) of the 911 calls were responded to within 4 minutes, and more than 9 out of 10 (.92) were within 8 minutes (implying that only .08 (or $1 - .92$) of the 911 calls took more than 8 minutes to respond to).

The next column of numbers in Table 3–7 is the percentage for each value. Recall that a percent is simply a standardized proportion, standardized in units of 100, and is calculated as Percent = $(f/N) \times 100$, or the value of the proportion of a value multiplied by 100. We can determine from Table 3–7 that 10 percent of the 911 calls were responded to within 1 minute, nearly 20 percent (18 percent) were responded to between 2 and 3 minutes, and only 4 percent took between 8 and 9 minutes to respond to.

The final column in Table 3–7 is a column of **cumulative percentages** ($c\%$). These are generally more useful than cumulative proportions because they are easier for most people to comprehend. The cumulative percents are calculated in exactly the same manner that the cumulative frequencies and cumulative proportions were. Take the percent of the first value (the 10 percent of the calls that were responded to within 1 minute) and add that to the percent for the second value (12 percent). We then see that 22 percent of the fifty 911 calls were responded to in 2 minutes or less. Now, add the percent for the third value, response times between 2 and 3 minutes, and we can see that 4 in 10 (40 percent) of the calls were responded to within 3 minutes. By subtraction, 60 percent of the calls took longer than 3 minutes to respond to. Finally, we can see that over 9 in 10 of the 911 calls (92 percent) were responded to in 8 minutes or less. The final entry in a column of cumulative percents should be 100 percent or close to that if there is rounding error.

Table 3–7, then, provides a great deal of information about our sample of fifty 911 calls to the police. For some, this numerical presentation of data in tabular form may be a bit daunting. We could, therefore, attempt to portray this information in a non-numerical or graphical way, as we did with our qualitative data in the previous section. One of the ways we can graph quantitative data is with something called a histogram.

Histograms   A **histogram** is very much like a bar chart. It is a graph of bars where the width of each bar on the x axis is equal to unity (1.0) and the height of the bar on the y axis is equal to the value's frequency, percent, or proportion. There are two important differences between a bar chart (shown in Figures 3-6 and 3-7) and a histogram. The first is that in the histogram the bars are connected to one another, indicating that the underlying measurement continuum is continuous and quantitative. Recall that in a bar chart the bars are

> A **histogram** is a graphical way to display interval-ratio-level variables. A histogram can include frequencies, proportions, or percents.

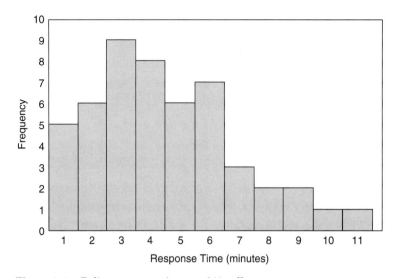

Figure 3–9   Police response times to 911 calls

separated by a space or gap to indicate the fact that the underlying measurement is discrete and qualitative rather than quantitative. Second, the bars on a histogram are placed on the graph from lowest score to highest score. In the bar chart, the placement of the values along the *x* axis was arbitrary.

Figure 3–9 shows a histogram for the ungrouped frequency distribution reported in Table 3–7. This graphical form allows you to easily see that the most frequent response time was 3 minutes and that the data really cluster around the 3–6 minute response time. You also can see that the reported response times fall off fairly substantially after 6 minutes. At least in this sample, the police do seem to respond to a 911 call within 6 minutes.

Line Graphs or Polygons   If we have continuous data we also can use other graphs to illustrate the frequency, proportion, or percent distribution. One such graph is a **line graph** or **polygon** (frequency polygon, proportion polygon, or percent polygon). The difference between a histogram and a polygon is that in the latter the frequency (or percent or proportion) is represented by a point or dot above each score, rather than a rectangular bar, where the height of the point corresponds to the magnitude of the frequency. The points or dots are then connected by a series of straight lines. Figure 3–10 illustrates the use of a frequency polygon for the 911 response call data in Table 3–7.

Like the histogram, this frequency polygon clearly shows that the response times to 911 calls cluster in the range of 3–6 minutes. It also clearly shows that there are far fewer response times that are 7 minutes or more. In other words, although there are some response times that are 8, 9, 10, and 11 minutes, there are not very many of them. Figure 3–11 demonstrates that you could also create a polygon with the percent data (or even the proportion data), and the story would be the same. The most likely response time (18

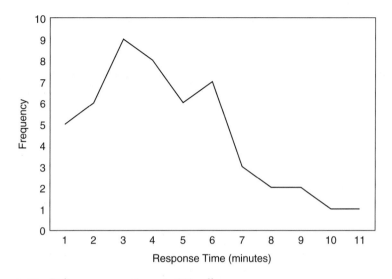

Figure 3–10   Police response times to 911 calls

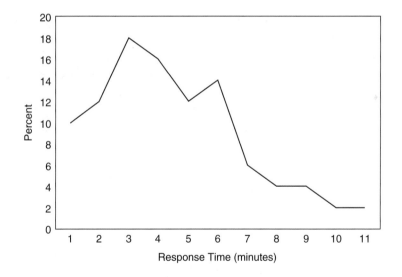

Figure 3–11   Police response times to 911 calls

percent of the time) was 3 minutes, followed by 4 minutes, with a clustering of cases in the 3–6 minute response time range.

Finally, it is possible to graph the cumulative data as well—cumulative frequencies, cumulative percents, and cumulative proportions—in the form of a line graph or polygon. We will illustrate for you a cumulative percent polygon in Figure 3–12, but keep in mind that we could just as easily have graphed the cumulative frequencies or cumulative proportions. In the cumulative percent polygon, the entry for each value of the variable

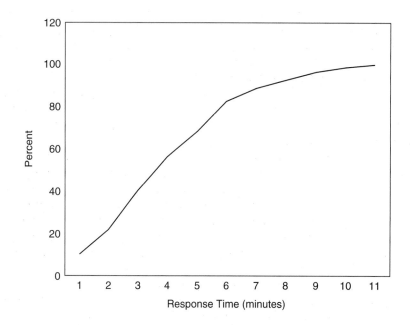

Figure 3–12   Police response times to 911 calls

corresponds to the percent of cases or scores which correspond to that value or are less. To interpret this cumulative percent graph, simply move up from a value on the *x* axis until you hit the line, and then move over to the *y* axis to find the percent of the cases that are at that value or less. For example, start at the value of 3 minutes, move up to hit the line and then over to the *y* axis, and you will discover that 40 percent of the response times were in 3 minutes or less. Approximately 80 percent of the response times were within 6 minutes, and 90 percent were within 8 minutes. Of course, 100 percent of the calls were responded to in 11 minutes or less. You should know that since cumulative percents are calculated by summing the successive percents for each value, the line on a cumulative percent polygon should never fall; it should always be rising or flat. This holds true for graphs of cumulative frequencies and cumulative proportions as well.

Grouped Distributions

Case Study: Recidivism   We provide you with another example of continuous quantitative data in Table 3–8. This table consists of a sample of 120 male offenders released from a penitentiary and followed until they were rearrested for a new offense. For each person we have recorded the number of days they were "free" until they committed a new offense. The first value of "25" in Table 3–8 implies that someone was out in the community for 25 days until he committed a new offense, the second person was free for 37 days until he was rearrested, and the last person in Table 3–8 was free for 34 days un-

TABLE 3–8

Number of Days Until Rearrest for Sample of 120 Released Offenders

25	30	31	33	19	36
37	34	39	32	33	37
20	27	38	29	23	36
29	39	30	28	33	35
27	27	25	24	29	38
28	26	34	23	36	17
40	31	29	28	33	38
28	26	34	23	36	17
40	31	29	28	33	38
26	31	32	35	37	32
30	29	37	33	33	25
18	19	33	40	31	29
27	23	40	24	36	38
24	27	35	33	32	32
34	30	31	31	36	36
24	25	25	26	27	28
34	32	28	35	33	29
35	29	35	31	28	27
31	34	37	36	36	35
40	29	31	34	34	33
30	32	30	29	29	30
31	33	33	34	35	34

til he was rearrested. This variable is measured at the ratio level. All 120 released offenders were rearrested at some time, and we have data on how long they were free before their first offense after release. Criminologists sometimes refer to this variable as a "time until failure" variable (because a rearrest is considered a failure). Since our interest here is the time it took until they were rearrested, all 120 of the offenders in this sample were rearrested. Of course, not everyone released from prison is arrested again.

As you can see, the data in Table 3–8 are pretty disorganized and chaotic. We cannot tell very easily how much time it took for someone to be rearrested. It is even difficult to determine very simple information, such as how quickly the first person was arrested and how long it was until the last offender was rearrested. The first thing we would like to do to our data, therefore, is to organize it. So far, we have learned how to organize Table 3–8 into an ungrouped frequency distribution.

Table 3–9 provides you with the ungrouped frequency distribution for these data. This ungrouped frequency distribution gives us some clarity. We can now easily see, for example, that one person was rearrested in 17 days

TABLE 3–9

Time Until Rearrest—Ungrouped Frequency and Percent Distribution Days Until Rearrest

Rearrest	f	%	c%
17	1	0.8	0.8
18	1	0.8	1.7
19	2	1.7	3.3
20	1	0.8	4.2
21	0	0.0	4.2
22	0	0.0	4.2
23	3	2.5	6.7
24	4	3.3	10.0
25	5	4.2	14.2
26	3	2.5	16.7
27	7	5.8	22.5
28	6	5.0	27.5
29	11	9.2	36.7
30	7	5.8	42.5
31	10	8.3	50.8
32	7	5.8	56.7
33	12	10.0	66.7
34	8	6.7	73.3
35	8	6.7	80.0
36	8	6.7	86.7
37	6	5.0	91.7
38	4	3.3	95.0
39	2	1.7	96.7
40	4	3.3	100.0

while four offenders lasted 40 days until they were rearrested. From the cumulative percent column we also can see that about one-half (50.8 percent) of the 120 offenders were rearrested within 31 days. Although this ungrouped frequency distribution is somewhat helpful in organizing the data, it still looks a little cluttered. This is because we have so many different values to report—there are 24 different values reported for the variable—and with few exceptions, the frequency for each value is fairly low. We provide a histogram of these ungrouped data in Figure 3–13. It is clear from this presentation that the graphed frequency distribution is not very helpful in organizing the data and helping us visualize its patterns or features. There is simply too much information. We need to reorganize these data in another way to make the picture a little clearer.

What we will first do is create a **grouped frequency distribution.** Unlike an ungrouped distribution, which reports all scores in a distribution, a

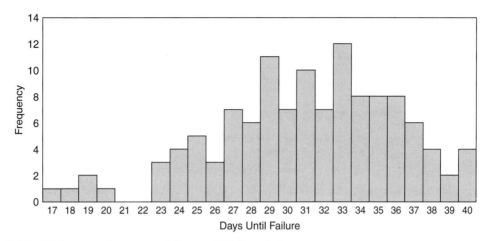

Figure 3–13 Histogram of ungrouped time until failure data

grouped distribution organizes the data by grouping scores into groups of values or class intervals and then listing the frequency, proportion, and percents associated with each interval rather than each separate value. A **class interval** is simply a range of values. For example, rather than reporting the individual values 17, 18, 19, 20 . . . days until rearrest, in a grouped distribution we may have a class interval that goes from 17–20 days. We would then determine the number or frequency of cases that fell within this interval. What we are going to do is take the ungrouped distribution reported in Table 3–9 and construct a grouped distribution. Before we do this, however, we need to discuss some rules and guidelines in the construction of grouped frequency distributions.

> **A grouped frequency distribution** reports the values of a quantitative continuous variable in intervals or a range of values rather than reporting every distinct value.

Before we get to these rules and guidelines, however, one general point needs to be made. The construction of a grouped frequency distribution is as much art as it is science. By this we mean you must keep in mind that your goal in creating a grouped distribution is to organize your data and communicate important characteristics and features about it. A good grouped frequency distribution does this, and a poor one does not. Unfortunately, there is frequently not a single or "correct" way to organize data into a grouped distribution. What you have to do is make some tentative decisions about how to make your grouped distributions, make the distribution under those decisions, and then look at the distribution you have made. You then must determine if this distribution adequately conveys the features of your data (e.g., its shape, most typical score) or if it obscures them. If you think the grouped distribution you have made is inadequate or fails to show the features of your data, simply construct another one and go through the same process. Keep the grouped frequency distribution that you are convinced appropriately reveals the features of your data.

There are a couple of "hard" rules in the creation of a grouped frequency distribution. These hard rules should not be broken:

1. Make your class intervals so that they are mutually exclusive. Make sure that each value falls into one and only one interval. Do not, therefore, have overlapping intervals like the following: 17–20 days, 20–24 days. Under this incorrect scheme, someone who was rearrested in 20 days could be placed in either the first or the second interval.

2. Make your class intervals so that they are exhaustive. In other words, make sure that each value falls into an interval. Do not make intervals that leave some values off. For example, in our time-until-rearrest data do not have your first two intervals like this: 18–21 days, 22–25 days. Although these intervals are mutually exclusive, they are not exhaustive; the value of 17 days in your data would be excluded.

3. Make your intervals all the same width. The **interval width,** symbolized as w_i, is the number of values that the class interval contains. For example, a class interval of 17–20 days has an interval width of 4 because it includes four values: 17, 18, 19, and 20 days until rearrest. The class interval 21–29 days has an interval width of 9. You would not want to have a grouped distribution that has the two intervals 17–20 days and 21–29 days because these class intervals do not have the same width. Class intervals of different widths will distort the appearance of your distribution.

4. Make sure that your first class interval contains your lowest value and your last class interval contains your highest value. In other words, do not make your first or last interval so that no cases fall into it. In the time-until-rearrest data, we would not want to make our first class interval 13–16 days and our second class interval 17–20 days. Although both class intervals have a width of 4 and they are mutually exclusive, with the data we have, the first interval would have a frequency of 0 since the earliest rearrest time was in 17 days. For the same reason, we would not want to have as our last class interval 41–44 days, since it too would have a frequency of 0.

We think these hard rules for the construction of a grouped frequency distribution should be followed at all times. This is the science part, but beyond this, it all becomes art.

Let us try to make a grouped frequency distribution from the rearrest time data shown in Table 3–9. There are really only three steps to follow in making a grouped frequency distribution. Keeping the hard rules in mind, the three steps are as follows.

Step 1. Determine the number of class intervals you want. Here we directly confront the "art" part of grouped frequency distributions. There is no hard rule about how many class intervals you should have—it depends entirely on your data. You should not have too few intervals so that you lose most of the information in your data. You should not have too many intervals because what you are trying to do is organize and make sense out of your data. A guide to follow is that you should have somewhere between 5 and 15 class intervals. After examining your data, determine what you think might be a good number of class intervals. A good place to start if you are stuck is to say you want 10 class intervals. For our time-until-rearrest data, then, we will start with the decision to have 10 class intervals.

Step 2. Determine the width of the class interval. Once you have determined the number of class intervals you want, you have to decide what your interval width should be. Keep in mind the hard rule that each class interval must be the same width. To estimate an approximate interval width, the following simple routine is useful. First, find the range in your data, where the range is simply the difference between your highest and lowest scores. In our time-to-rearrest data the range is 23, since the longest time until rearrest was 40 days and the quickest was 17 days ($40 - 17 = 23$). With this, an estimate of the interval width can be obtained by taking the ratio of the range to the number of class intervals you selected in step 1. The formula for the interval width is:

$$w_i = \frac{\text{Range}}{\text{Number of intervals}}$$

In this example:

$$w_i = \frac{23}{10}$$

$$w_i = 2.3$$

Given the fact that our data consist of whole numbers, we would not really want to have an interval width with a decimal place. What we can do now is round down and have a class interval width of 2 or round up and have an interval width of 3. Again, this is the "art" part. We will round up.

We now have two critical pieces of information. We know we would like to have approximately 10 class intervals, and we want each interval width to be 3.

Step 3. Make your class intervals. Now we are ready to make our class intervals, with the understanding that they must be mutually exclusive, exhaustive, and must include the lowest score in the first interval and the highest score in the last interval. In making our grouped frequency distribution with the time-until-rearrest data, we have to make sure that our first interval contains the value 17 days. One way we can ensure this is to have the first interval begin with 17. The first score that defines the beginning of a class interval is called the *lower limit* of the interval. Now if the first interval begins with 17, what should the last value of this interval be? The last value of any class interval is the *upper limit*. Many students make the mistake of adding the interval width to the lower limit to determine what the upper limit of the interval would be. They think that since we are using an interval width of 3, the first class interval should be 17–20 days, since 17 + 3 (the interval width) = 20. Unfortunately this is not correct because this interval actually has an interval width of 4 rather than 3 since it contains the values 17, 18, 19, and 20 days until rearrest.

A helpful hint in making your class intervals is to do the following. First, select the lower limit of your first class interval. In this case it is 17. Instead of figuring out what the upper limit is, leave it unknown for the moment:

First class interval 17–?

What you now should do is figure out what the lower limit of the second class interval should be. This is easy, because it can be determined by adding the interval width to the lower limit of the first class interval. The lower limit of the second class interval, therefore, should be 20 (Lower limit of first class interval + Interval width = 17 + 3).

17–?

20–?

Since the lower limit of the second interval is 20, the upper limit of the first interval must be 19 days. The first class interval, then, is 17–19, and it contains three values—17, 18, and 19 days. This is as it should be with an interval width of 3. You can complete your class intervals very easily now by adding the interval width to the lower limit of each class interval to find out what the lower limit of the next class interval should be. Repeat this procedure until you have a class interval that includes your highest score.

For our time-until-rearrest data, the class intervals are shown for you in the first column of Table 3–10 under the heading "Stated Class Limits." The **stated class limits** define the range of values for each class interval in the grouped frequency distribution. As we mentioned, there are two components to any stated class interval, a lower class limit and an upper class limit. The first score in any class interval is the lower limit of the interval (LL) while the last score of the class interval is the upper limit of the interval (UL). For the first class interval, then, the lower limit is 17 days and the upper limit is 19 days. The lower limit of the second class interval is 20 days and the upper limit is 22 days.

Notice that because we rounded up our estimated interval width from 2.3 to 3.0 we have 8 class intervals rather than the 10 we thought we were going to have according to step 1. Had we rounded the estimated interval width down to 2.0, we would have had 12 class intervals rather than 10. For now, we will work with the 8 intervals and see if we like it. Notice also that each class interval has the same width, 3.0, that the intervals are both mutually exclusive and exhaustive, and that the first interval contains the lowest score and the last interval contains the highest score. Everything looks good so far.

Now that we have our class intervals created we can go ahead and make a frequency distribution by counting the number of cases that fall into each class interval. For example, looking at the data in Table 3–9 you can determine that there are four offenders who were rearrested between 17 and 19 days, only one who was rearrested between 20 and 22 days, 12 who were rearrested between 23 and 25 days, and so on until you find that there are 10 cases who were rearrested between 38 and 40 days. As was true with an ungrouped frequency distribution, the sum of the frequency column in a grouped frequency distribution should equal the total number of cases ($\Sigma f = N$), in this example, 120. We can use these frequencies now to determine the proportions (p) and percent of the total for each class interval, where $p = f/N$, and percent $= p \times 100$. Since there were 4 offenders out of 120 who were rearrested between 17 and 19 days, they comprise .03 of the total ($4/120 = .03$), or 3 percent. Similarly, since there were 28 offenders who were rearrested between 29 and 31 days, they comprise .23 of the total ($28/120 = .23$), or 23 percent. We also can meaningfully calculate the cumulative frequencies, cumulative proportions, and cumulative percent for each class interval.

One thing you should immediately notice about our grouped frequency distribution is that, while our ungrouped data were measured at the interval/ratio level by creating class intervals, we now have ordinal-level data. Our data now consist of rank-ordered categories rather than continuous data. In a sense, then, we "dumbed" our data down from interval/ratio to ordinal-level.

To see this clearly, assume we take one hypothetical person from each of the first two class intervals. What we now know is that the person who falls into the first class interval (17–19 days) was rearrested sooner than the person who is in the second class interval (20–22 days). What we do not know, however, is how much sooner the first person was rearrested. Since we only know they fall into the first interval—and not their precise number of days until rearrest—we can use only words like "rearrested sooner" rather than more precise words like "rearrested two days sooner." With our original continuous data in terms of the exact number of days until rearrest we could calculate precise things like "how much more than" or "how much less than"—statements we cannot make with ordinal-level data. In creating a grouped frequency distribution from continuous data, then, we lose some precision in our measurement. What we have to determine is how large a price we are paying for creating a grouped frequency distribution. In other words, how much precision have we lost in going from interval/ratio to ordinal-level measurement?. We will address this issue in later chapters.

TABLE 3–10

Grouped Distribution for Time Until Rearrest Data

Stated Class Limits	f	cf	p	cp	%	c%
17–19	4	4	.033	.033	3.33	3.33
20–22	1	5	.008	.041	.83	4.16
23–25	12	17	.100	.141	10.00	14.16
26–28	16	33	.133	.274	13.33	27.49
29–31	28	61	.233	.507	23.33	50.82
32–34	28	89	.233	.740	23.33	74.15
35–37	21	110	.175	.915	17.50	91.65
38–40	10	120	.083	.998	8.33	99.98
Total	120		.998*		99.98*	

*Does not sum to 1.0 or 100% because of rounding error.

Even though there is some loss of precision because we have created categories or class intervals rather than reporting every value, Table 3–10 shows the distribution of the data much better than the ungrouped distribution shown in Table 3–9. We can see here that not many cases immediately resulted in a rearrest. There were no rearrests for 16 days and then only a handful until 23 days after release (five, or less than 5 percent of the total). There were, however, a large number of cases that resulted in a rearrest between 29 and 37 days; in fact, 77 cases or nearly two-thirds (64 percent) of the total were rearrested by then. By the 37th day after their release, 110 offenders of the 120 had been rearrested. This comprised over 9 out of 10 released offenders—or over 90 percent of the total. Having constructed this grouped distribution, we will now construct a histogram of the frequency data, shown for you in Figure 3–14.

This histogram of the grouped frequency distribution is a little more informative than that for the ungrouped data in Figure 3–13. We clearly see that few persons were rearrested very early upon release and that it was not until approximately 29 days after release when most offenders began to be rearrested, after which point they were rearrested at a fairly steady level until the 37th day. One is immediately struck by the fact that a large proportion of rearrests occurred between 29 and 34 days—approximately one month after release.

In case we were not satisfied with the grouped frequency distribution that has eight class intervals and an interval width of 3, we might want to try constructing a different set of intervals. Rather than round the interval width up from 2.3 to 3.0, we now will round down and have class intervals with a width of 2. We go through the same procedures as before, and as practice you should stop reading any further and attempt to create this grouped frequency distribution on your own and then check it with what we have done.

The grouped frequency distribution where the width of each class interval is 2 is shown for you in Table 3–11, along with the percent distribution.

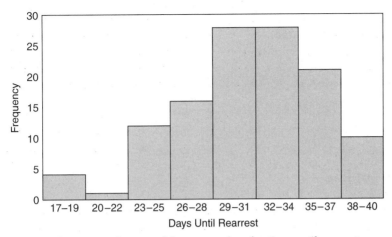

Figure 3–14   Histogram of grouped frequency data for time until rearrest

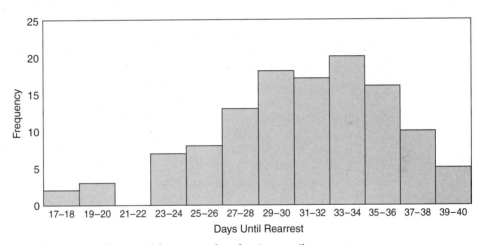

Figure 3–15   Histogram of grouped frequency data for time until rearrest

The corresponding histogram for the grouped frequency distribution is given in Figure 3–15. Because the interval width is 2.0 rather than 3.0, there are now 12 rather than 8 class intervals. But the story provided by the table and graph are virtually identical as when the interval width was 3.0, and both sets of tables and graphs are very easy to read, interpret, and understand. One would be hard-pressed to say that one set of tables/graphs is any better than the other. It looks as if they both are effective in showing the distribution of these time-until-rearrest data. You now have clear evidence that making a grouped frequency distribution does not have a clearly defined single answer and that making such distributions is "as much art as it is science."

TABLE 3–11

Grouped Distribution for Time-Until-Rearrest Data

Stated Class Limits	f	%
17–18	2	1.67
19–20	3	2.50
21–22	0	0.00
23–24	7	5.83
25–26	8	6.67
27–28	13	10.83
29–30	18	15.00
31–32	17	14.17
33–34	20	16.67
35–36	16	13.33
37–38	10	8.33
39–40	6	5.00
Total	120	100.00

Refinements to a Grouped Frequency Distribution   Recall that we created our grouped frequency distributions in the section above with data that were initially quantitative and continuous. The variable, time until rearrest, was measured at the interval/ratio level as the number of days a released offender was out in the community until he or she was rearrested. We then collapsed these data into ordinal-level categories. We see this categorization in our stated class limits. We would like to show you the difference between continuous data and the ordinal-level categories of the class intervals. First the interval/ratio level data measure time until rearrest in continuous increments of one day:

```
|-------|-------|-------|-------|-------|-------|------------|
one       two     three    four     five     six     seven      . . . forty
day      days     days    days     days     days    days . . .        days
```

This measurement of time until rearrest is continuous, and this continuity is seen in the gradual evolution of one day into two days into three days, and so on. When we collapsed the data into the ordinal categories of stated class intervals as in Table 3–10, however, our class intervals became discrete categories:

```
|------|    |------|    |------|    |------|    |------|    |------|
17–19 days   20–22 days   23–25 days   26–28 days . . . 35–37 days   38–40 days
```

There will be times, however, when we will want to maintain the continuous nature of our original interval/ratio measurement even though we have created ordinal-level categories. What we can do in order to reconstruct the original continuous nature of our class intervals is to construct something called real class limits. The creation of **real class limits** will both remind us that our underlying measurement is truly continuous, and allow us to perform certain statistical operations on the data (discussed in later chapters), which we could not do if the data were truly ordinal.

Constructing real class limits is very simple. Let's take as an illustration the first and second class intervals in Table 3–10. First, notice that there is a one unit "gap" between the upper limit of a given class interval and the lower limit of the next. For example, there is a one unit (one day) "gap" between the upper limit of the first stated class interval (19 days) and the lower limit of the next stated class interval (20 days). Notice that this one unit "gap" exists for each stated class limit, even the first class interval (the stated class interval 14–16 exists; we simply didn't use it because our first value is 17 days). What we are now going to do is extend the upper limit of the first stated class interval one-half of the distance of this "gap." Since the "gap" is one unit, that means we will increase the upper limit of the first stated class limit by one-half or .5 units. Now the upper limit of the first stated class interval will be .5 units closer to the lower limit of the next stated class interval. The real upper limit for the first class interval would then be 19.5 days. We now will decrease the lower limit of the second stated class interval one-half of the distance of the "gap," or .5 units, so that now it is .5 units closer to the upper limit of the previously stated class interval. The real lower limit for the second class interval would then be 19.5 days. We continue by decreasing the lower limit of each stated class interval by .5 (one-half of the distance of the "gap" between the stated class limits) and increasing the upper limit of each stated class interval by .5 (also one-half of the distance of the "gap"). The lower real limit for our first class interval would be 16.5 since we are decreasing the lower stated limit by .5, and the upper real limit would be 19.5. We do this for all class intervals, including the first and last. When we complete this, our real class limits are:

Real Class Limits
16.5–19.5 days
19.5–22.5 days
22.5–25.5 days
25.5–28.5 days
28.5–31.5 days
31.5–34.5 days
34.5–37.5 days
37.5–40.5 days

Notice that the upper real limit of each class interval is equal to the lower real limit of the next class interval. The intervals now merge imperceptibly together, reflecting the continuous nature of the underlying data. There are no "gaps" in this continuous data. Essentially, we have tried to recapture some of the measurement properties we lost when we created a grouped frequency distribution and made the originally continuous data categorical. What we are trying to recall, therefore, is that in spite of the fact that we created ordinal categories with our grouped frequency distribution, the underlying measurement of the original data was continuous. You can perhaps see this better below. With real class limits we now have:

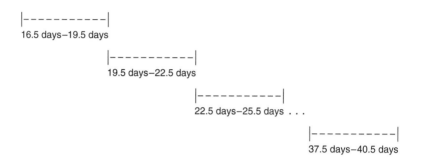

16.5 days–19.5 days

19.5 days–22.5 days

22.5 days–25.5 days . . .

37.5 days–40.5 days

We will use these real limits later to do some simple statistical calculations which normally would require us to have interval/ratio level data. You should notice that we cannot use these real class limits to calculate our frequency, proportion, or percent distributions for grouped data. Why not? Recall that one of the hard rules in making a grouped frequency distribution is that the class intervals should be mutually exclusive. That means that a given score should fall into one and only one class interval. This rule is violated with real class limits. Where, for example, would we place a score of 19 days? Would it go in the first or the second class interval?

Another piece of information we are now going to add to our grouped frequency distribution is something called the **midpoint** of the interval (the midpoint of a given class interval i is given by m_i). We will use the interval midpoints in the next two chapters when we discuss measures of central tendency and dispersion. The midpoint of a class interval is exactly what the term implies; it is a score that lies exactly at the midpoint of the class interval, exactly one-half of the distance between the lower limit and the upper limit. Each class interval has its own midpoint. The midpoint of a class interval is easy to calculate; simply take the sum of the lower limit and the upper limit and divide by two. Whether you use the lower and upper limits of the stated class limits or the lower and upper limits of the real class limits, the result will be the same:

$$m_i = \frac{\text{Lower limit} + \text{Upper limit}}{2}$$

For example, with our grouped frequency distribution in Table 3–10 we can calculate the midpoint of the first interval as $17 + 19/2 = 36/2 = 18$ using the stated limits and $16.5 + 19.5/2 = 36/2 = 18$ using the real class limits. Mid-

TABLE 3–12

Stated Class Limits, Real Class Limits, and Midpoints for Grouped Frequency Distribution in Table 3–10

Stated Class Limits	Real Class Limits	m_i	f
17–19	16.5–19.5	18	4
20–22	19.5–22.5	21	1
23–25	22.5–25.5	24	12
26–28	25.5–28.5	27	16
29–31	28.5–31.5	30	28
32–34	31.5–34.5	33	28
35–37	34.5–37.5	36	21
38–40	37.5–40.5	39	10
		Total =	120

points are always calculated for every class interval in a grouped frequency distribution, and in Table 3–12 we show you the real limits and midpoints for each class interval for the grouped frequency distribution data in Table 3–10, where the width of each stated class interval was 3.0.

THE SHAPE OF A DISTRIBUTION

One important piece of information that a graph of continuous data can tell you at a quick glance is the shape of your distribution. For statistical purposes, one important shape of a continuous distribution is normal. A **normal distribution** is a distribution that is symmetrical, which means that if you drew a line down the center of the distribution the left half would look exactly like the right half of the distribution. A normal distribution has a single peak in the middle of the distribution, with fewer and fewer cases as you move away from this middle. The ends of a distribution of continuous scores often are called the "tails" of the distribution. A distribution has both a left tail and a right tail.

> A **normal distribution** is a symmetrical distribution that has the greatest frequency of its cases in the middle, with fewer cases at each end or "tail" of the distribution. Because a normal distribution looks like a bell when drawn, it often is referred to as a bell-shaped distribution or curve.

A normal distribution often is referred to as a "bell-shaped curve" because it is shaped like a bell. An example of a normal distribution is shown for you in Figure 3–16, and we will take up the normal distribution in greater detail in Chapter 6 because many variables of interest in criminology and criminal justice are or are approximately normally distributed, and many of the statistics we apply to our data make the assumption that they are normally distributed.

When a distribution departs or deviates from normality it is said to be **skewed.** There are two forms of a skewed distribution. Figure 3–17 shows a distribution where there is a long

> A **skewed distribution** is a non-normal (nonsymmetrical) distribution. In a positively skewed distribution there is a long right tail, while in negatively skewed distribution there is a long left tail.

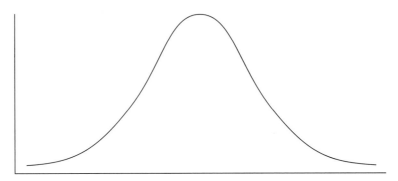

Figure 3–16   Example of a normal or symmetrical distribution

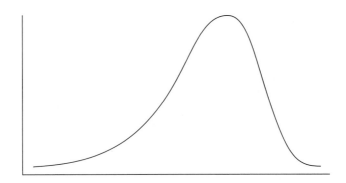

Figure 3–17   Example of a negatively skewed or left-tailed distribution

series of low scores, with most of the scores at the high end of the distribution. Notice that this distribution has a long left tail. This type of distribution is **negatively skewed** because the long tail of the distribution is to the left, and the left side of the number line moves toward negative numbers. In a distribution with a negative skew, then, most of the scores cluster at the high values of the variable and a long left tail indicates that there are a lot of low values with few cases at each value. Figure 13–18 shows a distribution where there is a long series of high scores, with most of the scores clustered at the low end of the distribution. Notice that this distribution has a long right tail. This type of distribution is **positively skewed** because the long tail of the distribution is to the right, and the right side of the number line moves toward positive numbers. In a distribution with a positive skew, therefore, most of the scores cluster at the low values of the variable and a long right tail indicates that there are a lot of high values with few cases at each value.

> An **outlier** is an unusually high or low value or score for a variable.

If you think of a very high or very low score as an **outlier,** a negatively skewed distribution has outliers at the left tail of the distribution (the long tail), while a positively skewed distribution has outliers at the right tail of the distribution.

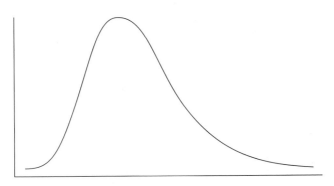

Figure 3–18   Example of a positively skewed or right-tailed distribution

TIME PLOTS

Frequently in criminology and other social sciences we are interested in the extent to which events change or remain stable over time. In other words, the values of some of our variables may change over time and we would like to have a convenient way to show this. We can do this by displaying our data in a table where we report the value of a variable at different time points, for example, every six months or every year. In addition to the tabular presentation of the value of a variable over time, we can graph the change in a **time plot.** A time plot is simply a graphical display of a variable's values over some unit of time (year, month, week, etc.). It is actually a type of line graph where the height of the line on the y axis reflects some attribute of the value (a frequency or a percent) and its length is marked off in units of time on the x axis.

A Trend Analysis of Crime Rates

Table 3–13 reports the annual rates of crime reported to the police for three "index offenses"—forcible rape, robbery, and aggravated assault—in the United States over the time period 1972–2000. There are, then, three variables—rape rates, robbery rates, and rates of aggravated assault—that are reported over a 29-year period. We reproduce these rates for each of the three crimes as a time plot in Figure 3–19. In Figure 3–19 notice that we have graphed all three crimes in one plot. We did this to make a point. Normally, we would not graph all three of these crime trends in a single plot. In a moment we will explain why.

Although with some time and careful reading of the table we can determine from the tabular data how the rates of these three index crimes have changed over the years, the graphical display of the time plots allows us to see this variation over time much more quickly and clearly. At least for armed robbery and aggravated assault, the trend in the rates is very clear over this nearly 30-year period. Let's concentrate on these two crimes for a moment.

TABLE 3–13

Annual Rates (per 100,000) of Rape, Robbery, and Aggravated Assault Known to the Police and Reported to the FBI's Uniform Crime Reporting Program: 1972–2000

Year	Rape Rate	Robbery Rate	Aggravated Assault Rate
1972	22.5	180.7	188.8
1973	24.5	183.1	200.5
1974	26.2	209.3	215.8
1975	26.3	220.8	227.4
1976	26.6	199.3	233.2
1977	29.4	190.7	247.0
1978	31.0	195.8	262.1
1979	34.7	218.4	286.0
1980	36.8	251.1	298.5
1981	36.0	258.7	289.3
1982	34.0	238.9	289.0
1983	33.7	216.5	279.4
1984	35.7	205.4	290.6
1985	37.1	208.5	304.0
1986	37.9	225.1	347.4
1987	37.4	212.7	352.9
1988	37.6	220.9	372.2
1989	38.1	233.0	385.6
1990	41.2	257.0	422.9
1991	42.3	272.7	433.4
1992	42.8	263.7	441.9
1993	41.1	256.0	440.5
1994	39.3	237.8	427.6
1995	37.1	220.9	418.3
1996	36.3	201.9	391.0
1997	35.9	186.2	382.1
1998	34.5	165.5	361.4
1999	32.8	150.1	334.3
2000	32.0	144.9	323.6

Source: Uniform Crime Reports, Federal Bureau of Investigaton, 1990, 1995, 2000.

As shown in Figure 3–19, crime rates for both armed robbery and aggravated assault started at low levels in the early 1970s, and there was a slight "bump" or increase in the rates of both crimes during the early 1980s. After this increase, there was a slight decline in the rates of robbery and assault during the middle to late 1980s, and then a fairly steady increase until the early 1990s, when both crime rates peaked (armed robbery in 1991 and aggravated

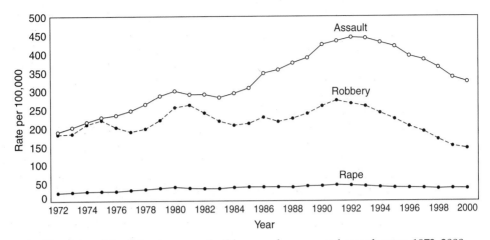

Figure 3–19 Time plot of forcible rape, armed robbery, and aggravated assault rates, 1972–2000

assault in 1992). After the peak in crime rates in the early 1990s, there is a gradual decline over the next 10 years. In fact, the rate for armed robbery has declined in the year 2000 to less than what it was in 1972. We can clearly see that while rates of armed robbery and aggravated assault started out nearly comparable, the difference between the two has increased over the years.

The trend over time is not so clear for rates of forcible rape, however. Here it appears as if rape rates have been almost flat over the 29 years, with a very slight increase in the early 1990s. Compared with the rates for armed robbery and aggravated assault, rates of forcible rape look almost stable. This is deceptive, however. To discover this, let us examine some percent change scores over different parts of the time trend. To calculate percent change scores, you perform the following calculations:

$$\% \text{ Change} = \left(\frac{\text{Finish value} - \text{Start value}}{\text{Start value}} \right) \times 100$$

If we calculate the percent change in the crime rate from 1972 until the peak rate for each crime in the early 1990s, we can determine that rates of forcible rape increased 90 percent, $(42.8 - 22.5)/22.5 \times 100 = 90.22\%$, while robbery rates increased by only 51 percent, $(272.7 - 180.7)/180.7 \times 100 = 50.9\%$, and rates of aggravated assault increased by 134 percent, $(441.9 - 188.8)/188.8 \times 100 = 134.1\%$. Thus, over the period from the early 1970s to the early 1990s, rates of forcible rape increased almost twice as much as those for armed robbery. You don't get this impression from the graph, do you? Now let's calculate the percent change in crime rates for each offense from its peak in the early 1990s until the end of the time period in 2000. When we do this we see that rape rates declined by 25 percent, $(32.0 - 42.8)/42.8 \times 100 = -25.2\%$, about the same decline as shown by aggravated assault rates,

$(323.6 - 441.9)/441.9 \times 100 = -26.8\%$, but approximately one-half as much as that for armed robbery rates, $(144.9 - 272.7)/272.7 \times 100 = -46.9\%$. As you can see from the calculation of these percent change scores, rates of forcible rape over the time period 1972–2000 were as volatile as those for armed robbery and aggravated assault, but it appears from the time plot in Figure 3–19 that rape rates were pretty constant. The reason the time plot in Figure 3–19 shows such a flat trend for forcible rape is that the base rate for rapes is much lower than the base rates for both armed robbery and aggravated assault. The base rate for forcible rape is in the 30–40 per 100,000 range, while the base rates for robbery and assault are in the 200–400 range. Relative to the crime rates for robbery and assault, then, the crime rate for forcible rape is restricted in a much more narrow range. As a result, when these three crimes are graphed together in a single time plot it is more difficult to see year-to-year fluctuations in rape rates. Graphing all three time trends in one plot, therefore, distorts the trend for forcible rape. This illustrates the importance of examining the y-axis on any graph or chart.

One way to remedy this distortion of the data is to provide a time trend for the forcible rape rates by themselves. We provide this graph for you in Figure 3–20. Notice that this time plot clearly shows the trend over time that we noticed from both our inspection of the raw data in Table 3–13 and our calculation of percent change scores. It also clearly shows that the general trend in rape rates over this 29-year period is comparable to the trends found for armed robbery and aggravated assault rates. Rates of forcible rape increased from the early 1970s to the early 1980s, there was a slight decline creating a small "bump" in the data, and then rates increased steadily until they peaked in the early 1990s, showing a gradual decline to 2000. In the year 2000, rates of forcible rape returned to the level they were in the late 1970s. Rather than be-

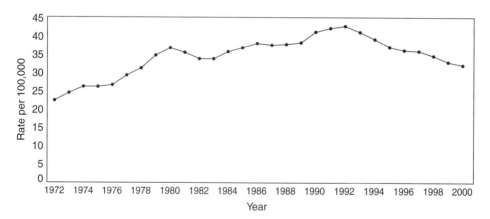

Figure 3–20   Time plot of forcible rape rates, 1972–2000. *Source:* Uniform Crime Reports, Federal Bureau of Investigation, 1990, 1995, 2000.

TABLE 3–14

Number of Executions in the United States: 1977–2001

Year	# of Executions
1977	1
1978	0
1979	2
1980	0
1981	1
1982	2
1983	5
1984	21
1985	18
1986	18
1987	25
1988	11
1989	16
1990	23
1991	14
1992	31
1993	38
1994	31
1995	56
1996	45
1997	74
1998	68
1999	98
2000	85
2001	49

Source: Death Row U.S.A. Fall 2002. NAACP Legal Defense and Education Fund, Inc. New York, NY.

ing stable over the period 1972–2000, rates of forcible rape followed approximately the same trend as the rates for armed robbery and aggravated assault.

Let's go through another example. In Table 3–14 we report the number of executions that have taken place in the United States from 1977 to the end of 2001. In 1977 the execution in Utah of Gary Gillmore ended an unofficial moratorium on the use of the death penalty in the United States. There are two things you might notice from this table: (1) the frequency of executions started out very low but has increased fairly steadily over time until dropping in 2000 and 2001, and (2) the frequency of executions has been very erratic and unstable from year to year. For example, there were only five executions in 1983, but this number bumped up to 21 in 1984. Fourteen

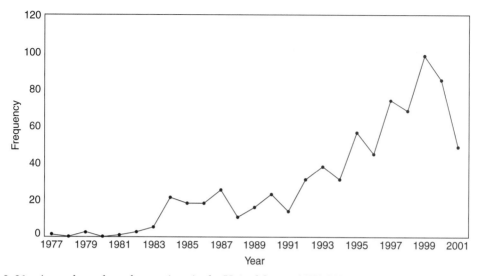

Figure 3–21   Annual number of executions in the United States: 1977–2001

executions in 1991 increased to 31 in 1992, and yet 85 executions in 2000 declined to only 49 executions in 2001. You can see both of these patterns in the execution data more clearly when you look at the time plot in Figure 3–21. This time plot illustrates well the value of the graphical display of data.

Since these execution frequency data show substantial year-to-year fluctuations, some researchers often elect to slightly modify the data so that any trends can be made more apparent. Such modification removes much of the severe short-term variability in the data and involves a technique called **smoothing.** In smoothing, a new data point is created by taking what is called a **moving average.** A moving average is simply the average frequency that an event occurred over some short-term time period. Using these execution frequency data, we are going to create a moving average of three years. In all smoothing techniques the values of the first and last scores in the time series remain the same. In our execution data, therefore, we would not smooth the number of executions that occurred in 1977 (1) nor those that occurred in 2001 (49). Beginning with the year 1978, however, we begin to create moving averages of three years. In this moving average of three, we take the frequency of executions for each year and then add to that number the frequency of executions for the years immediately before that year and immediately after that year; then we calculate the average of these three years by dividing this sum by 3. So, if f_2 is the frequency for the second year in the time series (recall that the first frequency, f_1, is not smoothed) and f_3 is the frequency for the third year, the first new data point we would calculate would be an average of the first, second, and third frequency as a moving average of three for $f_2 = f_1 + f_2 + f_3/3$. So the value of our first smoothed data point would be for the year

TABLE 3–15

Number of Executions in the United States: 1977–2001

Year	# of Executions	Smoothing Process	Smoothed # of Executions
1977	1	Endpoints remain	1
1978	0	$1 + 0 + 2/3$ $= 1$	1
1979	2	$0 + 2 + 0/3$ $= .66$	.66
1980	0	$0 + 2 + 1/3$ $= 1$	1
1981	1	$0 + 1 + 2/3$ $= 1$	1
1982	2	$1 + 2 + 5/3$ $= 2.6$	2.6
1983	5	$2 + 5 + 21/3$ $= 9.3$	9.3
1984	21	$5 + 21 + 18/3 = 14.6$	14.6
1985	18	$21 + 18 + 18/3 = 19$	19
1986	18	$18 + 18 + 25/3 = 20.3$	20.3
1987	25	$18 + 25 + 11/3 = 18$	18
1988	11	$25 + 11 + 16/3 = 17.3$	17.3
1989	16	$11 + 16 + 23/3 = 16.6$	16.6
1990	23	$16 + 23 + 14/3 = 17.6$	17.6
1991	14	$23 + 14 + 31/3 = 22.6$	22.6
1992	31	$14 + 31 + 38/3 = 27.6$	27.6
1993	38	$31 + 38 + 31/3 = 33.3$	33.3
1994	31	$38 + 31 + 56/3 = 41.6$	41.6
1995	56	$31 + 56 + 45/3 = 44$	44
1996	45	$56 + 45 + 74/3 = 58.3$	58.3
1997	74	$45 + 74 + 68/3 = 62.3$	62.3
1998	68	$74 + 68 + 98/3 = 80$	80
1999	98	$68 + 98 + 85/3 = 83.6$	83.6
2000	85	$98 + 85 + 49/3 = 77.3$	77.3
2001	49	Endpoints remain	49

1978 and it would be $1 + 0 + 2/3 = 3/3 = 1.0$. This value is the average number of executions for three years—1977, 1978, and 1979. The value of our second smoothed data point would be for the year 1979 and it would be the average number of executions for the years 1978, 1979, and 1980, or $0 + 2 + 0/3 = 2/3 = .67$. You then smooth each of the original frequency values for each year after this by taking the average of three data points (the year you are smoothing, plus the year before and the year after) until you reach the last data point in the series, which you leave unsmoothed.

Table 3–15 shows the value of the original execution frequency, how the smoothing technique was used, and the value of each smoothed frequency. We graph these smoothed frequencies and the unsmoothed raw frequencies as a time plot in Figure 3–22. You should note that we decided

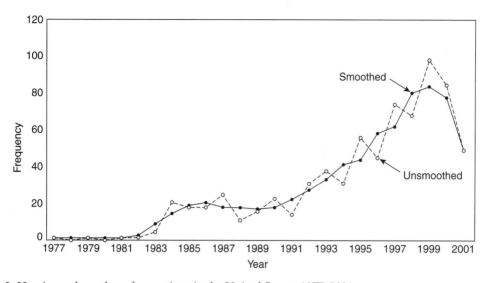

Figure 3–22 Annual number of executions in the United States: 1977–2001

to calculate a moving average of three years for these data. We also should mention that there was nothing sacred about a moving average of three; we could have calculated a moving average of two or four or even five years. Generally, the more years or data points that are included in the moving average, the more smoothed the data will be. In practice, your decision about the number of years to include in the moving average should be based on the characteristics and appearance of your data. And you might have to do a number of smooth time plots before you finally decide what the best moving average is.

Notice in Figure 3–22 that the smoothing of the data takes out the peaks and valleys in your data, as you would guess given the fact that the technique is called "smoothing." Without the erratic fluctuations, the trend in the smoothed data is a little easier to discern. You can see that executions remained at a very low level until the early 1980s, when they began to rise. The rate of annual executions was fairly flat throughout the decade of the 1980s, followed by a steady and consistent increase until its peak in 1999. In the two years since 1999, the number of executions per year has fallen, and fallen dramatically from 2000–2001.

SUMMARY

In this chapter we covered some of the ways to present our qualitative and quantitative data in tabular (or numerical) form and in graphs. An important point to take away from this chapter is that it is always a good idea to look at the appearance or distribution of your data before conducting any further statistical analyses. Qualitative data can be examined in both tabular and graphical form along with the calculation of some very simple descriptive information, such as the distribution of frequencies, proportions, and percents. A frequency distribution displays the values that the qualitative variable takes and how many cases fall into each value. The proportion and percents show the relative frequencies. Qualitative data can be graphed with either a pie chart or a bar chart.

Quantitative or continuous data also can be viewed in tabular or graphical form. With quantitative data there is a greater variety of descriptive information to report. With quantitative data we can meaningfully calculate cumulative frequencies, proportions, and percents. If every value of a quantitative variable is reported along with its frequency, proportion, and/or percent, the distribution is called an ungrouped frequency distribution. If the data are collapsed into a range of values rather than every single value, the corresponding distribution is referred to as a grouped frequency distribution. Continuous data can be graphed with a histogram or one of several different kinds of line graphs or polygons. Frequently in criminology and criminal justice we are interested in reporting the values of a variable over time. In such cases information can be displayed in a table or with a graph called a time plot. When there are sharp fluctuations in the data over a short period of time it is often helpful to first smooth the data before graphing the trend.

KEY TERMS

bar chart
class interval
cumulative frequency distribution
cumulative proportion distribution
cumulative percent distribution
grouped frequency distribution
histogram
interval width
line graph (polygon)
midpoint
moving average

negatively skewed distribution
normal distribution
outlier
pie chart
positively skewed distribution
real class limits
skewed distribution
stated class limits
smoothing
time plot
ungrouped frequency distribution

KEY FORMULAS

Midpoint of a Class Interval

$$m_i = \frac{\left(\text{lower class limit} + \text{upper class limit}\right)}{2}$$

Percent

$$\text{Percent} = \text{proportion} \times 100 \text{ or } \frac{f_i}{N} x100$$

Percent Change

$$\text{Percent Change} = \left(\frac{\text{finish value} - \text{start value}}{\text{start value}} \right) x100$$

Proportion

$$\text{Proportion} = \frac{f_i}{N}$$

Width of a Class Interval

$$w = \frac{\text{range in the data}}{\text{number of class intervals}}$$

PRACTICE PROBLEMS

1. Which of the two grouped frequency distributions is more effective in displaying the data on the number of prior offenses? Why?

Number of Prior Offenses for a Sample of Convicted Offenders

Stated Class Limits	f
0–5	0
7–10	35
10–15	40
16–30	50
	$\Sigma = 125$

Number of Prior Offenses for a Sample of Convicted Offenders

Stated Class Limits	f
7–9	35
10–12	25
13–15	15
16–18	20
19–21	10
22–24	5
25–27	10
28–30	5
	$\Sigma = 125$

2. If you had data on a variable called "the number of offenders sentenced to death in the United States from 1977–2001" and wanted to graph the frequency distribution, which type of graph would you use?

3. Imagine that you took a sample of 150 persons in a large lecture class from your university and asked each student the following question: "During the past 12 months, how many times did you use marijuana, cocaine, or some other illegal drug?" The possible response options were "never," "a few times," "more than a few times but not a lot," and "a lot." You found that 30 people reported "never" using drugs in the past year, 75 reported that they had used drugs "a few times," 35 said they had used drugs "more than a few times but not a lot," and 10 reported using drugs "a lot."

   a. What is the level of measurement for your variable, "self-reported drug use"?

   b. What is the ratio of "users" to "non-users"?

   c. What is the ratio of users who reported using drugs "more than a few times but not a lot" to those reporting "a lot"?

   d. Construct an ungrouped frequency distribution from your data and include both the proportion and the percent.

   e. What percent of your sample reported using drugs?

   f. What proportion of your sample reported using drugs "a lot"?

4. You are the director of a state's Department of Corrections. You have 20,751 inmates currently confined in four types of institutions: community correctional facilities ($n = 5,428$), minimum security institutions (3,285), medium security institutions (1,733), maximum security institutions ($n = 875$), and pretrial detention centers (9,430).

   a. Construct a frequency distribution with these data and include the percent and proportion.

   b. What percent of your inmates are housed in minimum security institutions?

   c. What proportion of your inmates are housed in maximum security institutions?

   d. What percent of your inmates are housed in pretrial detention facilities?

   e. Graph these data with the appropriate graph.

5. As the head of a state's police academy, you give a final examination to each class of recruits. This 20-question examination covers things that a rookie police officer should know, like safety rules, constitutional requirements in arrests, and other matters. The data below show the scores received on this exam by the last class of recruits, which had 25 people in it. They also show the gender of each recruit.

Scores on the Police Officer Recruit Test

Number Correct	Gender
15	Male
16	Female
11	Male
10	Male
14	Male
15	Male
15	Female
11	Female
10	Male
10	Male
20	Female
15	Female
14	Male
16	Male
15	Male
19	Female
11	Male
13	Male
15	Female
13	Female
10	Male
20	Male
15	Male
16	Female
10	Male

a. Construct an ungrouped frequency distribution of the test scores. In the table also include the proportion, percent, cumulative frequencies, cumulative proportions, and cumulative percents.

b. Construct a frequency distribution of the variable "gender," including both proportions and percents.

c. If a score of 14 or higher constituted a "pass" on the exam, how many and what percent of the recruits passed the test?

d. If a score of 18 or higher earned a rookie the distinction of "passing with honors," how many and what proportion of the recruits passed with honors?

e. If those who had a score of 13 or lower had to repeat their training, how many members of this class will have to repeat training?

   f. What was the proportion of males and females in this class?

   g. Graph the frequency data for the test scores and the percent data (with a pie chart) for the gender data.

   h. Graph the cumulative frequency data for the test scores.

6. You have a sample of 75 adults and have asked each one to report the age at which they committed their first delinquent or criminal act. The responses are shown for you below. With these data, construct a grouped frequency distribution. Make the lower limit of your first class interval 6, and have an interval width of 5. Then make a frequency distribution that includes the proportion, percent, cumulative frequencies, cumulative proportions, and cumulative percents.

Age at First Offense

17	22	13	24	15
12	30	17	27	16
21	14	12	13	18
18	27	19	18	25
11	19	11	26	30
28	28	23	14	35
8	13	26	22	21
17	20	15	39	15
26	24	16	30	31
31	25	24	23	6
15	32	29	38	36
34	16	12	34	12
20	12	33	35	34
7	21	11	37	19
11	21	20	43	35

Then answer the following questions:

   a. What are the real limits of these class intervals?

   b. What are the midpoints of each class interval?

   c. How many of these persons committed their first offense before the age of 31?

   d. What proportion committed their first offense between the ages of 11 and 15?

   e. What percent committed their first offense after age 20?

   f. What percent committed their first offense before the age of 16?

7. The data below show the total property crime victimization rate from the National Crime Victimization Survey for the time period 1973–2000.

Graph these data with a time plot. What time trend or trends do you detect in these data?

National Crime Victimization Survey Property Crime Trends, 1973–2000

Victimization Year	Rate per 1,000 Households
1973	519.9
1974	551.5
1975	553.6
1976	544.2
1977	544.1
1978	532.6
1979	531.8
1980	496.1
1981	497.2
1982	468.3
1983	428.4
1984	399.2
1985	385.4
1986	372.7
1987	379.6
1988	378.4
1989	373.4
1990	348.4
1991	353.7
1992	325.3
1993	318.9
1994	310.2
1995	290.5
1996	266.4
1997	248.3
1998	217.4
1999	190.0
2000	178.1

Source: Bureau of Justice Statistics website, www.ojp.usdoj.gov/bjs/.

8. The following data represent the estimated number of arrests over the time period 1970–2000 for drug abuse violations among adult males as determined by the FBI's Uniform Crime Reports. With these data, construct a time plot of the number of arrests with both the original data and then after smoothing the data with a three-year moving average.

Year	Number of Arrests
1970	322,300
1971	383,900
1972	407,300
1973	463,600
1974	474,900
1975	456,000
1976	464,100
1977	493,300
1978	480,000
1979	435,600
1980	471,200
1981	468,100
1982	584,900
1983	583,500
1984	623,700
1985	718,600
1986	742,700
1987	849,500
1988	1,050,600
1989	1,247,800
1990	1,008,300
1991	931,900
1992	980,700
1993	1,017,800
1994	1,192,800
1995	1,285,700
1996	1,295,100
1997	1,370,400
1998	1,360,600
1999	1,365,100
2000	1,375,600

Source: Federal Bureau of Investigation, Crime in the United States, Uniform Crime Reports—2001.

SPSS PRACTICE PROBLEMS

1. Access HOMICIDE.XPT. Under GRAPHS ask for PIE, and then SUM-MARIES FOR GROUPS OF CASES. Once the pie chart dialog box emerges, ask for the slices of the pie to represent % OF CASES, and then place the variable name in the DEFINE SLICES box. Construct a pie chart for the variable, MURCON, which is a variable that gives the disposition

of a homicide case according to three values: no conviction, a murder conviction, or some other felony conviction. What do you conclude about this sample of homicide cases after analyzing the pie chart for this variable?

2. Using the same data as in exercise (1), ask for a bar chart to be made for the variable giving the number of prior arrests the homicide defendant had (PRIARR). To do this, go under GRAPHS and ask for a SIMPLE bar chart for SUMMARIES FOR GROUPS OF CASES. When the bar chart dialog box emerges, ask for the bars to represent the % OF CASES, and then place the variable name (PRIARR) in the CATEGORY AXIS box. What do you conclude about the criminal history for this sample of homicide defendants?

3. Access YOUTH.XPT. Ask for a frequency distribution for the variable V63, which provides information on how often a respondent's parents know where he/she is when they are away from home using the following response options: 1—never, 2—sometimes, 3—usually, 4—always. To do this, go under ANALYZE, then DESCRIPTIVE STATISTICS, then FREQUENCIES. When the frequencies dialog box appears, you also can ask for a bar chart to be included in the output by selecting the CHARTS box, and then asking for a BAR CHART. What do you conclude about parents' knowledge of the whereabouts of their children from this sample of adolescents?

4. Access STATE.XPT. Under ANALYZE, ask for DESCRIPTIVE STATISTICS, then FREQUENCIES. Ask for a frequency distribution for the variable VIOLENT, which is the violent crime rate in each state per 100k population. Under the options for this procedure, you also can ask SPSS to produce a histogram of this variable distribution. Describe the shape of the distribution that emerges for this variable.

5. Using the same data as in exercise (4), under GRAPHS, ask for a HISTOGRAM for the variable DEATHSEN, which is the number of people sentenced to death as of December 31, 2000. Ask for a normal curve to be imposed over the histogram. Describe the shape of the distribution that emerges for this variable. Do you see any abnormalities or outliers?

6. Using the data in HOMICIDE.XPT, ask for a frequency distribution for the variable DAGE, which provides the age of each homicide defendant in the data set. Under ANALYZE, ask for DESCRIPTIVE STATISTICS, then FREQUENCIES. When the frequencies dialog box appears, you also can ask for a histogram to be included in the output by selecting the CHARTS box, and then asking for a HISTOGRAM. What do you conclude about the age at which most homicide defendants commit murder from this sample?

Measures of Central Tendency

> *N*ormal is in the eye of the beholder.
>
> —WHOOPI GOLDBERG
>
> *E*very normal person, in fact, is only normal on the average. His ego approximates to that of the psychotic in some part or other and to a greater or lesser extent.
>
> —SIGMUND FREUD

In addition to graphs and tables that show our data, it is also very useful to provide a summary measure of the important features of our data. Tables and graphs report a great deal of information, while a summary measure is usually a single number that captures one characteristic of our data. An example of such a summary measure is called a measure of central tendency. A measure of central tendency tells us what the most typical or most common score is. There are three measures of central tendency that we will discuss in this chapter: the mode, the median, and the mean. Each captures a somewhat different notion of "central tendency," and each requires a certain level of measurement. You will learn that the mode is the least demanding measure of central tendency, in that to identify the mode you do not need to do any calculations. The mode can be found by identifying the value of the variable that has the highest frequency. The mode, therefore, is the most frequent value of a variable. The mode can be found with data measured at any level, but it is the *only* appropriate measure of central tendency for nominal and purely ordinal-level data. If our data are measured at the interval/ratio level, there are two other measures of central tendency we can use. The second measure of central tendency you will learn about in this chapter is the median. The median is that score in a rank-ordered distribution of scores that is exactly in the middle, such that one-half of the scores are higher and one-half are lower. The third measure of central tendency is the mean. The mean is the arithmetic average of a group of scores. The mean has the advantage of taking all of the information in our data into account since it is calculated by summing all scores and dividing by the number of scores. This advantage is offset by the fact that since it takes all scores into account, the mean is often distorted when there are unusually high or low scores in the data (what are called *outliers*). You will learn to calculate the median and the mean with both grouped and ungrouped data.

INTRODUCTION

In the previous chapter we learned ways to present or show our data with tables and graphs. The use of tables and graphs is an effective way to report what our data look like in terms of both the number of different values a variable has along with their frequency and relative frequency. Tables and graphs, therefore, provide a great deal of important information about our variables to the reader. Sometimes, however, instead of or in addition to such detailed data, we also want to report more summary or concise features of our data. For example, in Problem (4) at the end of the previous chapter, the variable under consideration was the individual test scores received by police recruits. In that problem we asked you to create a table that reported the frequencies and other descriptive information for those 25 scores in table and graph form. The resulting table and graph, which we hope you completed, very nicely illustrated the features of those test scores.

In addition to this detailed information about the individual test scores for each of these 25 recruits, however, suppose we also want to know what the "average" or "most typical" score on the test was, as well as the extent to which the scores differ from this average or typical score. We usually want to express these features of our data in a very simple way; for example, with a single numerical value or just a few values. In other words, rather than creating another table of detailed information, sometimes a "summary measure" of our data is more helpful. There are two classes of such summary measures that are particularly important in statistics. Summary measures that capture the typical, average, or most likely score in a distribution of scores are referred to as **measures of central tendency.** Summary measures that reflect the extent to which the scores in a distribution are different from the typical or average score are referred to as *measures of dispersion.* Our concern in this chapter is with measures of central tendency and, although they are related, we defer our discussion of measures of dispersion until Chapter 5.

As we mentioned, a measure of central tendency is a summary descriptive statistic that captures the most typical score in a distribution of scores or the most typical value of a variable. They are called measures of central tendency because their purpose is to communicate what the "central" score or value is. That is, they attempt to measure the tendency in the data to be distributed about some central or typical score. There are different measures of central tendency, and each one has a slightly different understanding or conceptualization of exactly what is meant by a central or typical score. In addition to having a different sense of what a central score is, each measure of central tendency is calculated differently, each has its own advantages and disadvantages, and each makes a different assumption about the level of measurement of the variable. The three measures of central tendency that we discuss in this chapter are the mode, median, and mean.

THE MODE

The **mode** is one measure of central tendency. The mode conceptualizes "central tendency" in terms of what is the most likely, most common, or most frequent score in a distribution of scores. Putting it another way, the mode is the score or value that has the highest probability of occurring. The mode can be calculated with data measured at the nominal, ordinal, or interval/ratio level. However, if you have nominal or purely ordinal-level data (purely ordinal in the sense that it is not continuous data that has been made ordinal by making class intervals or grouping your data), then the mode is the only appropriate measure of central tendency. The mode is also very easy to calculate or determine. If the data are in numerical or tabular form, the mode can be identified by finding the score/value in a distribution that has: (1) the greatest frequency, (2) the highest proportion, or (3) the highest percent. If the data are in graphical form, the mode can be identified by finding the score/value in the graph that has: (1) the largest slice in a pie chart, (2) the longest bar in a bar chart, or (3) the longest bar in a histogram. So the way the mode understands central tendency is that it is the most likely or probable or the most frequent score or value in a distribution of values.

> > The **mode** is the value of a variable that occurs more often than another value; it is, therefore, the value with the greatest frequency. The mode is an appropriate measure of central tendency for nominal, ordinal, or interval/ratio-level data. With nominal and purely ordinal-level data, the mode is the only appropriate measure of central tendency.

Think of the mode like this: If you had information on the possible types of sentences for a sample of convicted offenders (probation, jail, a fine, prison) and you wanted to know which sentence was most often imposed, you would be asking about the mode.

The Modal Category of Hate Crime

Let's go through a couple of examples. In Table 4–1 we recall the data presented in Chapter 3 showing the distribution of different kinds of hate crimes that were reported to the police in the year 2000 (Table 3–2). As you can see, there were 8,019 hate crime incidents reported to the police that year, each of which fell into one of four distinct categories based upon their motivation or the type of hate that precipitated the crime: race, religion, sexual orientation, or ethnicity or national origin.

The variable "reported hate crime" is measured at the nominal level because the only distinction among the values of this variable is the qualitative distinction of "kind." In other words, a racially motivated hate crime is just a different kind of hate crime and not more or less of a hate crime than one motivated by religious or sexual bias.

Looking at the distribution of scores in this table, we can discern that the most frequently reported hate crime in 2000 was one motivated by racial hostility. We would conclude, therefore, that the mode for this variable is "racially motivated hate crime." There are a number of different ways we could come to this conclusion, each of which would converge on the same answer. First, we could look at the reported frequencies, discover that there were 4,337 racially motivated hate crimes, and note that this frequency is greater than the frequency for all other kinds of reported hate crimes. Second, we could look at the column of proportions to find that over one-half (.5408) of all hate crimes that were reported were racially motivated; this proportion is greater than the proportion for any other kind of hate crime. Third, we could examine the row of percentages to find that 54 percent of all hate crimes in 2000 were racially motivated hate crimes; this percent is greater than the

TABLE 4–1

Type of Hate Crime Incident Reported to Police in 2000

Type of Hate	*f*	Proportion	Percent
Racial	4,337	.5408	54.08%
Religious	1,472	.1836	18.36
Sexual orientation	1,299	.1620	16.20
Ethnicity/national origin	911	.1136	11.36
Total	8,019	1.000	100.00%

Source: *Hate Crimes Statistics—2000.* Federal Bureau of Investigation, Uniform Crime Reporting Program.

percent of hate crimes motivated by religion (18 percent), sexual orientation (16 percent), and ethnic/national origin (11 percent). Finally, we could use the information we have about proportions to determine the probability of each type of hate crime and then draw a conclusion about what the mode is. Since the proportion or relative frequency of a value/score also can be understood as its expected chance or probability of occurring, we can see that if we were to randomly select 1 out of the 8,019 hate crimes in 2000, the probability that it would be a racially motivated hate crime would be .5408, the probability that it would be one motivated by religious prejudice would be .1836, the probability that it would be a sexually motivated hate crime would be .1620, and the probability that the crime would be motivated by ethnic/national origin hatred would be .1136. The highest probability event, therefore, is a racial hate crime—nearly 55 out of every 100 hate crimes reported in 2000 were racial hate crimes, a probability that exceeds all other possible outcomes. All our different ways of capturing the mode tell us that the modal type of hate crime was racially motivated.

Another way of determining what the mode is for a nominal-level variable is to examine the graph of the frequency data (or the graphed proportions or percents). In Figure 4–1 we show the pie chart of the data in Table 4–1 with both the frequency and the percent of each value. In Figure 4–2 we show the same data with a horizontal bar chart. In both figures the easiest way to determine the mode is to find the value with the greatest area. Notice that both the largest slice in the pie chart and the longest bar in the bar chart are for the value "racial hate crime." This is the mode.

The modal type of hate crime reported in 2000, then, is a racially motivated hate crime. Notice that the mode is the *value* or *score* that is most frequent or most likely and not the value of the frequency, proportion, or percent. The

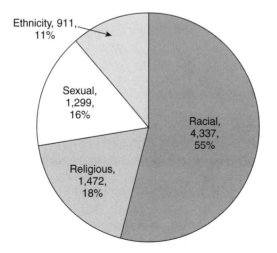

Figure 4–1   Type of Hate Crime Incident Reported to Police in 2000

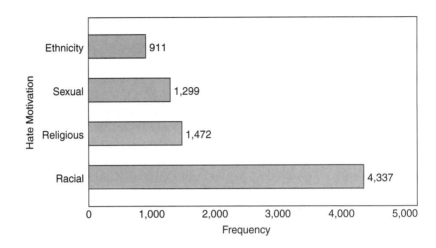

Figure 4–2   Type of Hate Crime Incident Reported to Police in 2000

mode for the variable "reported hate crime in the year 2000" is "racially motivated hate crime," not 4,337, or .5408, or 54.08 percent. The most frequent mistake that students make when they are first learning statistics is to conclude
that the mode is some frequency, proportion, or percent rather than the value
of a given variable. To avoid making this mistake just remember that the mode
refers to the value, score, or outcome of the variable that is most likely or frequent—not the actual frequency of that value. In our example, "racially motivated hate crime" is the value or outcome that is most frequent, and hence that
outcome is the mode—not 4,337 or 54.08 percent, which are not even values of
the variable "type of hate crime."

The Modal Number of Prior Arrests

In Table 4–2 we report the frequency distribution (and percents) of the number of prior arrests for a sample of 150 armed robbery suspects. The data are
in the form of an ungrouped frequency distribution, and the variable "number of prior arrests" is measured at the interval/ratio level. The histogram for
the frequency data is shown in Figure 4–3. Notice in the table that there are
two values that are more frequent than all of the others, "0 prior arrests" and
"1 prior arrest." The probability that a randomly selected armed robber from
this sample would have exactly 0 prior arrests is .2533 ($f = 38$), while the probability that the suspect would have exactly 1 arrest is .2333 ($f = 35$). These two
probabilities are very comparable and are much higher than any other outcome. This corresponds to the height of the two largest rectangular bars in the
histogram (Figure 4–3) for 0 and 1 prior arrests. Even though the frequencies
for "0" and "1" prior arrests are not exactly equal, they are comparable and
their frequencies are much greater than any of the other values or scores. It

TABLE 4–2

Number of Prior Arrests for a Sample of Armed Robbery Suspects

Number	f	%
0	38	25.33
1	35	23.33
2	10	6.67
3	9	6.00
4	14	9.33
5	7	4.67
6	11	7.33
7	8	5.33
8	10	6.67
9	5	3.33
10 or more	3	2.00
Total	150	99.99*

*Percentages may not sum to 100 percent due to rounding.

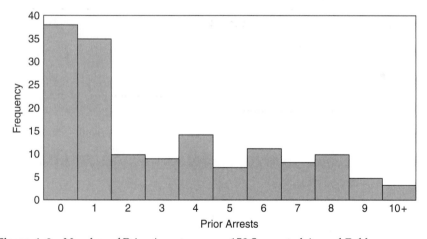

Figure 4–3   Number of Prior Arrests among 150 Suspected Armed Robbers

would appear that for this variable, then, there are two distinct modes, a mode of 0 prior arrests and a mode of 1 prior arrest. This distribution is called a **bimodal distribution.** A bimodal distribution is a distribution that has two distinct values with the greatest frequency or the highest probability of occurring, even though their frequencies are not exactly equal. This

> A **bimodal distribution** is a distribution that contains two distinct modes.

TABLE 4–3

Grouped Frequency Distribution Data for Time Until Rearrest for 120 Inmates

Stated Limits	f	Midpoint
17–19 days	4	18
20–22 days	1	21
23–25 days	12	24
26–28 days	16	27
29–31 days	28	30
32–34 days	28	33
35–37 days	21	36
38–40 days	10	39

type of distribution tells us that there are two scores that are roughly the most typical or most likely scores in the distribution.

The strategy for identifying the mode when the data are in the form of a grouped frequency distribution is pretty much the same as what we have just discussed. Table 4–3 provides the grouped frequency distribution for the variable "time until rearrest" for a sample of 120 inmates who were released from a penitentiary. We first presented these data in the previous chapter. Recall that each person's "score" reflects the number of days they were out in the community until the commission of a new offense. The histogram for these data is shown in Figure 4–4, where the class interval midpoints are shown on the x axis. Looking at this frequency distribution, it is apparent that these are bimodal data. The two modes are represented by the class intervals 29–31 days and 32–34 days. For both of these class intervals, the frequency is higher than for any other class interval. Exactly 28 inmates were arrested between 19 and 31 days and between 32 and 34 days—very close to one month after their release from prison. The two modes also can be seen from the histogram as the two highest peaks in Figure 4–4.

Advantages and Disadvantages of the Mode

As a measure of central tendency the mode has a number of advantages and disadvantages relative to other measures. One of the advantages of the mode

1. is that it is a measure of central tendency that is very simple and appealing conceptually—it is the score or value that is the most frequent and that has the greatest probability of occurring in a distribution of scores. This simple elegance also means that the mode is very easy for readers to comprehend and understand—a key quality that statistical measures should have. The mode also is very simple to calculate. In fact, there is no real arithmetic calculation

2. required to determine the mode, nothing to add or subtract; just identify the score with the highest frequency (or proportion or percent) in either a tabu-

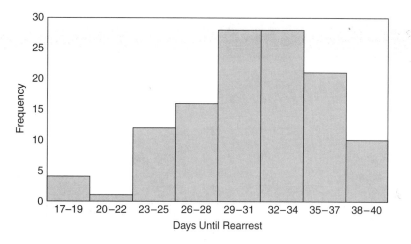

Figure 4–4 Histogram of Grouped Frequency Data for Time Until Rearrest

lar presentation of the data or a graph. Finally, the mode is a very general **3.** ~any level~ ~variable~
measure of central tendency since it can be determined for variables measured at any level. The mode is an appropriate measure of central tendency for nominal, ordinal, and interval/ratio-level data.

The simplicity of understanding and determining the mode is offset, however, by some disadvantages. Since the mode is based only upon the most frequent score or scores, it does not take into account all of the information available in a distribution. One thing statisticians do not like to do is ignore data or information, but that is exactly what the mode does; it requires us to ignore all other pieces of information in the data except the values/scores with the highest frequency. By ignoring or throwing out information, the mode may at times give us a very misleading notion of the central tendency of our data. For example, in Table 4–4 we report the number of subsequent charges of domestic violence accumulated over a one-year period by a sample of 60 men who had been arrested for domestic abuse. According to the table, the mode would be "0 new charges since arrest" since this value has the greatest frequency. Notice, however, that the ease of identifying "0 new charges" as the mode comes at the price of ignoring the fact that many of the men in this sample did have numerous new charges of being abusive toward their partner after their initial arrest. Although it is technically correct that the modal number of new charges is zero, this is somewhat misleading and does not represent the entire distribution of values. Maybe we need to consider alternative measures of central tendency.

If we have data measured at the nominal or truly ordinal level, then we have no real choice, as our only available (i.e., appropriate) measure of central tendency is the mode. If, however, we have ordinal data consisting of a grouped frequency distribution or data measured at the interval/ratio level, we have other measures of central tendency we can employ.

TABLE 4–4

Number of New Charges for Domestic Violence for 60 Men Arrested for Domestic Abuse

Number of New Charges	f
0	14
1	7
2	5
3	8
4	6
5	4
6	3
7	3
8	5
9	3
10 or more	2

+ Interval/ratio level measures

THE MEDIAN

> **> The median** is the score at the 50th percentile in a distribution of scores. As such, one-half of a variable's values are less than the median and one-half are greater than the median.

The **median** is an appropriate measure of central tendency for quantitative data measured at the interval/ratio level or for data that may have been measured at the interval/ratio level originally but now consist of grouped data (class intervals for grouped frequency distributions which are measured at the ordinal level). The easiest way to think of the median is that it is the score/value that is at the 50th percentile in a distribution of scores. The 50th percentile also is known as the second quartile when the data are divided into four quartiles. Since the median is at the 50th percentile, it is that score that divides a rank-ordered distribution of scores into two equal halves—one-half of the scores are lower than the median score and one-half are higher. The median score, in other words, is the score in the exact middle of a rank-ordered distribution of quantitative scores. You can think of the median as a balancing point in the distribution in that it is the score at which all scores on one side are less than the median and an exact number of scores on the other side are greater than the median.

When the data are continuous (not grouped), you can easily identify the median value by following these two steps:

Steps to Find the Median

Step 1: Rank-order all scores from lowest score to highest score.

Step 2: Find the position of the score (x) that is the median score by the following formula: Median position = $(n + 1)/2$. This formula says that the position of the median score is found by adding 1 to the total number of scores and then dividing by 2. *This formula will not give you the value of the median, but the* position *of the median score.* To find the value of the median, find the score in the position indicated by the formula in the rank-ordered array of scores.

When there are an odd number of scores, this formula is very easy to use.

Calculating the Median Number of Prior Convictions

Let us say that we have seven scores that represent the number of prior convictions for a sample of armed robbers: 9, 0, 3, 6, 12, 1, and 15. To find the median number of prior convictions, step 1 instructs us to first rank-order the scores from low to high:

Rank	Score
1	0
2	1
3	3
4	6
5	9
6	12
7	15

Next, we find the position of the median with our positional locator, $(n + 1)/2$, which in this case is $(7 + 1)/2 = 8/2 = 4$. The median score is thus in the fourth position in our rank-ordered scores. Again, we would like to emphasize that the median is not 4, but the median falls in the fourth position of our rank-ordered scores. In order to find the value of the median, find the score in the fourth position. We can do this either by starting at the top of the rank-ordered scores (the lowest score) and counting down until we find the fourth score or by starting at the bottom (the highest score) and counting up until we find the fourth score. The result is the same; the score in the fourth position of our rank-ordered scores is 6. The median number of arrests, therefore, is 6 prior arrests. Notice that as the median, exactly one-half of the scores in this distribution are lower (0, 1, and 3 prior convictions) and exactly one-half are higher (9, 12, and 15 prior convictions). The median score, then, sits in the exact middle of the distribution of rank-ordered scores. This is the interpretation of the median. We can say that 50 percent of the distribution of prior arrests fall below six prior arrests and 50 percent fall above this value.

Now let us add one more person to these data. This person has 18 prior arrests. We now have a total of eight scores, and the rank order of these eight scores would be:

Rank	Score
1	0
2	1
3	3
4	6
5	9
6	12
7	15
8	18

When we use our positional locator formula for the median, we find that the position of the median is $(8 + 1)/2 = 9/2 = 4.5$. What does a position of 4.5 mean? It means that the median score is the score that is in between, or the average of, the fourth and fifth scores. Since our fourth score (from the top) is 6 prior arrests and our fifth score (again from the top) is 9 prior arrests, the median score is the average of these scores. Had we found the fourth and fifth scores by starting at the bottom (or highest) score and counting up, the two scores still would have been 9 and 6. To find the average, recall that we simply sum all scores and divide by the number of scores. The average of 6 prior arrests and 9 prior arrests is $(6 + 9)/2 = 15/2 = 7.5$ prior arrests. The median number of prior arrests in this second set of scores, then, is 7.5. Notice that one-half of the scores are greater than and one-half are less than this value. The median, then, measures central tendency as the score in the middle or 50th percentile in a set of rank-ordered scores.

Another way to identify the median in a set of continuous scores is to find the 50th percentile in a cumulative percent distribution. Table 4–5 reports the distribution of scores for a variable called "number of times committing vandalism" for a sample of 150 boys. The values range from 0 times to 75 times. The first column in Table 4–5 reports the value or score (the number of times a boy reported committing an act of vandalism), the second column shows the frequency for each value, the third column reports the cumulative frequency, the fourth column is the percent for each value, and the fifth and final column provides a compilation of the cumulative percents.

There are two ways of finding the median number of acts of vandalism in this distribution. One is to use the formula for the position of the median we already know. Since we have $N = 77$ total scores, the median is in the $(77 + 1)/2 = 78/2 = 39$th position. To find the score at the 39th position, all we have to do is use the column of cumulative frequencies. We can see from this column that 30 scores are at the value of 2 or lower, and 41 scores are at the value of 3 or lower. This means that the 31st score is a 3, the 32nd score is a 3, . . . the 39th score is a 3, and the 40th and 41st scores are 3s as well. Since the median score is the 39th score, the median must be "3 acts of vandalism." We also could have discovered this by looking at the column of cumulative percents. Since the median is the 50th percentile, all we have to do is find the

TABLE 4–5

Reported Number of Times Committing Vandalism for 150 Boys

# of Times	f	cf	%	c%
0	15	15	19%	19%
1	10	25	13	32
2	5	30	7	39
3	11	41	14	53
4	7	48	9	62
5	8	56	10	72
6	5	61	7	79
7	4	65	5	84
8	5	70	7	91
9	4	74	5	96
10 or more	3	77	4	100

TABLE 4–6

Grouped Frequency Distribution Data for Time Until Rearrest for 120 Inmates

Stated Limits	Real Limits	f	cf
17–19 days	16.5–19.5 days	4	4
20–22 days	19.5–22.5 days	1	5
23–25 days	22.5–25.5 days	12	17
26–28 days	25.5–28.5 days	16	33
29–31 days	28.5–31.5 days	28	61
32–34 days	31.5–34.5 days	28	89
35–37 days	34.5–37.5 days	21	110
38–40 days	37.5–40.5 days	10	120

score at the 50th percentile. We can see that values of "2 acts of vandalism" are at the 39th percentile and that values of "3 acts of vandalism" go up to the 53rd percentile. Since the 50th percentile is contained in the latter percentile, then, the median is at the score of "3 acts of vandalism."

The Median for Grouped Data

What do we do when we have grouped data and want to find the median score? Things get a little more complicated, but with a formula we can locate the median with grouped data as well. Table 4–6 reports the grouped frequency distribution for the example of 120 inmates released into the community from whom we have the number of days they were "free" before being rearrested. Notice that this table reports the real limits of the class intervals. As you will see, you need to know the real limits when calculating the median for grouped data. The procedure for determining the value of the median for these grouped data is comparable to that for ungrouped data. First we have to rank-order the values of the variable. In Table 4–6 the values of the variable "time until rearrest" consist of class intervals, and they are already rank-ordered from low to high, as you can see. Now that the data have been rank-ordered, we need to find the class interval that contains the median. We can use our positional locator $(n + 1)/2$ and the column of cumulative frequencies to find the interval that contains the median. Since $n = 120$, the median is in the $(120 + 1)/2 = 121/2 = 60.5$th position, or the score that is the midpoint between the 60th and 61st scores. We now have to locate the class interval that has the median. The 34th score through the 61st score can be found in the class interval 29–31 days (see the column of cumulative frequencies). This is the interval that contains the median since the median score is the midpoint between the 60th and 61st scores. With this information we are now ready to calculate the actual value of the median. We can determine the value of the median (and not just the location in this case) with the following formula:

$$X_{median} = L + \left(\frac{\left(\frac{n+1}{2}\right) - cf}{f} \right) w_i \qquad (4\text{--}1)$$

where

X_{median} = the value of the median,

   L = the lower real limit of the class interval that contains the median,

   cf = the cumulative frequency of the class interval just before the class interval that contains the median,

   f = the frequency of the interval that contains the median,

   w_i = the width of the class interval, and

   n = the total number of observations in the sample.

Now let us calculate what the median number of days until rearrest is in these data:

$$X_{median} = L + \left(\frac{\left(\frac{n+1}{2}\right) - cf}{f} \right) w_i$$

$$X_{median} = 28.5 + \left(\frac{\left(\frac{120+1}{2} \right) - 33}{28} \right) 3$$

$$X_{median} = 28.5 + \left(\frac{60.5 - 33}{28} \right) 3$$

$$X_{median} = 28.5 + (.98)3$$

$$X_{median} = 28.5 + 2.94$$

$$X_{median} = 31.44 \text{ days until rearrest}$$

The median time until rearrest, then, is 31.44 days. In this distribution of grouped data, we can say that one-half of the inmates were rearrested within 31.44 days and one-half lasted more than 31.44 days before they were rearrested.

Advantages and Disadvantages of the Median

There are a number of advantages to the median as a measure of central tendency. First, while there may be several modes in a distribution, leading to some degree of confusion about exactly what the "central tendency" is in the data, there will always be only one median. Second, as the score in the exact middle of a rank-ordered distribution of scores, the median value has intuitive appeal—it is very easy to understand. Third, the median is a useful measure of central tendency that is used in some graphical displays of data. In Chapter 5, for example, we will be learning other ways to graphically display the distribution of a variable in something called a "box-and-whisker plot." In these graphs the median is the measure of central tendency in the data that we will use. Finally, because the median does not use all of the scores in our data, it is not influenced by extremely high or extremely low scores. Extremely high or low scores in a distribution often are referred to as **outliers,** Since the median locates the score in the middle of the distribution, or at the 50th percentile, it does not matter if there are outliers in the data. Let us explain.

Table 4–7 reports three columns of data. Each column represents the rate of forcible rape per 100,000 people for a sample of U. S. cities in 1999. There are seven cities in the first column, and the rape rates already have been rank-ordered for you. The median rape rate for these seven cities is 57.7 rapes per 100,000. In the next column of cities we simply add one more city, Minneapolis, with a rape rate of 126.7 per 100,000. This is an extremely high rape rate, and adding it to this list of seven cities makes it a high outlier. What happens to the value of the median? Well, with eight cases now in the distribution the median score is the midpoint between the 4th and 5th scores: (57.7 + 58.5)/2 = 58.1 rapes per 100,000. As you can clearly see, adding this very high outlier did not change the median rape rate that much at all, from 57.7 rapes

TABLE 4–7

Rape Rates per 100,000 People for Selected U.S. Cities in 1999

Rank	City	Rate	Rank	City	Rate	Rank	City	Rate
1	St. Louis	42.2	1	St. Louis	42.2	1	New York City	22.9
2	Milwaukee	46.8	2	Milwaukee	46.8	2	St. Louis	42.2
3	Denver	48.9	3	Denver	48.9	3	Milwaukee	46.8
4	Las Vegas	57.7	4	Las Vegas	57.7	4	Denver	48.9
5	Buffalo	58.5	5	Buffalo	58.5	5	Las Vegas	57.7
6	Boston	60.4	6	Boston	60.4	6	Buffalo	58.5
7	Kansas City	74.3	7	Kansas City	74.3	7	Boston	60.4
			8	Minneapolis	126.7	8	Kansas City	74.3

Source: U.S. Federal Bureau of Investigation, Crime in the United States—1999.

per 100,000 to 58.1 rapes per 100,000. As such, the median still gives a very accurate assessment of the central tendency of rape rates in these data.

In the next set of cites we remove Minneapolis and substitute New York City, which in 1999 had a rate of forcible rape of 22.9 per 100,000, one of the lowest rape rates for a major U.S. city. The rape rate for New York City is an example of a low outlier. We once again find the median for these eight scores as the midpoint between the 4th and 5th scores: $(48.9 + 57.7)/2 = 53.3$ rapes per 100,000. Comparing the three medians we calculated, with seven cities the median rape rate was 57.7 per 100,000. When we added Minneapolis with a high outlier the median rate was 58.1. And when we added New York City with a low outlier the median rape rate was 53.3. In each case, the measure of central tendency tells us that the median rape rate is in the low to high 50th percentile per 100,000. Even when there are outlying scores, then, the median is a very stable measure of central tendency since it is defined as the 50th percentile and does not take the value of each and every score into account. This is an important advantage of the median as a measure of central tendency. Moreover, the median really has no great disadvantage and, where appropriate, should always be reported as one of your measures of central tendency.

THE MEAN

The third and final measure of central tendency that we will examine is the mean. Like the median, the mean requires that the data be measured at the interval/ratio level. However, it too can be calculated if you have ordinal data in the form of a grouped frequency distribution where you have taken continuous data and created class intervals. An example of this is the time-until-rearrest data for our group of 120 released offenders.

Calculating the Mean

The **mean** is defined as the arithmetic average of a group of scores, and it is calculated by summing all of the scores and then dividing by the total number of scores. You are already very familiar with the mean. We calculated the mean of two scores when the median position of a distribution fell in between two values. Your college grade point average is also a mean. For example, suppose you took five classes last semester and earned two As, a B, a C, and a D (in math, of course). Let's assume that your college assigns a 4.0 for an A grade, a 3.0 for a B grade, a 2.0 for a C grade, and a 1.0 for a D grade. Your GPA or grade point *average* for last semester, then, would be $(4 + 4 + 3 + 2 + 1)/5 = 14/5 = 2.8$. This is the mean grade you received in all five of your classes. Your average would be almost a B, reflecting the fact that you did get two As but also received a C and a D.

> ▸ The **mean** is the arithmetic average of a group of scores and is calculated as the sum of the scores divided by the total number of scores. The mean is an appropriate measure of central tendency for interval/ratio-level data.

Before we get some practice in calculating the mean, we need to distinguish between the mean of a population and the mean of a sample. Recall from our discussion in Chapter 1 that a population consists of the universe of cases in which we are interested. For example, if we are interested in the relationship between IQ scores and delinquency among male youths between the ages of 12 and 18 in the United States, then our population would consist of all male youths between the ages of 12 and 18 who reside in the United States. The population we are interested in, then, is generally very large and both difficult and costly to study directly. In fact, our population of male adolescents would number in the millions. A sample, you will remember, is a subset of the population; we select and study a sample from the population with the intention of making an inference to the population based on what we know about the sample. The sample, then, is much smaller in size than the population itself, and it is the group that we actually study. In the study mentioned above, for example, we might first take a sample of states, then a sample of cities, and then finally a sample of youths between the ages of 12 and 18 from those cities.

It would be possible (although it would involve a great deal of work and money) to calculate the mean of a population. The mean of a population, therefore, is unknown but knowable. In statistics, the mean of a population is noted by the term μ (the Greek letter mu) and is defined as the sum of all scores in the population divided by the total number of observations in the population:

 $\mu =$ population mean

$$\mu = \frac{\sum_{i=1}^{N} X_i}{N} \qquad (4\text{--}2)$$

where

    X_i = each X score in the population, and
    N = the total number of observations in the population.

To calculate the population mean, therefore, sum all scores in the population starting with the first and ending with the last or Nth, and then divide by the total number of observations (N). Notice that the mean takes all scores into account since we have to sum all scores before calculating the mean.

When we have a sample and wish to calculate the mean of the sample, the formula we use is:

$$\overline{X} = \frac{\sum_{i=1}^{n} x_i}{n} \tag{4-3}$$

$\overline{X} =$ sample mean

where

  $\overline{X} =$ the symbol used for the sample mean (pronounced "x bar"),
  $x_i =$ the ith raw score in a distribution of scores,

$\sum_{i=1}^{n} x_i =$ the instruction to sum all x_i scores, starting with the first score
       $(i = 1)$ and continuing until the last score $(i = n)$, and

  $n =$ the total number of scores.

To calculate the sample mean, this formula is telling you to start by summing all of the scores in your distribution starting with the first score and ending with the last or Nth score, then divide this sum by the total number of scores in your sample. For example, if you had a distribution of 10 scores, you would calculate the mean of those scores by taking the sum of each of the 10 scores and then dividing by 10: $x = (x_1 + x_2 + x_3 + \ldots + x_{10})/10$. Unlike the median, the mean is not a positional measure of central tendency. Since the mean takes into account all of your scores, you do not need to rank-order them beforehand; you can simply start summing numbers from the very first score.

As an example of calculating the mean, let's begin by calculating the mean rape rate for the seven cities that comprise the first column of Table 4–7. The mean rate of forcible rape would be 55.54 rapes per 100,000:

$$\overline{X} = \frac{\sum_{i=1}^{n} x_i}{n}$$

$$\overline{X} = \frac{x_1 + x_2 + x_3 + x_4 + x_5 + x_6 + x_7}{7}$$

$$\overline{X} = \frac{42.2 + 46.8 + 48.9 + 57.7 + 58.5 + 60.4 + 74.3}{7} = \frac{388.8}{7} = 55.54$$

As practice, let's also calculate the mean rape rate per 100,000 for the second column of cities in Table 4–7:

$$\overline{X} = \frac{42.2 + 46.8 + 48.9 + 57.7 + 58.5 + 60.4 + 74.3 + 126.7}{8} = \frac{515.5}{8} =$$

64.44 rapes per 100,000

Like the median, the mean also is a sort of balancing score. Rather than balancing the exact number of scores in a distribution as the median, however, the mean exactly balances the distance of each score from the mean. If we were to subtract the mean of a distribution from each score in the distribution, the negative differences from the mean would exactly equal the positive differences. Let's take a simple example. We have a set of five scores (2, 4, 6, 8, and 10). We calculate the mean and it is equal to $\bar{X} = (2 + 4 + 6 + 8 + 10)/5 = 30/5 = 6$. We then subtract this mean from each score:

$$2 - 6 = -4$$
$$4 - 6 = -2$$
$$6 - 6 = 0$$
$$8 - 6 = 2$$
$$10 - 6 = 4$$

Subtracting the mean from each score is called the *mean deviation.* Notice that the sum of the negative differences is -6 and the sum of the positive differences is $+6$, so that the sum of all differences from the mean is equal to zero. When the mean is subtracted from each score, the sum of the differences from the mean always will be equal to zero because the negative differences will exactly equal the positive differences. This always will be true. It is in this sense that the mean is a balancing score of the differences. The mean is the only measure of central tendency that has this characteristic. The sum of the differences of each score from the mean, then, will always be zero. In mathematical terms, this means that $\Sigma(x - \bar{X}) = 0$.

Formula 4–3 for calculating the sample mean is very simple and easy to use when there are only a few scores. When there are a large number of scores, however, this formula is a bit cumbersome. To calculate the mean when there are many scores in a frequency distribution, the following formula is easier to use:

$$\bar{X} = \frac{\Sigma(x_i f_i)}{n} \tag{4-4}$$

where
  $\bar{X}$ = the mean,
  x_i = ith score,
  f_i = the frequency for the ith score
  $x_i f_i$ = the xth score multiplied by its frequency, and
  n = the total number of scores.

Formula 4–4 may seem a bit complicated, but we will illustrate its use with an example and will show you each step of the way.

Calculating the Mean Police Response Time

Table 4–8 shows you an ungrouped frequency distribution of response times to 911 calls to the police for assistance. Each response time was

TABLE 4–8

Response Times to 911 Calls for Police Assistance

Minutes	f_i	$X_i f_i$
1	5	5
2	6	12
3	9	27
4	8	32
5	6	30
6	7	42
7	3	21
8	2	16
9	2	18
10	1	10
11	1	11
		$\Sigma = 224$

rounded to the nearest minute. Just so there is no confusion, note that there were five occasions in which the police responded to a 911 call in 1 minute, six times they responded within 2 minutes, nine times they responded within 3 minutes, and so on, concluding with one time when they responded to a call for assistance within 11 minutes. You may recall that we used these data in the last chapter. The first step in calculating the mean is to create a new column of scores in which each entry in the column is the product of each x score multiplied by its frequency f (this column is labeled $x_i f_i$). For example, the first entry in the $x_i f_i$ column is 5, which represents the fact that the police responded to a 911 call in 1 minute five times. Normally, in order to calculate the mean we would add these five scores of "1" by doing $1 + 1 + 1 + 1 + 1 = 5$. But by taking the product of the score and its frequency $(x_i f_i)$, we are simply taking advantage of the fact that $1 + 1 + 1 + 1 + 1 = 1 \times 5 = 5$. For the second entry of the third column we are taking advantage of the fact that $2 + 2 + 2 + 2 + 2 + 2 = 2 \times 6 = 12$. We take each x_i score and multiply it by its frequency to form the column of $x_i f_i$. The second step in calculating the mean is then to sum all of these products. The sum of the column of $x_i f_i$ in Table 4–8 is 224. This is what we would have obtained had we taken the first approach and summed all x_i scores ($1 + 1 + 1 + \ldots 7 + 7 + 7 \ldots + 10 + 11 = 224$). The third step in calculating the mean is to divide the sum of the product $x_i f_i$ by the total number of scores. In this case, since there were 50 calls for police assistance we can calculate the mean or average response time to a 911 call as: $\bar{x} = 224/50 = 4.48$ minutes, and since .48 minutes is equal to 28.8 seconds (.48 × 60 seconds), the average response time was 4 minutes and 28.8 seconds, or about 4 1/2 minutes.

Steps to Calculate the Mean from an Ungrouped Frequency Distribution

Step 1: Multiply each x_i score by its frequency (f_i). This will give you a column of products ($x_i f_i$).

Step 2: Sum up the obtained products from step 1:

$$\Sigma(x_i f_i)$$

Step 3: Divide this sum by the total number of scores (n):

$$\overline{X} = \frac{\Sigma\left(x_i f_i\right)}{n}$$

Remember that the total number of scores is (n) and is the sum of the number of frequencies. Very often students will use the number of different scores in the frequency distribution rather than the total number of scores as the denominator for the mean. For example, rather than use 50 as the denominator in the above problem, since there were 50 response times recorded, many students are tempted to use 11 because there are 11 different values. There may be only 11 values for the variable "police response time," but these values occurred a total of 50 times, and this is the total number of observations.

The Mean for Grouped Data

The procedure for calculating the mean when the data are in a grouped frequency distribution is very similar to that used when the data are in an ungrouped frequency distribution. The first thing you have to determine is that the underlying measurement of the data is continuous even though the data are grouped. If you are satisfied that the data are continuous and have been put into a grouped frequency distribution simply for convenience and clarification, then you may proceed. Keep in mind that since the data are in the form of a grouped frequency distribution there are no individual x scores. Rather, the data are now in the form of class intervals, and while we know which class interval a score falls into, we do not know the exact score. In order to calculate a mean with grouped data, then, we are going to have to make a simplifying assumption. We are going to make the assumption that each score within a class interval is located exactly at its midpoint. Now, once we make this assumption we do not exactly have a distribution of x_i scores, but we have a distribution of m_i scores, where the m_i refers to the midpoint of the ith class interval.

Earlier in this chapter, Table 4–3 provided the grouped frequency distribution data for the time until rearrest for a sample of 120 offenders released into the community. Recall that these data provide a count of the number of days a released offender was in the community until being rearrested. These

are grouped data that were originally continuous, so we can legitimately calculate a mean. Our simplifying assumption is that each score within a class
interval is assumed to lie at its midpoint. So, for purposes of calculating the
mean, we are going to assume that all four cases in the first class interval are
at the midpoint of 18 days, the one score in the second class interval is at the
midpoint of 21, the 12 scores in the third class interval are at the midpoint of
24, and so on. Recall that we need to make this assumption because we must
have a specific score (18 days, for example) in order to calculate a mean,
rather than an interval within which a score lies (17–19 days). Since we are
making this assumption, we will be getting only an estimate of the mean for
these data. This estimate probably is not going to be exactly what the value
of the mean would be if we calculated it from the original continuous data.
In a moment, we will check and see how accurate we are in making this assumption.

Once we have made this assumption, we are ready to calculate our mean.
Recall that when we have data in the form of a frequency distribution, we can
use formula 4–3 to calculate the mean by taking the product of each x score
and its frequency ($x_i f_i$), summing these products over all x_i scores, and then
dividing by the total number of scores $\bar{X} = \sum x_i f_i / n$. We are going to modify
this formula only slightly and use it to calculate a mean from grouped data.
With grouped data, we do not have an individual x_i score, but we do have m_i
scores since we are assuming that each score within its class interval lies at its
midpoint (m_i). In order to calculate the mean from grouped data, then, we just
substitute m_i for x_i in formula 4–4 and take the product of each midpoint and
the number of scores that are assumed to lie at that midpoint:

$$\bar{X} = \frac{\sum m_i f_i}{n} \tag{4–5}$$

where

$\bar{X};$ = the mean,
m_i = the midpoint for the ith class interval,
f_i = the frequency for the ith class interval,
$m_i f_i$ = the m_i midpoint multiplied by its frequency, and
n = the total number of scores.

In words, to calculate the mean we are going to multiply the midpoint of each
class interval by the frequency of that class interval. Once we have done this
for each class interval, we are going to sum these products over all intervals
and then divide by the total number of scores. We will illustrate the use of the
mean formula for grouped data with the time until arrest data. Table 4–9 provides the information you need.

The sum of each midpoint multiplied by its frequency is 3,723. Now, to
calculate the mean all we have to do is divide this sum by the total number
of scores or observations. The mean number of days free until rearrest is
therefore 31.02 days:

TABLE 4–9

Calculating a Mean Using Grouped Data—Time Until Rearrest for 120 Inmates

Stated Limits	f	Midpoint	$f_i\, m_i$
17–19 days	4	18	72
20–22 days	1	21	21
23–25 days	12	24	288
26–28 days	16	27	432
29–31 days	28	30	840
32–34 days	28	33	924
35–37 days	21	36	756
38–40 days	10	39	390
	$\Sigma = 120$		$\Sigma = 3{,}723$

$$\overline{X} = \frac{3{,}723}{120} = 31.02 \text{ days}$$

On average, then, these offenders were free for 31.02 days before being arrested and returned to prison. When you calculate the mean from grouped data using this method, make sure that you use the correct sample size for the denominator. The "n" in the formula is the total number of observations or scores you have. In this example, our data consist of 120 observations.

> ### Steps to Calculate the Mean from a Grouped Frequency Distribution
>
> **Step 1:** Multiply each midpoint (m_i) by its frequency (f_i). This will give you a column of products ($m_i f_i$).
>
> **Step 2:** Sum the obtained products from step 1:
>
> $$\Sigma(m_i f_i)$$
>
> **Step 3:** Divide this sum by the total number of scores (n):
>
> $$\overline{X} = \Sigma\,(m_i f_i)/n$$

Recall that these time-until-arrest data were originally measured at the interval/ratio level from which we created class intervals. In the example above we estimated the mean number of days an offender was free in the community based on the class interval scores. The question to answer now is whether

TABLE 4–10

Calculating a Mean Using Ungrouped Data—Time Until Rearrest for 120 Inmates

x_i	f_i	$x_i f_i$
17 .	1	17
18	1	18
19	2	38
20	1	20
21	0	0
22	0	0
23	3	69
24	4	96
25	5	125
26	3	78
27	7	189
28	6	168
29	11	319
30	7	210
31	10	310
32	7	224
33	12	396
34	8	272
35	8	280
36	8	288
37	6	222
38	4	152
39	2	78
40	4	160
	$\Sigma = 120$	$\Sigma = 3{,}729$

or not we were accurate in our estimation of the mean using these grouped data. To determine our precision, let's calculate the mean number of days until arrest from the original variable measured at the interval/ratio level and compare it to our estimate with formula 4–4. Table 4–10 reports the frequency distribution for the time-until-arrest data in their original form; we provide the necessary column of ($f_i x_i$) for you. Using the ungrouped data, then, we can calculate the mean as: $\overline{X} = 3{,}729/120 = 31.075$ days. Our estimate of the mean with the grouped data was 31.02 days, so we were pretty close to the value of the mean had the data remained in their original interval/ratio form. In general, you will not lose much accuracy in estimating the mean when you use grouped rather than ungrouped data.

Advantages and Disadvantages of the Mean

The mean has a number of advantages as a measure of central tendency. First, it is intuitively appealing. Everyone is familiar with an average. The mean also uses all of the information in a data set, which is an advantage as long as there are no outliers in the data. The mean also is an efficient measure of central tendency. For example, let's say we had a population of scores (with a mean and median) and from this population we took many, many samples and calculated both the mean and the median for each sample. The medians of these samples would differ more from each other and the population median than the means would differ from each other and the population mean. Because we usually draw only one sample from a population, we want to have a measure of central tendency that is the most efficient. This is the mean.

The one disadvantage of the mean is a by-product of one of its strengths: Because it takes every score into account, the mean may be distorted by high or low outliers. When we sum every score to calculate the mean, we may at times be adding uncharacteristically high or low scores. When this happens, the value of the mean will give us a distorted sense of the central tendency of the data. To illustrate this point, let's return to Table 4–7, which provided three columns of rape rates per 100,000 people for selected U.S. cities. The first column consists of seven cities. If you were to calculate the mean rape rate for these cities, you would obtain a value of $\overline{X} = 388.8/7 = 55.5429$ rapes per 100,000. What happens to the mean when we include the high outlier of Minneapolis from the second column? The mean now is: $\overline{X} = 515.5/8 = 64.4375$ rapes per 100,000. Notice what happens to the value of the mean when we include this high outlier. The magnitude of the mean increases dramatically, and it is now over 64 rapes per 100,000. The inclusion of a high outlier, then, has the effect of inflating our mean. To get a sense of how this mean, while technically correct, might distort our sense of the central tendency of the data, you can see that are only two scores in the entire distribution that are even close to the mean—Minneapolis and Kansas City. It is, therefore, not really accurate to say that a mean rape rate of 64 per 100,000 represents the central tendency of these data.

Now look at the third column of cities in Table 4–7. What happens to the mean when we drop the high outlier of Minneapolis and add the low outlier of New York City, with a rape rate of 22.9 per 100,000? The value of the mean is now $\overline{X} = 411.7/8 = 51.4625$ rapes per 100,000. The mean has declined slightly, but it does not distort the central tendency as much as our high outlier did. As you can see, however, the effect of a low outlier is to lower the magnitude of the mean.

The purpose of this exercise is to show that sometimes the mean can provide a distorted sense of the central tendency in our data. Since the mean uses every score in our distribution, high outliers can inflate the mean and low outliers can deflate the mean, relative to what the value of the mean would be without the outliers. For this reason, it is generally a good idea to report *both* the mean and the median when you are discussing the central tendency in your data. With respect to Table 4–7 we saw how the mean moves rather substantially with the inclusion of outliers in the data. Remember that the median was much more stable, further illustrating this point.

Reporting both the mean and the median also can tell us something important about the shape of our data. In Chapter 3 we illustrated the difference between symmetrical and skewed distributions. In Chapter 6 we will be discussing the normal or bell-shaped distribution, a very important theoretical probability distribution in statistics. A normal distribution has one mode (it is single peaked), and it is symmetrical. If a line were drawn down the center of the distribution, the left half would be a mirror image of the right half. In a symmetrical or normal distribution, the mean, median, and mode all will be the same, located right at the center of the distribution. If a distribution is not normal, recall that it is said to be a **skewed distribution.** In a negatively skewed distribution the mean is less than the median. This is because there are low outlying scores on the left-hand side of the distribution pulling the value of the mean down. Stated differently, in a negatively skewed distribution the mean is lower in magnitude than the median because the low outliers are deflating the mean. This is what we saw in the third column of Table 4–7. Thus, knowing that in a distribution of scores the mean is much lower than the median, we might suspect that the distribution has a negative skew. The greater the difference between the mean and the median, the greater the negative skew. Conversely, in a positively skewed distribution the mean is greater than the median because there are high outliers that are inflating the magnitude of the mean relative to the median, as we saw in the second column of Table 4–7.

SUMMARY

Our focus in this chapter was on measures of central tendency. These measures of central tendency are used as summary indicators of the typical, usual, most frequent, or average score in a distribution of scores. There are three measures of central tendency: the mode, the median, and the mean.

The *mode* is the score or value with the highest frequency. It is, therefore, the score or value that has the highest probability or greatest likelihood of occurring. There may be more than one mode in a given distribution of scores. As a measure of central tendency the mode is probably the easiest to obtain since it requires no real calculations, and it is an appropriate measure of central tendency for nominal, ordinal, or interval/ratio-level data.

The *median* is the score at the 50th percentile. As such it is the score or value that divides a rank-ordered distribution of scores into two equal halves. A characteristic of the median, therefore, is that one-half of the scores will be greater than it and one-half will be less than it. The median requires continuous-level data (interval/ratio) or continuous-level data that have been made ordinal through the creation of a grouped frequency distribution. Since the median locates the score at the 50th percentile, it is not affected by outlying scores in a distribution. For this reason, it is a very good measure of central tendency when the data are skewed.

The *mean* is the arithmetic average of all scores. It is calculated by summing the value of all scores and dividing by the total number of scores. Calculation of the mean requires the same level of measurement as does the median. Because the mean uses all of the scores, it can be substantially affected by the presence of outliers in the data. In a normal distribution, the mode, median, and mean will be the same. In a negatively skewed distribution, the mean is less than the median, and in a positively skewed distribution, the mean is greater than the median. Because the presence of outliers may distort the mean as a measure of central tendency, it is generally a good policy to report both the median and the mean.

KEY TERMS

bimodal distribution	**mode**
mean	**outlier**
measure of central tendency	**skewed distribution**
median	

KEY FORMULAS

Sample median for grouped data (eq. 4–1):

$$X_{median} = L + \left(\frac{\left(\frac{n+1}{2} \right) - cf}{f} \right) w_i$$

where

$\bar{X}_{median}$ = the value of the median,

L = the lower real limit of the class interval that contains the median,

cf = the cumulative frequency of the class interval just before the class interval that contains the median,

f = the frequency of the interval that contains the median,

w_i = the width of the class interval, and

n = the total number of observations in the sample.

Sample mean (eq: 4–3):

$$\bar{X} = \frac{\sum_{i=1}^{n} x_i}{n}$$

where

$\bar{X}$ = the symbol used for the sample mean (pronounced "x bar"),

x_i = the ith raw score in a distribution of scores,

$\sum_{i=1}^{n} x_i$ = the instruction to sum all x_i scores, starting with the first score $(i = 1)$ and continuing until the last score $(I - n)$, and

n = the total number of scores.

Sample mean for data in a frequency distribution (eq. 4–4):

$$\bar{X} = \frac{\sum x_i f_i}{n}$$

where

$\bar{X}$ = the mean,

x_i = ith score,

f_i = the frequency for the ith score,

$x_i f_i$ = the xth score multiplied by its frequency, and

n = the total number of scores.

The sample mean for grouped data (eq. 4–5):

$$\bar{X} = \frac{\sum m_i f_i}{n}$$

where

$\bar{X}$ = the mean,

m_i = the midpoint for the ith class interval,

f_i = the frequency for the ith class interval,

$m_i f_i$ = the m_i midpoint multiplied by its frequency, and

n = the total number of scores.

PRACTICE PROBLEMS

1. As a measure of central tendency, the mode is the most common score. Below you have information on a variable called "the number of delinquent friends" someone has. What is the mode for these data, and what does it tell you? Why can't you calculate the "mean number of delinquent friends"?

Number of Delinquent Friends

x	f
None	20
Some	85
Most	30
All	10

2. You asked a random sample of seven correctional officers what their annual salary was, and their responses were as follows:

Salary ($)

25,900
32,100
28,400
31,000
29,500
27,800
26,100

What is the median salary and what is the mean salary for this sample?

3. The data below show the homicide rate per 100,000 people for 10 American cities. Given these data, which measure of central tendency would you use, and why?

City	Homicide Rate
Boston, MA	6.8
Cincinnati, OH	4.5
Denver, CO	6.0
Las Vegas, NV	8.8
New Orleans, LA	43.3
New York City, NY	8.7
Pittsburgh, PA	10.5
Salt Lake City, UT	5.6
San Diego, CA	4.3
San Francisco, CA	7.7

4. David Nurco and his colleagues (1988) have investigated the relationship between drug addiction and criminal activity. The hypothetical data below represent the number of crimes committed during a two-year period by 20 heroin addicts. Using ungrouped data, calculate the mean and the median for these 20 persons. Which measure of central tendency do you think best summarizes the central tendency of these data, and why?

Person Number	Number of Crimes Committed
1	4
2	16
3	10
4	7
5	3
6	112
7	5
8	10
9	6
10	2
11	4
12	11
13	10
14	88
15	9
16	12
17	8
18	5
19	7
20	10

5. In a study of 911 calls made to a large midwestern police department, Gilsinan (1989: 335) reported the following distribution of caller requests:

Request	Frequency
Information	65
Police assistance due to a crime	29
Police assistance for other reasons	82
Police assistance for a traffic problem	19
Police assistance because of an alarm sounding	9

What is the measure of central tendency most appropriate for these data? Why? What does this measure of central tendency tell you about the "most typical" reason for a 911 call?

6. The following hypothetical data show the distribution of the percent of total police officers who do narcotics investigation work in 100 American cities. Determine the mode, median, and mean.

% of Force Involved in Narcotics	Investigation Frequency
0–9%	5
10–19	13
20–29	26
30–39	38
40–49	14
50–59	2
60–69	2
70–79	0
80–89	0
90–99	0

7. The following data represent the number of persons executed in the United States over the years 1977–1983:

Year	Number of Executions
1977	1
1978	0
1979	2
1980	0
1981	1
1982	2
1983	5

What were the mean and median number of executions over this time period? What happens to the median and mean when we add the year 1984, in which there were 21 executions? Which measure of central tendency would you use to describe the 1977–1984 distribution?

8. One seemingly inconsistent finding in criminological research is that women have a greater subjective fear of crime than men, even though their objective risk of being the victim of a crime is lower. In one study, Kelly and DeKeseredy (1994) tried to explain this fact by suggesting that women are often the psychological or physical victim of a crime within their own homes by someone who is an intimate. The hypothetical data below represent the responses of a sample of 200 women who were asked to report to an interviewer the number of times that they had been hit by a spouse, partner, or intimate within the previous two years. Using these data, calculate the mean, median, and mode.

Number of Times Hit	Frequency
0–2	36
3–5	87
6–8	45
9–11	23
12–14	9

9. Research reported in Raine (1993) has suggested that there is a link between hypoglycemia (low blood sugar levels) and violent and aggressive behavior. He notes that the brain requires at least 80 milligrams of glucose per minute in order to function normally and that with reduced levels aggression may occur. In a random sample of 20 violent offenders currently incarcerated in a state penitentiary, the prison doctor finds the following levels of milligrams of glucose per minute. Calculate the mean and median for these data. Are the mean and median the same or different? Why do you think this is so?

Person	Level of Glucose Per Minute
1	65
2	68
3	69
4	62
5	69
6	70
7	73
8	74
9	71
10	67
11	65
12	72
13	66
14	75
15	68
16	71
17	67
18	72
19	70
20	72

SPSS PRACTICE PROBLEMS

Note: You can obtain the mean of a variable distribution by going under ANALYZE, then DESCRIPTIVE STATISTICS, and then asking for DESCRIPTIVES, which will provide you with the minimum, maximum, mean, and standard deviation for a variable. However, to obtain the median and the mode, you must ask for them under the STATISTICS option in the FREQUENCIES dialog box.

1. Access YOUTH.XPT. Under ANALYZE, then FREQUENCIES, ask for a frequency distribution of the variable V79, which is a variable asking respondents how wrong their best friends think it is to drink liquor under age using the response categories of 1—always wrong, 2—usually wrong, 3—sometimes wrong, and 4—seldom wrong. What is the mode for this variable?

2. Using the same data as in exercise (1), ask for a frequency distribution for the variable V1, which is respondent's gender (1—male, 0—female). Now under the STATISTICS box ask for the mode, the median, and the mean for this variable. Does it give you the mean and median values for this variable? Are they meaningful? How can you have a mean value of gender? (And you thought computers were smart!)

3. Access STATE.XPT. Under ANALYZE, then FREQUENCIES, ask for a frequency distribution of the variables MURDER and VIOLENT, which are the rates of murder and violent crime per 100k, respectively, in states. Under the STATISTICS box, ask SPSS to give you all three measures of central tendency for these variables: the mode, median, and mean. Interpret all three measures. Did the mode provide a good measure of center for these interval-/ratio-level variables? What can you deduce about the shape of each of these variable distributions simply by comparing the values of the median and the mean?

4. Access HOMICIDE.XPT. Obtain a frequency distribution along with the values of the mean and median for the variable PRITIME, which is the sentence length in days received by convicted defendants sentenced to prison. Describe this variables center. What measure of center is most appropriate for this distribution and why?

5. Using the same data set as in exercise (4), get a frequency distribution for the variable NUMVICT, which is the number of victims killed in the homicide incidents. What is the modal category for this variable? With the exception of the last category for this variable, which is five or more victims, you could assume this variable was measured at the interval level. Obtain a mean for this variable using either the DESCRIPTIVES or the FREQUENCIES command. How does this value differ from the mode?

6. Access STATE.XPT. Under ANALYZE, there is an option to COMPARE MEANS. After you click on this, select MEANS and a dialog box will appear asking you for a dependent variable and an independent variable. This procedure allows you to compare the means of an interval-level value across values of a qualitative variable (e.g., nominal). In this data set, you have a four-category variable denoting the region where a state resides (Northeast, South, Midwest, West). Ask for MURDER under the DEPENDENT LIST and REGION under the INDEPENDENT LIST. This will give you a list of mean murder rates for each of the four regions. What do you conclude about murder using these mean regional comparisons? How does each regional mean compare with the total mean rate of murder for the United States?

5

CHAPTER

Measures
of Dispersion

*R*esemblances are the shadows of differences. Different people see different similarities and similar differences.

—VLADIMIR NABOKOV

The purpose of this chapter is to introduce you to measures that capture the differences in a group of scores. These measures are called *measures of dispersion* or variability. Like the measures of central tendency we discussed in Chapter 4, measures of dispersion are summary measures that in one number reflect the differences among the values of a variable. In this chapter you will learn that there are different measures of dispersion, with the appropriate measure depending upon the level of measurement of your variable. For nominal and purely ordinal-level data, we will discuss a measure called the variation ratio. With interval-/ratio-level variables there are several measures: the range, the interquartile range, and the variance and standard deviation. The latter two measures of dispersion are particularly important because we use them frequently in later chapters. You will learn how to calculate and interpret each measure with both grouped and ungrouped data.

INTRODUCTION

In the last chapter we learned about ways of characterizing the most typical, middle score, or average score, in our distribution. Measures of central tendency are helpful in summarizing this important feature of our data. However, measures of central tendency do not provide all that we would like to know about the distribution. In addition to information about the central score, we also would like some information about how the scores differ from one another or differ from some measure of central tendency. Summary measures that reflect how different or variable scores are from each other or from some central score are called **measures of dispersion**, because they tell us how "dispersed" or scattered the scores in a distribution are. A measure of dispersion, then, tells us about the heterogeneity in the data. Heterogeneity exists whenever scores are dissimilar or different. The opposite is homogeneity, which exists when scores are similar or alike. Take the following group of five scores on an IQ test: 104, 102, 102, 104, 103. They are very similar to each other and are not very different from the mean of 103 (calculate this mean for yourself), so the homogeneity in the scores is high and the heterogeneity is low. Now consider the following five IQ scores: 74, 130, 80, 120, 111. These scores have the same mean as the first group ($\overline{X} = 103$), but these scores are very dissimilar both to each other and to the mean of the scores. In this second group the homogeneity of the IQ scores is low and the heterogeneity is high. Measures of dispersion capture this notion of the heterogeneity of scores.

Table 5–1 provides a more detailed illustration of the importance and kind of information a measure of dispersion provides to us. Table 5–1 reports the number of years of prison time given by two different judges to 40 defendants convicted of armed robbery. The data are rank-ordered for you already and put into a frequency distribution, so it is pretty easy to calculate the mean and median sentence

> **Measures of dispersion** capture how different the values of a variable are. The more dispersion there is in a variable, the more different the values are or the more heterogeneity in the data.

TABLE 5–1

Number of Years of Prison Time for Armed Robbery Defendants

Judge 1 Years	f	Judge 2 Years	f
5	1	1	1
7	5	2	2
8	4	3	3
9	3	4	2
10	1	5	1
11	3	8	1
12	2	9	1
14	1	10	1
		11	1
		14	1
		15	2
		16	1
		17	1
		18	1
		20	1
$n = 20$	$\Sigma = 180$	$n = 20$	$\Sigma = 180$

length given by these two judges. Each judge sentenced 20 different convicted armed robbers. The median sentence length for both judges is 8.5 years, and they have the same mean sentence length of 9.0 years. As far as these two measures of central tendency are concerned, therefore, the two judges are quite similar in how they sentence armed robbery defendants. But is this accurate? While the two judges may have the same median and mean sentence length, their sentencing behavior is very different. Judge 1's sentencing behavior is clustered narrowly around the mean of 9 years and the median of 8.5 years; her lowest sentence length is 5 years and her highest sentence length is 14 years. Judge 2, however, seems "all over the board" when it comes to sentencing. His sentences are not so tightly clustered around the mean and median. Judge 1's sentences are less different from each other and from her median and mean sentence length than are Judge 2's sentences. You can see this very clearly in Figure 5–1, which shows the sentence length given by the two judges along with their common mean and median sentence length. Notice that the line showing the sentences given by Judge 1 is much closer to the mean and median line than is the line showing the sentences given by Judge 2. What the table and figure both show is that even though they have the same median and mean sentence length, Judge 2 is much more different, dispersed, or heterogeneous in his sentencing behavior than Judge 1. We would, therefore, like to indicate the amount of heterogeneity or dis-

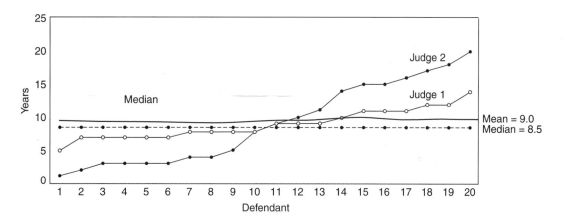

Figure 5–1   Sentence length given by two judges

persion in a variable. This is what measures of dispersion do—they are summary measures that capture the dispersion or heterogeneity in a variable. In addition to a measure of central tendency, then, a measure of dispersion helps us better understand our data. Just as there was more than one measure of central tendency, however, there is more than one measure of dispersion, and the appropriate measure of dispersion depends on the level of measurement of your variable.

MEASURING DISPERSION FOR NOMINAL- AND ORDINAL-LEVEL VARIABLES

The Variation Ratio

The **variation ratio** is a very simple measure of dispersion you can use whenever you have data measured at the nominal or ordinal level. Recall from our last chapter that when we have nominal or ordinal measurement the only measure of central tendency we can use is the mode, which is the score or value with the greatest frequency. The measure of dispersion for these data, the variation ratio, is based upon the mode. The variation ratio (VR) simply measures the extent to which the observations are not concentrated in the modal category. The lower the proportion of cases that are in the modal category, the higher the variation ratio will be. A high value of the variation ratio means that there is more variation in the data. The formula for the variation ratio is:

> ▸ The **variation ratio** is an appropriate measure of dispersion to use when you have data measured at the nominal or purely ordinal level. It measures the extent to which the values do not fall into the modal category. The greater the magnitude of the variation ratio, the more dispersion there is in the nominal or ordinal variable.

$$VR = 1 - \frac{f_{modal}}{n}$$

(5–1)

where

$$f_{modal} = \text{the frequency of cases in the modal category,}$$

$$n = \text{the total number of cases.}$$

This formula tells you to find the mode and then divide the frequency of cases in the modal category into the total number of cases. This gives you the proportion of cases that are in the modal value. Then subtract that proportion from 1.0, which gives you the proportion of the total number of cases that are not in the modal category. Notice that if all of the cases were to fall into one value or category, two things would happen: (1) there would be no variation or dispersion in the data since the "variable" would actually be a constant (all cases fall into only one value), and (2) the magnitude of the variation ratio would be zero, since f_{modal} would equal n and f_{modal}/n would be equal to 1.0.

In Table 5–2 we present a nominal-level variable that we used in Chapter 3. It is the number of hate crimes reported to the police in the year 2000. As we learned in Chapter 3, the variable "type of hate crime" is a nominal-level variable because the values represent only qualitative distinctions—one type of hate crime is simply different from another type of hate crime, rather than "more" of a hate crime.

The mode for this variable is "racial hate crime" since there was more of this kind of hate crime reported in 2000 than any other. More specifically, .54 of the total number of hate crimes were racially motivated hate crimes. We can calculate the value of the variation ratio for this variable as:

$$VR = 1 - \frac{4,337}{8,019}$$

$$VR = 1 - .54$$

$$VR = .46$$

The variation ratio, then, is .46, which tells us that slightly less than one-half of the cases (46 percent to be exact) are not in the modal category of racial hate crimes.

TABLE 5–2

Type of Hate Crime Incident Reported to Police in 2000

Type of Hate Crime	f	Proportion
Racial	4,337	.5408
Religious	1,472	.1836
Sexual orientation	1,299	.1620
Ethnicity/national origin	911	.1136
Total	8,019	1.000

Source: *Hate Crimes Statistics—2000.* Federal Bureau of Investigation, Uniform Crime Reporting Program.

TABLE 5–3

Hypothetical Hate Crime Data

Type of Hate Crime	f	Proportion
Racial	6,016	.75
Religious	974	.12
Sexual orientation	728	.09
Ethnicity/national origin	301	.04
Total	8,019	1.000

Table 5–3 gives you some made-up or hypothetical data of hate crimes. There are still 8,019 reported hate crimes, but in this example, there are 6,016 cases in the category "racial hate crimes." Notice that there is less dispersion or heterogeneity in these data than in Table 5–2 because there is a greater concentration of cases in one category (the mode of racially motivated hate crimes). Now when we calculate the variation ratio it is:

$$VR = 1 - \frac{6,016}{8,019}$$
$$VR = 1 - .75$$
$$VR = .25$$

There are now only .25 (or 25 percent) of the total number of cases *not* in the modal category. The fact that there is less heterogeneity than before is reflected in a lower magnitude of the variation ratio.

Now look at Table 5–4, where we show you another set of hypothetical data. In this example we still have 8,019 reported hate crimes, but now the cases are more evenly distributed across the four values. The mode would still be "racially motivated hate crimes," but there is more heterogeneity or dispersion in these data than in Table 5–3 or Table 5–2. Now when we calculate the magnitude of the variation ratio, we find it to be:

$$VR = 1 - \frac{2,005}{8,019}$$
$$VR = 1 - .25$$
$$VR = .75$$

There are now .75 or 75 percent of the cases that are not in the modal category, indicating that this distribution of hate crimes has more dispersion than the other two examples. The maximum amount of heterogeneity will be obtained when there is no mode and the cases are equally distributed in each of the values. The maximum value of the variation ratio, then, is determined by the number of categories the variable has. The maximum value of the VR will always be equal to

TABLE 5–4

Hypothetical Hate Crime Data

Type of Hate Crime	f	Proportion
Racial	2,005	.25
Religious	2,005	.25
Sexual orientation	2,005	.25
Ethnicity/national origin	2,004	.25
Total	8,019	1.000

$1 - \left(\dfrac{\frac{m}{k}}{n} \right)$ where k is equal to the number of values or categories a variable has and n is the total number of cases. In Tables 5–2 through 5–4, the maximum magnitude of the VR is .75. In Table 5–4 the obtained variation ratio was .75, which is 100 percent of the maximum amount of heterogeneity that could have existed. The important thing to keep in mind is that higher values of the variation ratio imply greater dispersion in the distribution of a nominal-level variable.

MEASURING DISPERSION FOR INTERVAL-/ RATIO-LEVEL VARIABLES

The Range and Interquartile Range

Let's now consider the case where we have data measured at the interval/ratio level, in other words, continuous data or data that can be considered to be continuous. When we have continuous data there are other ways that we can characterize dispersion other than the extent to which the cases fall into the modal value.

The simplest measure of dispersion with continuous data is called the **range**. For ungrouped data the range is the difference between the highest and lowest scores in a distribution: Range = Highest score − Lowest score. When we have data in a grouped frequency distribution, the range is the difference between the midpoint of the last class interval and the midpoint of the first class interval, or the difference between the highest and lowest midpoints.

Calculating the Range of Sentence Lengths

> **>** The **range** is a measure of dispersion appropriate for interval-/ratio-level data. It is calculated as the difference between the highest value or score and the lowest value: Range = Highest value − Lowest value

Referring back to Table 5–1, we can see that the range for Judge 1's sentences for armed robbery defendants is 9 years because the longest sentence she imposed was 14 years and the shortest sentence she imposed was 5 years (14 − 5 = 9 years). The range for Judge 2 is 19 years because his longest sentence was 20 years and his shortest was 1 year. Sometimes the range is expressed as the lowest and highest values

TABLE 5–5

Grouped Frequency Distribution Data for Time Until Failure for 120 Inmates

Stated Limits	f	Midpoint
17–19 days	4	18
20–22 days	1	21
23–25 days	12	24
26–28 days	16	27
29–31 days	28	30
32–34 days	28	33
35–37 days	21	36
38–40 days	10	39

rather than the difference between these values. In this use of the range, the range for Judge 1 would be "between 5 and 14 years" while for Judge 2 it would be "between 1 and 20 years." No matter how it is expressed, the range in sentencing is greater for Judge 2 than it is for Judge 1, a fact expressed by the greater magnitude of the range for Judge 2.

In Table 5–5 we revisit the grouped frequency distribution for the "time until arrest" data for our 120 offenders released into the community. Recall that these were originally continuous data which we made ordinal by creating a grouped frequency distribution. Since we have midpoints for our class intervals, we can calculate a range for the data. Since the midpoint of the last class interval is 39 days and the midpoint for the first class interval is 18 days, the range in these data is $39 - 18 = 21$ days. We also can say that the range is between 18 and 39 days. The range is a very simple measure of dispersion to calculate and is very easy to understand. But as in every other dimension of life, "there is no such thing as a free lunch." The ease of calculating the range may come at a high price: The range can distort a reader's impression of the dispersion in our data.

Since the range only includes two of the scores in our data, the highest and the lowest, it completely ignores the dispersion that may lie in between those two values. For example, let's look at Table 5–6, where we give you the sentencing data of two different judges. In both cases the judges sentenced 20 armed robbery defendants and, as in Table 5–1, the range in sentencing is 9 years for Judge 1 and 19 years for Judge 2. Using the range, then, we would get the impression that there is more dispersion or heterogeneity in the sentencing behavior of Judge 2 compared with Judge 1. Although the ranges of 9 and 19 years are technically correct, would we be accurate in inferring that Judge 2 has more dispersion in his sentencing than Judge 1? Judge 2 utilizes only two options—1 or 20 years—when he sentences armed robbery defendants, while Judge 1's sentences are much more dispersed. When we use the

TABLE 5–6

Number of Years of Prison Time for Armed Robbery Defendants

Judge 1			Judge 2	
Years	*f*		Years	*f*
5	1		1	10
6	1		20	10
7	3			
8	4			
9	3			
10	1			
11	3			
12	2			
13	1			
14	1			
Σ = 20			Σ = 20	

range in this example, therefore, we are overstating the amount of dispersion in the two judges' sentencing behavior. We might want to think of another measure of dispersion for continuous variables that takes more information into account than just the highest and lowest scores.

One alternative to the range is something called the **interquartile range (IQR)**. Since this is called the interquartile range, we can infer that it involves some kind of range, and it does. In calculating the interquartile range we still take the difference between two scores. However, unlike the range, rather than taking the difference between the highest and lowest scores, in the IQR we take the difference between the score at the 75th percentile and the score at the 25th percentile. Notice that since we are taking the range in scores between the 75th and 25th percentiles, this range covers the middle 50 percent of our distribution. In other words, one-half of all our scores can be found between the 75th and 25th percentiles.

> The **interquartile range** is a measure of dispersion appropriate for interval/ratio-level data. It measures the range of scores in the middle 50 percent of a distribution of continuous scores and is calculated as the difference between the score at the third quartile (the 75th percentile) and the score at the first quartile (the 25th percentile).

We can divide our distribution in a number of ways. One of the ways we already know. We can divide our scores into percentiles or units of 100 as we show in Table 5–7. We then can take these percentiles and group them into intervals of 10 or "deciles." There are 10 deciles for 100 percentiles. The first 10 percentiles comprise the first decile, the second 10 percentiles comprise the second decile, and so on. We also can group our percentiles into intervals of 25 percent or quartiles. Since the 100 percentiles are equally distributed into four quartiles, each quartile comprises 25 percentiles.

TABLE 5–7

The Relationship between Percentiles, Deciles, and Quartiles

Percentile	Decile	Quartile
100th	10th	4th Q4
99th		
98th		
90th	9th	
.		
80th	8th	
.		
.		
75th		3rd Q3
.		
.		
60th	6th	
.		
.		
50th	5th	2nd Q2
.		
30th	3rd	
29th		
28th		
25th		1st Q1
.		
.		
20th	2nd	
.		
3rd		
2nd		
1st	1st	

The first 25 percentiles comprise the first quartile (Q1), the second 25 percentiles make up the second quartile [Q2] (recall that the median is the second quartile), the next 25 percentiles from the 51st to the 75th percentile are contained in the third quartile (Q3), and the last 25 percent of the cases are in the fourth quartile (Q4). This information on percentiles, deciles, and quartiles is summarized in Table 5–7.

With this information we can see that the 25th percentile is the first quartile (Q1), and the 75th percentile is the third quartile (Q3). In order to find the interquartile range, we locate the score at the 75th percentile (Q3) and the score at the 25th percentile (Q1) and take the difference between them:

$$IQR = x_{Q_3} - x_{Q_1} \qquad\qquad (5\text{--}2)$$

Instead of taking the difference between the highest and lowest scores as the range does, the IQR is the difference between the x score at the 75th percentile (Q_3) and the x score at the 25th percentile (Q_1). As you can see, the interquartile range reflects the range in the data in between the 75th and 25th percentiles, or the middle 50 percent of the distribution. The calculation of the IQR is pretty straightforward. First we have to create a cumulative percent distribution, then identify the scores at the 75th and 25th percentile, and then take the difference.

Calculating the Interquartile Range of the Number of Escapes by Prison

For an example, let's use Table 5–8, which shows the number of escapes from 20 correctional institutions in two states, State A and State B. We can easily calculate the range in the number of escapes for the prisons in these two states. For State A the range is 23 because the highest number of escapes was 23 and the lowest was 0. For State B the range is 9 because there was a high of 10 escapes and a low of 1. Notice that according to the range there is substantially more dispersion in the number of escapes for State A. However, the range is greater for State A only because there was one prison that had an unusually high number of escapes (23), and this outlier is distorting the true dispersion in the data. Now what we want to do is take these data and calculate the IQR, and there are two ways we can do this.

One way is to first rank-order the data. After the data have been rank-ordered, you need to identify something called the *truncated median position*, or TMP. The truncated median position is simply the position of the median in the data with the decimal place truncated ("truncated" means that the decimal place is dropped or rounded down to the nearest integer). For example, we have 20 observations for each state in Table 5–8. Using our positional formula for the location of the median, the median is in the $(20 + 1)/2 = 10.5$th position. The truncated median position is 10, which was found by dropping the .5. With the value of the TMP we now can identify where the third and first quartiles can be found, or the quartile positions (QP): QP = (TMP + 1)/2. With a truncated median position of 10, we can determine that the position of the two quartiles is: $(10 + 1)/2 = 5.5$th position. The third and first quartiles, then, are at the midpoint of the 5th and 6th scores in the rank order of scores. More specifically, the first quartile is the midpoint between the 5th and 6th lowest score, while the third quartile is the midpoint between the 5th and 6th highest score. In Table 5–9 we provide the rank order of the number of escapes from each state, and the position of the first (Q_1) and third (Q_3) quar-

TABLE 5–8

Number of Escapes from 20 Correctional Institutions in Two States

Institution	State A	State B
1	3	3
2	2	4
3	4	1
4	9	2
5	2	3
6	5	6
7	6	5
8	4	3
9	1	4
10	3	4
11	4	5
12	5	2
13	2	3
14	0	5
15	7	8
16	1	1
17	7	6
18	6	8
19	23	9
20	3	10

tiles. To find the first quartile, we start from the lowest score, identify what the 5th and 6th scores are, and find the midpoint. To find the third quartile, we start from the highest score, identify what the 5th and 6th scores are, and find the midpoint. The first quartile for State A is 2, while the first quartile for State B is 3. The third quartile for both states is 6.

With this information we now can calculate the interquartile range for both states.

$$\text{IQR State A} = 6 - 2 = 4 \text{ escapes}$$

$$\text{IQR State B} = 6 - 3 = 3 \text{ escapes}$$

As you can see, the interquartile ranges for the two states are fairly comparable, thus indicating that in the middle 50 percent of the distributions of the number of escapes there is about an equal amount of variation in the two states. This is a different picture of the dispersion from the one we derived when we calculated the range.

TABLE 5–9

Rank-Ordered Number of Escapes from 20 Correctional Institutions in Two States

Institution	State A	State B
1	0	1
2	1	1
3	1	2
4	2	2
5	2	3
		Q_1
6	2	3
7	3	3
8	3	3
9	3	4
10	4	4
11	4	4
12	4	5
13	5	5
14	5	5
15	6	6
		Q_3
16	6	6
17	7	8
18	7	8
19	9	9
20	23	10

You also can find the interquartile range without identifying the truncated median position, using cumulative frequencies. Recall that the first quartile is the score at the 25th percentile and the third quartile is the score at the 75th percentile. We can find the scores at the 25th and 75th percentiles simply by calculating a column of cumulative percentages. Table 5–10 provides the frequency, percent, and cumulative percent distribution of escapes for the two states. For State A, the score at the 25th percentile is a 2. How do you know this? Notice that 15 percent of the scores are either 0 or 1, and 30 percent of the scores are either 0, 1, or 2. The score at the 25th percentile, then, is a 2. For State A the score at the 75th percentile is a 6, because 70 percent of the scores are 5 or lower and 80 percent of the scores are 6 escapes or lower. The 75th percentile, then, is 6 escapes. For State A the IQR is 6 − 2 = 4 escapes. For State B, the score at the 25th percentile is a 3, because 20 percent of the scores are 2 escapes or lower while 40 percent of the scores are 3 escapes or lower. The score at the 25th percentile, then, is a 3. The score at the 75th percentile is a 6, since 70 percent of the scores are 5 escapes or lower and 80 per-

TABLE 5–10

Frequency Counts, Percents, and Cumulative Percents for Escape Data from Two States

STATE A

# of Escapes	f	%	Cum %
0	1	5	5
1	2	10	15
2	3	15	30
3	3	15	45
4	3	15	60
5	2	10	70
6	2	10	80
7	2	10	90
9	1	5	95
23	1	5	100

STATE B

# of Escapes			
1	2	10	10
2	2	10	20
3	4	20	40
4	3	15	55
5	3	15	70
6	2	10	80
8	2	10	90
9	1	5	95
10	1	5	100

cent of them are 6 escapes or lower. The score at the 75th percentile, then, is a 6. The IQR for State B is $6 - 3 = 3$ escapes.

The Standard Deviation and Variance

The range and interquartile range are perfectly acceptable measures of dispersion if we have data measured at the interval/ratio level. Notice, however, that they both use a limited amount of information—both measures estimate the amount of dispersion in the data by taking the difference between only two scores. It might be nice to have a measure of dispersion that takes into account *all* the information for our variable. Recall that with interval/ratio-level data we can calculate a mean or arithmetic average as a measure of central tendency. Not surprisingly, there are measures of dispersion that use the mean as the reference point about which to measure dispersion.

These measures are based on the notion that one way to measure the amount of dispersion or heterogeneity for a variable is to determine how different a value is from the mean. The most common of these mean-based measures of dispersion are the variance and standard deviation.

> Both the standard deviation and the variance measure dispersion by taking differences or **deviations** of each score from the mean of a variable. As we mentioned, then, the mean is the reference point for the standard deviation and variance. Scores that are clustered very close to the mean are less dispersed or more heterogeneous than scores that are very far from the mean. The distance or deviation from the mean, therefore, might be a good way to capture the amount of dispersion in a variable. The simple formula for taking the distance of a score from the mean is: $x_i - \overline{X}$, where x_i is the

> **A mean deviation** is the distance between a score and the mean of the group of scores. The mean deviation for any score is found by taking the difference between the mean and that score:
$$x_i - \overline{X}$$

x score for the ith person.

Recall from the last chapter that $\overline{X}$ is the symbol for the mean of the sample. As we will see, using the distance or deviation from the mean as the basis for a measure of dispersion for continuous data will give us two pieces of information. The first is that the sign of the distance or deviation will tell us whether the score is less than or greater than the mean, while the magnitude of the deviation will tell us how far the score is from the mean, or its distance. Let's use this simple formula for the distance of a score from the mean and determine how it applies to the notion of dispersion.

In Figure 5–2 we show you two distributions of one variable. The mean of both distributions is 25. In the first distribution, shown in Figure 5–2(a), you can see that most of the values or scores are close to the mean. The farthest a score is away from the mean is 2 units (a score of 23 is −2 away from the mean, while a score of 27 is +2 units away). In other words, for this variable the distance of each score from the mean is not great, indicating that the scores are not very different from the mean (and by implication, from each other). You can see that there does not seem to be much dispersion in this distribution, and this fact is reflected in the short distance of each score from the mean. In the second dis-

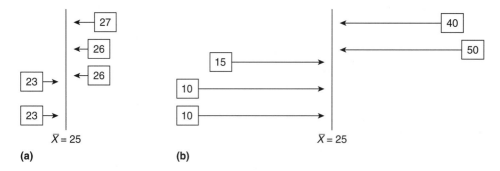

(a)   (b)

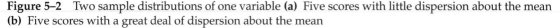

Figure 5–2   Two sample distributions of one variable **(a)** Five scores with little dispersion about the mean **(b)** Five scores with a great deal of dispersion about the mean

tribution, shown in Figure 5–2(b), however, the scores are much more different from the mean than those in Figure 5–2(a), and this is indicated by the fact that there is a greater distance between each of these scores and the mean. You should be able to determine, then, that the distribution shown in Figure 5–2(b) has more dispersion (the scores are more different from the mean or more heterogeneous) than the distribution of scores in Figure 5–2(a). We can get a hint from this that the notion of distance from the mean might be a good way to capture the dispersion of a variable measured at the interval/ratio level.

Let's take this example one step farther and calculate for each score the distance from the mean. We mentioned above that the distance of each score from the mean is also called a deviation from the mean. For the scores in Figure 5–2(a):

Score	Mean	Deviation from Mean
23	25	$23 - 25 = -2$
26	25	$26 - 25 = +1$
23	25	$23 - 25 = -2$
27	25	$27 - 25 = +2$
26	25	$26 - 25 = +1$

For the scores in Figure 5–2(b):

Score	Mean	Deviation from Mean
10	25	$10 - 25 = -15$
50	25	$50 - 25 = 25$
15	25	$15 - 25 = -10$
40	25	$40 - 25 = 15$
10	25	$10 - 25 = -15$

As we mentioned above, the deviation from the mean contains two pieces of information. Let's take the first x score, 23, in which the deviation from the mean is -2. The negative sign of the deviation tells us that a score of 23 is less than the mean, and the magnitude of 2 tells us that it is 2 units away from the mean. A negative mean deviation, then, means that the x score is less than the mean, while a positive mean deviation means that the score is greater than the mean. Moreover, the greater the magnitude of the mean deviation, the greater the distance the x score is from the mean. Finally, the greater the overall distance from the mean the scores are, the more dispersion or variability there is in the data. Knowing this, it's pretty easy to see that there is more dispersion in the second set of scores, and this is reflected in the fact that, taking all of the scores into account, the magnitude of the deviations is much greater in the second set of scores than in the first.

Rather than recording all of these deviation scores (imagine how messy things would look if we had 20 scores or 100!), however, it might be nice to create a summary measure that captures the average distance or deviation from the mean. That is, since we know that the mean is a good measure of central tendency, let's calculate the mean deviation score, which will provide us with one number that indicates the average distance of each score from the mean. This is easy to do. We know that the formula for the mean is $\dfrac{\sum_{i=1}^{n} x_1}{n}$ and that it is calculated by adding up all the scores and dividing by the number of scores. We can use this same formula for the mean here, the only difference is that our "score" is not an x_i but a difference score: $x_i - \overline{X}$. All we have to do is say $x_i = x_i - \overline{X}$, and calculate our mean distance or mean deviation score as:

$\overline{D} = \dfrac{\sum_{i=1}^{n} \left(x_i - \overline{X}\right)}{n}$ (just for now, let's let $\overline{D}$ be the symbol for the average deviation or distance score). This formula simply tells us to subtract the mean from each score (find the distance or deviation from the mean for each score), sum up these differences or deviations, and divide by the total number of scores. For the scores in Figure 5–2(a), the average deviation would be:

$$\overline{D} = \frac{(-2+1-2+2+1)}{5}$$

$$\overline{D} = \frac{0}{5}$$

For the scores in Figure 5–2(b), the average deviation would be:

$$\overline{D} = \frac{(-15+25-10+15-15)}{5}$$

$$\overline{D} = \frac{0}{5}$$

We've hit a snafu; the numerator of our formula for the average distance from the mean will always be zero. Recall that one of the properties of the mean that we learned in the last chapter is that the sum of the deviations about the mean will always be zero, that is, $\sum_{i=1}^{n} \left(x_i - \overline{X}\right) = 0$. The very idea of the mean as a measure of central tendency with continuous data was that it was a score that perfectly balanced the negative and positive differences from it. In other words, the sum of the negative scores from the mean is exactly equal to the sum of the positive scores from the mean. Because of this property of the mean, we are stuck.

One way to get unstuck would be to get rid of the negative signs for those values less than the mean. An easy way to do this would be to square the deviation or distance of each score from the mean, that is, take $(x_i - \overline{X})^2$. This squaring of deviations about the mean will ensure all positive values, allowing us to take the mean of these squared deviations. Now our formula for measuring dispersion looks like this: $\sum_{i=1}^{n} \dfrac{\left(x_i - \overline{X}\right)^2}{n}$ In words, this formula says to subtract the mean from each score (the "mean deviation"), square this deviation, sum up all of these squared deviations, and finally divide by the total number of scores. Let's use this formula with our data in Figures 5–2(a) and 5–2(b). For the scores in Figure 5–2(a):

Score	Mean	Deviation from Mean	Squared Deviation
23	25	$23 - 25 = -2$	4
26	25	$26 - 25 = +1$	1
23	25	$23 - 25 = -2$	4
27	25	$27 - 25 = +2$	4
26	25	$26 - 25 = +1$	1

The average squared deviation from the mean would be:

$$\overline{D} = \frac{(4+1+4+4+1)}{5} = \frac{14}{5} = 2.8$$

For the scores in Figure 5–2(b):

Score	Mean	Deviation from Mean	Squared Deviation
10	25	$10 - 25 = -15$	225
50	25	$50 - 25 = 25$	625
15	25	$15 - 25 = -10$	100
40	25	$40 - 25 = 15$	225
10	25	$10 - 25 = -15$	225

The average squared deviation from the mean would be:

$$\overline{D} = \frac{(225+625+100+225+225)}{5} = \frac{1,400}{5} = 280$$

Now we have one number for each set of scores which measures the amount of dispersion in the data by taking the average squared deviation from the mean. Using this, we can see quite clearly that there is substantially more dispersion in the second set of scores than in the first.

What you have actually just done is to calculate the measure of dispersion for continuous data, called the variance. The **variance** is defined as the average squared difference of each score in a set of scores from the mean of those scores. The greater the magnitude of the variance, the more dispersion there is. Now we need to complicate things a little because we need to distinguish between the variance of a population and the variance of a sample.

> The **variance** is the average of the squared deviations from the mean.

Recall from our discussion in Chapter 1 that a population consists of the universe of cases we are interested in. For example, if we are interested in the relationship between IQ scores and delinquency among male youths between the ages of 12 and 18 in the United States, then our population would consist of all male youths between the ages of 12 and 18 who reside in the United States. The population we are interested in, then, is generally very large and both difficult and costly to study directly. Our population of male adolescents, for example, would number in the millions. A sample, you will remember, is a subset of the population, and we select a sample from the population and study the sample with the intention of making an inference to the population based on what we know about the sample. The sample is much smaller in size than the population, and it is the group that we actually study. We might, for example, first take a sample of states, then a sample of cities, and then finally a sample of youths between the ages of 12 and 18 from those cities.

As was true for the mean, it would be entirely possible (though a great deal of work) to calculate the variance of a population. The variance of a population, therefore, is unknown but knowable. In statistics, the variance of a population is noted by the term σ^2 (the Greek letter sigma, squared), and it is defined as the average squared deviation of each score in a population from the mean of that population:

$$\sigma^2 = \frac{\sum_{i=1}^{N}(x_i - \mu)^2}{N} \tag{5-3}$$

where N is the total number of scores in the population and μ is the population mean.

If we do not have the entire population and have instead a sample from that population, then what we do is estimate the unknown population value with our sample data. Recall that for the mean, we estimated μ, the unknown population mean, with $\overline{X}$ the mean of the sample. Similarly, when we have sample data we estimate the variance of the population with the variance of our sample data. The formula for the variance of the sample is:

$$s^2 = \frac{\sum_{i=1}^{n}(x_i - \overline{X})^2}{n-1} \tag{5-4}$$

There are two differences between the formula for the variance of a population (eq. 5–3) and the formula for the variance of a sample (eq. 5–4). In the variance of a population, we take the sum of the squared deviations of each score from the population mean (μ) and divide by the population size (N). In the variance of a sample we take the sum of the squared deviations of each score from the sample mean ($\overline{X}$) and divide by the number of scores in the sample (n) minus 1. The reason we use $n - 1$ in the denominator of the sample variance is that it is a biased estimator of the population value σ^2. To correct for that bias we divide by $n - 1$ rather than n in our sample formula.

Notice that the practical effect of using $n - 1$ is to have a smaller denominator; this means that the estimate of the sample variance will be larger than if we simply used the sample size. It also means that the difference between $n - 1$ and n will be more substantial when the sample size is small.

Notice that in order to get rid of the negative signs in calculating the variance we took the squared deviations of each score from the mean. The variance, therefore, measures dispersion in the awkward terminology of "average squared deviation from the mean." The other measure of dispersion for continuous data that we will discuss, the **standard deviation**, adjusts for the squaring of the deviations about the mean. It does this by taking the square root of the variance (taking the square root of a value is the "opposite" operation of squaring it; 2 squared is 4 and the square root of 4 is 2). The symbol σ is given for the population standard deviation, and has the formula:

> The **standard deviation** is the square root of the squared deviations about the mean.

$$\sigma = \sqrt{\frac{\sum_{i=1}^{N}(x_i - \mu)^2}{N}} \quad \text{and} \quad \sigma = \sqrt{\sigma^2} \qquad (5\text{--}5)$$

The symbol s is given for the sample standard deviation, and it has the formula:

$$s = \sqrt{\frac{\sum_{i=1}^{n}(x_i - \overline{X})^2}{n-1}} \quad \text{and} \quad s = \sqrt{s^2} \qquad (5\text{--}6)$$

The standard deviation, therefore, is really the square root of the mean of the deviation scores, but it might be more useful for you to think of it as the typical distance of each score from the mean. The variance and standard deviation are the two most frequently used measures of dispersion for continuous data. To summarize what we have covered in this section, Table 5–11 shows the population and sample formulas for both.

Calculating the Variance and Standard Deviation of a Sample with Ungrouped Data: The Variation in Judges' Sentences

Let's practice using these sample formulas by calculating the variance and standard deviation for the sentencing data in Table 5–1. These are ungrouped data. Also, since these are samples of 20 sentences from the population of sentences that these judges handed down to convicted defendants, we will use the sample formulas for the variance (eq. 5–4) and standard deviation (eq. 5–6). Let's calculate the variance first, using the following steps:

TABLE 5–11

Definitional Formulas for Population and Sample Variance and Standard Deviation

---

Population

Variance (σ^2)

$$\sigma^2 = \frac{\sum_{i=1}^{n}\left(x_i - \mu\right)^2}{N}$$

Standard Deviation (σ)

$$\sigma = \sqrt{\frac{\sum_{i=1}^{n}\left(x_i - \mu\right)^2}{N}}$$

Sample

Variance (s^2)

$$s^2 = \frac{\sum_{i=1}^{n}\left(x_i - \overline{X}\right)^2}{n-1}$$

Standard Deviation (s)

$$s = \sqrt{\frac{\sum_{i=1}^{n}\left(x_i - \overline{X}\right)^2}{n-1}}$$

Steps in Calculating the Sample Variance

Step 1: Calculate the mean.

Step 2: Subtract the mean from each score ($x_i - \overline{X}$). This is called taking the deviation from the mean.

Step 3: Square the deviation of each score from the mean: $(x_i - \overline{X})^2$.

Step 4: Sum the squared deviations for all scores, starting with the first score ($x_i = 1$) and continuing to the last score ($x = n$):

$$\sum_{i=1}^{n}\left(x_i - \overline{X}\right)^2$$

This is called the sum of the squared deviations from the mean.

Step 5: Divide by the number of scores minus 1:

$$\frac{\sum_{i=1}^{n}\left(x_i - \overline{X}\right)^2}{n-1}$$

This is the sample variance.

TABLE 5–12

Calculations for the Variance and Standard Deviation in Judge 1's Sentencing

x	$(x - \overline{X})$	$(x - \overline{X})^2$
5	$5 - 9 = -4$	16
7	$7 - 9 = -2$	4
7	$7 - 9 = -2$	4
7	$7 - 9 = -2$	4
7	$7 - 9 = -2$	4
7	$7 - 9 = -2$	4
8	$8 - 9 = -1$	1
8	$8 - 9 = -1$	1
8	$8 - 9 = -1$	1
8	$8 - 9 = -1$	1
9	$9 - 9 = 0$	0
9	$9 - 9 = 0$	0
9	$9 - 9 = 0$	0
10	$10 - 9 = 1$	1
11	$11 - 9 = 2$	4
11	$11 - 9 = 2$	4
11	$11 - 9 = 2$	4
12	$12 - 9 = 3$	9
12	$12 - 9 = 3$	9
14	$14 - 9 = 5$	25
		$\Sigma = 96$

Now we will calculate the variance separately for each judge. First, the calculations for Judge 1 are shown for you in Table 5–12. We can see from Table 5–12 that the sum of the squared deviations is 96. In order to find the variance, we divide this by the number of scores (n) minus 1. The variance for Judge 1, therefore, is:

$$s^2 = \frac{96}{20 - 1}$$

$$s^2 = \frac{96}{19}$$

$$s^2 = 5.05$$

The calculations necessary to find the variance for Judge 2 are shown for you in Table 5–13. We can see from the table that the sum of the squared deviations about the mean for Judge 2 is 754. Again, in order to find the variance we divide this by the number of scores (n) minus 1. The variance for Judge 2, therefore, is:

TABLE 5–13

Calculations for the Variance and Standard Deviation in Judge 2's Sentencing

x	$(x - \overline{X})$	$(x - \overline{X})^2$
1	$1 - 9 = -8$	64
2	$2 - 9 = -7$	49
2	$2 - 9 = -7$	49
3	$3 - 9 = -6$	36
3	$3 - 9 = -6$	36
3	$3 - 9 = -6$	36
4	$4 - 9 = -5$	25
4	$4 - 9 = -5$	25
5	$5 - 9 = -4$	16
8	$8 - 9 = -1$	1
9	$9 - 9 = 0$	0
10	$10 - 9 = 1$	1
11	$11 - 9 = 2$	4
14	$14 - 9 = 5$	25
15	$15 - 9 = 6$	36
15	$15 - 9 = 6$	36
16	$16 - 9 = 7$	49
17	$17 - 9 = 8$	64
18	$18 - 9 = 9$	81
20	$20 - 9 = 11$	121
		$\Sigma = 754$

$$s^2 = \frac{754}{20 - 1}$$

$$s^2 = \frac{754}{19}$$

$$s^2 = 39.68$$

When we calculate the variance for Judge 1 and Judge 2, then, we find that the magnitude is much higher for Judge 2, confirming our suspicion that there is more dispersion or heterogeneity in this judge's sentencing behavior than in that of Judge 1.

Now let's calculate the sample standard deviation for the two judges. If you look at the formula for the sample standard deviation, you can see that all we have to do is take the square root of the variance. There is, then, only one more step involved in calculating the standard deviation. Since this is our first time calculating the standard deviation, however, we will outline each of the necessary steps:

Steps in Calculating the Sample Standard Deviation

Step 1: Calculate the mean.

Step 2: Subtract the mean from each score $(x_i - \overline{X})$. This is called taking the deviation from the mean.

Step 3: Square the deviation of each score from the mean: $(x_i - \overline{X})^2$.

Step 4: Sum the squared deviations for all scores, starting with the first score $(x_i = 1)$ and continuing to the last score:

$$\left(x_i = n\right): \sum_{i=1}^{n}\left(x_i - \overline{X}\right)^2$$

This is called the sum of the squared deviations from the mean.

Step 5: Divide by the number of scores minus 1:

$$\frac{\sum_{i=1}^{n}\left(x_i - \overline{X}\right)^2}{n-1}$$

Step 6: Take the square root of this:

$$\sqrt{\frac{\sum_{i=1}^{n}\left(x_i - \overline{X}\right)^2}{n-1}}$$

This is the sample standard deviation.

Since we already have the variances, let's quickly calculate the two standard deviations. First, for Judge 1:

$$s = \sqrt{s^2}$$

$$s = \sqrt{5.05}$$

$$s = 2.25$$

One way to interpret this would be to say that, for Judge 1, the typical distance of each of the 20 sentences from the mean is 2.25 months. The standard deviation for Judge 2 is:

$$s = \sqrt{s^2}$$

$$s = \sqrt{39.68}$$

$$s = 6.30$$

For Judge 2, the typical distance of each sentence from the mean is 6.30 months. The typical distance from the mean sentence for Judge 1 (2.25 months) is much closer than that for Judge 2 (6.30 months). Once again, we are led to the conclusion that there is more dispersion or heterogeneity in the sentencing behavior of Judge 2 than Judge 1. We will learn more about the interpretation of the variance and standard deviation in Chapter 6. For now, just understand that the standard deviation measures the average difference between a group of scores and the mean of those scores and that the greater the standard deviation (and variance), the more disperse the scores are. Recall that Judge 2 had a greater variance and standard deviation than Judge 1 in terms of his sentencing. We concluded that Judge 2 had more variability or dispersion in his sentencing behavior than Judge 1. In other words, Judge 2 was more inconsistent in his sentencing than Judge 1. Judge 1 stuck closely to her average (mean) sentence, but Judge 2 was "all over the place" in his sentencing, sometimes being very lenient and sometimes being very harsh.

Let's go through one more example of calculating the variance and standard deviation with ungrouped data before moving on to the grouped case. In Table 5–14 we have a sample of 25 IQ scores from a population of male

TABLE 5–14

IQ Scores for a Sample of 25 Incarcerated Youth

x	$(x - \overline{X})$	$(x - \overline{X})^2$
85	$85 - 91 = -6$	36
100	$100 - 91 = 9$	81
87	$87 - 91 = -4$	16
93	$93 - 91 = 2$	4
78	$78 - 91 = -13$	169
103	$103 - 91 = -12$	144
88	$88 - 91 = -3$	9
94	$94 - 91 = 3$	9
94	$94 - 91 = 3$	9
101	$101 - 91 = 10$	100
94	$94 - 91 = 3$	9
92	$92 - 91 = 1$	1
83	$83 - 91 = -8$	64
70	$70 - 91 = -21$	441
110	$110 - 91 = 19$	361
87	$81 - 91 = -4$	16
91	$91 - 91 = 0$	0
79	$79 - 91 = -12$	144
84	$84 - 91 = -7$	49
88	$88 - 91 = -3$	9
90	$90 - 91 = -1$	1
104	$104 - 91 = 13$	169
100	$100 - 91 = 9$	81
98	$98 - 91 = 7$	49
82	$82 - 91 = -9$	81
		$\Sigma = 2{,}052$

youths incarcerated in a state reform school. To determine the sample variance, we first need to find the mean. The mean IQ score for these 25 youths is 91.00. In the second column of Table 5–14 we provide the deviations from the mean, and in the third column we provide the squared deviations from the mean. If you were to sum the second column (the deviations from the mean) you would obtain a value of zero because by definition the sum of the deviations about the mean is equal to zero, that is, $\sum_{i=1}^{n}(x_i - \overline{X}) = 0$. The sum of the third column gives us the numerator for the sample variance, the sum of the squared deviations from the mean. In this example, the sum of the squared deviations is equal to 2,052. We can very easily obtain the sample variance by dividing this by $n - 1$. The variance of these IQ scores, then, is equal to:

$$s^2 = \frac{2,052}{24}$$

$$s^2 = 85.5$$

The average squared distance of each IQ score from the mean, then, is equal to 85.5 IQ points. The standard deviation is equal to:

$$s = \sqrt{\frac{2,052}{24}}$$

$$s = \sqrt{85.5}$$

$$s = 9.247$$

The typical distance of each IQ score from the mean of IQ scores, then, is equal to 9.247 IQ points.

Calculating the Variance and Standard Deviation of a Sample with Grouped Data

In previous chapters we have used continuous (interval/ratio)-level data to create categories in the form of class intervals. Once we created these categories we lost the interval/ratio property of our data and we recognized that we really had only ordinal data. The categories or class intervals could be rank-ordered, but we could not state, as we can with interval/ratio-level data, that someone had "twice" or "three" times as much of the variable as another. With ordinal-level data we could only state that someone had "more" or "less" of the variable than another. Strictly speaking, therefore, without interval/ratio-level (continuous) data we cannot really calculate a variance and standard deviation. However, also recall that in the last chapter we acknowledged that the underlying distribution of some grouped ordinal data was really continuous (the variable was measured at the interval/ratio level before we created categories or class intervals). Therefore, we reasoned, we could ignore the fact that it was ordinal and perform statistical operations that, strictly speaking, we could only do with interval/ratio-level data. For example, we calculated a mean with grouped data by making the simplifying assumption that each score within a class interval was at the midpoint. While this was not strictly true, it did allow us to recover the interval/ratio-level property of the data and we estimated a mean. We also discovered that this mean estimated from the grouped data was not far off from the mean we would have obtained had we calculated it from the original continuous data.

In this section of the chapter, we make the same assumption and regard each score in a class interval as lying at the midpoint of the interval in order to calculate a mean and a deviation from the mean. Once we calculate the deviation from the mean we also can easily calculate a variance and standard deviation. In order to calculate a variance and standard deviation with grouped sample data we need to make only two minor modifications to our formulas. Here is the formula to calculate a variance with grouped data:

$$S^2 = \frac{\sum_{i=1}^{k} f_i (m_i - \overline{X})^2}{n-1} \tag{5-7}$$

where

k = the number of class intervals or categories,

m_i = the midpoint of the ith interval, and

f_i = the frequency of the ith interval.

In words, here is what equation 5–7 is telling you to do. Start with the first class interval, ($k = 1$), and subtract the mean from the midpoint of this interval. Square this difference or deviation, then multiply that squared difference by the number of scores that are in that class interval, and then go to the next class interval and do the same thing, continuing until you do the last class interval. Finally, sum these values, and divide by the total number of scores minus 1.

There are two differences between this equation for the variance of grouped sample data and the equation for the variance of ungrouped sample data (eq. 5–4). The first difference is that we do not have an x_i score but an m_i score, since we use the midpoint of each class interval (m_i) as the x_i score from which we subtract the mean. Second, we have to take into account that there may be more than one score in a given class interval. In fact, there are f_i scores in each class interval—all of which are assumed to lie at the midpoint. Hence, rather than take $(m_i - \overline{X})^2$ f_i times, what we do is multiply $(m_i - \overline{X})^2$ by the number of scores at the midpoint, or f_i. Once we have the variance of a sample of grouped data, we can very easily find the standard deviation by taking the square root of the variance:

$$s = \sqrt{\frac{\sum_{i=1}^{k} f_i (m_i - \overline{X})^2}{n-1}} \tag{5-8}$$

TABLE 5–15

Stated Class Limits, Midpoints, and Frequencies for Grouped Frequency Distribution of Time-Until-Rearrest Data

Stated Class Limits	Midpoints m_i	f
17–19	18	4
20–22	21	1
23–25	24	12
26–28	27	16
29–31	30	28
32–34	33	28
35–37	36	21
38–40	39	10

Let's work through an example of calculating the variance and standard deviation with grouped data.

In Table 5–15 we show you a very familiar data set. It's the time-until-rearrest data for our 120 inmates released from a correctional institution and followed until they "failed" (were rearrested). Table 5–15 provides the stated class limits for each interval, the midpoint of the interval, and the frequency for each interval. In Chapter 4 we learned that the mean of this grouped data was 31.025 days. To make our calculations a little easier, let's calculate the variance and standard deviation with a mean of 31 days. Here are the steps involved in calculating the variance and standard deviation with grouped data.

Steps in Calculating the Sample Variance and Standard Deviation with Grouped Data

Step 1: Calculate the mean.

Step 2: Determine the midpoint of each class interval (m_i).

Step 3: Subtract the mean from the midpoint ($m_i - \overline{X}$) of the first interval.

Step 4: Square the deviation of the midpoint from the mean $(m_i - \overline{X})^2$.

Step 5: Multiply the squared deviation of the midpoint from the mean by the frequency for the class interval: $f_i (m_i - \overline{X})^2$.

Step 6: Repeat steps 2–4 for each class interval, starting with the first and ending with the last.

Step 7: Sum the $f_i (m_i - \overline{X})^2$ for all class intervals.

Step 8: Divide the result in step 6 by the number of scores minus 1:

$$\frac{\left(\sum_{i=1}^{k} f_i \left(m_i - \overline{X}\right)^2\right)}{n-1}$$

This is the variance for grouped data.

Step 9: Take the square root of this:

$$\sqrt{\frac{\left(\sum_{i=1}^{k} f_i \left(m_i - \overline{X}\right)^2\right)}{n-1}}$$

This is the sample standard deviation for grouped data.

We show the necessary calculations for you to calculate the variance in Table 5–16. The sum of the squared deviations about the mean for these grouped data is equal to 2,925. Now we are ready to calculate the variance:

$$s^2 = \frac{\left(\sum_{i=1}^{k} f_i \left(m_i - \overline{X}\right)^2\right)}{n-1}$$

$$s^2 = \frac{2,925}{119}$$

$$s^2 = 24.58$$

The average squared distance of each score from the mean, then, is 24.58 days. Since we have the variance, the standard deviation would be:

$$s = \sqrt{\frac{\left(\sum_{i=1}^{k} f_i \left(m_i - \overline{X}\right)^2\right)}{n-1}}$$

$$s = \sqrt{\frac{2,925}{119}}$$

$$s = 4.96$$

The typical distance of each score from the mean of 120 days until rearrest, then, is 4.96, or approximately 5 days.

You may be wondering how much precision we lost by categorizing the original interval/ratio-level time-until-rearrest data into ordinal- level class intervals. Recall from Chapter 4 that the mean with the time-until-arrest data when measured at the interval/ratio level was 31.075 days (and 31.025 days

TABLE 5–16

Calculations for Variance and Standard Deviation for Time-Until-Rearrest Data

Midpoint of Class Interval	$(m_i - \overline{X})$	$(m_i - \overline{X})^2$	f_i	$f_i(m_i - \overline{X})^2$
18	$18 - 31 = -13$	169	4	$4(169) = 676$
21	$21 - 31 = -10$	100	1	$1(100) = 100$
24	$24 - 31 = -7$	49	12	$12(49) = 588$
27	$27 - 31 = -4$	16	16	$16(16) = 256$
30	$30 - 31 = -1$	1	28	$28(1) = 28$
33	$33 - 31 = 2$	4	28	$28(4) = 112$
36	$36 - 31 = 5$	25	21	$21(25) = 525$
39	$39 - 31 = 8$	64	10	$10(64) = 640$
				$\Sigma = 2{,}925$

when the data were grouped). For the grouped data, we learned in the previous paragraph that the variance was 24.58 days and the standard deviation was 4.96. When these 120 observations were kept at their original interval/ratio level of measurement, the variance was 24.81 and the standard deviation was 4.98. Clearly, in this case we have not lost much precision in our data by grouping the values into class intervals.

Computational Formulas for Variance and Standard Deviation

In the last two sections we have provided you with what are called definitional formulas for the variance and standard deviation. We think that these definitional formulas show very clearly what both of these measures of dispersion capture. The variance is the average squared distance of each score from the mean of the scores, and the standard deviation is the square root of that average squared difference. Although these formulas are useful because we can see exactly what is being measured, some find them difficult to use. In this section we will provide you with several computational formulas which you might find easier to use in calculating the variance and standard deviation. We then will use these formulas with data presented earlier in the chapter to show you that we get the same result regardless of which formula we use.

When we have ungrouped data, the definitional formulas for the variance and standard deviation are:

$$\text{Variance} = s^2 = \frac{\left(\Sigma x_i^2\right) - \dfrac{\left(\Sigma x_i\right)^2}{n}}{n-1} \qquad (5\text{--}9)$$

$$\text{Standard deviation} = s = \sqrt{\frac{\left(\sum x_i^2\right) - \dfrac{\left(\sum x_i\right)^2}{n}}{n-1}} \qquad (5\text{--}10)$$

where

$\sum x_i^2$ = the sum of each squared x_i score,

$(\sum x_i)^2$ = the sum of the x_i scores squared, and

n = the total number of scores.

These computational formulas for ungrouped data require that we obtain three quantities. The first of these quantities is the sum of the squared x_i scores $(\sum x_i^2)$. To get this, we take each x_i score, square it (x_i^2), and then sum across all scores $(x_1^2 + x_2^2 + x_3^2 \ldots + \ldots x_n^2)$. The second quantity is the sum of the x_i scores squared. This is obtained by first summing across all x_i scores and then squaring the sum $(x_1 + x_2 + x_3 \ldots + \ldots x_n)^2$. The third quantity is simply the number of scores, or n. These computational formulas may not make as much intuitive sense as a measure of dispersion as the definitional formulas, but they may be easier for you to use since they involve fewer calculations. Rather than taking the square of each score from the mean, all you have to do with the computational formula is take the squares of the raw scores and the sum of the raw scores squared. If, however, you decide you don't like these computational formulas, stick with the definitional ones.

Steps for Using Computational Formulas for Variance and Standard Deviation with Ungrouped Data

Step 1: Square each of the x_i scores and sum these squared values: $\sum (x_i^2)$.

Step 2: Add all of the x_i scores, square this sum, and divide by the number of scores:

$$\frac{\left(\sum x_i^2\right)}{n}$$

Step 3: Subtract the results in Step 2 from the value in Step 1:

$$\sum\left(x_i^2\right) - \frac{\left(\sum x_i\right)^2}{n}$$

Step 4: Divide this by the number of scores minus 1:

$$\frac{\sum\left(x_i^2\right) - \dfrac{\left(\sum x_i\right)^2}{n}}{n-1}$$

This is the variance.

Step 5:   Take the square root of Step 4:

$$\sqrt{\frac{\Sigma\left(x_i^{2}\right)-\dfrac{\left(\Sigma x_i\right)^{2}}{n}}{n-1}}$$

This is the standard deviation.

Let's practice one problem with these computational formulas on ungrouped data before moving on to the computational formulas for grouped data. We will use the sentencing data from the two judges reported in Table 5–1. Since we calculated the variance and standard deviation of these data with our definitional formulas, we can compare those results with the results we get using the computational formulas. We reproduce these data along with the squared x_i scores in Table 5–17. Using the computational formula for Judge 1, we arrive at the following estimates of the variance and standard deviation:

$$s^{2}=\frac{\Sigma\left(x_i^{2}\right)-\dfrac{\left(\Sigma x_i\right)^{2}}{n}}{n-1}$$

$$s^{2}=\frac{1,716-\dfrac{(180)^{2}}{20}}{19}$$

$$s^{2}=5.05$$

$$s=\sqrt{s^{2}}$$

$$s=2.25$$

For judge 2, the variance and standard deviation are:

$$s^{2}=\frac{\Sigma\left(x_i^{2}\right)-\dfrac{\left(\Sigma x_i\right)^{2}}{n}}{n-1}$$

$$s^{2}=\frac{2,374-\dfrac{(180)^{2}}{20}}{19}$$

$$s^{2}=39.68$$

$$s=\sqrt{s^{2}}$$

$$s=6.30$$

TABLE 5–17

Data and Calculations for Variance and Standard Deviation (Judge Sentencing Data from Table 5–1)

Judge 1		Judge 2	
x	x^2	x	x^2
5	25	1	1
7	49	2	4
7	49	2	4
7	49	3	9
7	49	3	9
7	49	3	9
8	64	4	16
8	64	4	16
8	64	5	25
8	64	8	64
9	81	9	81
9	81	10	100
9	81	11	121
10	100	14	196
11	121	15	225
11	121	15	225
11	121	16	256
12	144	17	289
12	144	18	324
14	196	20	400
$\Sigma = 180$	$\Sigma = 1{,}716$	$\Sigma = 180$	$\Sigma = 2{,}374$

You can check for yourself, but these results with the computational formula are exactly the same as the estimated variance and standard deviation we got when we used the definitional formula earlier in the chapter.

We also have definitional formulas we can use when we have grouped data. With grouped data, the definitional formulas for the variance and standard deviation are:

$$\text{Variance} = s^2 = \frac{\Sigma\left(f_i m_i^{\,2}\right) - \dfrac{\Sigma\left(f_i m_i^{\,2}\right)}{n}}{n-1} \qquad \textbf{(5–11)}$$

$$\text{Standard deviation} = s = \sqrt{\frac{\Sigma\left(f_i m_i^{\,2}\right) - \dfrac{\Sigma\left(f_i m_i\right)^2}{n}}{n-1}} \qquad \textbf{(5–12)}$$

where

$\Sigma f_i m_i^2$ = the sum of each squared midpoint (m_i) times the frequency of the class interval (f_i),

$(\Sigma f_i m_i)^2$ = the sum of the product of each midpoint (m_i) multiplied by the frequency of the class interval (f_i), with the sum then squared, and

n = the total number of scores.

These computational formulas for ungrouped data require that we obtain three quantities. The first of these quantities requires us to square the midpoint of each class interval (m_i^2), multiply each squared midpoint by the frequency of the class interval [$f_i(m_i^2)$], and the sum across all intervals [$\Sigma f_i(m_i^2)$]. The second quantity is obtained by multiplying the midpoint of each class interval by its frequency, summing across all class intervals, and then squaring this sum $(\Sigma f_i m_i)^2$. The third quantity is simply the number of scores, or n.

Steps for Using Computational Formulas for Variance and Standard Deviation with Grouped Data

Step 1: Square each of the midpoints of the class intervals (m_i), multiply each of these squared midpoints by the frequency of its class interval (f_i), and then sum across all class intervals [$\Sigma f_i(m_i^2)$].

Step 2: Multiply each midpoint by the frequency of its class interval ($f_i m_i$), sum across all class intervals $\Sigma (f_i m_i)$, and square this sum:

$$\left[\Sigma \left(f_i m_i \right)^2 \right]$$

Step 3: Subtract the results in step 2 from the value in step 1:

$$\Sigma \left(f_i m_i^2 \right) - \frac{\Sigma \left(f_i m_i^2 \right)}{n}$$

Step 4: Divide this by the number of scores minus 1:

$$\frac{\Sigma \left(f_i m_i^2 \right) - \frac{\Sigma \left(f_i m_i^2 \right)}{n}}{n-1}$$

This is the variance.

Step 5: Take the square root of step 4:

$$\sqrt{\frac{\Sigma (f_i m_i^2) - \frac{\Sigma (f_i m_i)^2}{n}}{n-1}}$$

This is the standard deviation.

Let's use these computational formulas for grouped data to calculate the variance and standard deviation of our time-until-rearrest data that appeared in Table 5–5. We reproduce that data for you and all the necessary calculations for the variance and standard deviation in Table 5–17. The variance and standard deviation are:

$$s^2 = \frac{\Sigma(fi,i^2)\dfrac{(\Sigma f_i m_i)^2}{n}}{n-1}$$

$$s^2 = \frac{118,431 - \dfrac{(3,723)^2}{120}}{119}$$

$$s^2 = 24.58$$

$$s = \sqrt{s^2}$$

$$s = 4.96$$

These are exactly the same values for the variance and standard deviation that we obtained when we used the definitional formulas.

GRAPHING DISPERSION WITH EXPLORATORY DATA ANALYSIS

In this final section, we are going to introduce you to a class of techniques originally developed by the statistician John W. Tukey in the late 1970s. These techniques are subsumed under the name **exploratory data analysis (EDA)**. The name is fitting because this is what Tukey intended when he developed this type of analysis. The techniques of EDA allow us to "explore" the distributions of the variables in a data set; they facilitate our understanding of what our distributions look like, what abnormalities might be present (e.g., outliers), and what secrets they might hold.

In this section, we focus exclusively on the most widely used EDA technique, called the **boxplot**. It is difficult to categorize a boxplot as either numeric or graphical, since it is really both. A boxplot offers a visual display of the data and, in addition, provides the analyst with numerical information about the distribution's center, spread, and outliers. The novelty of a boxplot, however, is that all this information is available at a glance.

Constructing Boxplots

Boxplots, originally coined by Tukey (1977) as box-and-whisker plots, are a technique in the EDA family used to convey information about a variable distribution. Boxplots provide a very illuminating picture of the shape and variability of a distribution. At a glance, you can ascertain what the distribution looks like as a whole, how spread out the distribution is, where its center lies, and how far out any trailing data points (outliers) lie.

Constructing a Boxplot for Felony Conviction Data

Essentially, constructing a boxplot involves calculating particular values from your data and then forming the boxplot based on these values. The values upon which the boxplot is primarily based are the values of the median, the quartiles, and the interquartile range (IQR), which we have already discussed. Let's illustrate these steps by way of an example that utilizes the felony conviction data from Table 5–18. Specifically, we will construct a boxplot from the fourth column of data presented in Table 5–18, which lists in ascending order those convictions from felony arrests which resulted in a felony charge by each county.

   If this variable distribution was not already rank-ordered, the first necessary step would be to place the values in ascending order. Because all other points necessary to construct a boxplot can be obtained by knowing the median and the first (Q_1 = 25th percentile) and third (Q_3 = 75th percentile) quartiles, the next step is to find these values from our data. Since we have an even number of scores (34), the median can be found at the midpoint of the 17th and 18th $(34 + 1)/2 = 17.5$ positions. The score at the 17th position is 51 percent, and the score at the 18th position is 55 percent. The median, then, is $(51 + 55)/2 = 53$ percent.

   We can easily find the first and third quartiles (Q_1 and Q_3), respectively, by first finding the truncated median position. As you will recall, the truncated median position, or TMP, is the position of the median truncated at the decimal point. For example, the position of the median in this example is the midpoint between the 17th and 18th positions. In other words, the median is at the 17.5 position in our distribution of scores. When we drop the decimal place, the truncated median position is 17. We now can find the position of the first and third quartile with the simple formula:

$$\text{Quartile position} = \frac{(\text{TMP} + 1)}{2}$$

$$= \frac{(17 + 1)}{2}$$

$$= 9$$

Using the results of this formula, we see that the first quartile can be found 9 scores up from the bottom of the distribution (counting the lowest score as 1), and the third quartile can be found 9 scores down from the top of the distribution (counting the highest score as 1). The ninth score from the

TABLE 5–18

Percent of Felony Arrest Convictions That Resulted in Felony Charge and Percent That Resulted in a Misdemeanor Charge (N = 34 Counties)

Rank	County	State	% Felony	County	State	% Misdemeanor
1	Erie	NY	21.00	Tarrant	TX	.00
2	Washington	DC	21.00	Broward	FL	.00
3	Kings	NY	26.00	Essex	MA	1.00
4	Suffolk	MA	28.00	Wayne	MI	1.00
5	New York	NY	28.00	Cook	IL	3.00
6	Bronx	NY	28.00	Philadelphia	PA	3.00
7	Fairfax	VA	31.00	King	WA	3.00
8	Dade	FL	35.00	Suffolk	MA	4.00
9	Queens	NY	37.00	Harris	TX	4.00
10	Palm Beach	FL	41.00	Los Angeles	CA	4.00
11	Cook	IL	45.00	San Diego	CA	4.00
12	Hamilton	OH	45.00	St. Louis	MO	5.00
13	Philadelphia	PA	47.00	Fulton	GA	5.00
14	Shelby	TN	47.00	Hills	FL	5.00
15	Dallas	TX	48.00	Dallas	TX	6.00
16	Salt Lake City	UT	48.00	San Bernardino	CA	8.00
17	Duval	FL	51.00	Dade	FL	11.00
18	Tarrant	TX	55.00	Sacramento	CA	11.00
19	Essex	MA	58.00	Orange	CA	11.00
20	Allegheny	PA	58.00	Maricopa	AZ	15.00
21	St. Louis	MO	60.00	Erie	NY	16.00
22	Broward	FL	61.00	Santa Clara	CA	16.00
23	Wayne	MI	61.00	Duval	FL	17.00
24	Sacramento	CA	62.00	Queens	NY	26.00
25	Harris	TX	65.00	Hamilton	OH	27.00
26	Los Angeles	CA	69.00	Salt Lake City	UT	28.00
27	Maricopa	AZ	69.00	Allegheny	PA	28.00
28	San Bernardino	CA	70.00	New York	NY	32.00
29	Santa Clara	CA	70.00	Washington	DC	35.00
30	Orange	CA	72.00	Shelby	TN	35.00
31	King	WA	76.00	PalmBeach	FL	36.00
32	Fulton	GA	76.00	Kings	NY	38.00
33	Hills	FL	77.00	Fairfax	VA	38.00
34	San Diego	CA	79.00	Bronx	NY	39.00

Source: Adapted from Smith, P.Z. (1993). *Felony Defendants in Large Urban Counties, 1990* (Publication #NCJ—141872). Appendix table E. Bureau of Justice Statistics, U.S. Department of Justice.

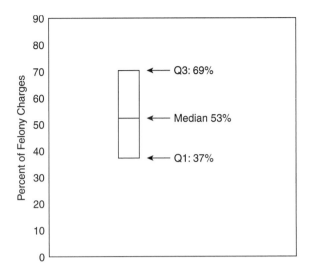

Figure 5–3 Skeleton boxplot for felony charge data

bottom is 37 percent (Queens, NY), and the ninth score from the top is 69 percent (Los Angeles, CA). The first quartile (Q_1), then, is 37 and the third quartile (Q_3) is 69.

Knowing the values of the quartiles and the median, we can calculate all of the other values we need. To construct our boxplot, we must calculate the interquartile range (IQR). Remember that this is simply the difference between the first and third quartiles (IQR = $Q_3 - Q_1$). For our data, then, the IQR is 69% − 37% = 32%. With this last piece of information, we can construct the box of our boxplot. Although a boxplot can be constructed either vertically or horizontally, computer programs usually display them with the axis running along the vertical axis; we will follow this guideline for the examples that follow.

The first element to be entered into our boxplot design is the vertical axis. Along the side of the paper, construct a vertical axis that will accommodate all of the data points for the felony adjudication variable in Table 15–18. Next, along this vertical axis, we construct the first part of our boxplot by simply drawing a box the length of the IQR from our first quartile to the third quartile. In our example, the box would extend from 69 percent to 37 percent of the vertical axis. Across this box, we place a line indicating where the median falls within the distribution. In our example, this line is drawn at 53. The box for the as yet unfinished boxplot from the felony conviction data of Table 15–18 is shown in Figure 5–3.

The next step is to add what Tukey termed the "whiskers" to the box. These whiskers are actually lines which extend out from the box on both the upper and lower ends, denoting how far the data extend up and down to a calculated value called a *fence*. There are four fences we must calculate from the following formulas:

The Calculation of Fences

Higher outer fence $= Q_3 + 3.0(IQR)$
High inner fence $\;\;= Q_3 + 1.5(IQR)$
Low inner fence $\;\;\;= Q_1 - 1.5(IQR)$
Lower outer fence $= Q_1 - 3.0(IQR)$

The inner fences are, then, placed at a distance one and one-half times the IQR above (high inner) and below (low inner) the edges of the box. The outer fences are placed at a distance three times the IQR above (higher outer) and below (lower outer) the edges of the box. Let's state this a different way. There are two inner fences in a boxplot, one coming out of the bottom of the box (the low inner fence) and one coming out of the top of the box (the high inner fence). These two inner fences extend a distance from the box equal to 1.5 times the value of the IQR [1.5(IQR)]. There are two outer fences, one coming out of the bottom of the box (the lower outer fence) and one coming out of the top of the box (the higher outer fence). These two outer fences extend a distance from the box equal to three times the value of the IQR, [3(IQR)]. Notice that the values for the two lower fences (low inner and lower outer) are found by *subtracting* 1.5(IQR) or 3.0(IQR) from the first quartile. We subtract because these fences are found below the box and are therefore below or less than the first quartile, and therefore, the median as well. The values for the two upper fences (high inner and higher outer) are found by *adding* 1.5(IQR) or 3.0(IQR) to the median because these fences are found above the box and are therefore above or greater than the third quartile, and therefore, the median as well. For our felony conviction data, we would obtain the following fence values:

$$\text{Higher outer fence} = [69 + 3.0(32)] = 69 + 96 = 165$$

$$\text{High inner fence} = [69 + 1.5(32)] = 69 + 48 = 117$$

$$\text{Low inner fence} = [37 - 1.5(32)] = 37 - 48 = -11$$

$$\text{Lower outer fence} = [37 - 3.0(32)] = 37 - 96 = -59$$

Again, notice that the values for the low and lower fences are obtained by subtracting the distance of each fence from Q_1, whereas the values for the high and higher fences are obtained by adding the distance of each fence to Q_3.

With these values, we can finish the boxplot by adding the whiskers. We use the values of our fences to determine the exact length of each whisker. There are two whiskers, a bottom one extending down from the bottom of the box (low end) and a top one extending up from the top of the box (high end). Before we can draw the whiskers from the box, however, we must find one more set of numbers. These are what are called the *adjacent values* in our distribution.

The adjacent values are the highest and lowest values in our variable distribution that do not fall outside either of the inner fences (either the low inner or the high inner fence). There are, then, two adjacent values, the *low adjacent value* and the *high adjacent value*. The low adjacent value is the lowest value in our distribution that does not fall outside of our low inner fence. In our example, the value of this low inner fence was −11. There is no value in our data that is lower than −11, so our low adjacent value would therefore be the lowest value in the distribution, which is 21 percent. The high adjacent value is the highest value in our distribution that does not fall outside the high inner fence. In our example, the value of this high inner fence was 117. Examining our felony conviction data, we see that there is no score higher than 117. The high adjacent value would therefore be the highest value in the distribution, or 79 percent.

These adjacent values denote how far out the whisker lines extend from each side of the box. The high whisker extends from the box up to the value of 79 percent on the vertical axis. Draw a line from the middle of the box up to that point, and then make another small perpendicular line the width of the box. There is one of your whiskers. The low whisker extends from the box down to 21 percent on the same vertical axis. Similarly, draw a line from the middle of the box down to 21 percent, and make another small perpendicular line the width of the box. There is the other whisker. These whisker lines added to our original box are displayed in Figure 5–4.

In addition to these whiskers, it is also possible to denote outliers in your boxplots. Outliers, you may remember, are unusually high or unusually low scores in a distribution. They do strange things to our statistical analyses at times—remember what an outlier can do to the value of the mean? In a boxplot, there are two types of outliers displayed: *mild outliers* and *extreme outliers*. As their respective terms imply, extreme outliers are even more unusual scores than mild outliers. Mild outliers, labeled with the symbol ○, are those values in the distribution that fall outside of the calculated inner fences but *do not* fall outside the calculated outer fences. Extreme outliers, labeled with the symbol ●, are those values in the distribution that fall outside of both the inner and outer fences. Because no values in the felony conviction data fall outside of either the inner or outer fences, we do not have any outliers to label for this boxplot. But be warned that outliers often exist, as we will see in the next example!

Now that we have created the masterpiece displayed in Figure 5–4, what can it tell us about our variable distribution? Think about it. What information

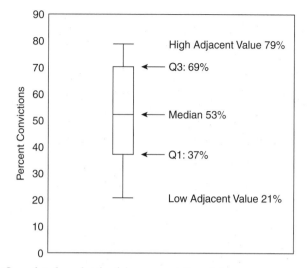

Figure 5–4   Complete boxplot for felony conviction data

makes up this boxplot? We know from looking at the display that the median in our distribution falls around 53 percent. We also know that the box represents the IQR marked off by the first and third quartiles. Thus, we know where the middle 50 percent of our cases lie and how spread out they are around the median. In addition, we have lines extending from the box that indicate where and to what extent the values fall beyond 1.5 IQRs below the first and above the third quartiles.

If the median fell exactly in the middle of the box and each whisker line was the same length, what would this tell us? It would tell us that our distribution is almost perfectly symmetrical, wouldn't it? Remember, this box represents the middle 50 percent of the cases only. Therefore, we can ascertain symmetry information at two levels: in the middle of the distribution and at the tails. The location of the median line in the box tells us about the shape of the middle of the distribution, and the length of the whiskers tells us about the distribution of the high and low 25 percent of our data.

If the median line were closer to the lower quartile than the higher one (that is, if the median line were lower than halfway down the box), there would be a greater concentration of scores on the lower side of the median. This would indicate a positive skew, or a long right tail of the distribution. Conversely, if the median line were closer to the third quartile in the box (that is, if the median line were higher than halfway up the box), this would indicate a higher concentration of cases falling on the lower end of the distribution. A long left tail, you will recall, indicates a negative skew.

Now let's examine the whiskers for signs of skew. If the whisker on the low or bottom end of the box were longer than the whisker at the top end, this would indicate a negative skew because scores would be pulling the left or lower tail out relative to the rest of the distribution. If the whisker at the high or top end of the box were longer than the lower whisker, this would indicate a higher concentration of cases falling on the upper end of the distribution, and hence, a positive skew. In Figure 5–4, the low whisker is slightly longer than the high whisker. This confirms our assessment of a slight positive skew in this distribution.

It might help you to see the shape of the distribution if you were to transpose the image in your head and place the box horizontally. In this way, you can impose a bell-shaped curve over the box to help you visualize what the distribution looks like. Of course, another fantastic tool that helps facilitate understanding is repetition, so let's go over another example. An outline of the steps used for boxplot construction is highlighted in the box that follows.

Steps for Boxplot Construction

Step 1: Rank the data in ascending order.

Step 2: Find the following values:

$$\text{Median [Median position} = (n + 1)/2]$$
$$Q_1 \text{ and } Q_3 \text{ [Quartile depth} = (TMP + 1)/2]$$
$$IQR = Q_3 - Q_1$$

Step 3: Draw a scale along the vertical axis to accommodate all data values.

Step 4: Draw a box indicating the width of the IQR from the first to third quartiles with a line drawn through the box indicating the median.

Step 5: Find fences:

$$\text{Higher outer fence} = Q_3 + 3.0(IQR)$$
$$\text{High inner fence} = Q_3 + 1.5(IQR)$$

$$\text{Low inner fence} = Q_1 - 1.5(IQR)$$
$$\text{Lower outer fence} = Q_1 - 3.0(IQR)$$

Step 6: Find adjacent values (those values that are closest to the inner fences but do not fall outside of them).

Step 7: Draw whisker lines to each adjacent value.

Step 8: Find the mild outliers (those values that fall outside of the inner fences but *not* outside of the outer fences). Mark with the symbol ○.

Step 9: Find the extreme outliers (those values that fall outside of the outer fences). Mark with the symbol ●.

Constructing a Boxplot for Prisoners Sentenced to Death

Table 5–19 provides a rank-order listing of the number of prisoners who were sentenced to death as of December 31, 2000, in the 38 states that authorized capital punishment at that time. We can tell just by glancing at the table that a few states sentenced many more people to death than the majority of states. In fact, the number of defendants sentenced to death ranges from a low of 0 (New Hampshire) to a high of 586 (California). Let's construct a boxplot of this variable distribution.

Since the data are already ordered for you, we can begin to calculate the values we need as follows:

$$\text{Median position} = (n + 1)/2 = (38 + 1)/2 = 19.5$$

$$\text{Median value} = (40 + 40)/2 = 40$$

$$\text{Quartile position} = (\text{TMP} + 1)/2 = (19 + 1)/2 = 10$$

$$Q_1 = 11 \text{ (Oregon)}$$

$$Q_3 = 120 \text{ (Georgia)}$$

$$\text{IQR} = (120 - 11) = 109$$

Higher outer fence $120 + 3(109) = 447$

High inner fence $120 + 1.5(109) = 283.5$

Low inner fence $11 - 1.5(109) = -152.5$

Lower outer fence $11 - 3(109) = -316$

High adjacent value = 238

Low adjacent value = 0

Mild outliers = 371 (Florida)

Extreme outliers = 450 (Texas), 586 (California)

To obtain a finished boxplot display, we must first construct the vertical axis to accommodate all of our values. Since we have such a large range in this variable distribution (586), we have labeled the axis at every 50th point, beginning with 0. The next step is to draw the box the length of the IQR from the first to the third quartile (11 to 120) and then place a line across the box where the median falls (40).

Adding the whiskers to the box is our next move. Our low adjacent value, which is the lowest value in our distribution that is closest to but not outside of the lower inner fence, is equal to 0 (New Hampshire); this is where the end of our low whisker line is marked off. Our high adjacent value, which is the highest value in our distribution that is closest to but not outside of the high inner fence, is 238 (Pennsylvania); this is where the end of our high whisker line is marked off.

TABLE 5–19

Number of Prisoners Under Sentence of Death by State, December 31, 2000

Rank	State	Number of Prisoners
1	New Hampshire	0
2	Wyoming	2
3	South Dakota	3
4	Kansas	4
5	New Mexico	5
6	Colorado	5
7	New York	6
8	Montana	6
9	Connecticut	7
10	Nebraska	11
11	Oregon	11
12	Utah	11
13	Washington	13
14	Delaware	15
15	New Jersey	15
16	Maryland	16
17	Idaho	21
18	Virginia	29
19	Arkansas	40
20	Kentucky	40
21	Indiana	43
22	Mississippi	61
23	South Carolina	66
24	Missouri	79
25	Nevada	88
26	Louisiana	90
27	Tennessee	97
28	Arizona	119
29	Georgia	120
30	Oklahoma	129
31	Illinois	163
32	Alabama	185
33	Ohio	201
34	North Carolina	215
35	Pennsylvania	238
36	Florida	371
37	Texas	450
38	California	586

Source: Snell, T.L. (2001). *Capital Punishment, 2000* (NCJ—190598), p. 6. Bureau of Justice Statistics, U.S. Department of Justice.

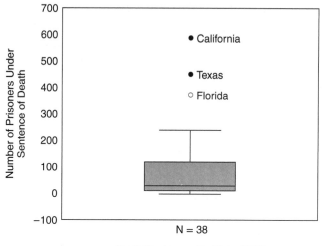

Figure 5–5   Boxplot of the number of prisoners sentenced to death by state, December 31, 2000

The final step we must take is to locate any outliers that exist in the distribution. We have three high values left in our distribution which are not represented in the boxplot: 371, 450, and 586. The first value of 371 (Florida) falls outside of the high inner fence but not outside of the higher outer fence; therefore, it is considered a mild outlier and marked on the boxplot with the symbol ○. The other two fall outside of the higher outer fence and are considered extreme outliers; therefore, they are marked on the boxplot with the symbol ●. The final boxplot, which displays the number of prisoners sentenced to death in the 38 states that authorized capital punishment at that time, is presented in Figure 5–5.

What can we say about the number of people under the sentence of death in the U.S. in 2000 based on the boxplot presented in Figure 5–5? We can say that the majority of states have sentenced less than 100 people to death; by the end of 2000, 50 percent of the states had sentenced less than 40 people to death while 50 percent had sentenced more than 40 people to die. The distribution of death sentences by state is positively skewed, indicating that only a few states have sentenced many people to die and these states are pulling the distribution upward toward the high end of the tail. In fact, there are three states that are classified as outliers in this distribution (one mild and two extreme). Florida, Texas, and California each sentenced over 300 people to death by the end of the 20th century (371, 450, and 586, respectively).

We hope that you have become a convert to EDA by now and agree that these techniques are very effective methods for examining the shape of variable distributions. Researchers often forget this crucial step in the process of statistical analysis and sometimes move on to inferential statistics—unaware that they may be working with variable distributions that are extremely skewed or have other abnormalities such as outliers. If, in the initial phase of your research, you use the EDA techniques we have just presented, you will avoid these mistakes. But hold on! There is even more we can do with these techniques. Not only are they effective for illuminating the univariate distributions of your data set, but they are also very useful for comparing variable distributions between different samples or distributions between subsets of the same sample.

SUMMARY

In this chapter we learned about measures of dispersion, which capture how different the values of a variable are from some reference point. Just as there were different measures of central tendency depending upon the level of measurement of a variable, there are also different measures of dispersion that correspond to the levels of measurement. For variables measured at the nominal or ordinal level, a common measure of dispersion is the variation ratio. The variation ratio measures dispersion with reference to the mode, and it reflects the extent to which the observations do not cluster in the modal category. When we have data measured at the interval/ratio level (or can assume we have this level of measurement), there are more measures of dispersion to employ. The simplest is the range, which is just the difference between the highest and lowest values of a variable. The interquartile range is the difference between the scores at the third quartile (the 75th percentile) and the first quartile (the 25th percentile). As such, the interquartile range captures the dispersion present in the middle 50 percent of a distribution of continuous scores. By far the most common measures of dispersion for continuous (interval/ratio)-level data are the variance and standard deviation. The variance and standard deviation use the mean as the reference point for measuring the amount of dispersion in a variable. Both are based upon the deviation from the mean, which is the difference between a given score and the mean of its distribution.

We also learned that the boxplot, a technique under the rubric of exploratory data analysis, is a useful tool for displaying the dispersion of a variable. With one glance at a boxplot, you can determine the shape of a distribution along with that distribution's center, variability, and any abnormalities that may exist in the distribution.

KEY TERMS

boxplot	measures of dispersion
deviation	range
exploratory data analysis (EDA)	standard deviation
interquartile range (IQR)	variance
mean deviation	variation ratio

REVIEW & PRACTICE

KEY FORMULAS

Variation ratio (eq. 5–1):

$$VR = 1 - \frac{f_{modal}}{n}$$

Range:
     Highest x_i score – Lowest x_i score

Interquartile range (eq. 5–2):

$$IQR = X_{Q_1} - X_{Q_3}$$

Variance of a population (eq. 5–3):

$$\sigma^2 = \frac{\sum_{i=1}^{N} \left(x_i - \mu \right)^2}{N}$$

Variance of a sample (eq. 5–4):

$$s^2 = \frac{\sum_{i=1}^{n} \left(x_i - \overline{X} \right)^2}{n-1}$$

Standard deviation of a population (eq. 5–5):

$$\sigma = \sqrt{\frac{\sum_{i=1}^{N} \left(x_i - \mu \right)^2}{N}}$$

Standard deviation of a sample (eq. 5–6):

$$s = \sqrt{\frac{\sum_{i=1}^{n} \left(x_i - \overline{X} \right)^2}{n-1}}$$

Variance of a sample with grouped data (eq. 5–7)

$$S^2 = \frac{\sum_{i=1}^{k} f_i \left(m_i - \overline{X} \right)^2}{n-1}$$

Standard deviation of a sample with grouped data (eq. 5–8):

$$s = \sqrt{\frac{\sum_{i=1}^{k} f_i \left(m_i - \overline{X} \right)^2}{n-1}}$$

Computational formula for sample variance with ungrouped data (eq. 5–9):

$$s^2 = \frac{\sum \left(x_i^2 \right) - \dfrac{\Sigma \left(x_i \right)^2}{n}}{n-1}$$

Computational formula for sample standard deviation with ungrouped data (eq. 5–10):

$$s = \sqrt{\frac{\sum \left(x_i^2 \right) - \dfrac{\left(\Sigma x_i \right)^2}{n}}{n-1}}$$

Computational formula for sample variance with grouped data (eq. 5–11):

$$s^2 = \sqrt{\frac{\sum \left(f_i m_i^2 \right) - \dfrac{\Sigma \left(f_i m_i \right)^2}{n}}{n-1}}$$

Computational formula for sample standard deviation with grouped data (eq. 5–12):

$$s = \sqrt{\frac{\sum \left(f_i m_i^2 \right) - \dfrac{\left(\Sigma \left(f_i m_i \right) \right)^2}{n}}{n-1}}$$

REVIEW & PRACTICE

PRACTICE PROBLEMS

1. What is the difference between the central tendency and the dispersion in a group of scores, and why is it important to know about and report both the central tendency and dispersion of our variables?

2. A sample of 1,040 youth who had been arrested for one of four offenses (property, violent, drug, and status offense) were asked what type of crime they committed previous to this one. The data are presented below. As you can see, of the 125 current property offenders, 75 reported that their last offense was also a property offense. Of the 110 current violent offenders, 30 reported that their last offense was also a violent offense. And so on.

   With these data, calculate the variation ratio for each type of current offense. Which type of current offense has the most variation/dispersion, and which has the least?

		Current Offense Is:			
		Property	Violent	Drug	Status
Previous Offense Was:	Property	75	50	40	120
	Violent	10	30	30	20
	Drug	20	10	110	115
	Status	20	20	50	320
	Total	125	110	230	575

3. A group of 205 high school males were asked to report the number of times in the past year that they had stolen something that was worth at least $25 in value. Their responses are shown in the following grouped frequency distribution. With these data, calculate the variance and standard deviation.

Number of Thefts	f
0–4	76
5–9	52
10–14	38
15–19	21
20–24	10
25–29	8

4. You take a random sample of 20 females from the population of female offenders incarcerated in a state prison system and find out how many years of school they have completed. Using the data below, calculate:

   a. The range.

   b. The interquartile range.

   c. Variance.

   d. Standard deviation.

Person	Years of Education
1	11
2	8
3	12
4	9
5	9
6	9
7	10
8	10
9	10
10	11
11	9
12	9
13	5
14	9
15	7
16	6
17	10
18	12
19	9
20	5

5. You have data on the race of the new inmates committed to a state's penitentiary for three years: 1980, 1990, and 2000. Is there a trend in the dispersion found in these data?

Year	Race	f
1980	White	852
	Black	675
	Hispanic	112
	Asian	25
	Other	59
1990	White	979
	Black	756
	Hispanic	262
	Asian	86
	Other	78
2000	White	1,211
	Black	925
	Hispanic	636
	Asian	310
	Other	120

6. The following data show the 1991 arrest rate for rape (per 100,000 persons) for a sample of 18 states. For these data, determine:

a. The range.

b. The interquartile range.

c. The variance.

d. The standard deviation.

State	Rape Arrest Rate
Arizona	42.4
Arkansas	44.6
Colorado	47.0
Georgia	42.3
Illinois	40.0
Kentucky	35.4
Louisiana	40.9
Maryland	45.9
Missouri	34.0
New York	28.2
North Carolina	34.6
North Dakota	18.3
Oregon	54.4
Pennsylvania	28.7
South Carolina	58.9
Texas	53.4
Utah	45.6
Wyoming	25.9

7. In the following table, murder rates are presented by state and by the four regions of the U.S. Construct separate boxplots for each regional distribution of murder. Compare and contrast how murder is distributed across the regions of the country.

Murder Rates per 100,000 by Region, Rank-Ordered by State, 1999

State	Murder Rate
South	
Delaware	3.2
West Virginia	4.4
Kentucky	5.4
Arkansas	5.6
Florida	5.7
Virginia	5.7
Texas	6.1
South Carolina	6.6
Oklahoma	6.9
Tennessee	7.1
North Carolina	7.2
Georgia	7.5
Mississippi	7.7
Alabama	7.9
Maryland	9.0
Louisiana	10.7
District of Columbia	46.4

West

Idaho	2.0
Utah	2.1
Wyoming	2.3
Montana	2.6
Oregon	2.7
Washington	3.0
Hawaii	3.7
Colorado	4.6
California	6.0
Arizona	8.0
Alaska	8.6
Nevada	9.1
New Mexico	9.8

Midwest

Iowa	1.5
North Dakota	1.6
South Dakota	2.5
Minnesota	2.8
Wisconsin	3.4
Ohio	3.5
Nebraska	3.6
Kansas	6.0
Indiana	6.6
Missouri	6.6
Michigan	7.0
Illinois	7.7

Northeast

New Hampshire	1.5
Massachusetts	2.0
Maine	2.2
Vermont	2.9
Connecticut	3.3
New Jersey	3.5
Rhode Island	3.6
Pennsylvania	4.9
New York	5.0

Source: Statistical Abstract of the United States: 2001, No. 293, p. 183. U.S. Census Bureau. See also U.S. Federal Bureau of Investigation, Crime in the United States, annual.

SPSS PRACTICE PROBLEMS

Note: As the statistical material we present in this book is inherently cumulative, we will often ask you to utilize statistics and techniques we have examined in earlier chapters as well as new ones learned in the current chapter. This reinforces the notion of the cumulative nature of this material and, since the results are almost instantaneous with SPSS, it is not that time-consuming!

1. Access STATE.XPT. Under ANALYZE, ask for DESCRIPTIVE STATISTICS, then FREQUENCIES. Ask for a frequency distribution of both MURDER and VIOLENT. Under the STATISTICS box, ask for the mean, the median, the quartiles, the standard deviation, and the range. Using the new measures of dispersion we have presented in this chapter, elaborate on the interpretation of these variable distributions.

2. Using the same variables, go under GRAPHS, then click on BOXPLOT, then ask for a SIMPLE boxplot for a SUMMARY OF SEPARATE VARIABLES, and then click on DEFINE to define your graph. In the boxplot dialogue box, place the variable you want to display as a boxplot in the BOXES REPRESENT box. You can also label any outliers that exist in your distribution with identifiers using the LABEL CASES BY box. For these boxplots, ask SPSS to label the cases using the alphanumeric variable called STATE. Describe both boxplots. What outliers show up that were not apparent in other graphical displays or through the use of univariate statistics?

3. We are now going to describe the variable called INMEXP, which is the annual expenditures in dollars spent on inmates per day for each state. Under ANALYZE, click on DESCRIPTIVE STATISTICS, then FREQUENCIES. Along with the frequency distribution, under the STATISTICS box, ask for a median and mean, the quartiles, and the variance and standard deviation for this variable. Using all of this information, describe this variable distribution. How would you characterize the amount of money we spend on incarceration in this country?

4. Using this same variable, let's examine the amount of money spent on incarcerating offenders across the regions of the country. Under ANALYZE, click COMPARE MEANS, then ask for MEANS. In the means dialog box, ask for INMEXP to be placed in the DEPENDENT list box and REGION to be placed in the INDEPENDENT list box. Interpret the means and the standard deviations for each region. After examining the dollar amount spent on inmates per day by region, how has your original interpretation changed?

5. Now let's get a bit fancy with the BOXPLOT function of SPSS. Under GRAPHS, ask for BOXPLOT. Then ask for a SIMPLE boxplot, but this time, ask for SUMMARIES FOR GROUPS OF CASES. In the VARIABLE box, place MURDER, which is the murder rate per 100k for each state. Under CATEGORY AXIS, place REGION, which will provide you with four boxplots for the distribution of murder rates for each of the four regions of the country. To identify any outliers that may exist by state, place the alphanumeric STATE variable in the LABEL CASES BY box. Interpret the variation of murder by region in the United States. How does this interpretation differ from the interpretation you made of murder for the entire country?

Probability, Probability Distributions, and an Introduction to Hypothesis Testing

CHAPTER

6

> *P*robable impossibilities are to be preferred to improbable possibilities.
>
> —ARISTOTLE
>
> *W*hat?
>
> —RAY PATERNOSTER

An important set of tools you will learn in this book are the tools of inferential statistics. In inferential statistics we have information that we have observed from our sample data and we wish to use this information to make an inference to a larger population. The foundation of inferential statistics is probability theory. You do not need to be an expert in probability theory in order to understand the statistical procedures in this book, but the background provided in this chapter should prove helpful.

In this chapter we will learn about two notions of probability—the chance that an event occurs in one trial, and the chance that an event occurs "over the long run." We will learn how to calculate the probability of events, including unconditional, conditional, and joint probabilities. To calculate these probabilities you will learn to apply some basic probability rules. You also will learn about probability distributions, which are extremely important because we use these theoretical distributions to conduct hypothesis tests. There are two probability distributions that you will learn in this chapter: a discrete distribution (binomial) and a continuous distribution (the standard normal distribution). You will find that the standard normal distribution is one of the most useful probability distributions because of a theorem in statistics called the Central Limit Theorem.

INTRODUCTION

In Chapters 2–5 of this book we have been discussing how to organize, display, and summarize important features of your data. Statistical tools like frequency and percent distributions, graphs and charts, measures of central tendency and dispersion, and the techniques of exploratory data analysis are all useful ways to describe variables. That is why this collection of statistical tools is often referred to as *descriptive statistics*. Descriptive statistics are useful in helping us to understand what our data look like and communicating the properties and characteristics of our data to others.

In addition to describing our variables, however, we often wish to do other things, such as use the information we have collected from our sample to make an inference about some unknown population value or make a decision about the relationship between two variables in a population. A very important part of statistical work in criminology and criminal justice, therefore, does not involve merely describing information gathered from a sample but using that sample data to make inferences about some unknown population value. As we noted in Chapter 1, these statistics are called *inferential statistics*, and they will be the focus of our attention for the remainder of this book.

PROBABILITY

The foundation of inferential statistics is probability theory, which is used in the creation of probability distributions. Probability theory can be a very difficult thing to understand, but in this chapter we will break it down into its most basic elements and rules. You probably already have some idea as to what the notion of probability is. You have asked yourself questions like, "What is the chance that I will pass a test if I go out partying the night before rather than studying?" or "What is the likelihood that I will win the Superball Lottery if I buy one ticket today?" or even "How likely is it that I will get stopped for running this kind of a yellowy-red traffic light?" Questions like these are all about the probability of an event. The answers to these questions are typically along the lines of: "not much of a chance," "a snowball's chance in hell," and "not very likely at all."

Persons in the criminal justice system frequently have to respond to probability questions. For example, in criminal cases a jury must determine that a defendant is guilty "beyond a reasonable doubt" before they convict her. The term "beyond a reasonable doubt" implies that there must be a very high probability that the person accused actually committed the offense before that person can be convicted. Wardens in correctional institutions often have to make a probability judgment as to how dangerous an inmate is before deciding if he can live in the regular inmate population or if he requires some additional restriction or custody. The concept of probability also forms the foundation for research and statistical work in criminology and criminal justice. In order to understand the concept of probability more precisely and how it applies to research problems in our field, we need to acquaint you with the mathematical notion of probability.

In mathematical terms, the probability of an event has a definite meaning. The **probability of an event** is defined as the number of times that a specific event can occur relative to the total number of times that any event can occur. The probability of an event (say, event A) is often written as $P(A)$, and the total number of times that any event can occur is often referred to as the number of trials. For simplicity's sake, let's think about the simple case of drawing an ace from a deck of cards. There are four aces in a standard deck of 52

> The **probability of an event** (event A) is defined as the number of times A can occur over the total number of events or trials. The formula for the probability of an event is:
>
> $$P(A) = \frac{\text{Number of times event } A \text{ can occur}}{\text{Total number of possible events or trials}}$$

cards. The probability of selecting one ace from the deck then is: $P(\text{Ace}) = 4$ (aces)/52 (cards) = .0769, since there are four possible ways of an ace occurring (an ace of hearts, diamonds, clubs, or spades) and there are 52 possible cards (52 possible outcomes) in the deck. Similarly, if we were to flip a coin, what is the probability that it would land heads? Since there are two possible outcomes in one flip of a coin (the coin can land on either heads or tails) and we want to know the probability of one possible outcome (a head), the probability would be: $P(\text{Head}) = 1$ (head)/2 (possible outcomes in one flip) = .50.

We need to maintain a distinction between two related but different notions of the concept of the probability of an event. The first conception of probability is the one we have just discussed. The probability of an event is the number of times an event can occur in a given number of trials. In our coin-flipping example, the probability of obtaining a head in one flip of a coin is .5. This does not mean, however, that if we flip a coin n number of times we should always expect to observe $n/2$ heads. For example, if we flip a coin 10 times we will not always find that we get five heads and five tails even though the probability of a head (and a tail, of course) is .5. In other words, just because the probability of observing a head in one flip of a coin is .5, this does not mean that we will always observe an equal number of heads and tails on any given number of trials. If you are not convinced of this, run an experiment in which you flip a coin 10 times. For each of the 10 trials, count the number of heads and tails. Notice that you did not get exactly five heads and five tails on every trial of 10 flips.

The second notion of probability—let's refer to this as the sampling notion of probability—tells us, however, that *in the long run* the most likely or most probable outcome when you flip a coin 10 times is that you will get five heads and five tails. Sometimes, but rarely, you will observe zero heads or zero tails in 10 flips. Sometimes, but less rarely, you will observe one head or one tail, but the most likely or most probable outcome will be five heads and five tails. If you were to repeat the coin flip experiment a large number of times (say, 10,000 times), the outcome with the highest frequency (and therefore the one with the highest probability) would be five heads and five tails.

THE RULES OF PROBABILITY

> The **bounding rule of probabilities** is that the probability of any event can never be less than zero or greater than 1.0:

$$0 \leq P(A) \leq 1.0$$

In working with probabilities there are a few simple rules to remember. The first is called the **bounding rule of probabilities** (Rule 1). Recall that the formula for determining a probability is P(A) = Number of times event A can occur/Total number of events. Let's designate the denominator, the total number of events, as n. Notice that we can have no fewer than 0 events of A out of n trials and no more than n events of A out of n trials. This means that the minimum value of a probability is $0/n$, or zero, while the maximum value is n/n, or 1.0. The minimum probability occurs when event A occurs zero times out of n while the maximum probability occurs when event A occurs n times out of n. This expresses the *bounding rule* of probabilities—the probability of any event is bounded by zero and 1.0. Any probability can never be less than zero or greater than 1.0. A probability of zero means that event A is impossible, probabilities close to zero imply that event A is unlikely to occur, probabilities close to 1.0 imply that there is a good chance that event A is likely to occur, and a probability of 1.0 implies that event A will always occur.

The probability of an event *not* occurring is called the **complement of an event.** Returning to our example, we have defined the probability of event A occurring as P(A). Therefore, the probability of event A not occurring, P(not A), is referred to as the complement of event A. Based on the bounding rule, if the probability of event A is P(A), then the probability that A will not occur or the probability of its complement must be $1 - P(A)$. For example, we found earlier that the probability of drawing one ace from a deck of cards is $4/52 = .0769$. The probability of not drawing an ace, therefore, must be $48/52 = .9231$, or $1 - .0769$. The bounding rule tells us, therefore, that the sum of an event and its complement is 1.0. Knowing about the complement of an event is important because it is part of the *odds* of an event occurring. We often hear about the odds of an event occurring; for example, we might hear that the odds of the New York Yankees winning the World Series this year are 7 to 3. We might then surmise that the odds of an event express how likely it is that the event will occur—without knowing exactly what it is. Well, the **odds** of event A occurring is simply the ratio of the probability of the event to its complement, Odds(A) = $P(A)/P(\text{not } A)$.

For example, let's say that the probability that a given defense lawyer will win an acquittal for her client is .80. The complement of this probability, or the probability that her client will be convicted, is .20. For this defense lawyer, then, the odds of an acquittal are .80/.20, or 4 to 1. If the probability that she would win an acquittal for her clients was .95, then the odds in favor of an acquittal would be .95/.05, or 19 to 1. Notice that the more likely the event is to occur, the higher the odds. For example, if the probability of an acquittal for possession of marijuana is .9, the odds are 9 to 1 in favor of acquittal over conviction. If the probability of a conviction for murder is .5, then the odds are even or 1 to 1 and no outcome is favored. Odds, therefore, are not the same thing as a probability, but probabilities and complements both go into the calculation of odds.

> The **odds** of an event occurring are equal to the ratio of the probability that the event will occur to the probability that it will not occur.
>
> $$\text{odds} = \frac{P(A)}{1 - P(A)}$$

Notice one more thing about the probability of an event and its complement—they cannot both occur at the same time. If the complement of event A consists of all occurrences of not-A, then we cannot have both A occurring and not-A occurring. For example, we cannot both select an ace from a deck of cards (event A) and select a card other than an ace (event not-A) in a single draw from the deck. In other words, an event and its complement are **mutually exclusive events.** The probability of two mutually exclusive events occurring at the same time, therefore, is zero. As another example, for a single criminal trial with a single criminal charge, the events of conviction and acquittal on the charge are mutually exclusive events (let's forget about the possibility of a "hung jury" or some other disposition). At the end of this trial you cannot observe both a conviction and an acquittal for the one criminal charge; they are mutually exclusive events. Figure 6–1 shows in a Venn diagram the notion of mutually exclusive events. Notice that the areas covered by the probability of event A and event B never overlap or intersect. This means that their joint

> **Mutually exclusive events** are events that cannot occur at the same time. In other words, there is no intersection of mutually exclusive events so that their joint probability is equal to zero.

Figure 6–1 Two mutually exclusive events, event A and event B

occurrence is impossible—they cannot both occur at the same time, so they are mutually exclusive events.

With our knowledge of mutually exclusive events we can now discuss the second rule of probabilities—the **addition rule of probabilities**. The addition rule will help us answer the question, "What is the probability of either event A or event B occurring?" There are actually two forms of the addition rule of probabilities, a general version and a more restricted or limited version. The restricted version covers instances where we can assume that all events are mutually exclusive. In the general version we cannot maintain the assumption that the events involved are mutually exclusive. We call this the *general form* of the addition rule because you can also use this rule in the case of mutually exclusive events and get the correct answer. If you are calculating the probability of events that are not mutually exclusive, however, you cannot use the restricted or limited rule. The restricted rule is a little simpler, so we will discuss it first.

> **Restricted addition rule of probabilities** (Rule 2a) states that if two events are mutually exclusive, the probability of event A occurring or event B occurring is equal to the sum of their separate probabilities:

$$P(A \text{ or } B) = P(A) + P(B)$$

The *restricted form* of the addition rule (Rule 2a) states that the probability of either of two mutually exclusive events occurring is equal to the sum of their separate probabilities. In other words, if event A and event B are mutually exclusive events, then the probability of event A or B occurring, written $P(A \text{ or } B)$, is equal to $P(A) + P(B)$. The addition rule is often referred to as the "*or*" rule because we want to know what the probability of one event "or" the other is. Let's use the information in Table 6–1 to help us understand the restricted form of the addition rule of probabilities.

Citizen Perceptions about Justice

The data in Table 6–1 come from a study of perceptual justice conducted by the social psychologist Tom Tyler (1990), who asked 1,575 citizens of Chicago about their perceptions of the police and court system. The first part of Table 6–1 reports respondents' answers to the question of whether they think the police are doing a good job, while the bottom panel of the table provides answers to a similar question about the court system. With these data, let's ask and answer some basic probability questions and some that require the restricted addition rule.

1. What is the probability that a person thought the police were doing a "good" job?

To answer this question, we need to know that 693 of the respondents thought that the police were doing a good job, out of a total of 1,575 respondents. The probability, therefore, is: P(good job) = 693/1,575 = .44.

2. What is the probability that a person thought the police were doing a "poor" job?

TABLE 6–1

Response to Questions about the Police and Courts of Chicago

"How good a job are the police doing?"	
Answer	*f*
Very good	158
Good	693
Fair	598
Poor	95
Very poor	31
Total	1,575
	n = 1,575
"How good a job are the courts doing?"	
Answer	*f*
Very good	63
Good	346
Fair	740
Poor	284
Very poor	142
Total	1,575
	n = 1,575

Source: Tom Tyler,*Why People Obey the Law*, p. 51, Table 4.7.

Since 95 of the 1,575 respondents thought that the police were doing a poor job, the probability is: P(poor job) = 95/1,575 = .06.

3. What is the probability that a person thought the police were doing a "fair" or "very poor" job?

This problem asks about the probability of either of two events occurring: the probability that a person thought the police were doing a fair job, or the probability that a person thought the police were doing a very poor job. We know that these two events are mutually exclusive, since a person can provide only one answer to the question and cannot, therefore, respond both "fair" and "very poor" to the question. The probability, then, is going to be equal to the sum of their separate probabilities:

$$P(\text{fair job or very poor job}) = \frac{598}{1,575} + \frac{31}{1,575} = \frac{629}{1,575} = .40$$

4. What is the probability that a person thought the police were doing a "very good," "good," or "poor" job?

There are two ways we can answer this question. One is to determine that these three events are mutually exclusive (because a person can provide only one answer to the police question) and then use the restricted form of the addition rule to calculate the sum of their separate probabilities:

$$P(\text{very good, good, or poor job}) = \frac{158}{1,575} + \frac{693}{1,575} + \frac{95}{5,175} = \frac{946}{1,575} = .60$$

Another way to answer this question would be to notice that these events are the complement of the previous problem, which asked for the probability of someone answering "fair" or "very poor" to the question ($P = .40$). Using the complement of an event, we can find the probability of very good, good, or a poor job as $1 - .40$, or $.60$. We arrive at the same answer.

5. What is the probability that a person thought the courts were doing a "very good" job or a "good" job?

Once again, these events are mutually exclusive, since a person could provide only one answer to the question. Using the restricted form of the addition rule, the probability is:

$$P(\text{very good job or good job}) = \frac{63}{1,575} + \frac{346}{1,575} = \frac{409}{1,575} = .26$$

6. Is it more likely that the respondents in the Tyler study thought that the police were doing either a "very good" or "good job" or that the courts were doing a "very good" or "good" job?

Using the addition rule for mutually exclusive events, the probability that the police were doing a very good or good job was:

$$P(\text{very good job or good job}) = \frac{158}{1,575} + \frac{693}{1,575} = \frac{851}{1,575} = .54$$

In other words, just over one-half of these Chicago citizens thought that the police were doing either a very good or good job.

Using the addition rule for mutually exclusive events, the probability that the courts were doing a very good or good job was:

$$P(\text{very good job or good job}) = \frac{63}{1,575} + \frac{346}{1,575} = \frac{409}{1,575} = .26$$

Just over one-quarter of the respondents thought that the courts were doing a very good or good job. Since a higher probability means that an event is more likely, it appears that it is more likely that the respondents think the police are doing a very good or good job than the courts.

Let's now discuss the case where we cannot assume that the events are mutually exclusive. Figure 6–2 provides a Venn diagram of two events, event A and event B, which are not mutually exclusive. Recall that **nonmutually exclusive events** can occur at the same time. The possibility of their joint occurrence is illustrated in the Venn diagram by the intersection of the two events. The intersection of the two

> **Nonmutually exclusive events** are events that can occur simultaneously. The joint probability of nonmutually exclusive events is, therefore, greater than zero.

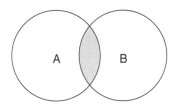

Figure 6–2   Two nonmutually exclusive events, event *A* and event *B*

events shows the area where both event *A* and event *B* are occurring. The greater the area of the intersection of the two events is, the higher the probability of their joint occurrence.

When two events are not mutually exclusive we cannot use the restricted version of the addition rule. We will see why in a moment. In the case of nonmutually exclusive events, we have to apply the **general addition rule of probabilities** (Rule 2b). This form of the addition rule states that, for two nonmutually exclusive events, events *A* and *B*, the probability of event *A* or event *B* occurring is equal to the sum of their separate probabilities minus the probability of their joint occurrence: P(*A* or *B*) = P(*A*) + P(*B*) − P(*A* and *B*). The new part of the addition rule is the last term, P(*A* and *B*), which is the probability of events *A* and *B* occurring at the same time or their joint probability. Another way to think of a joint probability is that it is the probability of two events occurring simultaneously. For example, the probability of drawing a heart from a deck of cards is 13 out of 52, and the probability of drawing a king is 4 out of 52. The joint probability of drawing a heart and a king is the probability of drawing the king of hearts, or 1 out of 52. The probability of the king of hearts is the joint probability of a king and a heart occurring at the same time. When two events are not mutually exclusive, this joint probability must be subtracted from the sum of the two separate probabilities because, as we will see, it is counted twice: once in determining the probability of event *A* and again in determining the probability of event *B*.

> **General addition rule of probabilities** (Rule 2b) states that if two events are not mutually exclusive, the probability of event *A* occurring or event *B* occurring is equal to the sum of their separate probabilities minus their joint probability:
>
> P(*A* or *B*) = P(*A*) + P(*B*) − P(*A* and *B*)

Let's answer some probability questions that require the use of this general addition rule and find out why it is more general than the restricted rule. One prominent theory in criminology is *general strain theory*, according to which participation in delinquent behavior is said to be more likely when youths experience strain in the form of stressful or unpleasant stimuli. In Table 6–2 we show some data pertaining to two variables, whether or not a youth's parents were separated or divorced in the past year (a stressful event) and whether one of the children committed a delinquent act in the subsequent year.

TABLE 6–2

Family Breakup and Delinquent Conduct

	Number of Delinquent Acts Committed			
Divorce/Separation	0	1–4	5 or more	Total
No	125	60	15	200
Yes	10	35	65	110
Total	135	95	80	310

1. What is the probability that a child committed 1–4 delinquent acts?

$$P(1\text{--}4\text{ deliquent acts}) = \frac{95}{310} = .31$$

2. What is the probability that parents were divorced/separated or the child did not commit a delinquent act?

Notice that these events are not mutually exclusive. How do we know this? To determine if two events are mutually exclusive, ask yourself if it is possible for them both to occur simultaneously. In this case, is it possible that the parents could have experienced a separation or divorce and also have a child who did not commit delinquent acts? Looking at Table 6–2, you should be able to see that the answer to that question is "yes"; in fact, there were 10 instances where there was both a separation/divorce and a nondelinquent child. There are instances, therefore, of separation/divorce and a child with no delinquent offenses. Since there is an intersection of the two events, separation/divorce and delinquency, they are not mutually exclusive. We cannot, then, use the restricted form of the addition rule but must instead appeal to the general form. The probability of having separated/divorced parents and a nondelinquent child is equal to the probability of separated/divorced parents plus the probability of a nondelinquent child, minus the probability of having both separated/divorced parents and a nondelinquent child:

$$P(\text{divorced/separated or no delinquent acts}) = \frac{110}{310} + \frac{135}{310} - \frac{10}{310} = \frac{235}{310} = .76$$

Why do we have to subtract the joint occurrence of divorced/separated parents and no delinquent acts from the sum of the separate probabilities? Notice that we included these 10 cases when we counted the number of divorced/separated parents and then again when we counted those with no delinquent acts. Since these nonmutually exclusive 10 cases include those with both a divorced/separated parent and no delinquent acts, they are counted twice. The final term removes the double addition.

3. What is the probability of having parents who are separated/divorced or a child with five or more delinquent acts?

These two events are not mutually exclusive events since there are 65 instances where there were divorced/separated parents and a child with five or more delinquent acts. The intersection of the two events is not zero, indicating that they are not mutually exclusive. To find the probability, then, we use the general version of the addition rule:

$$\text{P(divorced/separated or 5 + deliquent acts)} = \frac{110}{310} + \frac{80}{310} - \frac{65}{310} = \frac{125}{310} = .40$$

4. What is the probability of a child committing zero delinquent acts or committing five or more delinquent acts?

These events are mutually exclusive events since a child cannot commit both zero delinquent acts and five or more delinquent acts during the same time period. To determine this probability, therefore, we can use the restricted version of the addition rule:

$$\text{P(0 delinquent acts or 5+ deliquent acts)} = \frac{135}{310} + \frac{80}{310} = \frac{215}{310} = .69$$

To see why the general version of the addition rule is more general, let's use this rule to solve this problem. Recall that what we do is subtract the probability of the joint occurrence of the two events from the sum of their separate probabilities. What is the probability of the joint occurrence of zero delinquent acts in the subsequent year and five or more delinquent acts in the subsequent year? The answer is zero. The joint probability of these two events is zero because they are mutually exclusive events (see Figure 6–1). What we would do, therefore, is subtract zero from the .69 above and our answer would still be that there is a .69 probability that a child committed no delinquent acts or five or more delinquent acts. This shows that you can use the general addition rule in cases where there are mutually exclusive and non-mutually exclusive events and get the same answer as you would if you used the restricted rule. The reason is that if your events are mutually exclusive, you simply will be subtracting zero in the last term. However, if your events are not mutually exclusive, you cannot use the restricted rule of addition.

In our discussion of the addition rule of probabilities for events that are not mutually exclusive, we introduced the concept of **joint probability,** or the simultaneous occurrence of two events. Recall that nonmutually exclusive events are two or more events that can occur at the same time (see Figure 6–2), such as having divorced/separated parents (event A) and committing five or more delinquent acts (event B). We had to subtract the joint occurrence of the two events from the sum of the separate probabilities in applying the general form of the addition rule (the "or" rule).

> The **joint probability** of two or more events is the probability that they occur at the same time.

What we did not discuss, however, was exactly how one calculates the joint probability of two or more events, that is, the probability of event A *and* event B both occurring.

The joint probability of two or more events is determined with the application of the **multiplication rule of probabilities.** The multiplication rule of probabilities is often referred to as the "and" rule because with it we can determine the probability of events A "and" B occurring (recall that the addition rule was used to determine the probability of A "or" B occurring). The application of the multiplication rule to two events is written $P(A$ and $B)$. Like the addition rule, there are two forms of the multiplication rule; one is more general in its application, and the other is used under more restricted conditions.

> **Restricted multiplication rule of probabilities** (Rule 3a) states that if two events are independent of each other, the probability of both event A occurring and event B occurring is equal to the product of their separate probabilities:
>
> $P(A$ and $B) = P(A) \times P(B)$

The more restricted version of the multiplication rule concerns the case where the events are independent of one another. Two events are independent of each other when the occurrence of one event has no effect on (does not influence) the occurrence of another event. In other words, there is no relationship between independent events. For example, in two flips of a coin the fact that the first flip resulted in a head does not affect what the outcome of the second flip will be—a head is no more likely to follow a tail than another head. Later in this section we will give you a more formal test for the independence of two events. If two or more events are independent, then the probability of their joint occurrence is equal to the product of their separate probabilities. For example, assuming event A and event B are independent, the probability of both event A and event B occurring is equal to: $P(A$ and $B) = P(A) \times P(B)$.

Let's take as our first example a coin toss. The probability of a head (or tail) on any given flip of a fair coin is .5. In two flips of a coin, the probability of getting two heads P (head and head) is going to be $.5 \times .5 = .25$. In three flips of a coin, the probability of getting three heads is going to be $.5 \times .5 \times .5 = .125$.

What do we do when we cannot assume that the events whose joint probability we wish to determine are not independent? In the case of nonindependence we cannot use the restricted version of the multiplication rule but must use a more general version. This version of the multiplication rule is more general because, like the general form of the addition rule, it will always give you the correct answer.

> **General multiplication rule of probabilities** (Rule 3b) states that if two events are not independent of each other, the probability of event A occurring and event B occurring is equal to the product of the unconditional probability of event A and the conditional probability of event B given A:
>
> $P(A$ and $B) = P(A) \times P(B \,|\, A)$

The **general multiplication rule of probabilities** states that the probability of two nonindependent events, events A and B, occurring is equal to the probability of event A times the *conditional probability* of event B: $P(A$ and $B) = P(A) \times P(B \,|\, A)$. The last term of this formula, the **conditional probability**, is something new, and is read, "the conditional probability of event B given event A." We will learn about this and about the general multiplication rule by revisiting Table 6–2.

Previously, when we were interested in calculating a probability, we used as our denominator the total number of events. For example, in Table 6–2 the probability that any child will have committed 1–4 delinquent acts was found by dividing the total number of children who committed 1–4 delinquent acts (95) by the total number of children who theoretically could have committed 1–4 delinquent acts in our sample (310). This probability is called an unconditional probability. When we are interested in conditional probabilities, however, we are saying that some other event occurs first. The conditional probability of B given A asks, "What is the probability of event B occurring given that event A has already occurred?" In other words, the probability of B is now conditioned on A. In a conditional probability, the denominator is the number of events for event A, not the total number of events.

For example, in Table 6–2 the unconditional probability of 1–4 delinquent acts is .31, P(1–4 delinquent acts) = 95/310. Now, what is the conditional probability of 1–4 delinquent acts *given that* there is a divorced or separated parent [P(1–4 acts) | (divorced/separated parent)]? Before we calculate the probability of B (1–4 delinquent acts), event A (divorced/separated parent) has to occur first. So now let's look only at the subgroup of observations involving divorced/separated parents. There are 110 divorced/separated parents, and since we are conditioning on this event, this becomes the denominator of our probability. Of these 110 divorced/separated parents, 35 have children who committed 1–4 delinquent acts. The conditional probability of 1–4 delinquent acts given divorced/separated parents, therefore, is 35/110 = .32. In this case the conditional probability is not that much different from the unconditional probability, but as we will see, this will not always be the case.

Let's take one more example. What is the conditional probability of five or more delinquent acts given that the parents are not divorced/separated: P(5+ acts) | (no divorce/separation)? We are conditioning on the fact that the parents are not divorced. There are 200 cases of nondivorced parents. Of these cases, 15 have children who have committed five or more delinquent acts, so the conditional probability of 5+ delinquent acts given nondivorced/separated parents is 15/200 = .075.

We needed to learn about conditional probabilities in order to use the general version of the multiplication rule. Before we move on to this, however, we would like to discuss the notion of independence and its relationship to the multiplication rule. We have said that if we can assume that two events are independent of each other, then we can determine their joint probability, P(A and B), with the simpler, restricted version of the multiplication rule [P(A and B) = P(A) × P(B)]. If, however, our events are not independent, then we have to use the more general rule, [P(A and B) = P(A) × P(B|A)]. How do we know if two events are independent?

We said earlier that two events are independent if the occurrence of one event has no effect on the probability of the occurrence of the other event. Our example of two independent events was flipping a coin two times—the

> Two events, *A* and *B*, are **independent events** when the unconditional probability of *A* is equal to the conditional probability of *A* given *B*:

$$P(A) = P(A \mid B)$$

When two events are independent, knowledge of one event does not help predict the probability of the other event occurring.

outcome of the first flip has no effect or influence on the outcome of the second flip. This means that just because the first flip lands on heads, a heads on the second flip of a coin is no more or less likely to occur. When two events are not independent, however, then the outcome of one event influences the outcome of the other. If this is true, then knowing about the first event will help us predict the second event better. A more formal way to state this is that if two events (*A* and *B*) are independent, then the unconditional probability of *A* will be equal to the conditional probability of *A* given *B*, or $P(A) = P(A \mid B)$. In this instance, knowing that event *B* has occurred does not change the probability of event *A*. If two events (*A* and *B*) are not independent, however, the unconditional probability of *A* will not be equal to the conditional probability of *A* given *B*: [$P(A) \neq P(A \mid B)$]. In this case, knowing that event *B* has occurred does alter the probability of *A* occurring.

In Table 6–3 we present the joint distribution of two variables or events based on information collected from 100 youths. Variable or event *A* is whether the youth is right- or left-handed, and variable or event *B* is whether or not the youth has committed a delinquent act in the previous year. Let's first find the probability that a youth committed a delinquent act. Since 50 of the 100 youths committed at least one delinquent act, this unconditional probability of delinquency is equal to .50. Now let's find out if knowing whether or not someone is right- or left-handed helps predict whether or not they will be delinquent. What is the conditional probability of at least one delinquent act given that a youth was left-handed? Since there were 50 left-handed youths, and 25 of them had committed a delinquent offense in the past year, the conditional probability of delinquency given left-handedness is .50 (25 ǀ 50). Now, what is the conditional probability of at least one delinquent act given that a youth was right-handed? Since there were 50 right-handed youths, and 25 of them had committed a delinquent offense in the past year, the conditional probability of delinquency given right-handedness is .50 (25 ǀ 50). What we have discovered is that the unconditional probability of delinquency is equal to the conditional probability of delinquency given that the person is left-handed (and given the fact that they are right-handed). Does knowing whether or not someone is left-handed help us predict the probability that they will be delinquent? No, because the conditional probability of delinquency given left-handedness, .5, is the same as the unconditional probability of delinquency (.5).

Now let's look at Table 6–4, where we have the joint distribution of two events for the same 100 youths. We know whether or not they were delinquent; as before, 50 committed a delinquent act in the past year and 50 did not. We also know whether or not the youth was impulsive, according to the results of a psychological test. Fifty of them were deemed to be impulsive and 50 were not. As in Table 6–3, the unconditional probability that a youth committed a delinquent act is .50 since there were 50 who committed a delinquent

TABLE 6–3

Joint Frequency Distribution for Right-/Left-Handedness and Delinquency

Handedness	Committed Delinquent Act Last Year?		
	No	Yes	Total
Left-Handed	25	25	50
Right-Handed	25	25	50
Total	50	50	100

TABLE 6–4

Joint Frequency Distribution for Impulsivity and Delinquency

Youth Impulsive?	Committed Delinquent Act Last Year?		
	No	Yes	Total
No	40	10	50
Yes	10	40	50
Total	50	50	100

act out of 100 youths. Now, does knowing whether or not a youth was not impulsive affect this unconditional probability? The conditional probability of a delinquent act given the fact that a youth was not impulsive is: P(delinquency | not implusive) = 10/50 = .20. The conditional probability of delinquency for those who were not impulsive is much less than the unconditional probability of delinquency (.20 versus .50). Now, does knowing whether or not a youth was impulsive affect the unconditional probability? The conditional probability of a delinquent act given the fact that a youth was impulsive is: P(delinquency | impulsive) = 40/50 = .80. The unconditional probability of delinquency is not equal to the conditional probability of delinquency given being impulsive (.50 versus .80). A youth who is impulsive has a much higher risk of being delinquent. Does knowing the level of a youth's impulsivity affect the probability that he or she will be delinquent? The answer is yes, as youths are at a greatly reduced risk of delinquency if they are not impulsive and a greatly elevated risk of delinquency if they are impulsive. Knowing whether or not someone is impulsive does affect the outcome of delinquency, so the two events (delinquency and impulsivity) are not independent.

Now that we know about conditional probability and the independence of two events we are ready to apply the more general form of the multiplication rule, which states that if two events, *A* and *B*, are not independent, then the probability of A and B occurring is equal to the probability of A times the probability of B given A, or $P(A \text{ and } B) = P(A) \times P(B|A)$. Let's use this version of the multiplication rule to answer a few probability questions about Table 6–4. We already know that impulsivity and the commission of delinquent acts are not independent.

1. What is the probability that a youth has been rated not impulsive and has committed no delinquent offense?

The answer is found by determining the unconditional probability of being not impulsive times the conditional probability of having no delinquent acts given the fact that a youth was not impulsive: P(not impulsive) = 50/100 = .50, P(not delinquent | not impulsive) = 40/50 = .80. Therefore, P(not impulsive and not delinquent) = .50 × .80 = .40.

2. What is the probability that a youth has been rated impulsive but has not committed a delinquent act?

The unconditional probability that a youth will be impulsive is: P(impulsive) = 50/100 = .50; the conditional probability that a youth will not have committed a delinquent offense given that they are impulsive is: P(not delinquent | impulsive) = 10/50 = .20. Therefore, P(impulsive and not delinquent) = .50 × .20 = .10.

3. What is the probability that a youth has been rated impulsive and has committed a delinquent act?

The unconditional probability that a youth will be impulsive is: P(impulsive) = 50/100 = .50; the conditional probability that a youth will be delinquent given that they are impulsive is: P(delinquent | impulsive) = 40/50 = .80. Therefore, P(impulsive and delinquent) = .50 × .80 = .40.

The conditional probability version of the multiplication rule (Rule 3b) is more general because we can use this version both when our events are independent and when they are not. We cannot, however, use Rule 3a if our events are not independent, as that rule will give us the wrong answer. To see why multiplication rule 3b is more general, let's apply this rule to a probability problem from Table 6–3, where we know the events are independent.

What is the probability of being right-handed and delinquent? Using the restricted multiplication rule (Rule 3a) for independent events, the answer is equal to the product of the two probabilities: P(right-handed and delinquent) = P(right-handed) × P(delinquent) = 50/100 × 50/100 = .5 × .5 = .25. This is the correct answer. Now let's apply the more restricted multiplication rule (Rule 3b) for nonindependent events: P(right-handed and delinquent) = P(right-handed) × P(delinquent | right-handed) = 50/100 × 25/50 = .5 × .5 = .25. We still get the correct answer, and the reason is that with independent events the unconditional probability of being delinquent from Rule 3a is equal to the conditional probability of being delinquent given the fact that someone is right-handed from Rule 3b. Remember, when events are inde-

TABLE 6–5

Probability Rules

Rule 1: The Bounding Rule

The probability of an event (event *A*) must always be greater than or equal to zero and less than or equal to 1.0.

$$0 \le P \le 1$$

Rule 2: The Addition Rule

Rule 2a: The Restricted Addition Rule for Mutually Exclusive Events

If two events (events *A* and *B*) are mutually exclusive, the probability of either event *A* or event *B* occurring is equal to the sum of their separate probabilities.

$$P(A \text{ or } B) = P(A) + P(B)$$

Rule 2b: The General Addition Rule

If two events (events *A* and *B*) are not mutually exclusive, the probability of either event *A* or event *B* occurring is equal to the sum of their separate probabilities minus their joint probability.

$$P(A \text{ or } B) = P(A) + P(B) - P(A \text{ and } B)$$

Rule 3: The Multiplication Rule

Rule 3a: The Restricted Multiplication Rule for Independent Events

If two events (events *A* and *B*) are independent, the probability of event *A* and event *B* occurring simultaneously is equal to the product of their separate probabilities.

$$P(A \text{ and } B) = P(A) \times P(B)$$

Rule 3b: The General Multiplication Rule

If two events (events *A* and *B*) are not independent, then the probability of event *A* and event *B* occurring simultaneously is equal to the product of the unconditional probability of *A* and the conditional probability of *B* given *A*.

$$P(A \text{ or } B) = P(A) \times P(B \mid A)$$

pendent, the unconditional probability of an event is equal to its conditional probability.

All of the probability rules are summarized in Table 6–5.

PROBABILITY DISTRIBUTIONS

We now can apply our knowledge about probability to understanding a critically important concept in inferential statistics—a probability distribution. We already know from our study of descriptive statistics what a frequency distribution is. A frequency distribution is a tally of the number of times that we observe the different values of a variable. A frequency distribution, then, captures what we actually have observed or measured. A **probability distribution** is not something we actually observe; it is a theoretical distribution of what we *should* observe. In a probability distribution we report the probability that we should actually observe a given outcome in the long run. In other words, in a probability distribution we do not have the probability that each outcome actually occurred, but the theoretical probability that it will occur over the long run. This may sound a bit confusing, and a quick example might help before we go on.

Let's say we are interested in the number of times we get a head when we flip a coin two times. To calculate a probability distribution, we first determine what the possible outcomes are. If we flip a coin two times we could get:

1. A head followed by another head {H,H}—two heads.
2. A head followed by a tail {H,T}—one head.
3. A tail followed by a head {T,H}—one head.
4. A tail followed by another tail {T,T}—no heads.

So, on two flips of a coin we could get 0, 1, or 2 heads. Since flipping a coin once and then a second time are two independent events, we can use the restricted multiplication rule to determine the probability of each of the four outcomes:

1. P(head and head) = .5 × .5 =.25
2. P(head and tail) = .5 × .5 =.25
3. P(tail and head) = .5 × .5 =.25
4. P(tail and tail)   = .5 × .5 =.25

In Table 6–6 we show you the number of heads possible from flipping a coin twice and the probability of each outcome. Notice that we had to use our addition rule to find the probability of getting one head since we could obtain one head by first getting a head and then a tail on the second flip *or* by getting a tail on the first flip and a head on the second: P(head and tail) or P(tail and head) = .25 + .25 = .5.

Table 6–6 is a probability distribution. This probability distribution is a theoretical distribution based upon probability theory, and it shows us what

TABLE 6–6

Probability Distribution of the Number of Heads from Flipping a Coin Two Times

Number of Heads	P
0	.25
1	.50
2	.25

we should expect to see over the long run if we flip a coin twice. The sum of the probabilities is equal to 1.0, indicating that we have listed all possible outcomes and correctly calculated their probabilities. It is important to understand that this distribution is completely theoretical, based upon probability theory, and not what we observe. If we actually were to flip a coin twice and record the number of times we got a head, we would have a frequency distribution. We would like to do an experiment now. Take a coin and flip it twice, recording the number of heads you get. Then repeat this 10 times (for 10 trials). We did, and Table 6–7 shows you what we obtained.

We observed zero heads five times, one head three times, and two heads twice. What we observed from 10 trials of flipping a coin twice was a higher proportion of no heads than what we saw in Table 6–6. Based on probability theory, the probability of getting zero heads is .25, but one-half or .50 of our coin flips resulted in getting no heads. This illustrates the difference between a frequency distribution (Table 6–7), which is observed, and a theoretical probability distribution (Table 6–6), which is based on probability theory. If, instead of 10 trials of flipping a coin twice and recording the number of heads, you were to record the results of 100 trials, the probability of the observed frequencies would come closer to the theoretical probabilities in Table 6–6; if you had 1,000 trials of two flips it would come closer; and with 10,000 trials it would come even closer. In fact, as you increase the actual number of trials you observe to infinity, the closer the empirical (observed) distribution of probabilities would match the theoretical distribution. With 100,000 trials, our empirical distribution would look very much like the proportions in Table 6–6.

There are different kinds of probability distributions for different kinds of events or outcomes. In the remainder of this chapter we will discuss two important kinds of probability distributions. In the first, the event we are interested in has only two outcomes (heads or tails, guilty or innocent, rearrested or not rearrested) and is a type of discrete probability distribution. In the second, the event has an infinite possible number of outcomes (IQ scores, criminal propensity) and is a continuous probability distribution. While these are not all of the possible probability distributions, they do have wide applicability in criminology and criminal justice.

TABLE 6–7

Observed Results from Flipping a Coin Twice

Number of Heads	f	P
0	5	.50
1	3	.30
2	2	.20
Total	10	1.00

A DISCRETE PROBABILITY DISTRIBUTION—
THE BINOMIAL DISTRIBUTION

There are many instances in criminology and criminal justice research where we are interested in events that have only two outcomes. For example, whether a defendant appears for trial or jumps bail, whether an accused gets a public defender or retains her own lawyer, or whether someone who is arrested tests positively or negatively for the presence of drugs. In statistics a process that generates only two outcomes is called a *Bernoulli process*. The probability distribution based on a Bernoulli process is referred to as the **binomial distribution**. Let's examine the binomial probability distribution in some detail.

As our example, let's examine defendants who pay a cash bail after being arrested pending trial. We are interested in the event that they appear (or fail to appear) for their trial. The event we are looking at, therefore, has two outcomes—the defendant either shows up for trial or fails to do so. The probability that they appear for trial is denoted as p, while the probability that they fail to show up for their trial is $1 - p$, or q. Based on past experience, we know that the probability of showing up for trial if they have been released on a cash bail is .80, and the probability of failing to show up is, of course, .20. Let's say that we have five persons recently released on a cash bail, and we would like to calculate the probability distribution of the number of times that they would appear for trial. Let's use the term "success" for any defendant who shows up for trial and designate that with the letter r; we'll use the term "failure" for any defendant who fails to show up.

With five defendants, we could have none, one, two, three, four, or all five of them showing up for trial. We will assume that the event of one defendant showing up for trial is independent of the others, so that we have independent events. Using the restricted version of the multiplication rule, our knowledge that the probability of a success is .80 and the probability of a failure is .20, and letting r be the number of successes and n the total number of trials, we can use the following formula to calculate the probability of each outcome: $p^r q^{n-r}$. Let's use this formula to determine the probability that zero defendants will show up for trial (this means that we have no successes out of five defendants, or five failures):

$$P(0 \text{ successes}) = (.8)^0 (.2)^5 = .2 \times .2 \times .2 \times .2 \times .2 = .0003$$

The probability that one defendant will show up for trial would be:

$$P(1 \text{ success}) = (.8)^1 (.2)^4 = .8 \times .2 \times .2 \times .2 \times .2 = .00128$$

Now we need to stop here and point something out. The probability we calculated above is the probability of one success, followed by four failures. In other words, in this instance the first person out on cash bail showed up for trial, but the next four did not. But there are other ways of observing one success in five trials, aren't there? The first case could fail, the second one could be a success, and the next three could be failures (i.e., F,S,F,F,F). Or, the first two could fail, the next could show up for trial (be a success), and the two after that could fail (i.e., F, F, S, F, F).

What we need to do is figure out how to count all the different ways of having one success out of five trials. Fortunately, there is a very simple counting rule in probability that we can use to determine this. This is the counting rule for combinations, and the formula is:

$$\binom{n}{r} = \left(\frac{n!}{r!(n-r)!}\right)$$

The first expression, $\binom{n}{r}$, is read as "n choose r," and is the number of ways that r objects can be ordered out of n objects without regard to order. The expression that it is equal to, $[n!/r!(n-r)!)]$, is read as "n factorial" over "r factorial, $n - r$ factorial." A *factorial* is just an operation where the number we are taking the factorial of is multiplied by every whole number less than itself and greater than zero, so that 5! is equal to $5 \times 4 \times 3 \times 2 \times 1 = 120$. By convention, 0! = 1.

Let's use this combination formula to calculate the number of ways that we could get one success (defendant showing up for trial) out of five trials:

$$\frac{5!}{1!(5-1)!} = \frac{5!}{1!4!} = \frac{5\times4\times3\times2\times1}{1\times4\times3\times2\times1} = \frac{120}{24} = 5$$

We can verify this by noting that the success could appear in the 1st, 2nd, 3rd, 4th, or 5th case (the probability of each outcome is written next to it):

(S,F,F,F,F)	$P = (.8 \times .2 \times .2 \times .2 \times .2) = (.8)^1 \times (.2)^4 = .00128$
(F,S,F,F,F)	$P = (.2 \times .8 \times .2 \times .2 \times .2) = (.8)^1 \times (.2)^4 = .00128$
(F,F,S,F,F)	$P = (.2 \times .2 \times .8 \times .2 \times .2) = (.8)^1 \times (.2)^4 = .00128$
(F,F,F,S,F)	$P = (.2 \times .2 \times .2 \times .8 \times .2) = (.8)^1 \times (.2)^4 = .00128$
(F,F,F,F,S)	$P = (.2 \times .2 \times .2 \times .2 \times .8) = (.8)^1 \times (.2)^4 = .00128$

Now, if we want to know the probability of getting one success out of five failures we can do one of two things. We can use our addition rule and determine the probability of (S,F,F,F,F), (F,S,F,F,F), (F,F,S,F,F), (F,F,F,S,F), or (F,F,F,F,S), which would be $.00128 + .00128 + .00128 + .00128 + .00128 = .0064$. Or we can use our counting rule that we can get one success out of five trials five different ways. The probability of getting one success out of five trials in any order is .00128; multiplying the two together we get $5 \times .00128 = .0064$. No matter which way we do it, we get the same result.

If we use the counting rule, we now have a general formula to determine the probability of getting r successes out of n trials, where the probability of a success is p and the probability of failure is q:

$$P(r) = \left(\frac{n}{r} \right) p^r - q^{n-r}$$

$$P(r) = \left(\frac{n!}{r!(n-r)!} \right) p^r q^{n-r}$$

(6–1)

Formula 6–1 is known as the **binomial coefficient**. The binomial coefficient can be used to determine the probability of any number of r successes, so long as there are only two outcomes—success (p) and failure (q).

We will use the binomial coefficient to calculate the probability of zero, one, two, three, four, and five successes, where success is defined as a defendant who posts a cash bail and shows up for trial. We show both the calculations and the probabilities in Table 6–8, and we graph the probability distribution in Figure 6–3.

From Table 6–8 we can see that the probability of no defendant showing up for trial is quite small, as is the probability of only one or two of them ap-

TABLE 6–8

Probability Distribution of Appearance at Trial Where p (success) = .8, q (failure) = .2, and n = 5

Number of Successes	Calculation	P
0	$\left(\dfrac{5!}{0!(5-0)!} \right)(.8)^0 (.2)^5$	.0003
1	$\left(\dfrac{5!}{1!(5-1)!} \right)(.8)^1 (.2)^4$	.0064
2	$\left(\dfrac{5!}{2!(5-2)!} \right)(.8)^2 (.2)^3$	.0512
3	$\left(\dfrac{5!}{3!(5-3)!} \right)(.8)^3 (.2)^2$	.2048
4	$\left(\dfrac{5!}{4!(5-4)!} \right)(.8)^4 (.2)^1$	.4096
5	$\left(\dfrac{5!}{5!(5-5)!} \right)(.8)^5 (.2)^0$	.3277
Total		1.00

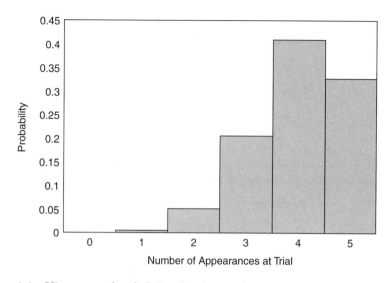

Figure 6–3 Histogram of probability distribution from Table 6–8

pearing at their trial. Based on probability theory we would expect to see three out of five appear for trial about 20 percent of the time, and almost 50 percent of the time four defendants would appear. Finally, if the probability of appearing at trial for a defendant released on a cash bail is .80, we would expect all five to show up about one-third of the time (P = .3277).

Just like a frequency distribution, a probability distribution has both a mean and a standard deviation. For a binomial probability distribution, the mean is given by (np − the number of trials or observations × the probability of a success). The mean of a theoretical probability distribution is generally referred to as the expected value E(x), so for a binominal distribution, E(x) = np. The formula for the variance of a binomial distribution is $\sigma^2 = npq$, and for the standard deviation we simply take the square root of the variance, $\sigma = \sqrt{npq}$. The mean of the probability distribution in Table 6–8 is 5(.8) = 4.0. This means that if the probability of a success is .8, and we have five observations, the expected value of the number of observed successes is 4. Out of five persons who post a cash bail, then, the average number who would be expected to appear at trial would be four. Notice from both the probability distribution and the histogram in Figure 6–3 that the greatest expected probability corresponds to 4 successes. This means that "over the long run" we would expect to see on average four people out of five show up for their trial if they posted a cash bail. You can use the formulas above to find that the variance of the probability distribution is .8 (5 × .8 × .2), and the standard deviation is .89 ($\sqrt{.8}$).

HYPOTHESIS TESTING WITH THE BINOMIAL DISTRIBUTION

One important value of probability distributions is that they allow us to make decisions under a situation of uncertainty. That is, they are critical in the testing of hypotheses. A hypothesis is simply a scientific "hunch" or question about something which is then put to empirical test. Researchers start with a question or hypothesis, collect data or information that pertain to that hypothesis, and then, with the help of a known probability distribution, come to some decision about the hypothesis. The process of hypothesis testing, therefore, is simply an empirical way to make a decision about a question or hunch that we have. Let's go through a brief example.

Predicting the Probability of Car Theft

Let's say we have recently purchased a car and we are concerned about the possibility of car theft. We hear from commercials that the car theft device "Lo-Jack" is effective in assisting the police in recovering your car should it get stolen. The Lo-Jack device is a hidden transformer in your car that you activate when the car is stolen. The transformer sends out an electronic transmission that the police are able to monitor in order to locate your car. The company claims that with Lo-Jack the police are better able to find and quickly recover stolen cars. You talk to the local police chief, and she claims that, based on 10 years' worth of evidence, the police department recovers about 40 percent of the stolen cars reported to it and returns them undamaged to the owner. You have a hunch that Lo-Jack might produce a recovery rate better than 40 percent. It's just a hunch or a hypothesis, however, and before you spend any of your money on installing Lo-Jack in your new car, you want to make sure that it will give you more protection from auto theft than you could otherwise expect from the police working without the assistance of Lo-Jack. Here's what you do.

You collect information from people who have Lo-Jack in their car and ask them: (1) if they have ever had their car stolen and (2) if stolen, whether their car was returned undamaged. You find 10 people who have had their cars stolen and who had Lo-Jack, and you learn that 8 of them were returned undamaged within 24 hours. What you observe, therefore, is an 80 percent recovery rate. You wonder if this means that Lo-Jack does result in a higher probability of recovery. You don't know for sure, however, because you did not ask everyone who had Lo-Jack about their theft experience, only 10 people. Maybe the eight people who had their cars returned quickly happened to be very lucky and are not typical of most car owners with Lo-Jack. Perhaps if you selected a different set of 10 people who had their cars stolen with Lo-Jack you would find that only two had their cars returned undamaged. In other words, perhaps the 80 percent recovery rate you observed from your sample of 10 people was due to luck or chance—and not the superiority of

Lo-Jack. How do you decide whether Lo-Jack is better than the police alone? How do you decide whether or not your observations are due to the chance selection of your 10 people (that is, due to sampling variation)? One way to be more sure that you have made the correct decision is to conduct a hypothesis test.

There are a number of steps involved in a hypothesis test, and the basic framework of these steps will be the same throughout this book. In the remainder of this section we will discuss the steps involved in a hypothesis test, but do not be too alarmed if you do not understand all of it right away. We will be conducting hypothesis tests under different situations in every chapter, so we will have a chance to review this material again.

The first step in a hypothesis test is to make a few assumptions. In our example with Lo-Jack, we are going to assume that Lo-Jack is no better than the police working alone in recovering stolen cars. Practically, this means that our starting assumption is that we can expect to find that 40 percent of the stolen cars equipped with Lo-Jack will be recovered undamaged. In making this assumption we are presuming that Lo-Jack is no more effective (nor less effective) than the police in recovering stolen cars. In other words, we presume that Lo-Jack does not work, and our hypothesis test will involve testing this assumption.

Researchers call this assumption the **null hypothesis** because of the implication that nothing is going on—or in our specific case that Lo-Jack does not work any better than the police. The null hypothesis usually is designated by: H_0. Since our null hypothesis involves the assumption that Lo-Jack's recovery rate is no better than the police working alone, this means that the expected probability of recovering a stolen Lo-Jack car is .40. Here, then, is our null hypothesis:

H_0: The probability of recovering a stolen car that has Lo-Jack is .40:
$$P(\text{recovery}) = .40$$

In addition to making an assumption in the null hypothesis, in testing a hypothesis we also make an assumption about an alternative. This assumption asks the question, "If the null hypothesis is not true, then what do we think is the true state of affairs"? This hypothesis is called the **research** or **alternative hypothesis**, symbolized with H_1. There are two general forms of stating the alternative hypothesis. It can be stated as a *directional* hypothesis or as a *nondirectional* alternative hypothesis.

In our example with Lo-Jack, the null hypothesis states that the probability of recovering a stolen car with Lo-Jack is no higher than the police working alone. Now, we think that Lo-Jack is likely to make the probability of recovering a stolen car undamaged higher than the police alone because the company claims that the transmitting device will enable the police to find the stolen car faster. With this *a priori* knowledge we can make the assumption in the alternative hypothesis that the probability of recovering a stolen car undamaged with Lo-Jack is greater than .40 (we do not have to say exactly how much greater in our alternative hypothesis, just that we think it is greater than that assumed in the null hypothesis):

H_1: The probability of recovering a stolen car that has Lo-Jack is greater than .40: P(recovery) > .40

This is a **directional alternative hypothesis** because we have assumed that the recovery rate with Lo-Jack is greater than .40 and, therefore, we have stated a specific direction (greater than) for Lo-Jack's recovery probability. Alternatively, we could have stated that the probability of recovery with Lo-Jack will be less than .40: P(recovery) < .40). This too is a directional alternative hypothesis because we have stated a specific direction in our alternative with respect to the null hypothesis (it is less than that assumed in the null). To support this alternative assumption we might have created a story that we think the police might be "put off" when someone reports that they have Lo-Jack in their car and therefore less than enthusiastic in trying to recover it. This seems a very unlikely state of affairs, however, and our alternative hypothesis of a greater probability of recovery seems more plausible.

We also could have created a **nondirectional alternative hypothesis**. In a nondirectional alternative hypothesis we simply state that the expected outcome is different from that assumed in the null hypothesis, not greater or less than, just different. So, for example, our nondirectional alternative would be that the rate of recovery for cars with Lo-Jack is not .40 − P(recovery) ≠ .40). However, for our example we are satisfied with our directional alternative hypothesis that the probability of recovery for cars with Lo-Jack is greater than .40.

We now have two hypotheses, a null hypothesis and a directional alternative hypothesis:

H_0: The probability of recovering a stolen car that has Lo-Jack is .40: P(recovery) = .40

H_1: The probability of recovering a stolen car that has Lo-Jack is greater than .40: P(recovery) > .40

In the process of hypothesis testing, only the null hypothesis is tested to determine its plausibility; the alternative is never directly tested. More specifically, what we do in a hypothesis test is ask how likely it is that the null hypothesis is true given our sample data. When we think the null hypothesis is very likely to be true given what we have observed, then we keep or retain it. In other words, we continue to believe that it is true. However, if we discover that it is "very unlikely" given our data (and we will discuss in a moment what we mean by "very unlikely"), then we reject the null hypothesis. When we reject the null hypothesis, we no longer believe that the assumption it contains is true; our faith in the truthfulness of the alternative hypothesis is strengthened. Therefore, while the alternative hypothesis is never directly tested, it becomes believable by implication in our rejection of the null hypothesis.

A useful analogy for the idea of hypothesis testing is the task given to a jury in a criminal trial. The jury starts with the assumption that the defendant is innocent; the alternative assumption is that the defendant is guilty. The jury then tests this assumption of innocence (the null hypothesis) by looking at the data, in this case the evidence presented by the prosecution and defense. After examining this evidence, the jury then makes a determination as to how likely it is that the defendant is innocent in the face of the evidence. If the jury thinks that the evidence does not make the defendant's innocence unlikely, it acquits. If, however, the jury thinks that the evidence raises grave suspicions about the defendant's innocence (meaning that it surpasses the burden of proof of beyond a reasonable doubt), then it rejects the null hypothesis and the assumption of innocence is abandoned in favor of the alternative.

Notice one very important thing about the jury's decision (and our own decisions about null hypotheses). In making its decision, the jury will almost never know that it is absolutely correct. That is, the jury will have a notion about how likely it is that the defendant is innocent, but it has no way of knowing for sure (only the defendant knows that). This means that the jury is making a decision under uncertainty and it might make the wrong decision.

There are two types of wrong decisions or errors a jury may make. First, it can reject the null hypothesis of innocence when in fact the defendant is innocent. In this error, the jury convicts an innocent person. The jury also could continue to accept the null hypothesis of innocence and acquit the defendant when in fact the person is guilty. In this error, the jury lets a guilty person go free. So, the jury has to make a decision about a person's innocence, but it does not and cannot know for sure whether it is making the correct decision. In our legal system we think the first error is worse the second. That is, we think it is more wrong to convict an innocent person than it is to acquit a guilty person. To ensure that we do not convict an innocent person, the legal system makes the standard of proof very high in criminal cases—the jury must believe "beyond a reasonable doubt" that the defendant is guilty before it may reject the null hypothesis of innocence. The phrase "beyond a reasonable doubt" means that the jury must determine that the null hypothesis of innocence is very, very unlikely before it may reject it.

In trying to answer our research question about car theft protection, we are very much like the jury. We will not know for sure whether or not Lo-Jack produces a higher recovery rate of stolen cars because we have information from only 10 owners of Lo-Jack, not from everyone who has it. In other words, we have a sample of Lo-Jack owners and not the entire population, and the success rate observed within this sample might be unique. When we make a decision about the null hypothesis, therefore, like the jury, we too are making it under uncertainty. Since we have incomplete information, we might err in our decision about the null hypothesis. We could reject a null hypothesis that happens to be true, or we could fail to reject a null hypothesis that is in fact false.

TABLE 6–9

Decision Making in Hypothesis Tests

	Decision Regarding Null Hypothesis	
True State of Affairs	**Fail to Reject**	**Reject**
Null hypothesis is true	Correct decision	Type I error
Null hypothesis is false	Type II error	Correct decision

> **A Type I error** occurs when we reject a null hypothesis that is really true.

> **A Type II error** occurs when we fail to reject a null hypothesis that is really false.

In research we have specific names for these two types of errors. Rejecting a null hypothesis that is true is referred to as a **Type I error**, while failing to reject a false null hypothesis is referred to as a **Type II error**. We show you the situation of a correct decision about the null hypothesis and the two types of errors we could make in Table 6–9.

It would be nice if we could minimize the risk of making both kinds of errors. Unfortunately, that is not possible. As we will learn, as we reduce the risk of making a Type I error, we simultaneously increase our risk of a Type II error. Think about this for a moment with respect to the jury's decision. One way that it can minimize the risk of a Type I error (convicting a person who is really innocent) is to make the burden of proof even higher than beyond a reasonable doubt. Such a standard might be something like, "do not convict someone unless you are 99.999 percent sure that they are guilty." Notice that while this will decrease the risk of convicting an innocent person, it also will increase the risk that a truly guilty person will be found innocent (a Type II error). If we minimize the risk of making a Type II error (acquitting a truly guilty person) by lowering the standard of proof to the standard in civil court of "a preponderance of the evidence," we will increase the risk of convicting an innocent person. What we have to do, therefore, is carefully balance the risks of making each type of error, and these risks differ depending upon the research situation.

What we actually do in research is establish beforehand some level of risk we are willing to take that we will make a Type I error. This level of risk is called a **level of significance** or **alpha level**. For example, if we set as our level of significance .05, we are saying that we are willing to risk rejecting a true null hypothesis 5 times out of 100. If we want to reduce that risk, we could adopt a significance level of .01 or even .001. Let's be clear about the concept of a level of significance.

Recall that we begin our hypothesis testing by assuming that the null hypothesis is true (that Lo-Jack is no better than the police working alone). We then say that we are going to continue to assume this is true unless our data (what we observe) tell us that the outcome we actually observed is "very unlikely" given the null hypothesis. What we do, then, is maintain our belief in the null hypothesis until we are informed by the data that this belief is improbable given what we have observed. What we mean by "very unlikely" or "improbable" is determined by the significance level. *What the significance level actually tells us is the probability of observing our data if the null hypothesis is true.* If this probability is very high, we have no reason to think our null hypothesis is false and we continue to assume it is true. If, however, the probability of observing what we did given that the null hypothesis is true is very low (where low is defined as less than or equal to our level of significance) or very unlikely, then it appears to us more probable that the null hypothesis is false and we reject it. This does not mean that we know the null hypothesis is wrong. It only means that the observed outcome is so unlikely that it's more likely that the null hypothesis is wrong or false rather than correct. Keep in mind that we are going with what we think is the most probable state of affairs because we do not and cannot know for sure what is actually true.

For example, let's say that with respect to our Lo-Jack example we are willing to accept a 5 percent risk of making a Type I error, giving us a .05 level of significance. We therefore are going to assume that the null hypothesis is true unless the outcome that we observe is unlikely, where "unlikely" now specifically means that it has a probability of occurring of .05 or less. If what we observe has a probability of occurring greater than .05, we continue to assume that the null hypothesis is true. If, however, what we observe has a probability of occurring less than or equal to .05, we reject the null hypothesis as false.

But how, you may ask, do we know what the probability is of observing what we have actually observed? More specifically, what is the probability of having 8 out of 10 stolen cars with Lo-Jack recovered undamaged if the true probability of recovery is .40? This is an excellent question. The answer is that we know this by referring to a probability distribution, and we have the tools in our toolbox now to calculate that probability distribution.

In our null hypothesis we are assuming that the probability of recovering a stolen car with Lo-Jack is no better than the police working alone, and from the information from the chief of police we know this probability to be .40. So we assume: P(recovery with Lo-Jack) = .40. Next, we ask the following question, "If the probability of recovering a stolen car with Lo-Jack is .40, what is the probability of observing 8 people out of 10 recovering their stolen cars undamaged?" (recall that this is what you have observed, so these are your data). Actually, since you have observed 8 out of 10 recoveries, you really want to know the probability of observing 8, 9, or 10 successful recoveries out of 10 if the true probability of recovering a stolen car undamaged is .40. This is because in our alternative hypothesis we expect Lo-Jack to result in more cars being recovered. So if we have observed 8 out of 10 undamaged recoveries, we want to know the probability of this event and more successful recoveries (i.e., eight or more). Notice that the event of recovering a stolen car can be considered a Bernoulli event—it is either recovered undamaged or it is not—which means that these two-outcome events are governed by a binomial process.

With our binomial formula in equation 6–1, we can determine the probability of 0, 1, 2 . . . 10 undamaged recoveries. Here is the binominal formula as it translates for this particular problem where $n = 10$ (the number of trials or the number of people we spoke with who had Lo-Jack when their car was stolen), $p = .40$ (the probability of recovery), and $q = .60$ (the probability of not recovering the car undamaged):

$$P(r) = \left(\frac{10!}{r!(10-r)!} \right)(.4)^r(.6)^{10-r}$$

where r = the number of successful recoveries of a stolen car. You should use this formula to calculate the probability of 0–10 successful recoveries. We report the results for you in Table 6–10 and graph the probability distribution in Figure 6–4.

TABLE 6–10

Probability Distribution of Recovering a Stolen Car with Lo-Jack Where p (success) = .4, q (failure) = .6, and n = 10

Number of Successes	Calculation	P
0	$\left(\dfrac{10!}{0!(10-0!)} \right)(.4)^0(.6)^{10}$	= .0060
1	$\left(\dfrac{10!}{1!(10-1!)} \right)(.4)^1(.6)^9$	= .0403
2	$\left(\dfrac{10!}{2!(10-2!)} \right)(.4)^2(.6)^8$	= .1209
3	$\left(\dfrac{10!}{3!(10-3!)} \right)(.4)^3(.6)^7$	= .2150
4	$\left(\dfrac{10!}{4!(10-4!)} \right)(.4)^4(.6)^6$	= .2508
5	$\left(\dfrac{10!}{5!(10-5!)} \right)(.4)^5(.6)^5$	= .2007
6	$\left(\dfrac{10!}{6!(10-6!)} \right)(.4)^6(.6)^4$	= .1115
7	$\left(\dfrac{10!}{7!(10-7!)} \right)(.4)^7(.6)^3$	= .0425
8	$\left(\dfrac{10!}{8!(10-8!)} \right)(.4)^8(.6)^2$	= .0106
9	$\left(\dfrac{10!}{9!(10-9!)} \right)(.4)^9(.6)^1$	= .0016
10	$\left(\dfrac{10!}{10!(10-10!)} \right)(.4)^{10}(.6)$	= .0001 Total 1.00

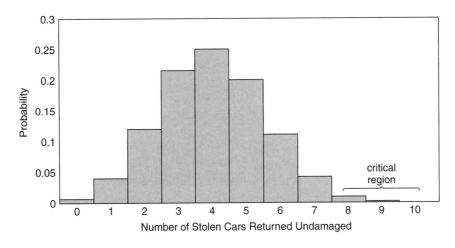

Figure 6–4   Histogram of probability distribution of stolen car recoveries

Notice that if the null hypothesis is true [i.e., P(recovery) = .40)], the probability of observing 8 out of 10 successfully recovered cars is .0106. Using our addition rule of probabilities, we can determine that the probability of 8, 9, or 10 recoveries, P(8, 9, or 10) is equal to .0123 (.0106 + .0016 + .0001). Understand what this means. It says that if the true probability of undamaged recovery is .40 (what we are assuming under the null hypothesis), then the probability of observing 8, 9, or 10 successful recoveries is .0123. Earlier we adopted a level of significance of .05. We said that we would reject the null hypothesis if what we observed was "very unlikely," where the term "very unlikely" meant an event with a probability of .05 or lower. We have just determined that the event of 8 or more undamaged recoveries out of 10 given a recovery probability of .40 has a probability of .0123. What we have observed, then, fits our definition of "very unlikely." We now have the information to conclude that 8 out of 10 recoveries is very unlikely given a recovery probability of .40, so we are going to reject the null hypothesis that P(recovery) = .40. We think that the alternative hypothesis is more likely to be true than the null hypothesis. (But keep in mind we might be wrong in rejecting the null hypothesis—we might be committing a Type I error.)

With a significance level of .05, notice from Table 6–10 that we would have rejected the null hypothesis had we observed 10 successful recoveries out of 10, 9 or 10 successful recoveries out of 10, or 8, 9, or 10 successful recoveries out of 10. We know that the cumulative probability of each of these events is equal to .0123, which is less than .05. In research we call this the **critical region** of our probability distribution. The critical region defines the set of outcomes which will lead us to reject the null hypothesis. In our case, the three outcomes 8,

> The **critical region** of a probability distribution defines the entire class of outcomes that will lead us to reject the null hypothesis. If the event we observe falls into the critical region, our decision will be to reject the null hypothesis.

9, or 10 successful recoveries will lead us to reject the null hypothesis because their cumulative probability is less than our .05 level of significance. Since the event that we observed, 8 out of 10 undamaged car recoveries, falls into this critical region, our decision is to reject the null hypothesis. We show you the critical region for this specific problem in Figure 6–4.

Had we observed 7 out of 10 successful recoveries, what would our decision have been? Using our addition rule and the information in Table 6–10, we can determine that the probability of 7, 8, 9, or 10 successful recoveries is equal to .0548 (.0425 + .0106 + .0016 + .0001 = .0548). Since our definition of a "very unlikely" event is an event with a probability of .05 or less, the event of seven or more successful recoveries is not unlikely enough to lead us to reject the null hypothesis. Had we observed 7 out of 10 successful car recoveries, therefore, we would continue to assume that the null hypothesis is true and would not reject it.

Now suppose that we had observed 8 out of 10 successful recoveries but instead of a significance level of .05 we decided earlier to adopt a significance level of .01. The selection of a level of significance is adopted *before* the hypothesis test is conducted, but we are changing the rules of the game to make a point here. By lowering the level of significance we are saying that what is to be considered a "very unlikely" event now must have an even lower probability of occurring before we are willing to reject a null hypothesis. In other words, we are reducing the risk we are willing to take that we will make a Type I error. Now, a "very unlikely" event (one that leads us to reject the null hypothesis) is one with a probability of .01 or lower (no longer one with a probability of .05 or lower). We know that the probability of observing 8, 9, or 10 successful car recoveries if P(recovery) = .40 is .0123. Since .0123 is greater than .01, our decision would have been to fail to reject the null hypothesis at a .01 level of significance. Notice that by lowering our level of significance, we are making it more difficult to reject the null hypothesis. With a .01 level of significance, the critical region becomes 9 or 10 successful recoveries out of 10.

The decision to either fail to reject or reject the null hypothesis is the final step of our hypothesis testing process. Since we now understand the process, we will outline each of the steps:

Steps of a Hypothesis Test

Step 1: Make an assumption about the null and alternative hypotheses.

Step 2: Determine what probability distribution you will use to find the probability of observing the event recorded in your sample data.

Step 3: Define what you mean by a "very unlikely" event by selecting a level of significance (the alpha level).

Step 4: Calculate the probability of observing your sample data under the null hypothesis.

Step 5: Make a decision about the null hypothesis (reject or fail to reject) and interpret your results.

In this section of the chapter we have been concerned with events that have only two possible outcomes—in this example, whether or not a stolen car is recovered undamaged (Bernoulli events). The binomial probability distribution that characterizes these events is a very useful one because many interesting events in criminology and criminal justice have only two outcomes. However, other interesting events are continuous rather than discrete. For example, rather than being interested in the Bernoulli event that someone goes to prison upon conviction or not, we might be interested in the number of months to which they are sentenced. Rather than being interested in whether or not someone gets rearrested after being released from prison, we might be interested in the number of days they were out before being rearrested. Rather than being interested in whether or not an adult has committed a crime, we might be interested in the number of crimes that the person has committed. There are, therefore, numerous instances in criminology and criminal justice where our interest is in continuous rather than Bernoulli events. Unfortunately, we cannot use the binomial distribution to characterize continuous events. We must learn another type of probability distribution—a continuous probability distribution.

A CONTINUOUS PROBABILITY DISTRIBUTION— THE STANDARD NORMAL DISTRIBUTION

In this section we are going to investigate another kind of probability distribution that has wide applicability in criminology and criminal justice research—the normal probability distribution. The **normal distribution** is a probability distribution for continuous events and looks like a smooth curve, unlike the binomial probability distribution, which looks like a series of steps. Figure 6–5 is an example of what a normal probability distribution might look like. Notice that the probability of an event occurring is higher in the center of the curve and that this probability declines for events at each of the two ends, or tails, of the distribution. Notice also that neither of the tails of the distribution touches the x axis, meaning that they go to both positive and negative infinity. It makes sense that the tails extend to infinity if we keep in mind that the normal distribution is a theoretical probability distribution. Like the binomial distribution, the normal distribution is defined by a mathematical equation, and while many characteristics can be assumed to be distributed as normal, the normal distribution is not an empirical distribution. However, there are some common features of any normal distribution. The

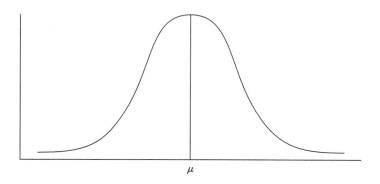

μ

Figure 6–5   Example of a normal distribution

normal distribution is a unimodal, symmetrical distribution and assumes the appearance of a bell-shaped curve. By a "symmetrical distribution" we mean that if we were to draw a line down the center of the curve, the left and right halves would be mirror images of each other. Compare this smooth curve to the histogram for a binomial probability distribution in Figure 6–4.

The normal distribution, like the binomial distribution, is a theoretical probability distribution defined by its mathematical formula. The mathematical formula for the normal distribution, or the normal probability density function, is:

$$f_x = \frac{1}{\sigma\sqrt{2\pi}} e^{\frac{-(x-\mu)^2}{2\sigma^2}} \tag{6–2}$$

where

μ = the mean (expected value) of the continuous variable x,
σ^2 = the variance of x, and
e and π = constants equal to 2.72 and 3.14, respectively.

Any normal distribution is defined by its two parameters, its mean (μ) or expected value, and its variance (σ^2). The mean defines the location of each normal distribution on the number line, while the variance defines its general shape. What this means is that there are many normal distributions, which may vary either in their means, their variances, or both. Figure 6–6 shows two normal distributions, each with a mean different from the other but with the same variance. Figure 6–7 shows two normal distributions with equal means but different variances, and Figure 6–8 shows two normal distributions with different means and different variances. That all of these figures are examples of a normal distribution implies that there is not one but a family of normal curves defined by μ and σ^2.

We could employ equation 6–2 and determine the probability distribution for any continuous variable. There is, however, one significant difference between determining the probability of a discrete variable and that of a con-

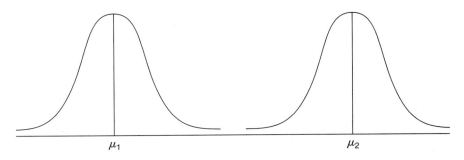

Figure 6–6 Two normal distributions with unequal means ($\mu_1 \neq \mu_2$) but equal variances ($\sigma^2_1 = \sigma^2_2$)

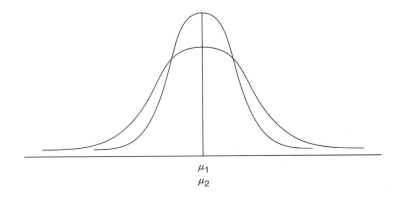

Figure 6–7 Two normal distributions with equal means ($\mu_1 = \mu_2$) but unequal variances ($\sigma^2_1 \neq \sigma^2_2$)

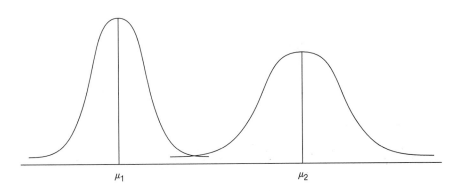

Figure 6–8 Two normal distributions with unequal means ($\mu_1 \neq \mu_2$) and unequal variances ($\sigma^2_1 \neq \sigma^2_2$)

tinuous one. When we calculated the probability of a discrete variable using the binomial probability distribution, we could employ the binomial formula to calculate the probability of a given event (i.e., the probability of recovering 8 or more stolen cars out of 10). We could do this because the events we were interested in were discrete—7 cars recovered, or 9 cars recovered. A continuous distribution, however, is comprised of events that are theoretically infinite. For example, response time to a 911 call could theoretically be measured in millionths of a second or an even finer gradation. Continuous events by their very nature are not discrete events, and this is reflected in the fact that the continuous probability distribution is a smooth curve. What we are interested in, therefore, is a point on a smooth curve. Recall from your college geometry, however, that the area of a point on a curve is zero—there is no area to a point; it is theoretically undefined. What we must do with continuous events, therefore, is determine the area between two points on a curve. What we will do, for example, is calculate the probability that a 911 response time will be between 2 and 4 minutes [$P(2 \leq x \leq 4)$], or the probability that it will be more than 6 minutes [$P(x > 6)$].

The Area under the Normal Curve

Since the normal distribution is a probability distribution, the area under the curve is 1.0. In other words, all possible outcomes are included in the area under a normal curve. One of the most important properties of a normal probability distribution is that there is a fixed area—or a fixed proportion of cases—that lies between the mean and any number of standard deviations to the left or right of that mean. Moreover, based upon mathematical theory, we can determine the exact proportion of cases between the mean and any point a given number of standard deviations away from the mean. For example, we know that for every normal distribution, .3413 (34.13 percent) of the area of the curve lies between the mean and a point that is 1.0 standard deviation to the right of that mean ($\mu + 1\sigma$). In other words, if we were to draw a line through any normal curve at its mean and another line through the curve 1.0 standard deviations to the right of the mean, the area between those two lines would be .3413 of the total area. This means that .3413 of the events in a normal probability distribution lie within 1.0 standard deviation to the right of the mean. We also know from mathematical theory that .4772 (or 47.72 percent) of the events in a normal probability distribution lie in an area from the mean to a point 2.0 standard deviations to the right of the mean, and .4987 (or 49.87 percent) of the cases lie within 3.0 standard deviations to the right of the mean. This property of the normal distribution is shown for you in Figure 6–9.

Combining this information with the fact that any normal distribution is symmetrical, we are ready to make some additional conclusions. If there is .3413 of the area of the normal curve from the mean to a point 1.0 standard deviation to the right of the mean, then, since a normal distribution is symmetrical, .3413 of the area of the curve must also lie from the mean to a point

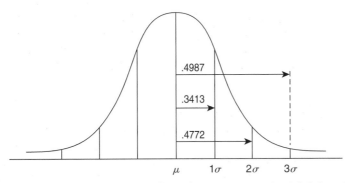

Figure 6–9   Area of the normal curve from the mean to a point 1.0, 2.0, and 3.0 standard deviations to the right

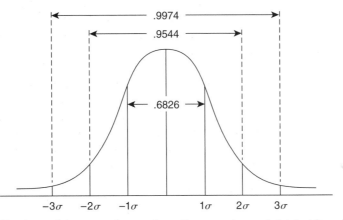

Figure 6–10   Area of the normal curve from the mean to a point ±1, ±2, and ±3 standard deviations away

1.0 standard deviation to the left of the mean. We can conclude from this that .6826 (.3413 + .3413) of the area (or 68.26 percent) of any normal distribution must lie within ±1 standard deviation of the mean. Similarly, if .4772 of the area of any normal curve lies between the mean and a point 2.0 standard deviations to the right of the mean, then .4772 of the area also lies between the mean and a point 2.0 standard deviations to the left of the mean. We can conclude from this that .9544 (.4772 + .4772) of the area of any normal curve lies within ±2 standard deviations from the mean. Finally, .9974 (or 99.74 percent) of the area of any normal curve lies within ±3 standard deviations of the mean. See Figure 6–10.

Now that we know this property of normal distributions, we have some way of determining and understanding the probability of continuous events. For example, in testing hypotheses with the binomial distribution we gave a specific interpretation for an event that was unlikely enough to lead us to reject the null hypothesis. A "very unlikely" event was, for example, an event with a probability of .05 or lower. With our knowledge of normal distributions and standard deviations, we can define a "very unlikely" continuous event. For example, suppose we were told that a given continuous x score was 2.4 standard deviations to the right of the mean. What would we conclude about its probability? Since we know that about 95 percent of all scores in a normal probability distribution lie within ± 2 standard deviations of the mean, an x score that is more than 2 standard deviations from the mean occurs with a probability of less than .05. This can be considered a "very unlikely event." An x score that is 3 standard deviations to the left of the mean is also a "very unlikely" event, since we know that approximately 99 percent of all scores lie within ± 3 standard deviations of the mean. An x score that is only .5 standard deviation to the right of the mean would not be considered a "very unlikely" score because we now know that approximately 65 percent of the area of the normal curve lies within 1.0 standard deviation from the mean. We can conclude from this, therefore, that "unlikely" or low probability scores are going to be those that are a number of standard deviations away from the mean, or out in the tails of the normal distribution.

With our knowledge of the relationship between the area under any normal curve and standard deviations we can use equation 6–2 to calculate probability problems with any continuous variable x. There is one practical difficulty with this, however. In addition to some complex mathematics we would have to do, since normal distributions differ depending upon the value of their two parameters, μ and σ^2, we would have to do new probability calculations for virtually every problem we confront (the mean and variance of response times, for example, would be different from the mean and variance of sentence length, IQ, the number of self-reported offenses committed, etc.). It would be nice if we had only one normal probability distribution with known values of μ and σ^2 to which we could appeal. Actually, there is, and this normal probability distribution is known as the **standard normal probability distribution**. As you can perhaps imagine, it is a very important probability distribution because it is so general.

The Standard Normal Distribution and Standard Scores

The standard normal distribution is a normal probability distribution that has a mean of 0 and a standard deviation of 1.0. Because of this fact, the standard normal distribution also is called the *unit normal distribution*. In order to use the standard normal probability distribution, however, we need to convert the scores of our continuous variable x, which is measured in terms of minutes of response times or months of a prison sentence with mean μ and standard deviation σ, into what is called a **standard score** or **z score**. A z score is simply a score for a continuous x variable that has been converted into standard units, in this case, standard deviation units rather than months or time or number of offenses. The formula for converting a raw x score into a standard or z score is:

TABLE 6–11

Number of Prior Arrests for Sample of 10 Persons Arrested in Past

Person	Number of Prior Arrests
1	3
2	2
3	0
4	8
5	0
6	6
7	13
8	4
9	10
10	5

$$z = \frac{x - \overline{X}}{s} \qquad (6\text{--}3)$$

where

x = a raw score for a continuous variable,
$\overline{X}$ = the sample mean of the empirical distribution, and
s = the standard deviation of the empirical distribution.

Let's go through an example.

Suppose we have an empirical distribution of 10 scores. These 10 scores represent the number of prior offenses committed by a sample of persons recently arrested by the local police department in the past year. The prior-arrest data for these persons are shown for you in Table 6–11. The mean number of prior arrests for this sample is 5.1, and the standard deviation is 4.25. Let's convert the first raw score, which is measured in units of "prior arrests," into a z score that has a mean of 0 and a standard deviation of 1:

$$z = \frac{3 - 5.1}{4.25}$$

$$z = -1.86$$

A raw score of 3, then, corresponds to a z score of $-.49$. Notice that the raw score of 3 prior arrests is less than the mean of 5.1 prior arrests. Notice also that the difference between 3 and 5 prior arrests is 2, and that this is approximately one-half of the standard deviation of 4.25.

There are two pieces of information we can get from any z score—its sign and its magnitude. The *sign* of our z score of $-.49$ is negative, telling us that it lies to the left of the mean of the standard normal distribution (remember, the mean of the standard normal distribution is 0). The *magnitude* of this z

score is .49, telling us that it is approximately one-half of 1 standard deviation away from the mean (remember, the mean of the standard normal distribution is 1). The sign of a z score, then, tells us whether it is to the left of the mean (less than) or the right of the mean (greater than), and the magnitude tells us how many standard deviation units away from the mean the score is. What is the corresponding z score for a raw score of 13?

$$z = \frac{3-5.1}{4.25}$$

$$z = -1.86$$

For this sample of 10 observations, then, a raw score of 13 prior arrests corresponds to a z score that is 1.86 standard deviation units to the right of the mean. In essence, what we are saying is that a raw score of 13 prior arrests corresponds to a score of 1.86 on the z scale.

Once we have converted our raw scores to z scores, we then can begin to answer probability questions. Like the binomial, the standard normal distribution is a known probability distribution. To answer probability questions, we need to refer to what is called a standard normal or z table. Table E–2 in Appendix E is such a z table, and we need to become very familiar with it because we will be using it throughout the rest of the text.

Table E–2 provides you with the area or proportion of the standard normal curve that lies between the mean and some given z score. The z scores in this table are always reported to 2 decimal places. The z score can be located by using the first column of the table, which lists the value of the unit's digit and the first decimal place, and the row of z scores at the top of the table, which lists the value of the second decimal place. The values reported in the body of the table represent the proportion of the standard normal distribution (also called the z distribution) that lies between the mean and that z score. This is probably a little confusing, so let's work through a couple of examples.

Suppose we had a z score of 1.47. How much of the standard normal curve lies between the mean and that score? To find this, we go down the first column of numbers until we find the value 1.4 (1 is our units digit and .4 is our first decimal place). You should be in the 15th row of the table (not counting the top row of z scores). Then, we use the row of z scores at the top of the table until we find the value of the second decimal place, .07. When the row of 1.4 converges with the column of .07 (our z score of 1.47), we see the table entry .4292. What this tells us is that .4292 (or 42.92 percent) of the area of the normal curve lies from the mean to a point .4292 standard deviation units to the right. We show this for you in Figure 6–11. This means that the probability that a z score is greater than or equal to zero or less than or equal to 1.47 is .4292: $P(0 \leq z \leq 1.47) = .4292$. Since the z distribution is symmetrical, we also know that .4292 of the normal curve lies between the mean and a z score of −1.47. Using this information, we can calculate that .8584 (or 85.84 percent) of the normal curve lies between a z score of −1.47 and +1.47.

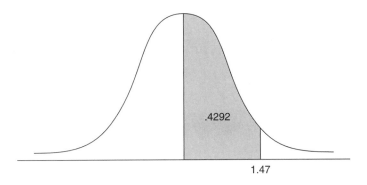

Figure 6–11 ■ Area of the normal curve from the mean to a point 1.47 standard deviations to the right

What proportion of the normal curve lies between the mean and a z score of −1.96? To find this we follow the same procedure as above. Since the z distribution is symmetrical, we can ignore the minus sign. We go down the first column until we find the values 1.9, and then we use the row of z scores at the top of the page to find .06. At the convergence of the 1.9 row and the .06 column we see the entry .4750, telling us that .4750 (or 47.50 percent) of the area of the normal curve lies between the mean and a z score of −1.96. The probability, therefore, that a z score is less than or equal to zero or greater than or equal to −1.96 is .4750: $P(-1.96 \leq z \leq 0) = .4750$.

What is the probability that a z score will be less than −1.96? We know that .50 of the normal curve lies to the right of the mean. We also know that .4750 of the curve lies from the mean to a z score that is 1.96 standard deviation units to the left of the mean. Combining this, then, we know that .9750 (.50 + .4750) of the curve lies to the right of $z = -1.96$. The probability that a z score is greater than or equal to −1.96, then, is .9750: $P(z \geq -1.96) = .9750$. Since the total area of the normal curve is 1.0, we can determine that 1 − .9750, or .025, of the curve lies to the left of $z = -1.96$. The probability that a z score is less than −1.96, therefore, is .025 (see Figure 6–12). A z score that is less than −1.96, then, can be considered a "very unlikely" or low probability event since it occurs less than 3 percent of the time. Because the z distribution is symmetrical, a z score of 1.96 or greater is also a low probability event because it occurs less than 3 percent of the time. A z score that is less than −1.96 or greater than 1.96 is a low probability event because it occurs only about 5 percent of the time (see Figure 6–13).

Now let's answer the following probability question: "What z scores are so unlikely that they fall into the top 1 percent of the standard normal probability distribution?" We show you the approximate top 1 percent of the z distribution in Figure 6–14. Let's use what we know to solve this problem. First, we know that .50 of the curve lies to the left of the mean, telling us that the

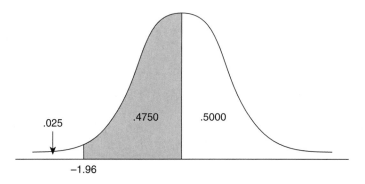

Figure 6–12 Area of the normal curve to the left of −1.96 standard deviation units from the mean

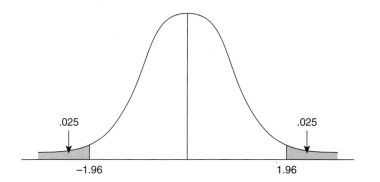

Figure 6–13 Area of the normal curve to the left and right of −1.96 standard deviation units from the mean

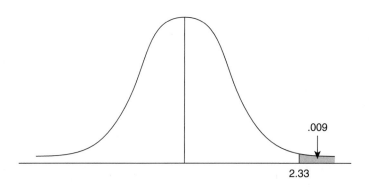

Figure 6–14 Area of the normal curve corresponding to the top 1 percent of the distribution

probability is .50 that a z score will be less than or equal to 0. Since .50 of the normal curve lies to the left of the mean, we know we have to find .49 of the area to the right of the mean (which with .50 to the left of the mean will sum to .99). Go into the body of the z table (Table E–2) and try to find .4900. You won't see .4900, but you should see .4901, which will be close enough. What we need, though, is not the area, but the z score. To find the z score that corresponds to this area, you must work backwards. First, find the z score for the row you are in (this will identify the units digit and first decimal place of your z score, which is 2.3), and then find the second decimal place by finding the column you are in (column .03). You now have a z score of 2.33. Combining all this information, you know that the probability that a z score will be less than 2.33 is .9901 (.50 + .4901). The probability that a z score will be greater than or equal to 2.33, therefore, is .009. Stated another way, a z score greater than or equal to 2.33 will fall in the upper 1 percent of the standard normal distribution. A z score greater than 2.33, then, as we hope you can see, is a low probability event.

We will not show you here how to conduct hypothesis tests using the standard normal distribution because we will be doing that in several later chapters. We do, however, hope you see how we would conduct such a hypothesis test by defining in probability terms what a "very unlikely" or low probability event is, and exactly what that means in terms of z scores. In the last section of this chapter we would like to briefly discuss why the standard normal distribution is so important for our statistical work.

SAMPLES, POPULATIONS, SAMPLING DISTRIBUTIONS, AND THE CENTRAL LIMIT THEOREM

A good understanding of the properties of the normal distribution is very important for statistical work. At some point in your reading of this chapter, though, you may have wondered just why the normal distribution is so important. You may have thought that while there certainly are some variables that are normally distributed in the population, many, if not most, are not. For example, population characteristics such as the number of crimes committed or the number of convictions experienced by persons are not likely to be normally distributed (most people commit zero or only a few crimes, and there is a long right tail of the distribution where few offenders commit many crimes). The same can be said as well for population characteristics such as neighborhood crime rates or the number of parole violations for those released from incarceration. If only a few variables are really normally distributed in the population, the utility of the normal distribution surely must be rather restricted. Not so!

The normal distribution has wide applicability, which makes it invaluable to aspiring researchers. The basis for the generality of the normal distribution can be traced to one of the most important and remarkable theorems of statistics: the **Central Limit Theorem**. It is because of the Central

Limit Theorem that we are able to employ the standard normal distribution in so much of our statistical work. Before we discuss this theorem and its implications, however, we need to discuss some preliminary issues.

Recall that in conducting our research we almost always draw a sample from a large population rather than study the entire population. We draw a sample from our population and collect data on characteristics of the sample, with the intention of making an inference about the corresponding, but unknown, characteristic in the population. The puzzle that the subject of inferential statistics attempts to solve is that, while we know a great deal about the characteristics of our sample (such as its mean, standard deviation, skew of the distribution, etc.), we know virtually nothing about the characteristics of the population. (If we knew about the characteristics of the population, why would we even bother to select a sample?) This is a problem because it is the population that we really want to know about. It is through inferential statistics that we can make some estimate about the characteristics of a population based on our knowledge of the characteristics of a sample. The connection between sample characteristics and population characteristics involves something called a **sampling distribution**.

As an example, let's assume that we are interested in the variable of height. Specifically, we want to know the mean height of the persons in some population. In this problem, we collect data on the height of those selected into our sample so that we can make an inference about the height of those in the larger population. Let's also assume for the moment that the distribution of height in the population is normal. We draw a random sample of 100 persons, so our sample size is 100 ($n = 100$). Both our sample of 100 persons and the larger population from which it was drawn have a mean value. Recall that for our sample the mean height is symbolized by $\overline{X}$, our *sample statistic*. The corresponding population value is called the *parameter*, and it is symbolized by μ. Not all of the values in our sample are equal to the mean value, however, since some scores are less than the mean and some scores are more than the mean. That is, although there is a mean height for our sample, not all 100 persons in our sample are that exact height. Some are taller, some are shorter, and some may actually be equal to the mean. We have, then, variation about our sample mean, which we measure with the sample standard deviation (s). Similarly, in our population there is variation about the population mean height, which is measured in terms of the population standard deviation (σ). Keep in mind that although the population is normally distributed (we have assumed that this is true), our sample of 100 heights that we have drawn from this population may not be. The distribution of height from our sample may be very skewed.

Now, instead of taking just one 100-person random sample from our population, let's imagine taking an infinite number of 100-person random samples one at a time. Remember, the number of samples is infinite, but the sample size is finite and equal to n, or 100 in this case. For each one of these samples, we can determine the mean ($\overline{X}$). That is, we draw a sample of size 100, and then we calculate the mean of that sample ($\bar{X}_1$). Next, draw a second random sample of size 100 and determine the mean of that sample ($\bar{X}_2$). We continue drawing a random sample from a population for an infinite number of samples, each of size 100, and calculate the mean of each sample ($\bar{X}_\infty$). If we do this for every sample we have drawn, we will have an infinite number of sample means. Since these infinite sample means are not all alike (that is, the value of the mean will vary from sample to sample because different people are in each 100-person sample), there is a corresponding distribution of means and a corresponding mean and standard deviation of this distribution of means. The fact that we are referring to an *infinite* number of sample means should alert you to the fact that we are speaking about a theoretical distribution and not a distribution that is based on empirical information. The distribution of this infinite number of sample means with a sample size of 100 ($n = 100$) is called a sampling distribution of means or just a sampling distribution. Keep in mind that in this sampling distribution, we have an infinite number of sample means ($\bar{X}$).

In this sampling distribution of infinite sample means, although the value of the means will vary from sample to sample, they will cluster about the true population mean (μ). The standard deviation of this distribution of sample means will be equal to ($\frac{\sigma}{\sqrt{n}}$). Based on this formula, you can see that the larger the size of the random sample we select from this normal population (n), the smaller the standard deviation of the sampling distribution will be, because the larger n gets, the larger the denominator of $\frac{\sigma}{\sqrt{n}}$ becomes. As our sample size increases, clustering of the sample means ($\bar{X}$) about the true population mean (μ) becomes more narrow. Stated another way, the means will have less variation from sample to sample with a large sample size (n.) Therefore, we will have more faith in each sample mean as an accurate or precise estimate of the population mean if we have a large sample size. Since the mean of the sample is our best estimate of the unknown mean of the population, we can draw two conclusions: (1) there is a certain amount of error in using a known sample mean to estimate an unknown population mean, since there is variation in the means from sample to sample, and (2) the amount of this error or imprecision decreases as the size of the sample (n) increases. Since it reflects the amount of error due to sampling variation, the standard deviation of the sampling distribution ($\frac{\sigma}{\sqrt{n}}$) is generally referred to as the **standard error** or the **standard error of the mean** ($\sigma_{\bar{x}}$).

Figure 6–15 shows what happens to the standard deviation of the sampling distribution when sample size is increased. Notice that the distribution of the sample means is narrower than the population distribution (except, of course, when $n = 1$, in which case it is the same), and the larger the sample size (n), the more narrow that sampling distribution becomes. As you can see, then, with a larger sample size, it is more likely that any randomly drawn sample of size n will be close to the population mean (μ). In other words, the larger the sample size, the less error there is in using our known sample statistic ($\bar{X}$) to estimate our unknown population parameter (μ). The general rule to remember is that larger samples are always better than smaller ones.

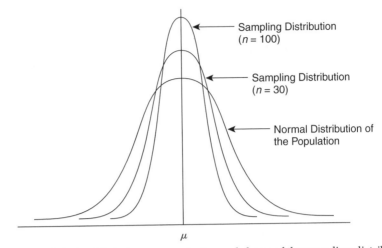

Figure 6–15   Relationship between sample size and shape of the sampling distribution

In addition to having a known mean and standard deviation (μ and ($\sigma / \sqrt{n}$), respectively), according to an important statistical theorem, the distribution of this infinite number of sample means drawn from a normal population also will also be normal. We will state this theorem explicitly:

> If an infinite number of random samples of size n are drawn from a normal population, with a mean equal to μ and standard deviation equal to σ, the sampling distribution of the sample means will itself be normally distributed with a mean equal to μ and a standard deviation equal to ($\sigma / \sqrt{n}$).

In other words, the theoretical sampling distribution of the means of an infinite number of random samples drawn from a normal population will have a normal distribution.

Before we resume our discussion of an even more useful and important statistical theorem, the Central Limit Theorem, you need to remember that in this section we have made reference to three distinct distributions, only two of which are normal. First, we have a distribution of raw scores from the single random sample that we actually draw and investigate. These scores are the heights of the individual persons in our random sample. The scores within our sample differ, so there is a distribution of sample scores with a mean ($\bar{X}$) and standard deviation (s). The distribution of our sample values is not presumed to be normal. The characteristic of interest (mean height) is referred to as a sample statistic.

The second distribution is the distribution of our population characteristic (height). The scores in this distribution vary one from the other, and they are presumed to be normally distributed with mean (μ) and standard deviation (σ). The characteristic of interest in this distribution (mean height) is called the population parameter. The third distribution discussed is the dis-

TABLE 6–12

Characteristics of Three Types of Distributions

	Mean	Standard Deviation	Distribution
Sample	$\overline{X}$	s	Empirical, and known
Population	μ	σ	Empirical, but not known
Sampling distribution	μ	$\dfrac{\sigma}{\sqrt{n}}$	Theoretical

tribution of sample means of an infinite number of random samples drawn from our normally distributed population. Based upon the theorem above, this distribution also is assumed to be normally distributed, with a mean equal to the population parameter (μ) and a standard deviation equal to ($\sigma / \sqrt{n}$). The three distributions and their associated characteristics are summarized in Table 6–12.

You should keep in mind that these are three distinct distributions. The first is a distribution of sample scores (empirical), and the second is a distribution of population scores (empirical but not known). What connects these two is the third distribution (theoretical), which is a distribution of sample means. That is, we can make inferences from our sample mean to the population mean by considering it as one sample mean from a theoretical distribution of all possible sample means (the sampling distribution). With our sampling distribution we can determine the probability of obtaining our sample statistic. Since the sampling distribution of means is normal and the population is assumed to be normal, we can make use of the standard normal distribution to determine this probability. This can be represented in the inference flow diagram presented below. We collect data from a random sample and use the theoretical sampling distribution to make inferences from these sample data to the unknown population parameter.

Sample data $\rightarrow$ Sampling distribution $\rightarrow$ Population parameter

You may be thinking to yourself right now, "What about in the vast majority of cases where we cannot reasonably make the assumption that the population characteristic is normally distributed? Does this mean that the normal distribution is inapplicable?" No. We can employ the normal distribution even if our population is not normally distributed. This is because of the remarkable nature of the Central Limit Theorem. The Central Limit Theorem states that:

> If an infinite number of random samples of size n are drawn from *any population* with mean μ and standard deviation σ, then as the sample size (n) becomes large, the sampling distribution of sample means will approach normality, with mean μ and standard deviation $\frac{\sigma}{\sqrt{n}}$, even if the population distribution is not normally distributed.

The importance of this theorem is that the sampling distribution does not depend upon normality in the population. No matter what the shape of the distribution in the population, the theoretical probability distribution of sample means will approximate a normal distribution as the sample size becomes large. Not only will the sampling distribution be normal, it will have a mean equal to the population mean μ and a standard deviation equal to $\frac{\sigma}{\sqrt{n}}$. This is quite an important theorem because it suggests that even if our population distribution is quite skewed (like the number of arrests in the population), we still can assume that our sampling distribution of means will be normal as the size of the sample becomes large. Since it is the sampling distribution that links our sample estimate to the population parameter, we can employ the normal probability distribution in instances where our population is not normal.

> ### Three Characteristics of the Sampling Distribution of the Mean Based on the decedent
>
> Whenever the sample size is large:
>
> 1. We can assume that the mean of the sampling distribution is equal to the population mean, μ.
> 2. We can assume that the standard deviation of the sampling distribution is equal to $\frac{\sigma}{\sqrt{n}}$.
> 3. We can assume the sampling distribution is normally distributed even if the population from which the sample was drawn is not.

The important and practical question to ask now is, "How large is large enough so we can relax the normality assumption and appeal to the Central Limit Theorem?" A good rule of thumb (and only a rule of thumb) is that the assumption of normality can almost always be relaxed when the sample size is 100 or more ($n \geq 100$). If there is some empirical evidence to suggest that the population is not terribly skewed, then it is recommended that the sample size be at least 50 ($n \geq 50$). With sample sizes of less than 50, the normality assumption should not generally be relaxed unless there is fairly strong empirical evidence that indicates that the population is normally distributed. In the case of small samples, statistics that do not appeal to the Central Limit Theorem and normal distribution must be employed. Before we leave this chapter, however, let's look at an example of the Central Limit Theorem at work.

Earlier in this chapter we worked with an example involving car theft recovery with Lo-Jack. Under the null hypothesis we assumed that the probability of getting a stolen car recovered undamaged was .40. You can see that the event of having a stolen car returned without damage is definitely not a normally distributed event. In fact, it follows a binomial distribution. Let's take a sample of $n = 1$, and calculate the probability distribution for this size sample. Figure 6–16 illustrates this probability distribution, which we can see is a very non-normal distribution. There is a .60 probability that the car will not be returned undamaged and a .40 probability that it will be returned

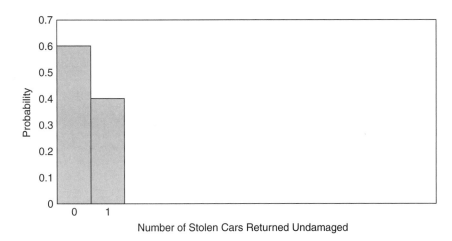

Figure 6–16 Probability distribution of stolen car recoveries where $n = 1$

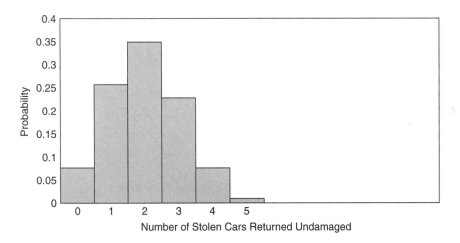

Figure 6–17 Probability distribution of stolen car recoveries where $n = 5$

undamaged. Now let's increase our sample size to 5. In this case, shown in Figure 6–17, we take a random sample of five people who had Lo-Jack in their cars when they were stolen and ask if their cars were recovered undamaged. We then calculate the probability of 0, 1, 2, 3, 4, or 5 undamaged car recoveries. This probability distribution is also not very normal in its appearance. In Figure 6–18 we increase the sample size to 10 and calculate the probability distribution. It too is non-normal but you can see that, even when the population distribution is very skewed, the probability distribution is starting to

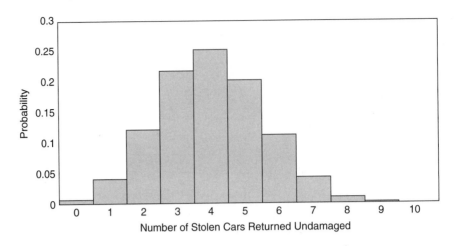

Figure 6–18   Probability distribution of stolen car recoveries where $n = 10$

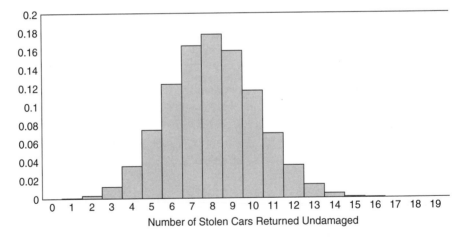

Figure 6–19   Probability distribution for stolen car recoveries where $n = 20$

approximate normality as we increase our sample size. In Figure 6–19 the sample size is increased to 20, and the appearance of normality becomes even more pronounced. Finally, in Figure 6–20 we have a sample size of $n = 50$, and this probability distribution is approximately normal. You can see that by increasing our sample size from 1 in Figure 6–16 to 50 in Figure 6–20 our sampling distribution comes closer and closer to being normal. This is the Central Limit Theorem at work.

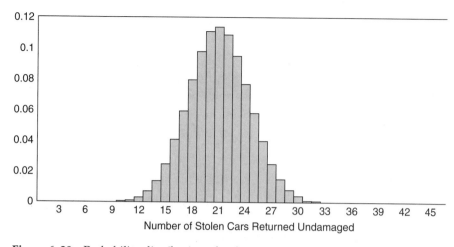

Figure 6–20   Probability distribution of stolen car recoveries where $n = 50$

SUMMARY

We have covered a lot of important ground in this chapter, ground that will serve as the foundation for our discussion of inferential statistics, which makes up the remainder of this text. At the core of this foundation is the notion of probability. We have discussed two senses of the idea of probability: (1) the chance or likelihood that a single event will occur in a given trial and (2) the chance of an event occurring over the long term with an infinite number of trials. We used probability to develop the notion of probability distributions—a distribution of theoretical outcomes determined by the laws of probability. One of these probability distributions is the binomial probability distribution, which governs events that have only two possible outcomes, called Bernoulli events. The binomial probability distribution is an important one for us since many of the events we are interested in have only two outcomes.

We then discussed a probability distribution that describes continuous events, the normal distribution. This distribution is a unimodal, symmetrical distribution that we often refer to as the bell-shaped curve. We learned that there is a large family of normal distributions which would make for some cumbersome probability calculations were it not for the standard normal distribution. The standard normal distribution is a normal distribution with a mean of zero and a standard deviation of 1. In order to use the normal distribution to figure out the probability of continuous events, we learned we must convert our raw x scores into what are called standard normal z scores. Once we have a z score, the determination of probabilities is relatively simple with the use of a z table.

Finally, we learned about the difference between a sample, a sampling distribution, and a population. We usually take one sample of size n from a single population and use the information from that sample to make an inference about some unknown population value. We are able to do this with the knowledge of sampling distributions. A sampling distribution is simply a theoretical distribution of an infinite number of sample values. Like any other distribution, a sampling distribution has a mean and a standard deviation. We know that if our population is normally distributed then the sampling distribution from that population also will be normal. We also introduced the Central Limit Theorem, which says that as our sample size increases, the sampling distribution will begin to approximate normality no matter what the shape of the population from which the samples have been drawn. Therefore, we can use the standard normal probability distribution for our probability calculations so long as we make sure that we select a large enough sample.

KEY TERMS

addition rule of probabilities
alpha level (level of significance)
alternative hypothesis (research hypothesis)
binomial coefficient
binomial distribution
bounding rule of probabilities
Central Limit Theorem
complement of an event
conditional probability
critical region
directional alternative hypothesis
general addition rule of probabilities
general multiplication rule of probabilities
independent events
joint probability
multiplication rule of probabilities
mutually exclusive events

nondirectional alternative hypothesis
nonmutually exclusive events
normal distribution
null hypothesis
odds
probability distribution
probability of an event
restricted addition rule of probabilities
restricted multiplication rule of probabilities
sampling distribution
standard error (standard error of the mean)
standard normal probability distribution
standard score (z score)
Type I error
Type II error

KEY FORMULAS

The probability of success—the binomial coefficient (eq. 6–1):

$$P(r) = \left(\frac{n}{r} \right) p^r q^{n-r}$$

$$P(r) = \left(\frac{n!}{r!(n-r)!} \right) p^r q^{n-r}$$

The mathematical formula for the normal distribution (eq. 6–2):

$$f(x) = \frac{1}{\sigma\sqrt{2\pi}} e^{\frac{-(x-\mu)^2}{2\sigma^2}}$$

Formula for converting a raw score into a z score (6–3):

$$z = \frac{x - \overline{X}}{s}$$

PRACTICE PROBLEMS

1. The data shown below consist of the starting salaries for police officers in 110 police departments in the state of Maryland.

Salary ($)	f
25,000	6
26,000	8
27,500	9
28,000	10
30,000	16
31,500	19
32,000	12
32,500	15
34,000	8
35,000	7
Total	110

With this information, calculate:

a. The probability that a starting salary will be exactly $30,000.

b. The probability that a starting salary will be exactly $35,000.

c. Whether the starting salaries of $30,000 and $35,000 are mutually exclusive events. Explain.

d. The probability that a starting salary will be at least $31,000.

e. The probability that a starting salary will be $30,000 or less.

f. The probability that a starting salary will be between $27,800 and $33,000.

g. The probability that a starting salary will be less than $25,000.

h. The probability that a starting salary will be either $28,000, $32,000, or $35,000.

2. The probability of being acquitted in criminal court in Baltimore, Maryland, is .40. Based on a random sample of the past 10 criminal cases where the defendant had a public defender, you find that there were seven acquittals and three convictions. What is the probability of observing seven or more acquittals out of 10 cases if the true probability of an acquittal is .40? Using an alpha of .05, test the null hypothesis (that the probability of an acquittal is .40 for defendants with public defenders) against the alternative hypothesis that it is higher than .40.

3. Assume that you have a normal distribution of IQ scores with a mean of 100 and a standard deviation of 10:

a. What is the z score for a raw score of 115?

b. What is the z score for a raw score of 83?

c. What is the z score for a raw score of 70?

d. What proportion of the cases have an IQ score above 115?

e. What proportion of the cases have an IQ score between 90 and 110?

f. What is the probability that you would find an IQ score of 70 or below?

g. What is the probability that you would find an IQ score of 125 or above?

4. In a recent article, Greg Pogarsky (2002) examined the relationship between criminal propensity (incorrigibility), deterrence, and criminal offending. He found that the fear of punishment deterred the criminal behavior only for those who were not incorrigible. Let's say you are interested in the same idea with the concept of impulsivity. You think that the impulsive cannot be deterred. You do some research and find the following joint distribution between impulsivity and whether or not someone was deterred by the certainty of punishment.

Impulsivity	Was the Person Deterred?		
	Deterred	Not Deterred	Total
Not impulsive	75	15	90
Impulsive	5	25	30
Total	80	40	120

a. What is the probability that someone was deterred?

b. Is this a conditional or an unconditional probability? Explain.

c. What is the probability that someone was not deterred?

d. What is the probability that someone was impulsive?

e. What is the probability that someone was impulsive or not deterred by punishment? Are these mutually exclusive events? Explain.

f. What is the probability that someone was deterred given that they were not impulsive?

g. What is the probability that someone was deterred given that they were impulsive?

h. Are impulsivity and being deterred by punishment independent events? Explain.

i. What is the probability that someone was implusive and not deterred?

j. What is the probability that someone was not impulsive and deterred?

5. The department of corrections in the state where you live has a policy whereby it accepts as correctional officers only those who score in the top 5 percent of a qualifying exam. The mean of this test is 80, and the standard deviation is 10.

a. Would a person with a raw score of 95 be accepted?

b. Would a person with a raw score of 110 be accepted?

c. What is the minimum score you would have to have on the test in order to be accepted?

6. Explain the difference between a sample, a sampling distribution, and a population. What are the means and standard deviations for each of these?

7. Draw a picture indicating what proportion (area) of the normal curve lies:

a. To the right of a z score of 1.65.

b. To the left of a z score of -1.65.

c. Either to the left of a z score of -1.96 or to the right of a z score of 1.96.

d. To the right of a z score of 2.33.

e. Is a z score of -2.56 a rare or low probability score? Explain.

8. There has been some controversy about school violence and how to prevent it. To study measures that might prevent school violence, you take a random sample of 250 schools that differ in what they do to prevent school violence. In addition, you collect information on the number of violent acts that were committed in each school during the previous school year. The information you have collected is shown below:

Number of Violent Acts	No Measures	Metal Detectors Only	Guards Only	Guards and Metal Detectors	Total
		Type of Preventive Measure			
None	5	10	15	30	60
1–4 acts	25	20	15	15	75
5+ acts	50	30	25	10	115
Total	80	60	55	55	250

With these data, answer the following probability questions:

   a. What is the probability that a school had no violent acts last year?

   b. What is the probability that a school had guards only as part of its violence prevention measures?

   c. What is the probability that either metal detectors or guards were used but not both?

   d. What is the probability that no measures were used?

   e. What is the probability that a school used both guards and metal detectors together or had 1–4 violent acts committed last year?

   f. What is the probability that a school used metal detectors only or had five or more acts of violence committed last year?

   g. What is the conditional probability of no violent acts in a school given that there were no preventive measures used?

   h. What is the conditional probability of no violent acts in a school given that some type of preventive measure was used?

   i. What is the conditional probability of five or more violent acts given that metal detectors only were used?

   j. What is the conditional probability of five or more violent acts given that both guards and metal detectors were used together?

   k. Are the two events, type of preventive measure used and number of violent acts in the school, independent events? Explain.

   l. What is the probability of no violent acts and the presence of guards only as a preventive measure?

   m. What is the probability of no preventive measures and five or more violent acts?

   n. What is the probability of both guards and metal detectors used together and 1–4 violent acts in the school?

9. A jail has an inmate population where the mean number of prior arrests is 6 and the standard deviation is 2.

   a. Would a new inmate with 9 prior arrests have an unusually high number, where unusual is in the top 5 percent?

   b. Would a new inmate with 11 prior arrests have an unusually high number, where unusual is in the top 5 percent?

   c. Would an inmate with 2 prior arrests have an unusually low number, where unusual is in the bottom 5 percent?

10. What is the Central Limit Theorem? What does it allow us to assume about sampling distributions given the fact that we have a large enough sample?

SPSS PRACTICE PROBLEMS

1. SPSS allows you to conduct a binomial test that compares the observed frequencies of a two-category dichotomous variable to the frequencies expected under a binomial distribution with a specified probability parameter. By default the probability parameter for both groups is 0–.5. To change the probabilities, you can enter a test proportion for the first group. The probability for the second group will be 1 minus the specified probability for the first group. Using the data set HOMICIDE.XPT, let's examine the univariate distribution for the life sentence variable, LIFE, coded 1 for all defendants who received a life sentence and 0 for those who didn't. Under ANALYZE, click NONPARAMETRIC TESTS, then BINOMIAL. Then place LIFE into the variable test box. What are your results?

2. SPSS also allows you to convert raw scores into standardized z scores. When these z scores are saved, they are added to the data in the Data Editor and are available for charts, data listing, and analyses. This procedure is helpful if you want to compare several variables that are measured in different units (e.g., crimes per 100,000 compared to crimes per 1,000). A z score transformation places the variables on a common scale for easier visual comparison. Let's transform the sentence length variable into a z score distribution. Click on ANALYZE, then DESCRIPTIVES, then place PRITIME in the variables box. Now click on the box that tells SPSS to save the standardized values as variables, and then click on OK. When you return to the Data Editor, there will be a new variable added at the end of the list called "ZPRITIME" that denotes the new variable.

3. Examine a frequency distribution and a histogram for the original PRITIME variable and the transformed z score distribution. Comment on the shape and variability of both distributions.

REVIEW & PRACTICE

7

Point Estimation and Confidence Intervals

Confidence, like art, never comes from having all the answers; it comes from being open to all the questions.

—EARL GRAY STEVENS

I was brought up to believe that the only thing worth doing was to add to the sum of accurate information in this world.

—MARGARET MEAD

In this chapter, we take our first steps into the world of inferential statistics by generalizing the results we obtain in a sample to the population of interest. We concentrate on two sample statistics in this chapter, the *mean* and the *proportion*. The estimates of the mean and the proportion that we obtain from a sample are referred to as *point estimates.* To generalize these estimates to the entire population, we have to construct what are called confidence intervals around them. These intervals allow us to make generalizations to the population with a known degree of certainty (e.g., confidence), and therefore they are frequently used not just in criminological research, but in the news media as well. By the end of the chapter, you will be able to construct and interpret confidence intervals on your own. In addition, you will be a more informed consumer of the point estimates that you encounter in the media on a daily basis.

INTRODUCTION

We are about to enter the world of inferential statistics. Recall that the objective of **inferential statistics** is to make inferences about a population characteristic based on information obtained from a sample. In this chapter, we examine different ways of estimating a population parameter based on a sample statistic. Estimation is a common interest among many criminologists. "How many children become the victims of abuse and neglect annually in this country?" "What proportion of the U.S. population agrees with the use of capital punishment instead of life in prison?" "How often do teenagers use alcohol or other drugs?" The answers to each of these questions begin with estimation.

In this chapter, we apply what we have learned so far about probability theory and begin making inferences about population parameters based on information we obtain from sample statistics. We want to evaluate how accurate our sample statistic (mean or proportion) is as an estimate of the true population value. The sample mean (or other sample statistic, such as the proportion) is referred to as our **point estimate** of the population mean. Because this estimate is subject to some measurement error, we want to surround it with a margin of error. This margin of error consists of a range of values or an interval into which we believe, with some established degree of confidence, the population value falls. That is, instead of estimating just one value for our population characteristic (our point estimate), we estimate a range of values or an interval within which we believe the population value falls. This interval is called a **confidence interval.** Think of a confidence interval as an estimated interval that we are reasonably confident contains the true population value "over the long run." The advantage of creating a confidence interval is that, by stipulating a range of values instead of a point estimate, the population parameter is more likely to be included.

Each of you has undoubtedly heard this type of interval being referred to, perhaps without even realizing that it was a statistical confidence interval. For example, when the media covers the results of an opinion poll, it will often caveat the story with a phrase like "A Gallup poll released today indicates that 79 percent (plus or minus 2 percent) of Americans believe that crime is the most important problem for the current administration to address." The 79 percent is the point estimate of the population value. In this case, the 79 percent is an estimate of the percent of Americans who believe that crime is the most important problem. The "plus or minus 2 percent" in this case is the interval the

Question: Do you approve or disapprove of the way that George W. Bush is handling the U.S. military action abroad to fight terrorism?

	Percent
Approve	71
Disapprove	24
No opinion	5

Question: How worried are you that you or someone in your family will become a victim of a terrorist attack?

	Percent
Very worried	10
Somewhat worried	30
Not too worried	28
Not worried at all	31
No opinion	1

Question: Do you think the government warnings of further terrorist attacks have mostly—

	Percent
Helped people	55
Just scared people	40
No opinion	5

Results are based on telephone interviews with a national probability sample of 1,012 adults, aged 18 and over, conducted November 2–4, 2001. For results based on the total sample of National Adults, one can say with 95 percent confidence that the margin of sampling error is ±3 percentage points.

Figure 7–1   *USA Today*/CNN/Gallup poll asking Americans their opinions on developments after the September 11, 2001, terrorist attacks. *Source:* http://www.usatoday.com/news/po11001.htm. Retrieved July 30, 2002.

researchers drew around the point estimate of 79 percent. With this confidence interval, these pollsters are saying that the true percent may be as low as 77 percent or as high as 81 percent.

Figure 7–1 displays the results of a *USA Today*/CNN/Gallup poll conducted after the September 11, 2001, terrorist attacks. The results of this poll were published by all three sponsors. Notice the sentence stating, "For results based on the total sample of National Adults, one can say with 95 percent confidence that the margin of sampling error is ±3 percentage points." What this is really telling readers is that, in order to be 95 percent confident that the true population parameter (percent) is included in the estimate, you must add 3 percent and subtract 3 percent from the point estimate to create an interval—this interval then becomes a 95 percent confidence interval. For example, in response to the question that asks whether respondents approve of how George W. Bush is handling U.S. military action abroad to fight terrorism, the point estimate of those who approved was 71 percent. The confidence interval of this, however, would be 71 percent ±3 percent. What does this tell us? Well, it says that we can be 95 percent confident that the true percent of adults in the U.S. who approve of the president's military action abroad to fight terrorism is somewhere between 68 and 74 percent. What is important about this statement is that a level of confidence, 95 percent, accompanies it. Without creating a confidence interval around the point estimate of 71 percent, researchers would not be able to provide any confidence claims in their inferences. (Also note that researchers had to start with a probability sample in order to do this in the first place!)

Let's describe the concept of a confidence interval in a different way. Think of a confidence interval in "long run" terms, similar to sampling distributions. For example, let's say we took repeated samples of the same size from the same population. For each sample we calculated the proportion of those who believe crime to be the most important problem in America today. We also created a 95 percent confidence interval around that sample proportion. A 95 percent confidence interval indicates that approximately 95 percent of these estimated intervals contain the true population proportion and approximately 5 percent do not.

Figure 7–2 illustrates the concept of a 95% confidence interval graphically. It shows a hypothetical example in which 20 samples ($n = 100$) are drawn from the same population. From each sample, the mean number of times individuals from each sample ran a stop sign per month was calculated and 95 percent confidence intervals were drawn around each mean. The horizontal lines across the figure represent these 95 percent confidence intervals, and the vertical line running down the middle of the figure represents the true population mean of stop sign violations. From Figure 7–2, you can see that 95 percent (19) of these confidence intervals actually contain the true population mean, while 5 percent (1) do not. Even though each of these confidence intervals varies from sample to sample, 95 percent of them nevertheless contain the true **population parameter.** This is the goal of inferential statistics. You also should notice that the true population parameter does not change, although the estimated interval varies from sample to sample. What we are 95 percent confident about, then, is the procedure itself—not the particular confidence interval we estimate with our sample data. That is, we should interpret our confidence interval as saying that, over the long run, 95 percent of the confidence intervals we estimate from this procedure will include the true population parameter. This is the goal of inferential statistics: to make inferences to the target population with some degree of confidence.

Of course, in the real world, we never take repeated samples from the population and we never really know whether we have contained the "true" population parameter within our confidence intervals. But if we have drawn our sample using probability sampling techniques (e.g., a simple random sample), we can utilize probability theory to estimate a population parameter from only one sample. And probability theory allows us to make numerical statements about the accuracy of our estimates.

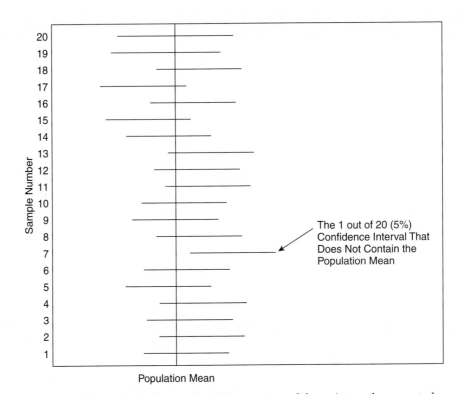

Figure 7–2   A hypothetical example of 95 percent confidence intervals computed from 20 different samples of the same size drawn from the same population

In the sections that follow, we begin by examining the properties that any good estimate should have. We then examine confidence interval estimation procedures for sample means based on large samples ($n > 100$). We utilize the z distribution to do this. Next, we will introduce the t distribution, which is used for estimating means from small-sized samples ($n < 100$). We conclude the chapter by examining estimation procedures used for proportions and percentages.

PROPERTIES OF GOOD ESTIMATES

The first parameter we estimate is a population mean, which is symbolized with the Greek letter μ. We are going to use the sample mean as our point estimate of the population mean. Why use the sample mean? Why not the sample median or the average of the mean and the median value as our point estimator? The sample mean is chosen as our estimator because it is an unbiased estimate of the population mean. Any given estimate of a population parameter is unbiased if the mean of its sampling distribution is equal to the parameter being estimated. In the last chapter we learned that the mean of the sampling distribution of means $(\mu_{\overline{X}})$ is the population mean (μ). Of course, this does not mean that any given sample mean ($\overline{X}$) will be equal to the population mean. Think of bias in the long run. With an infinite number of samples of size n the mean of the samples will be equal to the population mean.

We also know from the Central Limits Theorem (Chapter 6) that if the sample size is large enough, the distribution of the sample means will be approximately normal. We can, then, determine the probability that our sample statistic lies within a given number of standard deviation units from the population mean. We will know, for example, that there is a 68 percent chance that our sample mean is within 1 standard deviation unit of the population mean and a 95 percent chance that it is within ±2 standard deviation units. It is important, therefore, that our estimate be unbiased. The sample mean and proportion are unbiased estimates of their respective population values. In addition to being unbiased, a second important property of an estimate is that it be efficient.

The efficiency of an estimate refers to the degree to which the sampling distribution is clustered about the true population value. In this case, an efficient estimate is one where the sampling distribution of means is clustered close to the population mean. The greater the clustering, the greater the efficiency of the estimate. Recall from Chapter 6 that sampling distributions are simply the theoretical distributions we would obtain if we were to draw many random samples of the same size from the same population and calculate the statistic of interest. In this case, we are talking about the mean. As with any theoretical distribution such as the normal distribution, there are theoretical properties of the sampling distribution of the mean. These properties are displayed in Table 7–1.

TABLE 7–1

Properties of the Sampling Distribution of $\overline{X}$

---

1. The mean of this sampling distribution of $\overline{X}$ is μ.
2. The standard deviation of the sampling distribution of $\overline{X}$ is where σ is the standard deviation of the original population and n is the sample size. $\sigma_{\overline{x}}$ is used to denote the standard deviation of the sampling distribution. This entire term is called the **standard error of the mean**:

$$\sigma_{\overline{X}} = \frac{\sigma}{\sqrt{n}}$$

3. Because of the Central Limit Theorem, when n is large (safely, when $n \geq 100$), the sampling distribution of $\overline{X}$ is normally distributed, regardless of the distribution of the population from which the sample was drawn.
4. As the sample size increases, the standard deviation of the sampling distribution (the standard error of the mean) decreases.

You will recall from the previous chapter that the standard deviation of the sampling distribution of means is equal to $(\sigma /\sqrt{n}$. The standard deviation of the sampling distribution, therefore, is in proportion to n or the sample size. As sample size increases, the standard deviation of the sampling distribution decreases. This means that the sample means themselves differ less from one another and cluster more tightly about the population mean. The last chapter also illustrated that as sample size increases, the sampling distribution of means becomes more narrow. The practical implication of this is that our sample estimate becomes more efficient when sample size increases. We will repeat this important lesson throughout this and other chapters.

ESTIMATING A POPULATION MEAN FROM LARGE SAMPLES

We now know that a sample mean is an unbiased estimate of the population mean, and that the efficiency of the sample mean as an estimate is increased by increasing sample size. Therefore, we are ready to get down to the business of constructing confidence intervals. Based upon the properties of the sampling distribution of the mean and what we know about the normal distribution and probability theory, we can utilize the following formula to construct a confidence interval around a sample mean ($\overline{X}$):

$$\overline{X} \pm z_\alpha\left(\sigma_{\overline{X}}\right) = \overline{X} \pm z_\alpha\left(\frac{\sigma}{\sqrt{n}}\right) \qquad (7\text{--}1)$$

where

$\overline{X}$ = the mean of our sample,

z_α = the z score corresponding to the level of alpha we are using to construct our interval (i.e., the level of confidence we will have in our estimate), and

$\sigma_{\overline{X}}$ = the standard deviation of the sampling distribution (i.e., the standard error).

The confidence interval, then, is determined by going out in both a positive and negative direction from the point estimate (the mean in equation 7–1), a specified multiple of standard errors $(\sigma /\sqrt{n})$. How many standard errors we go out from the point estimate is a function of the confidence level we select.

The first order of business, therefore, is to select the size of our confidence interval or the strength of our confidence. What size should our confidence interval be? Expressed differently, how confident do we want to be that the population parameter is captured within our interval? Typically, criminologists choose an alpha level of .05 or .01 and construct 95 percent or 99 percent confidence intervals, although the choice is yours. The alpha we select will determine our **confidence level.** If $\alpha = .05$, we have a 95 percent confidence level; if $\alpha = .01$, we have a 99 percent confidence level. A 95 percent confidence level means that over the long run, we are willing to be wrong only 5 percent of the time. A 99 percent confidence level means that over the long run, we are willing to be wrong only 1 percent of the time. Being wrong in this case means having the population mean not within the boundaries established by the confidence interval. We will later see that the size of the confidence interval is a function of how confident you want to be and how large your sample is.

All this will make more sense to you once we demonstrate with a real example. Let's begin with a 95 percent confidence interval. No matter what confidence interval we select, we must determine the corresponding z score for that level of confidence. The z score corresponding to an alpha of .05 is 1.96 (see Appendix E, Table E–2). Why is it 1.96? With a 95 percent confidence interval, we are concerned with 5 percent of the tail of the standard normal distribution. Since, however, we do not know if our sample statistic ($\bar{X}$) is less than or greater than the true population value (μ), we really are concerned about both tails of the distribution. Hence, we divide 5 percent into two equal halves (2.5 percent) and place them at each tail of the distribution. The proportion of the normal curve corresponding to 2.5 percent is .025. The z score that corresponds to .4750 of the normal curve (.50 − .025) is (from Table E–2 of Appendix E) 1.96. To find this z score, simply go into the body of the table until you see the proportion .4750; the z score for this proportion is 1.96. Since we are interested in both tails of the distribution, our z score is ±1.96. In Table 7–2 we provide a list of some common confidence intervals and their corresponding z score.

You know from the previous chapter that the term ($\sigma_{\bar{X}}$) in formula 7–1 is the standard deviation of the sampling distribution, or the standard error. In cases where the standard deviation of the population is known, we can easily determine the standard error of the sampling distribution by dividing the population standard deviation by the square root of the sample size ($(\sigma / \sqrt{n})$). When we know the population standard deviation, then, the standard error of the sampling distribution can be directly determined, and we can create our confidence intervals from formula 7–1.

TABLE 7–2

Common Confidence Intervals and Their Corresponding Critical Values of z from the Sampling Distribution of z

Confidence Level (%)	Alpha/Significance (α)	z Score
90	.10	1.65
95	.05	1.96
99	.01	2.58
99.9	.001	3.27

It is rarely the case, however, that we know the standard deviation of our population. If we knew it, we probably would also be in a good position to know the mean, so our point estimate and confidence interval construction would be unnecessary. Most of the time, then, we do not know our population standard deviation and the standard error of the sampling distribution must be estimated. If the sample size is large enough, we can use our sample standard deviation (s) to estimate the population standard deviation (σ), and then use the z distribution to obtain the critical value needed for our confidence interval. The sample estimate of the standard deviation of the sampling distribution is now $\frac{s}{\sqrt{n}}$, and the formula for our confidence interval is:

$$\overline{X} \pm z A\left(\frac{s}{(\sqrt{n})}\right) \hspace{3cm} (7\text{--}2)$$

Estimating Alcohol Consumption

Suppose that we conducted a survey from a random sample of 140 state university students, asking them about the number of drinks of alcohol they consumed during the last 30 days. One of the objectives of the study was to estimate (make an inference about) the average number of drinks per month ingested by university students across the country. The sample statistics we obtained were as follows:

$$\overline{X} = \ 12.4$$
$$s = \ \ 3.2$$
$$n = 140$$

The sample mean above tells us that, on average, the students from our sample drink an average of 12.4 drinks per month. To remind you, this sample statistic ($\overline{X}$) is referred to as our point estimate of the true population parameter (μ). What does our sample mean tell us about the mean of the entire population of metropolitan residents? This is the question we are really trying to answer. We want to make our point estimate of 12.4 more reliable and, at the same time, give ourselves the ability to make a probability statement about the confidence we have in our estimate. To do this, we use formula 7–2 to construct a 95 percent confidence interval around the sample mean estimate of 12.4.

95% Confidence Interval (c.i.) of Drinks per Month for University Students

$$95\% \text{ c.i.} = 12.4 \pm 1.96\left(\frac{3.2}{\sqrt{140}}\right)$$

$$= 12.4 \pm 1.96\left(\frac{3.2}{11.83}\right)$$

$$= 12.4 \pm 1.96(.27)$$

$$= 12.4 \pm .53$$

To find the interval, we simply add .53 to the mean of 12.4 and subtract .53 from the mean of 12.4:

$$12.4 - .53 = 11.87$$

$$12.4 + .53 = 12.93$$

$$95\% \text{ c.i.} = 11.87 \text{ to } 12.93$$

So, what does this interval tell us? It tells us that, based on our sample data, we can be 95 percent confident that the mean number of drinks university students consume per month lies between 11.87 and 12.93. The end points of our estimated confidence interval (11.87 and 12.93) are referred to as our **confidence limits.** This indicates that we are 95 percent confident that our interval contains the population mean number of drinks. That is, theoretically speaking, if we had taken a large number of random samples from this same population (all state university students) and calculated 95 percent confidence intervals around the means obtained from each sample, approximately 95 percent of these intervals would include the true population mean (μ) and 5 percent would not. Another way to express this confidence interval would be:

$$11.87 \leq \mu \leq 12.93$$

We are 95 percent confident that the population mean number of drinks is greater than or equal to 11.87 and less than or equal to 12.93.

Let's say for the sake of argument that we only wanted a 90 percent confidence interval around our sample mean, rather than a 95 percent confidence interval. With the same data as above, we will calculate a 90 percent confidence interval for our point estimate of 12.4. From Table 7–2 we see that the z score corresponding to an alpha level (α) of .10, or a 90 percent confidence interval, is 1.65. As before, using formula 7–2 we construct our confidence interval as follows:

$$90\% \text{ c.i.} = 12.4 \pm 1.65 \left(\frac{3.2}{\sqrt{140}} \right)$$

$$= 12.4 \pm 1.65(.27)$$

$$= 12.4 \pm .44$$

$$90\% \text{ c.i.} = 11.96 \text{ to } 12.84$$

This interval indicates that we are 90 percent confident that the true population mean number of drinks for state university students falls between 11.96 and 12.84. Notice that the interval for a 90 percent confidence interval is narrower than the 95 percent confidence interval. You can see, then, that we are less confident (90 percent vs. 95 percent confident) that our true population mean falls into this interval. By lowering our level of confidence, however, we gained some precision in our estimate. We could reduce the width of our confidence interval even more, but we would have to pay the price in levels of confidence.

Of course, one way that we could decrease the width of our interval without compromising our level of confidence would be to increase our sample size. Why? Remember that a large standard error (like a large standard deviation) indicates that the mean varies a great deal from sample to sample, whereas a small standard error indicates that there is little variation from sample to sample. Intuitively, then, as the size of the standard error decreases, the level of confidence we have in sample estimates typically increases. This is reflected in the formula. The larger the sample size (n), the smaller the standard error will be (or our estimate of the standard error). Less sample-to-sample variation indicates that we can be more confident that our sample statistic actually reflects the population parameter we are trying to estimate. Let us state this another way. If the standard error of the sampling distribution of means is small, then all samples drawn from a given population will have fairly similar means. The means from these samples will cluster tightly about the true population mean (μ). In this case, any given sample mean will be a relatively good estimate of the population mean. We therefore will have a smaller (narrower) confidence interval.

However, if the standard error is large, then the means obtained from these same-sized samples will tend to be very different. Some may be close to the true population mean, and some may be far away. In this case we will be less confident that any sample mean, is a good estimate of the true population mean, and the confidence interval will be larger (wider). For example, let's construct the same 95 percent confidence interval around the university data, but instead of a sample size of 140, let's cut the sample size in half, to only 70. The confidence interval would now be calculated as follows:

$$95\% \text{ c.i.} = 12.4 \pm 1.96 \left(\frac{3.2}{\sqrt{70}} \right)$$

$$= 12.4 \pm 1.96 \left(\frac{3.2}{8.4} \right)$$

$$= 12.4 \pm 1.96 \,(.38)$$

$$= 12.4 \pm .74$$

$$95\% \text{ c.i.} = 11.66 \text{ to } 13.14$$

The smaller the sample size, the larger the standard deviation of the sampling distribution (the standard error), and the larger the standard error, the larger the confidence interval. So if you want to increase your precision (decrease the width of your interval), but you do not want to change your level of confidence, acquiring a larger sample is the key. Since virtually every statistic we will cover in this text includes a term in the formula to quantify the standard error of its sampling distribution, we will return to this concept again and again and again . . .You get the idea!

Estimating the Onset of Crack/Cocaine Use

Because repetition is the key to acquiring skill, let's go through another example from the literature. Deborah Baskin and Ira Sommers (1998) published *Casualties of Community Disorder: Women's Careers in Violent Crime,* a book that reported the results of their research investigating violent crime committed by female offenders. For this research, Baskin and Sommers interviewed 170 women who had committed nondomestic violent felony crimes (robbery, assault, homicide) in New York City. For the sake of example, let's assume that this is a random sample of 170 female offenders. A majority of these women used crack cocaine (83 percent), almost three-quarters of them on a regular basis (72 percent). The mean age at which these women began using crack cocaine was 19.16 years of age. Suppose that the standard deviation around this mean age was equal to 4.2. The sample statistics necessary to construct a confidence interval around this mean would be: $\overline{X} = 19.16$, $s = 4.2$, and $n = 170$. Let's construct a 95 percent confidence interval around this sample mean:

$$95\% \text{ c.i.} = 19.16 \pm 1.96 \left(\frac{4.2}{\sqrt{170}} \right)$$

$$= 19.16 \pm 1.96 \left(\frac{4.2}{13} \right)$$

$$= 19.16 \pm 1.96 \, (.32)$$

$$= 19.16 \pm .63$$

$$95\% \text{ c.i.} = 18.53 \text{ to } 19.79$$

How would you interpret this interval? As we explained in the beginning of the book, we believe that the ability to interpret statistical results is just as important as the ability to calculate them. So even though we have asked it before, the question, "How would you interpret this?" is not merely rhetorical. This 95 percent confidence interval indicates that we can be 95 percent confident, based on our sample statistics, that for those violent female offenders who use crack cocaine, the mean age at which they began using this drug was between 18.53 and 19.79. Baskin and Sommers (1998) conclude that it is not a single factor, but a set of processes that are responsible for inner-city women becoming involved in violent street crime. They conclude, "Within a community context characterized by economic and social dislocation, growing drug markets, and a marked disappearance of males, situational factors related to family, school, and peer relations combine to create social and economic opportunity structures open to women's increasing participation."[1]

Let's now take the same data, and instead of constructing a 95 percent confidence interval, let's increase the confidence we have in our interval estimate by calculating a 99 percent interval. The only change that is necessary in the formula is the critical value of z. Because we have increased the level of confidence we wish to have about our point estimate $(\overline{X})$, the critical value of z increases from 1.96 to 2.58 (Table 7–2). Using formula 7–2, the calculation of the 99 percent interval is shown below:

$$99\% \text{ c.i.} = 19.16 \pm 2.58 \left(\frac{4.2}{\sqrt{170}} \right)$$

$$= 19.16 \pm 2.58 \left(\frac{4.2}{13} \right)$$

$$= 19.16 \pm 2.58 \,(.32)$$

$$= 19.16 \pm .82$$

$$99\% \text{ c.i.} = 18.34 \text{ to } 19.98$$

Based on our sample statistics, then, we are 99 percent confident that the mean age at which female violent offenders who use crack first start using the drug lies between 18.34 and 19.98. Notice that this 99 percent confidence interval (18.34 to 19.98) is wider than the one we derived from the same data with only a 95 percent confidence interval (18.53 to 19.79). Since we want to be more confident that our interval contains the population mean, this increased confidence comes at the price of a wider confidence interval. By now, this should be making sense to you. It suggests that if we want to be more confident that the true population mean falls into our estimated interval, we have to make the interval wider (other things being equal). To reiterate, greater confidence comes at a price, and the price we pay is the width of the confidence interval.

Think for a minute about this question: "If we want to be more confident without increasing the size of the interval, what can we do?" If your answer was to increase our sample size, you were right! A confidence interval will be smaller with a larger sample size because when the standard deviation of the sampling distribution (standard error) is reduced, the sample value is a more accurate estimate of the true population mean. The lessons to be learned from this are as follows:

- The larger the sample size, the smaller the standard deviation of the sampling distribution of means (the standard error).
- The smaller the standard error, the more accurate our sample mean is as an estimate of the population mean.
- To increase the confidence that our interval contains the population mean, we can increase the confidence level (and widen the confidence interval) or increase the sample size.

After all of this discussion of different confidence levels, you may be asking yourself now, "When do we want to use a 99 percent confidence interval compared to a 95 percent interval or a 90 percent interval? What guides our decision to select a specific level of confidence?" Unfortunately, there are no hard and fast rules for this. The decision you make is in part a judgment call that depends on the nature of your research. Just remember that there is usually a trade-off between confidence and precision. Generally speaking, at a fixed sample size you will get a smaller interval and therefore more precision with lower levels of confidence. The lower your confidence, however, the less sure you will be that your interval contains the true population mean. If you want to attain greater confidence that your interval actually contains the population mean, increase your confidence level. The trade-off you make in doing this is a larger confidence interval (unless you increase sample size). In general, however, the 95 percent level of confidence is the most typical in the criminology and criminal justice literature.

ESTIMATING CONFIDENCE INTERVALS FROM SMALL SAMPLES

In constructing confidence intervals with formula 7–2, we used the sample standard deviation to estimate the population standard deviation. When our sample size is large (recall from Chapter 6 that when the sample size is at least 100 the assumption of a normal population can almost always be relaxed, and that it can generally be relaxed whenever $n > 50$), the standard deviation is a fairly good estimate of σ. This is not true, however, when our sample size is small. In the case of small sample sizes, the sample standard deviation shows substantial variation from sample to sample. For small samples, therefore, the standard deviation of the sampling distribution (standard error) is greater than for large samples. The practical implication of this is that the z distribution cannot be used for constructing confidence intervals in instances where the sample size is small.

There are many times in criminological research, however, when we must rely on small samples. In instances such as this, therefore, the assumptions we make about the normal distribution do not apply. Why? Well, recall that the properties of the Central Limit Theorem (described in the last chapter) only apply to large-sized samples. Therefore, if our sample is small, we must utilize statistics that violate this "large sample" assumption. When our research dictates that we have no choice and must utilize a small sample, the Student's t distribution is typically used to make inferences from the sample mean, $\bar{X}$, to the population mean, μ.

The theoretical sampling distribution called Student's t was calculated by W. E. Gosset and published in 1908. Gosset was a statistician for the Guinness brewing company. Although Guinness did not usually allow its employees to publish their own work, Gosset was permitted to do so under the nom de plume of "Student." Hence, his distribution has been called **Student's t distribution.**

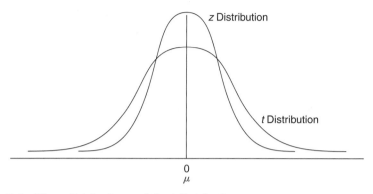

Figure 7–3 The z distribution and the t distribution

TABLE 7–3

Properties of the Sampling Distribution of t

1. The t distribution is bell-shaped and symmetrical and centers around $\mu = 0$.

2. The t distribution has more variability than the z distribution. It is flatter and has wider tails than the z distribution.

3. There are many different t distributions, which are based on sample size. More specifically, the distribution of t we utilize for our statistical test is based on a parameter called the *degrees of freedom (df)*. The degrees of freedom are calculated to be one less than the sample size $(n - 1)$.

4. With a sample size of 100 or more, the t distribution becomes virtually identical to the z distribution.

The t distribution is flatter and has a greater spread than the z distribution, which indicates that there is more sample-to-sample variation in the former. The two sampling distributions are shown in Figure 7–3. The smaller the sample size, the flatter the t distribution is compared to the normal distribution. Just as with the standard normal distribution of z, the t distribution also has several known properties, which are listed in Table 7–3.

As noted in Table 7–3, there are actually several different t distributions depending upon the degrees of freedom (df) present in the sample. The degrees of freedom are equal to one less than the sample size $(n - 1)$. As the sample size (and df) becomes larger, the t distribution more closely approximates the standard normal distribution (z distribution). When $n > 100$, the two distributions are virtually identical, but the t distribution will always be flatter than the z. The values of t associated with these degrees of freedom and different levels of alpha (α) are displayed in Table E–3 in Appendix E. Remember that, by definition, confidence intervals are two-tailed tests, because we do not know if our sample statistic is greater than or less than the true population value. For confidence intervals, then, we always use values of t

associated with a two-tailed test (see Appendix E, Table E–3) since we are creating an interval by going around a sample statistic and, therefore, utilizing both tails of the sampling distribution.

Let's say we had a sample size of $n = 10$ and wanted to make an inference to the population mean at the 95 percent level. We would begin by going into the t table using $t_\alpha = .05$ for a two-tailed test. Next we would find the degree of freedom associated with our sample data, which is $n - 1$ and in this case equal to 9 ($10 - 1 = 9$). Going down the alpha column of .05 for a two-tailed test to the row that lists 9 degrees of freedom, we would obtain a critical value of $t = 2.262$.

In Appendix Table E–3, notice that when the sample size is greater than 100, the critical values of t are about the same as those for z, and that when the sample size is greater than 120, they are identical. This reflects the fourth property listed in Table 7–3, which states that as the sample size approximates 100, the t distribution begins to look more and more like the z distribution. This should make intuitive sense to you based on our discussion in the last chapter. Remember that with large samples (over 100) the assumption of a normal population can almost always be relaxed. The sampling distribution of the mean can now be assumed to be approximately normal, which would allow us to utilize the z distribution to make inferences.

The formula for calculating a confidence interval around a mean using the t distribution is shown below. It looks almost exactly like the formula we used to calculate confidence intervals using the z distribution, doesn't it?

$$\overline{X} \pm t_\alpha \left(\sigma_{\overline{X}} \right) = \overline{X} \pm t_\alpha \left(\frac{s}{\sqrt{n}} \right) \tag{7-3}$$

Estimating the Effects of Arrest on Employment

Let's go through an example of making inferences about μ with a small sample using the t distribution. There is somewhat of a controversy in the criminological literature concerning the interrelationship between delinquency, arrest, and future employment success. For example, Hagan (1993) advances the idea that youths involved in crime do not develop the necessary social and human capital necessary to succeed in the legal labor market. Sampson and Laub (1997), on the other hand, contend that formal sanctions by the criminal justice system (e.g., arrest) lead employers to avoid individuals who might otherwise succeed in the labor market. To test these competing implications, Bushway (1998) examined the employment status of young men interviewed in the National Youth Survey (NYS) over a three-year period. In this way, Bushway was able to examine the effects of delinquency on employment status for those individuals who were both arrested and not arrested for their delinquent acts. His research adds support to Sampson and Laub's position because he found that formal contact with the criminal justice system, rather than criminal activity itself, directly damages job prospects.

Suppose that we conducted our own survey of young men, asking them about both their involvement in delinquent activities (e.g., vandalism, theft, taking drugs) and their involvement with the criminal justice system (e.g., arrest, conviction, probation, incarceration). After dividing the sample into delinquents who had been arrested and those who had not, let's say we found the following sample statistics, including the mean length of time (in weeks) they had retained employment during the past year:

Delinquents Who Were Arrested	Delinquents Who Remained Undetected
$\bar{X} = 22$	$\bar{X} = 31$
$s = 3$	$s = 4$
$n = 14$	$n = 21$

First, let's construct a 95 percent confidence interval around the sample mean for those delinquents who were arrested. The first step involves calculating the degrees of freedom you have and finding the critical value of t. With a sample size of 14, our degrees of freedom are equal to 13 ($n - 1$). Going down the appropriate column and across the appropriate row in the t table (Appendix E, Table E–3), you find the critical value needed is 2.160. Remember that the selection of the confidence level (and corresponding critical value) is up to you. Once you have this, you can construct your confidence interval with formula 7–3 as shown below:

$$95\% \text{ c.i.} = 22 \pm 2.160 \left(\frac{3}{\sqrt{14}} \right)$$

$$= 22 \pm 2.160 \left(\frac{3}{3.74} \right)$$

$$= 22 \pm 2.160(.80)$$

$$= 22 \pm 1.73$$

$$95\% \text{ c.i.} = 20.27 \text{ to } 23.73$$

As before, to find the lower and upper confidence limits, we add 1.8 to our mean of 22 and subtract 1.73 from 22. This interval tells us that based on our sample data, we can be 95 percent confident that the mean number of weeks arrested delinquents held down a job lies somewhere between 20.27 and 23.73 weeks. If we had taken a large number of random, same-sized samples from this same population of young men and calculated 95 percent confidence intervals around the means obtained from each sample, approximately 95 percent of these intervals would include the true population mean, μ, and 5 percent would not.

Notice the difference between the critical value in this confidence interval for small samples and the critical value for the same 95 percent confidence interval we calculated earlier for large samples. If we had a larger sample in this case, we could have used the critical z value of 1.96 instead of the larger t value of 2.160 that was necessary here. To reiterate the reasoning behind this, remember that since the t distribution is flatter than the z distribution, we have to go farther out in the tail to find our critical region. Again, the smaller the sample size, the flatter the t distribution is and the farther we will have to move out in the tail to find our critical region. At the same alpha level, the critical value of t will be much larger with very small sample sizes than the large sample z.

For the t distribution, the relationships between confidence levels, sample sizes, and confidence intervals are still the same. At a fixed sample size, decreasing the confidence level will narrow the confidence interval while increasing the confidence level will widen the confidence interval. The confidence interval can be narrowed (even when increasing the confidence level) by increasing the sample size.

Estimating Rape Offending Patterns

Let's go through another example. Research has shown that men convicted of rape usually commit the crime of rape once if not several times before they are eventually caught and incarcerated. Suppose that you are a criminologist interested in the number of rapes committed by rapists before they are arrested. One way to examine this issue would be to calculate the average number of self-reported rapes that incarcerated rapists committed before they were caught. To do this, you conduct interviews with a sample of 15 convicted rapists who are incarcerated in a state prison.[2] You find that the mean number of rapes committed by these men before they were convicted on the count they are currently serving time for is 5.3. You calculate the standard deviation of this distribution to be 3.4. Because you want to infer this sample information to the population of all incarcerated rapists, you decide to calculate a 95 percent confidence interval around the $\overline{X}$.

The first step in this procedure is to calculate the degrees of freedom you have and find the critical value of t. With a sample size of 15, our degrees of freedom are equal to 14 ($n - 1$). Going down the appropriate column and across the appropriate row in the t table (Appendix E, Table E–3), you find the critical value needed is 2.145. The confidence interval is calculated here:

$$95\% \text{ c.i.} = 5.3 \pm 2.145 \left(\frac{3.4}{\sqrt{15}} \right)$$

$$= 5.3 \pm 2.145 \left(\frac{3.4}{3.87} \right)$$

$$= 5.3 \pm 2.145 (.88)$$

$$= 5.3 \pm 1.89$$

$$95\% \text{ c.i.} = 3.41 \text{ to } 7.19$$

This interval tells us that, based on our sample data, we can be 95 percent confident that the mean number of self-admitted rapes committed by incarcerated rapists lies somewhere between 3.41 and 7.19 offenses. If we had taken a large number of random same-sized samples from this same population of incarcerated rapists and calculated 95 percent confidence intervals around the means obtained from each sample, approximately 95 percent of these intervals would include the true population mean μ, and 5 percent would not.

The degrees of freedom necessary to find the critical value of t for a 99 percent confidence interval still would be 14 ($n - 1$), but we would select an alpha (α) level of .01 instead of the .05 level of alpha we used for the 95 percent confidence interval. From Table E–3 we see that the critical value of t for this interval becomes 2.977. The computation of the confidence interval is as follows:

$$99\% \text{ c.i.} = 5.3 \pm 2.977 \left(\frac{3.4}{\sqrt{15}} \right)$$

$$= 5.3 \pm 2.977 \left(\frac{3.4}{3.87} \right)$$

$$= 5.3 \pm 2.977 (.88)$$

$$= 5.3 \pm 2.62$$

$$99\% \text{ c.i.} = 2.68 \text{ to } 7.92$$

Notice that the interval got much wider with this change from a 95 percent to a 99 percent level of confidence. Now we can say, however, that we are 99 percent confident that the population mean of self-reported rapes for convicted rapists is between 2.68 and 7.92. We are risking only a 1 percent ($\alpha = .01$) chance of being wrong—of not including the true population mean number of rapes. In exchange for this increased level of confidence, however, notice that we have increased the width of our interval.

Let's now estimate this same 99 percent confidence level but assume that we have a sample size of 40 rather than 15. To find the necessary critical value of t, we now enter Table E–3 with 39 degrees of freedom ($40 - 1 = 39$). But, as you can see, there is no specific t value for 39 degrees of freedom. Again, this is because the t distribution begins to approximate a normal distribution with large samples and, as our sample size increases, the critical values of t begin to change very little. In fact, after you reach a sample size over 120 ($n = 120$), they do not change at all and become equal to those of the z distribution ($\alpha = .05, z = 1.96$). When there is not a specific value of t listed in the table, simply take the closest degrees of freedom, which in this case would be equal to 40 degrees of freedom. The critical value necessary for this confidence interval is 2.704 (df = 40, $\alpha = .01$). The confidence interval in this case would be:

$$99\% \text{ c.i.} = 5.3 \pm 2.704 \left(\frac{3.4}{\sqrt{40}} \right)$$

$$= 5.3 \pm 2.704 \left(\frac{3.4}{6.3} \right)$$

$$= 5.3 \pm 2.704 (.54)$$

$$= 5.3 \pm 1.46$$

$$99\% \text{ c.i.} = 3.84 \text{ to } 6.76$$

As shown, with a 99 percent confidence level and $n = 40$, our confidence interval is 3.84 to 6.76. This interval is smaller than the interval at the same confidence level for an n of 15. The reason the interval is smaller is because the estimated standard deviation of the sampling distribution ($s/\sqrt{n}$) gets smaller when the sample size is increased. In the example with $n = 15$, the standard error was .88. When we increased our sample size to 40, the standard error was reduced to .54. The confidence intervals for each level of confidence and sample size were as follows:

$n = 15$, 95% confidence interval = 3.41–7.19

$n = 15$, 99% confidence interval = 2.68–7.92

$n = 40$, 99% confidence interval = 3.84–6.76

By increasing our sample size, then, we have decreased the standard deviation of the sampling distribution (standard error), and we have increased the precision of our estimate.

ESTIMATING CONFIDENCE INTERVALS FOR PROPORTIONS AND PERCENTS

Compared to the confidence intervals around means we have just examined, you are perhaps more familiar with confidence intervals constructed around proportions and percents. The media bombards us with examples of these all the time. As we said earlier, results of opinion polls are usually quickly followed by a phrase that says something like "plus or minus 3 percent." This is one way of presenting a confidence interval in a way the public will better understand. For our purposes here, the confidence intervals we will discuss in this section are for large samples only. The calculation of a confidence interval around a proportion is done by using the following formula:

$$\text{Confidence interval} = \hat{p} \pm z_\alpha \left(\sigma_p \right) \tag{7-4}$$

where

$\hat{p}$ = sample proportion,

$\sigma_{\hat{p}} = \sqrt{\dfrac{\hat{p}(1-\hat{p})}{n}}$, and

p = population proportion.

This formula is very similar to the confidence interval formula for sample means. With a large sample, sample proportions have sampling distributions that are approximately normal with a mean equal to the true population proportion (p) and a standard deviation (σ_p) equal to $\sqrt{p(1-p)/n}$. The latter term is referred to as the **standard error of the proportion.** In the confidence interval formula for proportions above, we simply replace the sample mean

($\overline{X}$) with the sample proportion ($\hat{p}$) and the <u>standard</u> error of the mean ($\sigma / \sqrt{n}$) by the standard error of the proportion $\sqrt{p(1-p)/n}$.

In formula 7–4, the value of $\hat{p}$ in the confidence interval is the sample proportion. It is the sample point estimate ($\hat{p}$) of the unknown population parameter (p). As with the confidence interval for the mean with large samples, the term z is the critical value of z we obtain from the standard normal table. As before, the precise value of z depends upon the particular confidence level we select. Notice, however, that the standard error of the proportion ($\sqrt{p(1-p)/n}$) is based upon the population proportion (p)—a quantity we do not know, and are in fact trying to estimate with our sample statistic ($\hat{p}$). Since p is not known, it must be estimated, and consequently, the standard error of the proportion also must be estimated. The symbol for the estimate of the standard error of the proportion is $\sigma_{\hat{p}}$. How do we estimate this quantity?

We will use the sample proportion ($\hat{p}$) to estimate the population proportion (p). In most instances where you have a large sample, this will be a reasonable solution, and the sample proportion will provide a good estimate of the population proportion. Simply substitute $\hat{p}$ for p in formula 7–4 and proceed with the construction of the confidence interval. In this approach, the estimated standard error of the proportion is:

$$\sigma_{\hat{p}} = \sqrt{\frac{\hat{p}(1-\hat{p})}{n}}$$

where $\hat{p}$ = sample proportion. This is generally a reasonable estimate for the standard error of the proportion.

Estimating the Effects of Community Policing

A relatively recent innovation in policing is called "community oriented policing," or COP for short. Community oriented policing is designed to increase the frequency of police-citizen encounters and to simultaneously increase the level of discretion officers have in making arrests. Officers' frequent use of discretion, coupled with the importance of their decision to invoke the criminal justice system, has led police researchers to increasingly examine the use of arrest by police officers. Recently, Novak, Frank, Smith, and Engel (2002) examined the influence of both situation- and community-level variables on the arrest decisions of two groups of officers: traditional patrol/beat officers and COP officers. To gather this information, these researchers actually accompanied officers during their shifts. The units of analysis for this study were the interactions between the police and a member of the public. The sample consisted of encounters where probable cause to believe the citizen committed a criminal offense was present during the encounter. Results indicated that 34 percent of these encounters resulted in an arrest by beat officers ($n = 230$), compared to 26 percent of similar encounters between COP officers and citizens ($n = 104$).

Let's construct 95 percent confidence intervals around both sample estimates. Since we have large samples, we can use the critical value of z at the α = .05 level. To use the formula, we have to convert the percents back into proportions by dividing them by 100. The calculations for both intervals are presented in Figure 7–4.

95% Confidence Interval for Beat Officers:

$$95\% \text{ c.i. } = .34 \pm 1.96 \sqrt{\frac{.34(1-.34)}{230}}$$

$$= .34 \pm 1.96 \sqrt{\frac{.34(.66)}{230}}$$

$$= .34 \pm 1.96 \sqrt{\frac{.22}{230}}$$

$$= .34 \pm 1.96 \sqrt{.00096}$$

$$= .34 \pm 1.96(.03)$$

$$= .34 \pm .059$$

$$95\% \text{ c.i. } = .28 \text{ to } .40, \text{ or } 28\% \text{ to } 40\%$$

95% Confidence Interval for Community Police Officers:

$$95\% \text{ c.i. } = .26 \pm 1.96 \sqrt{\frac{.26(1-.26)}{104}}$$

$$= .26 \pm 1.96 \sqrt{\frac{.26(.74)}{104}}$$

$$= .26 \pm 1.96 \sqrt{\frac{.192}{104}}$$

$$= .26 \pm 1.96 \sqrt{.0018}$$

$$= .26 \pm 1.96(.04)$$

$$= .26 \pm .078$$

$$95\% \text{ c.i. } = .18 \text{ to } .34, \text{ or } 18\% \text{ to } 34\%$$

Figure 7–4 95% confidence intervals for proportion of beat officers and community oriented police officers making an arrest

To find the upper and lower confidence limits for the interval for beat officers, we simply add .19 to our sample estimate of .34 and subtract .19 from .34. This gives us an interval of .28 to .39. Once this is complete, we can easily convert the proportions back into percents by multiplying them by 100 to get an easier-to-comprehend 28 to 39 percent. What does this tell us? We can now say that we are 95 percent confident that the true percent of arrests that involve probable cause in beat officer and citizen encounters lies somewhere between 28 and 39 percent.

What about the interval for COP officers? This tells us that we are 95 percent confident that the true percent of arrests that involve probable cause in COP officer and citizen encounters lies somewhere between 18 and 33 percent. Notice that the intervals actually overlap. That is, the true percent of encounters that may result in arrest for both beat and COP officers may well be 28 percent (the lower limit for beat officers), 29, 30, 31, 32, or 33 percent (the upper limit for COP officers). In this way, we can say that there was no significant difference between the arrest decisions made by beat officers and COP officers. In fact, this is what Novak and his colleagues found. The factors that did predict arrest were the demeanor of the citizen (hostile and not deferential), signs of intoxication, the availability of evidence, and gender (males were more likely to be arrested than females).

Gender Differences on Attitudes toward Crime Control

Let's go through another quick example. Attitudinal differences between men and women on issues of crime control policies have always been of interest to criminologists and policymakers alike. To examine whether gender differences exist in attitudes about such things as support for rehabilitation and punishment, Applegate, Cullen, and Fisher (2002) analyzed survey data from 1,000 Ohio residents. To determine respondents' attitudes toward rehabilitation, they were asked to respond to a number of statements including, "It is a good idea to provide treatment for offenders who are in prison," and "It is important to try to rehabilitate juveniles who have committed crimes and are now in the correctional system." The survey also replicated a question previously included in several polls conducted by Louis Harris and Associates that asked, "Now what do you think should be the main emphasis in most prisons—punishing the individual convicted of a crime, trying to rehabilitate the individual so that he might return to society as a productive citizen, or protecting society from future crimes he might commit?" While both men and women in the survey tended to rate rehabilitation as an important goal for prisons, women were significantly less likely to support capital punishment for murderers compared to men.

Suppose that, wanting to replicate these findings, we conduct a survey of our own, randomly selecting 150 male and 150 female U.S. adults to participate. To determine attitudes toward capital punishment, we ask respondents if they are in favor of the death penalty for all murderers, or instead, in favor of life in prison without the possibility of parole. Our results indicate that 58 percent of the men and 51 percent of the women are in favor of capital punishment for all murderers. Let's construct a 99 percent confidence interval around the percent for men. With $\hat{p} = .58$ and a critical value of z equal to 2.58 ($\alpha = .01$), the steps for calculating the 95% confidence interval for the male sample are as follows:

$$95\% \text{ c.i. } = .58 \pm 1.96 \sqrt{\frac{.58(1-.58)}{150}}$$

$$= .58 \pm 1.96 \sqrt{\frac{.58(.42)}{150}}$$

$$= .58 \pm 1.96 \sqrt{\frac{.24}{150}}$$

$$= .58 \pm 1.96 \sqrt{.0016}$$

$$= .58 \pm 1.96(.04)$$

$$= .58 \pm .078$$

$$95\% \text{ c.i. } = .50 \text{ to } .66, \text{ or } 50\% \text{ to } 66\%$$

To complete the interval, we simply add .078 to the sample proportion of .58 and subtract .078 from .58 to find the lower and upper confidence limits of the interval of .50 to .66, or 50 to 66 percent. We are 95 percent confident that the true population percent of men who favor the death penalty over life in prison without the possibility of parole lies somewhere between 50 and 66 percent. How about the women? The 99 percent confidence interval for their sample proportion is as follows:

$$99\% \text{ c.i. } = .51 \pm 2.58 \sqrt{\frac{.51(1-.51)}{150}}$$

$$= .51 \pm 2.58 \sqrt{\frac{.51(.49)}{150}}$$

$$= .51 \pm 2.58 \sqrt{\frac{.25}{150}}$$

$$= .51 \pm 2.58 \sqrt{.0017}$$

$$= .51 \pm 2.58(.04)$$

$$= .51 \pm .10$$

$$99\% \text{ c.i. } = .41 \text{ to } .61, \text{ or } 41\% \text{ to } 61\%$$

With this interval, we can say we are 99 percent confident that the true percent of women who favor the death penalty over life in prison without the possibility of parole lies somewhere between 41 and 61 percent. This is quite a large interval. How could we reduce its width while not losing any confidence? We hope your immediate answer was, *"increase sample size!"*

SUMMARY

In this chapter we have examined the procedures used to estimate population parameters using confidence intervals. To estimate confidence intervals around a $\overline{X}$ obtained from a large sample, we examined estimation procedures based on the z distribution. We also examined the formula based on the t distribution used to construct confidence intervals around means obtained from small samples. We concluded the chapter by examining the estimation procedures used to construct confidence intervals around proportions and percents.

Each of the above types of intervals could have been constructed using any level of confidence (e.g., 75 percent, 88 percent, 95 percent, etc.). However, we focused almost exclusively on confidence levels of 95 percent since this is the typical level used in criminological research. We discussed the trade-offs made when adopting particular levels of confidence: higher levels of confidence (e.g., 99 percent compared to 95 percent) produce wider intervals. So while you gain confidence in your estimation, you also lose precision. In this chapter, the importance of sample size was illuminated as well. Smaller samples always inflate the standard error of the sampling distribution you are working with, thereby increasing the width of a confidence interval. Thus, larger samples are more desirable than smaller ones.

KEY TERMS

confidence interval
confidence level
confidence limits
inferential statistics
point estimate
population parameter

standard error of the mean
standard error of the proportion
t distribution (Student's t distribution)
z distribution

REVIEW & PRACTICE

KEY FORMULAS

Confidence interval around a sample mean with large samples (eq. 7–2):

$$\bar{X} \pm z_\alpha \left(\sigma_{\bar{X}} \right) = z_\alpha \left(\frac{s}{\sqrt{n}} \right)$$

Confidence interval around a sample mean with small samples (eq. 7–3):

$$\bar{X} \pm t_\alpha \left(\sigma_{\bar{X}} \right) = \bar{X} \pm t_\alpha \left(\frac{s}{\sqrt{n}} \right)$$

Confidence interval around sample proportion with large samples (eq. 7–4):

$$\hat{p} \pm z_\alpha \left(\sigma_{\hat{p}} \right) = z_\alpha \sqrt{\frac{\hat{p}(1-\hat{p})}{n}}$$

PRACTICE PROBLEMS

1. What is the purpose of confidence intervals?
2. Describe the differences between the z distribution and the t distribution. When is it appropriate to use the z distribution for estimation procedures?
3. A hypothetical study concerned with estimating the amount of marijuana use per year among a teenage population obtained a sample of 110 high school students. With the following sample statistics, construct a 95 percent confidence interval around the mean number of times this sample uses marijuana in a given 6-month period:

$$\bar{X} = 4.5 \text{ times per year}$$

$$s = 3.2$$

$$n = 110$$

    What does the interval you constructed tell us about marijuana use in the population? Interpret these results.
4. Using the same mean and standard deviations in problem (3) above, change the sample size to 55 and construct a confidence interval around the mean using the appropriate procedures. How does the interval change? Provide an interpretation for your interval.
5. What does the standard deviation of the sampling distribution of the mean tell us? What affects the size of the standard error?

6. In a 1993 article, Terri Moffitt identified a group of young offenders, called "life course persistent" offenders, who commit both frequent and serious offenses throughout their lives. Let's say you have a sample of 20 young males who have been in juvenile institutions at least twice. The mean age of their first arrest is 11, and the standard deviation is 1.7. Build a 99 percent confidence interval around this point estimate.

7. The mayor of a large city wants to know how long it takes the police in his city to respond to a call for service. In a random sample of 15 citizens who called the police for service, the mayor's research director has found that the average response time was 560 seconds, with a standard deviation of 45 seconds. Construct a 95 percent confidence interval around your point estimate. How will the research director respond to the mayor's question?

8. Greenwood and Turner (1993) investigated the extent to which recidivism rates differed between convicted delinquents who were assigned to a small experimental program, called the Paint Creek Youth Center, and those who were assigned to a traditional training school. The Paint Creek Youth Center was designed to provide the youths with a comprehensive and highly structured array of intervention services and activities. Recidivism in this study was operationalized by computing the percent of youths who had been arrested for any crime within 12 months of their release from the programs. About .61 of the youths assigned to the traditional program ($n = 75$) were rearrested within 12 months, compared to .51 of the youths assigned to the Paint Creek Center ($n = 73$). Construct a 95 percent confidence interval around each of these sample proportions.

9. If you constructed a 99 percent confidence interval around the proportions in problem (8), how would this change the intervals? Why?

SPSS PRACTICE PROBLEMS

1. For this question, use the data from Homicide.sav, which contains information from a sample of murder defendants in 33 counties. We want to know about the mean sentence length in days given to defendants found guilty of murder (PRITIME). To examine this variable in detail, it is probably a good idea to obtain a frequency distribution (ANALYZE, DESCRIPTIVES, FREQUENCIES). Under the statistics box in the frequency dialogue box, ask for a mean and a standard error of the mean (S.E. of the mean) to be given. You also should obtain a graphical display of this distribution by asking for a boxplot and/or histogram under the GRAPHS menu. What does the univariate distribution for this variable look like?

2. Now construct a 95 percent confidence interval around the mean in exercise (1) using the appropriate critical value of z and the sample size. The

standard error you obtain in your calculations should be very close to the one calculated by SPSS. Interpret your confidence interval.

3. Notice that your sample size is very large. Now estimate a confidence interval using the same data as in exercise (1) with a much smaller sample. To do this, you must go under the DATA menu, then click on SELECT CASES, then tell SPSS to select a RANDOM SAMPLE OF CASES from your data. You will be asked to select your sampling method; ask for a random sample of 3 percent of your sample. This should give you an approximate sample size of just over 30 homicide defendants. Now follow the same procedures as above. How different are the means? How different are the confidence intervals and why? What does this say about sample size?

4. Now click on DATA, then SELECT CASES, and tell SPSS to use the entire sample again. Now, let's examine the percent of defendants who received a life sentence (LIFE). Using the results of a frequency distribution, construct a confidence interval around the proportion of your sample that received a sentence of life in prison. Interpret your results.

5. Now calculate the same interval for male and female defendants separately. To do this, you will have to go under DATA, SELECT CASES, and select, IF CONDITION IS SATISFIED. You will have to first tell SPSS to select cases for males by specifying when the variable SEX is equal to 1. Then perform your analysis. Then go under DATA, SELECT CASES again, and tell SPSS to select cases for females by specifying when the variable SEX is equal to 0. Interpret both intervals.

8
CHAPTER

From Estimation to Statistical Tests:

Hypothesis Testing
for One Population Mean
and Proportion

*I*n order to shake a hypothesis,
it is sometimes not necessary
to do anything more than push
it as far as it will go.

—DENIS DIDEROT

*S*moking is one of the leading
causes of statistics.

—FLETCHER KNEBEL

In the preceding chapter, we focused exclusively on techniques of point and confidence interval estimation. We examined how to utilize confidence intervals based on information from samples in order to place boundaries on our estimates of population parameters. In Chapter 7, then, we were primarily interested in finding out what the value of the population mean (proportion) was. In this chapter, we focus on a somewhat different type of question. We begin by making an assumption about what the value of the population parameter is, and then we ask whether this assumption is realistic given the particular sample statistic we observe from our data. Specifically, our focus in this chapter is on the following question: "Is it likely that the unknown population mean (proportion) is equal to what we have presumed it to be, given what we know about our sample mean (proportion)?"

We want to know whether we can continue to assume that our population parameter is equal to a hypothesized value in the face of the evidence we have from our sample. We presume something about our population characteristic (that the population mean or proportion is equal to some given value), and we have some real information from our sample (that the sample mean or sample proportion is actually equal to some value). What we want to know is whether our assumption about the value of the population parameter is reasonable, given the sample value. Either it is—and we conclude that our presumption about the population parameter is true—or it is not, and we conclude that our presumption about the population parameter is not true. Stated differently, we either reject or fail to reject our initial assumption. By the end of this chapter, you will have a deeper understanding of hypothesis testing.

INTRODUCTION

As we did in Chapter 6 when we performed a hypothesis test using the binomial distribution, in this chapter we again compare information we have from our sample with what we presume to be true about our population. We then use probability theory to provide a decision rule to determine the validity of our presumption. The decision we make, however, is not without some risk of error. Recall the Lo-Jack example from Chapter 6—no matter what we decide, there is always a chance that we have made the wrong decision. What probability theory permits us to do, then, is to estimate the probability of making the wrong decision. It lets us make our decision with some level of confidence.

Suppose, for example, that you have been hired by the warden of a correctional institution to evaluate a literacy program in the prison. After reviewing records at the State Department of Corrections, you know that the reading level for the entire population of incarcerated inmates in the state is 7.5 years, with a standard deviation of 2.2. You take a random sample of 100 "graduates" of the literacy program and find that their mean reading level is 9.3 years. You want to know whether the mean reading level for the sample of literacy program graduates is equal to the general population mean, that is, whether the population mean of literacy program graduates is equal to 7.5 years. The question you must ask is, "Is it reasonable to assume that the population mean for program graduates is 7.5 years, given that my sample mean is 9.3 years?"

If, instead of a sample of 100 graduates, you had information about every graduate who had ever completed the program (the population of program graduates), you would be better able to answer your question. In this case, you could simply compute the average reading level for your population of program graduates and see if it is equal to 7.5 years. Either it would be or it would not be. You would have no doubt, and there would be no risk of error in your conclusion because you would have the information about the entire population. In the real world, however, we rarely have information about the entire population; instead, we must make inferences about the population from information we acquire from a sample of the population.

Of course, with sample information, we can never be 100 percent positive about our conclusion. Even if your sample mean is very different from the presumed value of the population mean, you cannot automatically conclude that your assumption about the value of that population mean is wrong. The difference between your sample mean and the presumed population mean might be due simply to sampling variation, the fact that the means of repeated samples from the same population are invariably different from the true population value. Enter probability theory! With the information provided by your sample and the presumed value of the population mean, you can determine the likelihood of obtaining the sample mean if, in fact, the null hypothesis is true. We do this through the formal procedures of conducting a hypothesis test.

The remainder of this chapter examines the various ways to test a hypothesis about a single population mean using both large and small samples and a population proportion using a large sample. We also examine the differences between hypothesis testing using nondirectional (two-tailed or nondirectional) tests versus directional (one-tailed or directional) tests. Before we begin this new section, let's refresh our memory of the steps involved in any hypothesis test (presented in Chapter 6) by examining Figure 8–1. In the following sections, we apply these steps to the prob-

Step 1. Formally state your null (H_0) and research (H_1) hypotheses.
Step 2. Select an appropriate test statistic and the sampling distribution of that test statistic.
Step 3. Select a level of significance (alpha = α), and determine the critical value and rejection region of the test statistic based on the selected level of alpha.
Step 4. Conduct the test: Calculate the obtained value of the test statistic and compare it to the critical value.
Step 5. Make a decision about your null hypothesis and interpret this decision in a meaningful way based on the research question, sample, and population.

Figure 8–1 Formal steps for hypothesis testing

lems of testing a hypothesis first about a sample mean and then about a sample proportion.

TESTING A HYPOTHESIS ABOUT A SINGLE POPULATION MEAN: THE z TEST

Case Study: Testing the Mean Reading Levels from a Prison Literacy Program

Let's begin our discussion of hypothesis testing using the reading levels for the sample of prison literacy program graduates and the general population of inmates. We can summarize what we know about the two groups as follows:

	Population	Sample
Mean reading level	$\mu = 7.5$	$\bar{X} = 9.3$
Standard deviation	$\sigma = $ unknown	$s = 2.2$
		$n = 100$

What we know for sure, then, is that the mean reading level of our sample of 100 literacy program graduates ($\bar{X} = 9.3$) is different from the mean for the entire population of incarcerated inmates ($\mu = 7.5$). But is the mean reading level of the literacy program graduates really different from the population mean? In statistical terms, are the means *significantly* different? To conduct a formal hypothesis test to answer this question, we will initially assume that the population of literacy program graduates has the same mean reading level as the rest of the inmates, that is, 7.5 years. How valid is this assumption given the fact that our sample value (9.3 years) is quite different from the presumed population mean of 7.5? Because we have only a *sample* of literacy program graduates, we can account for this apparent difference in one of two ways.

One explanation for the difference between our sample mean of 9.3 and the population mean of 7.5 years is that the population mean is not really 7.5 years. This means that our assumption about the value of the population mean is incorrect and that the true population mean for the literacy program graduates is actually different from 7.5. The implication of this is that literacy program graduates come from a different population with a different mean than nonprogram inmates. By this we mean that our sample did not come from the same population as all other incarcerated offenders but from another population, the population of literacy program graduates, which has a different mean.

Figures 8–2 and 8–3 illustrate this explanation by showing the distribution of reading levels for the two populations. In Figure 8–2 the curve on the left is the population of incarcerated offenders with a mean reading level of 7.5 years ($\mu = 7.5$). The one on the right is a different population with a higher population mean ($\mu = 10$). One explanation for the differences between our sample

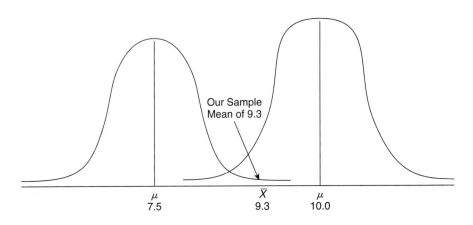

Figure 8–2   Two populations with different mean reading levels

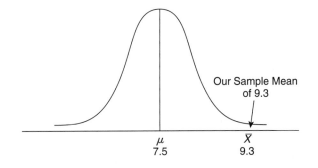

Figure 8–3   One population with mean 7.5 and the location of a sample from that population with a higher mean

mean (9.3) and what we have assumed as the true population mean (7.5) is that our sample was actually drawn from a different population. Perhaps our sample was drawn from the population on the right, where the population mean is 10 rather than 7.5. If this is true, our assumption that the population mean reading level for literacy program graduates is 7.5 years is not correct.

A second explanation for the difference between the presumed population mean (7.5 years) and the observed sample mean (9.3 years) is based on sampling variation—that the difference in means is due simply to the fact that we just happened to acquire a sample with a high mean, even though the true population mean is really equal to 7.5. Figure 8–3 illustrates this explanation. If we assume that this explanation is true, we conclude that the population mean for both program graduates of the literacy program and nongraduates is, in fact, 7.5 years. We then conclude that there is only one population and that that population has a mean reading level of 7.5 years. If this is true, our assumption that the population mean is 7.5 years is correct.

Well, you may wonder, "If the true population mean is 7.5, why is our sample mean different from this?" The second explanation is that the only reason the sample mean (9.3 years) is different from the presumed population mean (7.5) is that not every sample selected from a population will have a mean equal to that population's mean. Based on chance alone, we may sometimes select a sample that has a very different mean than the true population mean. It was just the "luck of the draw," so to speak. There always will be variation in the proximity of the many sample means to the true population mean. In other words, simple sampling variation can account for the difference between a sample mean and the mean of the population from which that sample was drawn.

Recall from our discussion of the **sampling distribution of the mean** in Chapter 7 that, if we take a very large or infinite number of samples of size n from a population whose mean is (μ), the individual sample means will differ from one another but the mean of the infinite number of sample means will still be (μ). Well, this supports our second explanation for the difference between the presumed population mean and the observed sample mean; we have selected one of those samples from the population in which the sample mean is quite different from the population mean. In this case, the sample we have was drawn from a population with a mean reading level of 7.5 years, but the sample mean just happens to be quite different from that (9.3 years). The reason they are different, then, is not because the means are actually different, but because of sampling variation—chance alone.

There is a standard deviation for the distribution of sample means, also called the **standard error of the mean.** A glance back at Figure 7–2 in Chapter 7 illustrates this fact. In that figure, confidence intervals were drawn around sample means taken from 20 different samples, all of which were different. In sum, it may be possible for a sample mean to be very different from a population mean and still have been drawn from the same population.

As you can perhaps imagine, the implications of the two explanations are quite different. In the first explanation, the implication is that there are two different populations with two different population means. In this scenario, our sample mean differs from the presumed population mean because the sample was drawn from an entirely different population. If this explanation is correct, we would conclude that the observed difference between the sample and population means is "statistically significant." In other words, it is a difference due to a difference in population means, and not chance factors, such as sampling variation. In drawing this conclusion, we would be saying that our initial assumption that the population mean is equal to 7.5 years was incorrect. In a word, we would *reject* this assumption.

If the second explanation is correct, however, the observed difference between our sample and population mean is more likely attributable to the fact that we just happened to pick a sample whose mean reading level was different from the population mean, but the sample still came from this same population. As such, there is really no significant difference between the sample mean and the population mean. In this case, the observed difference is not "statistically significant"—it is not due to a real difference between the two groups; it is just due to chance based on **sampling variation.** In drawing this conclusion, we have not rejected our initial assumption that the population mean is 7.5 years. Stated in statistical terms, we have *failed to reject* our initial assumption or hypothesis.

In sum, we have two possible and equally compelling explanations for the difference between our sample mean and population mean—two explanations with very different implications. Which explanation is correct? Unfortunately, because we have sample data, and not information from a population, we cannot know for certain which explanation is correct. Remember that we did not know what the population mean reading level was for literacy program graduates. Rather, we assumed that it was a given value and wondered how safe an assumption that was, given what we observed our sample mean to be. In cases such as these, where we cannot know for certain which explanation is correct, we set up a decision-making rule that will help us decide whether one of the explanations is more likely than the other. This decision rule also will tell us how confident we can be in determining which explanation is "more likely." The basis of this decision rule is the subject matter of **hypothesis testing.**

In making a hypothesis test about our two explanations, we begin by assuming that the second explanation is correct, that is, that the sample actually was drawn from the population in question. We are assuming, then, that the population mean is a particular value—in our example, that the mean reading level in the population is equal to 7.5 years. We have suggested to you that this assumption implies that the literacy program graduates come from the same population as the nonprogram inmates. In essence, we assume that the two groups come from the same population. We want to be very conservative in our decision making and not jump to any conclusion that the two groups are different. We proceed, then, by initially assuming that they are not different and see whether that assumption can be maintained given the sample information.

The assumption that there is one population with a mean of 7.5 years constitutes our **null hypothesis.** The word "null" implies that the entity considered is "of no consequence or value." We stated that the null hypothesis is the hypothesis of no difference. Our hypothesis that the population mean is 7.5 years is a null hypothesis because we are assuming that there is no "real" difference between the observed sample mean of 9.3 years and the population mean of 7.5 years. The difference is "null" or "of no consequence" because it is due simply to sampling variation or chance, not to any "real" difference between the sample and the population. The starting point of the process of hypothesis testing, then, is an assumption of no differences—a null hypothesis. In a hypothesis test, we determine whether this assumption is reasonable given the evidence we have from our sample data.

In Chapter 6 we made an analogy between the null hypothesis and the presumption of innocence in criminal proceedings. Just as a defendant is presumed to be innocent, a null hypothesis is presumed to be true. Similarly, just as the state must present considerable evidence ("beyond a reasonable doubt") to overcome this presumption of innocence and convince the jury to convict the defendant, the research scientist must present considerable evidence to overcome the presumption that the null hypothesis is not true. If there is enough evidence to suggest that the null hypothesis is probably not true, the scientist rejects it. Let us remind you, however, that both the jury and the scientist can make an error in rejecting their initial presumptions. The jury may convict an innocent person, and a researcher may reject a null hypothesis that happens to be true. However, the legal procedures of the criminal trial and the methodological and statistical rigor of science are there to keep this risk of error small.

In our research example, the null hypothesis is the hypothesis that the true population mean is equal to 7.5 years. It specifically refers to the fact that the sample mean and the population mean are not really different. So our assumption or null hypothesis is:

H_0: The population mean is equal to 7.5 years. The sample mean is not different from the population mean.

Since the null hypothesis is symbolized by a capital H with a subscript of zero (the zero symbolizes the null condition of no difference), there are actually two ways to symbolically state this:

$$H_0: \mu = 7.5 \text{ years.}$$

or

$$H_0: \overline{X} - \mu = 0$$

After stating this null hypothesis, we ask whether this assumption or hypothesis is true. What is the probability of getting the particular sample mean ($\overline{x}$) that we observe in our data? In other words, we want to know how likely it is that we would observe the value of our sample mean if the population mean is what we have assumed it to be. In our specific example, we want to determine the probability of selecting a sample with a mean reading level of 9.3 years from a population whose mean is 7.5. If the null hypothesis is true, we can determine the probability of observing the given value of our sample mean. Moreover, we can state in advance that, if this probability is very small (say 5 chances out of 100, which translates to an alpha level of .05 [$\alpha = .05$, or 1 chance out of 100, $\alpha = .01$]), we will conclude that the assumption behind the null hypothesis must be false. In other words, if it is very unlikely that we will observe the sample mean if the population mean is what we have presumed it to be under the null hypothesis, we will reject the null hypothesis.

This is exactly the procedure we used in Chapter 6 with our Lo-Jack example. Recall that we determined that the probability of having a stolen car returned 8 out of 10 times was very unlikely. Therefore, we rejected the assumption that the return rate of stolen cars with Lo-Jack would be the same as from the return rate of stolen cars without Lo-Jack. Forgive our repetition, but we again remind you that because we are asking questions about a sample, there is no way of knowing for sure whether the decision we make is the correct one. What we do know when we reject the null hypothesis is that the outcome (in this case, the sample mean) we have observed is so unlikely that "chances are" it came from a different population. The risk or chance that we are wrong is determined by the alpha level we set in our hypothesis test.

Although we have previously suggested that .05 and .01 are commonly selected levels of alpha, this is just conventional practice. There are at times compelling reasons why you may want to use a larger (.10) or much smaller alpha level (.001). Recall that in choosing a particular alpha level, we are selecting the risk we are willing to take in making a Type I error, that is, of rejecting a null hypothesis that is actually true. In this case, in rejecting a null hypothesis that is true, we are saying that the sample mean is significantly different from the population mean when, in fact, it is not.

Sometimes the cost of a Type I error may be very great and we may want to be very sure before we reject the null hypothesis. Suppose, for instance, that we know of a treatment program that successfully reduces a person's level of violence. This treatment, however, is expensive and we want to determine if a slightly cheaper treatment is just as effective. In this case, because we have a treatment program with proven success, we do not want to abandon it in favor of another program that is only marginally less expensive. In addition, reducing violence is more important than saving a little money, so we want to be very careful not to reject our null hypothesis of no difference between the two treatments if it is really true. Given these interests, we might want to set our alpha at a lower level than usual, say .001 instead of .05. If we do this, the probability that we will reject a null hypothesis that is really true will be only 1 out of 1,000, rather than 5 out of 100. Selecting a lower alpha level will make it more difficult for us to reject the assumption that the proven treatment program is no different from the less expensive program.

Case Study: Foot Patrols and Crime Rates

Consider a different research situation. As a police chief you have instituted a policy of foot patrols in a high crime area in an attempt to reduce crime. These foot patrols do not create any real added expense and, after a few months, residents in the affected neighborhoods report that they feel safer. After a year of trying foot patrols you request that some research be done on whether or not crime in these areas is significantly lower than it was without foot patrols. Because there have been many favorable by-products of these foot patrols (among them, that residents feel safer) and no increase in cost, you are more willing to risk a Type I error. In this situation, you might want to have a more generous level of alpha, such as .10. Just remember that the decision regarding what level of significance or alpha to use is one the researcher must make after very careful thought about the respective costs of making a Type I or Type II error. Unfortunately, there is no way you can minimize the cost of both errors simultaneously. As you reduce the risk of one error, you increase the risk of making the other (see Chapter 6 to refresh your memory if this makes no sense to you!).

There are a few remaining questions before we begin the nitty-gritty work of hypothesis testing with one sample mean. One concerns how we determine the likelihood of observing a particular sample mean ($\bar{X}$) given an observed population with mean (μ). How do we know whether a sample mean of 9.3 from a population with a mean of 7.5 is likely to occur or not? We can determine this likelihood or probability based on what we know about the theoretical sampling distribution of means, the central limit theorem, and the standard normal distribution (the z distribution). From the central limit theorem, we know that, with a large enough sample ($n \geq 100$), the sampling distribution of an infinite number of sample means from a population with mean μ and standard deviation σ will be normally distributed and have a mean of μ and standard deviation of $\sigma_{\bar{X}}(\sigma_{\bar{X}} = \sigma_{\bar{X}}/\sqrt{n})$. We also know that, if the sampling distribution of means is normally distributed with a known mean and standard deviation, we can convert our sample mean into a standard normal score called a z score. With our given sample mean expressed as a z score, we can then use our knowledge of the standard normal distribution (the z distribution) and determine the probability of observing a mean of this value given the known population mean. If this probability is very small, based on our selected alpha level, we will reject the null hypothesis. If the probability is greater than our selected alpha level, we must fail to reject the null hypothesis.

The only piece of information we lack now is how to translate our sample mean ($\bar{X}$) into a z score. We transformed a raw score into a z score in Chapter 6 with the following formula:

$$z = \frac{x - \bar{X}}{s} \qquad (8\text{--}1)$$

where

x = our raw score,

$\bar{X}$ = the mean for the sample, and

s = the sample standard deviation.

To transform our sample mean into a z score, all we need to do is modify slightly equation 8–1:

$$z = \frac{\bar{X} - \mu}{\sigma/\sqrt{n}} \qquad (8\text{--}2)$$

In this equation our raw score is replaced by the sample mean, the sample mean in formula 8–1 is replaced by the mean of the sampling distribution (which is μ, the population mean), and the standard deviation of the sample is replaced by the standard deviation of the sampling distribution of means (the standard error).

As you should guess by now, however, the population standard deviation rarely is known. If it is not known, and if our sample size is large ($n \geq$ 100), we can use the sample standard deviation (s) to estimate the population standard deviation (σ). As mentioned in the last chapter, however, the sample standard deviation is a biased estimate of the population standard deviation. As before, we correct for this bias by using the term $n - 1$ rather than n in the denominator of the standard error. Whenever σ is not known and the sample size is large, then, the estimate for the standard deviation of the sampling distribution becomes $s / \sqrt{n-1}$. The formula for the z **test** when the population standard deviation is not known and our sample size is large enough, then, becomes:

$$z_{obt} = \frac{\overline{X} - \mu}{s / \sqrt{n}}$$

(8–3)

We are now ready to conduct our hypothesis test with our hypothetical data about mean reading levels.

To refresh your memory, we have a sample of 100 graduates from a prison literacy program where the sample mean is 9.3 years. The population of incarcerated inmates[1] mean reading level is 7.5 years with a standard deviation of 2.2. We want to know if our sample comes from a population whose mean is 7.5.

Step 1. We begin our hypothesis test by stating the null and the research, or alternative, hypotheses:

H_0: The two means are equal ($\overline{X} = \mu$). We also could state this null hypothesis by giving the value of the population parameter ($\mu \neq 7.5$). Our hypothesis test seeks to determine whether the sample, whose mean we have observed, comes from this population.

H_1: The two means are not equal ($\overline{X} \neq \mu$; in our example, $\mu = 7.5$).

Notice that the alternative, or research, hypothesis (H_1) simply states that the two means are not equal. Remember that this is called a *nondirectional* (or two-tailed) *alternative hypothesis* because it does not state that the mean of the population from which the sample was drawn is greater than or less than the population mean referred to in the null hypothesis. It simply assumes that they are different. We have more to say about directional and nondirectional tests later in this chapter.

Step 2. The next step in hypothesis testing is to select an appropriate test statistic and obtain the sampling distribution for that statistic. Because the population standard deviation is known ($s = 2.2$), we can use the z score formula in equation 8–2. Accordingly, we use the standard normal distribution (z distribution) as our sampling distribution. By calculating the test statistic z with equation 8–2, what we are actually doing is obtaining a measurement of the distance in *standard error units* between the sample statistic (the sample mean, $\overline{X}$) and the hypothesized population parameter (the population mean, μ). If, for example, we obtained a z score of 1.5, this would indicate that our sample mean was 1.5 standard errors above the population mean (μ). An obtained z score of -2.3 would indicate that our sample mean was 2.3 standard errors below μ, and so on.

Step 3. The next step in formal hypothesis testing is to select a level of significance, termed our alpha level (α), and identify the critical region. Remember that the alpha level we set determines our risk of making a Type I error, that is, of rejecting a null hypothesis that is really true. Also remember that the selection of an alpha level is a judgment call. However, the alpha levels in criminology and most other social sciences are usually .05 and .01. Based on our selected level of alpha, we must then find the **critical value** of our test statistic, which we refer to as z_{crit}. This critical value determines the rejection region for our hypothesis test.

For the sake of illustration, let's opt for an alpha level of .05 ($\alpha = .05$). Because we are testing a nondirectional hypothesis, we have to divide our selected alpha level into two equal halves and place one half in each tail of the distribution (hence it is referred to as a two-tailed test). With an alpha level of .05, we are interested in identifying the z score that corresponds to $.05/2 = .025$ of the area at each tail of the normal curve. This .025 of the area at each tail of the normal distribution defines our *critical region*. The remaining area of the curve up to the mean is equal to $.50 - .025 = .4750$, so we need to find the z score that corresponds to .4750 of the curve. We find this from the z table in Table E–2 in Appendix E. Going into the body of the table until we find .4750, we can determine that the corresponding z score is 1.96. Because the normal curve is symmetrical, we do the same thing for the other tail of the distribution where the corresponding z score is -1.96. The critical value of z for a two-tailed test with an alpha level of .05, then, is ±1.96 ($z_{crit} = \pm1.96$). This means that, in order to reject the null hypothesis at the .05 level based on our sample data, the value of z we obtain from our test (z_{obt}) must fall either 1.96 standard errors or more above the population mean (μ) or below the population mean (μ). Stated another way, our decision rule is to reject the null hypothesis if $z_{obt} \leq -1.96$ or $z_{obt} \geq +1.96$, and to fail to reject the null hypothesis if $-1.96 < z_{obt} < 1.96$. For future reference, we have provided the most often used critical values of z in Table 8–1.

Now that we have our critical value of z, we can define the critical region in the sampling distribution. The **critical region** defines the area of the sampling distribution that contains all unlikely sample outcomes, based on the selected alpha level. We use the word "region" because the critical value of our test statistic defines the class of all obtained values that would lead us to reject the null hypothesis. For example, if we defined our critical value of z as ±1.96, one critical region would consist of all obtained z scores under -1.96. The second critical region would consist of all obtained z scores greater than $+1.96$. The critical value of z at ±1.96 and the corresponding rejection regions are illustrated for you in Figure 8–4.

TABLE 8–1

Alpha (α) Levels and Critical Values of z for One- and Two- Tailed Hypothesis Tests

Type of Hypothesis Test	Significance/ Alpha Level	Critical Area in Each Tail	Critical$_z$
Two-tailed	.10	.05	1.65
One-tailed	.10	.10	1.29
Two-tailed	.05	.025	1.96
One-tailed	.05	.05	1.65
Two-tailed	.01	.005	2.58
One-tailed	.01	.01	2.33
Two-tailed	.001	.0005	3.27
One-tiled	.001	.001	3.08

Because we selected an alpha level equal to .05 and are conducting a two-tailed hypothesis test, the critical region is equal to .025 (.05/2) of the area of the normal curve at each tail. You can see from Figure 8–4 that, if we obtained a z score of 2.3 from our statistical test, we would be able to reject the null hypothesis because our obtained value would fall inside the rejection region on the right tail of the z distribution. Similarly, if the value of z we obtained from our test was −2.3, we also would be able to reject the null hypothesis because this value would fall inside the rejection region on the left side of the distribution.

If you are getting a little lost (and even a bit hysterical), try to remain calm and continue through the entire example. The small pieces of the picture are often illuminated by observing the picture in its entirety. So let's move on with the remaining steps.

Step 4. Using the data we obtained from our sample, the fourth step is to calculate the obtained test statistic, in this case $z_{obt.}$ We have the sample size ($n = 100$), sample mean ($\bar{X} = 9.3$), and known population standard deviation ($s = 2.2$), so we can simply plug them into equation 8–3. The value of μ that is used in our calculations is always the value of μ we are testing in the null hypothesis; in this case it is 7.5. The calculation of the z_{obt} statistic is:

$$z_{obt} = \frac{\bar{X} - \mu}{s / \sqrt{n}}$$

$$= \frac{9.3 - 7.5}{2.2 / \sqrt{100}}$$

$$= \frac{1.8}{2.2 / 9.95}$$

$$= \frac{1.8}{.25}$$

$$z_{obt} = 7.2$$

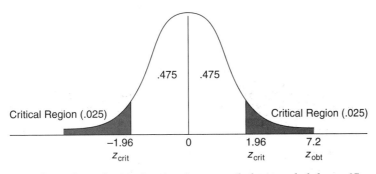

.475 .475

Critical Region (.025)   Critical Region (.025)

−1.96   0   1.96   7.2
z_{crit} z_{crit} z_{obt}

Figure 8–4 Critical z and critical region for two-tailed test and alpha $= .05$

Step 5. The obtained value of z, then, is 7.2. Using this value, the final step of our hypothesis testing enterprise involves making a decision about the validity of the null hypothesis based on the results of our statistical test. We do this by comparing our critical value of z ($z_{crit} = \pm 1.96$) with the value we obtain from our statistical test ($z_{obt} = 7.2$). We see that the obtained z value of 7.2 is greater than 1.96. In fact, it falls well into the critical region, over 7 standard error units above the hypothesized μ. This outcome is highly unlikely if the null hypothesis is really true. Because $z_{obt} > 1.96$, we will reject the null hypothesis that the population mean is equal to 7.5. We will conclude instead that the sample of literacy program graduates comes from a population where the mean reading level is not equal to 7.5 years. In fact, based on our sample statistic ($\bar{X}$), we also can infer that our sample comes from a population where the mean reading level is greater than 7.5 years. Stated differently, we can be 95 percent confident that the mean reading level of inmates who graduate from the literacy program is higher than the mean reading level of inmates who do not graduate from the program.

Case Study: Testing the Mean Sentence Length for Robbery

Let's work through another example. Suppose we are interested in the mean sentence length given to convicted armed robbers in a given state after the passage of a new firearms law. This new legislation provides for an automatic three-year additional prison term for those convicted offenders sentenced for a felony in which a gun was used during the commission of a crime. We know that the mean sentence length given to convicted armed robbers in the three years before the new legislation was passed was 52.5 months. This is our population mean (μ). We take a random sample of 110 armed robbers who were convicted under the new law and sentenced to prison. The mean sentence length given to these 110 offenders was 53.2 months, with a standard deviation of 6. The information we know, then, is as follows:

Population Parameters for Armed Robberies Before New Legislation	Sample Statistics for Armed Robberies After Legislation
$\mu = 52.5$	$\bar{X} = 53.2$
$\sigma = $ Unknown	$s = 6$
	$n = 110$

We want to know if this sample mean is significantly different from the known population mean. Of course, we know that it is different, but is it *significantly* different? To find out, we must conduct a hypothesis test. Again, let's state each step along the way.

Step 1. The first step is to state our null and research hypotheses. Our null hypothesis in this example is that the mean sentence length for our sample of armed robbers sentenced under the new law is the same as the mean sentence length for the population of previously sentenced armed robbers. Formally, the null hypothesis is that our sample is drawn from a population with a mean of 52.5 months:

$$H_0\text{: } \mu = 52.2$$

For our research hypothesis, we will state the nondirectional alternative that the population from which our sample was drawn has a mean that is not equal to 52.5. We are not stating direction in this research hypothesis because we do not know for sure whether the mean sentence length under the new law will be more than or less than the previous mean sentence. We are hesitant to predict direction because other things are working to affect the mean sentence length of armed robbers in addition to the new legislation. For example, the state may be experiencing tremendous prison overcrowding and judges might be responding to this by decreasing the average prison sentence they impose in all cases. In addition, judges might not like the fact that the state legislators are "meddling" in their sentencing domain. They might respond to the automatic three-year addition to a sentence length by taking three years off the sentence they normally would have imposed. Because of these countervailing effects, the only alternative hypothesis we feel comfortable in asserting is that the mean sentence length for newly convicted armed robbers is not 52.5.

$$H_1\text{: } \mu \neq 52.5$$

Step 2. Step 2 requires that we select our test statistic and the sampling distribution of that statistic. In this example, our test statistic is the z test and the sampling distribution is the standard normal (z) distribution. The population standard deviation (σ) is not known, so we will use Equation 8–3.

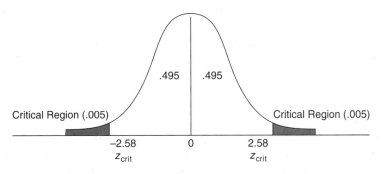

Figure 8–5 Critical z and critical region for two-tailed test and alpha = .01

$$z_{obt} = \frac{\overline{X} - \mu}{s / \sqrt{n}}$$

Step 3. Our third step in hypothesis testing is to select a level of significance (alpha level, α) and determine the critical value and critical region(s) of our test statistic. We select a .01 alpha level for this example. As we have stated, for a nondirectional research hypothesis, we place one-half of our selected alpha level (.01/2 = .005) in each tail of the z distribution. This area comprises our critical region, and it is marked for you in Figure 8–5.

Referring back to Table 8–1, the z score corresponding to this alpha level using a nondirectional (two-tailed) test is 2.58. This is the critical value of our z (z_{crit}), and the critical region is any z score less than or equal to −2.58 or greater than or equal to +2.58. Any obtained z score that falls into the critical region will lead us to reject the null hypothesis. Thus, our decision rule is to reject the null hypothesis if either $z_{obt} \leq -2.58$ or $z_{obt} \geq +2.58$, or to fail to reject the null hypothesis if $-2.58 < z_{obt} < 2.58$.

Step 4. Now that we have our critical value of z ($z_{crit} = \pm 2.58$), we need to compute our test statistic (z_{obt}). Using equation 8–3, we can transform our sample mean into a z score as follows:

$$z_{obt} = \frac{\overline{X} - \mu}{s / \sqrt{n}}$$

$$= \frac{53.2 - 52.5}{6 / \sqrt{110}}$$

$$= \frac{.7}{6 / 10.49}$$

$$= \frac{.7}{.57}$$

$$z_{obt} = 1.23$$

Step 5. With our sample data, we have an obtained z score of 1.23. Using this obtained value of z, our fifth and final step is to make a decision about our null hypothesis. Because our obtained z score of 1.23 is less than our critical z score of 2.58 ($z_{obt} < z_{crit}$), we must fail to reject the null hypothesis and conclude that the sample mean does, in fact, come from a population where the mean sentence length is 52.5 months. Thus, it appears that the sentencing enhancement (an additional 3 years) stipulated by the new law has not significantly increased the length of sentences for those convicted of armed robbery compared to the population mean sentence length before the law was enacted. Remember, it is not only necessary to make a decision about your null hypothesis, but it is equally important to interpret this decision based on the data and research issues you are working with.

DIRECTIONAL AND NONDIRECTIONAL HYPOTHESIS TESTS

The choice between a directional or a nondirectional hypothesis test depends on the researcher's beliefs about the population from which the sample is being drawn. **Directional hypothesis tests** are referred to as "one-tailed" statistical tests, and **nondirectional hypothesis tests** are called "two-tailed" statistical tests. In our one sample mean problem above, the null hypothesis stated that the sample came from a population with a known mean (μ). In general, the research hypothesis always states our beliefs about what we think to be the "truth." This truth has three possibilities:

1. The sample was drawn from a population with a different mean,
2. The sample was drawn from a population with a higher mean,
3. The sample was drawn from a population with a lower mean.

Notice that the last two of these possibilities are subsets of the first. The first possibility simply states a difference, but the latter two state a more specific direction of difference.

The first possibility is a nondirectonal hypothesis. As we have seen, nondirectional hypotheses are tested by a **two-tailed hypothesis test.** The second two possibilities are variations of a directional research hypothesis. Directional hypotheses are tested with **one-tailed hypothesis tests.**

In each of the preceding examples, the research hypothesis has been stated as a nondirectional alternative. In both cases, although we did not think that our sample came from the null hypothesis population, we did not know whether the population from which the sample was drawn had a mean higher or lower than that stated in the null hypothesis. For example, in the most recent example, the population of convicted armed robbers from which we drew our sample may have had a mean sentence length higher

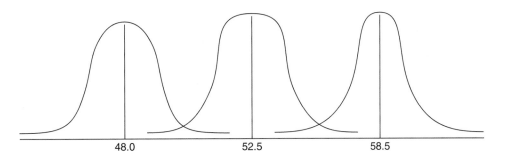

48.0   52.5   58.5

Figure 8–6   Three populations of convicted armed robbers with different mean sentence lengths

than 52.5, or it may have had a mean sentence lower than that. These two possibilities are shown in Figure 8–6. You can perhaps see from this figure why we are interested in both tails of a sampling distribution when we have a nondirectional research hypothesis—we have to cover both possibilities.

Unlike this scenario, directional research hypotheses state a more precise relationship between the sample and null hypothesis parameter (in this case, population mean). When we use directional hypotheses, we believe not only that the sample and population means are different, but also that we can define the exact direction of that difference. For example, in the same example, if we were more firm in our belief that the effect of the firearm law was to increase the prison terms of those convicted of a felony involving a weapon, we could have stated our alternative hypothesis more specifically as H_1: $\mu > 52.5$. This is a directional hypothesis because we are specifically stating what type of difference the population mean has from our sample mean. In this case, we are saying that our sample was drawn from a population whose mean is greater than the population mean expressed in the null hypothesis. This is illustrated for you in Figure 8–7, which shows two curves. The curve on the left is the curve for the population defined by the null hypothesis with a mean of 52.5. The curve on the right is the population defined by the directional alternative hypothesis (H_1: $\mu > 52.5$). In this population, the mean is hypothesized to be greater than that for the population of the null hypothesis. Had our directional research hypothesis stated that the sample mean came from a population whose mean was less than 52.5 (H_1: $\mu < 52.5$), our two curves would look like those in Figure 8–8. Thus, when stating a directional alternative or research hypothesis, we are stating a direction in which, we believe, lies the population from which our sample was drawn, either above (Figure 8–7) or below (Figure 8–8) the mean specified by the null hypothesis.

You may be wondering what possible difference it makes if we make our research hypothesis nondirectional or directional. If you can, it is to

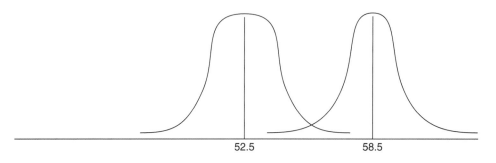

Figure 8–7   Two populations of convicted armed robbers, one with mean = 52.5 and one with mean = 58.5

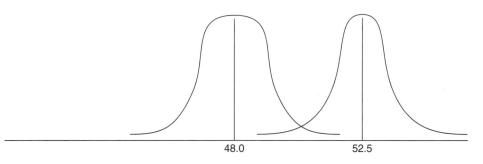

Figure 8–8   Two populations of convicted armed robbers, one with mean = 48.0 and one with mean = 52.5

your advantage as a researcher to specify a direction for your research hypothesis. This does not mean that in the absence of prior knowledge you should always make a directional research hypothesis—only that if you can, it is to your advantage to do so. Like most answers, however, this one is not very satisfactory because it only leads to another question. "Why is testing a directional rather than a nondirectional hypothesis to my advantage?" Well, let's think about this for a minute.

When we state a nondirectional research hypothesis, we hypothesize that our sample was drawn from a population with a mean that is different from that specified in the null hypothesis. We do not know, then, whether our real population mean is larger or smaller than that found in the null hypothesis. These two possibilities, and the null hypothesis, are illustrated in Figure 8–6. As you can see, in the nondirectional case we are interested in both tails of the distribution for the null hypothesis. That is why we divide our alpha level into two equal halves and place one-half in the right tail and one-half in the left tail of the distribution. Notice that, when we divide our alpha level in half, we are cutting the area of the critical region in the tail of the sampling distribution in half. Instead of .05 of the area of the curve in one tail, we have .025 (.05/2) of the area in both tails. Because we are interested in a smaller area of the curve, the effect of this is to push the critical region further out into the tail of the distribution. As you can see, it is not that our critical region is smaller in the two-tailed (nondirectional) research hypothesis; our critical area (alpha level) is still .05 of the curve. The important point is that this total area is now divided into two equal halves.

When we state a directional research hypothesis, however, we make the much more specific statement that we believe that the true population mean is higher (or lower) than that specified in the null hypothesis. Examples of a directional research hypothesis are shown in Figures 8–7 and 8–8. In these directional hypotheses we are interested in only one tail. Figure 8–7 illustrates the case when we hypothesize that the sample comes from a population with a higher mean than that specified in the null hypothesis. Because we suspect a higher population mean, our attention is directed at the right tail. Figure 8–8 illustrates the case when we hypothesize that the sample comes from a population with a lower mean than that stated in the null hypothesis. Both instances are examples of one-tailed hypothesis tests. Unlike the case with the nondirectional hypothesis, we do not have to divide our alpha level into two parts. In the one-tailed case, all of our alpha level is in one tail of the distribution.

When using a two-tailed hypothesis test, then, we are pushed out further into the tail of the distribution. Therefore, in order to reject the null hypothesis, our obtained z must be greater compared to a directional (one-tailed) alternative hypothesis at the same alpha level. Figures 8–9 and 8–10 illustrate this point.

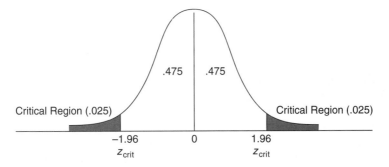

Figure 8–9 Critical z and critical region for two-tailed test and alpha = .05

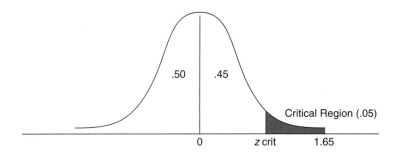

Figure 8–10   Critical z and critical region for one-tailed test and alpha = .05

In Figure 8–9 we show the critical region for a two-tailed hypothesis test with an alpha of .05. Each critical region is equal to .025 of the area under the normal curve, and the critical value of z is ±1.96. Thus, to reject the null hypothesis, we would need to obtain a z score under −1.96 or above +1.96. This two-tailed hypothesis test would correspond to the situation in Figure 8–6. In Figure 8–10 we have a one-tailed hypothesis test at the same alpha level (α = .05). In this test all .05 of our critical region is in one tail of the sampling distribution. You can see that the critical region in the right tail of Figure 8–10 is much larger than that in Figure 8–9; in fact, it is twice as large. Because we do not have to go so far out into the right tail, our critical value of z is only 1.65 in comparison to the 1.96 z value for the nondirectional two-tailed test in Figure 8–9.

As you can see, then, at any given level of alpha, we will need a smaller z_{obt} to reject the null hypothesis in the one-tailed (directional) hypothesis test. Now you can see that it is to your advantage to specify a directional alternative hypothesis *if you can.*

The critical z values reported in Table 8–1 clearly reveal that at each level of alpha, you will need a smaller value of z_{obt} to reject the null hypothesis using a one-tailed versus a two-tailed test. Remember, though, that no matter which type of test you are conducting, directional or nondirectional, the steps necessary to conduct a hypothesis test remain the same. Let's go through an example.

Case Study: Mean Socialization Levels of Offenders

Some criminologists and psychologists have long contended that there are important and stable personality differences between criminal offenders and the nonoffending "normal" population. One of these supposed personality differences is psychopathology—the degree to which persons feel antisocial or lack any regard for the feelings of others. A frequently used psychological test that has been assumed to measure the trait of psychopathology is the socialization (SO) scale of the California Psychological Inventory.[1] The SO scale measures such things as one's ability to form close social relationships, the extent to which one is concerned with the rights and feelings of others, and a tendency for deliberately planned rather than impulsive behavior. As a measure of healthy socialization, then, we would expect that adult criminal offenders would score lower on the SO scale than nonoffenders. When the scale was first designed, Megargee (1972) reported a mean SO scale score of 35.99 for a large group of working class male adults. We will take this as our population value. Let's suppose that we collected a sample of 177 male prison inmates in California with a mean SO scale score of 27.76 and a standard deviation of 6.03. We want to know if our sample of California prison inmates comes from the population with a mean of 35.99. Because we expect the mean for the prisoners to be less than that for the nonincarcerated population, we can state a directional research hypothesis. We now explicitly go through our formal hypothesis test.

Step 1. Our null and research hypotheses are as follows:

$$H_0: \mu = 35.99$$

$$H_1: \mu < 35.99$$

Remember that the null hypothesis is always the same, regardless of making a directional or nondirectional alternative/research hypothesis. In the directional research hypothesis, we are specifically stating that the true population mean is less than 35.99, so we will conduct a one-tailed test.

Step 2. Our test statistic will be the z statistic, and our sampling distribution will be the standard normal distribution (z distribution).

Step 3. We will select .01 as our alpha level. The critical value of z for $\alpha = .01$ with a one-tailed test in this direction is -2.33 ($z_{crit} = -2.33$). The critical value of z is negative because in our research hypothesis, we have predicted that the true population mean is less than the mean expressed in the null hypothesis. We are, therefore, interested in the left tail of the sampling distribution. If it helps, think of the numerator of formula 8–3. When the sample mean is less than the hypothesized population mean (μ), the numerator value will be negative. If you are making a directional hypothesis test stating this difference ($\bar{X} < \mu$), the critical value of your test statistic also should be negative. For this example, then, the critical region will consist of all z_{obt} scores less than or equal to -2.33. Our decision rule, therefore, is to reject H_0 if $z_{obt} \leq -2.33$.

Step 4. The value of z_{obt} is:

$$z_{obt} = \frac{\bar{X} - \mu}{s / \sqrt{n}}$$

$$= \frac{27.76 - 35.99}{6.03 / \sqrt{177}}$$

$$= \frac{-8.23}{6.03 / 13.30}$$

$$= \frac{-8.23}{.45}$$

$$z_{obt} = -18.29$$

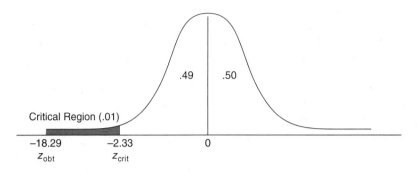

Figure 8–11   Critical z and critical region for one-tailed test and alpha = .01

Step 5. Because the obtained value of z falls inside the rejection region ($z_{obt} < z_{crit}$) and because we are dealing with a negative critical value, we would reject the null hypothesis. If this is confusing, simply remember that the absolute value of the obtained z must be larger than the critical value of z if we are to reject the null hypothesis. This is illustrated for you in Figure 8–11. We would therefore conclude that the population of incarcerated offenders has a mean SO scale score that is less than 35.99. Based on this test, then, we also can conclude that incarcerated offenders demonstrate greater psychopathology than nonoffenders.

Because hypothesis testing involves probabilities and not certainties, let us acknowledge yet again that there is some known risk of error in rejecting the null hypothesis. Our alpha level of .01 serves notice that, in the long run, there is 1 chance in 100, or a 1 percent chance, that we could have observed a sample mean of 27.76, even if the true population mean was 35.99. Because the probability of that occurring is very small, however, we have opted to reject the null hypothesis. Nevertheless, there is no way of knowing for sure whether we are correct. Keep in mind that the risk of rejecting a true null hypothesis is always present and is equal to alpha.

HYPOTHESIS TESTING FOR POPULATION MEANS USING SMALL SAMPLES

In the previous section we discussed hypothesis testing about one sample mean when our sample size was large enough that we could use the sample standard deviation (s) to estimate the standard error and proceed with the z score as our test statistic. When we have small samples ($n < 100$), however, the sample standard deviation is a more biased estimate of σ and we cannot take advantage of the Central Limit Theorem and employ the standard normal distribution as our sampling distribution. As with the differences we observed between calculating confidence intervals when we have large and small samples, the techniques we use when testing a hypothesis about a population mean also are a little different when we are utilizing a small sample. With small samples, the appropriate test statistic is the *t* **test** we used in Chapter 7 with confidence intervals. Our sampling distribution, then, is the Student's *t* distribution.

As we discussed in Chapter 7, the *t* distribution is somewhat different from the *z* distribution. The *t* distribution is flatter than the *z* distribution, and it is much flatter when the sample size is small. This means that the critical value of *t* at a given alpha level will be greater than the comparable critical value of *z* and can be much greater when *n* is small. As an example, you know that the critical value of *z* for a one-tailed test at $\alpha = .05$ is 1.65. Let's take the same alpha level and find the critical value of *t* with an *n* of 10. As before, to find the critical value of *t*, go to the table of *t* values in Table E–3 of Appendix E. First locate the appropriate alpha (significance) level and type of test (one- or two-tailed) at the top of the table. Then determine the correct degrees of freedom (df), where df is equal to $n - 1$. With a sample size of 10, therefore, we have 9 degrees of freedom. Keep in mind that, unlike the *z* table, the numbers in the body of the *t* table correspond to critical values of *t*, not to areas under the curve. We can see from the table that the critical value of *t* for a one-tailed test and an alpha of .05 with 9 degrees of freedom is 1.833. This is greater than the critical value of *z* at the same alpha level (1.65).

As an exercise, stay in the same column of *t* and move down the page. Notice what happens when the size of the sample increases. The size of critical *t* decreases. At a sample size of 121 (120 df) the critical value of *t* (1.658) is almost the same as the critical value of *z* (1.65). Therefore, you can see that, as the sample size increases, the more the *t* distribution approximates the shape of the *z* distribution. When our sample size has reached about 100, the two distributions are virtually identical.

The formula for the *t* test used to conduct a hypothesis test about a population mean using small samples is identical to the formula used for the *z* test when the population standard deviation is unknown:

$$t_{obt} = \frac{\overline{X} - \mu}{s / \sqrt{n}} \tag{8–4}$$

The steps involved in conducting a hypothesis test with *t* are the same as in the previous section with the *z* test. We first state the null and research hypotheses. We determine our test statistic and sampling distribution. We select an alpha level and, based on this, we determine the critical value of our test statistic (t_{crit}) and the critical region of our sampling distribution. We calculate our test statistic (t_{obt}) and compare it to the critical value. Finally, we make a decision about our null hypothesis and interpret this decision in a way that is meaningful to the research question at hand. The main difference between hypothesis testing using the *t* test and hypothesis testing using the *z* test lies in these statistics' respective sampling distributions and, consequently, the critical values and rejection regions for a given level of alpha. Let's go through an example.

Case Study: Deadbeat Dads

On July 31, 2002, the U.S. Marshals Service, along with state and local police, arrested 63 fathers in a national crackdown on people who have chronically failed to pay child support. Sixty-three men, including a former pro football player, were arrested in 23 states, the District of Columbia, and Puerto Rico. Each had been indicted already or had a pending criminal complaint for failure to pay court-ordered support, and each man faced a maximum of two years in jail, plus restitution of the money owed. The average (mean) amount owed by each individual was $75,200. All arrested individuals had a demonstrated ability to meet their financial responsibilities but had not done so; many had not made payments for several years.[2] For the sake of example, let's assume that we obtain a sample of 14 individuals who were delinquent in making child support payments from one state and calculate the mean delinquent amount to be equal to $71,500, with a standard deviation of $3,900. The information we have, then, is:

National Sample of Arrested Delinquent in Child Support	Sample of 14 Delinquent in Child Support in State A
$\mu = \$75{,}200$	$\bar{X} = \$71{,}500$
	$s = \$3{,}900$
	$n = 14$

Step 1. With these data we want to test the null hypothesis that the population mean dollar amount per individual delinquent in child support is equal to $75,200. Our research hypothesis states that μ is not equal to $75,200. Since we are not stating the direction of this difference, our alternative hypothesis is nondirectional. Formally, both hypotheses would be stated like this:

$$H_0: \mu = \$72{,}500$$
$$H_1: \mu \neq \$72{,}500$$

Step 2. Because we have a small sample, the t statistic and the sampling distribution of the t will be used to perform the hypothesis test.

Step 3. We decide to adopt an alpha level of .01 to test the null hypothesis. The next step is to find the critical value of t and to map out our rejection region. We know that we are conducting a nondirectional test using $\alpha = .01$, but we also need to calculate how many degrees of freedom we have in our sample. Remember that this is equal to $n - 1$ $(14 - 1)$, which gives us 13 degrees of freedom. From Table E–3 of Appendix E we find that for a two-tailed test with an alpha of .01 and 13 degrees of freedom, our critical value of t is 3.012. Recall that when doing a nondirectional test we are interested in both tails of our sampling distribution. In a nondirectional test, then, the critical value corresponds to both positive and negative values. Our critical value of t, therefore, is $t_{crit} = \pm 3.012$. Our decision rule will be to reject the null hypothesis if t_{obt} is less than or equal to -3.012 or greater than or equal to $+3.012$. Stated differently, we must fail to reject the null hypothesis if $3.012 < t_{obt} < 3.012$.

Step 4. We are now ready to compute our test statistic:

$$t_{obt} = \frac{\overline{X} - \mu}{s / \sqrt{n}}$$

$$= \frac{71,500 - 75,200}{3,900 / \sqrt{14}}$$

$$= \frac{-3700}{3,900 / 3.74}$$

$$= \frac{-3,700}{1,042.78}$$

$$t_{obt} = -3.5$$

Step 5. The value of t we obtain from our statistical test is -3.5. Figure 8–12 shows the obtained value of t relative to the critical regions of the sampling distribution. Because our obtained test statistic falls into the critical region on the left side of the sampling distribution (the negative end), we must reject the null hypothesis that individuals who are delinquent in their child support payments in this state come from a population with a mean equal to $75,200. It appears that there is a significant difference between our sample mean and the population mean. In fact, the average dollar amount that individuals from this state are delinquent in child support appears to be lower than the national average.

Let's go through another quick example. You should have the steps down fairly well now so we will not go into as much detail, but make a mental note as we cross off each step accordingly. The Federal Bureau of Investigation (FBI) has reported that the average number of law enforcement officers per

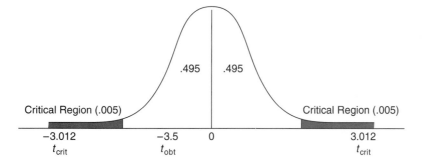

Figure 8–12 Critical t and critical region for two-tailed test and alpha = .01

1,000 inhabitants was generally around 3.3 in 2000. That is, there were an average of 3.3 police officers for every 1,000 inhabitants in cities and townships. Let's suppose that we represent a group of small town mayors who want to challenge this figure to demonstrate that rural towns have a lower number of officers to serve their population compared to the U.S. as a whole. To investigate this, we collect information about the number of sworn officers from a sample of nine rural communities ($n = 9$). From this sample of rural police departments, we find that the average number of police officers per 1,000 inhabitants is 2.9, with a standard deviation of .8.

To determine if this mean is significantly different from the population mean, we must conduct a hypothesis test. The null and research hypotheses are stated below:

$$H_0: \mu = 3.3$$

$$H_1: \mu < 3.3$$

For this test, we decide that an alpha level of .05 is sufficient. Because we are stating a directional research hypothesis, we will be conducting a one-tailed test. Given this information, along with our sample statistics, we define our critical value of t to be equal to -1.86 (df = 8, α = .05, one-tailed test). Our critical value of t is -1.86 because in our research hypothesis we have specifically hypothesized that the sample comes from a population with a lower mean than that expressed in the null hypothesis. Stated differently, we are predicting that the population mean will be less than 3.3 in the research hypothesis and, if this is correct, we should obtain a negative value of t. If t_{obt} is positive, we will fail to reject the null hypothesis even if it is greater than the absolute value of t_{crit} because it is in the wrong direction. Next we calculate the test statistic as:

$$t_{obt} = \frac{2.9 - 3.3}{.8 / \sqrt{9}}$$

$$= \frac{-.04}{.8 / 2.3}$$

$$= \frac{-.04}{.27}$$

$$t_{obt} = -.15$$

We are, therefore, only interested in the left tail of the t distribution and in negative values of t_{obt}. The obtained t value of $-.15$ does not fall within our stated rejection region. In Figure 8–13 we illustrate the critical value of t and the rejection region relative to the value of t that we obtained in our test. We must therefore fail to reject the null hypothesis and conclude that the mean number of law enforcement officers per capita in rural areas is not significantly different from the population mean number of police officers per capita for the U.S. as a whole. Contrary to the mayors' contention, then, there is not statistical evidence to conclude that rural communities have lower levels of police protection per capita than other areas of the country.

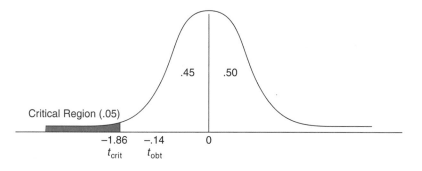

Figure 8–13 Critical *t* and critical region for one-tailed test and alpha = .05

So far, we have talked about hypothesis tests for population means only. We have conducted hypothesis tests for a population mean μ using data from both large samples (*z* test) and small samples (*t* test). Before we move on to hypothesis tests for proportions, let us summarize the types of tests that we can use when conducting hypothesis tests about a single population mean (μ). The three combinations of hypothesis tests that can be conducted when making an inference from a sample to the population about μ are summarized in the box on the next page.

HYPOTHESIS TESTING FOR POPULATION PROPORTIONS AND PERCENTS USING LARGE SAMPLES

Very frequently we find that our data cannot be measured at the interval or ratio level, and so we are unable to calculate a mean. Data of this type include such things as the percentage of the American public that supports the death penalty or owns firearms, the proportion of arrested defendants who test positively for drugs, and the proportion of arrested defendants who plead guilty in exchange for a lesser charge. Even though we have percent and proportion data, we still may be interested in the kind of problem we have been examining thus far in the chapter, namely, testing the difference between a sample statistic and a population parameter. What we want to know now is whether any observed difference between a sample proportion and population parameter is "significantly different" or whether this difference is due simply to chance or to sampling variation.

The general procedures used to conduct hypothesis tests about a single population proportion are almost identical to those used for a population mean, so we will not reiterate them here. As in the last chapter, we use $\hat{p}$ to denote the proportion obtained from our sample data and p to denote the population proportion. In this chapter, we focus exclusively on tests used for proportions obtained from large samples. With large samples, we can use our familiar *z* test. The general rule regarding sample size in tests of proportions is that the normal approximation (standard normal, or *z* distribution) can be used when both $n(\hat{p}) \geq 5$ and $n(\hat{p} - 1) \geq 5$. For example, if $\hat{p} = .5$, we would need a sample size of at least 10 to conduct a *z* test, because $10(.5) \geq 5$. If $\hat{p} = .10$, we would need a sample size of at least 50 [$50(.10) \geq 5$].

Formal Statements of the Null and Research/Alternative Hypotheses for Both Nondirectional (Two-Tailed) and Directional (One-Tailed) Tests with a Hypothetical Population Mean of 5

Nondirectional hypotheses for a population mean:

$$H_0: \mu = 5$$
$$H_1: \mu \neq 5$$

Directional hypotheses for a larger population mean:

$$H_0: \mu = 5$$
$$H_1: \mu > 5$$

Directional hypotheses for a smaller population mean:

$$H_0: \mu = 5$$
$$H_1: \mu < 5$$

To perform a hypothesis test about a population proportion using large samples, we again use the z test as our test statistic and the z distribution as our sampling distribution. If you are wondering why we are able to use the z or standard normal distribution with proportion data that clearly are not normally distributed, recall the central limit theorem from Chapter 6. This theorem states that, no matter what the shape of the population distribution, the sampling distribution of repeated random samples of size n will become normally distributed as n becomes large. Recall that we also used the z distribution when we estimated population proportions by calculating confidence intervals around sample proportions. The formula used to conduct a z test for proportions is comparable to the formula for hypothesis tests with a mean:

$$z = \frac{\hat{p} - p}{\sigma_{\hat{p}}}$$

(8–5)

where

$$\sigma_{\hat{p}} = \sqrt{\frac{p(q)}{n}} \, ,$$

$\hat{p}$ = the sample proportion,

p = the population proportion, and

$q = 1 - p$

The numerator of this formula simply is the difference between the sample and the population proportion. This represents the distance between the sample statistic and the hypothesized population parameter. The denominator $\left(\sqrt{pq/n} \right)$ is an estimate of the standard deviation of the sampling distribution. Remember that this standard deviation is also called the **standard error of the proportion,** which should be very familiar to you by now.

Case Study: Attitudes toward Gun Control

Let's go through the procedures involved in conducting a hypothesis test for a population proportion. Annually, the Gallup Polling Organization includes in one of its polls this question, "Do you think there should or should not be a law that would ban the possession of handguns except by the police and other authorized persons?" The proportion of the total population who believed there *should* be such a law during the early part of the 21st century was approximately 43 percent. This will be used as the population parameter in this exercise. Let's say we believe that attitudes regarding a law like this vary significantly by community. For example, we believe that individuals residing in communities like Littleton, Colorado, who have experienced traumatic mass murders (e.g., the Littleton High School mass murder), will be much more likely on average to favor such a law.

Step 1. To test our hypothesis, we collect a random sample of 107 individuals from communities that have experienced some form of mass murder (e.g., in a place of business or high school). As all good researchers do, we formally state our hypotheses (a directional or one-tailed research hypothesis) before conducting the statistical test:

$$H_0: p = .43$$

$$H_1: p > .43$$

Step 2. Since we have an appropriately large number in our sample, the z test along with the corresponding z sampling distribution will be used to conduct our test.

Step 3. We next specify the level of alpha at .05 and determine the critical region. The critical value of z with $\alpha = .05$ using a directional hypothesis is equal to 1.65 (see Table 8–1). The critical value is positive in this case because we believe the proportion of residents who live in a community that has experienced a firearm-related trauma will be much more likely to favor a gun control law. As such, we believe the population proportion for these residents will be greater than the null hypothesis proportion (making the obtained z score positive). We will reject the null hypothesis, then, if $z_{obt} \geq 1.65$.

Step 4. The results of our sample indicate that 66 of the 107 individuals from our sample believe that there should be a law banning the possession of handguns except by the police and other authorized persons. Remember, to obtain the proportion, we simply divide the frequency of interest, in this case those in favor of the law, by the total number in the sample ($f/n = 66/107$), which gives us a sample proportion of $\hat{p} = .62$. With this information, we calculate the obtained test statistic of z:

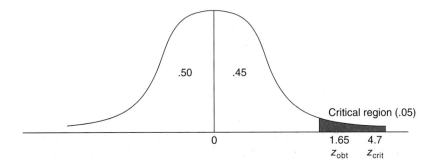

Figure 8–14   Critical z and critical region for one-tailed test and alpha $= .05$

$$z_{obt} = \frac{\hat{p} - p}{\sqrt{\dfrac{p(1-p)}{n}}}$$

$$= \frac{.62 - .43}{\sqrt{\dfrac{.43(1 - .43)}{107}}}$$

$$= \frac{.19}{\sqrt{\dfrac{.48(.52)}{107}}}$$

$$= \frac{.19}{\sqrt{\dfrac{.24}{107}}} = \frac{.19}{\sqrt{.002}} = \frac{.19}{.04}$$

$$z_{obt} = 4.7$$

The value of z we obtain from our statistical test indicates, just as all z scores do, that if the null hypothesis were true, the sample proportion $\hat{p} = .61$ would fall about 4.7 standard errors above the hypothesized population proportion p of .43. Since this value is greater than the critical value needed, it does fall within our rejection region. The obtained value of z relative to the critical value of z is displayed for you in Figure 8–14. Because $z_{obt} > z_{crit}$, we can reject the null hypothesis and conclude that the true proportion of residents who have experienced gun trauma and who favor such a ban on handguns is significantly greater than .43. We can state this in terms of percentages by simply multiplying the proportions by 100. Based on our hypothesis test, then, we can conclude that the percentage of residents who favor a ban on handguns and who reside in communities that have experienced a mass murder probably falls closer to 62 percent.

Case Study: Random Drug Testing of Inmates

Let's work through another example, this time using percents. Imagine that you passed your statistics course with flying colors, got your degree, and are now the research specialist for a municipal jail. During the course of your duties, you notice that in a random drug test of 100 new pretrial detainees, 36 percent tested positive for some form of cocaine. You begin to wonder whether perhaps the population of pretrial detainees contains a higher than normal percentage of cocaine users. You do a little background research and discover that, according to the National Institute on Drug Abuse, approximately 19 percent of young adults (age 18–25) have used cocaine at some time in their life (Akers, 1992: 50). You decide to test the hypothesis that the percent of cocaine use among pretrial detainees is significantly higher than the 19 percent found in the general population.

You have the following information:

Population	Sample
$p = .19$	$\hat{p} = .36$
	$n = 100$

With your well-honed statistical skills you identify this as a call for a hypothesis test of a one-sample proportion and go through each step in order.

Step 1. You state the null and research hypotheses:

$$H_0: p = .19, \text{ or } 19\%$$

$$H_1: p > .19, \text{ or } 19\%$$

As you suspect that the sample of pretrial detainees comes from a population where the percent of cocaine use is greater than 19 percent, you state a directional research hypothesis.

Step 2. Because you have a large sample ($n = 100$), you select the z test for proportions as your statistical test and the z distribution as your sampling distribution.

Step 3. You select an alpha level of .01. With a one-tailed test, the critical level of z at this level of alpha is 2.33 (see Table 8–1). Your decision is to reject the null hypothesis if $z_{obt} > 2.33$.

Step 4. You calculate the obtained value of your test statistic, z_{obt}, as follows:

$$z_{obt} = \frac{.36 - .19}{\sqrt{\dfrac{.19(1 - .19)}{100}}}$$

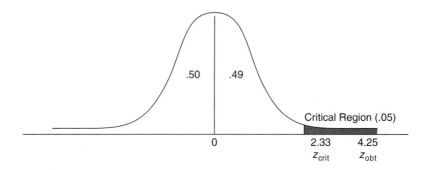

Figure 8–15 Critical z and critical region for a one-tailed test with an alpha = .05.

$$= \frac{.17}{\sqrt{\dfrac{.19(.81)}{100}}}$$

$$= \frac{.17}{\sqrt{\dfrac{.15}{100}}} = \frac{.17}{\sqrt{.001}} = \frac{.17}{.04}$$

$$z_{obt} = 4.25$$

Step 5. The location of the obtained value of z relative to the critical value and the critical region is illustrated in Figure 8–15. As z_{obt} > 2.33, you would reject the null hypothesis, knowing that there is a 1 in 100 chance that you are making the wrong decision (Type I error). From this hypothesis test, you can conclude that the percentage of pretrial detainees who have used cocaine is significantly greater than the percentage of those who have used cocaine in the general population of young adults.

SUMMARY

In this chapter, we have examined the procedures used to make inferences about two population parameters: inferences from the sample mean ($\bar{X}$) about a population mean (μ), and inferences from a sample proportion ($\hat{p}$) to a population proportion (p). We used a z test when making inferences about both sample means and sample proportions when we had large samples. When working with small samples, we demonstrated the steps necessary for hypothesis testing involving a mean using a t test.

Each of these hypothesis tests involved a series of decisions. The first decision is whether to state a directional or nondirectional research hypothesis.

If there are sound reasons to state your research hypothesis as a directional one, you should do so. The second decision to make concerns which test statistic and which corresponding sampling distribution to use. The third decision pertains to which level of significance (the alpha level) to use in conducting your hypothesis test. This is one of the most important decisions you will make in hypothesis testing because the alpha level determines the risk you accept of rejecting a null hypothesis that is really true (i.e., the risk of making a Type I error). Finally, the last and easiest decision you have to make is whether to fail to reject or to reject your null hypothesis. This is the easiest decision because, if you have properly conducted the hypothesis test and followed the order of the steps, this decision will have essentially been made for you. Once you have chosen your alpha level and found the critical value and critical region, all you need to determine is whether the obtained value of your test statistic falls in the critical region. If it does, you reject the null hypothesis; if it does not, you fail to reject the null hypothesis. What could be easier?

KEY TERMS

critical region	**sampling distribution of the mean**
critical value	**sampling variation**
directional hypothesis test	**standard error of the mean**
hypothesis testing	**standard error of the proportion**
nondirectional hypothesis test	**t test**
null hypothesis	**two-tailed hypothesis test**
one-tailed hypothesis test	**z test**

KEY FORMULAS

To find a z score (eq. 8–3):

$$z_{obt} = \frac{\overline{X} - \mu}{s / \sqrt{n}}$$

To find a t score (eq. 8–4):

$$t_{obt} = \frac{\overline{X} - \mu}{s / \sqrt{n}}$$

To conduct a hypothesis test for proportions (eq. 8–5):

$$z = \frac{\hat{p} - p}{\sigma_{\hat{p}}}$$

where $\sigma_{\hat{p}} = \sqrt{\dfrac{p(1-p)}{n}}$

PRACTICE PROBLEMS

1. When is it appropriate to use a t test for hypothesis testing instead of a z test?

2. We are interested in the average dollar amount lost by victims of burglary. The National Insurance Association has reported that the mean dollar amount lost by victims of burglary is $2,222. Assume that this is the population mean. We believe that the true population mean loss is different from this. Formally state the null and research hypotheses we would test to investigate this question. What if we believed the dollar amount to be higher?

3. The Internal Revenue Service has claimed that the mean number of times the average U.S. citizen has cheated on taxes in the last 10 years is 4.6 times. Assume that this is your population value. We believe the actual population mean (μ) of the number of times individuals cheat on their taxes is higher than this. We collect a random sample of 64 tax-paying citizens and find the following sample statistics: $\bar{X} = 6.3$, $s = 1.9$. Perform all of the procedures necessary for conducting a hypothesis test based on our assumption. Set your alpha level at .01. What do you conclude?

4. A major research study concluded that the mean number of times that adolescents engaged in vandalism during the previous 12 months was 3.5 times. We believe the true population mean to be less than this. After collecting our own sample of 59 adolescents, we find that the mean number of times they vandalized property during a one-year period was $\bar{X} = 2.9$, with a standard deviation equal to .7. Perform all of the procedures necessary for conducting a hypothesis test based on our assumption. What do you conclude? Set your alpha level at .05.

5. Over a 20-year period, the average sentence given to defendants convicted of aggravated assault in the United States was 25.9 months. Assume this to be your population mean. Because you think that it might be different in your home state, you conduct a little study to examine this question. You take a random sample of 75 jurisdictions in your home state and find that the mean aggravated assault sentence is 27.3 months, with a standard deviation of 6.5. Test the null hypothesis that the mean sentence is 25.9 months against the alternative hypothesis that it is different from that. Set your alpha level at .01.

6. A study conducted by the Research Institute of America has concluded that the average number of hours inmates at state correctional facilities spend in their cells during a day is 15. We believe the population mean number of hours to be different from this. Therefore, we contact a sample of 15 state correctional facilities and inquire about the mean number of hours inmates housed in their facilities spend in their cells. We come up with the following sample data:

Facility Number	Hours Spent in Cells
1	16.3
2	21.1
3	14.9
4	13.5
5	22.2
6	15.3
7	18.1
8	19.0
9	14.2
10	9.3
11	10.1
12	21.1
13	22.3
14	15.4
15	13.2

Calculate the mean number of hours inmates spend in their cells from the sample data. Test the research hypothesis that the mean number of hours inmates spend in their cells is 15 against the alternative research hypothesis that it is different from that. Set your alpha level at .05. Hint: You also will have to calculate the standard deviation. Remember, practice makes perfect! What do you conclude?

7. You are on the police force in a small town. During an election year, a candidate for mayor claims that fewer police are needed because the average police officer makes only four arrests per year. You think the population mean is much higher than that, so you conduct a small research project. You ask 12 other officers how many arrests they made in the past year. The average for this sample of 12 is 6.3, with a standard deviation of 1.5. With your sample evidence, test the null hypothesis that the population mean is four arrests against the alternative that it is greater than four. Set your alpha level at .01.

8. The American Bar Association reports that the mean length of time for a hearing in juvenile court is 25 minutes. Assume that this is your population mean. As a lawyer who practices in the juvenile court, you think that the average hearing is much shorter than this. You take a sample of 20 other lawyers who do juvenile work and ask them how long their last case in juvenile court lasted. The mean hearing length for this sample of 20 is 23 minutes, with a standard deviation of 6. Test the null hypothesis that the population mean is 25 minutes against the alternative that it is less than 25. Set your alpha level at .05.

9. A spokesperson for the National Rifle Association states that 45 percent of the households in the United States contain at least one firearm. Assume that this is your population value. You take a random sample of 200 homes and find that about 23 percent of them contain a firearm. Test the null hypothesis that the population proportion is 45 percent against the alternative that it is less than that. Set your alpha level at .01.

10. A friend of yours claims that 20 percent of the people in your neighborhood have been the victim of a crime. Take this as your population value. You take a random sample of 60 homes and find that about 31 percent of the homes have reported some kind of crime. Test the null hypothesis that the population proportion is 20 percent against the alternative that it is different from 20 percent. Set your alpha level at .05.

11. A public opinion study has concluded that the proportion of Americans agreeing with the statement, "Prisons should be for punishment, not rehabilitation," is .31. You believe the true population proportion agreeing with this statement is actually higher than this. After collecting your own sample of 110 individuals and asking them the same question, you find that 46 agree with the statement. Test the null hypothesis that the population proportion is .31 against the alternative that it is more than this. Set your alpha level at .05.

SPSS PRACTICE PROBLEMS

To obtain a one-sample t test from SPSS, you click on ANALYZE, then on COMPARE MEANS, then click on ONE-SAMPLE T TEST. In the variables box, you place the quantitative variable you want to test. This procedure will test the sample mean from your data against a numeric test value. In the ONE-SAMPLE T-TEST dialogue box, you must specify what that test value is (e.g., your null hypothesis mean).

1. Using the data set STATE2000, we want to determine if the amount of expenditures (dollars) spent per inmate per day in our sample is different from a hypothetical population mean. Assume this population mean is equal to $50. Conduct this hypothesis test. What do you conclude?

2. Using the same data set as in exercise (1), we now want to know if the mean rate of burglary per 100,000 population we have for this sample is significantly different from a hypothetical population mean equal to 800. Conduct this hypothesis test. What do you conclude?

3. Obtain the data set called YOUTH, which is a survey obtained from a sample of high school students. There is a delinquency variable (time 1 delinquency) in this data set. Test the hypothesis that the mean in this sample of high school youth is different from a hypothetical population mean delinquency rate equal to 22. What do you conclude?

Testing Hypotheses with Categorical Data

> *K*nowledge slowly builds up what Ignorance in an hour pulls down.
>
> —GEORGE ELIOT

In this chapter we will learn about the chi-square statistic. The chi-square statistic is useful when we have categorical variables—variables measured at the nominal or ordinal level. When we have one categorical variable, the chi-square statistic is used to test hypotheses about the frequency distribution of a categorical variable, for example, whether the frequencies are distributed proportionately across all categories of the variable, or whether the frequencies follow some form or distribution. When we have two categorical variables, the chi-square statistic will allow us to test the null hypothesis that the two variables are independent. This assumption of independence implies that there is no relationship between the variables. A relationship between two categorical variables can be seen also in the inspection of a contingency table, sometimes referred to as a cross-tabulation table. A contingency table shows the joint distribution of two categorical variables. With a contingency table we can look for the presence of a relationship between the two variables by comparing percentage differences on the dependent variable and by looking at relative risks. Finally, we will examine measures of association for the relationship between two variables. While the chi-square statistic can tell us whether or not there is a relationship between two categorical variables in the population, it tells us nothing about the possible strength of the relationship. Therefore, we conclude the chapter with a discussion of different statistics that measure the strength of the association between two categorical variables.

INTRODUCTION

In this chapter we are concerned with testing hypotheses and exploring relationships between categorical variables. Categorical variables are measured at either the nominal or the ordinal level, and the values of these variables consist of distinct categories. One example of a categorical nominal-level variable would be "family structure," with the values being "living with biological parents," "living with mother and stepfather," living with father and stepmother," "living with mother only," "living with father only," "living with neither biological parent." These are nominal categories because each value distinguishes only a different *type* of family structure; one value does not possess more "family" or more "structure" than any other value. An example of a categorical ordinal-level variable would be "number of delinquent acts committed in the past year," with the values being "none," "1–5 acts," "6–10 acts," and "11 or more delinquent acts committed."

We will study two kinds of tests, a one-variable and a two-variable hypothesis test. In the former, we ask if the distribution of a given categorical (nominal or ordinal) variable is consistent with some null hypothesis. For example, we will determine if the population distribution of some variable has a particular form (for example, if it is evenly distributed across the different values). These one-variable tests are often called **chi-square goodness of fit tests.** In the second, two-variable test, we test the null hypothesis that the two variables are independent. If we determine that the two variables are not independent but that there is in fact a relationship or association between them, we then ask how strongly they are related to each other. In this hypothesis test we will examine the joint distribution of the two variables because their joint distribution can tell us whether they are related to each other or are independent. These tests are often referred to as *tests of independence.*

In both of these problems we will be examining the chi-square statistic (χ^2), pronounced like "ki" (as in *kite*), where χ is the Greek letter chi. We also will learn about the chi-square distribution, which is the theoretical probability distribution of the chi-square statistic. The mathematical formula for the chi-square test is the same for both the one- and the two-variable case. We will introduce the chi-square goodness of fit test with one variable first and, with this as a foundation, move on to the more frequent two-variable chi-square test of independence.

THE ONE-VARIABLE GOODNESS OF FIT CHI-SQUARE TEST

Case Study: Satisfaction with Police Services

Suppose we are interested in how the citizens of a town feel about their police services. To find out about this, we take a public opinion poll of 200 people who live in the town. One of the questions we ask them is, "How satisfied are you with the quality of police services in this town?" with the four possible response options being "very satisfied," "satisfied," "dissatisfied," and "very dissatisfied." The responses to this question are reported in Table 9–1. We find that about 9 percent are very satisfied, 19 percent are satisfied, 32 percent are dissatisfied, and another 40 percent are very dissatisfied. From this distribution it might appear that the police are not viewed very favorably by the citizens of this town, but we don't really know for sure. Without any prior knowledge, we might have expected an even distribution of percentages in each of the four response categories (25 percent in each group), and maybe we are not far off from that. That is, maybe we have a particularly disgruntled sample and sampling variation, rather than true dissatisfaction, is producing these results. In other words, maybe the citizens are fairly satisfied with the police and just by chance we have selected these "grumps" into our sample. What we would like to do, therefore, is examine the possibility that the observed departure from an even distribution in our sample data is due to chance rather than true dissatisfaction with the police. In order to examine this, we need to conduct a hypothesis test, and this involves using the chi-square statistic.

The formula for the chi-square statistic is:

$$\chi^2 = \sum_{i=1}^{k} \frac{(f_o - f_e)^2}{f_e}$$

(9–1)

TABLE 9–1

Responses to Question about the Quality of Police Services

"How satisfied are you with the quality of police services in this town?"

	f	%
Very satisfied	18	9
Satisfied	38	19
Dissatisfied	64	32
Very dissatisfied	80	40
Total	200	

where

f_o = the observed frequencies from our sample data,

f_e = the expected frequencies we should get under the null hypothesis, and

k = the number of categories for the variable.

In words, this formula is telling us to subtract the expected frequencies (more about this soon) from the observed frequencies, square this difference, and then divide by the expected frequencies. We perform this calculation for each of the k categories and take the sum. This sum is our obtained value of the chi-square statistic. The chi-square statistic in equation 9–1 follows a chi-square distribution with $k - 1$ degrees of freedom. The chi-square distribution is simply a known probability distribution, just like the z and t distributions. As in our other hypothesis tests, we obtain a critical value of chi-square from our chi-square probability distribution, compare it to our obtained value, and ultimately come to a conclusion about the null hypothesis. Before we get to our hypothesis test, however, we need to go into some detail about the chi-square test.

We have said that the chi-square statistic follows a chi-square distribution with $k - 1$ degrees of freedom, where k is the number of categories for our variable. In our example involving police service satisfaction there are four categories, so we would have 3 degrees of freedom. But what exactly does the term "degrees of freedom" mean in this case? The term "degrees of freedom refers to the number of values in our data that are free to vary. Our data" consist of observed frequencies for the variable "satisfaction with the police." Table 9–1 shows our observed frequencies for the 200 citizens. To understand what degrees of freedom means in this context, assume that we have 200 responses and we need to distribute them in our four categories in such a way that the sum of the four categories must be 200 (our sample size). What value can the first frequency be? Theoretically, it can be any number so its value is free to vary. Therefore, we could have any value for the frequency of the "very satisfied" response. The only restriction we have is that the sum of the frequencies must be 200. So far, we have 1 degree of freedom because, theoretically, the frequency for "very satisfied" can be any number and we can still sum to 200.

	f
Very satisfied	?
Satisfied	?
Dissatisfied	?
Very dissatisfied	?
Total	200

Let's insert a number in place of the first question mark to indicate an observed frequency of the number of "very satisfied" responses, and let's just say that number is 18 (as in Table 9–1). Now we have the following:

	f
Very satisfied	18
Satisfied	?
Dissatisfied	?
Very dissatisfied	?
Total	200

What possible number of "satisfied" responses can we have? Keep in mind that we have determined that there are 18 "very satisfied" responses and that the total number of observations is restricted to 200. You should see that, theoretically, we are free to place any value we want as the frequency for "satisfied" responses. In fact, we can place any number into the "dissatisfied" category as well. Thus, we have a second and a third degree of freedom since these values are free to be anything we want. Again, using the data in Table 9–1, let's say we decide to make the number of "satisfied" responses equal to 38 and the number of "dissatisfied" responses equal to 64. Now we have:

	f
Very satisfied	18
Satisfied	38
Dissatisfied	64
Very dissatisfied	?
Total	200

Now, is the number of "very dissatisfied" responses also free to vary? No. It is not free to vary because the total must sum to 200, our sample size. This

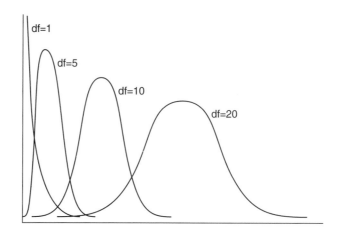

Figure 9–1   Chi-Square distribution with different degrees of freedom

means that the only possible number of "very dissatisfied" responses is 80. It is not free to vary since it can only be equal to 80. In this case, then, we have 3 degrees of freedom. Now you can see why the number of degrees of freedom for the chi-square statistic in the one variable case is $k - 1$, where k is the number of categories. In our example, the variable "satisfaction with the police" had four categories, and so we had $4 - 1 = 3$ degrees of freedom.

The importance of the degrees of freedom is that, like the t probability distribution, the chi-square distribution has a different shape depending upon the degrees of freedom. In Figure 9–1 we show how the shape of the chi-square distribution changes with different numbers of degrees of freedom. You can see that the chi-square distribution is very skewed when there are few degrees of freedom and that it approximates a normal distribution as the degrees of freedom increase. We will use the chi-square distribution to conduct our goodness of fit hypothesis test by getting a critical value of chi-square from the relevant chi-square distribution. In order to do this we need to know both the alpha level we are using for the problem (the level of significance or risk we are assuming of making a Type I error), and the degrees of freedom we have. The critical values of the chi-square statistic for different degrees of freedom and two alpha levels (.05 and .01) are given for you in Table E–4 of Appendix E.

Before we can get to the hypothesis test there is one more issue we need to discuss. Notice from equation 9–1 that in order to calculate the chi-square statistic we need to know something called the "expected frequencies." Recall that the **observed frequencies** are those that we actually see in our sample data, for example, that 18 citizens were "very satisfied" and 38 people were "satisfied" with the quality of police services (see Table 9–1). **Expected frequencies,** on the other hand, are determined on the basis of the null hypothesis. The null hypothesis we will eventually test in this example will as-

TABLE 9–2

Observed and Expected Frequencies—Responses to Question about the Quality of Police Services

"How satisfied are you with the quality of police services in this town?"

	Observed Frequencies	Expected Frequencies
Very satisfied	18	50
Satisfied	38	50
Dissatisfied	64	50
Very dissatisfied	82	50
Total	200	

sume that the responses to the question posed to the citizens regarding the quality of police services will be evenly distributed across the four possible response options. With four response options, we would expect that .25 of the total would fall into each category ($1/4 = .25$). This means that the expected frequency in each category, that is, the number expected under the null hypothesis, would be equal to our sample size (n) times this expected proportion ($200 \times .25$), or 50 responses in each category. Both the observed and expected frequencies are shown for you in Table 9–2. As we will see in our second example, different null hypotheses have different assumptions about what the expected frequencies should be. Now, let's continue with our hypothesis test involving citizens' views of police services.

As with all the hypothesis tests in this book, we will follow a series of five steps.

Step 1.
H_0: The response frequencies should be evenly distributed across each of the four response choices. In other words, there is no tendency for citizens to feel either disproportionately satisfied or dissatisfied with their police.

H_1: The response frequencies are unevenly distributed across the four response choices. In other words, there is a tendency for citizens to feel either disproportionately satisfied or dissatisfied with police.

Step 2. This is a chi-square test of the goodness of fit for one variable. We will use the chi-square sampling distribution.

Step 3. We will use an alpha level of .05 ($\alpha = .05$). Since we have 3 degrees of freedom and an alpha of .05 we can go to Table E–4 in Appendix E and find the critical value of chi-square. Finding the column at the top that corresponds to an alpha of .05 and then finding the row with 3 degrees of freedom, we can see that we have a critical chi-square value of 7.815. Since the chi-square statistic takes the difference between observed and expected frequencies and squares it, we are only concerned about positive values of the chi-square statistic; therefore, we are only concerned with the right tail of the chi-square probability distribution. The critical region of the chi-square distribution, therefore, is the area equal to and greater than a chi-square of 7.815. With a critical value of 7.815, our decision rule will be to reject the null hypothesis if our obtained value of chi-square is greater than or equal to 7.815.

Step 4. We calculate our obtained value of the chi-square statistic. Let's follow formula 9–1 very carefully, taking several steps. We present the results of the steps in Table 9–3.

Step 4a. Subtract the expected frequency from each observed frequency, $(f_o - f_e)$.

Step 4b. Square the difference between the observed and expected frequency, $(f_o - f_e)^2$.

Step 4c. Divide this by the expected frequency, $\frac{(f_o - f_e)^2}{f_e}$.

Step 4d. Sum the results across all categories.

From Table 9–3 you can see that the value of our obtained chi-square is 45.28 ($\chi^2_{obt} = 45.28$).

Step 5. We now compare the obtained to the critical value of chi-square and make our decision. Recall that our decision rule was to reject the null hypothesis if $\chi^2_{obt} \geq 7.815$. Since our obtained chi-square of 45.28 is greater than 7.815, our decision is to reject the null hypothesis and conclude that the responses are not evenly distributed across the four categories in the population.

TABLE 9–3

Observed and Expected Frequencies—Responses to Question about the Quality of Police Services

"How satisfied are you with the quality of police services in this town?"	f_o	f_e	$f_o - f_e$	$(f_o - f_e)^2$	$\dfrac{(f_o - f_e)^2}{f_e}$
Very satisfied	18	50	−32	1,024	20.48
Satisfied	38	50	−12	144	2.88
Dissatisfied	64	50	14	196	3.92
Very dissatisfied	80	50	30	900	18.00
Total	200				
					$\chi^2_{obt} = 45.28$

Notice that in taking the difference between the observed and expected frequencies, the greater this difference is, the larger our obtained value of the chi-square statistic is. Given this fact, we can examine the column of the observed minus the expected frequencies and find out which categories are contributing most to the magnitude of our obtained chi-square. For example, looking at Table 9–3, we can see that for the category of "very satisfied" we have a large negative number and for the category "very dissatisfied" we have a very large positive number. The large negative number means that there are much fewer cases observed in that category than we would expect under an equal distribution hypothesis; the large positive number means that there are much more cases observed in that category than we would expect under an equal distribution hypothesis. This means that, compared to a null hypothesis of an equal distribution of responses, we are observing fewer people who are "very satisfied" with their police services and more people who are "very dissatisfied."

Let's try another example. Suppose that we have obtained information about an identical question regarding citizens' satisfaction with local police services. This question was asked in the previous year and involved 300 persons who lived in the same town. These responses are summarized in Table 9–4. Notice the difference between the percentage of cases in each response category last year and this year (Table 9–1). It looks like there is a lower percentage who are "very satisfied" this year (9 percent) compared to the year before (11 percent). Likewise, a higher percentage are "very dissatisfied" (40 percent, compared to 38 percent the year before). What we would really like to know is if there is a statistically significant difference between the distribution of last year's and this year's responses, or if the observed differences in percentages between Table 9–1 and Table 9–4 are due to sampling variation or chance.

To find the answer to our question, we are going to conduct a formal hypothesis test to see if the distribution of cases in this year's question is the same as the distribution of cases in last year's question. We are going to use

TABLE 9–4

Response to Question about the Quality of Police Services, One Year Ago

"How satisfied are you with the quality of police services in this town?"

	f	%
Very satisfied	33	11
Satisfied	60	20
Dissatisfied	93	31
Very dissatisfied	114	38
Total	300	

TABLE 9–5

Expected Percentages and Expected Frequency of Responses If This Year's Responses Remain Unchanged from Last Year

"How satisfied are you with the quality of police services in this town?"

	Last Year's Percentage (%)	This Year's Expected Frequency
Very satisfied	11	22
Satisfied	20	40
Dissatisfied	31	62
Very dissatisfied	38	76
Total		200

the chi-square goodness of fit test to make this hypothesis test. Before we continue, however, we are going to create a table of expected frequencies. Since our null hypothesis is that the percentage of cases in each response category this year should be the same as last year, we are going to use the percentages in Table 9–4 to calculate how many of the 200 people questioned this year fall into each category. The presumed percentage of cases and the expected frequency (based on our sample size this year of 200) are shown for you in Table 9–5. Notice that if the percentages were the same, we would expect to find 22 (11% × 200) cases this year who were "very satisfied" with the quality of their police services. Likewise, the expected frequency of "satisfied" responses should be 40 (20% × 200), the expected frequency of "dissatisfied" cases should be 62 (31% × 200), and the expected frequency of "very dissatisfied" cases should be 76 (38% × 200). Table 9–5 shows the frequency we should expect to see if there is no change in the percentage of cases in each response category from last year's question to this year's. We see that there is a difference between the observed frequencies in Table 9–1 and the expected frequencies in Table 9–5. What we now have to determine is if this is a "real" or statistically significant difference, or if it is a difference due only to the chance nature of our sample. To help us decide which of these two possibilities is true, we will conduct a formal hypothesis test that the population of citizens' responses has the same distribution this year as last year.

Step 1.

H_0: The distribution of responses to the police satisfaction question should not be different between last year and this year. In other words, the responses to the question about satisfaction with the police show no change.

H_1: The response frequencies this year have a different distribution than those for last year. In other words, the expressed level of satisfaction or dissatisfaction with the police has changed over the one-year time period.

TABLE 9–6

Observed and Expected Frequencies: Responses to Question about the Quality of Police Services

"How satisfied are you with the quality of police services in this town?"	f_o	f_e	$f_o - f_e$	$(f_o - f_e)^2$	$\dfrac{(f_o - f_e)^2}{f_e}$
Very satisfied	18	22	−4	16	.73
Satisfied	38	40	−2	4	.10
Dissatisfied	64	62	2	4	.06
Very dissatisfied	80	76	4	16	.21
Total	200				$\chi^2_{obt} = 1.10$

Step 2. This is a chi-square test of the goodness of fit for one variable. This test has a chi-square distribution.

Step 3. For practice, let's use an alpha level of .01. We still have 3 degrees of freedom ($k - 1$). With 3 degrees of freedom and an alpha of .01 we can go to Table E–4 in Appendix E and find the critical value of chi-square. Finding the column at the top that corresponds to an alpha of .01 and finding the row with 3 degrees of freedom, we can see that we have a critical chi-square value of 11.345. With a critical value of 11.345, our decision rule will be to reject the null hypothesis if our obtained value of chi-square is greater than or equal to 11.345.

Step 4. We calculate our obtained value of the chi-square statistic. Let's follow formula 9–1 very carefully, taking several steps. We will show you the results of the steps in Table 9–6.

Step 4a. Subtract the expected frequency from each observed frequency, $(f_o - f_e)$.

Step 4b. Square the difference between the observed and expected frequency, $(f_o - f_e)^2$.

Step 4c. Divide this by the expected frequency, $\dfrac{(f_o - f_e)^2}{f_e}$.

Step 4d. Sum the results across all categories.

From Table 9–6 you can see that the value of our obtained chi-square is 1.10 $\chi^2_{obt} = 1.10$.

Step 5. Now we compare the obtained to the critical value of chi-square and make our decision. Our decision rule was to reject the null hypothesis if $\chi^2_{obt} \geq 11.345$. Since our obtained chi-square of 1.10 is less than 11.345 and not in the critical region, our decision is to fail to reject the null hypothesis and conclude that the responses to the police satisfaction question have not changed in one year. The differences we found between the observed frequencies from our sample data and the expected frequencies under the null hypothesis were due to sampling variation.

This illustration of the chi-square statistic for one variable should help to set the foundation for using the chi-square statistic to examine the relationship between two qualitatively measured variables.

CONTINGENCY TABLES AND THE TWO-VARIABLE CHI-SQUARE TEST OF INDEPENDENCE

When we are examining the relationship between two variables, we can usually distinguish between the independent variable and the dependent variable. Recall that an independent variable is a variable that we think has an influence on another variable, called the dependent variable. When we use causal language, we refer to the independent variable as the "cause" and the dependent variable as the "effect." In the rest of this chapter, then, we are going to be interested in determining two things: (1) if the independent and dependent variables are related to one another, and (2) if so, how strongly they are related. You may remember in our probability chapter that two events (i.e., the values of two variables) are independent if the outcome of one variable has no effect or influence on the outcome of the other. Similarly, our job in this chapter is to determine if our variables are independent of each other. With categorical variables, the tool we use to determine this is the chi-square test of independence. Before we get to this chi-square test, however, we need to examine in a little detail what the two categorical variable problem looks like and exactly how we are going to attack it.

Case Study: Gender and Emotions

> The **joint frequency distribution** of two categorical variables refers to the simultaneous occurrence of one event from the first variable and another event from the second variable. The joint distribution of two events, then, is the intersection of those two events. An examination of a joint frequency distribution of two categorical variables in the form of a contingency table can tell us something about whether or not a relationship exists between those two variables.

In looking at whether or not two categorical variables are related to each other, we examine their **joint frequency distribution.** The joint distribution of two variables is simply a description of how the values of the two variables occur simultaneously or jointly. In Table 9–7 we show the frequency distribution of two variables for a sample of 120 adolescents. One variable is the person's gender, while the second measures something called "negative emotionality." One of the most persistent facts in criminology is that males are more antisocial than females. The question is, why? In their research on gender differences in delinquency and antisocial behavior, Moffitt and her colleagues (2001) argue that one possible reason why males are more likely to commit criminal offenses than females is that males are more likely to experience neg-

TABLE 9–7

Distribution of Gender and Negative Emotionality, and Joint Distribution of Gender and Negative Emotionality in Contingency Table

Gender	*f*
Female	60
Male	60

Negative Emotionality	*f*
Low	90
High	30

Contingency Table of Observed Joint Frequency Distribution

Gender	**Negative Emotionality**		Total
	Low	**High**	**Total**
Female	46	14	60
Male	44	16	60
Total	90	30	120

ative emotions. In their theory, negative emotions are things like anger and anxiety. Of the 120 adolescents, the frequency distribution for gender shows that there are 60 males and 60 females. The 120 persons in Table 9–7 were given a personality test, and the frequency distribution for the negative emotionality variable shows that 90 of them were found to have "low" negative emotions and 30 were found to have "high" negative emotions. Notice from Table 9–7 that both of these variables are categorical variables, gender is a nominal-level variable, and negative emotions is an ordinal-level variable. Notice also that each variable has two values (male and female; low and high negative emotions).

The third distribution is actually the joint frequency distribution of two variables—gender and negative emotions. A joint frequency distribution of two variables shows the number of cases for each value of one variable at each value of the second variable. For example, there are 46 females who have low negative emotions. This is the joint distribution of the value "female" for the variable "gender" and the value "low negative emotions" for the variable "negative emotions." There are 14 females who have high negative emotions. This is the joint distribution of the value "female" and the value "high negative emotions." There are also 44 males with low negative emotions and 16 males with high negative emotions. Since there are two values of gender and two values of negative emotions, their joint distribution will result in four possible outcomes: (1) female and low negative emotions, (2) female and high negative emotions, (3) male and low negative emotions, and (4) male and high negative emotions. All four of these joint outcomes and the frequency of each are shown in Table 9–7.

> A **contingency table** shows the joint distribution of two categorical variables. A contingency table is defined by the number of rows and number of columns it has. A contingency table with three rows and two columns is a "3 by 2" contingency table. By looking at a contingency table we can make some judgment about whether or not a relationship exists between the two categorical variables.

A joint frequency distribution of categorical variables like that shown in Table 9–7 is called a **contingency table,** sometimes also referred to as a cross-tabulation table. Contingency tables generally are defined by the number of rows and columns that they have. Table 9–7 is called a 2 × 2 (read, 2 "by" 2) contingency table because there are two rows (female and male) and two columns (low and high negative emotions). Generally, contingency tables are referred to as R × C tables, where R is the number of rows and C is the number of columns. A contingency table with three rows and two columns, then, would be a 3 × 2 contingency table. The product of the number of rows in a contingency table and the number of columns is equal to the number of "cells." The number of cells corresponds to the total number of possible outcomes of the joint distribution of the two variables. For example, in Table 9–7 there are two rows and two columns, for a total of four (2 × 2 = 4) cells. These four cells of the contingency table correspond to the four possible outcomes of the joint distribution of the two variables: (1) female and low negative emotions, (2) female and high negative emotions, (3) male and low negative emotions, and (4) male and high negative emotions.

Table 9–8 provides important information that is contained in a contingency table. First there are the row (R_1 and R_2) and column marginals (C_1 and C_2). The **row marginals** correspond to the number of cases in each row of the table, while the **column marginals** correspond to the frequency in each column of the table. In the contingency table in Table 9–7, for example, the row marginals are 60 females and 60 males. The column marginals are 90 persons low in negative emotions and 30 persons high in negative emotions. The sum of the row marginals should equal the sum of the column marginals, and these sums should equal the total number of cases $(R_1 + R_2) = (C_1 + C_2) = n$. For example, in Table 9–7 the sum of the two row marginals (60 + 60) is equal to the sum of the two column marginals (90 + 30), both of which are equal to the total number of cases (120).

We look at joint frequency distributions, then, because they can provide us with information about the relationship between the two variables. As we stated earlier, it has been suggested that one reason why males are thought to be more likely to commit criminal offenses than females is that they are more likely to experience negative emotions. The question, then, is, "Are males more likely to experience negative emotions than females"? Can our joint frequency distribution in Table 9–7 provide us with any information about that hypothesized relationship?

TABLE 9–8

Labeling a 2 × 2 Contingency Table

	Number of Columns			
Number of Rows	1	2	Row Marginals	Total Sample Size
1	A*	B*	R_1	
2	C*	D*	R_2	
Column Marginals	C_1	C_2		n

*Cell frequencies.

In hypothesizing that there is a relationship between gender and negative emotions, we presume that gender is the independent variable and the experience of negative emotions is the dependent variable. Our null hypothesis would be that there is no relationship between gender and negative emotions, while our alternative hypothesis would be that males are more likely to experience negative emotional states. Later in this chapter we will learn about the chi-square test for independence, which is a formal hypothesis test, but first we will learn what a reading of the contingency table alone can tell us about the relationship between two variables.

Because our hypothesis is that one's gender has an impact or influence on the kinds of emotional experiences one is likely to have, what we would like to know is the extent to which males are more likely than females to have negative emotions. In other words, if gender varies, does the tendency to have negative emotions vary? One way to answer this question is to examine the percent of males who have negative emotions and compare that with the percent of females who have negative emotions. In examining percentages in contingency tables, we look at the percent of cases for *different* levels of the independent variable at a *fixed* level of the dependent variable. In other words, we calculate our percentages on the independent variable and compare percentages on the dependent variable. The marginal frequencies for our independent variable are the denominator we use in calculating these percentages, and this is true whether the independent variable is the row variable or the column variable. Let's go through an example.

In the contingency table shown in Table 9–7, gender is our independent variable. Therefore, we will use the row marginals for our percent calculations. In using the row marginals, we are saying that the percentages should sum to 100 percent at the end of each row or each value of the independent variable. We find that 77 percent [$(46/60) \times 100$] of the females are low in negative emotions, while 23 percent of the females are high in negative emotions [$(14/60) \times 100$]. Now, let's calculate the percentage of males who are low in negative emotions. Seventy-three percent of the males are low in negative

TABLE 9–9

Relationship between Gender and Negative Emotionality: Looking at Percentages

Gender	Negative Emotionality		
	Low (%)	High (%)	Total (%)
Female	77	23	100
Male	73	27	100

emotions [(44/60) × 100], and 27 percent of the males are high in negative emotions [(16/60) × 100]. Notice that we used the marginals for the independent variable to calculate our percentages. The relevant percentages for this contingency table are reported in Table 9–9.

Having calculated our percentages on the independent variable, we will now compare them at a fixed level of the dependent variable. Taking negative emotions, we find that 23 percent of the females and 27 percent of the males are high in negative emotions. Notice that we are comparing **percentage differences** found in different categories of the independent variable at the same category level of the dependent variable. Instead of using percentages, you could have left your calculations as proportions. Some people call this the **relative risk** of the dependent variable occurring. For example, the relative risk of having high negative emotions is .23 for females and .27 for males. Whether we compare percentages or relative risks, it appears that males are slightly more likely to have negative emotions than females.

> There are simple ways to look for a relationship between two categorical variables in a contingency table. One of them is to examine **percentage differences.** In looking at percentage differences we compare different levels of the independent variable at the same level or category of the dependent variable. If we compare proportions (probabilities) rather than percentages, then we are looking at the **relative risk** of the dependent variable.

It would appear that our hypothesis is supported; that is, it looks as though males are more likely to have negative emotions than females. But a percentage difference of 4 percent is not very impressive. Is a 4 percentage point difference enough for us to conclude that a relationship exists between gender and negative emotions? How large should the percentage difference be before we can with confidence conclude that there is a relationship? Five percent? Ten percent? What if the 4 percent difference we observed is due only to sampling variation, and the true difference is 0 percent? Maybe we just happened to select a sample by chance with a 4 percent difference. The probability of selecting such a sample might be high if the true percent difference in the population is zero (remember, we took only one sample from this population of an infinite number of samples). What we need is a formal hypothesis test of this difference of percentages or proportions with a known sampling distribution. The chi-square test gives us that formal hypothesis test. Before we discuss this two-variable chi-square test, however, let's look at another example of a contingency table.

TABLE 9–10

Relationship between Attitude toward School and Delinquency, Raw Frequencies

Number of Delinquent Acts	"Do you like school?"			
	Like	Neither Like nor Dislike	Dislike	
0	395	314	24	733
1	133	172	13	318
2+	52	162	35	249
Total	580	648	72	1,300

Source: Adapted from Travis Hirschi (1969), Table 33, p. 121. Reprinted by permission of the author.

Case Study: Liking School and Delinquency

Table 9–10 shows the joint distribution between two variables: (1) whether or not a respondent said that he or she "liked school," and (2) the number of delinquent acts he or she reported committing in the past year. This information was collected from a sample of 1,300 youths. We are interested in this joint distribution because we think that youths who like school are less likely to commit delinquent acts than are those who dislike school. A positive attitude toward school, we hypothesize, is a positive social bond that we think will inhibit an inclination to commit delinquent acts. In this example, attitude toward school is our independent variable and the number of delinquent acts is the dependent variable. Notice that in this contingency table our independent variable is the column variable and not the row variable, as it was in Table 9–7. In determining whether there is a relationship between one's attitude toward school and the number of delinquent acts committed, we will look at both percentage differences and relative risks.

You may have wondered in our last example why we compared percentages of cases across values of the independent variable and not the raw frequencies which we have right in our contingency table. Table 9–10 provides an answer to that question. Since attitude toward school is our independent variable, we are going to compare information at different categories of the independent variable at a fixed category of the dependent variable. Let's fix the category of the dependent variable at "2+ delinquent acts." If we were to compare raw frequencies, we would say that 52 youths who like school reported committing 2 or more delinquent acts in the past year, 162 youths who neither like nor dislike school committed 2+ delinquent acts, and only 35 of those who dislike school committed 2+ delinquent acts. It would appear, therefore, that those who dislike school are less likely to commit a lot of delinquent acts compared to those who are neutral and those who like school—a finding counter to our hypothesis. But notice that there are only 72 students out of 1,300 who dislike school. Maybe there are only 35 who committed 2+ delinquent acts because there are simply not that many kids who say they dislike school. Because the marginal frequencies for attitude toward school are so different ($C_1 = 580$, $C_2 = 648$, $C_3 = 72$), we cannot really compare raw frequencies but must standardize these column marginals by calculating percents. Remember that percents are standardized frequencies that show the frequency per 100 observations.

What we will do, then, is translate the cell frequencies into percentages. But what should we use as the denominator for our percentages? The rule for this was stated above: We will calculate our percentages based on the marginal frequencies of the independent variable, wherever it is. Since in this table the independent variable is the column variable, we use the column marginals to calculate the percentages. Our percentages, then, should sum to 100 percent at the end of each column. Table 9–11 reports both the cell frequencies and the cell percentages for Table 9–10. When we compare percentages we now come to a different conclusion. Of those who reported that they like school, only 9 percent committed two or more delinquent offenses in the past year; of those who neither like nor dislike school, 25 percent reported committing 2+ offenses; and of those who dislike school, almost one-half (48.6%) reported committing two or more offenses. Again, notice that we calculated our percentages within categories of the independent variable and compared percentages for different values of the independent variable at one category of the dependent variable (2+ delinquent offenses).

This should make intuitive sense. We are creating variation in the independent variable to see if this is related to different percentages in the dependent variable. If there is a relationship between our two variables, there will be variation; if there is no relationship, then the percent differences will be small or close to zero. This rule also applies if we look at the relative risk rather than percentages: the relative risk of two or more delinquent offenses is .09 when youths like school, it increases to .25 when they neither like nor dislike school, and it increases to .49 (.486) when they dislike school. Whether you look at the differences in percentages or relative risks, it appears that there is a relationship between attitude toward school and the number of delinquent acts committed. Those who dislike school are about five times more likely to report committing two or more delinquent acts than those who like school. More specifically, it looks like there is a negative relationship between liking school and delinquency. Having a positive attitude toward the school does seem to restrain the commission of delinquent acts.

Although we have a larger percentage difference across different values of the independent variable in Table 9–11 than we did in Table 9–7, we still cannot be confident that this difference is "real" and not due to sampling variation. In order to dismiss the probability that sampling variation has produced our observed results, we need to perform a formal hypothesis test involving a test statistic with a known sampling distribution. Fortunately, we have one, and it is called the chi-square test of independence.

TABLE 9–11

Relationship between Attitude toward School and Delinquency, Percentages Based on Column Marginals

Number of Delinquent Acts	"Do you like school?"			
	Like	Neither Like nor Dislike	Dislike	
0	395	314	24	733
	(68.1%)	(48.5%)	(33.3%)	
1	133	172	13	318
	(22.9%)	(26.5%)	(18.1%)	
2+	52	162	35	249
	(9%)	(25%)	(48.6%)	
Total	580	648	72	1,300
	(100%)	(100%)	(100%)	

Source: Adapted from Travis Hirschi (1969), Table 33, p. 121. Reprinted by permission of University of California Press.

THE CHI-SQUARE TEST OF INDEPENDENCE

The **chi-square test of independence** tests the null hypothesis that two categorical variables are independent of each other. In hypothesizing that they are independent, we are making the assumption that they are not related to one another; in causal terms, we are saying that the independent variable does not affect or influence the dependent variable. Recall from our discussion of probability in Chapter 6 that events are independent when they do not influence or affect the outcome of each other. If we cannot reject this null hypothesis, then we continue to presume that the events are not related. If, however, we reject the null hypothesis of independence, we are on firmer ground in concluding that the events are related to each other. We then can go on to examine how strongly the two variables are related.

The definitional formula for the chi-square test of independence is the same as that for the chi-square goodness of fit test, with some slight modification:

$$\chi^2 = \sum_{i=1}^{k} \frac{(f_o - f_e)^2}{f_e} \qquad (9\text{--}2)$$

where

f_o = the observed cell frequencies from our sample data,

f_e = the expected cell frequencies we should get under the null hypothesis, and

k = the number of cells in the table.

Notice that in describing this formula we are referring to the cells of a contingency table. More specifically, the chi-square test of independence is based upon the cell frequencies. In the one-variable independence problem we have observed and expected cell frequencies, and the chi-square statistic is based upon the difference between these observed and expected cell frequencies. The chi-square test of independence for two categorical variables is based upon the same principle. We create a table of expected cell frequencies where "expected" means the frequency we would expect to find in each cell if the two variables were in fact independent or not related to each other (which is the assumption of our null hypothesis). What we have, then, is a contingency table of observed cell frequencies and another contingency table of expected cell frequencies. For each cell, we take the difference between the observed and the expected cell frequency, square that difference, divide this squared difference by the expected frequency, and sum across all cells. What we do not know yet is where the values of expected cell frequencies come from. We need to explore this in a little detail before proceeding with our hypothesis test.

> The **observed frequencies** of a contingency table are the joint distribution of two categorical variables that we actually observed in our sample data. The **expected frequencies** of a contingency table are the joint frequency distribution we would expect to see if the two categorical variables were in fact independent of each other. The expected frequencies, therefore, are calculated under the assumption of no relationship or independence between the two variables. In the chi-square test of independence we compare the observed with the expected cell frequencies.

In the contingency table in Table 9–7, we have two categorical variables: a person's gender and whether that person is "low" or "high" in terms of negative emotionality. For now, think of the value of each variable as an event. Event A is gender, with event A_1 being a female and event A_2 a male. Event B is negative emotions, with event B_1 being low negative emotions and event B_2 high negative emotions. As we noted in a previous section, each cell in a contingency table represents the joint occurrence of a value of each of the two variables. As such, each cell represents the joint occurrence of two events, event A (gender) and event B (negative emotions). Another way to think of this is that each cell represents the occurrence of both event A and event B at the same time. For example, in Table 9–7, the uppermost cell on the left is the simultaneous or joint occurrence of a person who is both female *and* has experienced low negative emotions. The cell next to this one on the right is the joint occurrence of two other events, a person who is both female *and* has experienced high negative emotions. Each cell in this contingency table, then, is the joint occurrence of event A and event B.

What we want to know is what the expected cell frequency of any cell would be if the null hypothesis that the two variables are independent were true. Recall from our discussion of probability in Chapter 6 that given two independent events, A and B, the probability that both A and B will occur simultaneously (i.e., their joint probability) is equal to the product of their separate probabilities, $P(A \text{ and } B) = P(A) \times P(B)$. We are going to use this formula to calculate the expected cell frequencies under the null hypothesis of independence. While we do not know the expected cell frequencies (that is, we do not yet know their joint frequency distribution), we are restricted by the row and column marginals of our observed data (see Table 9–7). In other words, we are restricted by the fact that there were a total of 60 females and 60 males and 90 persons had low negative emotions and 30 had high negative emotions. We will use the restricted form of the multiplication rule to calculate the expected cell frequency for each cell in the table. Keep in mind that we are using the restricted form of the multiplication rule to determine this because it gives us the probability of two independent events. Under the null hypothesis, we are assuming that the events of gender and negative emotions are independent events.

Let's start our calculation of the expected cell frequencies for Table 9–7 in the uppermost cell on the left, the cell that contains the joint distribution of "females" and "low negative emotions." Under the assumption that these two events are independent events, then, we can use the restricted form of the multiplication rule to calculate that the probability that someone is both "female" and "low in negative emotions" is equal to the probability of being female times the probability of being low in negative emotions:

$$P(\text{female and low in negative emotions}) = \frac{60}{120} \times \frac{90}{120} = .50 \times .75 = .375$$

What we have is the probability of being female and low in negative emotions. In order to find the expected *frequency,* we need to multiply this probability by the total number of cases ($.375 \times 120 = 45$). What we know, then, is that if gender and negative emotions are independent events (i.e., not related to one another) we can expect to find 45 persons who are both female and have low negative emotions. The rule for determining the expected cell frequencies under the assumption of independent events, then, is to first calculate the probability of the joint event with the restricted form of the multiplication rule [$P(A \text{ and } B) = P(A) \times P(B)$] and then obtain the expected frequency by multiplying this joint probability by the total number of cases.

The expected number of persons who are both female and high in negative emotions is:

$$P(\text{female and high in negative emotions}) = \frac{60}{120} \times \frac{30}{120} = .50 \times .25 = .125$$

The expected frequency, then, is $.125 \times 120 = 15$ people. The expected number of persons who are both male and low in negative emotions is:

$$P(\text{male and low in negative emotions}) = \frac{60}{120} \times \frac{90}{120} = .50 \times .75 = .375$$

The expected frequency of finding this combination is $.375 \times 120 = 45$ people. And finally, the expected number of persons who are both male and high in negative emotions is:

$$P(\text{male and high in negative emotions}) = \frac{60}{120} \times \frac{30}{120} = .50 \times .25 = .125$$

The expected frequency of these two events is $.125 \times 120 = 15$ persons. We have thus calculated the expected cell frequencies for each of the four cells in our original contingency table. These expected cell frequencies are shown for you in the box below.

An Alternative Way to Calculate Expected Cell Frequencies

If you don't like to use the multiplication rule to calculate your expected cell frequencies in a contingency table, there is an alternative. A somewhat easier way to find expected cell frequencies is to use the following formula:

$$\text{Expected cell frequency of cell } f_{ij} = \frac{RM_i \times CM_j}{n}$$

where

RM_i = the row marginal frequency for row i,

CM_j = the column marginal frequency for column j, and

n = the total number of cases.

In words, to find the expected frequency of a given cell, multiply the frequency at the end of the row for this cell times the frequency at the bottom of the column for this cell and divide this product by the total number of cases.

Applying this simple formula to our observed frequencies in Table 9–7, we can calculate the expected cell frequencies (expected under the null hypothesis of independence) as:

$$\text{Female and low negative emotions} = \frac{60 \times 90}{120} = 45$$

$$\text{Female and high negative emotions} = \frac{60 \times 30}{120} = 15$$

$$\text{Male and low negative emotions} = \frac{60 \times 90}{120} = 45$$

$$\text{Male and high negative emotions} = \frac{60 \times 30}{120} = 15$$

Notice that in using this alternative formula we get the identical results for our expected cell frequencies.

We now have two tables of frequencies for gender and negative emotions. Table 9–7 is a table of observed frequencies. This shows the actual joint frequency distribution of our two variables that we have observed with our sample data of 120 persons. Table 9–12 is a table of expected frequencies. This

TABLE 9–12

Expected Cell Frequencies for the Joint Distribution of Gender and Negative Emotionality

	Negative Emotionality		
Gender	Low	High	Total
Female	45	15	60
Male	45	15	60
Total	90	30	120

table shows what the joint frequency distribution of gender and negative emotions should look like if in fact the two variables are independent. This is what we should see if our two categorical variables are not related to each other.

The chi-square test of independence asks the question, "Are the frequencies in the observed table different from the frequencies in the expected table?" More specifically, the chi-square test takes the difference between the observed and expected cell frequencies for each cell in the table. If the observed frequencies are equal to the expected frequencies (i.e., if the difference between them is zero), then we can be confident in concluding that the two variables are independent. If the difference between the observed and expected cell frequencies is zero, therefore, the chi-square test also will be zero. As the difference between the observed and expected cell frequencies increases, the magnitude of the chi-square test increases and our assumption of independence becomes more and more suspicious. Of course, the difference between the expected and observed cell frequencies is generally not going to be exactly zero, even when the two variables are independent simply due to sampling variation or chance. In other words, even if the two events are independent, we would still expect to find a non-zero value of the chi-square statistic. What we have to determine, therefore, is how large a difference we must find between the observed and expected cell frequencies, or how large a chi-square must we see, before we are willing to abandon the null hypothesis of independence.

The answer to this question is that the observed value of the chi-square statistic must be equal to or greater than the critical value of the chi-square we obtain from our chi-square table at a given alpha level (our selected level of significance) and a determined number of degrees of freedom. Just as in the one-variable chi-square test of goodness of fit, therefore, in order to find our critical value of chi-square and conduct our hypothesis test, we need to set our alpha level, determine our degrees of freedom, and then go to the chi-square table and identify our critical value and the critical region of the chi-square probability distribution.

In order to determine our level of significance we simply weigh the costs of making a Type I and a Type II error. Let's say we have done this and have

TABLE 9–13

Row and Column Marginals for Gender and Negative Emotions Data Found in Table 9–7

Gender	Negative Emotionality		
	Low	High	Total
Female	?	?	60
Male	?	?	60
Total	90	30	120

decided that an alpha level of .05 is reasonable for our current problem. The determination of the number of degrees of freedom in a chi-square test of independence is based on the following formula:

$$\text{Degrees of freedom} = (\text{\# of rows} - 1) \times (\text{\# of columns} - 1), \text{ or}$$

$$\text{Degrees of freedom} = (R - 1) \times (C - 1)$$

In the chi-square test of independence, then, the degrees of freedom are equal to the number of rows minus one × the number of columns minus one. In Table 9–7 we have two rows and two columns, so there is $1 \times 1 = 1$, or 1 degree of freedom. Let's look at Table 9–13 to see why we have 1 degree of freedom. Recall that a degree of freedom refers to a value that is free to vary, meaning that it is not fixed and can assume any number. In Table 9–13 we have question marks in each cell of our contingency table, with the row and column marginals provided. We need to figure out which cell frequencies are free to vary given the observed row and column marginals.

In determining how many degrees of freedom we have, the row and column marginals or frequencies are given; therefore, they are not free to vary. What *are* free to vary are the four cell frequencies which correspond to the joint distribution of the two variables. Let's start in the uppermost cell on the left side of Table 9–13 (female and low negative emotions) and ask what value this frequency can be, restricted only by the row and column marginals. Theoretically, this cell can have any frequency as long as we can still get sums of 60 for the row and 90 for the column. This cell frequency, therefore, is free to vary and we have 1 degree of freedom. Let's stick the number 46 in that cell (we could have used any number we wanted). In Table 9–14 we have a value of 46 for the frequency in the uppermost left cell and question marks for the remaining three cells. Let's now move one cell to the right. What value can this cell frequency be and still have a row total of 60 and a column total of 30? There is only one number that this cell frequency can be, and that is 14. A cell frequency of 14 and only 14 will make the row marginal equal to 60 and the column maginal equal to 30. This cell frequency is not, therefore, free to vary but must be equal to 14. Now let's go to the cell in the first column of the second row (male and low negative emotions). Is this cell frequency free to vary? No. It is not free to vary because the column marginal must sum to 90 and the

TABLE 9–14

Determining Degrees of Freedom in a 2 × 2 Table, Fixing the Frequencies for the First Cell

Gender	Negative Emotionality		
	Low	High	Total
Female	46		60
Male			60
Total	90	30	120

row marginal must sum to 60. The only way that this can happen is if the cell frequency is 44. It is fixed, then, and not free to vary. We conclude with the cell just to the right of this one (male and high negative emotions). Is this cell frequency free to vary? No. It is not free to vary either, because the row marginal must sum to 60 and the column marginal must sum to 30. The only value this frequency can be is 16. There is only one cell frequency that is free to vary then (and it could be the frequency in any of the four cells); once that cell frequency is determined, all the other cell frequencies are fixed (i.e., they can be only one value). Now you should understand what the concept of degrees of freedom means with respect to contingency tables and see why there is only 1 degree of freedom in the 2 × 2 contingency table.

We now have all the information we need to conduct our formal hypothesis test that our two categorical variables (gender and negative emotions) are independent of (unrelated to) each other. The null hypothesis is that the two variables are independent and the alternative hypothesis is that they are not independent and that there is a relationship between them. We will test this hypothesis with an alpha of .05. With an alpha of .05 and 1 degree of freedom, we can go to our chi-square probability distribution table (Table E–4 in Appendix E) and find our critical value of the chi-square statistic. Looking in the table, we see that the critical value of chi-square is 3.841, and the critical region is any chi-square value that is greater than or equal to 3.841. We are now ready to conduct our formal hypothesis test, one step at a time:

Step 1.

H_0: Gender and negative emotions are independent of each other. If they are independent, we would expect the value of our obtained chi-square statistic to be zero: $\chi^2 = 0$.

H_1: Gender and negative emotions are not independent of each other. If they are not independent, we would expect the value of our obtained chi-square statistic to be greater than zero: $\chi^2 > 0$.

Recall from our discussion of the chi-square goodness-of-fit statistic that the chi-square distribution is a positive distribution in that we will never have an obtained value that is less than zero. That is because we square the difference between the observed and expected frequencies.

The chi-square test of independence, therefore, always will be a directional or one-tailed test with the alternative stated as $\chi^2 > 0$.

Step 2. Our test statistic is the chi-square test of independence. The chi-square test has a chi-square distribution with $(R - 1) \times (C - 1)$ degrees of freedom.

Step 3. We have selected an alpha level of .05 and have 1 degree of freedom in our 2×2 table. We have discovered that the critical value of chi-square is 3.841. The critical region is defined as any chi-square greater than or equal to 3.841.

Step 4. We have our table of observed frequencies in Table 9–7 and our table of expected frequencies in Table 9–12. The definitional formula for the chi-square test of independence is:

$$\chi^2 = \sum_{i=1}^{k} \frac{(f_o - f_e)^2}{f_e}$$

where k = the number of cells. This formula tells us to subtract the expected cell frequency from the observed cell frequency, square this difference, divide this squared difference by the expected cell frequency, repeat the procedure for every cell in the table, and then sum the results over all cells. This is our obtained value of the chi-square statistic. The calculations for the independence of gender and negative emotions are shown in Table 9–15. As you can see, we have an obtained chi-square of .178.

Step 5. Since our obtained chi-square ($X^2_{obt} = .178$) is less than our critical chi-square ($X^2_{crit} = 3.841$) and does not fall into the critical region, our decision is to fail to reject the null hypothesis. Our conclusion, therefore, is that gender and negative emotions are independent; that is, there is no relationship between them. Our data do not support the hypothesis of Moffitt and her colleagues that males are more likely to experience negative emotions than females.

A SIMPLE-TO-USE COMPUTATIONAL FORMULA FOR THE CHI-SQUARE TEST OF INDEPENDENCE

You may find the definitional formula for the chi-square statistic in equation 9–2 to be somewhat cumbersome. There is an alternative, computational formula you can use to calculate your observed chi-square statistic which you might find easier to use since it involves fewer computations. The computational formula for the chi-square test of independence is:

$$\chi^2 = \sum \left(\frac{f_o^2}{f_e} \right) - n \qquad (9\text{–}3)$$

TABLE 9–15

Calculation of the Chi-Square Statistic for the Null Hypothesis that Gender and Negative Emotions Are Independent

f_o	f_e	$f_o - f_e$	$(f_o - f_e)^2$	$\dfrac{(f_o - f_e)^2}{f_e}$
46	45	1	1	.022
14	15	−1	1	.067
44	45	−1	1	.022
16	15	1	1	.067
				$\chi^2_{obt} = .178$

In this computational formula, the observed frequency for each cell is first squared, and then each squared observed frequency is divided by the expected cell frequency. This is done for each cell in the contingency table. These values are then summed and the total number of cases is subtracted. In steps:

Step 1. Square the observed frequency for each cell in your table.

Step 2. Divide each squared observed frequency by its expected frequency.

Step 3. Perform this operation on each cell in your contingency table and then sum over all cells.

Step 4. Subtract the sample size from this sum. This is your obtained chi-square statistic.

Let's use this computational formula to calculate the chi-square statistic for the gender and negative emotions data in Table 9–7. We show the necessary calculations in Table 9–16. The value of our obtained chi-square statistic is .178, which is exactly what we obtained using the definitional formula.

Case Study: Socioeconomic Status of Neighborhoods and Police Response Time

In Table 9–17 we give you the joint distribution for two categorical variables: (1) the socioeconomic status of a neighborhood and (2) the swiftness of police response time in reaction to a 911 call for assistance. Both variables are measured at the ordinal level. Neighborhood socioeconomic status has three levels or categories ("low status," "medium status," and "high status"), while police response time is also a three-categorical ordinal-level variable, with values of "less than 3 minutes," "between 3 and 7 minutes," and "more than 7 minutes." Our substantive problem is whether or not neighborhood socioeconomic status and police response time are related to each other. We

TABLE 9–16

Calculations for Chi-Square Statistic on Gender and Negative Emotions Data (Tables 9–11 and 9–12) Using the Computational Formula

f_o	f_o^2	f_e	$\dfrac{f_o^2}{f_e}$
46	2,116	45	$(2,116/45) = 47.022$
14	196	15	$(196/15) = 13.067$
44	1,936	45	$(1,936/45) = 43.022$
16	256	15	$(256/15) = 17.067$
			$\Sigma = 120.178$

$\chi^2 = 120.178 - 120$

$\chi^2 = .178$

think that the affluence of the neighborhood influences police response time and that the police respond faster to calls for assistance made from higher-status neighborhoods. In this case study, therefore, neighborhood socioeconomic status is the independent variable and police response time is the dependent variable.

Table 9–17 is a 3 × 3 (again, 3 "by" 3) contingency table because there are three rows and three columns. Each cell in this table represents the joint occurrence of neighborhood status and police response time. With three rows and three columns, there are a total of nine cells, with each cell comprising one possible outcome of the joint occurrence of the two variables. For example, in the uppermost cell on the left side of the table we see that there are 11 cases where there is a low-status neighborhood and a police response time of less than 3 minutes. This cell reflects the simultaneous occurrence of two events, a low-status neighborhood and a police response time of less than 3 minutes. The cell to the right of that indicates that there are 17 cases where there is a low-status neighborhood and a police response time of between 3 and 7 minutes.

Notice that there are a total of 191 cases, which is our total sample size. Notice also that there are 63 low-status neighborhoods, 53 medium-status neighborhoods, and 75 high-status neighborhoods in our data. Recall that these three numbers , 63, 53, and 75, are referred to as the "row marginals" because they tell us the total number of cases that fall into each row of our table. Similarly, there were 75 times when the police responded to a 911 call in less than 3 minutes, 61 times when they responded to a call between 3 and 7 minutes, and 55 times when they responded to a call in more than 7 minutes. These numbers, 75, 61, and 55, are referred to as the "column marginals" because they tell us the total number of cases that fall into each column of our table. The sum of the row marginals should equal the sum of the column marginals, and both of these should equal the total number of cases or observations we have $(63 + 53 + 75 = 75 + 61 + 55 = 191)$.

TABLE 9–17

Joint Distribution of Neighborhood Socioeconomic Status and Police Response Time to a 911 Call for Assistance

Neighborhood Socioeconomic Status	Police Response Time			
	Less than 3 Minutes	3–7 Minutes	More Than 7 Minutes	Total
Low	11	17	35	63
Medium	16	24	13	53
High	48	20	7	75
Total	75	61	55	191

We are now going to conduct the hypothesis test that neighborhood status and police response time are independent events. In other words, we believe that the socioeconomic status of the neighborhood is not related to how quickly the police respond to a 911 call for assistance. Before we conduct a formal hypothesis test, however, there are a number of very simple ways we can initially examine a contingency table to see if there might be a relationship between the two variables. One of the simplest ways is to compare percentages across values of the independent variable for a fixed value of the dependent variable. Recall that what we want to do is vary the independent variable to see if there is variation in the dependent variable. Since the socioeconomic status of the neighborhood is the independent variable, we will use the row marginals as the denominator of our percentages. Practically, this means that our percentages will sum to 100 percent at the end of the rows. We calculate these percentages in Table 9–18. Let's fix the value of the dependent variable at a response time of more than 7 minutes. From Table 9–18 we can see that 56 percent of the time, the police responded to a 911 call for assistance in a low-status neighborhood in more than 7 minutes. This drops to 25 percent of the time in medium-status neighborhoods and drops still further to only 9 percent of the time in high-status neighborhoods. As the social status of the neighborhood varies from low to high, then, it becomes less likely that the police will take a long time to respond to a 911 call (that is, that they will take more than 7 minutes). We get the same picture if we fix the value of the dependent variable at a quick police response time—less than 3 minutes. Police responded quickly only 17 percent of the time in low-status neighborhoods, 30 percent of the time in medium-status neighborhoods, and 64 percent of the time in high-status neighborhoods. Based on these percentage differences it looks like there is a relationship between the socioeconomic status of the neighborhood and how quickly the police respond to a 911 call; they are more likely to respond quickly and less likely to respond slowly in more affluent neighborhoods.

TABLE 9–18

Relationship between Neighborhood Socioeconomic Status and Police Response Time to a 911 Call for Assistance: Examining Percentages

Neighborhood Socioeconomic Status	Police Response Time			
	Less Than 3 Minutes (%)	3–7 Minutes (%)	More Than 7 Minutes (%)	Total (%)
Low	17	27	56	100
Medium	30	45	25	100
High	64	27	9	100

As we have already seen, another way to look at this is to examine what we called the relative risk or relative probability of an event. When we calculate a relative risk, we determine the probability of a value of the dependent variable occurring conditional on different values of the independent variable. What we do, then, is calculate the risk or probability of the dependent variable occurring and condition that probability on each level of the independent variable. Notice that we are doing the same thing as when we compare percentages; we are varying the level of the independent variable to see if that affects the risk or the probability of the dependent variable occurring.

For example, let's calculate the risk of the police responding to a 911 call for assistance in more than 7 minutes, conditional on each level of the independent variable. The probability of the police responding to a 911 call in more than 7 minutes for low-status neighborhoods is .56 (35/63), for medium-status neighborhoods the risk of responding in more than 7 minutes is .25 (13/53), and for high-status neighborhoods it is .09 (7/75). As you can see, the risk or probability of the police responding very slowly (in more than 7 minutes) to a 911 call for assistance varies in different kinds of neighborhoods. It is most likely to occur in low-status neighborhoods and least likely to occur in high-status neighborhoods. Let's now calculate the conditional probability of the police responding quickly (in less than 3 minutes) to a 911 call in the different neighborhoods. In low-status neighborhoods the probability that the police will respond quickly is .17 (11/63), in medium-status neighborhoods it is .30 (16/53), and in high-status neighborhoods it is .64 (48/75). The probability of the police responding quickly to a 911 call for assistance varies substantially across the three different neighborhood types; they are most likely to respond in less than 3 minutes in high-status neighborhoods and least likely to respond so quickly in low-status neighborhoods. It appears, therefore, that when we vary the independent variable (the socioeconomic status of the neighborhood) there does seem to be a dramatic change in the probability of the dependent variable (police response time). This *covariation* (i.e., the condi-

TABLE 9–19

Row and Column Marginals for Calculating Expected Cell Frequencies

Neighborhood Socioeconomic Status	Police Response Time			
	Less Than 3 Minutes	3–7 Minutes	More Than 7 Minutes	Total
Low				63
Medium				53
High				75
Total	75	61	55	191

tion that exists when varying one variable shows variation in the second variable) is the key indicator that our two variables are related.

Recall, however, that the problem with using the calculation of percentage differences or relative risks to determine whether or not there is a relationship between two variables is that there is no probability distribution associated with these statistics. We need a known probability distribution in order to determine whether the difference in relative risks for the independent variable we observed in our sample data is due to the fact that there is a relationship between the two variables in our population or simply due to sampling variability. Without a formal hypothesis test we have no way of knowing how large a difference there must be among our percentage differences or relative risks in order for us to conclude that there is in fact a relationship between the two variables. A formal hypothesis test avoids this ambiguity, and that is why we use the chi-square test of independence.

The first step in conducting a chi-square test of independence is to determine what the expected frequencies would be if the two variables were in fact independent. Using the restricted form of the multiplication rule and the row and column marginals in Table 9–19, we can calculate the probability of both a low-status neighborhood and a police response time of less than 3 minutes as:

$$P(\text{low neighborhood status}) = \frac{63}{191} = .330,$$

$$P(\text{less than 3 minutes response time}) = \frac{75}{191} = .393,$$

$$P(\text{low status and less than 3 minutes}) = (.330) \times (.393) = .130$$

The probability that a neighborhood both is low in socioeconomic status and has an average police response time of less than 3 minutes is .130. This is not, however, an expected cell frequency; it is just the probability of someone falling into that cell when the null hypothesis of independence is true. To find the expected cell frequency, recall that we need to multiply this probability by the total number of cases, or n. If the null hypothesis of independence is true, then, we should expect to find $.130 \times 191 = 25$ persons in that cell. We now can calculate the other expected cell frequencies using the same procedure.

$$P(\text{low status and } 3-7 \text{ mins. response time}) = \frac{63}{191} \times \frac{61}{191} = .330 \times .319 = .105;$$

$$\text{Expected cell frequency} = .105 \times 191 = 20$$

$$P(\text{low status and more than 7 mins. response time}) = \frac{63}{191} \times \frac{55}{191} = .330 \times .288 = .095;$$

$$\text{Expected cell frequency} = .095 \times 191 = 18$$

$$P(\text{medium status and less than 3 mins. response time}) = \frac{53}{191} \times \frac{75}{191} = .277 \times .393 = .109;$$

$$\text{Expected cell frequency} = .109 \times 191 = 21$$

$$P(\text{medium status and } 3-7 \text{ mins. response time}) = \frac{53}{191} \times \frac{61}{191} = .277 \times .319 = .088;$$

$$\text{Expected cell frequency} = .088 \times 191 = 17$$

$$P(\text{medium status and more than 7 mins. response time}) = \frac{53}{191} \times \frac{55}{191} = .227 \times .288 = .080;$$

$$\text{Expected cell frequency} = .080 \times 191 = 15$$

$$P(\text{high status and less than 3 mins. response time}) = \frac{75}{191} \times \frac{75}{191} = .393 \times .393 = .154;$$

$$\text{Expected cell frequency} \times .154 \times 191 = 29$$

$$P(\text{high status and } 3-7 \text{ mins. response time}) = \frac{75}{191} \times \frac{61}{191} = .393 \times .319 = .125;$$

$$\text{Expected cell frequency} = .125 \times 191 = 24$$

$$P(\text{high status and more than 7 mins. response time}) = \frac{75}{191} \times \frac{55}{191} = .393 \times .288 = .113;$$

$$\text{Expected cell frequency} = .113 \times 191 = 22$$

The expected cell frequencies under the null hypothesis that neighborhood socioeconomic status and police response time are independent of each other are given in Table 9–20. If you were to use the alternative formula for calculating the expected cell frequencies, you would obtain the following:

$$\text{Low status and less than 3 minutes response time: } \frac{63 \times 75}{191} = 25$$

$$\text{Low status and 3--7 minutes response time: } \frac{63 \times 61}{191} = 20$$

$$\text{Low status and more than 7 minutes response time: } \frac{63 \times 55}{191} = 18$$

$$\text{Medium status and less than 3 minutes response time: } \frac{53 \times 75}{191} = 21$$

$$\text{Medium status and 3 -- 7 minutes response time: } \frac{53 \times 61}{191} = 17$$

$$\text{Medium status and more than 7 minutes response time: } \frac{53 \times 55}{191} = 15$$

$$\text{High status and less than 3 minutes response time: } \frac{75 \times 75}{191} = 29$$

$$\text{High status and 3--7 minutes response time: } \frac{75 \times 61}{191} = 24$$

$$\text{High status and more than 7 minutes response time: } \frac{75 \times 55}{191} = 22$$

These expected frequencies are exactly what we obtained by using the multiplication rule for independent events.

TABLE 9–20

Expected Cell Frequencies Under the Null Hypothesis of Independence

| Neighborhood Socioeconomic Status | Police Response Time | | | |
	Less than 3 Minutes	3–7 Minutes	More Than 7 Minutes	Total
Low	25	20	18	63
Medium	21	17	15	53
High	29	24	22	75
Total	75	61	55	191

We now have two tables of cell frequencies. Table 9–17 is a table of observed cell frequencies. This table shows the joint distribution of the two variables we have observed with our sample data of 191 respondents. Table 9–20 is a table of expected cell frequencies. This table shows what the joint distribution would look like if the two variables were independent. This is the expected joint distribution we would find if neighborhood status and police response time were not related to each other. Recall that the chi-square test of independence is based upon the difference between the expected and the observed cell frequencies. In order to proceed with this hypothesis test, we need to determine our alpha level and our degrees of freedom. Let's use an alpha level of .01 for this hypothesis test. Using our formula for the correct degrees of freedom in a contingency table [df = $(R - 1) \times (C - 1)$], we can see that we have $(3 - 1) \times (3 - 1)$, or 4 degrees of freedom.

Now that we have selected an alpha level of .01 and 4 degrees of freedom, we can go to our chi-square probability distribution table (Table E–4 in Appendix E) and find our critical value of the chi-square statistic. Looking in the table, we see that the critical value of chi-square is 13.277, and the critical region is any chi-square value that is greater than or equal to 13.277. We are now ready to conduct our formal hypothesis test, one step at a time.

Step 1.

H_0: Neighborhood socioeconomic status and police response time are independent of each other. Our obtained value of chi-square should not be significantly different from zero: $\chi^2 = 0$.

H_1: Neighborhood socioeconomic status and police response time are not independent of each other. Our obtained value of chi-square should be significantly greater than zero: $\chi^2 > 0$.

Step 2. Our test statistic is the chi-square test of independence. The chi-square test has a chi-square distribution.

Step 3. We have selected an alpha level of .01 and have 4 degrees of freedom in our 3×3 table. We have discovered that the critical value of chi-square is 13.277. The critical region is defined as any chi-square greater than or equal to 13.277.

Step 4. We have our observed table of cell frequencies in Table 9–17 and our table of expected cell frequencies in Table 9–20. The formula for the chi-square statistic is:

$$\chi^2 = \sum_{i=1}^{k} \frac{(f_o - f_e)^2}{f_e}$$

where k = the number of cell frequencies. This formula tells us to subtract the expected cell frequency from the observed cell

TABLE 9–21

Calculation of the Chi-Square Statistic for the Null Hypothesis That Neighborhood Socioeconomic Status and Police Response Time Are Independent

f_o	f_e	$f_o - f_e$	$(f_o - f_e)^2$	$\dfrac{(f_o - f_e)}{f_e}$
11	25	−14	196	7.84
17	20	−3	9	.45
35	18	17	289	16.06
16	21	−5	25	1.19
24	17	7	49	2.88
13	15	−2	4	.27
48	29	19	361	12.45
20	24	−4	16	.67
7	22	−15	225	10.23
				$\chi^2_{obt} = 52.04$

frequency, square this difference, divide this squared difference by the expected cell frequency, repeat the procedure for every cell in the table, and then sum the results over all cells. This is our obtained value of the chi-square statistic. The calculations for this problem are shown in Table 9–21, and our obtained chi-square is 52.04.

Step 5. Since our obtained chi-square ($X^2_{obt} = 52.04$) is greater than our critical chi-square ($X^2_{obt} = 13.277$) and falls into the critical region, our decision is to reject the null hypothesis. Our conclusion, therefore, is that neighborhood socioeconomic status and police response time are not independent; that is, they are related to one another in the population. For comparison, we will also use the computational formula for chi-square. These results are provided in Table 9–22. The obtained chi-square statistic is 52.04, exactly what we obtained with the definitional formula.

While the chi-square statistic will allow us to reject the null hypothesis of independence in favor of the alternative hypothesis that there is a relationship between the two variables, it does not tell us anything about the magnitude or strength of the relationship. Two variables may be related to each other in the population, but the relationship may be very weak, of moderate strength, or very strong. In order to determine the strength of the relationship between two categorical variables, we need to learn about something called measures of association. We will do this in the next section.

TABLE 9–22

Computational Formula: Calculation of the Chi-Square Statistic for the Null Hypothesis That Neighborhood Socioeconomic Status and Police Response Time Are Independent

f_o	f_o^2	f_e	$\dfrac{f_o^2}{f_e}$
11	121	25	4.84
17	289	20	14.45
35	1,225	18	68.06
16	256	21	12.19
24	576	17	33.88
13	169	15	11.27
48	2,304	29	79.45
20	400	24	16.67
7	49	22	2.23

$$\Sigma = 243.04$$
$$\chi^2_{obt} = 243.04 - 191$$
$$\chi^2_{obt} = 52.04$$

MEASURES OF ASSOCIATION: DETERMINING THE STRENGTH OF THE RELATIONSHIP BETWEEN TWO CATEGORICAL VARIABLES

The chi-square statistic will allow us to determine whether two categorical variables (nominal or ordinal) are independent or related to each other in the population, but it tells us nothing about the strength of the relationship if in fact one exists. If we are interested in understanding the strength of the relationship between our variables, we need to be acquainted with something called measures of association. A **measure of association** is a summary measure that captures the magnitude or strength of the relationship between two variables. There are different kinds of measures of association depending on the level of measurement for our variables.

> **Measures of association** are statistics that inform us about the strength or magnitude as well as the direction of the relationship between two variables..

Nominal-Level Variables

Let's start with a very simple problem. In this problem we have a 2 × 2 contingency table with nominal-level data. For example, in Table 9–23 we have the joint distribution of two nominal-level variables, the gender of a police officer (male/female) and the type of job they do (desk job/patrol). We think that male and female police officers are given very different assignments. When we calculate the relative risk of having a patrol assignment, we see that male police officers are about two times more likely to have a patrol assignment (.64;

TABLE 9–23

Joint Distribution of Gender of Police Officer and Type of Work Performed

Gender	Desk Job	Patrol	Total
Male	45	80	125
Female	30	15	45
Total	75	95	170

80/125) than female officers (.33; 15/45). If we were to conduct a hypothesis test of the independence of these two variables, we would have an obtained chi-square of 12.25 (calculate this chi-square for practice). With 1 degree of freedom, we would reject the null hypothesis of independence at either a .05 or .01 level of significance. We would conclude that the two variables are not independent but related to one another.

A measure of association we could use in this problem to gauge the strength of the relationship is the phi coefficient. The phi coefficient (ϕ) is appropriate when we have nominal-level variables and a 2×2 table. The phi coefficient is very simple to calculate and uses the obtained value of our chi-square coefficient:

$$\phi = \sqrt{\frac{X^2}{n}} \qquad \textbf{(9–4)}$$

To obtain the phi coefficient, therefore, all we do is take the square root of our obtained chi-square divided by our sample size. The phi coefficient will equal zero when there is no relationship and will attain a maximum value of 1.0 with a perfect relationship. The phi coefficient will always be positive, and the magnitude of the relationship will tell us how strongly the two nominal-level variables are related. Magnitudes of phi near zero indicate a very weak relationship, while those nearing 1.0 indicate a very strong relationship. A helpful rule of thumb to follow with the phi coefficient and any measure of association is that relationships between 0 and ±.29 can be considered "weak," relationships between ±.30 and ±.59 can be considered "moderate," and relationships between ±.60 and ±1.00 can be considered "strong." However, this is only an informal guide. For the data in Table 9–23, we would have a phi coefficient of:

$$\phi = \sqrt{\frac{12.25}{170}}$$

$$\phi = .27$$

A phi coefficient of .27 tells us that there is a weak relationship between gender and type of assignment on the police force.

The phi coefficient cannot be used for nominal variables that have more than two levels or categories. One measure of association for tables that are larger than 2×2 is the **contingency coefficient (C)**. Like phi, the contingency coefficient is based upon the obtained value of the chi-square statistic. The formula for C is:

$$C = \sqrt{\frac{\chi^2}{n + \chi^2}}$$

(9–5)

Let's work through an example.

Case Study: Type of Counsel and Sentence   In Table 9–24 we show you the joint distribution of two nominal-level variables: (1) the type of lawyer a criminal defendant had and (2) the type of sentence they received after conviction. We think that the type of lawyer someone has may affect the kind of sentence they receive, so type of lawyer is the independent variable and type of sentence is the dependent variable. When we conduct a chi-square test of independence at an alpha level of .01 and 4 degrees of freedom, we reject the null hypothesis. Upon completing the calculations, we find: ($\chi^2_{\text{crit}} = 13.277$, $\chi^2_{\text{obt}} = 32.52$). We conclude from this that there is a relationship in the population between these two variables, although we do not know the strength of the relationship. We use the contingency coefficient to tell us that:

$$C = \sqrt{\frac{32.52}{160 + 32.52}}$$

$$C = .41$$

A contingency coefficient of .41 informs us that there is a moderate strong relationship between the type of lawyer one has and the type of sentence one receives when convicted.

Although it is easy to calculate, one of the disadvantages of the contingency coefficient is that it is not always anchored by a maximum value of 1.0. In fact, the maximum value of C will vary depending upon the size of the table, although it will never be greater than 1.0. Another measure of association for nominal-level variables that does not have this disadvantage is known as **Cramer's V.** Cramer's V also can be used with nominal-level data

TABLE 9–24

Joint Distribution for Type of Lawyer and Type of Sentence Received

Type of Lawyer	Type of Sentence Received			
	Probation	Fine Only	Fine and Jail Time	Total
Court Appointed	5	10	40	55
Public Defender	15	20	30	65
Private	25	10	5	40
Total	45	40	75	160

and with tables that are larger than 2×2. Like C and the phi coefficient, it is based on chi-square and it ranges in magnitude from 0 to 1.0. The formula is:

$$V = \sqrt{\frac{\chi^2}{n(k-1)}} \tag{9–6}$$

where k = the number of rows or the number of columns, whichever is smaller. For Table 9–24, the value of V would be:

$$V = \sqrt{\frac{32.52}{160(3-1)}}$$

$$V = .32$$

We would conclude from this that there is a moderate association between type of lawyer and type of sentence.

Another measure of association with nominal-level data is **lambda (λ).** Lambda can be used on tables that are larger than 2×2, and it is known as a proportionate reduction in error (PRE) measure of association. Recall that when two variables are independent, knowledge of one variable will not help us predict the occurrence of the other. When two variables are related to one another, however (that is, when they are not independent), then knowing something about one variable should help us predict the other, and the more strongly they are related the more help we get in using the independent variable to predict the dependent variable. A proportionate reduction in error measure can tell us exactly how much better we will be in predicting one variable based on our knowledge of the other. The calculation of lambda requires that we identify beforehand which variable is independent and which variable is dependent because its magnitude will be different depending on this identification. Because of this fact, lambda is known as an asymmetric measure of association.

The magnitude of our lambda coefficient will vary between zero and 1.0. A value of zero means that we cannot reduce our errors in predicting the dependent variable from knowledge of the independent variable, while a value of 1.0 means that we can reduce all of our errors—or that knowledge of the independent variable will allow us to predict with perfect accuracy the value of the dependent variable. Magnitudes of lambda close to zero suggest that the relationship between the variables is weak, and the strength of the relationship increases as the observed lambda value approaches 1.0. An easy way to interpret lambda is to multiply the obtained value by 100. This gives us the percentage amount that we can reduce our prediction errors in the dependent variable by having information about the independent variable. So, for example, if we have an obtained lambda of .70 we can claim that we can reduce our prediction errors in the dependent variable by 70 percent by having knowledge of the independent variable. For an obtained lambda of .15, we have reduced our prediction errors by only 15 percent. The whole notion of prediction errors and the reduction of these errors may be a bit vague, so let's carefully go through an example.

Let's use the data in Table 9–24. Suppose without any other information we have to predict what the sentence would be for each of these 160 criminal defendants. What would our best guess be? Our best guess for each case would be the mode of the dependent variable—a fine and jail time ($n = 75$). If we predicted that each of the 160 defendants would be sentenced to pay a fine and serve some jail time, we would be correct 75 times (the actual number who received this sentence) and we would have made 85 prediction errors (the 45 who received probation plus the 40 who received a fine only). With 75 correct predictions (and 85 incorrect predictions) out of 160, we would have a 47 percent correct rate of prediction. The question now is whether and the extent to which we can improve on this by having some knowledge of the independent variable.

In the calculation of lambda we ask the following question: "If I use the modal response for each level or category of the independent variable to predict the dependent variable, how many prediction errors will I make?" Among defendants who had court appointed lawyers, the mode is a fine with jail time. Using this mode to predict the dependent variable for defendants with court appointed lawyers, you would accurately predict 40 cases (because 40 defendants with court appointed lawyers received a fine with jail time) and make 15 prediction errors (because you predicted that they would receive a fine and jail time and, instead, 5 received probation and 10 received a fine only). The mode for those with public defenders is also a fine with jail time. If you predicted that all 65 of these cases would receive a fine with jail time, you would be correct 30 times and make 35 prediction errors. The mode for those defendants with private lawyers is probation. If you predicted that all 40 defendants with private lawyers would receive probation, you would be correct 25 times and make 15 prediction errors. Using the mode of each level of the independent variable to predict the category of the dependent variable, then, you would make a total of $15 + 35 + 15 = 65$ prediction errors. If you were not to use knowledge of the independent variable to predict the dependent variable, recall that you would make 85 errors. The formula for the lambda coefficient is:

$$\lambda = \frac{\begin{array}{c}\text{Number of errors} \\ \text{using mode of} \\ \text{dependent variable}\end{array} - \begin{array}{c}\text{Number of errors using mode} \\ \text{of dependent variable within} \\ \text{categories of the independent} \\ \text{variable}\end{array}}{\text{Number of errors using mode of dependent variable}} \qquad (9\text{–}7)$$

In our example, with type of counsel as the independent variable and type of sentence as the dependent variable (Table 9–24), the observed value of lambda is:

$$\lambda = \frac{85 - 65}{85}$$

$$\lambda = .23$$

Multiplying this by 100, we can conclude that we are able to reduce our errors in predicting the dependent variable (type of sentence received) by 23 percent when we use the independent variable. To see why we have a proportionate reduction in errors of 23 percent, remember that when we used only the mode of the dependent variable to predict sentence type, we made 85 errors out of 160 predictions, for an error rate of 53 percent. When we used knowledge of the independent variable to predict the type of sentence, we made 65 errors out of 160 predictions, for an error rate of 41 percent.

The percent difference in the error rates of 53 percent (without using the independent variable) and 41 percent (error rate when using the independent variable) is 12 percent. Twelve percent is equal to 23 percent of our error rate of 53 percent obtained when we did not use the independent variable. Hence the proportionate reduction in error is 23 percent—this is the value of our lambda statistic.

There is also a computational formula for lambda that is very easy to use:

$$\lambda = \frac{(\Sigma f_i) - f_d}{n - f_d} \qquad (9\text{--}8)$$

where

f_i = the largest cell frequency *in each* category of the independent variable,

d = the largest marginal frequency of the dependent variable, and

n = the total number of cases.

For the data in Table 9–24, the largest cell frequency for court appointed lawyers is 40, for public defenders it is 30, and for private counsel it is 25. The largest marginal frequency for the dependent values is 75, for the value "fine and jail time." With this information we can calculate the value of lambda as:

$$\lambda = \frac{(40 + 30 + 25) - 75}{160 - 75}$$

$$\lambda = .23$$

And this is the same value as we derived using our other, definitional formula.

Ordinal-Level Variables

When our variables are measured at the ordinal level, phi, the contingency coefficient, Cramer's V, and the lambda coefficient are no longer appropriate measures of association. With ordinal-level variables, one of the most popular measures of association in the literature is **Goodman and Kruskal's gamma.** Like lambda, gamma is a proportionate reduction in error measure, which takes on a minimum value of zero (when there is no relationship between the two ordinal variables) and a maximum value of ± 1.0 (for a perfect positive and a perfect negative relationship). As we noted with respect to the phi coefficient, a helpful rule of thumb to follow with any measure of association—but only as an informal guide—is that relationships between zero and $\pm .29$ can be considered "weak," relationships between $\pm .30$ and $\pm .59$ can be considered "moderate," and relationships between $\pm .60$ and ± 1.00 can be considered "strong." Unlike lambda, gamma is a symmetric measure of association, meaning that it does not matter which variable we designate as the independent and dependent variable.

In the special case of a 2 × 2 table (a table with two rows and two columns), gamma is often referred to as **Yule's Q** instead. With the four cells labeled as:

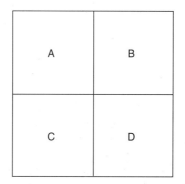

Yule's Q or gamma for a 2 × 2 table is defined as:

$$Q = \frac{(f_{\text{cell a}} \times f_{\text{cell d}}) - (f_{\text{cell b}} \times f_{\text{cell c}})}{(f_{\text{cell a}} \times f_{\text{cell d}}) + (f_{\text{cell b}} \times f_{\text{cell c}})} \qquad (9\text{–}9)$$

To calculate the Q coefficient, then, all you do is take the product of the frequency in cell A times the frequency in cell D, and the product of the frequency in cell B times the frequency in cell C. In the numerator of Q we take the difference between these two values, and in the denominator we take the sum.

Let's use this formula to calculate the value of Q for our two variables in Table 9–7, which showed the joint distribution of gender and negative emotions. Recall that we failed to reject the null hypothesis when we conducted our chi-square test of independence. The value of Q is:

$$Q = \frac{(46 \times 16) - (44 \times 14)}{(46 \times 16) + (44 \times 14)}$$

$$Q = \frac{120}{1,352}$$

$$Q = .09$$

The value of Yule's Q here is very small—not that much different from zero—confirming our chi-square test that there is no relationship in the population between gender and negative emotions.

Case Study: Adolescents' Employment and Drug and Alcohol Use   Let's try another example. In Table 9–25 we show you the joint distribution of two variables. One variable is the number of hours that a youth spends working during the school year, and the second is the number of times during the year that he or she reports using drugs or alcohol. In this example we will take the num-

TABLE 9–25

Joint Distribution of Number of Hours Worked per Week During the School Year and Number of Times a Youth Has Used Drugs or Alcohol

	Number of Times Used Drugs/Alcohol		
Number of Hours Worked	0	1 or More	Total
Less than 20	15	60	75
20 or More	40	20	60
Total	55	80	135

ber of working hours as the independent variable and the level of drug/alcohol use as the dependent variable. If we conduct a chi-square test of independence, we obtain a chi-square of 31.85, which with 1 degree of freedom is significant at either a .05 or a .01 level. Therefore, we reject the null hypothesis of independence and conclude that there is a relationship between the two variables. We can then determine the strength of the relationship with Yule's Q:

$$Q = \frac{(15 \times 20) - (40 \times 60)}{(15 \times 20) + (40 \times 60)}$$

$$Q = \frac{-2,100}{2,700}$$

$$Q = -.78$$

We see that we have a Yule's Q of $-.78$, implying that there is a strong negative relationship between working while in school and substance use. What does a negative relationship imply here?

In a **negative relationship,** increasing the level of one variable has the effect of decreasing the level of the other, while in a **positive relationship,** increasing the level of one variable has the effect of increasing the level of the other. Notice that in Table 9–25 the two variables are arranged in increasing order in the sense that drug/alcohol use increases from left to right (zero use to using it one or more times) and working increases from less than 20 hours per week in the

> In a **negative relationship** between two variables, an increase in the value of one variable is related to a decrease in the value of the other. In a **positive relationship** between two variables, an increase in one variable is related to an increase in the other.

top row to working 20 or more hours per week in the lower row. A negative relationship between two ordinal-level variables means that increasing the independent variable decreases the dependent variable. In this case, increasing the level of working from under 20 hours per week to 20 or more hours has the effect of decreasing the level of the dependent variable (using drugs/alcohol) from one or more times to zero. Had we obtained a Q coefficient of $+.78$, then we would have concluded that increasing the level of working from under 20 to more than 20 hours per week increases the risk of drug/alcohol use from zero times to one or more times.

In contingency tables that are larger than 2 × 2, we cannot use Yule's Q, but must use a more general formula for Goodman and Kruskal's gamma that can be used on any table. The formula for gamma is:

$$\gamma = \frac{CP - DP}{CP + DP} \qquad (9\text{--}10)$$

where

CP = the number of concordant pairs of observations, and

DP = the number of discordant pairs of observations.

Before we get to the application of the gamma coefficient, it is first necessary that we understand exactly what a concordant and discordant pair of observations is.

Case Study: Age of Onset for Delinquency and Future Offending   Let's begin with two variables measured from a sample of adult offenders. Both variables are measured at the ordinal level and have three levels or categories. The first variable is the age at which delinquent offending first started:

Variable 1 (V_1) : Age of First Delinquent Act:

Level 1: 8–10 years old

Level 2: 11–13 years old

Level 3: 14–16 years old

The second variable is the number of years into adulthood that the person offends:

Variable 2 (V_2): Years of "Criminal Career":

Level 1: 1–4 years

Level 2: 5–8 years

Level 3: 9 years or more

Since these two variables are measured at the ordinal level, those at a higher level or category have more of the variable than those at a lower level. Let's now take five people from our sample who fall into different categories of the two ordinal variables. The following table shows the level or "score" on both variables for each of these five people.

Person Number	Level on V_1	Level on V_2
1	1	2
2	2	3
3	3	2
4	3	3
5	3	2

Two pairs of observations are said to be *concordant* when the scores on the two variables are consistently higher or consistently lower. For example, let's take person 1 and person 2. In comparing person 1 and person 2 on the two variables, we see that the second person scores higher on both V_1 and V_2 (2 vs. 1 on V_1 and 3 vs. 2 on V_2). This pair of persons or pair of observations, then, is concordant because person 2 scores consistently higher on both variables compared with person 1. Person 4 is concordant with person 1 also, because that person also scores higher than person 1 on both variables (3 vs. 1 on V_1 and 3 vs. 2 on V_2).

Now let's compare person 2 and person 3. Person 2 is lower on V_1 compared with person 3 (2 vs. 3) but higher on V_2 (3 vs. 2). Person 2 is not, therefore, consistently higher (or lower) on both variables than person 3, but is higher on one variable and lower on another. Pairs of observations like these, where one case is higher on one variable but lower on another, are called *discordant*. Think of discordant pairs of cases as those where the scores on the two variables are dissimilar. A person is higher than the other person on one variable but lower than that person on another variable. Person 5 is also discordant with person 2.

Now let's compare person 3 with person 4. In this pair of observations, persons 3 and 4 are tied on V_1 and person 4 is higher than person 3 on V_2. Person 4 also is tied with person 2 on the second variable (V_2). Person 3 is tied with person 5 on both variables. These three comparisons are neither concordant nor discordant; rather, they are referred to as *tied* pairs of observations because they have the same score on at least one variable.

In comparing a pair of cases, then, there are three possible outcomes: concordant pairs, discordant pairs, or tied pairs. In a given contingency table, if concordant pairs outnumber discordant pairs, we will find a positive relationship because the predominance of concordant pairs implies that as one variable increases so does the other. If we have instead a predominance of discordant pairs, then we will find a negative relationship between the two variables because this implies that as one variable increases the other decreases. If there are approximately the same number of concordant as discordant pairs, then our variables are not related to one other or are not related very strongly.

Now that we know what concordant and discordant pairs are, we can reintroduce the gamma coefficient and apply it to a few of our examples. Recall that the formula for gamma is:

$$\gamma = \frac{CP - DP}{CP + DP}$$

Gamma, therefore, simply takes the ratio of the difference between the number of concordant pairs of cases (CP) and the number of discordant pairs (DP) to the sum of the concordant and discordant pairs.

Like Yule's Q, gamma ranges in magnitude from zero to ± 1.0, with zero indicating no relationship between our ordinal-level variables, -1.0 indicating a perfect negative relationship, and $+1.0$ indicating a perfect positive relationship. As you can perhaps see from the formula, gamma takes into account only concordant and discordant pairs of cases; it ignores all those tied on one or both of the variables. Notice also that when $CP > DP$ gamma will be positive and when $CP < DP$ gamma will be negative. Finally, notice that the magnitude of gamma will increase as the number of CP or DP cases increases relative to the other. Now, the only question remaining is how to go about calculating gamma.

Let's use as an example the data in Table 9–26, which shows the relationship between the grades a student received in school during the past year and the number of times a student reported stealing something. When calculating gamma you should make sure that both values are arranged in ascending order. In this example, we take school grades as the independent variable and theft as the dependent variable. In order to calculate gamma, we need to identify and count the number of concordant and discordant pairs. Fortunately, there is a very simple algorithm for doing this. To calculate the number of concordant pairs, start in the top left-most cell (mostly Ds or Fs and zero acts of theft). Then ignore all cases that are in the same row or the same column as this cell (because these cases are tied), and multiply this cell frequency by the sum of all cell frequencies that are both *below* and *to the right of* this cell. The number of concordant pairs with this cell is equal to: $23 \times (157 + 123 + 345 + 155 + 166 + 56) = 23,046$. We show the cells that are concordant with the top left-most cell in the shaded area of Table 9–27. Next, move to the cell to the right of this first cell and repeat the same procedure. Multiply this cell frequency by the sum of all cell frequencies that are both below and to the right of this cell: $19 \times (123 + 155 + 56) = 6,346$ concordant pairs. We cannot go to the next cell to the right because there would be no cases both below and to the right of this, so we go down to the first cell of the second row (mostly Cs). Multiply this cell frequency by the sum of all cell frequencies both below and to the right of this: $307 \times (345 + 155 + 166 + 56) = 221,654$ concordant pairs. Moving to the cell immediately to the right and performing the same operation, we have: $157 \times (155 + 56) = 33,127$ concordant pairs. Then follow the same procedure for the first cell of the third row (mostly Bs), multiplying the cell frequency by the sum of the cell frequencies that are both below and to the right of that cell: $762 \times (166 + 56) = 169,164$ concordant pairs. Moving to the cell to the right, we find: $345 \times (56) = 19,320$ concordant pairs. Summing this, we have a total of $23,046 + 6,346 + 221,654 + 33,127 + 169,164 + 19,320 = 472,657$ concordant pairs.

To calculate the number of discordant pairs of observations, do the following. Start in the lower left-most cell, the cell that is "low" on the column variable but "high" on the row variable (in this case, zero acts of theft and mostly As). Ignore all cells that are in the same row or the same column (again, because these observations are tied on one or both of the variables). Multiply this cell frequency by the sum of the cell frequencies for all cells that are both *above* and *to the right of* this cell. The number of discordant pairs with those in this cell is equal to: $418 \times (345 + 155 + 157 + 123 + 19 + 20) = 342,342$. We show the cells that are discordant to the cell in the lower left cor-

TABLE 9–26

Grades in School and Self-Reported Acts of Petty Theft

Grades in School	Self-Reported Acts of Theft			
	0	1–5	6+	Total
Mostly Ds and Fs	23	19	20	62
Mostly Cs	307	157	123	587
Mostly Bs	762	345	155	1,262
Mostly As	418	166	56	640
Total	1,510	687	354	2,551

TABLE 9–27

Cells That Are Concordant with Those in the Top Left-Most Cell

Grades in School	Self-Reported Acts of Theft			
	0	1–5	6+	Total
Mostly Ds and Fs	23	19	20	62
Mostly Cs	307	157	123	587
Mostly Bs	762	345	155	1,262
Mostly As	418	166	56	640
Total	1,510	687	354	2,551

ner in the shaded area of Table 9–28. Move to the cell immediately to the right of this and multiply this cell frequency by the sum of all cell frequencies that are both above and to the right of this: $166 \times (155 + 123 + 20) = 49{,}468$ discordant pairs. If we move to the next cell to the right (56), there are no cells both above and to the right, so we move to the first cell in the row above this. Multiply this cell frequency by the sum of all cell frequencies that are both above and to the right of this: $762 \times (157 + 123 + 19 + 20) = 243{,}078$ discordant pairs. Continue multiplying each cell frequency by the sum of all cell frequencies that are both above and to the right:

$$345 \times (123 + 20) = 49{,}335$$

$$307 \times (19 + 20) = 11{,}973$$

$$157 \times (20) = 3{,}140$$

There are a total of $342{,}342 + 49{,}468 + 243{,}078 + 49{,}335 + 11{,}973 + 3{,}140 = 699{,}336$ discordant pairs.

With the number of both concordant and discordant pairs determined, we are now ready to calculate our gamma coefficient for Table 9–26:

TABLE 9–28

Cells That Are Discordant with Those in the Lower Left-Most Cell

Grades in School	Self-Reported Acts of Theft			Total
	0	1–5	6+	
Mostly Ds and Fs	23	19	20	62
Mostly Cs	307	157	123	587
Mostly Bs	762	345	155	1,262
Mostly As	418	166	56	640
Total	1,510	687	354	2,551

$$\gamma = \frac{472,657 - 699,336}{472,657 + 699,336}$$

$$\gamma = -.19$$

We have an obtained gamma coefficient of $-.19$, telling us that there is a weak negative relationship between school grades and self-reported theft. Recall that the presence of a negative relationship means that an increase in the independent variable is associated with a decrease in the dependent variable. Looking at Table 9–26, this means that as a student's grades "increase" (that is, improve by going from Ds and Fs to As) they are less likely to commit acts of theft. In other words, having good grades acts to inhibit theft.

One more example might be helpful. In Table 9–29 we have the joint distribution of two ordinal-level variables, the number of years that a police officer has been on the police force, and the number of arrests in the past year that were thrown out by the courts for legal technicalities. We think that as the number of years that an officer is on the force increases, so does the number of arrests that are thrown out of court. This is because we believe that new recruits have more up-to-date knowledge of the law, while the knowledge of older police officers is more likely to be outdated, resulting in arrests that violate suspects' constitutional rights. The independent variable here is the number of years on the force, and the dependent variable is the number of arrests thrown out of court. You should do the calculations yourself, but the obtained value of the chi-square statistic for this example is 79.5, and with 4 degrees of freedom the obtained chi-square is greater than the critical chi-square at either a .05 or a .01 alpha level. We would, therefore, reject the null hypothesis of independence and conclude that there is a relationship between years of police experience and having an arrest thrown out by the courts.

We will now calculate the gamma coefficient to determine the strength of this relationship. Using the algorithm we learned above, we find there are a total of 18,180 concordant pairs (10,080 + 2,000 + 3,300 + 2,800):

TABLE 9–29

Number of Years on the Police Force and the Number of Arrests Thrown Out of Court

| Number of Years on Force | Number of Arrests Thrown Out by the Courts | | | |
	0	1–2	3 or More	Total
1–5 Years	56	20	9	85
6–10 Years	30	40	30	100
11 Years or More	15	40	70	125
Total	101	100	109	310

$$56 \times (40 + 30 + 40 + 70) = 10,080$$

$$20 \times (30 + 70) = 2,000$$

$$30 \times (40 + 70) = 3,300$$

$$40 \times (70) = 2,800$$

The number of discordant pairs is equal to 4,275 (1,485 + 1,560 + 870 + 360):

$$15 \times (40 + 30 + 20 + 9) = 1,485$$

$$40 \times (30 + 9) = 1,560$$

$$30 \times (20 + 9) = 870$$

$$40 \times (9) = 360$$

Finally, our value of gamma is:

$$\gamma = \frac{18,180 - 4,275}{18,180 + 4,275}$$

$$\gamma = .62$$

The gamma coefficient tells us that there is a strong positive relationship between the number of years that an officer has been on the police force and the number of arrests they have had thrown out of court. Officers on the force for a longer time have more arrests thrown out of court than do those officers who have more recently been schooled in the constitutional rights of suspected criminals.

SUMMARY

In this chapter we learned about two kinds of significance tests for categorical variables. In the first, we tested the null hypothesis that the distribution of a categorical variable in the population followed some specified form. We used the chi-square goodness of fit test for this. In the second, we tested the null hypothesis that two categorical variables (nominal or ordinal) were independent against the alternative that there was a relationship between them. We used the chi-square test of independence for this hypothesis test. In both tests, we examined the difference between some observed frequency and that expected under the null hypothesis. We also examined measures of association, which capture information about the strength of the relationship between two categorical variables. The appropriate measure of association depends upon the level of measurement of our variables.

KEY TERMS

chi-square goodness-of-fit test
chi-square test of independence
column marginal or column frequency
contingency coefficient (C)
contingency table
Cramer's V
expected frequencies
Goodman and Kruskal's gamma
joint frequency distribution

lambda
measure of association
negative relationship
observed frequencies
percentage differences
positive relationship
relative risk
row marginal or row frequency
Yule's Q

KEY FORMULAS

Definitional formula for chi-square statistic (eq. 9–1) and (eq. 9–2):

$$\chi^2 = \sum_{i=1}^{k} \frac{(f_o - f_e)^2}{f_e}$$

Computational formula for expected cell frequencies (p. 330)

$$f_{ij} = \frac{RM_i \times CM_j}{n}$$

Computational formula for chi-square statistic (eq. 9–3):

$$\chi^2 = \sum \left(\frac{f_o^2}{f_e} \right) - n$$

Phi coefficient (eq. 9–4):

$$\phi = \sqrt{\frac{\chi^2}{n}}$$

Contingency coefficient (eq. 9–5):

$$C = \sqrt{\frac{\chi^2}{n + \chi^2}}$$

Cramer's V (eq. 9–6):

$$V = \sqrt{\frac{\chi^2}{n(k - 1)}}$$

Lambda (eq. 9–7):

$$\lambda = \frac{\begin{array}{c}\text{Number of errors} \\ \text{using mode of} \\ \text{dependent variable}\end{array} - \begin{array}{c}\text{Number of errors using mode} \\ \text{of dependent variable within} \\ \text{categories of the independent} \\ \text{variable}\end{array}}{\text{Number of errors using mode of dependent variable}}$$

Computational formula for lambda (eq. 9–8):

$$\lambda = \frac{(\Sigma f_i) - f_d}{n - f_d}$$

Yule's Q (eq. 9–9):

$$Q = \frac{(f_{\text{cell a}} \times f_{\text{cell d}}) - (f_{\text{cell b}} \times f_{\text{cell c}})}{(f_{\text{cell a}} \times f_{\text{cell d}}) + (f_{\text{cell b}} \times f_{\text{cell c}})}$$

Gamma (eq. 9–10):

$$\gamma = \frac{CP - DP}{CP + DP}$$

PRACTICE PROBLEMS

1. The following contingency table describes the joint distribution of two variables, the type of institution a correctional officer works in, and whether or not the officer reports being satisfied with his or her job. Your hypothesis is that those who work in medium security facilities will be more satisfied with their jobs.

| | Satisfied with Job? | | |
Type of Institution	No	Yes	Total
Medium Security	15	30	45
Maximum Security	100	40	140
Total	115	70	185

a. What is the independent and what is the dependent variable?

b. How many observations or cases are there?

c. What are the column marginals?

d. What are the row marginals?

e. What is the size of this contingency table?

f. How many correctional officers are in medium security facilities and are satisfied with their jobs?

g. How many correctional officers are in maximum security facilities and are not satisfied with their jobs?

h. How many degrees of freedom are there in this table?

i. Calculate the relative risk of not being satisfied with your job for each of the two types of facilities. What does this suggest?

j. Test the null hypothesis that the two variables are independent. Use an alpha level of .05, and state each step of your hypothesis test. If you reject the null hypothesis, how strongly are the two variables related?

2. Social disorganization theorists have argued that neighborhoods that lack the capacity to solve their own problems (i.e., are socially disorganized) have higher rates of crime and other social problems than neighborhoods that are organized. To test this hypothesis you take a random sample of 250 communities and determine if they are socially organized or disorganized and whether they have low or high crime rates. Here are your data.

| | Social Organization | | |
Crime Rate	Socially Organized	Socially Disorganized	Total
Low Crime Rate	90	98	188
High Crime Rate	10	52	62
Total	100	150	250

a. What is the independent and what is the dependent variable?

b. How many observations or cases are there?

c. What are the column marginals?

d. What are the row marginals?

e. What is the size of this contingency table?

f. How many socially disorganized neighborhoods have a high crime rate?

g. How many socially organized neighborhoods have a low crime rate?

h. How many degrees of freedom are there in this table?

i. Calculate the relative risk of a high neighborhood crime rate for both socially organized and socially disorganized communities. What does this suggest?

j. Test the null hypothesis that the two variables are independent. Use an alpha level of .01, and state each step of your hypothesis test. If you reject the null hypothesis, how strongly are the two variables related?

3. You think that there is a relationship between where a defendant's case is tried and the type of the sentence they receive. To test this hypothesis you collect data on 425 defendants convicted in rural, suburban, and urban courts in your state. Here are your data.

	Where Defendant Was Tried			
Type of Sentence Received	Rural Court	Suburban Court	Urban Court	Total
Jail Only	18	30	94	142
Fine and Jail	22	37	36	95
Less Than 60 Days of Jail Time	24	38	50	112
60 or More Days of Jail Time	16	20	40	76
Total	80	125	220	425

a. What is the independent and what is the dependent variable?

b. How many observations or cases are there?

c. What are the column marginals?

d. What are the row marginals?

e. What is the size of this contingency table?

f. How many defendants from suburban courts received a sentence of less than 60 days of jail time?

g. How many defendants from rural courts received a sentence of a fine and jail time?

h. How many degrees of freedom are there in this table?

i. Calculate the relative risk of getting a sentence of 60 or more days of jail time for defendants from the different court jurisdictions. What does this suggest?

j. Test the null hypothesis that the two variables are independent. Use an alpha level of .01, and state each step of your hypothesis test. If you reject the null hypothesis, how strongly are the two variables related?

4. You think that there might be a relationship between race and the number of property crimes a defendant has committed. To test this hypothesis you

take a random sample of 360 defendants convicted of a crime, examine their criminal records, and count the number of property crimes they have committed. Here are your data.

Race	Number of Property Crimes		Total
	0–4	5 or More	
Non-White	77	33	110
White	180	70	250
Total	257	103	360

a. What is the independent and what is the dependent variable?

b. How many observations or cases are there?

c. What are the column marginals?

d. What are the row marginals?

e. What is the size of this contingency table?

f. How many non-white offenders have committed 5 or more property offenses?

g. How many white offenders have committed 0–4 property offenses?

h. How many degrees of freedom are there in this table?

i. Calculate the relative risk of having 5 or more property crime arrests for each race. What does this suggest?

j. Test the null hypothesis that the two variables are independent. Use an alpha level of .05, and state each step of your hypothesis test. If you reject the null hypothesis, how strongly are the two variables related?

5. In their book *Crime in the Making,* Robert Sampson and John Laub (1993) argue that strong social bonds established later in life serve as effective social controls to adult crime. Let's say you were interested in this notion and studied the post-release behavior of random samples of three groups of formerly incarcerated offenders: (1) those who had a stable and satisfying job, (2) those with intermittent or sporadic employment, and (3) those unable to find a job. For each group you were able to determine how many were rearrested after three years of their release from prison. Here is what you found.

Number of Arrests After Three Years	Type of Employment			Total
	Stable Employment	Sporadic Employment	Unemployed	
None	30	14	10	54
One or More	15	16	30	61
Total	45	30	40	115

a. What is the independent and what is the dependent variable?

b. How many observations or cases are there?

c. What are the column marginals?

d. What are the row marginals?

e. What is the size of this contingency table?

f. How many persons with sporadic employment had one or more arrests after three years?

g. How many persons who were unemployed had no arrests after three years?

h. How many degrees of freedom are there in this table?

i. Calculate the relative risk of having one or more arrests for those with different types of post-release employment. What does this suggest?

j. Test the null hypothesis that the two variables are independent. Use an alpha level of .05, and state each step of your hypothesis test. If you reject the null hypothesis, how strongly are the two variables related?

6. Terri Moffitt (1991) has argued that there are two different types of offenders, life course persistent offenders who commit crimes early in life and throughout life, and adolescent-limited offenders who start offending in early adolescence and desist by the time they are young adults. To test the notion that life course persistent offenders commit more crimes as adults, you take a random sample of 320 adults currently on probation. You determine when they started offending (early in life or as adolescents) and then get a count of the number of adult crimes they have committed. Here are your data.

	Number of Crimes Committed				
Offender Type	0–4 Adult Offenses	5–9 Adult Offenses	10–14 Adult Offenses	15 or More Adult Offenses	Total
Adolescent-Limited	78	56	34	15	183
Life Course Persistent	15	22	37	63	137
Total	93	78	71	78	320

a. What is the independent and what is the dependent variable?

b. How many observations or cases are there?

c. What are the column marginals?

d. What are the row marginals?

e. What is the size of this contingency table?

f. How many life course persistent offenders have 10–14 adult offenses?

g. How many adolescent-limited offenders have 15 or more adult offenses?

h. How many degrees of freedom are there in this table?

i. Calculate the relative risk of having only 0–4 adult offenses for both offender types. What does this suggest?

j. Calculate the relative risk of having 15 or more adult offenses for both offender types.

k. Test the null hypothesis that the two variables are independent. Use an alpha level of .01, and state each step of your hypothesis test. If you reject the null hypothesis, how strongly are the two variables related?

SPSS PRACTICE PROBLEMS

1. There are many factors that affect the willingness of crime victims to report their victimization to police. Female victims of violence, particularly violence perpetrated by known offenders such as intimate partners, are generally the least likely to report their victimizations to police. The data in NCVS93 contains violent victimizations against women obtained from the National Crime Victimization Survey in 1993. The question we want to explore with these data is, "What are the factors that affect a woman's willingness to report her victimization to police?" Let's obtain a frequency distribution for the variables of interest: REPORTED, SOSTRANG, and INJURY using the FREQUENCIES subcommand under DESCRIPTIVE STATISICS.

   Notice that there are some missing cases for these data, so the appropriate percents to examine in the frequency output are under the "valid percents" column. The SOSTRANG variable indicates the relationship between the victim and the offender for each victimization as "knew before," "stranger," or "don't know." Let's recode this variable into strangers and nonstrangers by clicking on TRANSFORM, then RECODE, and then INTO DIFFERENT VARIABLE. When you are in the recode dialogue box, simply follow the procedures for recoding the values. Let's tell SPSS we want to call the new variable RELATE. You can recode the categories of 1 (knew before) and 2 (stranger) into the same or different values, but the main goal is to reclassify those "don't know" (3 and 8) responses into missing values to create a two-category variable. Check your newly created variable using the frequencies command to make sure it was recoded correctly.

2. Now let's examine the bivariate relationship between police-reporting behavior (REPORTED) and the relationship between the victim and the offender. Click on ANALYZE, then DESCRIPTIVE STATISTICS, and then CROSSTABS. You will be asked to place a variable in a "column" box and one in a "row" box. Let's keep with the practice of placing the independent variable (RELATE) in the columns and the dependent variable (REPORTED) in the rows. Now click on the CELLS box and ask for the appropriate percentages to be calculated (column), as well as the ob-

served counts. Now click on the STATISTICS box and tell SPSS to calculate the CHI-SQUARE statistic. Using the cross-tabulation table and the chi-square test, what do you conclude about the null hypothesis that these two variables are independent or not related?

3. Now let's examine the bivariate relationship between police-reporting behavior (REPORTED) and whether or not the victim sustained an injury as the result of her victimization (INJURY). Click on ANALYZE, then DESCRIPTIVE STATISTICS, and then CROSSTABS. You will be asked to place a variable in a "column" box and one in a "row" box. Let's keep with the practice of placing the independent variable (INJURY) in the columns and the dependent variable (REPORTED) in the rows. Now click on the CELLS box and ask for the appropriate percentages to be calculated (column), as well as the observed counts. Now click on the STATISTICS box and tell SPSS to calculate the CHI-SQUARE statistic. Using the cross-tabulation table and the chi-square test, what do you conclude about the null hypothesis that these two variables are independent or not related?

4. As you learned in this chapter, a significant relationship found between two variables does not always tell the entire story. We also want to know how strong the relationship is. Redo the chi-square tests you just performed, but this time, in the STATISTICS option box of the CROSSTABS dialogue box, ask for all appropriate measures of association that we have examined in this chapter. Interpret your results.

10

Hypothesis Tests Involving Two Population Means or Proportions

*E*very normal person, in fact, is only normal on the average. His ego approximates to that of the psychotic in some part or other and to a greater or lesser extent.

—SIGMUND FREUD

*W*hat a weak barrier is truth when it stands in the way of a hypothesis!

—MARY WOLLSTONECRAFT

In this chapter we examine the statistical procedures that allow us to test hypotheses about the differences *between* two population means ($\mu_1 - \mu_2$) and two population proportions ($p_1 - p_2$). We examine two types of mean difference tests: one for independent samples and one for dependent or matched samples.

The independent samples test is designed to measure mean differences between *two* samples or *two* subsets within the same sample. The key here is that the two groups are assumed to be independent in nature, and not related in any way. In contrast, the matched group or dependent samples test is designed to measure the difference between means obtained for the same sample over time or for two samples that are matched on certain characteristics so as to be as much alike as possible.

We also examine a test for the difference between two sample proportions in this chapter. We will see that a test for the difference between proportions is a special case of a test for mean differences. In this chapter, we use the terms "sample" and "group" interchangeably. Let's get started.

EXPLAINING THE DIFFERENCE BETWEEN TWO SAMPLE MEANS

In hypothesis tests like these, we have two variables to consider. One of them is a two-level or dichotomous categorical variable, and the other is a continuous variable. The categorical variable is generally thought of as the independent variable, and the continuous variable is considered to be the dependent variable. For example, one of the most persistent findings in criminology is the relationship between gender and the number of delinquent offenses committed. Consistently, males report having committed more delinquent acts than females. In a random sample of young males and females, then, the mean for the males will be expected to be greater than the mean for the females. In the language of causal analysis, gender is the independent variable that is predicted to "cause" high levels of delinquency, the dependent variable. In this example, gender is the dichotomous independent variable (male/female) and number of committed delinquent acts is the dependent variable. Let's follow this example through to illustrate the kinds of problems we will encounter in this chapter.

If we were to take a random sample of 70 young males and independently select an equal number of young females and then ask each youth to report the number of times in the past year that they committed each of four delinquent offenses (theft, vandalism, fighting, use of drugs), we would have two means: a mean number of delinquent offenses for the sample of young men ($\bar{X}_{men}$) and a mean for the sample of young women ($\bar{X}_{women}$). We also have two population means, one from the population of men (μ_{men}) and one from the population of women (μ_{women}). Both the sample and the population also have standard deviations. To keep these different components of samples and populations straight, we show each and their respective notations in Table 10–1. Let's say that, consistent with previous research, the mean number of offenses for the sample of young males is greater than the mean for the sample of young females ($\bar{X}_m > \bar{X}_w$). As we learned in the last chapter, however, we can account for the difference between these two sample means in two different ways.

TABLE 10–1

Characteristics and Notations for Two-Sample Problems

	Population 1	Population 2
Population mean	μ_1	μ_2
Population standard deviation	σ_1	σ_2
Sample mean	$\overline{X}_1$	$\overline{X}_2$
Sample standard deviation	S_1	S_2
Sample size	n_1	n_2

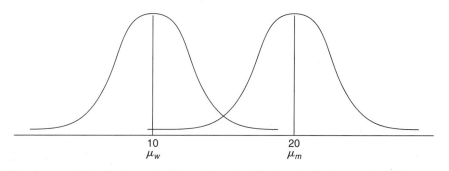

Figure 10–1 Distribution of male and female delinquent offending with different population means

One explanation for the difference between the male and female sample means is that there really *is* a difference between the rate at which young men and women offend. What this explanation implies is that males and females come from different offending populations with different population means. In Figure 10–1 we show two distributions of the rate of delinquent offending, one for females, on the left, and one for males, on the right. The population mean for the number of delinquent acts committed is greater for men (μ_m = 20) than it is for women (μ_w = 10). Notice that if this is true, then when we randomly select a sample of men and record their mean and randomly select a sample of women and record their mean, more frequently than not the sample mean for men will be greater than the sample mean for women.

A second explanation for the observed difference in sample means between young men and women is that, while each sample comes from a different population, the two population means are equal ($\mu_m = \mu_w$). This is illustrated in Figure 10–2, which shows two distributions of offending, one for the population of males and one for the population of females. Although

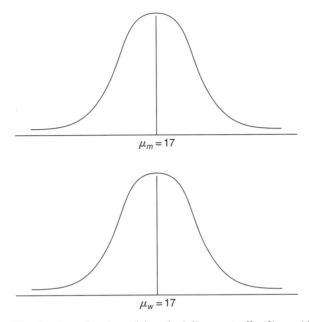

$\mu_m = 17$

$\mu_w = 17$

Figure 10–2   Distribution of male and female delinquent offending with equal population means

they may differ in some respects (their respective standard deviations may be different, for example), the two population means are the same. In this explanation, when we draw random samples from both populations, the two sample means will sometimes differ. In some samples we will happen to select very delinquent males or very delinquent females simply because of chance and sample variation.

These two explanations have very different implications. If the first explanation is true, then we will conclude that the mean number of delinquent offenses committed by males is significantly different from the mean number of offenses committed by females. Because the frequency of committing delinquent acts is significantly different between males and females, we will say that there is a "statistically significant" relationship between gender and delinquency. What we are saying here is that the difference between the male and the female mean is so large that "chances are" the samples have come from different populations. On the other hand, if the second explanation is true, then we will conclude that the observed difference between means is no greater than what we would expect to observe by chance alone, in spite of the fact that the sample means are different.

Because we have sample data, not population data, any difference we observe in our sample means may be due to "real differences" between males and females in how frequently they commit delinquent acts, or just due to

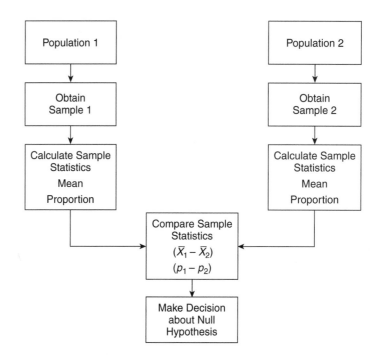

Figure 10–3   Hypothesis test for difference between two means or proportions

chance. We do not and cannot know for sure which explanation is really true. But with the help of probability theory, we can determine which explanation is more likely. In deciding which of these two possible explanations is more likely, we will proceed exactly as we have in the last two chapters.

We will begin by assuming that there is no difference between the two population means. That is, we will assume that the populations from which each of the two samples were drawn have equal means ($\mu_m = \mu_w$). With the use of probability theory and a new kind of sampling distribution, we will then ask the question, "If the population means are equal, how likely is it that we would have observed the difference between the two sample means?" If it is very unlikely, we will conclude that our presumption of equal population means is not true.

In this chapter, we are interested in the sampling distribution of sample mean and proportion differences. We illustrate the process of hypothesis testing with two sample means and proportions in Figure 10–3.

SAMPLING DISTRIBUTION OF MEAN DIFFERENCES

To understand what a sampling distribution of sample mean differences is, imagine that we take a sample of males and a sample of females from their

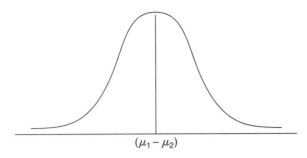

$(\mu_1 - \mu_2)$

Figure 10–4 Sampling distribution of the difference between two sample means

respective populations, compute a mean for each sample, and then calculate the difference between the two means. Imagine that we do this for an infinite number of samples, calculating the mean for each group and the difference between the means. We then plot this frequency distribution of an infinite number of mean differences. This theoretical distribution of all differences between an infinite number of sample means is our sampling distribution of *differences* between sample means, or **sampling distribution of sample mean differences.** We illustrate what this distribution might look like in Figure 10–4 and provide a summary of its characteristics here:

1. The mean of the sampling distribution of the difference between two means, $\mu_1 - \mu_2$, is equal to the difference between the population means.

2. The standard deviation of the sampling distribution of the difference between two means is called the **standard error of the difference between means** and reflects how much variation exists from sample to sample.

This sampling distribution of mean differences is analogous to the sampling distribution of the mean that we discussed in Chapters 7 and 8. The differences are that the sampling distribution in Figure 10–4 is composed of the *difference* between sample means rather than single means. Second, it is centered around the difference between the two population means ($\mu_1 - \mu_2$), rather than a single population mean (μ).

The mean of this distribution of mean differences is determined by the difference between the two population means. If the two population means are equal ($\mu_m = \mu_w$) as in Figure 10–2, the mean of the sampling distribution of mean differences will be zero ($\mu_1 - \mu_2 = 0$). As we stated above, even if this is true, not every sample difference is expected to be equal to zero. Sometimes the male mean will be greater than the female mean, and sometimes the female mean will be greater. What will be true, however, is that with an infinite number of samples, the mean of the distribution of sample differences will be zero.

If the two population means are different, as they are in Figure 10–1 with the population mean for men being greater than that for women ($\mu_m > \mu_w$), then most of the sample mean differences $\overline{X}_m - \overline{X}_f$ will be positive. This will be true because in most of the samples, the male mean will be greater than the female mean. In this case the mean of the sampling distribution of differences will be greater than zero. More specifically, the mean of the sampling distribution will be equal to the difference between the population means ($\mu_m - \mu_w$).

Up to now, we have repeatedly stated that no matter what the value of the means for the two populations, when repeated random samples are taken, means calculated, and differences taken, not every mean difference will be exactly the same. There will, then, be dispersion about the mean of the sampling distribution of differences. You can see the spread about the mean of the sampling distribution of differences in Figure 10–4. This dispersion is measured by the standard deviation of sample mean differences or the standard error of the difference $(\sigma_{(\overline{X}_1 - \overline{X}_2)})$, which is defined as:

$$\sigma_{(\overline{X}_1 - \overline{X}_2)} = \sqrt{\frac{\sigma_1^2}{n_1} + \frac{\sigma_2^2}{n_2}} \qquad (10\text{–}1)$$

where

$\sigma_1^2 = $ the variance of the first population, and

$\sigma_2^2 = $ the variance of the second population.

Not only do we know the mean and standard deviation of the sampling distribution of differences, we also are in a position to know its shape. This important statistical theorem states that:

If two independent random samples of size n_1 and n_2 are drawn from normal populations, then the sampling distribution of the difference between the two sample means $(\overline{X}_1 - \overline{X}_2)$ will be normally distributed.

We now can use the Central Limit Theorem to generalize this to include any population whenever the sample sizes are large. That is, no matter what the shape of the two populations, if independent random samples of size n_1 and n_2 are drawn, the sampling distribution of the difference between the two sample means will approximate a normal distribution as n_1 and n_2 become large (both sample sizes over 50). With normal populations or with large enough samples from any population, then, the sampling distribution of differences will approximate normality.

This should sound familiar to you because it is similar to what we did in Chapter 8. An appropriate statistical test for the difference between two means is either a z test or a t test. Therefore, an appropriate sampling distribution would be either the z or the t distribution. The z test for two means is appropriate whenever the two population variances (σ_1, σ_2) are known. If these values are unknown, the t test for two means is the appropriate statistical test. Since we are seldom in a position to know the value of the population variances, the t test is the more frequently applied test. For that reason, we will discuss only t tests for the difference between two means in this chapter. Now, let's go through some examples of different types of hypothesis tests involving two population means.

TESTING A HYPOTHESIS ABOUT THE DIFFERENCE BETWEEN TWO MEANS: INDEPENDENT SAMPLES

In this section, we will discuss the case of hypothesis tests for the difference between two *independent* sample means. In the independent samples case, we have two samples whose elements are randomly and independently selected. Random and independent selection occurs whenever there is a known probability of any other element being selected into a sample, and the selection of an element into one sample has no effect on the selection of any other element into the other sample. In other words, both samples are randomly selected and are independent of one another.

In our example, independence would occur if the selection of a male into one sample had no effect on the selection of a female into the other sample. The independence assumption is violated in the case of matched or dependent samples, where an element is deliberately selected into a sample or when the same observations are found in both samples. We will review the special case of hypothesis testing presented by matched and dependent samples later in this chapter.

The statistical test we will conduct here is different from the t test we used in Chapter 8 in three ways: (1) our sample statistic is not the sample mean but the difference between two sample means $(\overline{X}_1 - \overline{X}_2)$; (2) the mean of the sampling distribution is not the population mean but the difference between two population means $(\mu_1 - \mu_2)$; and (3) the estimated standard deviation of the sampling distribution is the estimated standard deviation of the sampling distribution of the difference between sample means $(\sigma_{\overline{X}_1 - \overline{X}_2})$. The general formula for the t test involving the difference between two sample means can be expressed as:

$$t_{\text{obt}} = \frac{\overline{X}_1 - \overline{X}_2}{\hat{\sigma}_{(\overline{X}_1 - \overline{X}_2)}} \qquad (10\text{--}2)$$

This t test requires that the two samples be independent random samples selected from normally distributed populations, and that the dependent variable be measured at the interval/ratio level.

As you can see from equation 10–2, the t statistic is obtained by dividing the difference between the two sample means by the estimated standard deviation of the sampling distribution (the standard error of the difference). There are, however, two cases of the t test between two means. In one test we can assume that the unknown population standard deviations are equal $(\sigma_1 = \sigma_2)$; in the second case we cannot make that assumption $(\sigma_1 \neq \sigma_2)$. The importance of this is that our estimate of the standard error of the difference

$(\hat{\sigma}_{(\bar{X}_1 - \bar{X}_2)})$ is different for the two cases. We will examine the t test for both of these cases separately.

Model 1: Pooled Variance Estimate ($\sigma_1 = \sigma_2$)

If we can assume that the two unknown population standard deviations are equal ($\sigma_1 = \sigma_2$), then we can estimate the standard error of the difference using what is called a pooled variance estimate. As the population standard deviations are not known, the decision as to whether or not they are equal is made based upon the equality of the sample standard deviations (s_1 and s_2). Something called an F test is the appropriate test for the significance of the difference between the two sample standard deviations. Without going into too much detail here, the F test tests the null hypothesis that $\sigma_1^2 = \sigma_2^2$. If we fail to reject this null hypothesis, we can assume that the population standard deviations are equal. If, however, we are led to reject this hypothesis, we cannot make the assumption that the two population standard deviations are equal and we must estimate the standard error using what is called a *separate variance estimate*, which we will discuss later.

We will continue in this section under the assumption that $\sigma_1 = \sigma_2$ and demonstrate the use of a pooled variance estimate of the standard error of the difference. Recall from formula 10–1 that the standard error of the difference was:

$$\sigma_{(\bar{X}_1 - \bar{X}_2)} = \sqrt{\frac{\sigma_1^2}{n_1} + \frac{\sigma_2^2}{n_2}}$$

If we can assume that the two population standard deviations are equal ($\sigma_1 = \sigma_2$), then we have a common value of σ. Using the common value of the population standard deviations, we can then rewrite the formula above as:

$$\sigma_{(\bar{X}_1 - \bar{X}_2)} = \sqrt{\frac{\sigma_1^2}{n_1} + \frac{\sigma_2^2}{n_2}}$$

$$= \sigma \sqrt{\frac{1}{n_1} + \frac{1}{n_2}}$$

$$= \sigma \sqrt{\frac{n_1 + n_2}{n_1 n_2}}$$

We must, of course, find an estimate of this common standard deviation (σ). Since we are assuming that the two population standard deviations are equal, we can obtain an estimate of the common standard deviation by pooling or combining the two sample standard deviations. By combining the two sample values, we get a better estimate of the common population standard deviation. Since in many instances the samples are of unequal size, we must weight each sample standard deviation by its respective degrees of freedom ($n - 1$). Since we are still using the sample standard deviation to estimate the population value, we will continue to employ the degrees of freedom $(n - 1)$ in the denominator. Our pooled sample estimate of the common population standard deviation, then, becomes:

$$\sigma = \hat{\sigma}$$

$$\hat{\sigma} = \sqrt{\frac{(n_1 - 1)s_1^2 + (n_2 - 1)s_2^2}{n_1 + n_2 - 2}}$$

As the formula demonstrates, our estimate of the pooled population standard deviation $(\hat{\sigma})$ uses the weighted average of the two sample standard deviations. More weight is therefore given to larger-sized samples. You should also note that our pooled estimate $\hat{\sigma}$ will normally be in between the two sample values of s_1 and s_2.

Now that we have our estimate of the common population standard deviation $(\hat{\sigma})$, we can multiply it by $\sqrt{\dfrac{n_1 + n_2}{n_1 n_2}}$ here to obtain our **pooled variance estimate of the standard error of the difference:**

$$\hat{\sigma}_{(\overline{X}_1 - \overline{X}_2)} = \sqrt{\frac{(n_1 - 1)s_1^2 + (n_2 - 1)s_2^2}{n_1 + n_2 - 2}} \sqrt{\frac{n_1 + n_2}{n_1 n_2}}$$

For the grand finale, the formula for our pooled variance t test then becomes:

$$t_{obt} = \frac{\overline{X}_1 - \overline{X}_2}{\sqrt{\dfrac{(n_1 - 1)s_1^2 + (n_2 - 1)s_2^2}{n_1 + n_2 - 2}} \sqrt{\dfrac{n_1 + n_2}{n_1 n_2}}} \qquad \textbf{(10–3)}$$

Once we have our obtained value of t (t_{obt}), we will compare it to our critical value (t_{crit}) and make a decision about the null hypothesis. The critical value of t is based upon our chosen alpha level and is obtained from the t table (Table E–3 of Appendix E). You will remember from Chapter 8 that before using the t table, we first needed to determine the appropriate degrees of freedom. In the one-sample case, the degrees of freedom were equal to $n - 1$. Not surprisingly, when testing the difference between two sample means, the degrees of freedom are equal to $(n_1 - 1 + n_2 - 1)$. Another way to express this is to say that we have $(n_1 + n_2 - 2)$ degrees of freedom in the two-sample case for the t test. Once we have determined our degrees of freedom, we can go to the t table with our chosen alpha level and find our critical value.

Let's go through an example of a formal hypothesis test using the t test. In this example, we will assume that we have conducted our F test and did not reject the null hypothesis. Because we can therefore assume that the population standard deviations are equal, then, we can use the pooled variance estimate of the standard error of the difference.

Case Study: State Prison Expenditures by Region Suppose that we are interested in regional differences in the cost of housing state prison inmates. Table 10–2 displays data from state prisons for two regions (West

TABLE 10–2

Prison Expenditures per Inmate per Day by State and Region, 1999

	Mean State Prison Operating Expenditures per Inmate
West	
Nevada	42.1
Idaho	44.6
Arizona	52.3
Wyoming	53.3
Montana	56.9
Colorado	57.5
California	58.5
Hawaii	63.8
Washington	73.0
New Mexico	80.8
Oregon	87.2
Alaska	88.1
Utah	88.6

Sample statistics for the West:

$$\overline{X}_1 = 65.1$$
$$s_1^2 = 272.2$$
$$n_1 = 13$$

Northeast	
New Hampshire	57.1
Massachusetts	71.2
Pennsylvania	76.8
New York	77.8
New Jersey	84.3
Vermont	85.1
Connecticut	87.4
Maine	92.3
Rhode Island	97.9

Sample statistics for the Northeast:

$$\overline{X}_1 = 81.1$$
$$s_2^2 = 146.4$$
$$n_2 = 9$$

Source: Statistical Abstract of the United States: 2001, U.S. Census Bureau, Table no. 333, p. 201.

TABLE 10–3

Steps Taken When Conducting a Hypothesis Test

Step 1. Formally state your null (H_0) and research (H_1) hypotheses.

Step 2. Select an appropriate test statistic and the sampling distribution of that test statistic.

Step 3. Select a level of significance (alpha = α) and determine the critical value and rejection region of the test statistic based on the selected level of alpha.

Step 4. Conduct the test: Calculate the obtained value of the test statistic and compare it to the critical value.

Step 5. Make a decision about your null hypothesis and interpret this decision in a meaningful way based on the research question, sample, and population.

and Northeast. The dependent variable of interest is the mean operating expenditure per inmate per day, which is measured at the interval/ratio level. Let's say we believe that the average annual cost to house an inmate in state prisons will differ between the West and the Northeast. In this scenario, region would be the independent variable (West v. Northeast) and cost would be the dependent variable. We review the steps necessary to conduct a hypothesis test in Table 10–3. We will go through each of these steps using this example.

Step 1. Since we have no real idea about the nature of the relationship between region and cost, a nondirectional (two-tailed) hypothesis test is appropriate. The null hypothesis (H_0) will state that the mean annual cost to house inmates in the West is equal to the mean cost in the Northeast. The research hypothesis (H_1) will represent our belief that the regional means are not equal to each other. These are formally stated below:

H_0: $\mu_{\text{West}} = \mu_{\text{Northeast}}$
H_1: $\mu_{\text{West}} \neq \mu_{\text{Northeast}}$

Step 2. To determine the validity of the null hypothesis above, we will rely on the t statistic along with its corresponding sampling distribution. Because we will assume that the unkown population standard deviations are equal, we can estimate the standard error of the difference using a pooled variance estimate.

Step 3. Let's adopt an alpha level equal to .05 (α = .05). Referring to Table E–3 in Appendix E, with this level of alpha and using a nondirectional test and ($9 + 13 - 2 = 20$) degrees of freedom, the critical value of t is equal to ± 2.086 ($t_{\text{crit}} = 2.086$). The value of t we obtain from our statistical test must therefore be equal to or greater than 2.086 or equal to or less than -2.086 in order to reject the null hypothesis of equal means. This means that

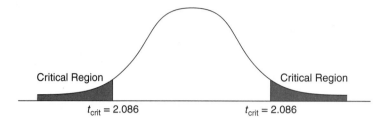

Critical Region   Critical Region

$t_{\text{crit}} = 2.086$ $t_{\text{crit}} = 2.086$

Figure 10–5   Critical t and critical region for alpha = .05 (df = 20) and a two-tailed test

we will fail to reject the null hypothesis if $-2.086 < t_{\text{obt}} < 2.086$. We show the two critical values and critical regions in Figure 10–5.

Step 4. As in the previous example, we will assume that the population standard deviations are equal and that we can use a pooled variance estimate of the standard error of the difference. The calculation of t_{obt} from this sample data is presented below.

$$t_{\text{obt}} = \frac{\overline{X}_1 - \overline{X}_2}{\sqrt{\dfrac{(n_1 - 1)s_1^2 + (n_2 - 1)s_2^2}{n_1 + n_2 - 2}}\sqrt{\dfrac{n_1 + n_2}{n_1 n_2}}}$$

$$t_{\text{obt}} = \frac{65.1 - 81.1}{\sqrt{\dfrac{(13 - 1)272.2 + (9 - 1)146.4}{9 + 13 - 2}}\sqrt{\dfrac{9 + 13}{(9)(13)}}}$$

$$t_{\text{obt}} = \frac{-16}{\sqrt{\dfrac{(12)272.2 + (8)146.4}{20}}\sqrt{\dfrac{22}{117}}}$$

$$t_{\text{obt}} = \frac{-16}{\sqrt{\dfrac{3266.4 + 1171.2}{20}}\sqrt{\dfrac{22}{117}}}$$

$$t_{\text{obt}} = \frac{-16}{\sqrt{\dfrac{4437.6}{20}}\sqrt{.188}}$$

$$t_{\text{obt}} = \frac{-16}{\sqrt{221.8}\ \sqrt{.188}} = \frac{-16}{(14.89)(.43)} = \frac{-16}{6.4}$$

$$t_{\text{obt}} = 2.5$$

Step 5. The obtained value of t ($t_{\text{obt}} = 2.5$) as calculated above does fall in the critical region. The data obtained from our sample, then, provide enough evidence for us to reject the null hypothesis that the population means are actually equal. We conclude that there is a significant relationship between region and annual cost to house inmates. The results of our test indicate that region, at least the West versus the Northeast, does affect the cost of incarcerating offenders housed in state prisons. In addition, the direction of this difference indicates that it is much more expensive to house prison inmates in the Northeast compared to the West. Let's go through another example.

Case Study: Social Disorganization and Crime　Since the days of the Chicago School in the 1920s (Clifford Shaw and Henry McKay), criminologists have long postulated that conditions of social disorganization within a residential community increase the likelihood of various kinds of social problems and pathologies, including criminal victimization. One indicator that has been used to measure social disorganization within communities is the extent to which people move in and out of the community. Communities wherein very few families move in and move out are considered more stable and more organized than those wherein there is a great deal of population "turnover." This is because in communities with relatively little turnover, residents live in the same place for a long time and get to know their neighbors, and, as a result, a sense of community becomes established. It is hypothesized that this sense of community and the social relationships between community members are responsible for the lower crime rates in these kinds of stable neighborhoods. In this hypothesis, the population turnover in a community is the independent variable and the rate of crime is the dependent variable.

Suppose that we wanted to investigate the relationship between social disorganization and household crime. To do so, we collect a random sample of residents and ask them whether or not anything has been stolen from or around their home (including their automobile) within the last six months. In addition, we ask them how long they have lived at their present address. From this survey, we divide our sample into two groups according to the length of time they have resided at their address: (1) those residing at their current address for less than one year, whom we will term "transient," and (2) those residing at their address for more than one year, whom we will term "stable." We then calculate the mean number of times each group experienced a household theft. For this hypothetical example, we obtain the following sample statistics:

Less Than One Year	More Than One Year
$\overline{X}_1 = 22.4$	$\overline{X}_2 = 16.2$
$s_1^2 = 4.2$	$s_2^2 = 4.1$
$n_1 = 49$	$n_2 = 53$

Step 1.　Because we have some idea about the nature of the relationship between residential stability and risk of household victimization, we adopt a directional (one-tailed) hypothesis test. Since

we believe that those residing in an area for less than one year will be more vulnerable to becoming the victims of household crime, our research hypothesis states that the mean number of household victimizations experienced by residents who have lived at their current address for less than one year will be greater than the mean for those who have lived in their residences for more than one year. Both the null and research hypothesis are formally stated below:

H_0: $\mu_{\text{Less than 1 year}} = \mu_{\text{More than 1 year}}$

H_1: $\mu_{\text{Less than 1 year}} > \mu_{\text{More than 1 year}}$

Step 2. To determine the validity of the null hypothesis above, we will rely on the t statistic along with its corresponding sampling distribution. Because we can assume that the unkown population standard deviations are equal, we can estimate the standard error of the difference using a pooled variance estimate.

Step 3. For this test, let's select an alpha level of .01. With $\alpha = .01$, using a directional test and degrees of freedom equal to $(n_1 + n_2 - 2) = (49 + 53 - 2) = 100$, the critical value of t that defines the rejection region can be found in Table E–3 of Appendix E. Using the degrees of freedom of 120 listed in the table (since that is the closest value), we see that the critical value of t which defines the lower limit of the rejection region is 2.358. Therefore, in order to reject the null hypothesis, we must obtain a t value which is equal to or greater than 2.358. We use a positive value of t in this case because our research hypothesis states that the value of the first mean will be greater than the value of the mean for the second group; the obtained value of t is therefore predicted to be positive. If we obtain a negative value of t, we must fail to reject the null hypothesis. We show the critical value of t and the critical region for this problem in Figure 10–6.

Step 4. The next step of our hypothesis test is to convert the difference between our sample means into a t value. This is done below:

$$t_{obt} = \frac{22.4 - 16.2}{\sqrt{\frac{(49-1)4.2 + (53-1)4.1}{49+53-2}}\sqrt{\frac{49+53}{(49)(53)}}}$$

$$t_{obt} = \frac{6.2}{\sqrt{\frac{(48)4.2 + (52)4.1}{100}}\sqrt{\frac{102}{2597}}}$$

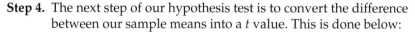

$$t_{obt} = \frac{6.2}{\sqrt{\frac{201.6 + 213.2}{100}}\sqrt{.039}}$$

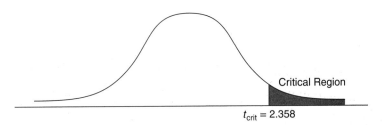

Critical Region

$t_{crit} = 2.358$

Figure 10–6 Critical t and critical region for alpha = .01 (df = 120) and a one-tailed test

$$t_{obt} = \frac{6.2}{\sqrt{\frac{414.8}{100}} \, \sqrt{.039}}$$

$$t_{obt} = \frac{6.2}{\sqrt{4.1} \, \sqrt{.039}} = \frac{6.2}{(2.02)(.197)} = \frac{6.2}{.398}$$

$$t_{obt} = 15.58$$

Step 5. The t value we obtained of 15.58 is substantially greater than the critical value of t (2.358) that was needed in order to reject the null hypothesis. Since $t_{obt} > t_{crit}$ we will reject the null hypothesis that the population means are equal. This suggests that the observed sample mean difference is too large to be attributed to chance or sampling variation and we can therefore assume that the mean rate of household victimization experienced by those who have recently moved is greater than the mean rate experienced by those who have lived in their places of residence for one year or more. The results of our statistical test lend support to one of the premises of social disorganization theory; we have found that individuals who have just recently been in a state of transiency (e.g., have moved within the last year) are more likely to become the victims of household crime than are those who have been more residentially stable (e.g., have not moved within the last year).

Case Study: Boot Camps and Recidivism Since their beginning in 1983 in Georgia, the use of correctional boot camps, sometimes called shock incarceration programs, has skyrocketed in both state and federal prison systems. Many questions remain, however, about the value of boot camps. Do they work? This is difficult to answer because there are so many different types of boot camps. Moreover, despite their increased popularity, there have been only a few systematic attempts to evaluate their efficacy in reducing recidivism. Some of the most ambitious evaluations of boot camps have been conducted by Doris MacKenzie and her colleagues, who have tracked and compared individuals who have graduated from boot camps to individuals who have been convicted of the same crimes but sent to prison.[1]

Suppose we want to conduct our own experiment on the issue. We get the help of a local judge and randomly select from a group of young adult offenders those who will go to a military style boot camp and those who will be sent to the state prison. After their release, individuals are followed for two years. To collect information on offending behavior, we conduct interviews with the individuals themselves and also obtain official arrest data. Mean levels of offending behavior (for all crimes including violent, property, and drug offenses) are calculated for both groups as follows:

Boot Camp Group	Prison Group
$\overline{X}_1 = 15.2$	$\overline{X}_2 = 15.9$
$s_1^2 = 4.7$	$s_2^2 = 5.1$
$n_1 = 32$	$n_2 = 29$

To determine whether or not there is a significant difference in the mean rates of offending between the boot camp graduates and those released from prison, we must conduct a hypothesis test to determine the difference between the two means. To help you learn the steps of formal hypothesis testing, we ask that you check off each step as we go through them.

Because there has been so little research on the efficacy of boot camps, let's say that we select a nondirectional hypothesis test. The formal hypothesis statements are as follows:

H_0: $\mu_{\text{Boot camps}} = \mu_{\text{prison}}$

H_1: $\mu_{\text{Boot camps}} \neq \mu_{\text{prison}}$

The t test, along with its corresponding sampling distribution, is an appropriate statistical test for our data. Let's select an alpha level of .05. With a nondirectional hypothesis test, an $\alpha = .05$, and 59 degrees of freedom [(32 + 29 − 2) = 59], we will use the critical value of t for 60 degrees of freedom because that is the closest value in Table E–3. We will reject the null hypothesis if our obtained t is either less than or equal to −2.00 or greater than or equal to +2.00. The critical values and corresponding critical regions are displayed in Figure 10–7. The obtained value of t is calculated below:

$$t_{obt} = \frac{15.2 - 15.9}{\sqrt{\frac{(32 - 1)4.7 + (29 - 1)5.1}{32 + 29 - 2}}\sqrt{\frac{32 + 29}{(32)(29)}}}$$

$$t_{obt} = \frac{-.7}{\sqrt{\frac{(31)4.7 + (28)5.1}{59}}\sqrt{\frac{61}{928}}}$$

$$t_{obt} = \frac{-.7}{\sqrt{\frac{145.7 + 142.8}{59}}\sqrt{.066}}$$

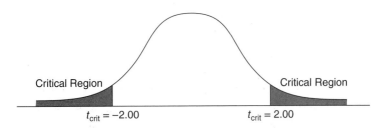

Critical Region   Critical Region

$t_{crit} = -2.00$ $t_{crit} = 2.00$

Figure 10–7 Critical t and critical regions for alpha = .05 (df = 57) and a two-tailed test

$$t_{obt} = \frac{-.7}{\sqrt{\frac{288.5}{59}} \sqrt{.066}}$$

$$t_{obt} = \frac{-.7}{\sqrt{4.89} \sqrt{.066}} = \frac{-.7}{(2.2)(.26)} = \frac{-.7}{.57}$$

$$t_{obt} = -1.23$$

Our statistical test results in an obtained t value of -1.23. An obtained t of -1.23 does not lie within the critical region. Since $t_{obt} > -t_{crit}$ and $t_{obt} < +t_{crit}$, we must fail to reject the null hypothesis. Because we failed to reject the null hypothesis, we must conclude that the mean offending rates in which similar offenders from boot camp and state prison recidivate after release are not significantly different from one another. This would be in line with much of the research to date on boot camps. As MacKenzie states, "Results clearly show that the core elements of boot camp programs—military-style discipline, hard labor, and physical training—by themselves [do] not reduce offender recidivism—but it is likely that some mixture of rehabilitation and intensive follow-up supervision plays an important role."[2]

Model 2: Separate Variance Estimate ($\sigma_1 \neq \sigma_2$)

In the previous examples, we have assumed that the two population standard deviations are equal. Under this assumption, we can take advantage of this equality and use a common estimate of the population standard deviation (σ) to calculate a pooled variance estimate for the standard error of the difference ($\sigma_{\overline{X}1} - \sigma_{\overline{X}2}$). Of course, it will not always be possible for us to do this. In many instances, our F test will lead us to *reject* the null hypothesis that $\sigma_1 = \sigma_2$. When this occurs, we conclude that the two population standard deviations are different. If we cannot maintain the assumption that the two population standard deviations are equal, we cannot use a pooled estimate of that standard deviation. Instead, we must estimate what is called a **separate variance estimate of the standard error of the difference.** The formula for this estimate is:

$$\sigma_{\overline{X}1} - \sigma_{\overline{X}2} = \sqrt{\frac{s_1^2}{n_1 - 1} + \frac{s_2^2}{n_2 - 1}}$$

As you can see, unlike the estimated standard error based on a pooled standard deviation, the separate variance estimate is based on just that: separate contributions from each sample standard deviation. This should make sense, since we have determined that the two standard deviations are significantly different from each other.

With a separate variance estimate of the standard error of the difference, the formula for our t test becomes:

$$t_{\text{obt}} = \frac{\overline{X}_1 - \overline{X}_2}{\sqrt{\frac{s_1^2}{n_1 - 1} + \frac{s_2^2}{n_2 - 1}}} \tag{10–4}$$

The steps necessary to conduct a hypothesis test remain the same as before except for determining the degrees of freedom. The correct degrees of freedom for the separate variance t test are not equal to $n_1 + n_2 - 2$. In fact, the formula for the degrees of freedom for a t test using a separate variance estimate is quite a bit more complicated. The following formula has been suggested to obtain the appropriate degrees of freedom for this test (Blalock 1979; Hays 1994):

$$df = \left[\frac{\left(\frac{s_1^2}{n_1 - 1} + \frac{s_2^2}{n_2 - 1} \right)^2}{\left(\frac{s_1^2}{n_1 - 1} \right)^2 \left(\frac{1}{n_1 + 1} \right) + \left(\frac{s_2^2}{n_2 - 1} \right)^2 \left(\frac{1}{n_2 + 1} \right)} \right] - 2 \tag{10–5}$$

Wow! And you thought the degrees of freedom were relatively unimportant! The results of the formula above should be rounded to the nearest integer to obtain the approximate degrees of freedom. Let's go through two examples using the separate variance estimate approach for the t test.

Case Study: Formal Sanctions and Intimate Partner Assault In 1981, the first large scale experiment to test the deterrent effects of arrest on batterers, called the Minneapolis Domestic Violence Experiment, was conducted by Sherman and Berk (1984a, 1984b). The theoretical impetus for this experiment was guided by notions of specific deterrence. The primary research question driving the study was, "Does arresting a man who has assaulted his partner decrease the probability that he will assault her in the future compared to interventions which are typically used, such as separating the parties?" From this, the researchers concluded that arrest provided the strongest deterrent to future violence and consequently was the preferred police response.

To test the validity of experimental findings, an important canon of science is replication. Accordingly, the National Institute of Justice funded replication experiments of the Minneapolis experiment in six cities. Unlike the original Minneapolis experiment, the published findings from these replications, which became known as the Spouse Assault Replication Program (SARP), have not uniformly found that arrest is an effective deterrent in spouse assault cases.[3] Maxwell, Garner, and Fagan (1999) analyzed the common data elements of each experiment and did find a modest effect for arrest in decreasing recidivism. However, they concluded that a minority of women were still repeatedly victimized by their intimate partners regardless of arrest.

Let's say we attempted to conduct our own study on a much smaller scale. We randomly assigned arrested suspects who had assaulted their intimate partners to either short-term (no more than three hours) or long-term (four or more hours) detention. We then followed them for a 120-day period and recorded the number of new victimizations their partners reported to interviewers along with the number of calls to police or arrests for domestic assault during that period. The hypothetical mean number of post-detention assaults, along with the other sample statistics for each group, are as follows:

Short-Term Detention	**Long-Term Detention**
$\overline{X}_1 = 6.4$	$\overline{X}_2 = 8.1$
$s_1^2 = 4.84$	$s_2^2 = 15.21$
$n_1 = 14$	$n_2 = 42$

In this example, the length of detention (short-term v. long-term) is the independent variable and the number of post-detention domestic assaults is the dependent variable. We would like to test the hypothesis that the population means for the two groups are equal. In saying this, we are suggesting that the length of detention has no effect on the frequency with which intimate partner assault is committed. Let's suppose that, based upon an F test, we have rejected the null hypothesis that the population standard deviations are equal, and therefore we must use the separate variance t test as our statistical test.

Step 1. Because the literature on the efficacy in deterring intimate partner assault is equivocal, we will conduct a nondirectional (two-tailed) research hypothesis which states that the two population means are different. Our null hypothesis states that the two population means are equal. Both are formally stated below:

H_0: $\mu_{\text{short detention}} = \mu_{\text{long detention}}$

H_1: $\mu_{\text{short detention}} \neq \mu_{\text{long detention}}$

Step 2. As mentioned above, our statistical test will be the separate variance t test, and our sampling distribution will be the t distribution.

Step 3. We will select an alpha level of .01. In order to find our critical value of t and the critical region, we first need to determine the appropriate degrees of freedom. Based on equation 10–5, we can approximate our degrees of freedom as equal to:

$$df = \left[\frac{\left(\dfrac{4.84}{14-1} + \dfrac{15.21}{42-1} \right)^2}{\left(\dfrac{4.84}{14-1} \right)^2 \left(\dfrac{1}{14+1} \right) + \left(\dfrac{15.21}{42-1} \right)^2 \left(\dfrac{1}{42+1} \right)} \right] - 2$$

$$= \left[\frac{\left(\dfrac{4.84}{13} + \dfrac{15.21}{41} \right)^2}{\left(\dfrac{4.84}{13} \right)^2 \left(\dfrac{1}{15} \right) + \left(\dfrac{15.21}{41} \right)^2 \left(\dfrac{1}{43} \right)} \right] - 2$$

$$= \frac{(.37 + .37)^2}{(.37)^2(.07) + (.37)^2(.02)} - 2$$

$$= \frac{(.74)^2}{.010 + .003} - 2$$

$$= \frac{.55}{.013} - 2$$

$$= 42.3 - 2$$

$$= 40.3$$

With 40 degrees of freedom and an alpha of .01 for a two-tailed test, our critical value of t is ± 2.704 (Table E–3, Appendix E). Our critical region, then, will consist of any t_{obt} less than or equal to -2.704 or greater than or equal to 2.704. We will fail to reject the null hypothesis if $-2.704 < t_{obt} < 2.704$. We show the critical values and critical region in Figure 10–8.

We now calculate our obtained value of t as shown here:

$$t_{obt} = \frac{\overline{X}_1 - \overline{X}_2}{\sqrt{\dfrac{s_1^2}{n_1 - 1} + \dfrac{s_2^2}{n_2 - 1}}}$$

$$= \frac{6.4 - 8.1}{\sqrt{\dfrac{4.84}{14 - 1} + \dfrac{15.21}{42 - 1}}}$$

$$= \frac{-1.7}{\sqrt{\dfrac{4.84}{13} + \dfrac{15.21}{41}}}$$

$$= \frac{-1.7}{\sqrt{.37 + .37}}$$

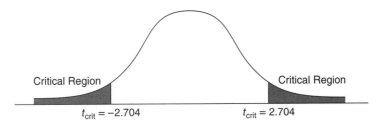

Figure 10–8 Critical t and critical region for alpha = .01 (df = 40) and a two-tailed test

$$= \frac{-1.7}{.86}$$

$$= -1.98$$

Our obtained t statistic is -1.98. Because this negative value does not fall below the critical value of t, we fail to reject the null hypothesis. Our conclusion then, based on our sample results, is that there is no significant difference between the mean number of post-detention assaults for those who are given short-term detention and those who are given long-term detention. Thus, it appears that there is no significant relationship between time in detention and a batterer's propensity to commit acts of violence in the future. Let's go through another quick example.

Case Study: Gender and Sentencing　A great deal of research has focused on the idea of gender disparity in sentencing (Daly, 1987; Steffensmeier et al., 1993). The controversy still exists, however, over whether disparity in sentencing truly exists or is an artifact of poor methodology. Some research has found that female defendants are more likely to have all the charges against them dismissed and are sentenced less harshly than males (Boritch, 1992; Keitner, 2002; Stalans, 1996; Spohn and Spears, 1997). Others, however, have found little or no evidence of gender disparity (Daly, 1994; Rapaport, 1991; Steffensmeier et al., 1993). Steffensmeier and his colleagues, for example, have gone so far as to conclude, "When men and women appear in (contemporary) criminal court in similar circumstances and are charged with similar offenses, they receive similar treatment" (Steffensmeier et al., 1993:411). You should immediately recognize that gender in this scenario is the independent variable and the sentence received is the dependent variable.

　　Let's assume that we have a random sample of 50 male and 25 female defendants who have been found guilty of burglary. The mean sentence lengths received for both male and female defendants, along with their respective standard deviations and sample sizes, are as follows:

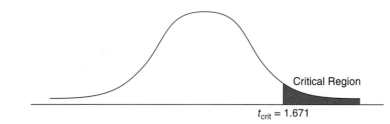

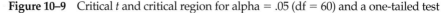

$t_{crit} = 1.671$

Figure 10–9 Critical t and critical region for alpha = .05 (df = 60) and a one-tailed test

Male Defendants

$\overline{X}_1 = 12.02$

$s_1^2 = 72.68$

$n_1 = 50$

Female Defendants

$\overline{X}_1 = 3.32$

$s_1^2 = 11.31$

$n_1 = 25$

Step 1. Let's say we believe that males will be sentenced more harshly than females. Accordingly, we state a directional (one-tailed) research hypothesis that the population mean sentence length is greater for male defendants than for female defendants. The null hypothesis is that the population means are equal:

H_0: $\mu_{Males} = \mu_{Females}$

H_1: $\mu_{Males} > \mu_{Females}$

Step 2. Our test statistic is the separate variance t test, and our sampling distribution is the t distribution.

Step 3. We choose an alpha level of .05 ($\alpha = .05$). Based on equation 10–5 above, we determine that the approximate degrees of freedom is 56 (we will not show the work here, but it would be a good idea to compute this for yourself). With 56 degrees of freedom, an $\alpha = .05$, and a one-tailed test, we can see from the t table that our critical t value is 1.671 (actually, this t score corresponds to 60 degrees of freedom, but it is the closest value we have to 56 df in Table E–3). Since we have predicted that the population mean for males will be greater than the population mean for females, we will reject the null hypothesis if $t_{obt} \geq$ 1.671, and we will fail to reject the null hypothesis if $t_{obt} < 1.671$. We show the critical value and the critical region in Figure 10–9.

Step 4. We will now calculate our obtained t value, using the separate variance estimate as shown below:

$$t_{obt} = \frac{12.02 - 3.32}{\sqrt{\dfrac{(72.68)}{50-1} + \dfrac{(11.31)}{25-1}}}$$

$$= \frac{8.07}{\sqrt{\dfrac{72.68}{49} + \dfrac{11.31}{24}}}$$

$$= \frac{8.07}{\sqrt{1.48 + .47}}$$

$$= \frac{8.07}{\sqrt{1.4}}$$

$$= 5.76$$

Our obtained t score of 5.76 is considerably greater than the critical t of 1.671. Our decision, then, will be to reject the null hypothesis that there is no difference in the population means. We will conclude that, based on our sample data, there is a significant relationship between sentence length received and gender of defendant. Thus, it appears the sentences handed down by judges for males convicted of robbery are greater than the sentences received by females convicted of the same offense.

In this section, we have illustrated the use of two different types of t tests. One, the pooled variance t test, is appropriate when we can assume that the population standard deviations are equal ($\sigma_1 = \sigma_2$). The estimated standard error of the difference $(\sigma_{(\overline{X}_1 - \overline{X}_2)})$ in this t test is based upon a pooled estimate of the common population standard deviation. The second, the separate variance t test, is used whenever we cannot assume that the two population standard deviations are equal ($\sigma_1 \neq \sigma_2$). As the name implies, the standard error of this t test is based upon two separate standard deviation estimates.

So far, we have examined ways of comparing means across two different samples or groups of cases. In the next section we will examine a procedure called the *matched-groups t test*, which is used to compare two means within the same or comparable group or sample.

MATCHED-GROUPS OR DEPENDENT SAMPLES t TEST

In our application of the t test for the difference between two means in the preceding section, we assumed that the two samples were independent of each other. That is, we assumed that the selection of the elements of one sample had no effect on the selection of the elements of the other. There are times when this assumption is deliberately violated. One instance of this occurs when we have a "treatment" and a "control" group. In order to make sure that the two groups are comparable to one another, each observation in one group is "matched" with an observation in the other group on relevant characteristics. Typically, this is done so that the only thing that differentiates them is that one group has received a certain type of treatment or has been exposed to some phenomena and the other group has not.

For example, one way to determine the effects of counseling on future delinquency would be to collect data from two samples that are very similar in nature, with the exception that one receives counseling (treatment group) and the other does not (control group). In such a study, an 18-year-old minority male who lives in an urban area and who has no prior criminal history might be placed in a sample that is to receive treatment (counseling) while another 18-year-old minority male who lives in an urban area and who has no prior criminal history would be "matched" to this treatment male but placed in a sample that is to receive no treatment (no counseling). If the members of the two groups are effectively matched on important characteristics, such as age, criminal history, minority status, and location of residence, then any observed differences between the two groups on the dependent variable (future delinquency) are unlikely to be due to these demographic characteristics. Rather, they are more likely to be due to the treatment, which in this example is counseling. The important point here is that by matching someone in one sample with a counterpart in a second sample, we have violated our assumption that the two samples are independent.

A second common use of matched or dependent samples occurs with "before–after" research designs, more generally referred to as "pre and post" designs. In this type of study, there is only one sample, but measures of the dependent variable are taken at two different points in time. An example of this design is when persons are measured with respect to a variable of interest before and after some experimental variable is introduced. For example, using the preceding scenario of counseling and delinquency, suppose we have access to only one group and all of its members are going to receive counseling. In this case, there can be no matched control group; instead, we have access only to the individuals before and after they have received the counseling. In this case, we may use self-report data before and after counseling to determine if counseling actually has decreased rates of offending. However, this type of sample also violates our assumption of independence since the same persons appear in both groups.

If we were to use either the matched sample or the pre–post design in a study, we might be tempted to use a difference of means *t* test in order to determine if the groups were significantly different on some continuous variable of interest. It should be clear to you, however, that the two previously described *t* tests would not be appropriate because we would not have independent samples. Since the elements of each sample have been deliberately selected to be alike, we really only have *n* independent observations. In both the matched-groups and pre–post design, the independent observation is actually a *pair of cases*, not two independent groups. If we now consider each pair as an independent observation, we can conduct a statistical test based on the difference between the scores for each pair. In other words, we will make a pair-by-pair comparison by obtaining a difference score for each pair. Unlike the t test for independent samples that tests for the difference between two sample means $(\overline{X}_1 - \overline{X}_2)$, the matched-groups t test (also called the **matched-groups t test**) will test the difference between the scores for each pair $(x_2 - x_1)$.

In the null hypothesis of the t test for dependent samples, we will assume that the two populations are equal; that is, we will assume the treatment or intervention has no effect. If this is true, the two scores will be equal, so that the difference between them will be zero. If, under the null hypothesis, we take the difference between each pair of observations, each difference will be expected to be zero, and the mean of the differences will be zero. The null hypothesis, then, presumes that the population mean of group differences will be zero. We will symbolize the mean of the population of group differences as μ_D, with the subscript D indicating that this is the difference between the two populations. The statistical test in a dependent samples t test, then, is really a single-sample test of the hypothesis that $\mu_D = 0$.

Our procedure will be to determine the difference between each sample pair of scores $[X_D = (x_2 - x_1)]$, calculate the mean of those differences $(\overline{X}_D)$, and then test whether this sample mean difference is equal to the expected population mean difference (μ_D) of zero. If the null hypothesis is true, then most of these X_D differences will be close to zero, as will the mean of the differences $\overline{X}_D$. If, however, the null hypothesis is not true, then the two scores will tend to be different and the mean difference score will be greater than or less than zero. The greater the difference between the pairs of scores, the greater the mean difference will be, and the more likely we will be to reject the null hypothesis.

The formula for the t test with dependent samples is:

$$t = \frac{\overline{X}_D - \mu_D}{s_D / \sqrt{n-1}} \tag{10–6}$$

Remember that we have analogized the t test for matched samples to a hypothesis test involving a single population mean (μ_D). In the t test in Chapter 8 where we dealt with one-sample problems, we subtracted the population mean from the sample mean and divided by the standard deviation of the sampling distribution. This is exactly what we do in the matched-groups t test in equation 10–6 above. We subtract the population mean (μ_D) from the sample mean $(\overline{X}_D)$ where the sample mean is the *mean of the differences between each pair of scores,* and we divide by the estimated standard deviation of the sampling distribution, which is the standard deviation of the observed difference scores. Notice that the dependent samples t test is based solely upon the difference scores X_D (where $\overline{X}_D = x_2 - x_1$) and the standard deviation of the difference scores (S_D).

Since the null hypothesis assumes that the population mean is zero ($\mu_D = 0$), the formula for the dependent samples t test can be reduced to:

$$t_{\text{obt}} = \frac{\overline{X}_D}{s_D \,/\, \sqrt{n-1}} \tag{10--7}$$

where

$$s_D = \sqrt{\frac{\sum (x_D - \overline{X}_D)^2}{n}}$$

Once we have our obtained t value, we do the same thing as with any t test discussed thus far. We compare t_{obt} with t_{crit} and make a decision about our null hypothesis. We go to the same t table as for independent-samples t tests (Table E–3 of Appendix E). The difference is that in the case of matched samples, since we have only n pairs of independent observations (rather than $n_1 + n_2$ observations, as in the case of independent samples, and the elaborate degrees of freedom estimate for the separate variance t test), we have $n - 1$ degrees of freedom in the matched t test, where n is equal to the number of *pairs* of observations. A couple of examples will help illuminate what is going on here. In each example we will conduct a formal hypothesis test.

Case Study: Problem-Oriented Policing and Crime

Several recent studies have found that over half of all crimes in a city are committed at a few criminogenic places within communities. These places have been called "hot spots" by some criminologists (Braga et al., 1999; Sherman, Gartin, & Buerger, 1989; Weisburd et al., 1992). Even within the most crime-ridden neighborhoods, it has been found that crime clusters at a few discrete locations while other areas remain relatively crime-free. The clustering of violent crime at particular locations suggests that there are important features or dynamics at these locations that give rise to violent situations. As such, focused crime prevention efforts have recently sought to modify these criminogenic conditions and reduce violence.

Problem-oriented policing strategies (similar to community policing) have been increasingly utilized by urban jurisdictions to reduce crime in these high-activity crime places. Problem-oriented policing challenges officers to identify and analyze the causes of problems behind a string of criminal incidents. Once the underlying conditions that give rise to crime problems are known, police officers can develop and implement appropriate responses. For example, some of these strategies include using community members as information sources to discuss the nature of the problems the community faces and the possible effectiveness of proposed responses, as well as to assess the implemented responses. Other strategies target the social disorder problems inherent in these neighborhoods, such as cleaning up the environment of the place and making physical improvements such as securing vacant lots or removing trash from the street.

Suppose we are interested in the efficacy of these policing strategies in reducing acts of violence in neighborhoods plagued by high rates of crime. We target 20 neighborhoods within a city and send out teams of community police officers to implement problem-oriented policing strategies in these neighborhoods. Before the program begins, we obtain the number of arrests for violent offenses that have been made in each neighborhood within the 60 days prior to the program's implementation. After the program has been in place for three months, we again obtain the number of arrests for violent offenses that have been made in each neighborhood for a 60-day period. In this case, the program of problem-oriented policing is the independent variable and the number of violent offenses before and after the program is the dependent variable. We want to know whether the average number of violent arrests has increased or decreased after implementation of the policing program. The hypothetical number of arrests for each time point is reported in the second and third columns of Table 10–4. We are now ready to conduct our hypothesis test.

TABLE 10–4

Number of Violent Arrests in Neighborhoods Before (First Score) and After (Second Score) Problem-Oriented Policing Implementation

Pair Number	First Score X_1	Second Score X_2	X_D $(X_2 - X_1)$
1	25	21	− 4.00
2	29	25	− 4.00
3	32	32	.00
4	42	39	− 3.00
5	21	25	4.00
6	29	25	− 4.00
7	33	29	− 4.00
8	35	36	1.00
9	32	29	− 3.00
10	36	35	− 1.00
11	39	40	1.00
12	25	21	− 4.00
13	27	25	− 2.00
14	41	35	− 6.00
15	36	35	− 1.00
16	21	23	2.00
17	38	31	− 7.00
18	25	21	− 4.00
19	29	25	− 4.00
20	25	20	− 5.00
			$\sum X_D = -48$
			$\bar{X}_D = -2.4$

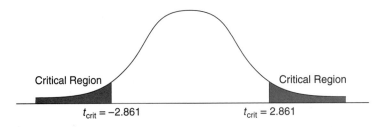

Figure 10–10   Critical t and critical regions for alpha = .01 (df = 19) and a two-tailed test

Step 1. First, we state our assumptions and the null and research hypotheses. Our null hypothesis is that the mean difference score in the population is equal to zero. This implies that the problem-oriented policing has no effect on the number of violent arrests within neighborhoods. Because there is very little research that examines the efficacy of problem-oriented policing strategies in reducing violence, we also will state a nondirectional research hypothesis stating our belief that, on average, the number of arrests in neighborhoods after the new policing strategy will be different from the number of arrests before problem-oriented policing was implemented in neighborhoods. Both the null and research hypotheses are formally stated below.

H_0: $\mu_D = 0$
H_1: $\mu_D \neq 0$

Step 2. The next step is to state our test statistic and the sampling distribution of that test statistic. Because we have dependent samples, we use the dependent samples t test as the statistical test and the t distribution as our sampling distribution.

Step 3. The third step is to select our alpha level and determine the critical value and region. We select an alpha level of .01 (α = .01). Because we have 20 pairs of independent observations (n = 20), we have $20 - 1$, or 19 degrees of freedom. We go to Table E–3 of Appendix E and find that, for a two-tailed hypothesis test with α = .01 and 19 degrees of freedom, the critical value of t is ± 2.861. We will, therefore, reject the null hypothesis if t_{obt} is less than or equal to $- 2.861$ or if t_{obt} is greater than or equal to 2.861. We illustrate this in Figure 10–10.

Step 4. The fourth step of our hypothesis testing procedure is to calculate the test statistic and compare it to our critical value. Since this is our first example of a matched-groups t test, we will illustrate the calculations in detail. From equation 10–7, we see that we need to determine the mean of the difference scores and the estimated standard deviation of the difference scores. In Table 10–4, we report the sum of the difference scores is equal to −48 ($\Sigma X_D = -48$). Notice how these difference scores are created. For each neighborhood, we subtract the first score from the second. For example, the first pair of cases had 21 arrests after the problem-oriented policing strategy was implemented and 25 arrests before the strategy. The difference, then, is $21 - 25 = -4$. We do this for each neighborhood (each pair), sum across the cases, and then divide by the number of cases to obtain a mean difference score. All scores are added in calculating this mean difference score, including zeros and scores with negative signs. With 20 pairs of scores, the mean difference score for these data is −48/20, or −2.4 ($\overline{X}_D = -2.4$).

We now calculate the estimated standard deviation of the difference scores. This is just like calculating the standard deviation for any other group of scores, except the raw data are the difference scores and the mean is the mean of the difference scores. In this example we use the definitional formula for the standard deviation. First, subtract the mean difference score from each difference score, then square this difference, sum these squared differences, divide by the number of pairs, and take the square root. To get the standard deviation of the sampling distribution, divide this result by the square root of the sample size minus 1. The calculations necessary to find this are shown in Table 10–5.

We can place this into our definitional formula for the standard deviation (Chapter 5):

$$s = \sqrt{\frac{\sum (X_D - \overline{X}_D)^2}{n}}$$

The standard deviation of the difference scores is symbolized as s_D, and for this example it is calculated using the standard deviation formula above:

$$s_D = \sqrt{\frac{152.8}{20}}$$

$$= \sqrt{7.64}$$

$$= 2.76$$

Now that we have the standard deviation of the difference scores, we can calculate our test statistic:

$$t_{obt} = \frac{\overline{X}_D}{s_D / \sqrt{n-1}}$$

TABLE 10–5

Standard Deviations of the Sampling Distribution for the Number of Neighborhood Violent Arrests Before (First Score) and After (Second Score) Problem-Oriented Policing Implementation

Pair	$(D - \overline{X}_D)$		$(D - \overline{X}_D)^2$
1	$(-4 - -2.4)$	$= -1.60$	2.56
2	$(-4 - -2.4)$	$= -1.60$	2.56
3	$(\ 0 - -2.4)$	$= -2.40$	5.76
4	$(-3 - -2.4)$	$= -\ .60$	.36
5	$(\ 4 - -2.4)$	$=\ \ 6.40$	40.96
6	$(-4 - -2.4)$	$= -1.60$	2.56
7	$(-4 - -2.4)$	$= -1.60$	2.56
8	$(\ 1 - -2.4)$	$=\ \ 3.40$	11.56
9	$(-3 - -2.4)$	$= -\ .60$	.36
10	$(-1 - -2.4)$	$= -1.40$	1.96
11	$(\ 1 - -2.4)$	$= -3.40$	11.56
12	$(-4 - -2.4)$	$= -1.60$	2.56
13	$(-2 - -2.4)$	$= -\ .40$	.16
14	$(-6 - -2.4)$	$= -3.60$	12.96
15	$(-1 - -2.4)$	$= -1.40$	1.96
16	$(\ 2 - -2.4)$	$= -4.40$	19.36
17	$(-7 - -2.4)$	$= -4.60$	21.16
18	$(-4 - -2.4)$	$= -1.60$	2.56
19	$(-4 - -2.4)$	$= -1.60$	2.56
20	$(-5 - -2.4)$	$= -2.60$	6.76
$n = 20$			$\Sigma(D - \overline{X}_D)^2 = 152.8$

$$= \frac{-2.4}{2.76 / 4.36}$$

$$= \frac{-2.4}{.63}$$

$$= -3.81$$

Step 5. Finally, we compare our obtained value of t (-3.81) with our critical value (± 2.861) and the critical region. Since t_{obt} falls within the critical region ($-3.81 > -2.861$) we must reject the null hypothesis that the mean of the differences is equal to zero. We will conclude that the number of post-arrests for violence is significantly different from the number of pre-arrests. The implementation of problem-oriented policing within our sample of neighborhoods does appear to have had a significant impact on the number of violent arrests made within each neighborhood.

Case Study: Siblings and Delinquency

One of the most comprehensive studies undertaken regarding the causes of delinquent behavior was reported over 40 years ago by Sheldon and Eleanor Glueck (1950). The Gluecks compared 500 institutionalized chronic delinquents with a matched group of 500 nondelinquents. Among their findings, the Gluecks reported that those in the delinquent group were more likely to come from broken homes and economically disadvantaged families, were more likely to have friends who also were delinquents, and were more likely to have parents who were cruel and erratic in their discipline than the group of nondelinquents.

Let's presume that like the Gluecks we have a group of 15 delinquents and a matched group of 15 nondelinquents who are matched with respect to social class, gender, age, race, and whether or not both natural parents are in the home. For each youth we also have data regarding the number of siblings who have been arrested for a crime. What we want to know is if the delinquent youth have more delinquent siblings than the nondelinquent youth. The data from the two groups are reported in the second the third columns of Table 10–6.

TABLE 10–6

Number of Delinquent Siblings for 15 Delinquent Youths and a Matched Group of 15 Nondelinquent Youths and the Calculations Necessary for a Matched Samples t Test.

Pair	Nondelinquent Score	Delinquent Score	$(x_2 - x_1)$ D			$(D - \overline{X}_D)$	$(D - \overline{X}_D)^2$
1	1	3	2	$(2 - -1.40)$	$=$	.60	.36
2	0	2	2	$(2 - -1.40)$	$=$	.60	.36
3	0	1	1	$(1 - -1.40)$	$=$	$-$ .40	.16
4	1	4	3	$(3 - -1.40)$	$=$	1.60	2.56
5	2	1	-1	$(-1 - -1.40)$	$=$	-2.40	5.76
6	0	3	3	$(3 - -1.40)$	$=$	1.60	2.56
7	2	2	0	$(0 - -1.40)$	$=$	-1.40	1.96
8	1	4	3	$(3 - -1.40)$	$=$	1.60	2.56
9	0	1	1	$(1 - -1.40)$	$=$	$-$ .40	.16
10	0	2	2	$(2 - -1.40)$	$=$	.60	.36
11	0	0	0	$(0 - -1.40)$	$=$	-1.40	1.96
12	1	2	1	$(1 - -1.40)$	$=$	$-$ .40	.16
13	0	2	2	$(2 - -1.40)$	$=$	.60	.36
14	1	3	2	$(2 - -1.40)$	$=$	.60	.36
15	0	0	0	$(0 - -1.40)$	$=$	-1.40	1.96
$n = 15$			$\sum X_D = 21$				
			$\overline{X}_D = 21/15 = 1.40$				$\sum (D - \overline{X}_D)^2 = 21.60$

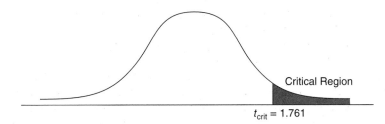

Figure 10–11   Critical t and critical region for alpha $= .05$ (df $= 14$) and a one-tailed test

Step 1. As always, our null hypothesis is that the number of delinquent
siblings is not different between the two groups. In other
words, we hypothesize that the population mean for the difference between the pair of scores is zero. Based on our knowledge of the delinquency literature, our directional (one-tailed)
research hypothesis is that the delinquent group will have more
delinquent siblings than the nondelinquent group. Our prediction, therefore, is that the difference scores will generally be
positive and that the population mean for the differences will
be greater than zero. Both are formally stated below:

$H_0: \mu_D = 0$
$H_1: \mu_D > 0$

Step 2. Our test statistic will be the dependent samples t test, and the
sampling distribution will be the t distribution.

Step 3. For our hypothesis test we will choose an alpha level of .05.
Since our research hypothesis states that the true population
mean is greater than zero, our critical region will lie in the
right tail of the sampling distribution. With $n - 1$ or 14 degrees of freedom, $\alpha = .05$, and a one-tailed test, we find in
the t table (Table E–3) that $t_{crit} = -1.761$. The critical region
consists of all obtained t scores that are equal to or greater
than 1.761. We will, therefore, fail to reject the null hypothesis if $t_{obt} < 1.761$. We show the critical t value and critical region in Figure 10–11.

Step 4. In Table 10–6 we provide the necessary calculations to determine both the mean and the standard deviation of the difference scores for the data in the second and third columns. The
value of t_{obt} is calculated below:

$$t_{obt} = \frac{\overline{X}_D}{\sqrt{\dfrac{\sum (D - \overline{X}_D)^2}{n}} \Big/ \sqrt{n-1}}$$

$$= \frac{1.40}{\sqrt{\dfrac{21.60}{15}} \,/\, \sqrt{15-1}}$$

$$= \frac{1.40}{\sqrt{1.44} \,/\, \sqrt{14}}$$

$$= \frac{1.40}{1.20 \,/\, 3.74}$$

$$= \frac{1.40}{.32}$$

$$= 4.38$$

Step 5. The obtained value of our test statistic is 4.38. Because $t_{obt} > t_{crit}$, we are led to reject the null hypothesis that the mean population difference is zero. We would conclude that there is a significant relationship between delinquency and the number of delinquent siblings that a youth has; delinquents have significantly more delinquent siblings than nondelinquents.

In this and the previous two sections of this chapter, we have examined several different types of statistics to test a hypothesis about two population means. This must present a somewhat bewildering picture to you, and we will admit that it might seem a bit overwhelming right now. In selecting the appropriate test statistic for the two-sample mean problem, however, a good deal of confusion can be eliminated if you can remember that you need to answer only a few fundamental questions before deciding which test is appropriate for your problem. We have tried to summarize these decisions for you in Figure 10–12. Think of this figure as a road map for deciding which statistical test for two-sample mean problems you should use. In the next section, we will examine hypothesis tests about the difference between two sample proportions.

HYPOTHESIS TESTS FOR THE DIFFERENCE BETWEEN TWO PROPORTIONS: LARGE SAMPLES

Up to this point, we have examined testing hypotheses that involve the difference between two population means. In this section, we will examine a statistical test for the significance of the difference between two population *proportions* (p_1 and p_2). Think of the difference of proportions test as a special case of the difference of means test.

Let's say we have a sample of 100 persons and we ask each of them whether or not they favor the death penalty for those who commit first degree murder. We arbitrarily assign a score of "0" for those who say no and "1" for those who say yes. Let's assume that 89 of the 100 say they approve of the

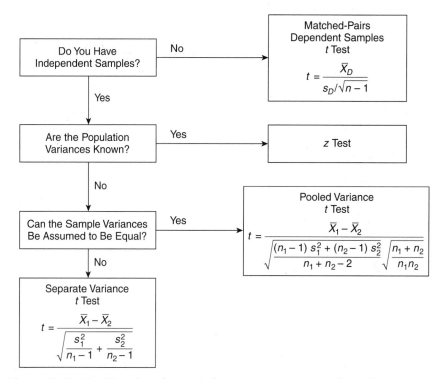

Figure 10–12   Decision chart for using the appropriate statistical test for two mean problems

death penalty under that circumstance, while 11 say that they do not. Since there are only two values (0/no and 1/yes) we can treat this variable as being measured at the interval level. We can determine the mean of this variable by counting the number of "1" scores (or "0" scores) and dividing by n. Since we have 89 "1" scores, the mean would be 89/100, or .89. The mean for a dichotomized variable (a variable with only two values) that has been coded "0" and "1," then, is the proportion of "1" scores, in this case, the proportion of our sample who were in favor of the death penalty. The mean, therefore, is actually the proportion of "1" scores. Even though the population is dichotomous (it is made up of zeros and ones), we know from the Central Limit Theorem that with a large enough sample, the distribution of sample means and the difference between two sample means will be approximately normal. Hence, we can use a z test and the z distribution to test hypotheses about the difference between two proportions.

In this chapter, we will consider only those tests appropriate for data obtained from large independent samples. If $np \geq 5$ and $nq \geq 5$ for each of the two samples (where p is the population proportion and $q = 1 - p$), the sampling distribution of the difference between proportions will be approximately normal, and we can use a z test as our test statistic.

In the t test for two sample means, we subtracted one sample mean from the other and divided by the standard error of the difference between means. We will conduct the same procedure in our test for the difference between two proportions. In our z test for two proportions, we will subtract the two sample proportions ($\hat{p}_1 - \hat{p}_2$) and divide by the standard deviation of the sampling distribution of the difference between ($\sigma_{(p_1-p_2)}$). This standard deviation is also referred to as the **standard error of the difference between proportions.** The z test for the difference between proportions is:

$$z_{\text{obt}} = \frac{\hat{p}_1 - \hat{p}_2}{\sigma_{(p_1-p_2)}} \qquad \text{(10–8)}$$

where

$$\hat{p}_1 = \text{the sample proportion for the first sample,}$$
$$\hat{p}_2 = \text{the sample proportion for the second sample, and}$$
$$\sigma(p_1 - p_2) = \text{the standard error of the difference between proportions.}$$

Since the two sample proportions ($\hat{p}_1 - \hat{p}_2$) are known, the only remaining unknown is the denominator, the standard error of the difference between two proportions. Since the null hypothesis states that there is no difference between the two population proportions, we can assume that $p_1 = p_2$. We have already seen in Chapter 8 that the standard deviation of a population proportion $\sigma_p = \sqrt{pq/n}$. If, by the null hypothesis, $p_1 = p_2$, then it will be true that $\sigma_1 = \sigma_2$ because $\sqrt{p_1q_1} = \sqrt{p_2q_2}$. In the difference of proportions test, then, we can assume that the population standard deviations are equal and we can simplify our hypothesis test by using a pooled variance estimate for the standard error of the difference between proportions. The formula for the pooled standard error is:

$$\sigma_{(p_1-p_2)} = \sigma \sqrt{\frac{n_1 + n_2}{n_1 n_2}}$$

where

$$(\sigma = \sqrt{pq})$$

However, as the population proportion (p) is unknown, we need to estimate the pooled standard deviation ($\sigma = \sqrt{pq}$) by calculating a pooled estimate of p ($\hat{p}$). The formula for our pooled estimate of the population proportion p, is:

$$\hat{p} = \frac{n_1\hat{p}_1 + n_2\hat{p}_2}{n_1 + n_2} \qquad \text{(10–9)}$$

where

$\hat{p}_1$ = the sample proportion for the first sample,

$\hat{p}_2$ = the sample proportion for the second sample, and

Once we have found $\hat{p}$, we can then determine $\hat{q}$ by subtraction, since $\hat{q} = 1 - \hat{p}$. Our estimate of the standard error of the difference between two proportions can then be calculated from the following formula:

$$\hat{\sigma}_{(p_1 - p_2)} = \sqrt{\hat{p}\hat{q}} \sqrt{\frac{n_1 + n_2}{n_1 n_2}}$$

(10–10)

Our obtained value of z now can be estimated using the formula shown below:

$$z_{\text{obt}} = \frac{\hat{p}_1 - \hat{p}_2}{\sqrt{\hat{p}\hat{q}} \sqrt{\dfrac{n_1 + n_2}{n_1 n_2}}}$$

(10–11)

As with all the preceding hypothesis tests, once we have obtained the test statistic, we compare our z_{obt} with z_{crit} and make a decision about the null hypothesis. Let's go through an example.

Case Study: Education and Recidivism

One of the primary questions in the correctional literature regards what programs within the correctional setting either increase or decrease inmates' rates of recidivism once they are released. Stevens and Ward (1997) tracked two groups of inmates after their release from the North Carolina Department of Corrections: in one group, inmates had earned their associate and/or baccalaureate degrees while incarcerated; in the other group, no inmate had been a student at any time while incarcerated. Not surprisingly, Stevens and Ward found that rates of recidivism were significantly lower for the group of inmates who had received education compared to the group of inmates who had not.

Let's say we have independent random samples of 120 inmates from a correctional institution; 60 inmates in this group have received either their associate and/or baccalaureate degrees while the remaining 60 inmates have received no educational curriculum whatsoever. Of the 60 who have received an education, 18 percent ($\hat{p}_1 = .18$) are rearrested within one year of release. Of the 60 who have not received any education, 38 percent ($\hat{p}_2 = .38$) are rearrested within the same time period. We wonder whether there is a significant difference in the percent of released inmates who have been rearrested (our measure of recidivism) between the two groups. To answer this question, we need to conduct an explicit hypothesis test.

Step 1. Our null hypothesis is that the two samples come from populations with the same proportion of inmates rearrested after release. To be on the safe side, we test a nondirectional (two-tailed) research hypothesis that the two proportions are different. Both are stated as:

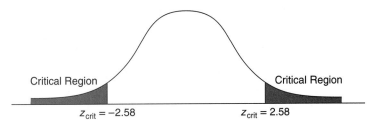

Figure 10–13   Critical z and critical regions for alpha = .01 and a two-tailed test

$H_0: p_1 = p_2$
$H_1: p_1 \neq p_2$

Step 2. To test these hypotheses, we select as our test statistic the z test for a difference of proportions. Since we have a large sample size, the z distribution will be our sampling distribution.

Step 3. We will select an alpha level of .01. For a two-tailed test, the critical level of z at $\alpha = .01$ is $z_{crit} = \pm 2.58$ (see Table E–2 in Appendix E or Table 8-1 in Chapter 8 for the critical values of z for common levels of alpha). Since this is a two-tailed test, the critical region lies in both tails of the z distribution and consists of all obtained z scores less than or equal to -2.58 and greater than or equal to 2.58. We will fail to reject the null hypothesis if $-2.58 < z_{obt} < +2.58$. We illustrate the two critical regions and the critical z values in Figure 10–13.

Step 4. To make the calculations more manageable, we will find our obtained value of z in a series of steps.

Step 4.1. We find the estimated value of the pooled population proportions:

$$\hat{p} = \frac{(60)(.18) + (60)(.38)}{60 + 60}$$

$$= \frac{10.8 + 22.8}{120}$$

$$= \frac{33.6}{120}$$

$$= .28$$

$$\hat{\sigma} = 1 - .28$$

$$\hat{\sigma} = .72$$

Step 4.2. We find the standard error estimate of the difference between population proportions:

$$\hat{\sigma}_{(p_1-p_2)} = \sqrt{\hat{p}\hat{q}}\sqrt{\frac{n_1+n_2}{n_1 n_2}}$$

$$= \sqrt{(.28).72}\sqrt{\frac{60+60}{60(60)}}$$

$$= \sqrt{.20}\sqrt{\frac{120}{3600}}\cdot$$

$$= (.45)\sqrt{.033}$$

$$= (.45)(.18)$$

$$= .081$$

Step 4.3. Finally, plugging our sample proportions into the numerator and this standard error estimate into the denominator of equation 10–11, we calculate the value of our obtained z test:

$$z_{obt} = \frac{\hat{p}_1 - \hat{p}_2}{\sqrt{\hat{p}\hat{q}}\sqrt{\frac{n_1+n_2}{n_1 n_2}}}$$

$$= \frac{.18-.38}{.081}$$

$$= \frac{-.20}{.081}$$

$$= -2.47$$

Step 5. Our obtained z statistic is −2.47. This value of z_{obt} just misses falling into our rejection region. It does not lie within the critical region $-2.58 < -2.47 < 2.58$, and so we must therefore fail to reject the null hypothesis. We cannot conclude, based upon our sample data, that the proportion of inmates who recidivate is significantly different between those inmates who receive education in prison and those who do not. Despite our failure to reject the null hypothesis in this case, notice that there is a 20 percent difference between our sample proportions. What could we do to increase the likelihood of rejecting the null hypothesis? The answer is the same thing we can always do to improve our inferences from a sample to the population—increase our sample size.

SUMMARY

In this chapter, we have examined techniques used to perform hypothesis tests to determine the difference between two means and two proportions. With unknown population variances, the statistical test for the difference between two means is conducted with a t test. If the test involves two independent random samples, there are two different kinds of t tests from which we can choose. The first type is called a pooled variance t test. This test for two sample means is appropriate when we can assume that the population standard deviations are equal. When we cannot maintain that assumption, the correct t test to use is the separate variance t test.

In addition to these tests for independent samples, we also examined a t test for matched or dependent samples. In this kind of t test, rather than being interested in the difference between two means, we are interested in testing whether or not the difference between two sets of scores is equal to zero.

Finally, we also learned how to test for the significance of the difference between two proportions and discovered that this is a special instance of the two-sample mean test.

KEY TERMS

dependent-groups t test

independent variable

matched-groups t test

pooled variance estimate of the standard error of the difference

sampling distribution of sample mean differences

separate variance estimate of the standard error of the difference

standard error of the difference between means

standard error of the difference between proportions

KEY FORMULAS

Pooled variance t test (eq. 10–3):

$$t_{obt} = \frac{\overline{X}_1 - \overline{X}_2}{\sqrt{\dfrac{(n_1 - 1)s_1^2 + (n_2 - 1)s_2^2}{n_1 + n_2 - 2}} \sqrt{\dfrac{n_1 + n_2}{n_1 n_2}}}$$

Separate variance t test (eq. 10–4):

$$t_{obt} = \frac{\overline{X}_1 - \overline{X}_2}{\sqrt{\dfrac{s_1^2}{n_1 - 1} + \dfrac{s_2^2}{n_2 - 1}}}$$

REVIEW & PRACTICE

Degrees of freedom for separate variance t test (eq. 10–5):

$$df = \left[\frac{\left(\frac{s_1^2}{n_1 - 1} + \frac{s_2^2}{n_2 - 1} \right)^2}{\left(\frac{s_1^2}{n_1 - 1} \right)^2 \left(\frac{1}{n_1 + 1} \right) + \left(\frac{s_2^2}{n_2 - 1} \right)^2 \left(\frac{1}{n_2 + 1} \right)} \right] - 2$$

Dependent samples t test (eq. 10–7):

$$t_{obt} = \frac{\overline{X}_D}{s_D / \sqrt{n - 1}}$$

where

$$S_D \sqrt{\frac{\sum (X_D - \overline{X}_D)^2}{n}}$$

Difference between proportions z test (eq. 10–8):

$$z_{obt} = \frac{\hat{p}_1 - \hat{p}_2}{\sigma_{(p_1 - p_2)}}$$

where

$$\hat{\sigma}_{(p_1 - p_2)} = \sqrt{\hat{p}\hat{q}} \sqrt{\frac{n_1 + n_2}{n_1 n_2}}$$

PRACTICE PROBLEMS

1. Explain the difference between independent and dependent variables. If you think that low self-control affects crime, which is the independent and which is the dependent variable?

2. When is it appropriate to use an independent-groups t test versus a t test for dependent samples or matched groups?

3. Thomas Peete and his colleagues (1994) found that the fear of losing the good opinion of others kept people from breaking rules, particularly if the person was very strongly attached to the social group. Let's say that we have two independent random samples of people, those who think that their coworkers would disapprove of them for stealing things from their employer, and those who think that their coworkers either would not care or would approve of their stealing from their employer. We ask each person in each group to self-report the number of times that they have stolen from their employer in the past 12 months:

Would Not Approve of Stealing	Would Approve of Stealing
$n_1 = 40$	$n_2 = 25$
$\overline{X}_1 = 5.1$	$\overline{X}_2 = 8.2$
$s_1 = 1.8$	$s_2 = 1.9$

Test the null hypothesis that the two population means are equal against the alternative hypothesis that the group whose coworkers would not approve of stealing has a lower mean rate of theft. In your hypothesis test, assume that the unknown population standard deviations are equal and use an alpha level of .01.

4. The use of monetary fines as a criminal sanction is being considered as one possible solution to the problem of prison overcrowding. Supporters of the use of fines contend that it would be both an effective deterrent to crime and a way to punish even moderately severe crimes without imprisonment. Critics argue that giving criminal offenders only fines increases their motivation to commit more crimes in order to pay their fine. You want to test the effect of fines versus incarceration on criminal behavior. You take a random sample of 150 convicted offenders who have been given a fine as punishment and follow up on them for three years. You take a second independent random sample of 110 offenders recently released from prison and follow up on them for three years. At the end of the three-year follow-up period you find that 33 percent of those given a fine have been rearrested and 38 percent of those given a prison sentence have been rearrested. Test the null hypothesis that the proportion rearrested in the two groups is equal against the alternative hypothesis that the proportions are different. Use an alpha level of .05.

5. Alissa Worden (1993) has conducted some research on the perceptions that female and male police officers have of their role, the public, and their department. She concluded that female and male police officers do not view their jobs very differently. Let's say that we wanted to continue her work and were interested in how female and male police officers view one component of police work, the handling of domestic disputes. To do this research, we have created a scale that measures how important settling domestic disputes is and whether it is perceived to be part of "police work." Those who score high on this scale think that the fair settling of domestic disturbances is of high priority and that it should be an important part of a police officer's duties. We then take two random samples. One is a sample of 50 male police officers, and the second is an independent random sample of 25 female police officers. We give each officer a questionnaire that includes our domestic dispute scale. The mean score for the male officersis 18.8 (with a standard deviation of 4.5) and the mean for the female officers is 21.3 (with a standard deviation of 3.0). Test the null hypothesis that the two population means are equal against the alternative hypothesis that the male mean is lower than the female mean.

In your hypothesis test *do not* presume that the population standard deviations are equal and use an alpha level of .05.

6. Capital punishment law is among the most complex bodies of law in our legal system. As a result, judges make frequent errors in capital cases in terms of their rulings regarding a change of venue, the decision to sequester jurors, questions of *voir dire*, suppression of evidence, and so on. When these errors are made, cases are often won on appeal and have to be retried or have a second penalty phase hearing. The Trial Judges Association thinks that only those judges who have received special training should sit on capital cases because these judges would commit fewer errors and there would be fewer cases lost on appeal. You decide to test this hypothesis. You take a random sample of 15 judges who have received extensive training in capital punishment law. You match these judges with 15 other judges who have not received such training but are matched in terms of their number of years on the bench, experience as trial lawyers, gender, and age. You want the two groups of judges to be alike in every way except in the experience of capital punishment law training. The data on your matched groups of judges are as follows:

Number of Cases Lost on Appeal

Judge	Untrained	Trained
1	3	0
2	1	3
3	2	4
4	7	4
5	5	2
6	4	5
7	6	1
8	2	1
9	7	0
10	5	6
11	3	4
12	4	2
13	5	5
14	6	3
15	2	1

Test the null hypothesis, that the mean difference in the number of cases lost on appeal for the two groups of judges is zero, against the alternative hypothesis, that the untrained judges lose more cases on appeal. Use an alpha level of .01.

7. In a recent book, Adrian Raine (1993) discusses some research in biological criminology that suggests that children with criminal parents are more likely to be criminals themselves than are children with noncriminal parents. Suppose you conducted a study on a random sample of 100 delinquent youths

confined in a correctional institution with a random sample of 75 nondelinquent youths. You find that 43 percent of the delinquent youths have at least one criminal parent, but only 17 percent of the nondelinquent youths have a criminal parent. Test the null hypothesis that the two population proportions are equal against the alternative that the delinquent group has a higher proportion of criminal parents. Use an alpha level of .01.

8. It is common wisdom to believe that dropping out of high school leads to delinquency. For example, Travis Hirschi's (1969) control theory might predict that those with little or no commitment to education are delinquent more often than those with strong educational commitments. In his general strain theory, however, Robert Agnew (1992) might predict that dropping out of school lowers one's involvement in delinquency because it gets youths out of an aversive and painful environment. You want to examine the relationship between dropping out of high school and delinquency. You have a random sample of 11 students. For each student you have the number of delinquent offenses they reported committing in the year before they dropped out of school and the number of offenses they reported committing in the year after they dropped out of school:

Number of Delinquent Acts

Person	Before	After
1	5	7
2	9	5
3	2	3
4	7	7
5	8	11
6	11	13
7	8	4
8	8	10
9	5	7
10	2	1
11	9	3

Test the null hypothesis that the mean difference between the two sets of scores is zero against the alternative hypothesis that it is different from zero. Use an alpha level of .05.

SPSS PRACTICE PROBLEMS

1. Using the data from HOMICIDE, which is a sample of information on homicide defendants from 33 counties in the U.S., the question we want to address is, "Are convicted male and female homicide defendants treated

differently? Specifically, do they receive different prison sentences?" The dependent variable, then, is sentence length received (PRIMTIME) and the independent variable is gender of defendant (SEX). The null hypothesis you will be testing is that the mean sentence lengths received by males and females are equal in the population of all convicted homicide defendants. To perform this test, click on ANALYZE, then COMPARE MEANS, then on an INDEPENDENT-SAMPLES *T* TEST. When you are in the dialogue box, you will see two boxes, a "test variable" box and a box called "grouping variable." The former is where the dependent variable is placed, and the latter is for the independent variable. However, in addition to placing the independent variable in the grouping variable box, you must also tell SPSS exactly how this variable is coded. For example, gender in this data set is coded 1 for males and 0 for females. You must enter these two values in the spaces provided. What do you conclude?

2. The question we next want to address using the data in exercise (1) is, "Do defendants with prior criminal records receive longer sentences than those with no criminal records?" The variable that provides information on prior records, however, is not a two-categorical variable, so you must recode it first, coding all those defendants who had no prior records as different (say 0) from those who had one or more prior records (say 1). Remember to run a frequency distribution on the newly created variable to make sure that it has been recoded correctly! Now you can click on ANALYZE, then COMPARE MEANS, then on an INDEPENDENT-SAMPLES *T* TEST, and place PRITIME in the test variable box and your new PRIOR variable in the grouping variable box along with your new codes. What do you conclude about the null hypothesis that states that the mean sentence length received by defendants with priors is equal to the mean sentence length received by those defendants without criminal records?

3. For this question, we will be conducting a *t* test for samples that are matched or paired. To do this, bring up the data set called YOUTH, which contains data from a survey of high school youth. Two variables will be used in these data, DELINQ1 and DELINQ2. Both are self-reported acts of delinquency (e.g., stealing, destroying property, drinking, taking or selling drugs) engaged in by the respondents during two time periods. Thus, we have two measures of self-reported involvement in delinquency from the same respondents taken at two different points in time. The question we are interested in is, "Did respondents' involvement in delinquent activities change from time 1 to time 2?" Let's say we believe that the students' delinquency will not remain the same, but will increase. The null hypothesis, of course, states that the difference in mean rates of delinquency for time 1 and time 2 will remain the same. To test this hypothesis, click on ANALYZE, then COMPARE MEANS, then on PAIRED-SAMPLES *T* TEST. In the PAIRED VARIABLES box, place the variables for both delinquency scores, DELINQ1 and DELINQ2. What do you conclude?

Hypothesis Tests Involving Three or More Population Means: Analysis of Variance

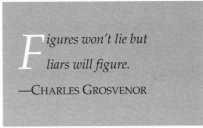

Figures won't lie but liars will figure.

—CHARLES GROSVENOR

In this chapter, we will examine the case where we have an independent variable with two or more categories and a quantitative dependent variable. As in the last chapter, we also are interested in the difference between the means of three or more groups, but for reasons we will explain, the application of the *t* test to more than two groups is not appropriate. In this chapter, you will learn about another technique, called analysis of variance, or ANOVA for short,

411

which relies on the sampling distribution of F. In addition, because we have more than two means in this case, the results of a null hypothesis test that states three or more population means are equal can only tell us that at least one pair of the means may be different—but it cannot tell us which one. You also will learn how to conduct a test called Tukey's Honest Significant Difference (HSD) test to determine which of your group means are significantly different from each other. What neither the F test nor Tukey's HSD test can do, however, is tell us about the *strength* of the relationship between our independent and dependent variables. Therefore, we will conclude our discussion by learning how to calculate eta squared, which measures the strength of the relationship between an independent and dependent variable in an analysis of variance.

INTRODUCTION

In the previous chapter we conducted a hypothesis test about the equality between two population means ($\mu_1 = \mu_2$) by examining the difference between two sample means $(\overline{X}_1 - \overline{X}_2)$. In this kind of problem we had a continuous dependent variable (measured at the interval/ratio level) and a categorical independent variable (nominal or ordinal) that had only two levels or values. This t test is a very valuable tool to have in our statistical toolbox because many issues we confront in criminology and criminal justice concern a comparison of means between two distinct groups (for example, males vs. females, those put on probation vs. those given jail time, life sentences vs. death sentences). There will be many times, however, when our independent variable is a categorical variable but has more than three values.

For example, suppose we were interested in finding out if the sentence given to armed robbers (measured in months) varied by the race of the defendant. Suppose also that our independent variable (race of defendant) consisted of the following categories: white, black, Hispanic, and Asian. With the tools we now have in our toolbox, we might be tempted to just do a series of pairwise t tests. That is, we could use our t test for independent samples and conduct the hypothesis test at some level of significance (say, $\alpha = .05$) that each pair of sample means is equal, against the alternative that each pair is not equal. Notice that if we were to do this, we would have a lot of pair-wise t tests to perform. With four groups, we would have to do $(4 - 1)/2$, or 6 different t tests: $\overline{X}_{white} - \overline{X}_{black}$, $\overline{X}_{white} - \overline{X}_{hispanic}$, $\overline{X}_{white} - \overline{X}_{asian}$, $\overline{X}_{black} - \overline{X}_{hispanic}$, $\overline{X}_{black} - \overline{X}_{asian}$, $\overline{X}_{hispanic} - \overline{X}_{asian}$. We would, therefore, have a lot of work to do. That's not the real problem with this strategy, however.

The real problem of doing a series of t tests with the same data is that the significance level of our hypothesis test assumes that the sample means are independent. When we use the same sample means for multiple significance tests (notice that the white group mean in the example above is used in three separate hypothesis tests), this assumption of independence is violated. The real problem with this is that our alpha level increases. That is, while our first *t* test hypothesis test is done with an alpha level of .05, because the assumption of independence is violated, the overall or combined alpha level for all six hypothesis tests is higher than this. What this means is that for our six separate hypothesis tests referred to above, the probability of making a Type I error in rejecting a true null hypothesis is not .05, but greater than that. In conducting multiple means tests with the same data, therefore, we do not have a true alpha level.

Because of this, we need to have a tool in our toolbox that can conduct multiple tests of population means and maintain a true alpha level. This tool, which we will learn in this chapter, is called an **analysis of variance,** or **ANOVA** for short. The analysis of variance test is to be used when we are interested in conducting a hypothesis test where we have a continuous (interval/ratio) dependent variable and an independent variable that is categorical (nominal or ordinal), and where there are three or more levels (values) of that independent variable.

THE LOGIC OF ANALYSIS OF VARIANCE

Let's assume we have three population means whose equality we are testing ($\mu_1 = \mu_2 = \mu_3$). Our hypothesis test is called the analysis of variance because in testing this hypothesis we are not going to examine the means directly, but examine the variances. That is why the test is called an analysis of *variance.* Now, it may seem to you very odd to do a hypothesis test about population means by examining variances, so allow us to explain.

Case Study: Police Responses to Domestic Violence

We will use the substantive problem in this section as an example. We are interested in the differential effect of three different kinds of police response to a domestic violence call: (1) simply separate the couple and do nothing else, (2) separate the couple and require counseling for the offender, and (3) arrest the offender. The outcome in which we are interested is the number of times the police are called back to the address on another domestic violence call involving the same offender in the subsequent year. Our nominal-level independent variable is the police response to domestic violence, and there are three values or categories: separate, counsel, and arrest. Our interval-/ratio-level dependent variable is the number of return calls to the address involving the same offender. Let's assume that we have a sample of 100 persons in each group, for a total sample size of 300, and after a year we calculate the mean number of return calls for each group.

Figure 11–1(a) shows a hypothetical distribution of return calls for each of the three groups. Notice that the three group means are very different. The mean number of return calls is highest for the separate-only group, next highest for the counsel group, and lowest for the arrest group. Notice also that while the three group means are very different from each other, the scores within each group are not that different from their own unique group mean. In other words, each score within a group clusters fairly tightly around its group mean. In sum, scores do not vary that much within groups, but the mean scores vary a great deal between groups. Based on this figure, we would be tempted to conclude that how the police respond to a domestic violence call does indeed make a difference in terms of the effect on the suspect (i.e., there is a "treatment effect"). Suspects who have been arrested seem least likely to repeat their offense in the subsequent year compared with those who have been counseled and those who have been separated. In addition, the counseled group of suspects seems to do better than those who are simply told to leave the scene; in fact, the latter group has the highest number of new offenses. In other words, it looks as if $\overline{X}_{arrest} \neq \overline{X}_{counsel} \neq \overline{X}_{separate}$.

Figure 11–1(b) shows a different set of distributions for the same data. In this case, although the three group means are the same as in Figure 11–1(a), there is much greater variability within each group. The scores within each group no longer cluster tightly about the group mean but are highly variable, overlapping with the scores of the other groups. It looks like there is as much or more variability within a group as there is between groups. In this set of distributions, we are less tempted to conclude that there is a "treatment effect"

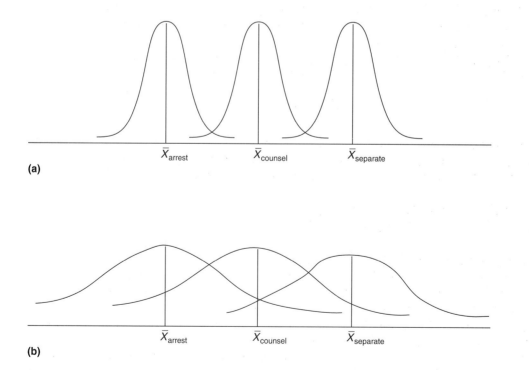

(a)

(b)

Figure 11–1   Distribution of the number of new offenses for three groups of domestic violence suspects

due to the different police responses to domestic violence. Now it looks like $\overline{X}_{arrest} = \overline{X}_{counsel} = \overline{X}_{separate}$. We came to this tentative conclusion by comparing the variability within each group to that which exists between the groups. This comparison of within-group to between-group variability is at the heart of the analysis of variance. All we have to do is change the word "variability" to "variance" and we can see that an analysis of variance is based on comparing the variance within groups to the variance between groups in order to draw a conclusion about the equality of group means.

TOTAL, BETWEEN-GROUP, AND WITHIN-GROUP VARIANCE

In the analysis of variance test we calculate three different types of variance: the total variance, the between-group variance, and the within-group variance. To refresh your memory, here is the formula we have used for a variance:

$$s^2 = \frac{\Sigma(x - \overline{X})^2}{n - 1}$$

(11–1)

To calculate a variance, therefore, we simply take the difference between a score and its mean, square that difference, sum over all scores, and divide by the degrees of freedom ($n - 1$). As you can see, we can calculate a variance for any group of scores where we have a mean of those scores. Technically, the test for an analysis of variance is called the F test, which is actually a ratio of two variances, the variance between groups over the variance within groups. It is the F test that we use to test the null hypothesis about the equality of three or more population means. Let's first examine the different sorts of variability we have in this three or more population mean problem.

Continuing with our example from the previous section, let's assume we want to test the null hypothesis about the equality of the mean number of new offenses for our three groups of domestic violence offenders. In that example we had a group of suspects who were arrested by the police in response to a 911 call for domestic violence, a group of suspects who were given mandatory counseling, and a group who were only physically separated from their victim. Our dependent variable was the number of new domestic violence offenses committed by the same offender in the subsequent year. For simplicity's sake, let's say we have a sample of five offenders in each of our three groups. The number of new offenses for each offender and the mean for each group are shown for you in Table 11–1.

You can see that the mean number of new offenses differs across the three groups. On average, those arrested have committed one new offense, those counseled have committed on average five new offenses, and those separated have committed nine new offenses in the subsequent year. We cannot, of course, conclude on the basis of this sample data that the police response affects the number of new offenses in the population. That is, we cannot

TABLE 11–1

Number of New Offenses for Suspects Arrested, Counseled, or Separated by Police in Response to a 911 Call for Domestic Violence

Arrested	Counseled	Separated
0	6	8
2	4	10
1	4	9
1	6	10
1	5	8
$\overline{X}_{arrest} = 1.0$	$\overline{X}_{counseled} = 5.0$	$\overline{X}_{separated} = 9.0$

automatically conclude from these different sample means that $\mu_{arrest} \neq \mu_{counseled} \neq \mu_{separated}$ because our observed sample means may differ from each other by chance alone. That is, sampling variation may account for the observed differences in our sample means, instead of a real difference between the population means. Our decision to rule out the possibility of sampling variation is going to be based on a formal hypothesis test using the analysis of variance.

For the data in Table 11–1 we can calculate a couple of means. First we will calculate the mean number of new offenses for each group separately—that is, a mean number of new offenses for the arrested, counseled, and separated treatment groups. We have already done this in Table 11–1, and the three means are reported at the bottom of each group. Let's call these three means the group means. Now let's calculate another mean by ignoring the fact that someone belongs in a particular group. We will add together all 15 scores and divide by 15. Let's call this mean the "grand mean" because it is the overall mean for all the scores. The grand mean is calculated as:

$$\overline{X}_{grand} = \frac{0+2+1+1+1+6 \ldots +9+10+8}{15}$$

$$\overline{X}_{grand} = 5.0$$

Ignoring the group that an offender falls into, then, the average number of new offenses for these 15 offenders is 5. We could have calculated the grand mean another way. Since we have the same number of cases in each group, we could have obtained the grand mean by adding the three group means together and dividing by three:

$$\overline{X}_{grand} = \frac{1+5+9}{3}$$

$$\overline{X}_{grand} = 5.0$$

With these means we are now going to calculate a couple of different measures of *variability,* where variability is defined as the difference between a given score and the mean of those scores. First, we are going to calculate a measure of **total variability,** which is the difference between an individual score (x_i) and the grand mean $x_i - \overline{X}_{grand}$. This total variability can be divided into two separate components. One component of the total variability is the difference between an individual score and the mean of the group to which an individual belongs $(x_i - \overline{X}_k)$, where $\overline{X}_k$ here is the mean for the kth group. This is a measure of **within-group variability**. According to this component of total variability, there is variation within a group not because the people within it have received a different treatment (because all persons within a group have received the same treatment), but for other reasons.

The second component of total variability is the difference between the group mean and the grand mean $(\overline{X}_k - \overline{X}_{grand})$. This is a measure of **between-groups variability**. According to this component, there is variation between groups because offenders in different groups have received a different "treatment" (police response). In other words, there is a group "treatment effect." For example, there are on average a different number of offenses committed between the groups because offenders respond to being arrested differently than they do to being counseled or separated in a case of domestic violence. By separating the two types of variability, we can determine which type contributes more to the total variability.

Let's illustrate this with our data. The total variability for the first case (with a score of new offenses) in the arrested group is equal to: $(0 - 5) = -5$. He has five fewer offenses than the overall average number of offenses (the grand mean, $\overline{X}_{grand}$. We will now break this variability down into two components. First is the within-group variability, which is the difference between the individual score and the group mean $(0 - 1 = -1)$. Part of the total variability for person 1, then, is due to the fact that the number of new offenses for this person is 1 less than the average for the group that person is in (the arrested group). The between-group variability is -4 $(1 - 5 = -4)$. Most of the variability for this person is due to the fact that those in the arrested group have fewer new offenses than the overall average. In sum:

Total Variability		**Within-Group Variability**		**Between-Group Variability**
$(x_i - \overline{X}_{grand})$	$=$	$(x_i - \overline{X}_k)$	$+$	$(\overline{X}_k - \overline{X}_{grand})$
$(0 - 5)$	$=$	$(0 - 1)$	$+$	$(1 - 5)$
-5	$=$	-1	$+$	-4
-5	$=$	-5		

Another way to describe this is: (Individual score − Grand mean) = (Individual score − Group mean) + (Group mean − Grand mean).

Let's now do the same thing for the first case in the counseled group in Table 11–1. We will divide the total variability (the difference between the individual's score and the grand mean) into both within-group (the difference between the individual's score and the group mean) and between-group differences (the difference between the group mean and the grand mean):

Total Variability		Within-Group Variability		Between-Group Variability
$(x_i - \overline{X}_{grand})$	$=$	$(x_i - \overline{X}_k)$	$+$	$(\overline{X}_k - \overline{X}_{grand})$
$(6 - 5)$	$=$	$(6 - 5)$	$+$	$(5 - 5)$
1	$=$	1	$+$	0
1	$=$	1		

In this case, all of the variability is due to within-group variability. Finally, let's take the first person in the separated group and decompose that person's total variability into its two components:

Total Variability		Within-Group Variability		Between-Group Variability
$(x_i - \overline{X}_{grand})$	$=$	$(x_i - \overline{X}_k)$	$+$	$(\overline{X}_k - \overline{X}_{grand})$
$(8 - 5)$	$=$	$(8 - 9)$	$+$	$(9 - 5)$
3	$=$	-1	$+$	4
3	$=$	3		

The total variability for this person is a +3, and most of this is due to the fact that this person's group (suspects separated by police) has a higher mean number of new offenses than the other two groups (i.e., it's due to variability between groups).

What the analysis of variance does, therefore, is calculate the overall or total variability for each observation and then divide it into the within and between components. You should be able to see that if the lion's share of the total variability for these domestic violence data is due to variability within groups and the variability between groups is relatively small (see Figure 11–1[b]), we are not as likely to conclude that the group means are different and, thus, not so likely to conclude that the population means are different (that is, reject the null hypothesis). If, however, most of the total variability is due to variability between groups and the variability within groups is relatively small (see Figure 11–1[a]), then we suspect that there really is a group "treatment effect" and that the population means really are different from each other.

The analysis of variance F test is based on the two types of variance that we will demonstrate next. First, we are going to take each of our three sources of variability—total, within, and between groups—and square them to obtain the variances of each component. These components are therefore called the *sum of squares.* For example, let's take the simple formula we have for total variability ($x_i - \overline{X}_{grand}$) and do two things to it: (1) square the difference, and (2) require that we take this squared difference for every score or observation. If we do this, the squared difference between each score and the grand mean has a special term, called the **total sum of squares,** or (SS_{total}). This formula is:

$$SS_{total} = \sum_i \sum_k \left(x_{ik} - \overline{X}_{grand} \right)^2 \tag{11-2}$$

where i references the individual x score, and k references the group. This formula says that the total sum of squares is obtained by subtracting the grand mean from each individual score, squaring that difference, and then summing over all scores (the summation signs, $\sum_i \sum_k$, instruct us to start with the first i score in the first of k groups, and continue until the last i score in the last of k groups). Notice that this total sum of squares looks a lot like the numerator of an estimate of the variance in equation 11–1—it's a squared difference of the mean from some score.

We are now going to take our within-group variability and with this derive an estimate of the squared difference of each score in a group from the mean of the group. This squared difference of each score from the mean of the group is called the **within-group sum of squares,** or (SS_{within}):

$$SS_{within} = \sum_i \sum_k (x_{ik} - \overline{X}_k)^2 \tag{11-3}$$

In words, this formula tells us to start with the first group ($k = 1$) and take the first person in this group ($i = 1$), subtract the group mean from this x_i score, square this difference, repeat this for each person in the first group, and then sum the squared differences. Then, go to the first person in the second group ($k = 2$) and do the same thing for each person in this group. Continue until you have squared the difference between the score for the last person in the last group and that group mean. Notice that this within-group sum of squares also looks a lot like the numerator of an estimate of the variance in equation 11–1. Like the total sum of squares, it too is a squared difference of the mean from some score.

Finally, we are going to take our measure of the variability between groups and derive an estimate of the squared difference of each group mean from the grand mean. This squared difference of each group mean from the grand mean is called the **between-groups sum of squares,** or ($SS_{between}$):

$$SS_{between} = \sum_i \sum_k (\overline{X}_k - \overline{X}_{grand})^2 \tag{11-4}$$

In words, this formula tells us to take the first group mean, subtract the grand mean from that, square the difference, and then do the same for each of the i persons in that group and sum over the number of cases in that group. Then do the same thing for each of the other k groups and sum over groups. Notice that this between-groups sum of squares also looks a lot like the numerator of an estimate of the variance in equation 11–1. Like the total and within-group sums of squares, the sum of squares between groups also is a squared difference of the mean from some score.

The three sum of squares have this property:

$$SS_{total} = SS_{within} + SS_{between}$$

As such, we need to calculate only two sources of the sum of squares and the third can be found by subtraction (i.e., $SS_{total} - SS_{within} = SS_{between}$) or addition ($SS_{within} + SS_{between} = SS_{total}$).

We now have three sum of squares measures: total, within-group, and between-groups. Each of these sums of squares is the numerator of an estimate of a source of variance—total variance, within-group variance, and between-group variance. Looking at equation 11–1, in order to complete our formulas for each of these three variances, we need to divide each sum of squares by its respective degrees of freedom. Just as there are three different sum of squares, there are three corresponding degrees of freedom:

$$\textbf{Total degrees of freedom} = df_{total} \quad = n - 1$$

$$\textbf{Within-group degree of freedom} = df_{within} \quad = n - k$$

$$\textbf{Between-groups degrees of freedom} = df_{between} = k - 1$$

where

$$n = \text{total number of observations, and}$$

$$k = \text{number of groups.}$$

As with the sum of squares:

$$df_{total} = df_{total} + df_{between}$$

So we have to calculate only two sources of degrees of freedom and then can obtain the third by subtraction or addition.

We now have three different variance estimates:

$$\textbf{Total variance} = \frac{SS_{total}}{df_{total}} \quad = \frac{\sum_i \sum_k (x_{ik} - \overline{X}_{grand})^2}{n - 1}$$

$$\textbf{Within-group variance} = \frac{SS_{within}}{df_{within}} \quad = \frac{\sum_i \sum_k (x_{ik} - \overline{X}_k)^2}{n - k}$$

$$\textbf{Between-groups variance} = \frac{SS_{between}}{df_{between}} \quad = \frac{\sum_i \sum_k (\overline{X}_k - \overline{X}_{grand})^2}{k - 1}$$

The F test that is the test statistic for the analysis of variance is simply the ratio of the between-groups to the within-group variance:

$$F = \frac{SS_{between} / df_{between}}{SS_{within} / df_{within}} = \frac{\text{Variance between groups}}{\text{Variance within group}}$$

Notice that this **F statistic** will become larger as the variance between groups becomes greater relative to the variance within groups. This corresponds to Figure 11–1(a). Large values of the F statistic, then, will lead us to reject the null hypothesis of equal population means. What we do not yet know, however, is how large our obtained F must be in order for us to reject the null hypothesis of equal population means.

Like any test statistic we have discussed thus far (the t, z, or chi-square test, for example), in order to conduct our hypothesis test we need to select a level of significance or alpha level and then find a critical value of our test statistic from the appropriate probability distribution. In this case involving a hypothesis test of three or more population means, we know that our test statistic is the analysis of variance F test. The F statistic follows an **F distribution**. Critical values of F can be obtained from Table E–5 in Appendix E. There are two F tables here, one table in which the alpha level is .05 and another in which there is a .01 level of significance. In order to find the critical value of F at some alpha level, we also need to know two types of degrees of freedom. The between-groups degrees of freedom are found at the top of each of the two tables, forming columns, while the within-group degrees of freedom are found along the left side of the tables, forming rows. In order to find the correct critical value of F, then, you need to identify the column corresponding to your between-groups degrees of freedom and identify the correct row corresponding to your within-group degrees of freedom. The value of F found at the convergence of that column and row is your critical F. Since the obtained F statistic is based upon a sum of *squares* (deviations from some mean, squared) we will have only positive values. Our decision, then, will always be to reject the null hypothesis when our obtained F is greater than or equal to our critical F.

Since we have all the necessary tools to do an analysis of variance, we will now move on and actually test a hypothesis about equal population means. Let's use the data in Table 11–1, which reported the number of new offenses for three groups of offenders who were given a different treatment by the police in response to a 911 call for domestic violence.

CONDUCTING A HYPOTHESIS TEST WITH ANOVA

In an analysis of variance, the hypothesis test involves the equality of three or more population means. In our example, we want to know if the mean number of new offenses for the arrested, counseled, and separated populations is equal. The null hypothesis is expressed as: $\mu_{arrest} = \mu_{counsel} = \mu_{separate}$. When we fail to reject the null hypothesis, therefore, we are assuming that the population means are equal. This conclusion implies that the different "treatments" or police responses to domestic violence make no difference in terms of the number of new offenses committed—that arresting the offender is no better than counseling or separating in terms of reducing the number of new offenses. The alternative hypothesis in an analysis of variance always states that the population means are simply different from each other (i.e., that they are not equal): $\mu_{arrest} \neq \mu_{counsel} \neq \mu_{separate}$. When we reject the null hypothesis, we are concluding that at least two of the population means are different. There is no directional alternative hypothesis test in an analysis of variance; instead, the alternative is always stated that the population means are not equal. Notice in the alternative hypothesis that we have stated only that the population means for the three groups are not equal. When we reject the null hypothesis, therefore, the only thing we know for sure is that at least one population mean is significantly different from at least one other population mean. We do not know from the analysis of variance test which specific population means are different from each other. This will require an additional step, which we will get to later in the chapter.

Let's now do our hypothesis test with the police response to domestic violence data. As always, we follow a series of five steps:

Step 1.

H_0: $\mu_{arrest} = \mu_{counsel} = \mu_{separate}$. In other words, the different police responses to domestic violence have no effect on the number of new offenses.

H_1: $\mu_{arrest} \neq \mu_{counsel} \neq \mu_{separate}$. The alternative or research hypothesis states that the type of response the police make to a call for domestic violence does make a difference in terms of the number of new offenses.

Step 2. Since we are testing a hypothesis about the quality of more than two population means, we recognize this as an analysis of variance test. Our test statistic is the F test, which has an F distribution.

Step 3. For this problem we are going to select an alpha level of .05. In order to find our critical value of F we need to determine our 2 degrees of freedom: within-group and between-groups. The within-group degrees of freedom are equal to $n - k$, where n is the total number of observations and k is the number of groups. In our problem, $n = 15$ and $k = 3$, so the within-group degrees of freedom are equal to $15 - 3 = 12$. The between-groups degrees of freedom are equal to $k - 1$. With three groups, the between-groups degrees of freedom for this problem are equal to: $3 - 1 = 2$. We can now go to the appropriate F table, with an alpha of .05, and 12 within-group and 2 between-groups degrees of freedom. We use the 2 between-groups degrees of freedom in

Table E–5 to find the correct column, and we use the 12 within-group degrees of freedom to find the correct row. We can see that with an alpha of .05 and 2 and 12 degrees of freedom, the critical value of F is 3.88. The critical region consists of all values of F equal to or greater than 3.88, and our decision rule is to reject the null hypothesis when $F_{\text{obtained}} \geq 3.88$.

Step 4. We now need to calculate our obtained value of F. To do this we need to calculate our three sources of variance. We will do this in a series of steps as well. Our first step will be to find the three sums of squares. We show all the calculations in Table 11–2. We provide the calculations to obtain all three sum of squares, but recall that we could have calculated only two and gotten the third by subtraction or addition. For example, we could have calculated the total and within-group sums of squares and then subtracted these two to get the between-groups sum of squares:

$$SS_{\text{total}} - SS_{\text{within}} = SS_{\text{between}}$$

$$170 - 10 = 160$$

Now that we have our sum of squares, we need to determine the degrees of freedom:

$$df_{\text{within}} = n - k = 15 - 3 = 12 \text{ degrees of freedom within groups,}$$

$$df_{\text{between}} = k - 1 = 3 - 1 = 2 \text{ degrees of freedom between groups,}$$

$$df_{\text{total}} = n - 1 = 15 - 1 = 14 \text{ total degrees of freedom.}$$

We can verify that these are correct because the sum of the within-group and between-groups degrees of freedom should equal the total degrees of freedom.

Now we are ready to calculate the estimates of our within-group variance and between-groups variance, which goes into the F statistic. Recall that the estimate of each source of variance is obtained by dividing the sum of squares by its respective degrees of freedom. We will put this information into what is frequently called an F test summary table. This summary table shows the sum of squares, the degrees of freedom, the estimated variance (also called the mean square), and the obtained F statistic. For our example we provide this F table in Table 11–3. The value of the F statistic reported in Table 11–3 is obtained by taking the ratio of the between-groups variance to the within-group variance (80/83).

Step 5. Since $F_{\text{obtained}} > F_{\text{critical}}$ (96.38 > 3.88), our decision is to reject the null hypothesis in favor of the alternative. We would conclude, then, that $\mu_{\text{arrest}} \neq \mu_{\text{counsel}} \neq \mu_{\text{separate}}$. We are saying two things in

TABLE 11–2

Calculations of Sum of Squares for Analysis of Variance Test

Total sum of squares:	$(x_i - \overline{X}_{grand})$	$(x_i - \overline{X}_{grand})^2$
	$(0 - 5) = -5$	25
	$(2 - 5) = -3$	9
	$(1 - 5) = -4$	16
	$(1 - 5) = -4$	16
	$(1 - 5) = -4$	16
	$(6 - 5) = 1$	1
	$(4 - 5) = -1$	1
	$(4 - 5) = -1$	1
	$(6 - 5) = 1$	1
	$(5 - 5) = 0$	0
	$(8 - 5) = 3$	9
	$(10 - 5) = 5$	25
	$(9 - 5) = 4$	16
	$(10 - 5) = 5$	25
	$(8 - 5) = 3$	9
		$\Sigma = 170$

Within-group sum of squares:	$(x_i - \overline{X}_k)$	$(x_i - \overline{X}_k)^2$
	$(0 - 1) = -1$	1
	$(2 - 1) = 1$	1
	$(1 - 1) = 0$	0
	$(1 - 1) = 0$	0
	$(1 - 1) = 0$	0
	$(6 - 5) = 1$	1
	$(4 - 5) = -1$	1
	$(4 - 5) = -1$	1
	$(6 - 5) = 1$	1
	$(5 - 5) = 0$	0
	$(8 - 9) = -1$	1
	$(10 - 9) = 1$	1
	$(9 - 9) = 0$	0
	$(10 - 9) = 1$	1
	$(8 - 9) = -1$	1
		$\Sigma = 10$

(Continued)

TABLE 11–2

(Continued)

Between-groups sum of squares:	$(x_k - \overline{X}_{grand})$	$(x_i - \overline{X}_{grand})^2$
	$(1 - 5) = -4$	16
	$(1 - 5) = -4$	16
	$(1 - 5) = -4$	16
	$(1 - 5) = -4$	16
	$(1 - 5) = -4$	16
	$(5 - 5) = 0$	0
	$(5 - 5) = 0$	0
	$(5 - 5) = 0$	0
	$(5 - 5) = 0$	0
	$(5 - 5) = 0$	0
	$(9 - 5) = 4$	16
	$(9 - 5) = 4$	16
	$(9 - 5) = 4$	16
	$(9 - 5) = 4$	16
	$(9 - 5) = 4$	16
		$\Sigma = 160$

TABLE 11–3

Summary F Table for Police Response to Domestic Violence Data

Source	Sum of Squares	df	Variance	F
Between-groups	160	2	80.00	96.38
Within-group	10	12	.83	
Total	170	14		

making this conclusion. First, we are saying that the independent variable, type of police response to domestic violence, is related to the number of new domestic violence acts an offender subsequently commits. Second, the only thing we can conclude is that some combination of these population means is not equal to the others. In other words, we know that the three populations of arrested, counseled, and separated suspects have different means; we do not, however, know which specific population means are different. We could be rejecting the null hypothesis because $\mu_{arrest} \neq \mu_{counsel} \neq \mu_{separate}$, or because $\mu_{arrest} \neq \mu_{counsel}$, or because $\mu_{arrest} \neq \mu_{separate}$, or because $\mu_{counsel} \neq \mu_{separate}$. We simply don't know on the basis of our F test. In order to decide which particular population means are different, we have to do another kind of statistical test.

AFTER THE *F* TEST: TESTING THE DIFFERENCE BETWEEN PAIRS OF MEANS

Once we have rejected the null hypothesis in an analysis of variance, our attention turns to the next question: "Which means are significantly different from which other means?" To answer this question we will conduct a statistical test about the difference between two population means. There are several different statistical tests in the literature that can do this, and each is appropriate in different situations. For our purposes here, however, we will learn one of the most frequently used tests, **Tukey's Honest Significant Difference (HSD) test.** Tukey's HSD test requires that we calculate something called the **critical difference (CD) score:**

$$CD = q \sqrt{\frac{\text{Within-group variance}}{n_k}} \qquad (11\text{--}5)$$

where

n_k = the number of cases *in each of the k groups,* and

q = the studentized range statistic.

Values of the studentized range statistic can be found in Table E–6 in Appendix E. You need three pieces of information in order to identify the correct value of q to use: (1) your selected alpha level (α), (2) your degrees of freedom within groups (df_{within}), and (3) the number of groups you have (k). What the critical difference gives us is the minimum absolute value of the difference between two sample means which would lead us to reject the null hypothesis (that they are equal). Now this last sentence, while accurate, is entirely too cryptic to be helpful. We can best explain things by going through an example using the HSD test.

In our analysis of variance in the last section, we rejected the null hypothesis that $\mu_{arrest} = \mu_{counsel} = \mu_{separate}$ in favor of the alternative hypothesis that $\mu_{arrest} \neq \mu_{counsel} \neq \mu_{separate}$. We now want to know which of these three population means is significantly different from the others. To do this we will use our sample means and conduct a Tukey HSD test of *each pair* of sample means. That is, we will examine the difference between our sample means to make an inference about the equality of the unknown population means. Unlike a series of independent sample t tests, however, Tukey's HSD will give us an honest level of significance for each of our sample mean comparisons.

First, we will list our null and alternative hypotheses for each population mean comparison:

H_0: $\mu_{arrest} = \mu_{counsel}$

H_1: $\mu_{arrest} \neq \mu_{counsel}$

H_0: $\mu_{arrest} = \mu_{separate}$

H_1: $\mu_{arrest} \neq \mu_{separate}$

H_0: $\mu_{counsel} = \mu_{separate}$

H_1: $\mu_{counsel} \neq \mu_{separate}$

Second, we will calculate the value of the critical difference (CD) using equation 11–5. In Tukey's HSD test we use the same level of significance we employed in the analysis of variance F test in the preceding example ($\alpha = .05$). In order to calculate the CD we need to get the value of q or the studentized range statistic, and to obtain this we need to go to Table E–6 in Appendix E with our alpha level (.05), the within-group degrees of freedom ($df_{within} = 12$), and the number of groups ($k = 3$). With this information, we can see that the value of q is equal to 4.60. We can now put this value into equation 11–5 for the CD with the other values (the within-group variance and the number of people in each group):

$$CD = 3.77 \sqrt{\frac{.83}{5}}$$

$$CD = 1.54$$

We have a critical difference score of 1.54. This means that the absolute value of the difference between any two sample means that we test must be greater than or equal to 1.54 in order for us to reject the null hypothesis of equal population means. Keep in mind that we need to compare the CD score to the *absolute value* of the difference between two sample means.

With our critical difference score of 1.54, let's calculate the absolute value of the difference between each of the three pairs of sample means. First, the difference in the mean number of new offenses between the arrested and counseled groups is:

$$\left| \frac{\begin{array}{r} 1 \\ -5 \end{array}}{4} \right|$$

Since the absolute value of the difference between these two sample means is greater than the critical difference score of 1.54, we can conclude that the two population means are significantly different from each other. We will decide, therefore, that $\mu_{arrest} \neq \mu_{counsel}$, and that the population of offenders who are arrested for domestic violence have fewer new offenses on average than those who are counseled.

Second, let's calculate the absolute value of the difference in the mean number of new offenses between the arrested and the separated groups:

Since the absolute value of the difference between these two sample means is greater than our critical difference score of 1.54, we will conclude that these two population means are significantly different from each other. We will decide that $\mu_{arrest} \neq \mu_{separate}$, and that domestic violence offenders who are arrested have significantly fewer new offenses on average than those who are merely separated from their partners.

Finally, let's calculate the absolute value of the difference between the mean number of new offenses for the counseled and separated groups:

$$\frac{\begin{array}{r} 5 \\ -9 \end{array}}{|\ 4\ |}$$

Since the absolute value of the difference between these two sample means is also greater than the critical difference score of 1.54, we will conclude that the population mean number of new offenses is significantly different for those offenders who are counseled and those who are simply separated from their partners. It seems that counseling offenders of domestic violence is more effective in reducing the number of new offenses than merely separating the couple.

In sum, the analysis of variance test and the series of Tukey's Honest Significant Difference tests tell us that how the police respond to an incidence of domestic violence does make a difference. At least in terms of reducing the number of new offenses committed by the same offender, arrest leads to the fewest new offenses on average, counseling leads to significantly more new offenses than arrest but significantly fewer offenses than just separating the couple, and separating the pair is the least effective police response in curbing future acts of domestic violence.

A MEASURE OF ASSOCIATION WITH ANOVA

In the previous sections we used the F test of an analysis of variance and Tukey's HSD test to assess the relationship between the type of police response to domestic violence and the number of new offenses committed by an offender. When we rejected the null hypothesis in the analysis of variance, we concluded that there was a relationship between the type of response that the police make to domestic violence and the number of new offenses subsequently committed. What neither the F test nor Tukey's HSD test told us, however, was the *strength* of the relationship between our independent and dependent variables. As we have learned in previous chapters, concluding that there is a relationship between two variables gives no clue as to the magnitude or strength of the relationship between them. In order to assess the strength of a relationship we must use an appropriate measure of association.

Recall that in the analysis of variance we calculated three sources of sum of squares—total, between-groups, and within-group. The total sum of squares measures the total amount of variability that exists among the scores. The between-groups variability measures the amount of variability due to group membership. This variability reflects the extent to which the groups differ from each other on the dependent variable. If there is a substantial amount of this variability, then it would appear that the group one is in matters, at least as far as the dependent variable is concerned. Finally, the within-group variability measures the amount of variability that is unaccounted for by group membership. Since everyone within a group shares the same group membership, members cannot differ because of different group effects. In fact, we do not know exactly why the scores within a group are different since they have the same level of the independent variable, so this variability is unexplained or unaccounted for. With this in mind, think of the total sum of squares as consisting of total variability, the between-groups sum of squares as consisting of explained variability (variability explained by membership in the group), and the within-group sum of squares as consisting of unexplained variability.

Recall also that the sum of the between-groups and within-group sum of squares is equal to the total sum of squares. The total variability in the scores, or the total sum of squares, then, is equal to two components, an explained component (the between-groups sum of squares) and an unexplained component (the within-group sum of squares). If we take the ratio of the between-groups to the total sum of squares, then, we get an estimate of the proportion of the total variability that is explained. The greater the amount of the total variability that is explained or due to variation in the independent variable, the stronger the relationship between it and the dependent variable.

This discussion of explained, unexplained, and total variability is the conceptual basis behind one measure of association with ANOVA called **eta squared,** or the **correlation ratio:**

$$\eta^2 = \frac{SS_{between}}{SS_{total}} \qquad (11\text{–}6)$$

Eta squared measures the strength of the relationship between an independent and a dependent variable in an analysis of variance. More specifically, it measures the amount of variability in the dependent variable that is explained by the independent variable. Eta squared can range from zero, indicating no relationship between the independent and dependent variables, and 1.0, indicating a perfect relationship between the two. A perfect relationship means that all of the variability among the scores is due to differences in group membership and there is no within-group variability. We can follow our old rule of thumb about measures of association and state that values of eta squared between zero and .29 can be interpreted as a "weak" relationship, values between .30 and .59 indicate a "moderate" relationship, and values greater than .60 reflect a "strong" relationship.

Let's use our police response to domestic violence data and calculate the value of eta squared:

$$\eta^2 = \frac{160}{170}$$

$$\eta^2 = .94$$

We have a very strong relationship between type of police response and the number of subsequent offenses. Multiplying eta squared by 100 tells us that 94 percent of the variability in the number of offenses committed is due to difference in police response.

A SECOND ANOVA EXAMPLE: ADOLESCENT EMPLOYMENT AND DELINQUENCY

In our second example, we are interested in the relationship between adolescent employment and the number of delinquent acts one commits. There has been some controversy in the criminological literature regarding this issue, with some studies finding that youths who work long hours during the school year (20 or more hours per week) are at higher risk for involvement in delinquency and other "problem behaviors" than youths who work fewer hours or who do not work at all. To examine the relationship between adolescent employment and delinquency, you take a sample of 10 youths who did not work two years ago and who this year either (1) continued not work-

TABLE 11–4

Number of Different Delinquent Offenses Committed by Adolescents Who Were Nonworkers, Moderate Workers, or Intensive Workers

Nonworkers	Moderate Workers	Intensive Workers
7	10	11
12	14	8
13	8	7
5	7	10
8	9	9
11	11	9
10	13	7
14	12	8
9	8	3
6	8	3
$\overline{X}_{nonworker} = 9.5$	$\overline{X}_{moderate} = 10.0$	$\overline{X}_{intensive} = 7.5$

ing (nonworkers), (2) started working but were employed for fewer than 20 hours per week (moderate workers), or (3) started working and were employed for 20 or more hours per week (intensive workers). You ask each of these youths to self-report the number of different delinquent acts they have committed from a list of 20 offenses. The data are shown in Table 11–4.

We want to test the null hypothesis that $\mu_{nonworker} = \mu_{moderate} = \mu_{intensive}$ against the alternative hypothesis that $\mu_{nonworker} \neq \mu_{moderate} \neq \mu_{intensive}$. We will use an alpha of .01 for this hypothesis test. All of the steps are shown below.

Step 1.

H_0: $\mu_{nonworker} = \mu_{moderate} = \mu_{intensive}$

H_1: $\mu_{nonworker} \neq \mu_{moderate} \neq \mu_{intensive}$

Step 2. This is a problem involving the equality of three population means, so the correct statistical test is the F test of an analysis of variance. The F test has an F distribution.

Step 3. We will use an alpha of .01. Our within-group degrees of freedom $(n - k)$ is equal to 27, and our between-groups degrees of freedom $(k - 1)$ is equal to 2. With 2 and 27 degrees of freedom, our critical value of F is 5.49 (see Table E–5, Appendix E), and the critical region is comprised of all F values greater than or equal to that. Our decision rule is to reject the null hypothesis if $F_{obtained} \geq 5.49$.

Step 4. The calculations for the total, between-groups, and within-group sums of squares are shown for you in Table 11–5. With the sums of squares and degrees of freedom, we can calculate the between-groups and within-group variance and the F statistic. The analysis of variance summary table in shown in Table 11–6.

Step 5. We have an obtained F value of 2.374. Since this is less than our critical value of $F_{critical} = 5.49$, our decision is to fail to reject the null hypothesis. We will conclude that $\mu_{nonworker} = \mu_{moderate} = \mu_{intensive}$, and that the intensity of youths' employment is not related to their risk of delinquent offenses. Since we failed to reject the null hypothesis, we do not need to examine our individual pairs of sample means with Tukey's HSD. The HSD test is appropriate only if we have rejected the null hypothesis in an analysis of variance. We can, however, calculate eta squared:

$$\eta^2 = \frac{35}{234}$$

$$\eta^2 = .15$$

A magnitude of .15 is small, strengthening our conclusion that the intensity of youth employment is not related to the number of delinquent offenses committed.

TABLE 11–5

Calculations for Second Analysis of Variance Example

Total Sum of Squares		Within-Group Sum of Squares		Between-Groups Sum of Squares	
$(xi - \bar{X}_{grand})$	$(xi - \bar{X}_{grand})^2$	$(xi - \bar{X}_k)$	$(xi - \bar{X}_k)^2$	$(\bar{X}_k - \bar{X}_{grand})$	$(x_k - \bar{X}_{grand})^2$
7 − 9 = −2	4	7 − 9.5 = −2.5	6.25	9.5 − 9 = .5	.25
12 − 9 = 3	9	12 − 9.5 = 2.5	6.25	9.5 − 9 = .5	.25
13 − 9 = 4	16	13 − 9.5 = 3.5	12.25	9.5 − 9 = .5	.25
5 − 9 = −4	16	5 − 9.5 = −4.5	20.25	9.5 − 9 = .5	.25
8 − 9 = −1	1	8 − 9.5 = −1.5	2.25	9.5 − 9 = .5	.25
11 − 9 = 2	4	11 − 9.5 = 1.5	2.25	9.5 − 9 = .5	.25
10 − 9 = 1	1	10 − 9.5 = .5	.25	9.5 − 9 = .5	.25
14 − 9 = 5	25	14 − 9.5 = 4.5	20.25	9.5 − 9 = .5	.25
9 − 9 = 0	0	9 − 9.5 = −.5	.25	9.5 − 9 = .5	.25
6 − 9 = −3	9	6 − 9.5 = −3.5	12.25	9.5 − 9 = .5	.25
10 − 9 = 1	1	10 − 10 = 0	0.00	10 − 9 = 1	1.00
14 − 9 = 5	25	14 − 10 = 4	16.00	10 − 9 = 1	1.00
8 − 9 = −1	1	8 − 10 = −2	4.00	10 − 9 = 1	1.00
7 − 9 = −2	4	7 − 10 = −3	9.00	10 − 9 = 1	1.00
9 − 9 = 0	0	9 − 10 = −1	1.00	10 − 9 = 1	1.00
11 − 9 = 2	4	11 − 10 = 1	1.00	10 − 9 = 1	1.00
13 − 9 = 4	16	13 − 10 = 3	9.00	10 − 9 = 1	1.00
12 − 9 = 3	9	12 − 10 = 2	4.00	10 − 9 = 1	1.00
8 − 9 = −1	1	8 − 10 = −2	4.00	10 − 9 = 1	1.00
8 − 9 = −1	1	8 − 10 = −2	4.00	10 − 9 = 1	1.00
11 − 9 = 2	4	11 − 7.5 = 3.5	12.25	7.5 − 9 = −1.5	2.25
8 − 9 = −1	1	8 − 7.5 = .5	.25	7.5 − 9 = −1.5	2.25
7 − 9 = −2	4	7 − 7.5 = −.5	.25	7.5 − 9 = −1.5	2.25
10 − 9 = 1	1	10 − 7.5 = 2.5	6.25	7.5 − 9 = −1.5	2.25
9 − 9 = 0	0	9 − 7.5 = 1.5	2.25	7.5 − 9 = −1.5	2.25
9 − 9 = 0	0	9 − 7.5 = 1.5	2.25	7.5 − 9 = −1.5	2.25
7 − 9 = −2	4	7 − 7.5 = −.5	.25	7.5 − 9 = −1.5	2.25
8 − 9 = −1	1	8 − 7.5 = .5	.25	7.5 − 9 = −1.5	2.25
3 − 9 = −6	36	3 − 7.5 = −4.5	20.25	7.5 − 9 = −1.5	2.25
3 − 9 = −6	36	3 − 7.5 = −4.5	20.25	7.5 − 9 = −1.5	2.25
	$\Sigma = 234$		$\Sigma = 199$		$\Sigma = 35$

TABLE 11–6

Summary F Table for the Relationship between Adolescent Employment and Delinquency

Source	Sum of Squares	df	Variance	F
Between-groups	35	2	17.50	2.37
Within-group	199	27	7.37	
Total	234	29		

TABLE 11–7

Rate of Murders and Non-Negligent Manslaughters (per 100,000) by Four Regions of the United States

Northeast		Midwest		South		West	
Connecticut	3.3	Illinois	7.7	Florida	5.7	Arizona	8.0
Maine	2.2	Indiana	6.6	Georgia	7.5	Idaho	2.0
Massachusetts	2.2	Michigan	6.0	North Carolina	7.2	Montana	2.6
New Hampshire	1.5	Ohio	3.5	South Carolina	6.6	Nevada	9.1
Rhode Island	3.6	Wisconsin	3.4	Virginia	5.7	New Mexico	9.8
Vermont	2.9	Iowa	1.5	Alabama	7.9	California	6.0
New Jersey	3.5	Kansas	7.0	Louisiana	10.7	Oregon	2.7
New York	5.0	Minnesota	2.8	Texas	6.1	Washington	3.0
Pennsylvania	4.9	Missouri	6.6	Mississippi	7.7	Utah	2.1
$\overline{X}_{northeast} = 3.23$		$\overline{X}_{midwest} = 5.01$		$\overline{X}_{south} = 7.23$		$\overline{X}_{west} = 5.03$	

A THIRD ANOVA EXAMPLE: REGION OF THE COUNTRY AND HOMICIDE

Let's work on one more example of an analysis of variance. In this last example, our independent variable is the region of the country and our dependent variable is the homicide rate. We have information on the homicide rate for 36 states, and we have classified each state as belonging to one of four regions of the country: Northeast, Midwest, South, and West. There are nine states that fall into each region, and we calculate the average homicide rate per 100,000 population in each of the four regions. These data are shown in Table 11–7. You can see that the sample means indicate that the homicide rate is lowest in the northeastern states, that the midwestern and western states have comparable rates of homicide on average, and that the southern states have the highest average homicide rate. We will test the hypothesis that the population mean homicide rates for the four regions are the same, and we will use an alpha of .05 in our hypothesis test. As always, we follow a series of five steps.

> **Step 1.**
>
> H_0: $\mu_{northeast} = \mu_{midwest} = \mu_{south} = \mu_{west}$
>
> H_1: $\mu_{northeast} \neq \mu_{midwest} \neq \mu_{south} \neq \mu_{west}$
>
> **Step 2.** Since this is a test involving the equality of three or more population means, the correct statistical test is the analysis of variance F test. The F test has an F distribution.
>
> **Step 3.** We will use an alpha of .05. We have 32 within-group degrees of freedom ($n - k$; $36 - 4 = 32$), and we have 3 between-groups degrees of freedom ($k - 1$; $4 - 1 = 3$). There is no row for 32 within-group degrees of freedom in Table E–5, so we will use 30 degrees of freedom. With 30 and 3 degrees of freedom and an alpha of .05, our critical value of F is 2.92. The critical region consists of all values of F equal to or greater than 2.92. Our decision rule is to reject the null hypothesis if $F_{obtained} \geq 2.92$.
>
> **Step 4.** The calculations necessary to find the total, within-group, and between-groups sum of squares are reported in Table 11–8. With the sum of squares and degrees of freedom, we also can calculate the between-groups and within-group variance and the F statistic. The analysis of variance summary table is shown in Table 11–9.
>
> **Step 5.** We have an obtained F value of 5.08. Since this is greater than our critical value of $F_{critical} = 2.92$, our decision is to reject the null hypothesis. We will conclude that $\mu_{northeast} \neq \mu_{midwest} \neq \mu_{south} \neq \mu_{west}$, and that there is a statistically significant difference in the rate of homicide across some regions of the United States. We now will use Tukey's HSD test to determine which pair of population means is significantly different.

We first need to determine the value of CD, the critical difference score:

$$CD = q\sqrt{\frac{\text{Within-group variance}}{n_k}}$$

To find the value of q, the studentized range statistic, we consult Table E–6 in Appendix E. With an alpha of .05, 30 within-group degrees of freedom (there is no row for 32 degrees of freedom), and 4 groups ($k = 4$), we find that $q = 3.84$. We are now ready to find our critical difference score:

$$CD = 3.84\sqrt{\frac{4.75}{9}}$$

$$CD = 2.79$$

Our critical difference score is 2.79. This means that when we compare each pair of our sample means, the absolute value of the difference between the

TABLE 11–8

Calculations for Third Analysis of Variance Example

Total Sum of Squares		Within-Group Sum of Squares		Between-Groups Sum of Squares	
$(x_i - \overline{X}_{grand})$	$(x_i - \overline{X}_{grand})^2$	$(x_i - \overline{X}_k)$	$(x_i - \overline{X}_k)^2$	$(x_k - \overline{X}_{grand})$	$(x_k - \overline{X}_{grand})^2$
$3.3 - 5.13 = -1.83$	3.35	$3.3 - 3.23 = .07$	.005	$3.23 - 5.13 = -1.90$	3.61
$2.2 - 5.13 = -2.93$	8.58	$2.2 - 3.23 = -1.03$	1.06	$3.23 - 5.13 = -1.90$	3.61
$2.2 - 5.13 = -2.93$	8.58	$2.2 - 3.23 = -1.03$	1.06	$3.23 - 5.13 = -1.90$	3.61
$1.5 - 5.13 = -3.63$	13.18	$1.5 - 3.23 = -1.73$	2.99	$3.23 - 5.13 = -1.90$	3.61
$3.6 - 5.13 = -1.53$	2.34	$3.6 - 3.23 = .37$	.14	$3.23 - 5.13 = -1.90$	3.61
$2.9 - 5.13 = -2.23$	4.97	$2.9 - 3.23 = -.33$	.11	$3.23 - 5.13 = -1.90$	3.61
$3.5 - 5.13 = -1.63$	2.66	$3.5 - 3.23 = .27$	.07	$3.23 - 5.13 = -1.90$	3.61
$5.0 - 5.13 = -.13$	.02	$5.0 - 3.23 = 1.77$	3.13	$3.23 - 5.13 = -1.90$	3.61
$4.9 - 5.13 = -.23$	.05	$4.9 - 3.23 = 1.67$	2.79	$3.23 - 5.13 = -1.90$	3.61
$7.7 - 5.13 = 2.57$	6.60	$7.7 - 5.01 = 2.69$	7.24	$5.01 - 5.13 = -.12$	.01
$6.6 - 5.13 = 1.47$	2.16	$6.6 - 5.01 = 1.59$	2.53	$5.01 - 5.13 = -.12$	.01
$6.0 - 5.13 = .87$	3.50	$7.0 - 5.01 = 1.99$	.98	$5.01 - 5.13 = -.12$	.01
$3.5 - 5.13 = -1.63$	2.66	$3.5 - 5.01 = -1.51$	2.28	$5.01 - 5.13 = -.12$	.01
$3.4 - 5.13 = -1.73$	2.99	$3.4 - 5.01 = -1.61$	2.59	$5.01 - 5.13 = -.12$	.01
$1.5 - 5.13 = -3.63$	13.18	$1.5 - 5.01 = -3.51$	12.32	$5.01 - 5.13 = -.12$	.01
$7.0 - 5.13 = 1.87$	.76	$6.0 - 5.01 = .99$	3.96	$5.01 - 5.13 = -.12$	.01
$2.8 - 5.13 = -2.33$	5.43	$2.8 - 5.01 = -2.21$	4.88	$5.01 - 5.13 = -.12$	.01
$6.6 - 5.13 = 1.47$	2.16	$6.6 - 5.01 = 1.59$	2.53	$5.01 - 5.13 = -.12$	.01
$5.7 - 5.13 = .57$	.32	$5.7 - 7.23 = -1.53$	2.34	$7.23 - 5.13 = 2.10$	4.41
$7.5 - 5.13 = 2.37$	5.62	$7.5 - 7.23 = .27$	.07	$7.23 - 5.13 = 2.10$	4.41
$7.2 - 5.13 = 2.07$	4.28	$7.2 - 7.23 = -.03$	.001	$7.23 - 5.13 = 2.10$	4.41
$6.6 - 5.13 = 1.47$	2.16	$6.6 - 7.23 = -.63$	.40	$7.23 - 5.13 = 2.10$	4.41
$5.7 - 5.13 = .57$	.32	$5.7 - 7.23 = -1.53$	2.34	$7.23 - 5.13 = 2.10$	4.41
$7.9 - 5.13 = 2.77$	7.67	$7.9 - 7.23 = .67$	.45	$7.23 - 5.13 = 2.10$	4.41
$10.7 - 5.13 = 5.57$	31.02	$10.7 - 7.23 = 3.47$	12.04	$7.23 - 5.13 = 2.10$	4.41
$6.1 - 5.13 = .97$	.94	$6.1 - 7.23 = -1.13$	1.28	$7.23 - 5.13 = 2.10$	4.41
$7.7 - 5.13 = 2.57$	6.60	$7.7 - 7.23 = .47$	.22	$7.23 - 5.13 = 2.10$	4.41
$8.0 - 5.13 = 2.87$	8.24	$8.0 - 5.03 = 2.97$	8.82	$5.03 - 5.13 = -.10$	.01
$2.0 - 5.13 = -3.13$	9.80	$2.0 - 5.03 = -3.03$	9.18	$5.03 - 5.13 = -.10$	.01
$2.6 - 5.13 = -2.53$	6.40	$2.6 - 5.03 = -2.43$	5.90	$5.03 - 5.13 = -.10$	.01
$9.1 - 5.13 = 3.97$	15.76	$9.1 - 5.03 = 4.07$	16.56	$5.03 - 5.13 = -.10$	.01
$9.8 - 5.13 = 4.67$	21.81	$9.8 - 5.03 = 4.77$	22.75	$5.03 - 5.13 = -.10$	.01
$6.0 - 5.13 = .87$	.76	$6.0 - 5.03 = .97$	.94	$5.03 - 5.13 = -.10$	.01
$2.7 - 5.13 = -2.43$	5.90	$2.7 - 5.03 = -2.33$	5.43	$5.03 - 5.13 = -.10$	.01
$3.0 - 5.13 = -2.13$	4.54	$3.0 - 5.03 = -2.03$	4.12	$5.03 - 5.13 = -.10$	.01
$2.1 - 5.13 = -3.03$	9.18	$2.1 - 5.03 = -2.93$	8.58	$5.03 - 5.13 = -.10$	.01
	$\Sigma = 224.51$		$\Sigma = 152.11$		$\Sigma = 72.40$

TABLE 11–9

Summary F Table for the Relationship between Region of the Country and Homicide Rates

Source	Sum of Squares	df	Variance	F
Between-groups	72.40	3	24.13	5.08
Within-group	152.11	32	4.75	
Total	224.51	35		

two means must be 2.79 or greater for us to reject the null hypothesis that they are equal.

Let's state explicitly each null hypothesis and its alternative and then conduct the necessary hypothesis test. Since we have four groups, there are six different mean comparisons to make.

H_0: $\mu_{northeast} = \mu_{midwest}$

H_1: $\mu_{northeast} \neq \mu_{midwest}$

$$\begin{array}{r} 3.23 \\ \underline{-5.01} \\ |\ 1.78\ | \end{array}$$

This difference in sample means is not greater than or equal to the CD score of 2.79, so we conclude that the population mean homicide rate for the northeastern states is not significantly different from that for the midwestern states. We would fail to reject the null hypothesis.

H_0: $\mu_{northeast} = \mu_{south}$

H_1: $\mu_{northeast} \neq \mu_{south}$

$$\begin{array}{r} 3.23 \\ \underline{-7.23} \\ |\ 4.00\ | \end{array}$$

This difference in sample means is greater than the CD score of 2.79, so we would conclude that the population mean homicide rate for the northeastern states is significantly different from that for the southern states. We would reject the null hypothesis. On average, southern states have significantly higher homicide rates than northeastern states.

H_0: $\mu_{northeast} = \mu_{west}$

H_1: $\mu_{northeast} \neq \mu_{west}$

$$\begin{array}{r} 3.23 \\ \underline{-5.03} \\ |\ 1.80\ | \end{array}$$

This difference in sample means is not greater than or equal to the CD score of 2.79, so we conclude that the population mean homicide rate for the northeastern states is not significantly different from that for the western states. We would fail to reject the null hypothesis.

H_0: $\mu_{midwest} = \mu_{south}$

H_1: $\mu_{midwest} \neq \mu_{south}$

$$\begin{array}{r} 5.01 \\ -7.23 \\ \hline |\ 2.22\ | \end{array}$$

This difference in sample means is not greater than or equal to the CD score of 2.79, so we conclude that the population mean homicide rate for the midwestern states is not significantly different from that for the southern states. We would fail to reject the null hypothesis.

H_0: $\mu_{midwest} = \mu_{west}$

H_1: $\mu_{midwest} \neq \mu_{west}$

$$\begin{array}{r} 5.01 \\ -5.03 \\ \hline |\ 0.02\ | \end{array}$$

This difference in sample means is not greater than or equal to the CD score of 2.79, so we conclude that the population mean homicide rate for the midwestern states is not significantly different from that for the western states. We would fail to reject the null hypothesis.

H_0: $\mu_{south} = \mu_{west}$

H_1: $\mu_{south} \neq \mu_{west}$

$$\begin{array}{r} 7.23 \\ -5.03 \\ \hline |\ 2.20\ | \end{array}$$

This difference in sample means is not greater than or equal to the CD score of 2.79, so we conclude that the population mean homicide rate for the southern states is not significantly different from that for the western states. We would fail to reject the null hypothesis.

In sum, we rejected the analysis of variance null hypothesis of equal population mean homicide rates for the northeastern, midwestern, southern, and western states only because the homicide rates in the northeastern states are significantly different from those in the southern states. None of the other mean comparisons were significantly different from each other. The northeastern states have significantly lower rates of homicide on average than the midwestern, southern, and western states.

Finally, we can calculate the value of eta squared to determine the strength of the relationship between region of the country and homicide rates:

$$\eta^2 = \frac{72.40}{244.51}$$

$$\eta^2 = .30$$

This value demonstrates a moderate relationship between region of the country and homicide rates in the population.

SUMMARY

In this chapter we studied the analysis of variance. Although the technique is called an analysis of *variance*, it is used to test a hypothesis about the equality of three or more population means. In an analysis of variance we have an independent variable that is measured at the nominal or ordinal level and has three or more values or levels, and we have a continuous (interval/ratio) dependent variable. The test statistic is the F statistic, which is a ratio of the variance that exists between groups to that which exists within a group. A high F statistic means that there is more between-groups than within-group variance, a finding which would lead us to reject the null hypothesis of equal population means.

When we reject the null hypothesis in an analysis of variance, we conclude that some of the population means are equal, although the F test does not tell us which specific ones. In order to identify which population means are significantly different, we used Tukey's Honest Significant Difference (HSD) test. Finally, we learned about a measure of association in an analysis of variance, eta squared. Eta squared measures the amount of variability in the dependent variable that can be explained by the independent variable. The larger the magnitude of eta squared, the stronger the relationship between the independent and dependent variables.

KEY TERMS

analysis of variance (ANOVA)
between-groups degrees of
  freedom
between-groups sum of squares
between-groups variability
between-groups variance
critical difference (CD) score
eta squared (correlation ratio)
F distribution
F statistic
F test

total degrees of freedom
total sum of squares
total variability
total variance
Tukey's Honest Significant
  Difference (HSD) test
within-group degrees of freedom
within-group sum of squares
within-group variability
within-group variance

KEY FORMULAS

Total sum of squares (SS_{total}) (eq. 11–2):

$$SS_{total} = \sum_i \sum_k \left(x_{ik} - \overline{X}_{grand} \right)^2$$

Within-group sum of squares (SS_{within}) (eq. 11–3):

$$SS_{within} = \sum_i \sum_k (x_{ik} - \overline{X}_k)^2$$

Between-groups sum of squares ($SS_{between}$) (eq. 11–4):

$$SS_{between} = \sum_i \sum_k (\overline{X}_k - \overline{X}_{grand})^2$$

Tukey's Honest Significant Difference test: Critical difference score (eq. 11–5):

$$CD = q\sqrt{\frac{\text{Within-group variance}}{n_k}}$$

Eta squared or the correlation ratio (eq. 11–6):

$$\eta^2 = \frac{SS_{between}}{SS_{total}}$$

PRACTICE PROBLEMS

1. When is it appropriate to perform an analysis of variance with our data? What type of variables do we need?

2. What statistical technique should we use if we have a continuous dependent variable and a categorical independent variable with only two categories?

3. Why do we call this statistical technique an analysis of *variance* when we are really interested in the difference among population *means*?

4. What two types of variance do we use to calculate the F ratio?

5. How do we determine the df_{total}, $df_{between}$, and df_{within}?

6. In 1995, Robin Ogle and her colleagues published a paper in which they argued that some women experience great stress (for instance, in physically abusive relationships), and that if this stress is not released in some healthy fashion, they are likely to strike out in violent and homicidal ways. The targets of this aggression, they argue, are likely to be those in close proximity to them—for example, partners and children. Let's say you want to test this hypothesis. You have a random sample of 30 women with small children living at home. Based on questions about their home life and possible sources of stress, you are able to place them into one of three groups: "high stress," "medium stress," and "low stress." You then ask each of the women how many times they have physically punished their children in the past month. You think that stress might be related to the use of physical punishment. The following are the data from your sample:

Number of Times Physically Used Punishment Last Month

Level of Stress		
High	**Medium**	**Low**
x	*x*	*x*
4	2	3
6	4	1
12	5	2
10	3	0
5	0	2
9	3	2
8	2	4
11	5	1
10	5	0
8	4	1

With these data, do the following:

a. Identify the independent and dependent variables.

b. Calculate the total, between-groups, and within-group sums of squares.

c. Determine the correct number of degrees of freedom, calculate the ratio of sum of squares to degrees of freedom, and determine the F ratio.

d. With an alpha of .05, test the null hypothesis that the three population means are equal against the alternative hypothesis that some of them are different.

e. If appropriate, conduct a mean comparison for each pair of means using Tukey's HSD test.

f. Calculate the value of eta squared and make a conclusion about the strength of the relationship between a mother's stress level and the frequency with which she punishes her child.

7. One of the most pressing social problems is the problem of drunk driving. Drunk driving causes untold human suffering and has profound economic effects. States have tried various things to inhibit drunk driving. Some states have tried to cut down on drunk driving within their borders by "getting tough" with drunk drivers (e.g., suspending driver's licenses, imposing heavy fines, and serving jail and prison sentences). Other states have tried a "moral appeal" by mounting public relations campaigns that proclaim the harm and injury produced by drunk driving. You want to determine the effectiveness of these strategies. You calculate the rate of drunk driving per 100,000 residents for each of 45 states and then classify each state into one of three categories: a "get tough" state, a "moral appeal" state, or a "control" state. The latter states do nothing special to those who get caught drinking and driving. Your summary data look like the following:

Get Tough States	Moral Appeal States	Control States
$n_1 = 15$	$n_2 = 15$	$n_3 = 15$
$\overline{X}_1 = 125.2$	$\overline{X}_2 = 119.7$	$\overline{X}_3 = 145.3$

Part of your summary F table looks like the following:

	Sum of Squares	df	SS/df	F
Between-groups	475.3			
Within-group	204.5			
Total	679.8			

With these summary data, do the following:

a. Identify the independent and dependent variables.

b. Determine the correct number of degrees of freedom, calculate the ratio of sum of squares to degrees of freedom, and determine the F ratio.

c. With an alpha of .01, test the null hypothesis that the three population means are equal against the alternative hypothesis that some of them are different.

d. If appropriate, conduct a mean comparison for each pair of means using Tukey's HSD test.

e. Calculate the value of eta squared and make a conclusion about the strength of the relationship between sanction policy and the rate of drunk driving.

8. In a 1995 article, Fisher and Nasar suggested that there are areas of the city that might be characterized as "fear spots." These fear spots are defined geographical areas where people feel vulnerable to criminal victimization. As a research project, you want to find out why particular areas are feared more than others. You think it is because people's perceptions of their risk of criminal victimization are strongly related to their actual risk of being the victim of a crime. Let's say that you identified five geographical areas in your city that vary in terms of how much fear people feel going into those areas ("high fear" spot to "very low fear" spot). You then go into each of these areas and ask a random sample of 50 people how many times they have been the victim of a crime in the last five years. You find the following mean number of victimizations for each area:

	Very High Fear Spot	High Fear Spot	Medium Fear Spot	Low Fear Spot	Very Low Fear Spot
Means	14.5	14.3	14.7	13.4	13.9
n	50	50	50	50	50

REVIEW & PRACTICE

Part of your summary F table looks like the following:

	Sum of Squares	df	SS/df	F
Between-groups	12.5			
Within-group	616.2			
Total	628.7			

With these summary data, do the following:

a. Identify the independent and dependent variables.

b. Determine the correct number of degrees of freedom, calculate the ratio of sum of squares to degrees of freedom, and determine the F ratio.

c. With an alpha of .05, test the null hypothesis that the four population means are equal against the alternative hypothesis that some of them are different.

d. If appropriate, conduct a mean comparison for all pairs of means using Tukey's HSD test.

e. Calculate the value of eta squared and make a conclusion about the strength of the relationship between fear spots and the number of actual criminal victimizations.

9. In his study of the influence of delinquent peers, Mark Warr (2002) has suggested that females who are in the company of males are more at risk for delinquency than those who associate primarily with other females. In other words, he suggests that "bad boys help make bad girls." To test his notion you take a random sample of girls and classify them into one of three groups: those who (1) "hang around with boys mostly," (2) "hang around with boys and girls," and (3) "hang around with girls mostly." You then ask each girl to self-report the number of delinquent offenses she has committed in the past year. The table below shows the number of delinquent acts committed by each girl in each of the three groups.

Number of Delinquent Acts Committed

	Hangs Around with:	
Mostly Boys	**Boys and Girls**	**Mostly Girls**
5	7	2
8	5	3
9	4	0
4	9	3
7	6	1
10	4	3
6	7	2

With these data, do the following:

a. Identify the independent and dependent variables.

b. Calculate the total, between-groups, and within-group sums of squares.

c. Determine the correct number of degrees of freedom, calculate the ratio of sum of squares to degrees of freedom, and determine the F ratio.

d. With an alpha of .05, test the null hypothesis that the three population means are equal against the alternative hypothesis that some of them are different.

e. If appropriate, conduct a mean comparison for each pair of means using Tukey's HSD test.

f. Calculate the value of eta squared and make a conclusion about the strength of the relationship between the gender makeup of a girl's friends and the number of delinquent acts she commits.

SPSS PRACTICE PROBLEMS

1. To demonstrate using ANOVA with SPSS, we will use the data set called "STATE2000," which contains a number of variables at the state level, including rates of murder and violence, along with independent variables thought to affect state levels of violence like poverty and social disorganization. It is always important to conduct a univariate analysis of the variables you are using, so click on ANALYZE, then DESCRIPTIVE STATISTICS, and then FREQUENCIES, and ask SPSS to construct a frequency distribution for each of these variables: MURDER, VIOLENT, REGION, and POVERTY. In the STATISTICS box, also ask SPSS to provide the following univariate statistics: median, mean, and standard deviation. After examining the output, how would you describe the distribution for each of these variables?

2. We now want to determine if murder rates are significantly different across the four regions of the country. To conduct an analysis of variance, click on ANALYZE, then COMPARE MEANS, and then ONE-WAY ANOVA. This will place you in the ANOVA dialogue box. In the DEPENDENT LIST box, place the dependent variable MURDER. In the FACTOR box, place the independent variable region. This is a four-category variable denoting the regions: Northeast, South, West, and Midwest. In the POST HOC dialogue box, ask SPSS to give you TUKEY'S post hoc tests. The output will provide you with an ANOVA box listing the sum of squares, their degrees of freedom, the obtained F value, and the exact level of significance (alpha) that corresponds with this value of F. The bottom box provides you with Tukey's Honest

Significant Difference test results. Assuming the null hypothesis is that the regional means for murder are equal, what do you conclude?

3. We now want to determine if rates of violent crime in general are significantly different across the four regions of the country. To conduct an analysis of variance, click on ANALYZE, then COMPARE MEANS, and then ONE-WAY ANOVA. This will place you in the ANOVA dialogue box. In the DEPENDENT LIST box, place the dependent variable VIOLENT. In the FACTOR box, place the independent variable region. This is a four-category variable denoting the regions: Northeast, South, West, and Midwest. In the POST HOC dialogue box, ask SPSS to give you TUKEY'S post hoc tests. The output will provide you with an ANOVA box listing the sum of squares, their degrees of freedom, the obtained F value, and the exact level of significance (alpha) that corresponds with this value of F. The bottom box provides you with Tukey's Honest Significant Difference test results. Assuming the null hypothesis is that the regional means for violent crime are equal, what do you conclude?

4. Now we want to examine the regional variability of a variable thought to affect rates of violence: poverty. The null hypothesis states that the mean rates of poverty for the South, Midwest, West, and Northeast are equal. To conduct an analysis of variance, click on ANALYZE, then COMPARE MEANS, and then ONE-WAY ANOVA. This will place you in the ANOVA dialogue box. In the DEPENDENT LIST box, place the dependent variable POVERTY. In the FACTOR box, place the independent variable region. This is a four-category variable denoting the regions: Northeast, South, West, and Midwest. In the POST HOC dialogue box, ask SPSS to give you TUKEY'S post hoc tests. The output will provide you with an ANOVA box listing the sums of squares, their degrees of freedom, the obtained F value, and the exact level of significance (alpha) that corresponds with this value of F. The bottom box provides you with Tukey's Honest Significant Difference test results. What do you conclude?

Bivariate Correlation and Regression

> *If A is a success in life, then A equals x plus y plus z. Work is x; y is play; and z is keeping your mouth shut.*
>
> —ALBERT EINSTEIN
>
> *I hung about the dangerous frontier of "guess," avoiding with infinite trouble to myself and others the broad valley of reason.*
>
> —HELEN KELLER

In this chapter we examine the association between two variables measured at the interval/ratio level. Usually whenever there are interval-/ratio-level variables the association or relationship between variables is referred to as the **correlation** between two variables. When we have only one independent variable and one dependent variable, it is referred to as *bivariate correlation.* We will adopt this convention as well. Our discussion of correlation covers many of the same issues that we discussed when examining the relationship between other types of variables. For example, we examine the strength and direction of a relationship, as well as whether the magnitude of the relationship is significantly different from zero. In this chapter, you first will learn how to construct a scatterplot depicting the linear relationship between a quantitative independent and a quantitative dependent variable. You then will learn about the statistics that quantify this linear relationship, including the correlation coefficient, the coefficient of determination, and the ordinary least-squares regression equation. Our attention in this chapter will be limited to the bivariate case, where we have one independent variable (x) and one dependent variable (y). In Chapter 13 we examine the multivariate case, where we have more than one independent variable.

GRAPHING THE BIVARIATE DISTRIBUTION BETWEEN TWO QUANTITATIVE VARIABLES: SCATTERPLOTS

Throughout this book we have stressed the importance and usefulness of displaying data graphically. Let us again remind you that it is no less true in statistics as in "real life" that "a picture is worth a thousand words." When you are first examining two interval-/ ratio-level variables, one of the most instructive things you can do is draw a picture of what the two variables look like when graphed together. In the bivariate case, the graphical display of two interval-/ ratio-level variables is called a **scattergram,** or **scatterplot.** It is called this because the picture looks like points scattered across the graph. The pattern or scatter of data points provides you with valuable information about the relationship between the variables.

At this point, you may be wondering how you go about constructing a scatterplot and what it can tell you about the relationship between two interval-/ ratio-level variables. Let's begin this discussion with a simple illustration. In the list that follows, we have data on two variables for 10 observations:

Observation	x Score	y Score
1	3	3
2	5	5
3	2	2
4	4	4
5	8	8
6	10	10
7	1	1
8	7	7
9	6	6
10	9	9

We can construct a scatterplot for these data by first drawing a graph with two axes. The first axis of this graph is the horizontal axis, or abscissa. The second axis of the graph is formed at a right angle to the first axis and is the vertical axis, or ordinate. We will label the horizontal axis the x axis and display the data for the x variable on that axis. To do this, simply place the original measurement scale for the x variable at equal intervals along the axis. We will label the vertical axis the y axis and display the data for the y variable along that axis. Again, place the measurement scale for the y variable along the vertical axis.

Once you have done this, you can begin to graph your data points. For each observation, find the position of its x score along the horizontal axis. Then, follow in a straight line up from that point until you find the corresponding position of its y score along the vertical axis. Place a dot or point here. For example, for the first observation, go along the x axis until you find "3." Then go straight up from that point until you reach the "3" on the y axis. Place a point here. This point represents the position on the graph for the xy score of the first observation. Continue to do this for each of the 10 observations, placing a point where you have found the intersection of each x and y score. You can see the collection of data points, called the scatterplot, in Figure 12–1.

What does this scatterplot tell us about the x and y scores? Notice that all the scores fall on a straight line that ascends from the bottom left of the scatterplot

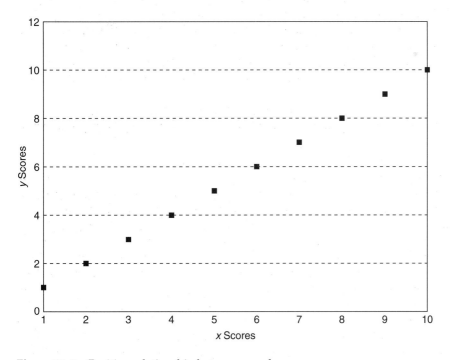

Figure 12–1 Positive relationship between x and y.

to the top right. This is because there is a unique relationship between the x and y scores. The y score is always the same as its corresponding x score. That is, if the y score is 4, the corresponding x score is 4, and if the y score is 6, the x score is 6. Therefore, those observations that have high x scores also have high y scores, and those with low x scores have low y scores. Notice also that when the x score increases one unit, the y score also increases by one unit. For example, when the x score changes from 4 to 5, the corresponding score for the y variable changes from 4 to 5, an increase of one unit. Whenever two variables are related in this manner—when high scores on one variable (x) also have high scores on a second variable (y) and an increase in one score is associated with an increase in the other score—we have a **positive correlation** or relationship between x and y.

In the list that follows and in Figure 12–2 we have a different set of x and y scores for 10 observations:

Observation	x Score	y Score
1	2	9
2	4	7
3	9	2
4	7	4
5	8	3
6	1	10
7	5	6
8	6	5
9	10	1
10	3	8

In this case the data points are still on a straight line, but the pattern is different from that in Figure 12–1. In Figure 12–2, the pattern of the points is one that descends from the top left to the bottom right. This is because those observations that have high scores on the x variable have *low* scores on the y variable. Whenever high scores on one variable (x) have low scores on a second variable (y) we have a **negative correlation** or relationship between x and y. There is, then, a clear pattern to the scatterplot of scores whenever the two variables are negatively correlated—there is a band or line of descending scores that runs from the top left to the bottom right of the scatterplot.

In regard to the data in Figures 12–1 and 12–2, we can say that when two variables are correlated their scores vary together; this is termed *covariation* in statistics. As the scores on the x variable change or vary, the scores on the y variable also change or vary. How, or the direction in which they change, is a function of the direction of the correlation. With the positive correlation in Figure 12–1, as the x scores increase, the y scores also increase (similarly, as x decreases, y also decreases). With the negative correlation in Figure 12–2, as

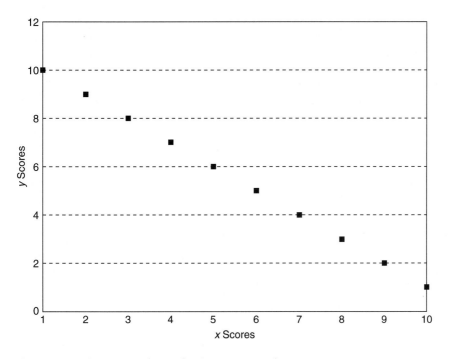

Figure 12–2 Negative relationship between x and y

the x scores increase, the y scores decrease (similarly, as x decreases, y increases). In a positive correlation, then, the two variables covary in the same direction (x increases and y increases; x decreases and y decreases). In a negative correlation, the two variables covary in the opposite direction (x increases and y decreases; x decreases and y increases).

In the list that follows we have a third set of x and y scores for 10 observations:

Observation	x Score	y Score
1	6	4
2	9	4
3	2	4
4	7	4
5	3	4
6	4	4
7	1	4
8	8	4
9	5	4
10	10	4

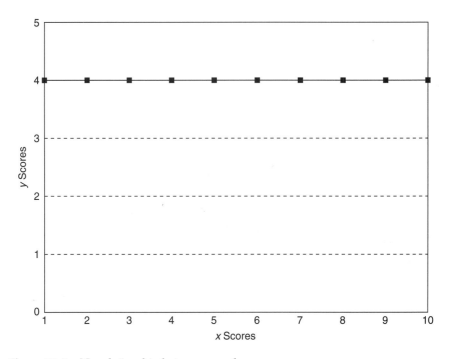

Figure 12–3   No relationship between x and y

Figure 12–3 presents the scatterplot of these scores. Notice that, unlike the previous two figures, there is no ascending or descending pattern to the scores in this scatterplot. In fact, the scores are perfectly horizontal because for different values of x, the y score is the same ($y = 4$). In other words, the x variable and the y variable do not seem to covary; there is no relationship between x and y. As x increases or decreases, the value of y stays the same. To state this one more way, variations in x (increases and decreases) do not seem to result in systematic variations in y.

One of the things that we can learn from a scatterplot, then, is the *direction* of a relationship between two variables. By the direction of a relationship, we mean whether it is positive or negative. When the scatterplot looks like Figure 12–1, where the pattern of scores resembles an upward slope, we can conclude that the two variables are positively related. In this case, there is positive covariation. When the scatterplot looks like Figure 12–2, where the pattern of scores has a downward slope, we can conclude that the two variables are negatively related. There is negative covariation. And finally, when the scatterplot resembles Figure 12–3, and there is no clear upward or downward slope, we can presume that the two variables are not correlated with one another.

In addition to the direction of a relationship, what else can we determine by examining a scatterplot of x and y scores? Let's return to the data illus-

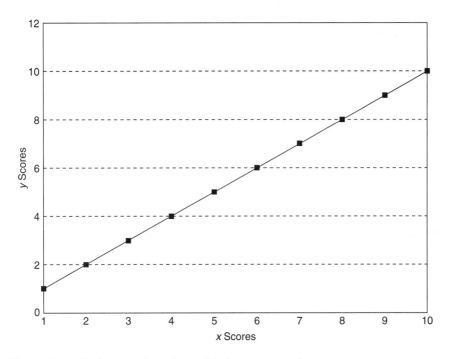

Figure 12–4 Perfect positive relationship between x and y

trated in Figure 12–1. Without being too precise, let's draw a straight line that goes through each data point. We have shown this for you in Figure 12–4. In looking at this figure, we can see that if we were to connect the data points, the straight line would go through each data point in its upward slope. In other words, each point would fall exactly on that straight upward-moving line. Later in this chapter we will have more to say about how to fit this straight line to our data points. For now we will simply note that this line is called the **regression line.** In the example presented in Figures 12–1 and 12–4, where all the data points fall exactly on a straight upward-sloping line, we can say that the two variables have a *perfect positive correlation*, positive because the regression line slopes upward and perfect because all the points fall exactly on the line.

Notice that we also can draw a straight line through the data points in Figure 12–2, as shown in Figure 12–5. Here, all the data points lie precisely on this line, but in this case the line slopes downward. This figure illustrates a *perfect negative correlation* between two variables.

We also have drawn a line for the data points in Figure 12–3, shown in Figure 12–6. Notice that this straight line does not have an upward slope (like Figure 12–4) or a downward slope (like Figure 12–5) but is instead a flat line that is horizontal to the x axis. This line has no slope. As we suggested earlier, in this example there is no correlation between x and y. It

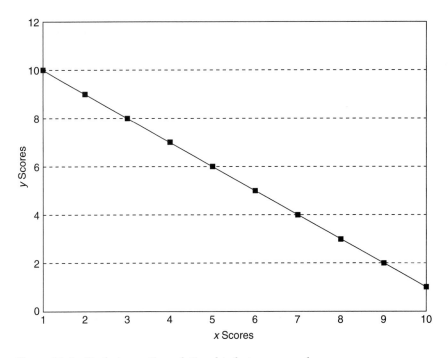

Figure 12–5 Perfect negative relationship between x and y

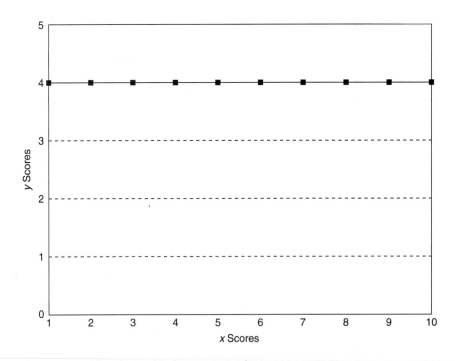

Figure 12–6 No relationship between x and y

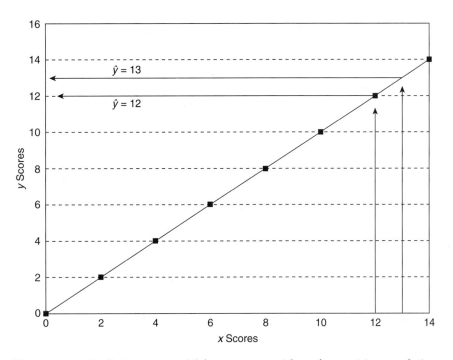

Figure 12–7   Predicting y scores ($\hat{y}$) from x scores with perfect positive correlation

might be said that Figure 12–6 presents an example of two variables with absolutely no correlation.

In addition to direction, the second valuable thing we can learn from a scatterplot, then, is an indication of the *strength* or *magnitude* of the relationship. The strength of a relationship can be judged by examining the spread of the data points around a straight line, called the regression line, which passes through them. The closer the data points are to this line, the stronger the relationship or correlation between the two variables is. In a perfect positive or perfect negative relationship, all of the data points will fall exactly on a straight regression line that passes through each data point. The further the data points are from the line, the weaker the correlation between the two variables. When the two variables are not correlated at all (perfect noncorrelation), the points will also lie on a straight line, but this line will be perfectly horizontal to the x axis. Of course, as you will see, in reality we never have perfect relationships. We have used these examples of perfect relationships simply to illustrate the concept of the direction regarding a relationship.

There is one other very important thing we can learn from a scatterplot, and that is how to predict the score on one variable (the y variable) from the score on another variable (the x variable). Figures 12–7 and 12–8 show the previous examples of a perfect positive correlation and no correlation between x and y, respectively. In these figures the two axes and the straight

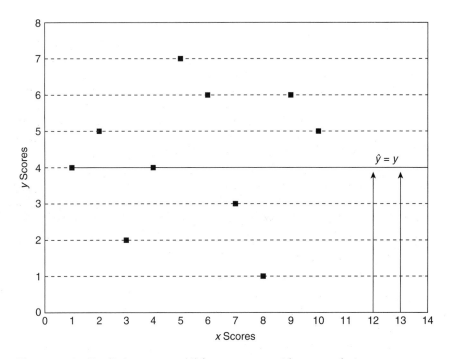

Figure 12–8   Predicting y scores($\hat{y}$) from x scores with no correlation

regression line have been extended to include additional scores. Let's first look at Figure 12–7. In this figure we want to predict what someone's y score would be if they had an x score of 12. To find the predicted value of y (denoted by the symbol $\hat{y}$ to distinguish it from its actual value) we first find the value of x on the x axis (x = 12), then draw a straight line up to the regression line, and from that point, draw another straight line parallel to the x axis across to the y axis. The predicted value of y ($\hat{y}$) is the value of y where this line touches the y axis. In this case our predicted value of y with x = 12 would be 12 ($\hat{y}$ = 12). We could follow the same procedure and determine that for an x = 13, our predicted y score would also be 13.

   In Figure 12–8, which shows no strong correlation between x and y, we also could make predictions about y based on information about x, but in this case the predictions would all be the same. That is, no matter what the observed x score, if we were to draw a straight line up from the x axis to the regression line and then another line over to the y axis, we would have the same predicted y score ($\hat{y}$ = 4). With an observed x score of 12, our predicted y would be 4, and with an observed x score of 13, our predicted value of y also would be 4. In the case of no correlation between two variables, it seems that there is no unique predicted score for y at different values of x. Instead, no matter what the x score is, the predicted y score will always be the same. In other words, knowledge of x does not help us predict the value of y.

TABLE 12–1

Murder Rate per 100,000 and Percent of State Population Living Below the Poverty Level for 15 States, 2000

State	Murder Rate y	Poverty Level x
Alabama	7.9	15.1
Arkansas	5.6	14.7
California	6.0	13.8
Delaware	3.2	10.4
Florida	5.7	12.4
Georgia	7.5	12.9
Hawaii	3.7	10.9
Illinois	7.7	9.9
Maine	2.2	10.6
Maryland	9.0	7.3
Nevada	9.1	11.3
New Jersey	3.5	7.8
New Mexico	9.8	20.7
North Carolina	7.2	13.5
Tennessee	7.1	11.9

Source: Statistical Abstract of the United States: 2001, U.S. Census Bureau.

Relationships or correlations between variables in the real world rarely have such obvious patterns. When real crime data are utilized, patterns become a little less clear.

Case Study: Causes of State-Level Crime

Now that you understand what can be learned from a scatterplot, let's examine some real data. Let's say that we are interested in the factors related to violent crime. From our review of the literature, we determine that poverty and economic deprivation often are found to be related to murder. One way to look at this relationship between poverty and murder would be to examine the correlation between a state's poverty rate (we will designate this our x or independent variable) and its rate of homicide (our y or dependent variable). More specifically, we use the percent of the state's population that lives below the poverty level as our independent variable (x) and the homicide rate for each state obtained from the FBI's Uniform Crime Reports as our dependent variable (y).

To examine this issue, we take a random sample of 15 states ($n = 15$) and record the murder rate in the state along with the state's rate of poverty for the year 2000. These data are shown in Table 12–1. Based on these data, we create the scatterplot displayed in Figure 12–9. This was created the same

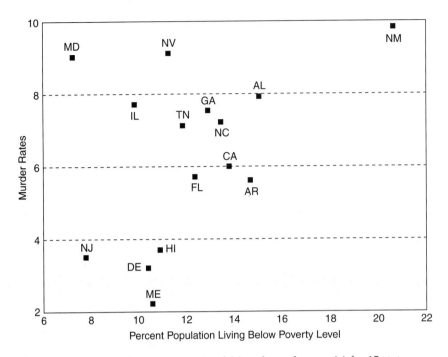

Figure 12–9   Scatterplot of poverty level (x) and murder rate (y) for 15 states

way the other scatterplots were, first by drawing the x and y axes to accommodate both variables, and then simply finding the bivariate data point for each case. For example, for the first state, Alabama, we go over 15.1 on the horizontal or x axis and then up to 7.9 on the vertical or y axis. This point then becomes the point that represents Alabama on our scatterplot.

What kind of relationship do you see in Figure 12–9? By eyeballing the data, we can draw a straight line that we think runs though the data points; however, unlike our hypothetical data, the data points do not all fall perfectly on any one line. Instead, we will have to draw our line in such a way that it comes as close to all the data points as possible. A line that appears to fit the data is drawn through the scatterplot and displayed in Figure 12–10. As before, we will use this line to summarize the pattern and strength of the relationship between our two variables.

Based on what we have learned so far in this chapter, we can conclude two things from this scatterplot. First, there does seem to be a positive correlation between poverty and murder rates. The general pattern of the data points, and the line that runs through them, is an upward slope, indicating that as the rate of poverty increases (as x increases), the murder rate also increases (y increases). States that have high poverty rates, then, also tend to have high rates of murder. Second, the correlation between the two variables is far from perfect. None of the data points fall exactly on the straight line. In

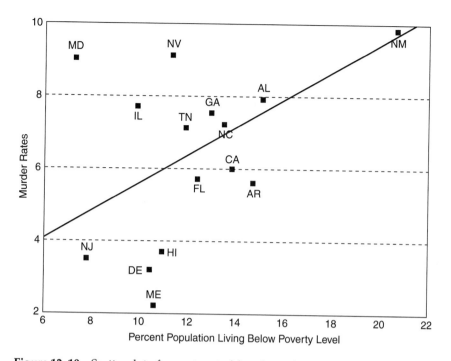

Figure 12–10 Scatterplot of poverty rate (x) and murder rate (y) for 15 states with regression line

fact, many of these points lie fairly far below the line (Maine) and above it (Maryland). What we can tell from this scatterplot, then, is that we have a nonperfect positive correlation between a state's murder rate and its poverty rate. These types of relationships are more typical of real crime data compared to the hypothetical data we examined earlier.

In Table 12–2 we have the same random sample of states but two different variables. In this table the x variable is the percent of the population in the state that lives in a nonmetropolitan (rural) area and the y variable is the rate of violent crime. We examine this relationship because we suspect that there is a correlation between how rural or nonmetropolitan a state is and its rate of violent crime. We think that rural states have lower rates of violent crime than urban states because we think they are more cohesive, homogeneous, and less socially disorganized. This is a prediction based on the early "Chicago School" of crime and social disorganization.

Figure 12–11 depicts the scatterplot of the data in Table 12–2. Here we see a downward-sloping pattern of data points. This indicates the existence of a negative correlation between rural population and violent crime. States that are more rural, such as Alabama and Arkansas, have lower rates of violent crime than the less rural states of California and Maryland. As in the last example, the negative correlation between rural population and violent crime

TABLE 12–2

Violent Crime Rate per 100,000 and Percent of State Population Residing in Nonmetropolitan (Rural) Areas for 15 States, 2000

State	Violent Crime Rate y	Rural Area (%) x
Alabama	490	30
Arkansas	425	50
California	627	3
Delaware	734	20
Florida	854	7
Georgia	534	31
Hawaii	235	28
Illinois	733	15
Maine	112	63
Maryland	743	7
Nevada	570	12
New Jersey	412	0
New Mexico	835	43
North Carolina	542	32
Tennessee	695	32

Source: Statistical Abstract of the United States: 2001, U.S. Census Bureau.

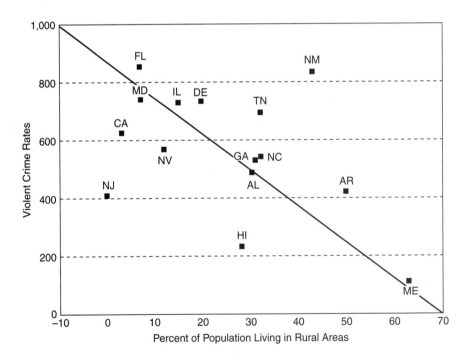

Figure 12–11   Scatterplot of percent rural (*x*) and violent crime rate (*y*) for 15 states

TABLE 12–3

Violent Crime Rate per 100,000 Population and the Divorce Rate per 1,000 Population for 15 States, 2000

State	Violent Crime Rate	Divorce Rate
Alabama	490	5.9
Arkansas	425	6.3
California	627	4.5
Delaware	734	4.9
Florida	854	5.3
Georgia	534	4.8
Hawaii	235	4.6
Illinois	733	3.2
Maine	112	4.4
Maryland	743	2.9
Nevada	570	6.8
New Jersey	412	3.0
New Mexico	835	6.5
North Carolina	542	4.8
Tennessee	695	6.0

Source: Statistical Abstract of the United States: 2001, U.S. Census Bureau.

is less than perfect. Not all of the points lie exactly on the regression line. Some states, like New Mexico, are far above the line, while others, such as Hawaii, are far below it.

Let's say we make a third conjecture about our random sample of 15 states. Let's hypothesize that states with high divorce rates also will have high rates of violent crime. In Table 12–3 we record the number of divorces per 1,000 residents of each state and the violent crime rate. We create a scatterplot for this data in Figure 12–12. Unlike the other two scatterplots using the state-level crime data, however, this one has no clear or discernable pattern. That is, it slopes neither upward nor downward. Also, unlike our hypothetical data, these data points do not lie on a perfectly horizontal line. The line that probably best describes this pattern of data would generally be flat, running through the middle of the data. Moreover, most data points in this scatterplot would be far from the straight line we drew. From this, we would conclude that there probably is very little correlation between these two variables.

In sum, by graphically representing the relationship between two interval-/ratio-level variables, we can learn about both the direction and the strength of the relationship or correlation between x and y. If the pattern of the data points and a line drawn through them is an ascending one, we can conclude that the correlation between x and y is positive. If the pattern is a descending one, we can conclude that the correlation is negative. If there is no pattern to

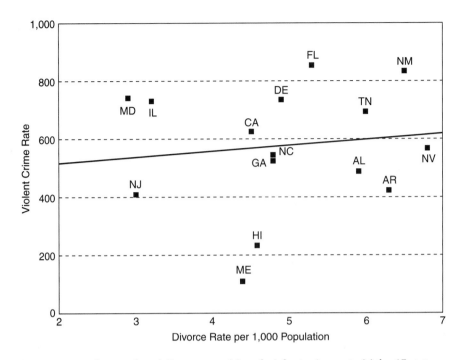

Figure 12–12   Scatterplot of divorce rate (*x*) and violent crime rate (*y*) for 15 states with regression line

the data and the line we draw through the data points is almost horizontal, we may conclude that there is very little correlation between the two variables. We can estimate the strength of the relationship by examining the distance between the actual data points and the straight line. The closer the data points cluster to this line, the stronger the correlation between *x* and *y*. Correlations that are not strong generally have data points that fall far above and below the line. It would be nice to have a numerical indicator that told us the extent of the correlation between two variables, wouldn't it? Fortunately there is, and we discuss it next.

PEARSON CORRELATION COEFFICIENT

The statistic used to measure the correlation between two interval-/ratio-level variables is called the **Pearson correlation coefficient,** or *Pearson product–moment correlation coefficient.* We will refer to this statistic simply as *Pearson's r,* named after its originator, the statistician Karl Pearson. Pearson's *r* measures the strength of the *linear* correlation between two continuous (interval/ratio) level variables. The statistic *r* is our sample estimate of the correlation between the two variables in the population. The population correlation coefficient is designated by ρ, the Greek letter rho.

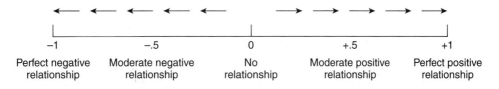

Figure 12–13 Pearson's r values closer to positive or negative 1 indicate stronger relationships

Pearson's correlation coefficient is standardized. By that we mean that the magnitude of r does not depend upon the natural units of measurement of the x and y variables. No matter what the unit of measurement, Pearson's r assumes a value of zero whenever there is no correlation between two variables, and it attains a maximum value of ± 1.0 when there is a perfect correlation between two variables. Figure 12–13 displays a guide to aid you in the interpretation of Pearson's r. A correlation of ± 1.0 occurs when all points fall exactly on a straight regression line. A Pearson correlation coefficient of $+1.00$ means that there is a perfect positive correlation between two variables (as in Figure 12–1), while an r of -1.00 means that there is a perfect negative correlation (as in Figure 12–2). The closer the data points cluster around the regression line, the stronger the correlation will be between the two variables and the higher the value of r will be. If there is no linear pattern in data points, the value of r will be closer to zero, indicating very little linear relationship between the two variables.

The calculation of Pearson's r is relatively straightforward and involves arithmetic operations you are already very familiar with. As with other statistical formulas, we will provide you with both a definitional formula, which more clearly defines the foundation of the statistic, and a computational formula, which is easier to use. The definitional formula for Pearson's r is as follows:

$$ r = \frac{\sum (x - \overline{X})(y - \overline{Y})}{\sqrt{[\sum (x - \overline{X})^2][\sum (y - \overline{Y})^2]}} \tag{12–1} $$

The first term of this expression is simply the difference between an x score and its mean, while the second is the difference between a y score and its mean. In the definitional formula for the correlation coefficient, we multiply these difference scores by each other, do the same for each difference score, and then sum over all scores. Since the mean is defined in statistical terms as the *first moment*, the terms $(x - \overline{X})$ and $(y - \overline{Y})$ are referred to as the first moments about the mean. The correlation coefficient, then, is based upon the product of the first moments about the mean of x and y; hence it is often referred to as the *product–moment* correlation coefficient.

The product of $(x - \overline{X})$ and $(y - \overline{Y})$ measures the *covariation* between x and y. That is, it measures the extent to which the x and y scores vary together, or covary. The stronger the relationship between the two variables, the greater the covariance. A covariation of zero implies that the two variables are not correlated, a positive covariation implies positive correlation, and a negative covariation implies negative correlation.

We cannot simply use the size of the covariation as our measure of correlation, however. First of all, the magnitude of the covariation is a function of the measurement units of the variables. For example, other things being equal, we would obtain a much greater covariation if one of our variables was measured in pennies rather than dollars. Second, the covariance often can be greater than 1.0, so we have no clear interpretation for it.

We can, however, standardize the covariation, that is, make its value independent of the units of measurement. We do this by dividing the covariation in x and y by a term that includes both the variation in x and the variation in y. This term is the denominator of the correlation coefficient and should also look very familiar to you. It is simply the product of two terms: the amount of variation in the x variable and the amount of variation in the y variable. The **correlation coefficient,** then, expresses the ratio of the covariation in x and y to the product of the variation in x and the variation in y. It has a lower limit of -1.0 and an upper limit of $+1.0$.

As you can imagine from going over formula 12–1 in your head, the necessary calculations to estimate r are enough to make you faint. There is, fortunately, a computational formula that involves fewer operations and, therefore, fewer chances of making computational errors. The computational formula for Pearson's correlation coefficient is:

$$r = \frac{n\sum xy - (\sum x)(\sum y)}{\sqrt{[n\sum x^2 - (\sum x)^2][n\sum y^2 - (\sum y)^2]}} \tag{12–2}$$

Even this formula may appear forbidding to you, but fear not, we can break it down into five simple elements that we can then plug into the formula and solve. The computational formula requires the following five sums:

1. $\sum xy$ = the sum of each x score times its corresponding y score.

2. $\sum x$ = the sum of the x scores.

3. $\sum y$ = the sum of the y scores.

4. $\sum x^2$ = the sum of the squared x scores $(x_1^2 + x_2^2 \dots + x_n^2)$.

5. $\sum y^2$ = the sum of the squared y scores $(y_1^2 + y_2^2 \dots + y_n^2)$.

We will use this computational formula to calculate the value of r for the state data in Table 12–1, Table 12–2, and Table 12–3. In calculating the value of r, it will be helpful if you first calculate each of the five sums above and then insert them into the formula. A listing of the sums in separate columns will make keeping track of the different components of the formula easier. We have provided these calculations in Tables 12–4 through 12–6, although you should first try to calculate them yourself.

TABLE 12–4

Calculation of Pearson Correlation Coefficient, r, for Correlation between State Murder Rate and Poverty Level (Table 12–1)

State	Poverty Level x	Murder Rate y	x^2	y^2	xy
Alabama	15.1	7.9	228.01	62.41	119.29
Arkansas	14.7	5.6	216.09	31.36	82.32
California	13.8	6.0	190.44	36.00	82.80
Delaware	10.4	3.2	108.16	10.24	33.28
Florida	12.4	5.7	153.76	32.49	70.68
Georgia	12.9	7.5	166.41	56.25	96.75
Hawaii	10.9	3.7	118.81	13.69	40.33
Illinois	9.9	7.7	98.01	59.29	76.23
Maine	10.6	2.2	112.36	4.84	23.32
Maryland	7.3	9.0	53.29	81.00	65.70
Nevada	11.3	9.1	127.69	82.81	102.83
New Jersey	7.8	3.5	60.84	12.25	27.30
New Mexico	20.7	9.8	428.49	96.04	202.86
North Carolina	13.5	7.2	182.25	51.84	97.20
Tennessee	11.9	7.1	141.61	50.41	84.49
$n = 15$	$\sum x = 183.2$	$\sum y = 95.2$	$\sum x^2 = 2,386.2$	$\sum y^2 = 680.9$	$\sum xy = 1,205.3$

For the state-level data in Table 12–4, which reports the murder rates and poverty rates for 15 randomly selected states (first presented in Table 12–1), we calculate the value of r as:

$$r = \frac{n\sum xy - (\sum x)(\sum y)}{\sqrt{[n\sum x^2 - (\sum x)^2][n\sum y^2 - (\sum y)^2]}}$$

$$= \frac{(15)(1,205.3) - (183.2)(95.2)}{\sqrt{[(15)(2,386.2) - (183.2)^2][(15)(680.9) - (95.2)^2]}}$$

$$\frac{18,079.5 - 17,440.6}{\sqrt{[35,793 - 33,562.2][10,213.5 - 9,063.0]}}$$

$$= \frac{638.9}{\sqrt{(223.8)(1,150.5)}}$$

$$= \frac{638.9}{\sqrt{2,566,535.4}}$$

$$= \frac{638.9}{1,602}$$

$$= .39$$

TABLE 12–5

Calculation of Pearson Correlation Coefficient, r, for Correlation between Percent of State Population Residing in Rural Areas and Rate of Violent Crime for 15 States (Table 12–2)

State	Rural Area (%) x	Violent Crime Rate y	x^2	y^2	xy
Alabama	30	490	900.0	240,100.0	14,700.0
Arkansas	50	425	2,500.0	180,625.0	21,250.0
California	3	627	9.0	393,129.0	1,881.0
Delaware	20	734	400.0	538,756.0	14,680.0
Florida	7	854	49.0	729,316.0	5,978.0
Georgia	31	534	961.0	285,156.0	16,554.0
Hawaii	28	235	784.0	55,225.0	6,580.0
Illinois	15	733	225.0	537,289.0	10,995.0
Maine	63	112	3,969.0	12,544.0	7,056.0
Maryland	7	743	49.0	552,049.0	5,201.0
Nevada	12	570	144.0	324,900.0	6,840.0
New Jersey	0	412	.0	169,744.0	.0
New Mexico	43	835	1,849.0	697,225.0	35,905.0
North Carolina	32	542	1,024.0	293,764.0	17,344.0
Tennessee	32	695	1,024.0	483,025.0	22,240.0
$n = 15$	$\sum x = 373$	$\sum y = 8,541$	$\sum x^2 = 13,887$	$\sum y^2 = 5,492,847$	$\sum xy = 187,204$

What does this correlation between a state's murder rate and a poverty level of .39 tell us? Well, the sign of the correlation coefficient informs us that there is a positive correlation between a state's murder rate and the percent of the population that lives below the poverty level. Those states with high murder rates also tend to have high rates of poverty.

How do we interpret the magnitude of this correlation? Recall that the value of a Pearson correlation coefficient varies between −1.0 (a perfect negative correlation) and +1.0 (a perfect positive correlation), with zero indicating no correlation. One thing we can say about our correlation of .39 is that it is a bit closer to zero than it is to 1.0, and therefore it is weak to moderately strong. Unfortunately, there are no clear and agreed upon rules that tell us what constitutes a "weak," "moderate," or "strong" correlation. It is entirely subjective. We provide a more exact interpretation of the magnitude of r in the following section, but for now, we use less precise terms like "moderately strong" or "weak." We can conclude from this, then, that there is a weak to moderately strong positive correlation between the poverty rate in a state and its rate of murder.

Using the data first presented in Table 12–2, Table 12–5 reports the calculations necessary to estimate the correlation between the percent of a state's population that lives in a nonmetropolitan area and its rate of violent crime. The correlation between these two variables is calculated as follows:

$$r = \frac{(15)(187,024) - (373)(8,541)}{\sqrt{[(15)(13,887) - (373)^2][(15)(5,492,847) - (8,541)^2]}}$$

$$\frac{2,808,060 - 3,185,793}{\sqrt{[208,305 - 139,129][82,392,705 - 72,948,681]}}$$

$$= \frac{-377,733}{\sqrt{(69,176)(9,444,024)}}$$

$$= \frac{-377,733}{\sqrt{653,299,804,200}}$$

$$= \frac{-377,733}{808,269.6}$$

$$= -.46$$

This coefficient (r = −.46) indicates that there is a moderate negative correlation between a state's percent of rural population and its level of violent crime. States with a higher rural population percentage have lower rates of violent crime than do more urbanized states.

Using the data first presented in Table 12–3, Table 12–6 reports the calculations necessary to estimate the correlation between the divorce rate in a state and its rate of violent crime. The correlation is:

$$r = \frac{(15)(42,461.2) - (73.9)(8,541)}{\sqrt{[(15)(385.59) - (73.9)^2][(15)(5,492,847) - (8,541)^2]}}$$

$$\frac{636,918 - 631,179.9}{\sqrt{[5,783.8 - 5,461.2][82,392,705 - 72,948,681]}}$$

$$= \frac{5,738.1}{\sqrt{(322.6)(9,444,024)}}$$

$$= \frac{5,738.1}{\sqrt{3,146,642,142}}$$

$$= \frac{5,738.1}{55,196.3}$$

$$= .10$$

How would you interpret this correlation of .10? It is closer to zero than the other correlation coefficients; this indicates that there is a very weak positive correlation between the divorce rate in a state and its rate of violent crime. Consistent with the appearance of our scatterplot, then, there is not a very strong linear relationship between these two variables.

In our examination of the three relationships, we have found a weak to moderately strong positive correlation between a state's murder rate and its poverty rate, a moderately strong negative correlation between a state's

TABLE 12–6

Calculation of Pearson Correlation Coefficient, r, for Correlation between the Divorce Rate and Rate of Violent Crime for 15 States (Table 12–3)

State	Divorce Rate x	Violent Crime Rate y	x^2	y^2	xy
Alabama	5.9	490	34.81	240,100.0	2,891.0
Arkansas	6.3	425	39.69	180,625.0	2,677.5
California	4.5	627	20.25	393,129.0	2,821.5
Delaware	4.9	734	24.01	538,756.0	3,596.6
Florida	5.3	854	28.09	729,316.0	4,526.2
Georgia	4.8	534	23.04	285,156.0	2,563.2
Hawaii	4.6	235	21.16	55,225.0	1,081.0
Illinois	3.2	733	10.24	537,289.0	2,345.6
Maine	4.4	112	19.36	12,544.0	492.8
Maryland	2.9	743	8.41	552,049.0	2,154.7
Nevada	6.8	570	46.24	324,900.0	3,876.0
New Jersey	3.0	412	9.00	169,744.0	1,236.0
New Mexico	6.5	835	42.25	697,225.0	5,427.5
North Carolina	4.8	542	23.04	293,764.0	2,601.6
Tennessee	6.0	695	36.00	483,025.0	4,170.0
$n = 15$	$\sum x = 73.9$	$\sum y = 8,541$	$\sum x^2 = 385.59$	$\sum y^2 = 5,492,847$	$\sum xy = 42,461.2$

percent of rural population and its rate of violent crime, and a very weak positive correlation between a state's divorce rate and its violent crime rate.

Although we can interpret a perfect positive correlation as +1.0, a perfect negative correlation as −1.0, and no linear correlation at all as zero, what do correlations that fall between these extremes mean? These interpretations are left to a researcher's judgment. However, there is another statistic that allows us to make a more precise interpretation of the strength of the relationship between two variables. This statistic is called the *coefficient of determination*. We examine this statistic in the next section.

INTERPRETING A CORRELATION: THE COEFFICIENT OF DETERMINATION

The **coefficient of determination** (r^2) allows us to definitively interpret the strength of the association between two variables. It is very easy to obtain once we have already calculated the correlation coefficient. As the symbol r^2 suggests, the coefficient of determination is simply the square of the Pearson correlation coefficient. It is interpreted as the proportion of the variation in the y variable that is explained by the x variable. When the value of r^2 is multiplied by 100 to get a percent, it is interpreted as the *percent of the variance* in the y variable that is explained by the x variable.

For example, our correlation between the poverty rate and the murder rate for our 15 states was .39. The coefficient of determination is $(.39)^2$, or .15, and it can be understood as the amount of variance in murder rates that is explained by the rate of poverty. In this example, 15 percent of the variance in states' murder rates is explained by state-level rates of poverty. The correlation between percent of rural population and rate of violent crime was $-.46$. The coefficient of determination is $(-.46)^2$, or .21, which indicates that 21 percent of the variance in violent crime rates for these 15 states is explained by the percent of the states' population that lives in a rural area. Finally, the correlation between a state's divorce rate and its rate of violent crime is $(.10)^2$, or .01. This indicates that just 1 percent of the variance in violent crime rates is explained by the divorce rate in states.

The amount of variance explained varies from zero to 100 percent. The more variance explained, the stronger the association between the two variables. If two variables are perfectly related, the amount of explained variance is 100 percent $(+1.0^2 = -1.0^2 = 1.0)$. If two variables are perfectly unrelated (independent) the amount of variance one variable explains in the other will be zero percent. The more variance one variable explains in another, the more accurate the predictions of a y variable from an x variable will be. The magnitude of r^2, the coefficient of determination, then, is the proportion of variance in y that is explained by x. As the amount of explained variance increases, r^2 increases. The greater the proportion of total variance that is explained, the stronger the **linear relationship** between x and y.

As you can see, the coefficient of determination (r^2) is a very useful measure of association between two continuous variables. Unlike the correlation coefficient (r), values of the coefficient of determination between zero and 1.0 are readily interpretable. R^2 values reflect the amount of variance in the y variable explained by the x variable, or the improvement in our predictive accuracy. There is an even more precise way, however, to describe a linear relationship between x and y. The least-squares regression line, which we will discuss next, not only provides information about the strength and direction of the relationship between x and y, it also allows us to predict more precisely values of y from values of x.

THE LEAST-SQUARES REGRESSION LINE

Case Study: Age and Delinquency

In order to understand the idea behind the **least-squares regression line,** we first need to discuss how the line is constructed and why it is called the "least-squares" regression line. Let's begin our discussion of the least-squares regression line by looking at the hypothetical data in Table 12–7. This table shows the age of a random sample of 20 youths and the number of self-reported acts of delinquency committed by each youth in the previous year. Age is our designated independent (x) variable and the number of self-reported delinquent acts is our dependent (y) variable.

TABLE 12–7

Hypothetical Data for 20 Students

Student	Age x	Self-Reported Delinquency y
1	12	0
2	12	2
3	12	1
4	12	3
5	13	4
6	13	2
7	13	1
8	14	2
9	14	5
10	14	4
11	15	3
12	15	4
13	15	6
14	15	8
15	16	9
16	16	7
17	16	6
18	17	8
19	17	10
20	17	7

The first thing to notice in Table 12–7 is that for any given x value, there is more than one value of y. This means that there are several youths who are the same age who have not committed the same number of delinquent acts. For example, of the four 12–year-old youths in the sample, one committed no delinquent acts, one committed 1 delinquent act, one committed 2 delinquent acts, and one committed 3 delinquent acts. The three 13-year-old youths each committed a different number of delinquent acts as well. For each value of x, then, there are a number of different y values. Think of these different y values at each value of x as constituting a distribution of y scores. Since there are six different x scores, there are six different distributions of y scores. Another way to say this is that at every fixed value of x, there is a corresponding distribution of y scores. In statistics, these distributions of y scores are often called **conditional distributions,** since the distribution of y scores depends or is conditional upon the value of x. This is similar to a conditional probability where the probability of one event $P(A)$ depends upon another event (B).

Figure 12–14 is the scatterplot illustrating these data. We can tell from "eyeballing" this scatterplot that age and self-reported delinquency seem to be positively related to one another, and that this relationship looks reasonably strong. The data form an ascending pattern. We would now like to fit a

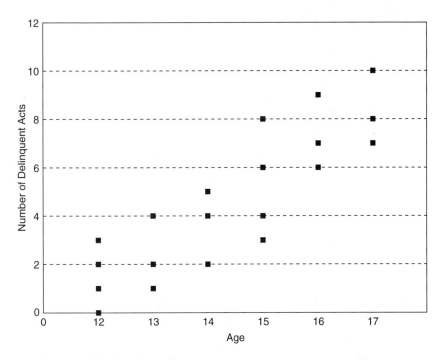

Figure 12–14 Age (x) and number of self-reported delinquent acts (y)

straight line to these data in such a way that the line comes as close to the original data points as possible. Moreover, instead of simply eyeballing the fit of the line to the data, we would like our determination of "the closest fit" to have some objective basis.

Recall from Chapter 4 that we can determine a central score within a distribution of scores that arithmetically varies the least from all other scores in the distribution. This point of minimum variation, you will remember, is the *mean*. The mean is that one score around which the variation of the other scores is the smallest or is minimized. In mathematical terms, the mean satisfies the expression:

$$\sum (x - \overline{X})^2 = \text{Minimum variance}$$

This expression means that the sum of the squared differences (deviations) around any mean is the minimum variance that can be defined. Arithmetically, we know that if any value other than the mean were used in the expression, the variance would be greater. In other words, in any distribution of scores the mean will be that score that is closest to all of the other scores.

This property of the mean holds true even for a conditional distribution of scores, such as that shown in Table 12–7. If we calculate a mean of y at each value of x (called the **conditional mean of y**), this mean will be that score

TABLE 12–8

Conditional Means (Means of y for Fixed Values of x) for the Age and Self-Reported Delinquency Data

Age	y Scores	Conditional $\overline{Y}$
12	0, 1, 2, 3	1.5
13	4, 2, 1	2.3
14	2, 5, 4	3.7
15	3, 4, 6, 8	5.2
16	9, 7, 6	7.3
17	8, 10, 7	8.3

which is closest to all other y scores at that given value of x. We have calculated each of these conditional y means for you and report the results in Table 12–8. These conditional means were calculated like any other mean, by summing all values of y at a fixed value of x, and then dividing by the total number of these y scores. For example, in Table 12–7 there were four y scores (number of self-reported delinquent acts) for those at age 12: 0, 2, 1, and 3. The mean number of self-reported delinquent acts for these four 12-year-old youths is therefore: $(0 + 2 + 1 + 3)/4 = 1.5$. This mean indicates that the 12–year-old youths from this sample reported committing an average of 1.5 delinquent acts. We can similarly calculate conditional means of y for each of the other ages, as shown in Table 12–8. In Figure 12–15 we show the scatterplot that includes points for both the original scores and each of the conditional means (shown by $\overline{Y}$).

Since the conditional means ($\overline{Y}$) minimize the variance of the y scores for each value of x, the regression line that comes the closest to going through each value of ($\overline{Y}$) here will be our best-fitting line. By "best-fitting" we mean that it is the line that will minimize the variance of the conditional y scores about that line. Because the variance is measured by the squared deviations from the mean $(y - \overline{Y})^2$, this regression line is the *least-squares* regression line, and the estimation procedure is referred to as **ordinary least squares,** or OLS regression. The least-squares regression line, therefore, is the line where the squared deviations of the conditional means for the y scores ($\overline{Y}$) are the least. Figure 12–16 is the scatterplot of the conditional $\overline{Y}$ values from Figure 12–15. We also have included the regression line and the distance (drawn with a vertical line) between each conditional mean and the regression line. This regression line is the best-fitting line in the sense that it is calculated in such a way that this vertical distance is at a minimum.

Mathematically, the equation that defines this least-squares regression line takes the general linear form:

$$y = \alpha + \beta x \qquad (12\text{–}3)$$

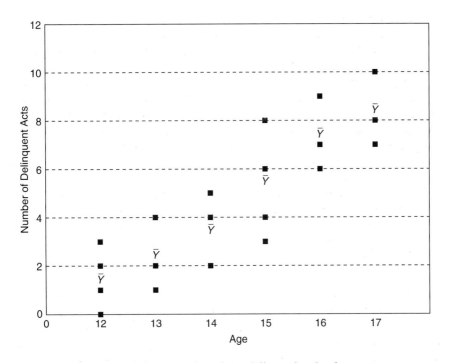

Figure 12–15 Conditional mean value of y at different levels of x

where

   y = the score on the y variable,

   α = the y intercept,

   β = the slope of the regression line, and

   x = the score on the x variable.

There are two new terms in this equation, the intercept and the slope, that must be defined and explained. The **y intercept** (α) is the point where the regression line crosses the y axis. As you can determine from the equation, it is equal to the value of y whenever $x = 0$. The **slope** of the regression line, β, also known as the **beta coefficient** or the **regression coefficient,** measures the amount of change produced in the y variable by a 1 unit increase in the x variable, and the sign indicates the direction of that change. For example, a slope of 2 indicates that a 1 unit increase in x produces a 2 unit increase in y. A slope of -2 would indicate that a 1 unit change in x produces a 2 unit decrease in y. If the slope in our age and delinquency example above were 2, this would indicate that a 1 year increase in age (a 1 unit change in x) would increase the number of self-reported delinquent acts by 2 (2 units change in y).

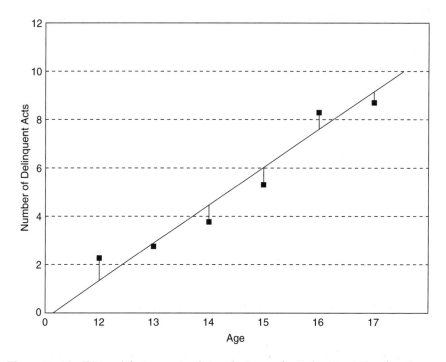

Figure 12–16   Distance between conditional means of y and estimated regression line

In equation (12–3), alpha (α) is the symbol for the population intercept, and beta signifies the slope coefficient in the population. As you should immediately know by now, these two values are virtually always unknown. Thus, we again have to use the sample data to estimate their respective values. The sample intercept is symbolized by the letter a, and the slope in the sample is symbolized by the letter b. The sample statistic is an estimate of the unknown population parameter alpha, and b is an estimate of the unknown population parameter beta. The sample **regression equation** can thus be rewritten as:

$$y = a + bx \qquad (12\text{–}4)$$

From our sample data, we can determine our regression equation when we know the values of the intercept and slope. Both values are derived from the original data points. We determine the intercept (a) by first computing the value of the slope (b). The definitional formula for estimating the slope of a regression line is:

$$b = \frac{\sum (x - \overline{X})(y - \overline{Y})}{\sum (x - \overline{X})^2} \qquad (12\text{–}5)$$

This should look very familiar to you by now. The numerator of the equation is simply the product of each x score minus its mean and each y score minus its mean. Remember that the product of these two mean differences is referred to as the *covariation* between x and y. It measures the extent to which x and y vary together, or *covary*. If we divide this sum by n, what we get is called the *covariance* between x and y.

The denominator of formula 12–5 is the squared deviation of each x score about its mean (the sum of squares for x). When divided by n, this is the variance. The slope coefficient, then, can be understood as the ratio of the covariance between x and y to the variance in x. Since the n terms in both the numerator and the denominator cancel each other out, the equation above is written in terms of the ratio of covariation between x and y to the variation in x.

Notice that the covariation between x and y, the numerator in the formula for b, can be either positive or negative. We already know that when x and y are positively correlated, large values of x ($x > \overline{X}$) also tend to correspond to large values of y ($y > \overline{Y}$), and low values of x ($x < \overline{X}$) are associated with low values of y ($y < \overline{Y}$). In the first instance, each term of the product $(x - \overline{X})(y - \overline{Y})$ is likely to be positive—as would, of course, the product and the sum of these products. In the second instance, each term of the $(x - \overline{X})(y - \overline{Y})$ is likely to be negative, but the product of two negative terms would be positive, as would the sum of these products. The term describing the covariation then would be positive, and the stronger the positive correlation between x and y, the greater the magnitude of this covariation. Correspondingly, when x and y are negatively correlated, high values on x ($x > \overline{X}$) will be associated with low values on y ($y < \overline{Y}$), and low values on x ($x < \overline{X}$) will be associated with high values on y ($y > \overline{Y}$). In this case, one term of the product will be negative and one term will be positive. With negative correlation, then, the product would generally be negative, as would the sum of these products. The term describing the covariation would be negative, and the stronger the negative correlation between x and y, the greater the magnitude of this covariation. When the correlation between x and y is near zero, then approximately half of the products will be positive, half will be negative, and the corresponding sum products will be zero. In this case, the term describing the covariation also will be zero, indicating that x and y do not covary.

Calculating the slope (b) from this definitional formula would be a tiresome (and error-prone) task. Fortunately, as with the Pearson correlation coefficient, there is a much easier computation formula for b:

$$b = \frac{n\sum xy - (\sum x)(\sum y)}{n\sum x^2 - (\sum x)^2} \qquad (12\text{–}6)$$

At first glance this formula looks no more easy to use than the definitional formula (equation 12–5). But it, too, should be familiar to you by now. We can break this monster up into six component parts that are really quite simple to compute:

1. $\sum xy$ = the sum of the product formed by multiplying each x score by each y score, and then summing over all scores.

2. $\sum x$ = the sum of the x scores.

3. $\sum y$ = the sum of the y scores.

4. $\sum x^2$ = the sum of the squared x scores $(x_1^2 + ... x_2^2 + ... x_n^2)$.

5. $\left(\sum x\right)^2$ = the sum of the x scores squared $(x_1 + ... x_2 + ... x_n)^2$.

6. n = the number of observations, or sample size.

We first illustrate the calculation of b using the hypothetical age and self-reported delinquency data, and then return to our real state-level data.

The necessary calculations for b for the data in Table 12–7 are provided in Table 12–9. In this table, the component elements of the formula are represented by separate columns. With this information, we can calculate the slope using formula 12–6:

$$b = \frac{n\sum xy - \left(\sum x\right)\left(\sum y\right)}{n\sum x^2 - \left(\sum x\right)^2}$$

$$= \frac{(20)(1,409) - (288)(92)}{(20)(4,206) - (288)^2}$$

$$= \frac{28,180 - 26,496}{84,120 - 82,944}$$

$$= \frac{1,684}{1,176}$$

$$= 1.43$$

The slope coefficient, b, in this example is 1.43. It is positive, indicating that there is a positive relationship between age and the number of self-reported delinquent acts. The value of 1.43 indicates that as age increases by one year, the number of self-reported delinquent acts increases by 1.43 units.

Once we have obtained our estimated slope coefficient, we can find the intercept (a) in our regression equation. The first step is to find the mean values of both the x and y distributions. We do this by dividing $\sum x$ by n, and then doing the same for the y scores. For the self-reported delinquent acts data, $\overline{X}$ = 14.4 (288/20) and $\overline{Y}$ = 4.6 (92 / 20). Because the regression line

TABLE 12–9

Calculations for Determining the Slope (b) for the Age and Self-Reported Delinquency Data

ID #	Age x	Self-Reported Delinquency y	x^2	xy
1	12	0	144	0
2	12	2	144	24
3	12	1	144	12
4	12	3	144	36
5	13	4	169	52
6	13	2	169	26
7	13	1	169	13
8	14	2	196	28
9	14	5	196	70
10	14	4	196	56
11	15	3	225	45
12	15	4	225	60
13	15	6	225	90
14	15	8	225	120
15	16	9	256	144
16	16	7	256	112
17	16	6	256	96
18	17	8	289	136
19	17	10	289	170
20	17	7	289	119
$n = 20$	$\Sigma x = 288$	$\Sigma y = 92$	$\Sigma x^2 = 4,206$	$\Sigma xy = 1,409$

will always pass through the mean value of both x and y, represented by $\overline{X}$ and $\overline{Y}$, we simply have to substitute these terms into the equation:

$$\overline{Y} = a + b\overline{X}$$

Then, by substitution, we obtain:

$$a = \overline{Y} - b\overline{X}$$

For our example, the solution would be:

$$a = 4.6 - (1.43)(14.4)$$

$$= 4.6 - 20.59$$

$$= -15.99$$

Thus, the regression line will cross the y axis at the point where $y = -15.99$ when the value of x equals zero. We now can specify our complete regression equation as:

$$y = a + bx$$

$$y = -15.99 + (1.43)x$$

Using the Regression Line for Prediction

After we have computed the regression equation, we can use it to determine the **predicted value of y (ŷ)** for any value of x. For example, using the estimated regression equation for age and self-reported delinquent acts, the expected number of delinquent acts for a 19-year-old youth would be:

$$\hat{y} = -15.99 + (1.43)(19)$$

$$= 11.18$$

This predicted value indicates that we would expect approximately 11 self-reported delinquent acts to be reported by a 19-year-old youth. In reality, this predicted y value is simply our "best guess" based on the estimated regression line. It does not mean that every 19 year old will report 11 delinquent acts. Since age and delinquency are linearly related, however, it does mean that our best guess when using the regression equation is better than guessing the number of delinquent acts without it. The stronger the linear relationship between age and self-reported delinquency, the better or more accurate our estimate will be.

We now know two data points that lie exactly on our estimated regression line, the one corresponding to the mean of the x and y values ($\overline{X} = 14.4$, $\overline{Y} = 4.6$) and the one corresponding to the predicted value of y when $x = 19$ ($\hat{y} = 11.18$) from our prediction equation above. Knowing these two data points allows us to more accurately draw the regression line without having to "eyeball" the data. We simply draw a straight line that runs through these two data points. This is shown in Figure 12–17. This line represents the "best fitting" regression line that we could obtain to describe the relationship between age and self-reported delinquency.

Case Study: Predicting State Crime Rates

Let's return now to our state-level data and estimate the value of the slope coefficient for each of the three relationships we examined earlier. In Table 12–1 we reported the poverty level (x) and the murder rate (y) for 15 randomly selected states. When we plotted these data in a scatterplot (Figure 12–9), we observed an apparent positive relationship between these two variables. This was confirmed by the calculation of the correlation coefficient, $r = .39$, which told us there was a weak to moderate positive relationship between poverty and murder in these 15 states. We also know that poverty rates explain 15 percent of the variation in rates of murder ($r^2 = .15$, or 15 percent).

Now we will fit a regression line to these data by first determining the slope (b) and then the intercept (a). Because we needed the same information to calculate the correlation coefficient, the calculations necessary to calculate

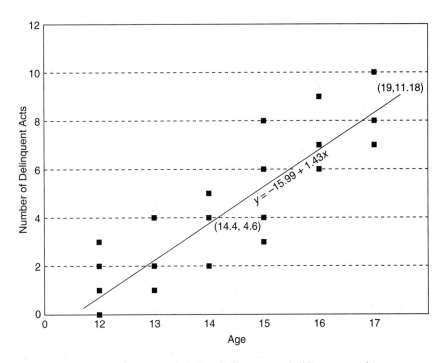

Figure 12–17 Fitting a regression line to the age and delinquency data

the slope have already been provided in Table 12–4. With these calculations and formula 12–6, we can estimate the slope coefficient as:

$$b = \frac{15(1,205.3) - (183.2)(95.2)}{15(2,386.2) - (183.2)^2}$$

$$= \frac{18,079.5 - 17,440.6}{35,793 - 33,562.2}$$

$$= \frac{638.9}{2,230.8}$$

$$= .28$$

As with the correlation coefficient, the slope coefficient is positive, indicating that there is a positive linear relationship between a state's murder rate and its poverty rate. The magnitude of the slope is .28, which tells us that a 1 unit increase in the rate of poverty (a 1 percent increase in poverty, since the poverty variable is measured as the percent of the population living below the poverty level) increases the murder rate by .28 units (by .28 per 100,000). There is, then, a positive linear relationship between the poverty level in a state and its murder rate. This is a bit difficult to understand since it is hard to comprehend an increase of .28 units of the murder rate. To increase our understanding, we can add units to x to determine the change in y. For example, if a 1 unit increase in poverty increases the murder rate by .28 units, we know that a 5 unit increase in poverty will increase the rate of murder by 1.4 units ($5 \times .28 = 1.4$). This allows us to more meaningfully demonstrate the effect of x on y—increasing the poverty rate by 5 percent, in this case, will serve to increase the rate of murder by 1.4 murders per 100,000 population.

Let's move on to solve for the entire regression equation. Knowing the value of b and the mean values of x (poverty rate) and y (murder rate), we can now solve for the intercept (a). The mean homicide rate for these 15 states is 6.3 (95.2/15), and the mean rate of poverty is 12.2 (183.2/15). The intercept then, is equal to:

$$a = \overline{Y} - b\overline{X}$$

$$= 6.3 - (.28)(12.2)$$

$$= 6.3 - 3.41$$

$$= 2.89$$

The point where the regression line crosses the y axis when x is equal to zero is where $y = 2.89$. We now can write our full regression equation for these data as:

$$y = a + bx$$

$$y = 2.89 + .28(x)$$

With this regression equation, we now can estimate the predicted value of y ($\hat{y}$) at any given value of x. For example, the predicted murder level for a state with a poverty rate of 21 would be:

$$y = a + bx$$

$$y = 2.89 + .28(21)$$

$$y = 2.89 + 5.88$$

$$y = 8.77$$

Exactly what does this predicted value mean? It means that we would predict that a state with 21 percent of its population living below the poverty level would have a murder rate of 8.77 per 100,000. Keep in mind that this is our predicted value of y based upon our regression equation estimated from the sample data. It represents our best guess of what y will be at a given value of x. It does not mean that the y score will be that exact value. In fact, let's use the regression equation to get a predicted y score (murder rate) for an x score that we have in our data—a poverty rate of 10.9 (Hawaii):

$$y = a + bx$$

$$Y = 2.89 + .28(10.9)$$

$$Y = 2.89 + 3.05$$

$$Y = 5.94$$

Thus, if the percent of the population living below the poverty level in a state were equal to 10.9, based upon our regression equation, we would predict that its murder rate would be 5.94 per 100,000. Notice in Table 12–4, however, that the state of Hawaii, which has a poverty rate of 10.9, has a murder rate of 3.7 per 100,000. Our predicted y is not the same as our observed y. This means, of course, that we have some amount of error in our prediction. Unless all of the sample data points lie exactly on the regression line (which would mean that our two variables are perfectly correlated), our predicted y values $(\hat{y})$ usually will be different from our observed y values. In regression analysis, this error in predicting the dependent variable is often called the **residual**. In the case of perfect correlation we can predict one score from another without error. The closer the data points are to the estimated regression line, therefore, the more accurate our predicted y scores will be. Conversely, the further the data points are from the line, the less accurate our predicted y scores will be.

Because we always have error in prediction, we must rewrite the regression equation as:

$$\hat{y} = a + bx + \varepsilon$$

where ε (the Greek letter **epsilon**) is the symbol for the error term. The error term reflects measurement error in the y variable, the fact that we have a sample of observations and thus sampling error, and other factors that explain or account for the y variable besides the x variable we have measured. The latter refers to the fact that there usually are several factors that explain a given y variable. If we are only examining one of them, we will not be able to predict y with perfect precision. In other words, in looking only at x and ignoring other factors that influence y, our predictions will contain some amount of error. The more that y is determined solely by x, the less error we will have. We have more to say about this in the next chapter, which is about multiple regression. For now, let's return to our problem.

With our predicted value of $\hat{y} = 8.77$ with an x score of 21, we now have two data points that fall exactly on our regression line, including the value for the means of x and y ($\overline{X} = 12.2$, $\overline{Y} = 6.3$). Connecting these two points with a straight line will give us the best-fitting regression line that describes the relationship between a state's murder rate and poverty level. This is shown in Figure 12–18. Notice that this regression line crosses the y axis at approximately $y = 2.8$. Recall that this is the y intercept, symbolized by the letter a in the regression equation.

Let's go through another example. In Table 12–2 we reported data for 15 states regarding the percent of each state's population living in a nonmetropolitan area (x) and its rate of violent crime (y). In the scatterplot we constructed from these data (Figure 12–11), we observed a negative relationship between these two variables. This, too, was confirmed by the sign of the correlation coefficient ($r = -.46$). The magnitude of the correlation coefficient indicated that knowing the percent of a state's rural population could explain 21 percent of the variation in violent crime ($r^2 = .21$). Now we will fit a regression

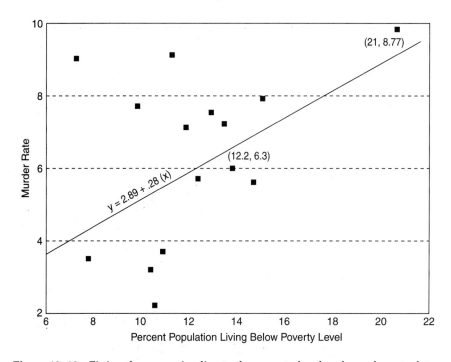

Figure 12–18   Fitting the regression line to the poverty level and murder rate data

line to these data by first determining the slope (b), and then the intercept (a). The calculations necessary to calculate the slope have already been provided in Table 12–5. With these calculations and formula 12–6, we can estimate the slope coefficient to be:

$$b = \frac{n\sum xy - (\sum x)(\sum y)}{n\sum x^2 - (\sum x)^2}$$

$$= \frac{(15)(187,204) - (373)(8,541)}{15(13,887) - (373)^2}$$

$$= \frac{2,808,060 - 3,185,793}{208,305 - 139,129}$$

$$= \frac{-377,733}{69,176}$$

$$= -5.4$$

The sign of the slope is negative, indicating a negative relationship between the percent of a state's rural population and its rate of violent crime. This means that for every 1 unit increase in x, there is a b unit decrease in y. Thus, the magnitude of the slope tells us that for each 1 percent increase in the state's population that is rural, the violent crime rate declines by 5.4 units per 100,000. The greater the percentage of a state's population that lives in a rural area, the lower the rate of violent crime. States with larger percentages of urban residents, therefore, have higher rates of violent crime.

We next can calculate the mean for the x variable (percent nonmetropolitan) as $373/15 = 24.8$, and the mean of y (rate of violent crime) as $8,541/15 = 569.4$. With this information, we can determine the intercept:

$$a = 569.4 - (-5.4)(24.8)$$

$$= 569.4 + 133.92$$

$$= 703.3$$

The point where the regression line crosses the y axis when the value of x is equal to zero is $y = 435.4$. We now can write our full regression equation as:

$$y = a + bx$$

$$y = 703.3 + -5.4(x)$$

With this regression equation we can estimate a predicted value of the violent crime rate $(\hat{y})$ for a given value of a state's rural population percentage. If the population of the state that lives in a nonmetropolitan area is 10 percent, our predicted violent crime rate will be:

$$\hat{y} = 703.3 + -5.4(10)$$

$$= 703.3 + -54$$

$$= 649.3$$

Given a state with a 10 percent rural population, then, we would predict a violent crime rate of 649.3 per 100,000. We now have two data points that lie exactly on the estimated regression line. One of these points is the mean of the x and y variable $(\overline{X}, \overline{Y})$, which is (24.8, 569.4), and the other is our x value of 10 and the predicted value of y $(\hat{y})$, equal to 649.3. With these two points we can draw a straight line that runs through both points to establish our regression line; this line represents the best-fitting regression line that describes the linear relationship between these data. We have drawn this line on the scatterplot presented in Figure 12–19.

Our final example using the state-level data involved the relationship between the divorce rate in a state and its violent crime rate. Recall that the original data for these variables along with the calculations necessary for determining b were presented in Table 12–6. In our scatterplot of these data (Figure 12–12), we could not discern any clear upward or downward linear pattern in the data points. This suggested to us that the two variables were not very strongly related to one another. The correlation coefficient we obtained of $r = .10$ confirmed this suspicion, indicating that the divorce rate

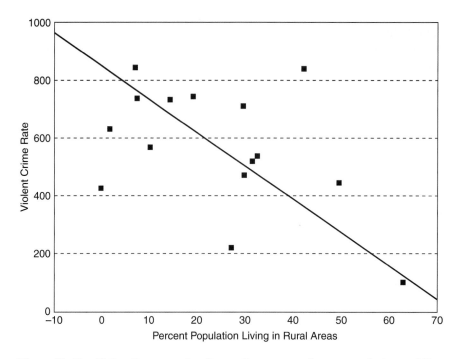

Figure 12–19   Fitting the regression line to the percent of state population residing in rural area and violent crime rate data

only explains about 1 percent of the variation in violent crime in states. Now, we will more precisely fit a least-squares regression line to the data.

As in our other examples, we will begin by estimating the slope of the regression line (b) using the calculations provided in Table 12–6. With these calculations we can derive an estimate of b as:

$$b = \frac{n\sum xy - (\sum x)(\sum y)}{n\sum x^2 - (\sum x)^2}$$

$$= \frac{(15)(42,461.2) - (73.9)(8,541)}{(15)(385.59) - (73.9)^2}$$

$$= \frac{636,918 - 631,179.9}{5,783.85 - 5,461.2}$$

$$= \frac{5,738.1}{322.6}$$

$$= 17.7$$

The sign and magnitude of the slope coefficient indicate that as the divorce rate in a state increases by 1 unit, the violent crime rate increases by 17.7 units per 100,000. There is, then, a positive linear relationship between the divorce rate in a state and its corresponding rate of violent crime. The mean value of the divorce rate is 4.9 (73.9/15), and the mean violent crime rate is 569.4 per 100,000 (8,541/15). With these values, the estimated value of the intercept can be determined as:

$$a = \overline{Y} - b\overline{X}$$

$$= 569.4 - 17.7(4.9)$$

$$= 569.4 - 86.7$$

$$= 482.7$$

The point where the regression line crosses the y axis (the y intercept) is where $y = 482.7$. Our complete regression equation for these data now can be defined as:

$$y = a + bx$$

$$y = 482.7 + 17.7(x)$$

For any value of x, we now can estimate a predicted value of y ($\hat{y}$). For example, the predicted violent crime rate for a state with a divorce rate equal to 9 per 1,000 would be:

$$\hat{y} = 482.7 + 17.7(9)$$

$$= 482.7 + 159.3$$

$$= 642$$

Thus, if a state's divorce rate was 9 per 1,000 residents, based on our estimated regression equation, we would predict that there would be approximately 642 violent crimes per 100,000 residents. Knowing this data point along with the mean values of both variables ($\overline{X} = 4.9$, $\overline{Y} = 569.4$), we now can draw our regression line by drawing a straight line through these two points. This is shown in Figure 12–20. Notice that this regression line is much more horizontal (flat) than the other two we have drawn using the state-level data.

COMPARISON OF b AND r

We have discussed two important statistics for continuous variables in this chapter, the slope coefficient (b) and the correlation coefficient (r)—and (r^2), which is based on (r). You may be wondering at this point why two statistics are necessary. Couldn't we estimate just one with our sample data and be done with it? The quick answer to your question (and you should know by now that there is *never* really a quick answer) is that while the two measures have some similar properties, they are not identical. In fact, they are far from identical since they tell us somewhat different things about our continuous variables.

Notice that the slope coefficient is interpreted in terms of the original units of measurement of the variables. That is, an increase of 1 in the x variable's unit of measurement (percent below the poverty level, percent rural

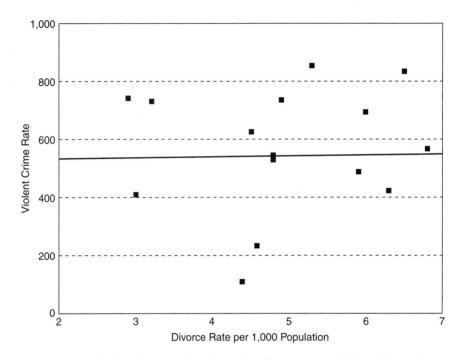

Figure 12–20   Fitting the regression line to the divorce rate and the violent crime rate data

population, divorce rate) changes (increases/decreases) the y variable by b units (murder rate per 100,000, violent crime rate per 100,000). Beyond this very general interpretation, however, there is no information that conveys the magnitude of the relationship. If, for example, we were to change units of measurement, say from dollars to pennies or from rates per 10,000 to rates per 100,000, the magnitude (but not the direction) of our slope coefficient would correspondingly change. That is why we cannot simply assume that a small slope coefficient indicates that the magnitude of the coefficient is also small. A small slope coefficient may carry quite a wallop in terms of how strongly related it is to the dependent variable! Notice, for example, that the slope co-efficient in the regression equation for the divorce rate and the rate of violent crime was equal to 17.7 ($b = 17.7$), but the slope coefficient in the regression equation for the poverty rate and the rate of murder was equal to .28 ($b = .28$). We cannot compare the magnitude of these two coefficients and conclude that the relationship between divorce and violent crime is stronger than the relationship between poverty and murder. The reason why the slope coeffi-cient is so much smaller in the latter example is that there is very little varia-tion in our rates of murder and the rates themselves are much smaller compared to rates of violent crime. For example, the murder rates for our 15 states range from 2.2 to 9.8 per 100,000, while the violent crime rates range from 112 to 854 per 100,000 population.

That is why we need the values of both the regression coefficient (b) and Pearson's correlation coefficient (r). The regression coefficient (b) gives us the more precise indicator of the change in y associated with a change in x, while the correlation coefficient (r) standardizes the magnitude of this relationship so that we can compare the relative strength of relationships across different cases and across different variables. When we examine the correlation coefficients for both cases, we see that the correlation is actually stronger for the relationship between murder and poverty ($r = .39$) compared to the relationship between divorce and violent crime ($r = .10$).

Let's illustrate this important measurement issue with an example. Take a close look at the definitional formula for the slope coefficient (equation 12–5). The numerator in this equation is the product of the mean deviations for both variables $[(x - \overline{X})(y - \overline{Y})]$. As this numerator increases, of course, the magnitude of the slope will increase. The magnitude of this numerator is, in turn, a partial function of the unit of measurement. Let's say that the y variable is measured in units of dollars and the mean for our data happens to be 5. A given y score of \$7, then, would have a mean deviation of 2 (\$7 − \$5). If the unit of measurement happened to be pennies rather than dollars, however, the mean would be 500 (500 pennies = \$5), the same x score of \$7 would be 700 pennies, and the mean deviation would now be 200 rather than 2. All else being equal, the magnitude of the slope coefficient would increase by a factor of 100 even though we are still talking about the same amount of money.

Remember that while the numerators for the slope and correlation coefficient are identical (the covariation of x and y), the denominators are not. The denominator for the slope reflects the variation in the x variable, while the denominator of the correlation coefficient reflects the product of the variation in both x and y. In fact, we can rewrite the correlation coefficient as follows:

$$r_{yx} = b_{yx}\left(\frac{s_x}{s_y}\right)$$

The important implication of expressing the correlation coefficient as the product of the slope and the ratio of the standard deviation of x to the standard deviation of y is that the value of the correlation coefficient will depend not only upon the linear relationship between the two variables (b_{yx}), but on a quantity that changes from sample to sample (s_x/s_y). We may, then, find relationships with very similar slopes but much different correlation coefficients because the sample standard deviations of x and y are very different.

In sum, the slope coefficient measures the *form* of the linear relationship between x and y but is expressed in terms of the units of measurement of the variables. While the correlation coefficient can tell us about the *strength* of the linear relationship between two continuous variables, it tells us nothing about the form or precise nature of that relationship. We cannot use the value of r to predict y values because we do not know how much of an impact x has on y, nor do we know the original measurement units of the variables. Again, this is because the correlation coefficient is standardized. For this reason, it is important to calculate and report both the slope coefficient (b) and the correlation coefficient (r). Knowing the values of both b and r, however, still does not tell us if there is a significant relationship between x and y. For this, we need to perform a hypothesis test.

TESTING FOR THE SIGNIFICANCE OF b AND r

Because the slope (b) and the correlation coefficient (r) are only sample estimates of their respective population parameters (β and ρ), we must test for the statistical significance of b and r. Returning to our state-level data, the question we want to address, then, concerns the relationship between x and y for the 50 states, not just our sample of 15. The null hypothesis used for the slope and correlation coefficient in the population assumes that there is no linear association between the x and y variables in the population. Remember that when there is no linear relationship between two variables, both the slope and the correlation coefficient will be equal to zero. Since the numerators for the slope and correlation coefficient are identical, a hypothesis test about the slope is also a hypothesis test about the correlation coefficient in the bivariate case. The alternative hypothesis assumes that there is a linear relationship between the x and y variables in the population and, thus, that the slope and correlation coefficient are significantly different from zero. Formally stated, the research and null hypotheses for the slope and regression coefficient would be:

H_0: β and $\rho = 0$

H_1: β and $\rho \neq 0$

H_1: β and $\rho > 0$

H_1: β and $\rho < 0$

Before we conduct our hypothesis test, however, we must be sure that our data meet certain assumptions. A few of these assumptions are familiar to you. For example, we must assume that the data have been randomly selected. Second, we must assume that both variables are normally distributed. Third, we must assume that the data are continuous, and that they are measured at the interval or ratio level. Fourth, we must assume that the nature of the relationship between the two variables is linear. The fifth assumption is really a set of assumptions about the error term. It is assumed that the error component of a regression equation is independent of and therefore uncorrelated with the independent or x variable, that it is normally distributed, that it has an expected value of zero, and that it has constant variance across all levels of x. The last assumption is called the assumption of **homoscedasticity.** The assumption of homoscedasticity is simply that the variance of the conditional y scores is equal at each value of x.

Assumptions for Testing Hypotheses About β and ρ

1. The observations have been randomly selected.
2. Both variables have normal distributions.
3. The two variables are measured at the interval/ratio level.
4. The variables are related in a linear form.
5. The error component is independent of and therefore uncorrelated with the independent or x variable, is normally distributed, has an expected value of zero, and has a constant variance across all levels of x (assumption of **homoscedasticity**).

The assumption of homoscedasticity, as well as the assumption of linearity, may be assessed by examining the scatterplots. In Figure 12–21 the relationship between x and y is linear, and the assumption of homoscedasticity is met. At each value of x, the variance of y is the same. In other words, the conditional distribution of the y scores at fixed values of x shows the same dispersion. No value of x has a variance that is significantly higher or lower compared to the other values of x.

In Figure 12–22, however, the assumption of homoscedasticity is violated. Although the relationship is linear, the variance of the y scores is much greater at higher values of x than at lower values. This can be seen from the fact that there is a "wedge" pattern in the y scores as x increases. The spread or dispersion of y scores is greater when x is greater than 15. When the assumption of linearity is violated, linear-based statistics such as the Pearson correlation and least-squares regression coefficient are not appropriate.

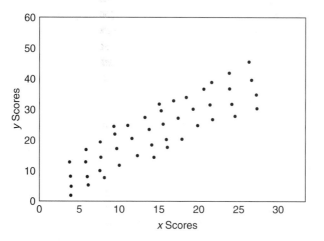

Figure 12–21   Linear relationship with equal variance of y at each level of x

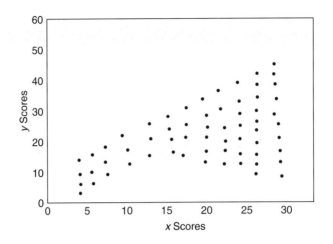

Figure 12–22   Linear relationship with unequal variance of y at each level of x

When the assumption of homoscedasticity is not supported, you may have to make transformations of your data. This topic, you will be relieved to learn, is beyond the scope of this book. You should be aware, however, that a careful inspection of your scatterplot is always the first order of business because it can warn you of potential problems with your data.

If all assumptions have been met, the significance test for r and b is relatively straightforward. With the null hypothesis of no linear relationship, the distribution of the sample rs (and bs) is approximated with the t distribution, with the degrees of freedom equal to $n - 2$. The t statistic for this test has the following formula:

$$t = r\sqrt{\frac{n - 2}{1 - r^2}}$$

(12–7)

where

r = the estimated sample r, and

n = the sample size.

For our sample of state-level data, let's test for the significance of a linear relationship between the three sets of variables. Because we have some idea about the relationship between each independent and dependent variable, we will use one-tailed tests with an alpha level of .05 (one-tailed) and 13 degrees of freedom ($15 - 2 = 13$). From Table E-3 of Appendix E, we can see that for a one-tailed test with an $\alpha = .05$ and 13 degrees of freedom, the critical t value is 1.771. Let's get going.

Case Study: Murder and Poverty

Step 1. For the relationship between poverty level and murder rates, we found that $r = .39$ and $b = .28$. Our null hypothesis is that the slope and correlation coefficient are zero or that there is no linear relationship between murder and poverty. Because we believe that there is a positive relationship between poverty and rates of murder, our research or alternative hypothesis is that both coefficients will be significantly greater than zero:

H_0: β and ρ for murder and poverty rates $= 0$.

H_1: β and ρ for murder and poverty rates > 0.

Step 2. To test this null hypothesis, we will utilize the t statistic and its respective sampling distribution. The question we are really asking is, "If there were no linear relationship between poverty level and murder rates in the population, how likely would it be to obtain a sample r of .39 or greater, or a sample b of .28 or greater?"

Step 3. We have already decided to use a one-tailed test with an alpha level of .05 ($\alpha = .05$). The critical value of t from Table E-3 in Appendix E tells us that our obtained value of t for this test must be greater than 1.771 to reject the null hypothesis.

Step 4. Calculate the obtained value of t:

$$t = .39 \sqrt{\frac{15 - 2}{1 - (.39)^2}}$$

$$= .39 \sqrt{\frac{13}{1 - .15}}$$

$$= .39 \sqrt{\frac{13}{.85}}$$

$$= .39 \sqrt{15.29}$$

$$= .39 (3.9)$$

$$= 1.5$$

Step 5. Since our obtained t of 1.5 is less than the critical t value of 1.771, we must fail to reject the null hypothesis and conclude that there is not a significant relationship between the poverty level and murder rates for the 50 U.S. states. Of course, being the astute methodologist that you now are, you immediately realize that the best way to improve your chances of rejecting the null hypothesis is to increase your sample size. (A sample of 15 is very small and not likely to represent the true population parameters!)

Case Study: Violent Crime and Rural Population

Let's move on to our data regarding the relationship between a state's rural population percent and its violent crime rate. With our sample of 15 states, we found a correlation of $r = -.46$ and a slope of $b = -5.4$. Because we believe that the rurality of a state will be negatively related to its rate of violent crime, we will assume that the values of β and ρ also will be negative. This is reflected in our research hypothesis below, which states that the values of β and ρ will be less than zero. The first step, then, is to formalize our null and research hypotheses:

H_0: β and ρ for violent crime and rurality $= 0$.

H_1: β and ρ for violent crime and rurality < 0.

In this case, our directional research hypothesis states that the coefficients will be less than zero because we believe rural areas will have lower rates of violent crime than urban areas. Therefore, using an $\alpha = .05$ with 13 degrees of freedom for a one-tailed test, we have a critical value of t equal to -1.771. We will reject the null hypothesis if t_{obt} is less than or equal to -1.771, and we will fail to reject the null hypothesis if it is greater than -1.771. We next can calculate the obtained value of t from the sample data and compare it to t_{crit}:

$$t = -.46\sqrt{\frac{15-2}{1-(-.46)^2}}$$

$$= -.46\sqrt{\frac{13}{1-.21}}$$

$$= -.46\sqrt{\frac{13}{.79}}$$

$$= -.46\sqrt{16.4}$$

$$= -.46(4.05)$$

$$= -1.86$$

Since the obtained t value of -1.86 is less than the critical t value of -1.771 (the absolute magnitude is greater), we can reject the null hypothesis of no linear relationship. We conclude that there is a significant negative linear relationship between rural population percent and rates of violent crime for the 50 states. States with higher population percentages in rural areas tend to have significantly lower rates of violent crime.

Case Study: Violent Crime and Divorce

Finally, let's test the null hypothesis that there is no significant linear relationship between the divorce rate and the rate of violent crime. The sample correlation for our data was $r = .10$, and the estimated sample slope coefficient was $b = 17.7$. Our research hypothesis assumes that there is a positive relationship between the divorce rate and rates of violent crime and, along with the null hypothesis, it is formally stated:

H_0: β and ρ for violent crime and divorce $= 0$.

H_1: β and ρ for violent crime and divorce > 0.

We are again using a one-tailed hypothesis. With 13 degrees of freedom and $\alpha = .05$ the critical value of t is 1.771. We will, then, reject the null hypothesis if $t_{obt} > 1.771$ and fail to reject it if $t_{obt} < 1.771$. The t statistic we would obtain for this relationship is:

$$t = .10\sqrt{\frac{15-2}{1-(.10)^2}}$$

$$= .10\sqrt{\frac{13}{1-.01}}$$

$$= .10\sqrt{\frac{13}{.99}}$$

$$= .10\sqrt{13.13}$$

$$= .10(3.6)$$

$$= .36$$

In this case, the obtained t statistic is almost equal to zero. The value of .36 is much less than the critical t value of 1.771. We would, therefore, fail to reject the null hypothesis. We must conclude that there is not a significant linear relationship between divorce and violent crime rates at the state level. Rates of divorce within states, then, do not appear to affect rates of violent crime.

THE PROBLEMS OF LIMITED VARIATION, NONLINEAR RELATIONSHIPS, AND OUTLIERS IN THE DATA

Before concluding this chapter on correlation and regression analysis, you need to be aware of some potential pitfalls. In general, you should always be suspicious of your data, and this suspicion should be overcome only by a careful understanding and inspection of your data at the univariate and bivariate levels—especially with graphical inspections. Exactly what kind of problems are lurking out there for the unsuspecting correlation and regression user?

One of these problems is the problem of limited variation in the independent or x variable. Let's say you have an x variable that is distributed in the population over a wide range of scores, say, from zero to 40. In collecting your sample data, however, your observed x scores range only from zero to 10. Figure 12–23 shows that it is possible that you may find no correlation between x and some y variable within a limited range of observed x scores

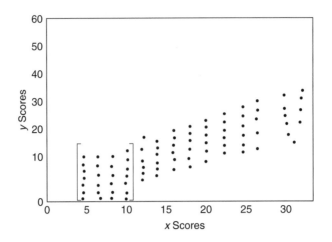

Figure 12–23   No correlation within a limited range of x (0–10) but strong positive correlation over the full range of scores

(0–10) when there is, in fact, a correlation in the full range of x scores. As you can see in Figure 12–23, the estimated correlation and slope coefficients for the obtained data where the x scores range only from zero to 10 would be close to zero, even though across the total range of x scores there is a positive correlation. In fact, within any *limited range* of x scores, as Figure 12–23 indicates, there may appear to be no correlation between x and y, and the sample correlation and slope coefficients will be close to zero. You should always be aware of the fact that limited variation in the x variable may lead to sample estimates of no correlation when a correlation may, in fact, exist in the population.

A second problem you may see after examining the relationship between two continuous variables is *nonlinearity*. Throughout this chapter we have tried to emphasize the fact that Pearson's correlation coefficient (r) and the regression coefficient (b) both presume that the relationship between the x and y variable is linear. In other words, it is presumed that the data points in a scatterplot fall in an approximate straight line so that the mathematical equation for the straight line ($y = a + bx$) can be used to both describe the data and obtain predicted values of y. When r and $b = 0$, there is no straight line that can fit the data, meaning that there is no linear relationship between the two variables.

However, be cautioned that if you do find that $r = b = 0$, this does not necessarily mean that there is no relationship between x and y. The two variables may have a very strong **nonlinear relationship,** in which case both the correlation coefficient and the slope coefficient are zero, but the conclusion of no relationship is false. In this case what you would be observing is not a linear relationship, but possibly a strong nonlinear relationship. Figure 12–24 illustrates this case.

The relationship between the x and y variables in Figure 12–24 is **curvilinear.** At low levels of x there is a moderate negative relationship with y, but

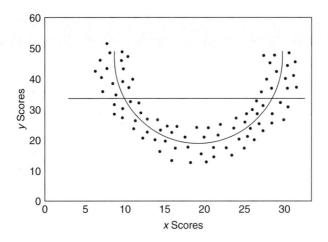

Figure 12–24 Nonlinear relationship between x and y

at higher x scores this relationship is positive. In this instance the estimated correlation coefficient would be near zero as would the slope, since the best-fitting straight line would go through the middle of the data as illustrated in the scatterplot. With such a flat line, neither b nor r would be significantly different from zero. A much better fitting line would be a curved one as shown. The curved line shows that there is actually a very strong relationship between x and y, but the relationship happens to be nonlinear.

Other examples of nonlinear relationships are shown in Figure 12–25. When the relationship between the variables is nonlinear, as in Figures 12–24 and 12–25, linear-based estimation techniques such as those discussed in this chapter are inappropriate. The least-squares approach of this chapter would underestimate the strength and nature of the true relationship. Unfortunately, the estimation of nonlinear relationships is beyond the scope of this book. Our strong advice is that if you find that $r = b = 0$, do not immediately jump to the conclusion that there is no relationship between your variables. There may be a nonlinear relationship. To avoid this mistake, we again urge you to carefully scrutinize your scatterplots. If there really is no relationship between the two variables, the scatterplot will show a random scatter of data points (no pattern). In this case the correlation coefficient will correctly be zero. If, however, the scatterplot shows evidence of marked nonlinearity, you should not use the linear statistics of this chapter.

As if these problems were not enough, there is another potential problem out there waiting to fool you. This is the problem posed by outliers. You are probably wondering, what is an outlier, and how can it mess with me? Recall from our discussion of EDA techniques that an outlier, as it suggests, is a data point that is "lying out there," far away from the other scores. An **outlier,** then, is an extremely low score or an extremely high score. The problem that an outlier poses to the unwary data analyst is that it can unduly influence the value

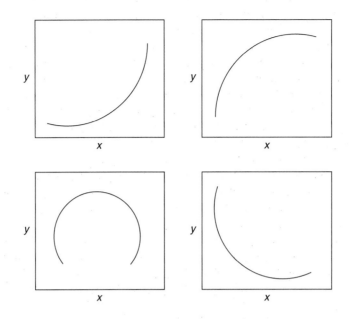

Figure 12–25   Other nonlinear relationships

of the slope and correlation coefficient. The presence of one or a few extreme scores may lead you to exaggerate the existence of a linear relationship by inflating the magnitudes of r and b.

As an example of this, Table 12–10 reports two pieces of information for 12 randomly selected states and the District of Columbia: the rate of violent crime per 100,000 (the x variable) and the incarceration rate per 100,000 (the y variable). The latter variable is the number of state prisoners with a prison sentence of more than one year, per 100,000 residents of the state. In this example we are interested in examining whether those states with high rates of serious crime also have high rates of incarceration. We might suspect that the response to high rates of violent crime is to "lock 'em up." You will note from Table 12–10 that the District of Columbia has both an unusually high rate of violent crime and a high rate of incarceration. In fact, the violent crime rate for the District of Columbia is more than twice that of the state with the second highest violent crime rate (New York). In addition, its incarceration rate is more than three times higher than that of the next highest rate (506 per 100,000 for Oklahoma). The District of Columbia, then, represents an extreme case for these two variables; it is an outlier.

You can see just how far out it lies from the other scores in Figure 12–26, which is a scatterplot of the 13 jurisdictions' violent crime and incarceration rate data given in Table 12–10. The 12 states lie in a relatively narrow range of values for both the violent crime rate and the incarceration rate. These data points cluster in the bottom left of the scatterplot. The data point representing the District of Columbia lies far away from these other points in the up-

TABLE 12–10

Rate of Violent Crime per 100,000 Population (x) in 1992 and the Rate of Incarceration per 100,000 Population (y) in 1993 for 12 States and the District of Columbia

State	Violent Crime Rate x	Incarceration Rate y
AL	871.1	431
CA	1,119.7	368
DE	621.2	397
DC	2,832.8	1,549
GA	733.2	387
IN	508.5	250
LA	984.6	499
MD	1,000.1	383
NY	1,122.1	354
OK	622.8	506
SC	944.5	489
TN	746.2	250
WA	534.5	196

Source: Data from Kathleen Maguire and Ann L. Pastore, eds., Sourcebook of Criminal Justice Statistics 1994. U.S. Department of Justice, Bureau of Justice Statistics. Washington, DC: USGPO, 1995; and Kathleen Maguire and Ann L. Pastore, eds., Sourcebook of Criminal Justice Statistics 1993. U.S. Department of Justice, Bureau of Justice Statistics, Washington, DC: USGPO, 1994.

per right-hand corner of the scatterplot. As you can see, for these data the District of Columbia is an outlier.

The crucial issue, though, is the effect that an outlying score such as this has on our analysis and interpretation of the data. We have estimated two regression equations, two slopes, and two correlation coefficients from these data, one including the District of Columbia and one excluding it. Based on the regression equations we also have drawn two regression lines in Figure 12–26. Looking at these two lines, you can immediately see the potential effect of an outlier. When the District of Columbia is excluded from the analysis, the slope of the regression line is gently ascending, with a slope coefficient of $b = .186$. The correlation coefficient is $r = .40$, with $r^2 = .16$. This would suggest that the relationship between rates of violent crime and rates of incarceration is positive, though not particularly strong. Only 16 percent of the variance in incarceration rates is explained by the rate of violent crime.

Notice what happens, however, when the District of Columbia is included in the analysis. The regression line that includes the District of Columbia is ascending much steeper, as reflected in the fact that the magnitude of the slope coefficient is almost three times higher ($b = .533$) than when it was excluded. The value of Pearson's correlation coefficient increases to .938, and the coefficient of determination (r^2) is now .88. With the District of Columbia included in the analysis, then, 88 percent of the variance in incarceration rates is explained

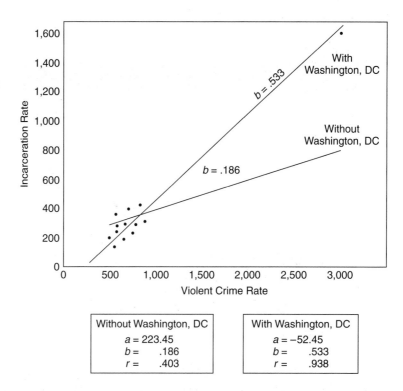

Figure 12–26   Effect of an outlier on the regression equation between rates of violent crime and incarceration

by the rate of violent crime. We would conclude in this case that there is a very strong positive linear relationship between the two variables.

Not surprisingly, given the dramatic difference in their magnitude, our test of the statistical significance of *r* and *b* for the two sets of data would lead us to draw different conclusions about the significance of the relationship between violent crime and incarceration rates. When the District of Columbia is not included in the data, we obtain a *t* value of:

$$t_{obt} = .403\sqrt{\frac{12-2}{1-.162}}$$

$$= .403\sqrt{\frac{10}{.838}}$$

$$= 1.392$$

With 10 (12 − 2) degrees of freedom for a one-tailed hypothesis test, an obtained *t* value of 1.392 would not be greater than the critical value at $\alpha = .05$ ($t_{crit} = 1.812$). In this situation, we would fail to reject the null hypothesis. Even though a positive correlation exists in the sample, we would conclude from our hypothesis test that there is no significant linear relationship in the population between violent crime rates and rates of incarceration.

When we include the District of Columbia in our analysis, however, the obtained t value becomes:

$$t_{obt} = .938\sqrt{\frac{13-2}{1-.88}}$$

$$= .938\sqrt{\frac{11}{.12}}$$

$$= 8.981$$

With 11 (13 − 2) degrees of freedom, an obtained t value of 8.981 would be significant at $\alpha = .05$ or $\alpha = .01$ for a one-tailed test. In this circumstance, we would reject the null hypothesis and conclude that there is a positive linear relationship between rates of violent crime and rates of incarceration in the population.

The lesson to be learned from this is that extreme scores or outliers may have a very pronounced effect on r and b and their associated significance tests. In the case of outliers such as the one in our example, it might be advisable to report the analysis both with and without the outlying score or scores. In detecting outliers and other possible problems, we once again urge you to carefully examine your scatterplot before rushing into any analysis. If you have not yet grasped a very important theme of this book, let us now unequivocally state it: *There is probably nothing more important than a very slow and careful inspection of your data, complete with descriptive statistics and graphical displays, before proceeding with your statistical analysis.*

SUMMARY

In this chapter we have been concerned with the relationship between two continuous (interval/ratio) level variables. This relationship is often expressed in terms of the correlation between variables. In examining the correlation between two continuous variables (x and y), a very important first step is to create a scatterplot or scattergram. The scatterplot is a graphical display of your joint xy data points. From the pattern of these data points you can discern if the relationship between your variables is linear (a pattern resembling a straight line), nonlinear (a pattern resembling a curved line), or if there is no relationship between them (no pattern, but a random scatter of points).

If the relationship is linear, you can tell from the scatterplot if it is positive (the line is ascending) or negative (the line is descending). You also can make a preliminary judgment from your scatterplot regarding the strength of the linear relationship by roughly sketching a straight line that passes as close to as many data points as possible and examining how close the points fall to the line. The closer the data points cluster to the line, the stronger the linear relationship between the variables.

A more precise way to draw your regression line and calculate predicted values of y ($\hat{y}$), however, is to use the mathematical equation for a straight line ($y = a + bx$). If your data are linearly related, this regression line is estimated in such a way that it provides the "best fit" to your data. Rather than "eyeballing" the data and drawing a line that seems to come closest to the data points, this equation for the straight line gives you the best fit in terms of minimizing the squared difference between each data point and the mean of y at fixed values of x. This is the idea of the "least-squares" regression line. One term in the regression equation is the slope (b), which measures the steepness of the line. The magnitude of the slope measures the effect of the x variable on the y variable, while its sign tells us the direction of the relationship.

Unfortunately, since the magnitude of the slope coefficient is in terms of the natural units of measurement of the x and y variable, it is not a very convenient measure of association. A standardized measure of association for continuous variables is the Pearson correlation coefficient (r). The sign of the correlation coefficient is the same as its corresponding slope. The value of the correlation coefficient is that its upper limit is unity, so that as the relationship between x and y gets stronger, the magnitude of r gets closer to ± 1.0. The drawback to the correlation coefficient as a measure of association is that, while an r of zero is indicative of no correlation and an r of ± 1.0 indicates a perfect correlation, magnitudes in between these values are not so easy to interpret, other than subjective assessments such as a "weak" or "moderately strong" correlation.

The squared value of r (r^2), the coefficient of determination, is, however, readily interpretable at all magnitudes. The value of r^2 reflects the amount of variance in the y variable that is explained by the x variable. Another way to understand this is to view the value of r^2 as an indication of how much we improve our prediction of y by knowing the value of x. Once we have estimated the direction and strength of the relationship between two continuous variables with our sample data, we then can test for the existence of a significant relationship in the population by using a t test.

Finally, in this chapter we have emphasized the importance of carefully examining a scatterplot of your data before estimating correlation and regression coefficients. The fact that $r = b = 0$ should not lead you to the immediate conclusion that there is no relationship between x and y. It may be that while there is no linear relationship between the two, there is a very strong nonlinear relationship. Furthermore, the value of our correlation and regression coefficients may be dramatically affected by the presence of one or more extreme scores or outliers in our data. By examining the scatterplot we can determine if we have a nonlinear relationship between x and y or perhaps some extreme scores trying to lead us astray.

KEY TERMS

beta coefficient
bivariate correlation
coefficient of determination (r^2)
conditional distributions
conditional mean of y
correlation
correlation coefficient
curvilinear relationship
epsilon
homoscedasticity
least-squares regression line
linear relationship
negative correlation
nonlinear relationship

ordinary least squares (OLS)
outlier
Pearson correlation coefficient
positive correlation
predicted value of y ($\hat{y}$)
regression coefficient
regression equation
regression line
residual
scattergram
scatterplot
slope
y intercept

KEY FORMULAS

Definitional formula for Pearson's r (eq. 12–1):

$$r = \frac{\sum(x - \overline{X})(y - \overline{Y})}{\sqrt{[\sum(x - \overline{X})^2][\sum(y - \overline{Y})]^2}}$$

Computational formula for Pearson's correlation coefficient (eq. 12–2):

$$r = \frac{n\sum xy - (\sum x)(\sum y)}{\sqrt{[n\sum x^2 - (\sum x)^2][n\sum y^2 - (\sum y)^2]}}$$

Ordinary least-squares regression line for the population (eq. 12–3):

$$y = \alpha + \beta x$$

Sample regression line (eq. 12–4):

$$y = a + bx$$

Definitional formula for the slope coefficient (eq. 12–5):

$$b = \frac{\sum(x - \overline{X})(y - \overline{Y})}{\sum(x - \overline{X})^2}$$

Computational formula for the slope coefficient (eq. 12–6):

$$b = \frac{n \sum xy - (\sum x)(\sum y)}{n \sum x^2 - (\sum x)^2}$$

t statistic for testing null hypothesis about b and r (eq. 12–7):

$$t = r \sqrt{\frac{n - 2}{1 - r^2}}$$

PRACTICE PROBLEMS

1. Interpret the following Pearson correlation coefficients.
   a. An r of $-.55$ between the crime rate in a neighborhood and the median income level per household.
   b. An r of .17 between the number of hours spent working after school and self-reported delinquency.
   c. An r of .74 between the number of prior arrests and length of sentence received for most recent conviction.
   d. An r of $-.12$ between number of jobs held when 15–17 years old and number of arrests as an adult.
   e. An r of $-.03$ between the divorce rate and a state's rate of violent crime.

2. Square each correlation coefficient in problem (1) and interpret the coefficient of determination.

3. Interpret the following regression slope coefficients.
   a. A b of $-.017$ between the dollar fines given by a federal court for white collar crimes and the number of citations for price fixing.
   b. A b of .715 between percent unemployed and property crime rates.
   c. A b of 1,444.53 between the number of years of education and police officers' salaries.

4. In their 1993 research, Grasmick and his colleagues found a moderately strong relationship between their low self-control scale and self-reported acts of crime. Persons with low self-control admitted committing more criminal acts. Let's say you wanted to replicate this study. With the following data for self-control (x) (assume that high scores on this scale mean low self-control) and self-reported delinquency (y), do the following:
   a. Draw a scatterplot of your data points.
   b. Calculate what the slope of the regression line would be.

c. Determine what the y intercept is.

d. What is the predicted number of self-reported offenses ($\hat{y}$) when the self-control scale is equal to 70?

e. Calculate the value of r, and test for its significance with an alpha level of .01.

f. How much of the variance in self-reported delinquency is explained by self-control?

g. What do you conclude about the relationship between self-control and delinquency? Are your findings consistent with those reported by Grasmick et. al.?

x Self-Control	y Self-Reported Delinquency
45	5
63	10
38	2
77	23
82	19
59	7
61	17
88	24
52	14
67	20

5. In their research, Kohfeld and Sprague (1990) found that the faster the police respond to crime (x), the lower the crime rate (y) may be in a given community. You have data below on the average time it takes the police to respond to a call for help by a citizen in a community, as well as that community's rate of crime. With these data, do the following exercises:

a. Draw a scatterplot of your data points.

b. Calculate what the slope of the regression line would be.

c. Determine what the y intercept is.

d. What is the predicted rate of crime ($\hat{y}$) when the police response time is 11 minutes?

e. Calculate the value of r, and determine if it is significantly different from zero with an alpha level of .05.

f. How much of the variance in the rate of crime is explained by police response time?

g. What do you conclude about the relationship between the police response rate and crime?

x Police Response Time in Minutes	y Community Rate of Crime per 1,000
14	82.9
3	23.6
5	42.5
6	39.7
5	63.2
8	51.3
7	58.7
4	44.5
10	61.2
12	73.5

6. A group of citizens has filed a complaint with the police commissioner of a large city. In this complaint they allege that poor neighborhoods receive significantly less protection than more affluent neighborhoods. The commissioner asks you to examine this issue, and you have the following data on the percent of the population in the neighborhood that is on welfare (x) and the number of hours of daily police patrols (y) for a sample of 12 communities in the city. With this data in mind, do the following:

a. Draw a scatterplot of the data points.

b. Calculate what the slope of the regression line would be.

c. Determine what the y intercept is.

d. What is the predicted number of hours of foot patrol ($\hat{y}$) when the percent unemployed is 30 percent?

e. Calculate the value of r, and test its significance with an alpha of .01.

f. How much of the variance in the number of hours of police patrol is explained by the percent of the population on welfare?

g. What do you conclude about the relationship between the percent of the population on welfare and the number of police patrols?

h. Calculate the value of b and r again, but this time leave out the data for community numbers 11 and 12. What do you conclude now? How do you explain these very different findings? Draw a scatterplot of these data and compare it with the one in part (a) above.

x Community Number	y Percent of Population on Welfare (%)	Hours of Daily Police Patrol
1	40	20
2	37	15
3	32	20
4	29	20
5	25	15
6	24	20
7	17	15
8	15	20
9	12	10
10	8	20
11	4	40
12	2	50

SPSS PRACTICE PROBLEMS

1. The substantive and theoretical issues we will explore in these excercises generally can be subsumed under the comparative crime literature. This field of study has been concerned with exploring the extent to which aggregate levels of crime are affected by other aggregate level conditions such as poverty, a culture that legitimates violence, social disorganization, and so on. Research in this area has examined many units of analysis or levels of aggregation, ranging from nations to states, to cities, to counties, and even to zip code areas. The units of analysis for the data we are going to examine are states. The general question we will investigate is, "Is there a relationship between homicide rates within states and indicators of poverty and social disorganization?" The first thing you need to do is bring up the data in the file called STATE2000, which contains many state-level variables for the year 2000. It is a good idea to examine the frequency distribution of the variables we will examine, including MURDER (the total murder rate per 100,000), POPDENS (the population density per square mile), PERRURAL (the percent of the state's population residing in rural areas), and INFMORT (the infant mortality rate per 1,000 live births). Murder will be our dependent variable, and the remaining will be used as independent variables. Click on ANALYZE, then DESCRIPTIVE STATISTICS, and then FREQUENICES, and obtain a frequency distribution for each of these variables along with the statistics of the median, mean, and standard deviation in the STATISTICS box. What do you conclude about the univariate distributions of these variables?

Are there any outliers or severely skewed distributions that you should take note of?

2.   One way to obtain several scatterplots in one picture is by asking for a MATRIX scatterplot under the SCATTER option of the GRAPHS menu. This will take you to a dialogue box that asks you to place all the variables you desire in a MATRIX box. It is a good idea to place the dependent variable first in the list so the first column will display the scatterplots of each of the independent variables with the dependent variable (MURDER). Along the diagonal of the matrix is a scatterplot of each variable with itself—as such, it is usually not displayed. The top and bottom halves of a matrix are mirror images of themselves, as you can see. Thus, it is only necessary to utilize the bottom diagonal of the box. This will give you a scatterplot for each of the possible pairs of variables you listed in the MATRIX box. Interpret each scatterplot of MURDER with each of the independent variables. What do you conclude? Comment on the direction of the relationship that appears in each of the scatterplots. What scatterplot depicts the strongest relationship?

You should have noticed that there was an outlier in almost all of the graphs. This was the District of Columbia. For the exercises below, run all analyses with DC included and then excluded. Note the differences that one simple outlier can produce! You can do this by clicking on DATA, then SELECT CASES, and then IF CONDITION IS SATISFIED. In the box that asks you to specify the condition, type "STATEID NE 9" (since the value for the DC in the STATEID variable is equal to 9, this will exclude DC because it is telling SPSS to select all cases that are not equal ("ne") to 9).

3.   To quantify each of these bivariate relationships with Pearson's correlation coefficient, we can also ask for a matrix that displays the correlation coefficient for each these relationships in a similar manner. Click on ANALYZE, then CORRELATE, and then BIVARIATE. Place all the variables in the variables box and SPSS will produce a matrix of correlations for each combination of variables along with the coefficient's corresponding significance level (a nondirectional two-tailed test is the default). Interpret your results.

4.   Now it's time to determine the OLS regression equation for each of the independent variables and our dependent variable of MURDER. Let's start with determining the linear relationship between MURDER and the population density of each state (POPDENS). Click on ANALYZE, then REGRESSION, and then LINEAR. Place MURDER in the dependent variable box and POPDENS in the independent variable box. What is the regression equation for these data? Interpret the slope coefficient. What is your decision about the null hypothesis that the slope coefficient is equal to zero in the population?

5. Let's determine the linear relationship between MURDER and the percent of the population living in rural areas (PERRURAL). Click on ANALYZE, then REGRESSION, and then LINEAR. Place MURDER in the dependent variable box and PERRURAL in the independent variable box. What is the regression equation for these data? Interpret the slope coefficient. What is your decision about the null hypothesis that the slope coefficient is equal to zero in the population?

6. Infant mortality rates often have been used as an indicator of economic deprivation in the literature. Let's determine the linear relationship between MURDER and the infant mortality rate in states (INFMORT). Click on ANALYZE, then REGRESSION, and then LINEAR. Place MURDER in the dependent variable box and INFMORT in the independent variable box. What is the regression equation for these data? Interpret the slope coefficient. What is your decision about the null hypothesis that the slope coefficient is equal to zero in the population?

13

Controlling
for a Third Variable:
Multiple Regression
and Partial Correlation

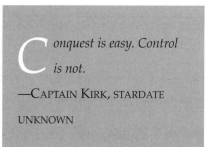

C onquest is easy. Control is not.

—CAPTAIN KIRK, STARDATE

UNKNOWN

U p to this point in the book, we have been examining the relationship that one independent variable has with a dependent variable. It is rarely the case, however, that one independent variable sufficiently explains the dependent variable, because in reality there are usually several factors that jointly influence the dependent variable. We need, therefore, to build on our knowledge of the bivariate regression model by adding more independent variables. When we examine the effect of more than one independent variable on a dependent variable, we employ what is called a *multivariate regression model*. As the name implies, in the *multi*variate model we have more than one independent variable whose effects on the dependent variable we wish to gauge. An implicit assumption of the multivariate regression model, therefore, is that there is more than one variable that explains the dependent variable. The corresponding correlation coefficient is called the *partial correlation coefficient*. In this chapter, we will introduce you to some of the most important features of the multivariate regression model and partial correlation.

CONTROLLING FOR OTHER IMPORTANT VARIABLES TO DETERMINE CAUSATION

Identifying causes of phenomena—figuring out *why* things happen—is the goal of most criminological research. Unfortunately, valid explanations for the causes of things, including crime, do not come easily. A **causal effect** is the finding that change in one variable leads to change in another variable, *ceteris paribus* (i.e., other things being equal). Establishing the existence of a causal effect between an independent and a dependent variable is often termed *causal validity*. The language we use in criminology and criminal justice often implies causality. For example, if a research study finds that men arrested for assaulting their intimate partners are less likely to assault their partners in the future compared to men who assault their partners and are not arrested, the researcher may conclude that arrest is causally related to this decrease in the likelihood of future violence. But establishing a **causal relationship** is actually very difficult. Specifically, we need to consider three criteria for deciding whether a causal connection exists:

1. Empirical association.
2. Appropriate time order.
3. Nonspuriousness.

The first criterion, demonstrating that there is a statistical association, is generally the easiest to demonstrate. The second and third are the most difficult. Establishing the second criterion, that the independent variable did indeed occur prior to the dependent variable, involves the research design. For example, if a researcher was trying to determine the effects of watching media violence on actual violent behavior, she would have to set up a study to monitor the behavior of study participants after they observed media violence, thereby establishing the correct time order of the independent and dependent variables. For a detailed discussion of research designs, of course, you should seek out a research methods text.

The third criterion of nonspuriousness, however, is inextricably related to the subject matter of this chapter. **Nonspuriousness** between two variables means that the relationship between them is not actually caused by a third factor that may be related to them both. When a third variable, called an extraneous variable, causes the original relationship between x and y, it is said to have created a spurious relationship between the independent and the dependent variable. Most often in criminological research, we use statistical control to satisfy the criterion of nonspuriousness. One technique used to statistically control the effects of other variables is multiple regression. Before we move on to this more advanced technique, however, we want to illustrate the concept of statistical control with a simpler to understand partial crosstabulation table.

Illustrating Statistical Control with Partial Tables

Case Study: Boot Camps and Recidivism   The top panel of Figure 13–1 depicts data from a hypothetical study examining the relationship between attending a boot camp prison (a highly regimented, discipline-focused correctional program) and the likelihood of committing crimes after prison (recidivism). As you can see, the 2 x 2 table reveals that prisoners who attend boot camp are less likely to recidivate (47 percent) compared to those who do not attend boot camp (55 percent). The bottom panel of Figure 13–1, however, depicts this same relationship between attending boot camp and recidivism

All Prisoners, $n = 350$

	Attended Boot Camp	Did Not Attend Boot Camp
Recidivated	75 47%	105 55%
Did not Recidivate	85 53%	85 44%
	160	190

	Female Prisoners, $n = 150$		Male Prisoners, $n = 200$	
	Attended Boot Camp	Did Not Attend Boot Camp	Attended Boot Camp	Did Not Attend Boot Camp
Recidivated	40 40%	20 40%	60 60%	90 60%
Did not Recidivate	60 60%	30 60%	20 40%	60 40%
	100	50	50	150

Figure 13–1   Data from a hypothetical study examining the relationship between attending a boot camp prison and the likelihood of committing crimes after prison.

while holding constant the offender's gender. This bottom table is referred to as a partial cross-tabs table—it examines the relationship between boot camp attendance and recidivism separately for males and females. When gender is held constant, a much different picture emerges. The original relationship between recidivism and boot camp attendance is found to be spurious. Attending boot camp just appears to reduce recidivism because females are more likely to attend boot camp and are less likely to commit crimes after prison, regardless of whether they attend boot camp or a regular correctional facility.

This illustrates the beauty of statistical control. If the original bivariate relationship between an independent variable and a dependent variable still holds even after controlling for other important variables, we can have more confidence that these variables may be causally related. This is exactly what the multivariate regression equation does.

THE MULTIPLE REGRESSION EQUATION

As we suggested above, the **multiple regression equation** (or model) is simply a straightforward extension of the bivariate regression model. One of the most important differences between the bivariate and multiple regression models is that the latter has more than one independent variable. In the case of multiple regression, we aim to estimate the effect of several independent variables on a dependent variable. Given that there are several independent variables, there will be more than one slope coefficient to estimate. Formally, the multiple regression model specifies the dependent variable (y) as being a linear function of more than one independent variable (x_1, x_2, and so on) plus an error term that encompasses various omitted factors:

$$y = \alpha + \beta_1 x_1 + \beta_2 x_2 + \ldots \beta_k x_k + \varepsilon \tag{13-1}$$

where

k = the number of independent variables, and
ε = the error term.

There are several similarities between this model and the bivariate regression model of the previous chapter. The α and β are population parameters that are estimated by sample data. The corresponding sample estimates are a and b. As before, the multivariate regression equation estimates the "best-fitting" regression line to the data. It is best-fitting according to the same principle of least squares—it minimizes the sum of the squared deviations between the predicted y values and the observed y values. Similar to the bivariate case, then, the goal of multiple regression is to provide the best-fitting line between a continuous dependent variable and several continuous independent variables.

In spite of these similarities, however, the multivariate regression model in equation 13–1 contains some new concepts, as well as different meanings for some old concepts. The multivariate regression model from sample data is represented as:

$$y = a + b_1 x_1 + b_2 x_2 + \ldots b_k x_k + \varepsilon$$

(13–2)

The intercept (a) in this multivariate equation is the predicted value of y when all independent variables equal zero. The interpretation of the slope coefficient (b), which is identified by subscripts, is somewhat different from the bivariate case. Technically, slope coefficients estimated with multiple regression equations are referred to as **partial slope coefficients** or **partial regression coefficients.** The first slope coefficient in the equation above, b_1, is the partial slope of the linear relationship between the first independent variable and the dependent variable, y. The second slope coefficient, b_2, is the partial slope of the linear relationship between the second independent variable and y. If you were using five independent variables to predict a dependent variable, there would be five partial slope coefficients, each denoted by its subscript (b_1, b_2, b_3, b_4, b_5).

Each slope coefficient indicates the change in the mean of the y variable associated with a 1 unit change in a given independent variable, when all other independent variables in the model are held constant. This last component of the interpretation, "when all other independent variables are held constant," is important. It is this statistical control that allows us to separate the effect of one independent variable from the effects of other independent variables. In other words, the partial slope coefficient measures the effect of one independent variable on the dependent variable when the effect of all the other independent variables on the dependent variable have been considered (e.g., statistically controlled).

The final term in the multiple regression equation is the error term, ϵ. As in the bivariate model, the error component in the multiple regression model reflects things like measurement error and explanatory variables that are excluded from the model. We should note that the order in which the independent variables are listed does not matter in a regular multiple regression analysis.[1] What does matter are the potential explanatory variables that are explicitly included in the model as x variables and that are left out and implicitly included in the error term.

The practice of good regression analysis consists of including in the model those explanatory variables that are most strongly related to the dependent variable and unrelated to one another. Although the multiple regression equation above can be estimated using a large number of independent variables, for ease of presentation, in this chapter we will concentrate on equations utilizing only two independent variables. The extension to more than two independent variables is relatively straightforward, and the interested reader is encouraged to examine other sources.[2]

The assumptions of the multiple regression model are identical to those in the one independent variable case, except for the addition of one new assumption (the final assumption in the following list):

1. The data have been randomly selected.
2. All populations are normally distributed.
3. The data are continuous, and they are measured at the interval or ratio level.
4. The nature of the relationship between the dependent variable and each of the independent variables is linear.
5. The error term (ϵ) is independent of and therefore uncorrelated with each of the independent or x variables, it is normally distributed, and it has an expected value of zero and constant variance across all levels of x (no homoscedasticity).
6. The independent variables are independent of or uncorrelated with one another. Having independent variables that are highly correlated is referred to as the problem of **multicollinearity.**

The assumption in point (6), that the independent variables are independent of or uncorrelated with one another, is a very important new assumption in the multivariate regression model. As we noted in the above discussion, good regression analysis involves selecting independent variables that are strongly related to the dependent variable *and weakly related or unrelated to each other.* This problem did not arise in the case of one independent variable, but it will be a constant concern as we add to the list of independent variables in our model. Why is it so important that the independent variables be uncorrelated with one another?

To answer this question, think carefully about what we want to do in our multiple regression analysis. We have a dependent variable that we are trying to explain. We have at least two independent variables that may explain this dependent variable. What we would like to know from our multiple regression analysis is two important things: (1) How much of the variance in the dependent variable are we explaining by our two independent variables together? and (2) How much of this combined explained variance can we say is uniquely due to each of the independent variables? The first question asks how much variance we can explain in the dependent variable. The second asks how much of what we explain is due to the unique contribution of each of our independent variables. It is this second question that is difficult to answer when the independent variables are correlated.

Think of two independent variables as lying on a continuum from being completely unique variables having nothing in common to being identical to one another and having everything in common. At one end of this continuum are two variables that are completely unique. These variables are not correlated; that is, the correlation between them is zero ($r = 0$). When two variables are correlated, however, it means that they share something in common. The lower the correlation, the more they are unique and the less they have in common. The higher the correlation, however, the less unique they are and the more they have in common. At the other end of the continuum, the two variables are indistinguishable, and have nothing unique. Therefore, one variable may be used in place of the other because they are essentially the same variable. In this extreme, the two independent variables are perfectly correlated ($r = 1.0$).

When two independent variables are completely uncorrelated, we are able to separate their combined explained variance of the dependent variable into separate and unique components. For example, we can specify that of the 60 percent of explained variance in the dependent variable (y), two-thirds of that is due to x_1 and the other one-third is due to x_2. As two independent variables become correlated, however, some of the explained variance to the dependent variable cannot be uniquely attributed to one or the other variable. That is, some of the explained variance cannot be said to be due to x_1 or x_2, but can only be said to be due to their shared influence. The stronger the correlation between the two independent variables, the less of the explained variance we can attribute to the unique effect of each variable, and the more we must attribute to the explained variance that they share. When the two variables are very highly correlated, we can contribute no unique explained variance to them, and all of the explained variance in the dependent variable is shared between the two.

When the independent variables in a regression equation are correlated with one another, they are said to be *collinear*. This means that there is a linear relationship among the independent variables. The problem of multicollinearity is something you want to avoid in multiple regression analysis. As we stated earlier, you want your independent variables to be strongly correlated with the dependent variable, but uncorrelated with each other.

You can detect problems of multicollinearity in your data. If you have only two independent variables, the easiest way to identify multicollinearity is to examine the correlation between them. The higher the correlation, the greater the problem of multicollinearity. Although this is not a "hard and fast" rule, be suspicious of multicollinearity when the correlation between two independent variables is .70 or higher. With more than two independent variables, the detection of multicollinearity becomes more of a problem. While this topic is beyond the scope of this text, one simple way to detect multicollinearity in such cases is to inspect the standard error of your regression coefficients. Multicollinearity will frequently manifest itself in high standard errors for two or more coefficients. If one variable is dropped from the model and the standard error of the other is substantially decreased, multicollinearity will frequently be the source. Another way to detect multicollinearity is to regress each independent variable on the other independent variables. In this analysis each independent variable becomes the dependent variable and the other independent variables serve as independent variables for it. If multicollinearity is not a problem, the amount of explained variance will be quite low.

We may have gotten a little ahead of ourselves with this detailed discussion of multicollinearity. It is important, however, for you to fully understand this very important assumption of the multiple regression model. Now let's return to the multiple regression model described in equation 13–2 and consider some data to illustrate and give meaning to the concepts we have discussed thus far.

Predicting Delinquency

Tables 13–1 through 13–3 present hypothetical data from a random survey of 23 high school students who were queried on a number of factors, including their self-reported delinquent activity (e.g., drinking, taking other drugs, truancy, stealing, vandalizing property), their attachment to their families (e.g., time spent with family, parents/guardians knowing respondent's whereabouts, perceived closeness to parents/guardians and siblings), and their age. Two indexes were created measuring students' self-reported delinquency and family attachments, which can be assumed to be measured at the interval/ratio level of measurement.

From these data, we are going to estimate the effect that both age and family attachments have on rates of delinquency. For the sake of this example, let's say we believe that age will be positively related to delinquency and that family attachments will be negatively related to delinquency. Thus, older students will tend to have higher delinquency scores, while those who are more strongly attached to their families will tend to have lower rates of delinquency. In this example, delinquency is our dependent variable (y), while age (x_1) and family attachments (x_2) are our two independent variables. It is also probably true that age and family attachments are not strongly correlated; thus, we do not expect multicollinearity to be a problem. Our two-variable regression model, then, looks like the following:

$$\text{Delinquency} = a + b_1\,(\text{age}) + b_2\,(\text{family attachments}) + \varepsilon$$

The mean, the standard deviation, and the bivariate correlation coefficients are presented at the bottom of each table.

The first step we need to take in computing our multiple regression equation is to calculate each partial slope. The formula used for calculating partial slope coefficients is presented below.

$$b_1 = \left(\frac{s_y}{s_{x_1}}\right)\left(\frac{r_{yx_1} - (r_{yx_2})(r_{x_1x_2})}{1 - r^2_{x_1x_2}}\right) \qquad \textbf{(13–3)}$$

$$b_2 = \left(\frac{s_y}{s_{x_2}}\right)\left(\frac{r_{yx_2} - (r_{yx_1})(r_{x_1x_2})}{1 - r^2_{x_1x_2}}\right) \qquad \textbf{(13–4)}$$

TABLE 13–1

Calculations Necessary to Compute the Partial Slope Coefficient between Delinquency and Age, n = 23

Delinquency y	Age x_1	y^2	x_1^2	x_1y
80	17	6,400	289	1,360
60	15	3,600	225	900
50	14	2,500	196	700
70	17	4,900	289	1,190
10	13	100	169	130
15	13	225	169	195
20	14	400	196	280
5	13	25	169	65
70	13	4,900	169	910
55	14	3,025	196	770
40	15	1,600	225	600
35	16	1,225	256	560
10	17	100	289	170
15	16	225	256	240
10	14	100	196	140
15	16	225	256	240
0	14	0	196	0
0	13	0	169	0
20	14	400	196	280
0	13	0	169	0
20	14	400	196	280
45	16	2,025	256	720
50	17	2,500	289	850
Totals:				
695	338	34,875	5,016	10,580

$$\overline{X}_{x_1} = 14.7$$

$$\overline{Y} = 30.22$$

$$s_{x_1} = 1.49$$

$$s_y = 25.11$$

$$r_{yx_1} = .445$$

$$r_{x_1x_2} = -.366$$

TABLE 13–2

Calculations Necessary to Compute the Partial Slope Coefficient between Delinquency and Family Attachments, $n = 23$

Delinquency y	Family Attachments x_2	y^2	x_2^2	x_2y
80	10	6,400	100	800
60	20	3,600	400	1,200
50	25	2,500	625	1,250
70	15	4,900	225	1,050
10	35	100	1,225	350
15	30	225	900	450
20	28	400	784	560
5	40	25	1,600	200
70	15	4,900	225	1,050
55	20	3,025	400	1,100
40	25	1,600	625	1,000
35	20	1,225	400	700
10	30	100	900	300
15	25	225	625	375
10	20	100	400	200
15	25	225	625	375
0	25	0	625	0
0	35	0	1,225	0
20	20	400	400	400
0	20	0	400	0
20	30	400	900	600
45	30	2,025	900	1,350
50	25	2,500	625	1,250
Totals:				
695	568	34,875	15,134	14,560

$$\overline{X}_{x_2} = 24.69$$

$$\overline{Y} = 30.22$$

$$s_{x_2} = 7.09$$

$$s_y = 25.11$$

$$r_{yx_2} = -.664$$

$$r_{x_1x_2} = -.366$$

$$r_{yx_2 \cdot x_1} = -.6017$$

TABLE 13–3

Calculations Necessary to Compute the Partial Slope Coefficient between Delinquency and Age and Deliquency and Family Attachments, $n = 23$

Age x_1	Family Attachments x_2	x_1^2	x_2^2	$x_1 x_2$
17	10	289	100	170
15	20	225	400	300
14	25	196	625	350
17	15	289	225	255
13	35	169	1,225	455
13	30	169	900	390
14	28	196	784	392
13	40	169	1,600	520
13	15	169	225	195
14	20	196	400	280
15	25	225	625	375
16	20	256	400	320
17	30	289	900	510
16	25	256	625	400
14	20	196	400	280
16	25	256	625	400
14	25	196	625	350
13	35	169	1,225	455
14	20	196	400	280
13	20	169	400	260
14	30	196	900	420
16	30	256	900	480
17	25	289	625	425
Totals:				
338	568	5,016	15,134	8,262

$$\overline{X}_{x_1} = 14.7$$

$$\overline{Y} = 30.22$$

$$s_{x_1} = 1.49$$

$$s_y = 25.11$$

$$r_{yx_1} = .445$$

$$r_{x_1 x_2} = -.366$$

$$r_{yx_1 \cdot x_2} = .29$$

where

b_1 = the partial slope of x_1 on y,

b_2 = the partial slope of x_2 on y,

s_y = the standard deviation of y,

s_1 = the standard deviation of the first independent variable (x_1),

s_2 = the standard deviation of the second independent variable (x_2),

r_{yx_1} = the bivariate correlation between y and x_1,

r_{yx_2} = the bivariate correlation between y and x_2, and

$r_{x_1y_2}$ = the bivariate correlation between x_1 and x_2.

Notice that you not only need the bivariate correlation coefficient between the independent variable and each of the dependent variables, you also need the bivariate correlation between the two independent variables. That is, to obtain a partial slope coefficient for each independent variable, the equation takes into account the bivariate relationship between that variable and the dependent variable (r_{yx_1}), between the other independent variable and the dependent variable (r_{yx_2}), and between both independent variables ($r_{x_1x_2}$). In our examples of the multiple regression model, we will go through the calculations of each component of the partial slope coefficient, but we will provide you with the bivariate correlation coefficients.

As can be seen in the tables, the bivariate correlation coefficients indicate that the relationship between age and delinquency (Table 13–1) is positive ($r = .445$) and the relationship between family attachments and delinquency (Table 13–2) is negative ($r = -.664$). In addition, age and family attachments also are negatively related to each other ($r_{x_1x_2} = -.366$). These correlation coefficients suggest that older students tend to have higher rates delinquency, but students with high rates of family attachments tend to have lower rates of delinquency. The correlation between our two independent variables ($r = -.366$) is not very high, so we do not have to worry about the problem of multicollinearity.

With these correlation coefficients, together with the standard deviation of each of the variables and formulas 13–3 and 13–4, we can calculate for each independent variable the partial slope coefficient. From these partial slope coefficients we will be able to ascertain the effect of each independent variable on the dependent variable while holding the other independent variable constant. These calculations are shown below:

Partial slope coefficient for the effect of age on delinquency:

$$b_1 = \left(\frac{25.11}{1.49}\right)\left(\frac{.445 - (-.664)(-.366)}{1 - (-.366)^2}\right)$$

$$= (16.85)\left(\frac{.445 - .243}{1 - .133}\right)$$

$$= (16.85)\left(\frac{.202}{.867}\right)$$

$$= (16.85)(.232)$$

$$= 3.9$$

Partial slope coefficient for the effect of family attachments on delinquency:

$$b_2 = \left(\frac{25.11}{7.09}\right)\left(\frac{-.664 - (-.445)(-.366)}{1 - (-.366)^2}\right)$$

$$= (3.54)\left(\frac{-.664 - .16}{1 - .133}\right)$$

$$= (3.54)\left(\frac{-.504}{.867}\right)$$

$$= (3.54)(-.58)$$

$$= -2.05$$

The partial slope coefficient for the effect of age on delinquency is $b_1 = 3.9$. This indicates that, on average, with every 1 unit increase in age, delinquency scores increase by 3.9 units, while simultaneously holding constant an individual's attachments to family. Similarly, the partial slope coefficient for the effect of family attachments on delinquency scores is $b_2 = -2.05$. This indicates that, on average, for every 1 unit increase in an individual's family attachment scores, there is a 2.05 unit decrease in delinquency scores, while simultaneously holding constant an individual's age.

Now that we have obtained the partial slopes, b_1 and b_2, for the independent variables of age and family attachments, we can compute the final unknown element in the least-squares regression equation, the intercept (a). This is done in the same way we obtained the intercept in the bivariate regression equation—by substituting the mean of the dependent variable ($\overline{Y}$) and the means of the two independent variables ($\overline{X}_1$ and $\overline{X}_2$) into the equation below and solving for a:

$$a = \overline{Y} - b_1\overline{X}_1 - b_2\overline{X}_2$$

$$= 30.22 - 3.9(14.7) - -2.05(24.69)$$

$$= 30.22 - (57.33) - (-50.61)$$

$$= 23.1$$

The intercept value in the equation above indicates that when both independent variables are equal to zero, the average value of y will be equal to 23.1. Now that we have solved for the intercept (a) and both partial regression slopes, our multiple regression equation for delinquency can now be expressed as shown on the next page:

$$\hat{y} = a + b_1 x_1 + b_2 x_2$$

$$= 23.1 + 3.9(x_1) + -2.05(x_2)$$

$$= 23.1 + 3.9(\text{age}) + -2.05(\text{family attachment})$$

As was the case with the bivariate regression equation we examined in the last chapter, this least-squares multiple regression equation provides us with the best-fitting line to our data. However, we can no longer represent the equation graphically with a simple straight line fitted to a two-dimensional (X, Y) scattergram. In a two independent variable multiple regression, we have to use our imagination to visualize the fitting of a regression plane to a three-dimensional scatter of points that is defined by each of the coefficients (a, b_1, b_2). As you can imagine, this exercise in imagery becomes even more complex as more independent variables are brought into the equation. With k independent variables, the regression equation is represented by a plane in k-dimensional space.

As was true for the bivariate equation, we can use this multivariate equation to predict scores on our dependent variable, delinquency, from scores on the independent variables of age and family attachments. For example, our best prediction of a delinquency score $(\hat{y})$ for an 18-year-old with a score on the family attachment index of 15 would be obtained by substituting these two x values into the least-squares regression formula as shown below:

$$\hat{y} = a + b_1 x_1 + b_2 x_2$$

$$= 23.1 + 3.9(18) + -2.05(15)$$

$$= 23.1 + 70.2 + -30.75$$

$$= 62.55$$

Our multiple regression equation predicts that an 18-year-old adolescent with a score on the family attachment index of 15 (relatively low) would have a predicted delinquency score of 62.55. Let's predict what the delinquency score would be for a younger student (13) with relatively strong attachments to his family (45). Using our regression equation, the predicted delinquency score would be:

$$\hat{y} = 23.1 + 3.9(13) + -2.05(45)$$

$$= 23.1 + 50.7 + -92.25$$

$$= -18.45$$

The predicted delinquency score for a student with these characteristics would, then, be 18.45, a relatively low delinquency score. In reality, of course, it is not possible to get a negative score since the lowest score is equal to zero.

As we found in the above example, the slope coefficient for age on delinquency scores was 3.9 while holding family attachments constant, and the slope coefficient for family attachments on delinquency scores was -2.05 while holding age constant. We would caution you not to conclude from this that the effect of age on delinquency is almost twice as great as the effect of family attachments. We cannot conclude on the basis of the size of these partial slope coefficients that age is a more important (more powerful) explanatory variable than family attachments when explaining delinquency. *In a multiple regression analysis, you cannot determine which independent variable has the strongest effect on the dependent variable by comparing partial slope coefficients.*

Remember from our discussion in the last chapter that the slope coefficient is measured in terms of the unit of measurement of the x variable—that a 1 unit change in x produces a b change in the y variable. The size of the partial slope coefficient, then, reflects the underlying units of measurement. As a result of this, the magnitude of the slope coefficient is not a good indicator of the strength of the variable.

In the bivariate model we solved this problem by calculating a standardized coefficient that was not dependent upon the independent variable's unit of measurement, the correlation coefficient. A similar standardized coefficient in multiple regression is called the *standardized partial slope* or *beta weight* (not to be confused with the beta, the population parameter for the slope coefficient). We will examine beta weights next.

BETA WEIGHTS

In order to compare the effects of two independent variables on a dependent variable, it is necessary to remove differences in the relative magnitudes of the slopes that are solely the function of differences in the units of measurement (e.g., dollars compared to cents, years compared to months, and so on). One way of doing this is to convert all of the variables in the equation to a common scale. For example, we could standardize all of our original variable distributions by converting our scores on the independent variables into z scores. If we did this, each variable distribution would have a mean of zero and a standard deviation of 1. Comparisons across independent variables, then, would be much more meaningful since differences in size would reflect differences in effect and not the underlying unit of measurement.

To obtain slope coefficients in this way, we first would have to convert all of our original data points for each variable into z scores, and then recompute the partial slopes and the Y intercept from these new z distributions. This would not only require a great deal of work, we would also lose the value of the original partial slope coefficient that was specific to each variable's original measurement unit. There is a way, however, to easily compute a standardized partial slope coefficient (a beta weight) from the obtained partial slope coefficient. If we do this, we will have two partial slope coefficients for each independent variable, one standardized (the beta weight) and one in the original measurement scale.

The formulas used to obtain **standardized partial slopes** or **beta weights,** symbolized b^*, from a multiple regression equation with two independent variables are shown on the next page:

$$b^*_{x_1} = b_{x_1}\left(\frac{s_{x_1}}{s_y}\right) \qquad\qquad (13\text{--}5)$$

$$b^*_{x_2} = b_{x_2}\left(\frac{s_{x_2}}{s_y}\right) \qquad\qquad (13\text{--}6)$$

As the formulas indicate, the computation of the beta weight involves multiplying the partial slope coefficient (b_1) obtained for an independent variable by the ratio of the standard deviation of that variable (s_{x_1}) to the standard deviation of the dependent variable (s_y). The interpretation of a beta weight is relatively straightforward. Like a partial slope coefficient, beta coefficients can be either positive or negative. A positive beta coefficient indicates a positive linear relationship between the independent and the dependent variable, while a negative beta weight indicates a negative relationship. The standardized partial slope will always have the same sign as the unstandardized slope. Similar to the interpretation of a correlation coefficient, the larger the beta weight, the stronger the relationship between the independent and the dependent variable. More specifically, the beta weights show the expected change in a standardized score on the dependent variable for a 1 unit change in a standardized score of the independent variable, while holding constant the other independent variable. If we want to know the *relative importance* of two variables, we can, then, compare the magnitude of their respective beta weights. The variable with the larger beta weight (absolute value) has the stronger effect on the dependent variable.

Let's go through an example using the delinquency data. Recall that the partial slope coefficient for age (b_1) was equal to 3.9 and the partial slope coefficient for family attachments (b_2) was equal to -2.05. The standard deviations for age and family attachments are 1.49 and 7.09, respectively (see Tables 13–1 and 13–2). To determine the beta weights for each independent variable, we simply plug these values into equations 13–5 and 13–6, as shown below:

$$b^*_{x_1} = (3.9)\left(\frac{1.49}{25.11}\right)$$

$$= .23$$

$$b^*_{x_2} = (-2.05)\left(\frac{7.09}{25.11}\right)$$

$$= -.579$$

Using these beta weights, we can compare the effect of one independent variable on the dependent variable with the effect of the other, without our comparison being distorted by a variable's unit of measurement. From the beta weights displayed above, we can immediately ascertain that family attachments have a much stronger relationship with delinquency ($b^*x_2 = -.579$) than does age ($b^*x_1 = -.23$). You should now see that even though the partial slope coefficient for the effect of age ($bx_1 = 3.9$) was almost twice as large as that for family attachments ($bx_2 = -2.05$), this was due to the different units of measurement for the two variables. When their standardized coefficients are examined, we can see that the variable that is more important in explaining delinquency is family attachment scores.

There are two other ways of assessing the relative importance of independent variables in a multiple regression analysis. One method with which you are already familiar from our treatment of bivariate regression is to calculate correlation coefficients and coefficients of determination. The second way is to compare the absolute value of the magnitude of the obtained t value for each independent variable from a hypothesis test that the slope coefficient is equal to zero. We will explore the multivariate equivalent of correlation coefficients and coefficients of determination in the next section, and then we will examine hypothesis tests for the significance of partial slope coefficients in the section following that.

PARTIAL CORRELATION COEFFICIENTS

Another way of addressing the relative effects of our independent variables is to compute *partial correlation coefficients.* With partial correlation coefficients, we also can compute the *multiple coefficient of determination (R^2).* Both of these coefficients allow us to investigate the question of the relative importance of independent variables, although they do so in somewhat different ways. The interpretation of the partial correlation coefficient and multiple coefficient of determination, however, is analogous to their bivariate equivalents, so you should have no problem with this section. We will begin our discussion with the partial correlation coefficient.

The magnitude of a **partial correlation coefficient** indicates the correlation or strength of the relationship between a given independent variable and the dependent variable when the linear effect of another independent variable is held constant or removed. In the example we are currently using, the partial correlation between age and delinquency would measure the relationship between these two variables when the linear effect of family attachments has been removed.

In referring to the partial correlation coefficient, we will continue with the same subscripts we have used throughout this chapter, with one additional twist. We will use the partial correlation symbol $r_{yx_1 \cdot x_2}$ to show the correlation between the dependent variable (y) and the first independent variable (x_1), while controlling for the second independent variable (x_2). The subscript to the right of the dot indicates the variable whose effect is being controlled. The formulas used to obtain partial correlation coefficients for two independent variables with a dependent variable are shown on the next page:

$$r_{yx_1 \cdot x_2} = \frac{r_{yx_1} - (r_{yx_2})(r_{x_1 x_2})}{\sqrt{1 - r^2_{yx_2}}\sqrt{1 - r^2_{x_1 x_2}}} \qquad (13\text{–}7)$$

$$r_{yx_2 \cdot x_1} = \frac{r_{yx_2} - (r_{yx_1})(r_{x_1 x_2})}{\sqrt{1 - r^2_{yx_1}}\sqrt{1 - r^2_{x_1 x_2}}} \qquad (13\text{–}8)$$

We now have all the values we need to calculate these coefficients for our delinquency data. Recall that the bivariate correlation between age and delinquency was (r_{yx_1} = .445), the correlation between family attachments and delinquency was (r_{yx_2} = −.664), and the correlation between age and family attachments was ($r_{y_1 x_2}$ = −.366). With this information, we can compute the partial correlation coefficients for both independent variables as shown below:

Partial correlation coefficient for age and delinquency controlling for family attachments:

$$r_{x_1 y \cdot x_2} = \frac{.445 - (-.664)(-.366)}{\sqrt{1 - (-.664)^2}\sqrt{1 - (-.366)^2}}$$

$$= .29$$

Partial correlation coefficient for family attachments and delinquency controlling for age:

$$r_{yx_1 \cdot x_2} = \frac{-.664 - (.445)(-.366)}{\sqrt{1 - (.445)^2}\sqrt{1 - (-.366)^2}}$$

$$= -.601$$

The partial correlation between age and delinquency is .29, while controlling for family attachments. The partial correlation between family attachments and delinquency is −.601, while controlling for age. Since the partial correlation for family attachments (−.601) is greater than the partial correlation for age (.29), family attachments has the stronger effect on a student's involvement in delinquent behavior. This is consistent with our conclusion when we used beta weights. In general, the relative explanatory power of two independent variables can be determined by comparing their partial correlation coefficients. The variable with the largest partial correlation coefficient has the strongest relationship with the dependent variable.

We should note here that the reason why the partial correlation coefficients for both independent variables are less than their respective bivariate correlations is that, since the two independent variables are themselves positively correlated ($r_{y_1 x_2}$ = −.366), they share a certain amount of the total explanatory power or explained variance. In other words, in this particular regression model, there are four sources that explain delinquency:

1. That which is due uniquely to the effect of age.
2. That which is due uniquely to the effect of family attachments.

3. That which is due to the *joint effect* of age and family attachments.

4. That which is due to all other factors not explicitly included in the model but whose effect is manifested through the error term (ϵ).

What the partial correlation (and partial slope) coefficients reflect is the unique effect of each independent variable on the dependent variable. That is, they reveal the effect of each independent variable that is not shared with the other independent variable. The greater the correlation between the two independent variables $(r_{x_1 x_2})$, the weaker the first two sources and the stronger the joint effect.

Multiple Coefficient of Determination, R^2

Another way to disentangle the separate effects of the independent variables on the dependent variable is to compute the increase in the amount of explained variance when each independent variable is separately added to the regression model. With two independent variables, this requires comparing the amount of variation in the dependent variable explained by both independent variables subtracted by the amount of variance explained by each independent variable when it alone is added to the model. This gives you the amount of variance that is explained uniquely by that independent variable ($R^2_{\text{Full}} - R^2_{\text{Reduced}}$).

To do this, of course, requires knowing how much of the variance in the dependent variable is explained by both independent variables together. We obtain this value by computing what is termed the **multiple coefficient of determination,** symbolized by a capital R^2 to differentiate it from the bivariate coefficient of determination r^2. The multiple coefficient of determination indicates the proportion of variance in the dependent variable that is explained by both independent variables combined. You might think of the multiple coefficient of determination as an indicator of how well your model fits the data, in terms of the combined ability of the independent variables to explain the dependent variable. The range of R^2 is from zero percent, which indicates that the independent variables explain no variance in the dependent variable, to a maximum of 100 percent, which indicates that the independent variables explain all of the variance. As the independent variables explain a larger amount of the variance (i.e., as R^2 approaches 100 percent), the estimated regression model is providing a better fit to the data.

To obtain the multiple coefficient of determination, we cannot simply add together the separate bivariate coefficients of determination. Why? Because the independent variables are also correlated with each other. If the independent variables in a multiple regression equation are correlated, the estimated value of R^2 reflects both the amount of variance that each variable uniquely explains and that which the variables share through their joint correlation. As a result, there will be a joint effect on the dependent variable that cannot be attributed to one variable alone. Again, the amount of this joint effect is a function of the extent to which the two independent variables are correlated themselves.

For a two-independent variable regression equation, the multiple coefficient of determination is found with the following formula:

$$R^2 = r^2_{yx_1} + (r^2_{yx_2 \cdot x_1})(1 - r^2_{yx_1})$$ **(13–9)**

where

R^2 = the multiple coefficient of determination.

$r^2_{yx_1}$ = the bivariate correlation between X_1 and Y, the quantity squared.

$r^2_{yx_2 \cdot x_1}$ = the partial correlation of X_2 and y while controlling for X_1, the quantity squared.

$r^2_{yx_1}$ = the bivariate correlation between X_1 and Y, the quantity squared.

Before we explain the different components of this formula, let's compute the multiple coefficient of determination with our delinquency data. We have already calculated all of the values we need, so we can simply plug them into formula 13–9, as shown below:

$$R^2 = (.445)^2 + (-.601)^2[1 - (.445)^2]$$

$$= (.198) + (.36)(.802)$$

$$= (.198) + .288$$

$$= .488$$

This R^2 indicates the proportion of variance explained in the dependent variable by both independent variables in the regression equation. The obtained R^2 of .488 indicates that combined, age and family attachment scores together explain almost 49 percent of the variation in delinquency scores.

Calculating Change in R^2

How can we disentangle the contribution of each independent variable to this total explained variance? Notice what the formula for the multiple coefficient of determination (formula 13–9) does. It first lets one independent variable do all the explaining in the dependent variable that it can. That is the first expression after the equals sign $(r^2_{yx_1})$. The value of this term is simply the square of the bivariate correlation coefficient between the first independent variable and the dependent variable. After the first independent variable has done all of the explaining that it can, the second variable is then given the chance to explain what it can of the remaining unexplained variation. That is the second term in the expression. This term is the squared partial correlation coefficient between the second independent variable and the dependent variable (controlling for the first independent variable), multiplied by the proportion of variance that the first variable cannot explain:

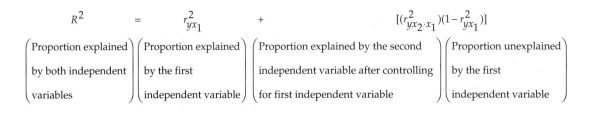

The magnitude of the R^2 will be the same no matter which of the two independent variables appears first. The following two formulas will, then, produce identical results:

$$R^2 = r^1_{yx_1} + (r^2_{yx_2 \cdot x_1})(1 - r^2_{yx_1})$$

and

$$R^2 = r^2_{yx_2} + (r^2_{yx_1 \cdot x_2})(1 - r^2_{yx_2})$$

In the first formula above we begin by letting x_1 explain all the variance it can in the dependent variable, and then we let x_2 explain what it can of the remaining variance. In the second formula, we first let x_2 do all the explaining it can in the dependent variable, and then we let x_1 explain what remains. The combined explanatory power of the two variables will always be the same. However, while the value of R^2 will be the same no matter which variable is considered first, the amount of explained variance that is attributed to a given variable will differ, depending upon the order in which it appears. The first variable considered will explain more variance, unless the two independent variables are not correlated. If there is a substantial correlation between the two independent variables, the first variable considered will be "given credit" for the explained variance that they share. In this circumstance, the variance explained by the second variable that is not already explained by the first will be small. It is, therefore, a good idea to estimate R^2 with each variable appearing first to see how much additional variance the second-considered variable can explain above that explained by the first-considered variable.

As you can now perhaps see, the expression for the multiple coefficient of determination can give us some idea of the contribution to the total explained variance made by each variable. To perhaps see this more clearly, we can rewrite our two expressions for the multiple coefficient of determination as follows:

$$R^2 - r^2_{yx_1} = (r^2_{yx_2 \cdot x_1})(1 - r_{yx_1})^2$$
$$R^2 - r^2_{yx_2} = (r^2_{yx_1 \cdot x_2})(1 - r_{yx_2})^2$$

In the first formula above, the expression on the left-hand side of the equals sign is the difference between the total amount of explained variance and that which is explained by the first variable alone in the regression equation. You can see that the latter is just the squared bivariate correlation between the first independent variable and the dependent variable. The expression to the right of the equals sign reflects the amount of variance explained by the second variable that is left unexplained by the first. This latter component of the total explained variance is often referred to as the R^2 **change,** because it reflects the change in the amount of variance explained when the second variable is entered into the regression model. If the change in variance explained is substantial, it tells us that the second variable is able to give us information about the dependent variable that we do not get from the first independent variable.

The second formula above is a corollary formula for R^2 change. The expression on the left-hand side of the equals sign is the difference between the total amount of explained variance and that which is explained by the second variable alone in the regression equation. The $r^2_{yx_2}$ term is just the squared bivariate correlation between the second independent variable and the dependent variable. The expression to the right of the equals sign reflects the amount of variance explained by the first independent variable that is left unexplained by the second. This formula measures the change in explained variance that we can uniquely attribute to the first independent variable because it reflects the amount of variance it explains over and above that explained by the second independent variable. We now will illustrate the R^2 change term with our delinquency data.

In our calculation of the multiple coefficient of determination for delinquency scores above, age was the independent variable considered first. It explained 19.8 percent of the total 48.8 percent explained variance in delinquency scores. Family attachments explained the remaining 29 percent. It would appear, then, that family attachments are much more important in explaining delinquency than age is.

In the calculation below, family attachment scores appear first. This variable is given the opportunity to explain all it can in delinquency, and then age is entered to explain the remaining variance left unexplained by family attachment:

$$R^2 = (-.664)^2 + (.29)^2[1-(-.664)^2]$$
$$= .44 + (.084)(.56)$$
$$= .44 + .047$$
$$= .48$$

The combined variance explained is still 48 percent; thus, no matter which variable is considered first, the total amount of explained variance remains the same. We find here that family attachment explains 44 percent of the variance when considered first, while age explains 4.7 percent of the variance above and beyond that explained by the family attachments variable. Again, we would conclude that family attachment is a more important variable in explaining delinquency than age is.

You should also note here that 52 percent of the variance in delinquency remains unexplained by age and family attachments ($1 - R^2 = .52$, or 52%). This gives us a clue that there are factors other than age and family attachment that explain why some kids are more likely to engage in delinquent activity compared to others. This would lead us on a search for suitable other independent variables to add to our regression model. To be a good explanatory model, other factors theorized or empirically found to be associated with the dependent variable should also be included. Next we would explicitly bring these other independent variables into our model and estimate a regression equation with three or more independent variables.

The next questions we need to address are: (1) "Is there a significant relationship between the combination of independent variables and the dependent variable?" and (2) "Is there a significant relationship between each of the independent variables and the dependent variable?" We will discuss issues of hypothesis testing with multiple regression in the next section.

HYPOTHESIS TESTING IN MULTIPLE REGRESSION

So far in this chapter we have focused on calculating and interpreting the various coefficients associated with multiple regression analysis. However, since we are really interested in knowing if the total amount of variance explained is significantly different from zero, and in estimating the value of the *population* partial slope coefficients (β_1 and β_2) from the sample coefficients (b_1 and b_2), we now must examine issues of hypothesis testing. In multiple regression analysis we are interested in testing hypotheses about the multiple coefficient of determination and the partial slope coefficients. The calculation of the standard error for these hypothesis tests, however, gets a bit labor-intensive and tricky. For this reason, we are going to rely on statistical output from SPSS to conduct the hypotheses tests for this chapter. In the remainder of this chapter, therefore, we will simply report the results of the calculations and work through the interpretation with you. Figure 13–2 presents the SPSS computer output for the multiple regression equation predicting delinquency that we have been examining.

The first null hypothesis of interest states that all slope coefficients in the regression equation are equal to zero. This is the same as saying that the multiple coefficient of determination R^2 is equal to zero. The alternative hypothesis states that the slopes for all independent variables when used together are not equal to zero. This can be expressed as shown below:

$H_0: \beta_1, \beta_2, \beta_3, \ldots, \beta_k = 0$ or $R^2 = 0$

$H_1: \beta_1, \beta_2, \beta_3, \ldots, \beta_k \neq 0$ or $R^2 \neq 0$

Regression

Variables Entered/Removed[b]

Model	Variables Entered	Variables Removed	Method
1	family attachments, age in years[a]		Enter

a. All requested variables entered

b. Dependent Variable: Delinquency Score

Model Summary

Model	R	R Square	Adjusted R Square	Std. Error of the Estimate
1	.699[a]	.488	.437	18.84

a. Predictors: (Constant), family attachments, age in years

ANOVA[b]

Model		Sum of Squares	df	Mean Square	F	Sig.
1	Regression	6,777.010	2	3,388.505	9.549	.001[a]
	Residual	7,096.903	20	354.845		
	Total	13,873.913	22			

a. Predictors: (Constant), family attachments, age in years

b. Dependent Variable: Delinquency Score

Coefficients[a]

Model		Unstandardized Coefficients		Standardized Coefficients	t	Sig.
		B	Std. Error	Beta		
1	(Constant)	23.102	50.199		.460	.650
	age in years	3.929	2.896	.233	1.357	.190
	family attachments	−2.050	.608	−.579	−3.369	.003

a. Dependent Variable: Delinquency Score

Figure 13–2 Multiple regression output from SPSS rredicting delinquency by age and family attachments

In order to reject the null hypothesis, only one of the partial slope coefficients needs to be different from zero. To determine the results of this hypothesis test, we need to examine the boxes in Figure 13–2 labeled "Model Summary" and "ANOVA." The former displays the results of our sample R^2, which we have already calculated by hand to be .488.

An *F* test is used to test this null hypothesis. This *F* test is comparable to the *F* test we conducted with the analysis of variance. It is based upon two sources of variability in our data, explained and unexplained variability. These correspond to two estimates of the population variance, explained/regression variance and unexplained/residual variance. These terms you should be familiar with from the previous chapter on bivariate regression models.

The regression variance is the variance in the data we can explain from our regression equation. Hence, this is often referred to as explained variance. It is estimated as the ratio of the regression sum of squares to its degrees of freedom. The regression sum of squares is the sum of the squared differences between the predicted value of y ($\hat{y}$) based upon the regression equation and the mean of y ($\overline{Y}$). The number of degrees of freedom for the regression sum of squares is equal to k, where k equals the number of independent variables in the regression model. This ratio of regression sum of squares to degrees of freedom is one estimate of the population variance. In Figure 13–2 this estimate of the variance is labeled as the Regression "Mean Square."

The residual variance is the variance in our data unexplained by the regression equation. It is estimated as the ratio of the residual sum of squares to its degrees of freedom. The residual sum of squares is the sum of the squared differences between the observed value of y and its predicted value ($\hat{y}$). The number of degrees of freedom for the residual sum of squares is equal to $n - k$. This ratio of residual sum of squares to degrees of freedom is the second estimate of the population variance, and in Figure 13–2 it is labeled as the Residual "Mean Square."

The *F* test for the significance of R^2 is based on the ratio of these two estimates of variance or mean squares, as shown below:

$$F = \frac{\text{Regression variance}}{\text{Residual variance}}$$

$$F = \frac{\text{Mean square for the regression}}{\text{Mean square for the residual}}$$

The obtained value of *F* can be directly compared with a critical *F* at a chosen alpha level with k and $n - k$ degrees of freedom. If $F_{obt} > F_{crit}$, your decision is to reject the null hypothesis. Again, many computer software programs report only the exact probability of the *F* statistic, under the assumption that the null hypothesis is true and $R^2 = 0$. If this exact probability is equal to or less than your chosen alpha level, your decision is to reject the null hypothesis. If the reported exact probability is greater than your alpha level, you fail to reject the null hypothesis.

Figure 13–2 reports the results of an *F* test for our delinquency, age, and family attachments example. Before we begin, we should formally state our null and alternative hypotheses as shown below:

$H_0 = \beta_{age}$ and $\beta_{attachments} = 0$ or $R^2_{age,\ attachments} = 0$

$H_1 = \beta_{age}$ and $\beta_{attachments} \neq 0$ or $R^2_{age,\ attachments} \neq 0$

Figure 13–2 reports the exact probability of our obtained F, and it is .001. This tells us that the probability of obtaining an F value of 9.54 if the null hypothesis is true is equal to .001. This probability is well below the alpha = .05, so we can safely reject the null hypothesis that both of the slope coefficients when used together to predict the dependent variable are equal to zero. We can instead conclude that there is a significant linear relationship between the independent variables of age and family attachments used together to explain delinquency scores for high school students.

If we reject the null hypothesis that $R^2 = 0$, we know only that at least one of the partial slope coefficients is significantly different from zero. If we want to know which specific partial slopes are significant, we must perform hypothesis tests on our individual slope coefficients. The hypothesis tests associated with partial slopes are very similar to the tests we conducted in the last chapter for bivariate slope coefficients. Specifically, we want to determine if each partial slope coefficient is significantly different from zero. The null hypothesis in this case would state that the true population parameter for each independent variable, β_i, is equal to zero.

Just as we did with the bivariate slope hypothesis tests in the last chapter, we utilize the t statistic and sampling distribution to test this hypothesis. The calculations for the t statistic in the multiple regression case are, however, much more complicated. The t statistic we use for our partial slope coefficient hypothesis test is simply the ratio of the partial slope to the standard error of the slope:

$$t = \frac{b_i}{s_{bi}}$$

The sampling distribution used for the t statistic above is the Student's t with $(n - k - 1)$ degrees of freedom, where k is the number of independent variables in the regression equation.

The formula above may look easy, but the complicated part is in estimating the denominator—the standard error of the partial slope! For a two-variable multiple regression problem (x_1, x_2), the estimate for the standard error of the slope can be derived from the following formulas:

$$s_{byx_1 \cdot x_2} = \sqrt{\frac{\text{Residual mean square}}{\sum x_1^2 (1 - r_{x_1 x_2}^2)}}$$

$$s_{byx_2 \cdot x_1} = \sqrt{\frac{\text{Residual mean square}}{\sum x_2^2 (1 - r_{x_1 x_2}^2)}}$$

where

$\sum x_1^2 = $ the sum of squares for x_1,

$\sum x_2^2 = $ the sum of squares for x_2, and

$R_{x_1 x_2}^2 = $ the squared correlation coefficient between x_1 and x_2.

Again, however, we will rely on the computer output to make our decision. The necessary information to make this hypothesis test is shown in Figure 13–2, displayed in the "Coefficients" box. In this box, you will find the partial slopes (B), the standard error of each slope, the beta coefficients (beta weights or standardized partial slopes), the resulting t values obtained for each slope, and the *exact* significance level (two-tailed) that corresponds to each t value. The row displaying the "constant" refers to the y intercept from the equation (a).

We are interested in testing the null hypothesis associated with each partial slope coefficient that there is no linear relationship between age and delinquency when holding family attachments constant and that there is no linear relationship between family attachments and delinquency when holding age constant. That is, we are testing the null hypothesis that the population parameters, β_{x_1} and β_{x_2} are both equal to zero. The alternative hypotheses state that the slope coefficients in the population are not equal to zero. These null and research hypotheses for each partial slope can be expressed as follows:

H_0: $\beta_{\text{age}} = 0$
H_1: $\beta_{\text{age}} \neq 0$

H_0: $\beta_{\text{family attachments}} = 0$
H_1: $\beta_{\text{family attachments}} \neq 0$

The next step in our hypothesis test is to select an alpha level with the appropriate degrees of freedom and determine what the critical value of t is. You now can select an alpha level (let's use an alpha of .05) and go to the t table (Table E–3) in Appendix E with $n - k - 1$ degrees of freedom and find the critical value of t. For this example, with $n = 23$ and $k = 2$, we have $23 - 2 - 1$, or 20 degrees of freedom. The critical value of t with $\alpha = .05$ for a two-tailed hypothesis test and 20 degrees of freedom is 2.086. If our obtained t is greater than or equal to 2.086 or less than or equal to -2.086, we will reject the null hypothesis.

Many computer software programs that do multiple regression analysis do not print the critical value of t for you. This is because the program does not know whether you are conducting a one- or a two-tailed test or what particular alpha level you have chosen. What these programs do usually print for you, however, is the *exact probability* of each t statistic (two-tailed) under the assumption that the null hypothesis is true. This exact probability is displayed for you in Figure 13–2 under the column labeled "Sig." (for the significance of t). The reported probability is the probability of getting the partial regression slope that you did if the null hypothesis were true and the population partial slope coefficient were equal to zero. Your decision to reject the null hypothesis is the same as before. If this reported probability is less than or equal to your chosen alpha level, your decision will be to reject the null hypothesis. If the reported probability is greater than your selected alpha level, your decision will be to fail to reject the null hypothesis. In order to conduct our hypothesis test, all we need now is the obtained t statistic for each partial slope coefficient. You can find the obtained t values under the heading t in Figure 13–2. We will now proceed with our test.

We can see from Figure 13–2 that the partial slope coefficient for the effect of age on delinquency is 3.929 and the obtained t value for that partial slope coefficient is 1.357. The critical value of t we got from the t table with an alpha of .05 was ± 2.086. Since $-t_{crit} < t_{obt} < t_{crit}$, we would not reject the null hypothesis that this partial slope coefficient is equal to zero. But we really don't have to make this comparison because you can see that the exact probability of a sample slope coefficient this large if the population coefficient is actually zero is .19. That means if we reject the null hypothesis, we will be wrong about 19 percent of the time. We are only willing to be wrong 5 percent of the time ($\alpha = .05$). Thus, we will fail to reject the null hypothesis. We would conclude, therefore, that there is no significant linear effect of age on delinquency once students' attachments to their families are controlled. We have illustrated making a decision about our null hypothesis using both the critical value of t and the exact significance displayed in the computer output to demonstrate that the results are exactly the same. From now on, we will utilize the computer output only.

The partial slope coefficient for family attachments is -2.02, and the obtained t value is -3.369. If we look at the exact probability, we can see that the probability of getting a t that large if the null hypothesis is true is only .003. Since the exact probability is less than .05 (.003 < .05), we will reject the null hypothesis. Let us put this another way. If the partial slope coefficient in the population was actually zero, we would obtain a sample value of -2.02 by chance alone less than 1 time out of 100. Since this is a very unlikely event, we would reject the null hypothesis that the slope coefficient in the population is equal to zero. We would instead conclude that there is a significant positive linear effect of family attachment on delinquency even after controlling for age.

We suggested to you earlier that, in addition to their use in conducting hypothesis tests, the obtained t statistic also can be used to compare the relative effects of two independent variables on the dependent variable. If you want to know which independent variable has the stronger effect, simply compare the absolute value of each variable's obtained t statistic. For a given regression equation, the greater the t_{obt}, the stronger the effect the variable has on the dependent variable.[3] In our example, the obtained t for the partial slope for age was .1.357, while the t_{obt} for family attachments was -3.369. Since the absolute value of 3.369 is greater than 1.357, we would conclude that family attachment has a stronger effect on delinquency than does age. This conclusion is consistent with our earlier findings using the standardized slope coefficients.

Let's move on to another example from the criminological literature. For the remainder of the chapter, we will place more emphasis on the interpretation of multiple regression analysis, rather than on the calculation of these coefficients.

ANOTHER EXAMPLE: PRISON DENSITY, MEAN AGE, AND RATE OF INMATE-TO-INMATE ASSAULT

Several researchers have examined the effect of prison overcrowding on the frequency with which inmates assault one another. Results of this research have remained equivocal, however, with some researchers finding a significant positive relationship between prison overcrowding and assaults between inmates (Gaes, 1985; Nacci et al., 1977), while others report finding no relationship (Innes, 1986; Sechrest, 1991).

Let's set up a hypothetical study investigating the extent to which prison overcrowding is related to the rate of inmate-to-inmate assault. To do this, we select a sample of prisons and collect data for three variables: inmate-to-inmate assault rates, prison density (which we will use as our measure of overcrowding), and the mean age of inmates in the facility. We operationalize overcrowding by a "prison density index," which is computed by dividing a prison's inmate population by the prison's official rated inmate capacity. For example, if a prison had a population of 500 and a rated capacity of 400, it would yield a density index of 1.25, indicating that the facility was 25 percent over capacity. That is, the prison was overcrowded by 25 percent. We suspect that the rate of inmate assault is positively related to the extent to which a prison is overcrowded. We collect information on age because previous research has found that, compared to facilities with older populations, prisons with younger inmates tend to have higher rates of inmate-to-inmate assault.

The hypothetical data we obtain from a random sample of 30 correctional facilities are presented in Table 13–4. Also reported in Table 13–4 are each of the component values necessary to calculate the bivariate correlation coefficients between each of the variables, in addition to the correlation coefficients themselves. We will not go through the labor of computing these correlation coefficients by hand here, but it would be a good exercise for you to do so on your own before moving on.

The bivariate correlation coefficients shown in Table 13–4 indicate that both independent variables have moderately strong relationships with the dependent variable. The relationship between overcrowding (prison density) and inmate-to-inmate assault rates is moderate and positive ($r = .62$), indicating that overcrowding within prisons tends to increase the number of assaults between inmates. The correlation between the mean age of inmates and inmate-to-inmate assault rates is negative and moderately strong ($r = -.76$), indicating that prisons with a younger inmate population tend to have higher assault rates compared to prisons with older inmate populations. The correlation between our two independent variables is $-.56$. Though not small, the R^2 value is only .31, indicating that 31 percent of the variance in one

TABLE 13–4

Hypothetical Inmate-to-Inmate Assault Rates per 100 Inmate Population, Prison Density Index, and Mean Age of Inmates for a Random Sample of 30 Prisons

Case	Prison	Assault Rate y	Density Index x_1	Mean Age x_2
1	Prison A	10.20	1.50	25.80
2	Prison B	8.20	1.00	32.10
3	Prison C	11.30	1.60	26.20
4	Prison D	9.20	1.20	29.60
5	Prison E	5.30	.98	34.50
6	Prison F	8.50	1.10	27.50
7	Prison G	8.60	1.30	30.20
8	Prison H	7.50	.88	33.20
9	Prison I	15.30	1.90	27.20
10	Prison J	10.50	1.50	26.30
11	Prison K	12.50	1.50	28.30
12	Prison L	5.40	1.10	32.30
13	Prison M	10.50	1.40	23.50
14	Prison N	15.40	1.40	24.50
15	Prison O	12.80	1.20	24.50
16	Prison P	13.50	1.30	27.50
17	Prison Q	17.50	1.80	25.80
18	Prison R	11.50	1.60	32.60
19	Prison S	19.00	1.40	21.20
20	Prison T	14.20	1.20	26.50
21	Prison U	11.40	1.60	32.00
22	Prison V	9.80	1.10	29.90
23	Prison W	6.60	.85	36.20
24	Prison X	8.90	.95	35.00
25	Prison Y	10.60	1.10	29.80
26	Prison Z	12.50	1.20	25.60
27	Prison AA	7.40	1.10	33.50
28	Prison BB	3.30	1.20	38.20
29	Prison CC	17.50	1.70	25.20
30	Prison DD	13.20	.90	33.10

$$\Sigma_y = 328.10 \qquad \Sigma x_1 = 38.56 \qquad \Sigma x_2 = 877.80$$
$$\overline{Y} = 10.94 \qquad \overline{X}_{x_1} = 1.29 \qquad \overline{X}_{x_2} = 29.26$$
$$s_y = 3.78 \qquad s_{x_1} = .28 \qquad s_{x_2} = 4.2$$
$$\Sigma y^2 = 4002.10 \qquad \Sigma x_1^2 = 51.85 \qquad \Sigma x_2^2 = 2{,}6193.2$$

$$\Sigma yx_1 = 440.6 \qquad \Sigma yx_2 = 9{,}250.9 \qquad \Sigma x_1 x_2 = 1{,}109.2$$
$$r_{yx_1} = .62 \qquad r_{yx_2} = -.76 \qquad r_{y_1 x_2} = -.56$$

independent variable is explained by the other. The correlation is not large enough to create a problem of multicollinearity.

With these bivariate correlation coefficients and the respective standard deviations of each variable, we can calculate the partial slope coefficients using equations 13–4 and 13–5:

Partial slope coefficient for prison overcrowding regressed on inmate assault rates:

$$b_1 = \left(\frac{3.78}{.28}\right)\left(\frac{.62-(-.76)(-.56)}{1-(-.56)^2}\right)$$

$$= (13.5)\left(\frac{.62-.42}{1-.31}\right)$$

$$= (13.5)\left(\frac{.2}{.69}\right)$$

$$= 3.92$$

Partial slope coefficient for mean age of prison inmate population regressed on inmate assault rates:

$$b_2 = \left(\frac{3.78}{4.2}\right)\left(\frac{-.76-(.61)(-.56)}{1-(-.56)^2}\right)$$

$$= (.9)\left(\frac{-.76-(-.34)}{1-.31}\right)$$

$$= (.9)\left(\frac{-.42}{.69}\right)$$

$$= -.549$$

The partial slope coefficient for overcrowding, b_1, indicates that on average, inmate-to-inmate assault rates increase by 3.92 with every 1 percent increase in prison overcrowding, while simultaneously holding constant the mean age of the inmate population. The partial slope coefficient for mean inmate age, b_2, indicates that on average, assault rates between inmates decrease by $-.549$ with every 1 year increase in mean age, while simultaneously holding constant prison density.

These partial slopes help us determine the form of the linear effect for a given independent variable. However, since their magnitude is affected by the underlying units of measurement, they are not very useful in comparing relative effects across independent variables. This is why it is necessary to calculate other statistics, such as the standardized partial slope coefficient or beta weights (b^*). Before we do this, however, we will solve the multiple regression equation for this model as shown below:

$$y = a + b_1 x_1 + b_2 x_2$$

$$= a + (3.92)x_1 + (-.549)x_2$$

Now that we have obtained the partial slopes for overcrowding (b_1) and age (b_2), we can compute the intercept value by substituting the mean of the dependent variable and the means of the two independent variables (Table 13–4) into the equation as follows:

$$a = \overline{Y} - b_1\overline{X}_1 - b_2\overline{X}_2$$

$$= 10.94 - (3.92)(1.29) - (-.549)(29.26)$$

$$= 10.94 - 5.06 - (-16.06)$$

$$= 21.94$$

The intercept value we obtain from the above equation indicates that when both independent variables are equal to zero, the average value of y, our inmate assault rate, will be equal to 21.94.

Now that we have solved for the intercept and both partial slope coefficients, the multiple regression equation for this model can be expressed as follows:

$$\hat{y} = 21.94 + 3.92(x_1) + -5.06(x_2)$$

Now let's return to the issue of comparing the relative magnitude of effects for our two independent variables. Recall that standardized partial slope coefficients, called beta weights (b^*), are one way to achieve this end. Using formulas 13–5 and 13–6, let's compute the beta weights for overcrowding and mean age:

$$b_1^* = 3.7\left(\frac{.28}{3.78}\right)$$

$$= (3.7)(.074)$$

$$= .274$$

$$b_2^* = (-.54)\left(\frac{4.19}{3.78}\right)$$

$$= (-.54)(1.108)$$

$$= -.598$$

The obtained absolute value of the beta weight obtained for age is almost double that of the beta weight obtained for prison overcrowding ($-.598$ v. .274). This indicates that mean inmate age in prison settings has a much stronger effect on inmate-to-inmate assaults compared to the extent to which a prison is overcrowded.

Another way of assessing the relative importance of the independent variables in predicting the dependent variable is through the partial correlation coefficients and a partitioning of the multiple coefficient of determination. Using formulas 13–7 and 13–8, let's compute $r_{yx_1 \cdot x_2}$ and $r_{yx_2 \cdot x_1}$.

Partial correlation coefficient for overcrowding and assault, controlling for age:

$$r_{yx_1 \cdot x_2} = \frac{.62-(-.76)(-.56)}{\sqrt{1-(-.76)^2}\sqrt{1-(-.56)^2}}$$

$$= \frac{.62-.426}{\sqrt{1-.58}\sqrt{1-.31}}$$

$$= .359$$

Partial correlation coefficient for age and assaults, controlling for overcrowding:

$$r_{yx_2 \cdot x_1} = \frac{-.76-(.62)(-.56)}{\sqrt{1-(.62)^2}\sqrt{1-(-.56)^2}}$$

$$= \frac{-.76-(-.35)}{\sqrt{1-.38}\sqrt{1-.31}}$$

$$= -.625$$

The partial correlation coefficient between age and assault when controlling for prison overcrowding is equal to $-.625$. Its absolute value is greater than the partial correlation between overcrowding and assault when controlling for inmate age (.359). This would lead us to conclude that age is more important than overcrowding in explaining inmate assault rates.

With these partial correlation coefficients, we can calculate the multiple coefficient of determination. Using formula 13–9, we obtain the multiple coefficient of determination for overcrowding and age on assault as follows:

$$R^2_{yx_1x_2} = (.62)^2 + (-.63)^2[1-(.62)^2]$$

$$= (.38)+(.40)(1-.38)$$

$$= .63$$

The obtained $R^2_{yx_1x_2} = .63$ indicates that both overcrowding and mean age, when used together, explain 63 percent of the variance in inmate-to-inmate assault rates within prisons.

With the multiple coefficient of determination calculated, we now can determine the relative contribution in explained variance made by each independent variable. Recall that we do this by subtracting the bivariate coefficient of determination for each variable from the multiple coefficient of determination. For example, to determine the relative contribution of age in explaining assault rates, we simply subtract the bivariate coefficient of determination for overcrowding on inmate assaults $(r_{yx_1})^2$ by the multiple coefficient of determination. This will give us the proportion of explained variance added to the total when mean age is added to the model explaining inmate assault rates.

In the calculated multiple coefficient of determination above, we found that prison density by itself explains 38 percent of the variance in inmate assault rates. When age is considered, it contributes an additional 25 percent to the total explained variance over and above that explained by prison density. The R^2 change value for age is, then, 25 percent ($63\% - 38\%$). This indicates that age contributes unique information about the dependent variable of assault rates that is not available through knowledge of overcrowding.

When age is the first variable considered we find the following:

$$R^2_{yx_2x_1} = (-.76) + (.36)^2[1 - (-.76)^2]$$

$$= (.58) + (.13)(.42)$$

$$= .58 + .05$$

$$= .63$$

By itself, age explains 58 percent of the total variance, while prison overcrowding explains only 5 percent additional variance beyond that explained by age. It would appear, then, that while both variables contribute to the total explained variance, the age of the inmates gives us more information about assault rates than does the extent of overcrowding.

After having examined the issue of the relative effects of the two variables, we need to perform hypothesis tests to determine if the multiple coefficient of determination and each partial regression slope are significantly different from zero. The information pertaining to these tests is provided for you in Figure 13–3. Before we proceed to the hypothesis tests, however, we would like to discuss a term in Figure 13–3 referred to as the "Adjusted R Square."

The **adjusted R^2** is often used in multiple regression problems because in some instances the unadjusted value gives an inflated estimate of how much variance is explained—and therefore, how good a particular regression model fits the data. The estimated R^2 is at times inflated because in calculating it, sample correlation coefficients are used to estimate population values. These sample coefficients, which vary from sample to sample, are treated as if they were error-free. In fact, the sample estimates are positively biased, inflating the sample estimate of R^2. Because of this bias, it is a good idea to examine the adjusted R^2 of your multiple regression model. Formally, the equation used to obtain the adjusted R^2 is:

$$R^2_{\text{Adjusted}} = R^2 - \frac{k(1 - R^2)}{n - k - 1} \qquad (13\text{–}10)$$

where k = the number of independent variables. Even though the adjusted value of R^2 is already displayed for you in Figure 13–3, you can see that if we plugged the appropriate values into the equation, we would obtain the same result:

Regression

Variables Entered/Removed[b]

Model	Variables Entered	Variables Removed	Method
1	MEANAGE, DENSITY[a]		Enter

a. All requested variables entered.
b. Dependent Variable: ASSAULT

Model Summary

Model	R	R Square	Adjusted R Square	Std. Error of the Estimate
1	.795[a]	.632	.605	2.374

a. Predictors: (Constant), MEANAGE, DENSITY

ANOVA[b]

Model		Sum of Squares	df	Mean Square	F	Sig.
1	Regression	261.556	2	130.778	23.201	.000[a]
	Residual	152.193	27	5.637		
	Total	413.750	29			

a. Predictors: (Constant), MEANAGE, DENSITY
b. Dependent Variable: ASSAULT

Coefficients[a]

Model		Unstandardized Coefficients		Standardized Coefficients	t	Sig.
		B	Std. Error	Beta		
1	(Constant)	22.169	5.469		4.053	.000
	DENSITY	3.721	1.891	.277	1.968	.059
	MEANAGE	−.547	.127	−.607	−4.317	.000

a. Dependent Variable: ASSAULT

Figure 13–3   Multiple regression output from SPSS predicting inmate-to-inmate assaults in prison by mean age in the prison and overcrowding

$$R^2_{\text{Adjusted}} = .63216 - \frac{(2)(1-.63216)}{30-2-1}$$

$$= .63216 - \frac{(2)(.3678)}{27}$$

$$= .6049$$

In this example, the unadjusted R^2 value is .63 and its adjusted value is .60, so the shrinkage in the amount of explained variance in this particular regression model is slight.

The coefficient of determination (R^2) always increases some or stays the same when additional independent variables are added into the equation. For this reason, some statisticians believe the adjusted R^2 is a more appropriate indicator of explained variance than its unadjusted value. The amount of the adjustment or shrinkage is dependent upon the ratio of the number of independent variables in the model to sample size. If there are many independent variables relative to the sample size, the adjustment will be large and the adjustment will amount to a substantial reduction in R^2. In larger samples with fewer independent variables, however, the adjustment makes a lesser difference. Some statisticians have recommended as a rule of thumb that there be 30 observations for each one independent variable. When using multiple regression, however, you should always examine both the unadjusted and the adjusted R_2 values.

Let's move on to testing the significance of our partial slope coefficients and the significance of the entire multiple regression equation. We first want to address the extent to which there is a significant linear relationship between the dependent variable, the number of inmate assaults, and our two independent variables, prison overcrowding and inmate age, considered in combination. The null and research hypotheses for this test can be expressed as follows:

$$H_0 = \beta_{\text{overcrowding}}, \beta_{\text{age}} = 0 \text{ or } R^2_{\text{overcrowding, age}} = 0$$
$$H_1 = \beta_{\text{overcrowding}}, \beta_{\text{age}} \neq 0 \text{ or } R^2_{\text{overcrowding, age}} \neq 0$$

As we stated before, this hypothesis test really determines if the R^2 value is significantly different from zero. If we reject this null hypothesis, we can conclude that at least one of the partial slope coefficients is significantly different from zero. Our next set of hypothesis tests will then determine which specific slopes are significantly different from zero.

We will use the F statistic and sampling distribution (refer to Table E–5 of Appendix E) to test the null hypothesis about R^2. We will adopt an alpha level of .01 for this test and find F_{crit} with the appropriate degrees of freedom. As before, however, we will also provide the exact probability level of F_{obt}. With a sample size of 30 and 2 independent variables, our F test has 2 and 27 degrees of freedom. For an alpha level of .01 with 2 and 27 degrees of freedom, our critical value of F is 5.49. Our decision rule, then, is to reject the null hypothesis if $F_{\text{obt}} > 5.49$, and to fail to reject if $F_{\text{obt}} < 5.49$.

All of the information necessary to make a decision about the null hypothesis is provided in the top portion of Figure 13–3. The obtained value of F for the entire equation is equal to 23.2. Since an F_{obt} of 23.2 is greater than the critical F of 5.49, our decision is to reject the null hypothesis. Figure 13–3 shows that if the null hypothesis were true and the population R^2 were really zero, the probability of observing a sample R^2 of .63 by chance would be less than 1 in 10,000. The exact probability level of .000 is much less than our chosen alpha level of .01, so we again would be led to reject the null hypothesis. We can conclude that there is a significant linear relationship between prison

overcrowding and the mean age of the inmate population when used together to predict rates of inmate-to-inmate assault.

We next will determine exactly which independent variable(s) is significant in predicting the dependent variable. The null hypotheses we are testing
are that the population parameters, β_1 and β_2, are each equal to zero. The research hypotheses state that the slope coefficients for the effect of inmate age
and prison overcrowding on inmate assaults in the population are not equal
to zero. These can be formally expressed as follows:

$H_0 : \beta_{overcrowding} = 0$
$H_1 : \beta_{overcrowding} \neq 0$

$H_0 : \beta_{age} = 0$
$H_1 : \beta_{age} \neq 0$

The next step in our hypothesis test is to select an alpha level, determine
our degrees of freedom, and identify the critical value of our test statistic.
Let's continue with the alpha of .01. The statistic we will use to test our null
hypothesis is the Student's t, and the sampling distribution we will utilize is
the t distribution with $n - k$ degrees of freedom. We will conduct this hypothesis test with the exact probability of t_{obt}.

From Figure 13–3 you can see that the partial slope coefficient for the effect of age on inmate assaults is $-.547$ and the t statistic is -4.317, with an
exact probability of this t_{obt} being equal to .000. Since this probability is less
than our critical alpha of .01, we are led to reject the null hypothesis. Our
conclusion will be that the age of the inmate population is significantly related to the rate of inmate-to-inmate assaults. As the mean age of the inmate
population increases, rates of assault between inmates decrease. In other
words, our sample data indicate that prisons with younger inmate populations tend to have significantly higher rates of assault between inmates than
do prisons with older inmate populations, even after controlling for the effects of overcrowding.

The slope coefficient for the effect of prison density on inmate assaults is
3.72, with a t value of 1.968. This corresponds to an exact probability level of
.059. Since this is greater than our alpha level of .01, we must fail to reject the
null hypothesis stating that the slope coefficient in the population for prison
overcrowding is equal to zero. We conclude that there is no significant linear
relationship between overcrowding and rates of inmate-to-inmate assault
within prisons. Finally, notice that the absolute value of t_{obt} for age (-4.317)
is greater than that for prison density (1.968). This also would lead us to believe that inmate age has more of an effect on the rate of inmate assaults than
does prison density.

SUMMARY

In this chapter we have examined techniques of multiple regression analysis. The multiple regression model is really a straightforward extension of the bivariate, or one-variable, model. The slope coefficient in the multiple regression model, the partial slope coefficient, reflects the change in the dependent variable for a 1 unit change in one independent variable while holding constant all other independent variables. The relative explanatory power of independent variables can be assessed by partial correlation coefficients, the value of R^2 change, and the absolute value of the t ratios. In deciding which explanatory variables to include in a multiple regression model, the optimal strategy is to include those variables that are strongly correlated with the dependent variable but uncorrelated with other independent variables.

KEY TERMS

adjusted R^2
beta weight
causal effect
causal relationship
multicollinearity
multiple coefficient of
  determination (R^2)
multiple correlation coefficient
multiple regression equation

nonspuriousness
partial correlation coefficient
partial regression coefficient
partial slope coefficient
R^2 change
standardized partial slopes
standardized regression
  coefficient

KEY FORMULAS

Multiple regression model (eq. 13–1):

$$y = \alpha + \beta_1 x_1 + \beta_2 x_2 + \ldots \beta_k x_k + \epsilon$$

Multivariate regression equation (eq. 13–2):

$$y = a + b_1 x_1 + b_2 x_2 + \ldots b_k x_k + \epsilon$$

Partial slope coefficients (eq. 13–3, 13–4):

$$b_1 = \left(\frac{s_y}{s_{x_1}} \right) \left(\frac{r_{yx_1} - (r_{yx_2})(r_{x_1 x_2})}{1 - r^2_{x_1 x_2}} \right)$$

$$b_2 = \left(\frac{s_y}{s_{x_2}} \right) \left(\frac{r_{yx_2} - (r_{yx_1})(r_{x_1 x_2})}{1 - r^2_{x_1 x_2}} \right)$$

Beta weights (eq. 13–5, 13–6):

$$b^*_{x_1} = b_{x_1}\left(\frac{s_{x_1}}{s_y}\right)$$

$$b^*_{x_2} = b_{x_2}\left(\frac{s_{x_2}}{s_y}\right)$$

Partial correlation coefficients (eq. 13–7, 13–8):

$$r_{yx_1 \cdot x_2} = \frac{r_{yx_1} - (r_{yx_2})(r_{x_1 x_2})}{\sqrt{1 - r^2_{yx_2}}\sqrt{1 - r^2_{x_1 x_2}}}$$

$$r_{yx_2 \cdot x_1} = \frac{r_{yx_2} - (r_{yx_1})(r_{x_1 x_2})}{\sqrt{1 - r^2_{yx_1}}\sqrt{1 - r^2_{x_1 x_2}}}$$

Multiple coefficient of determination, R^2 (eq. 13–9):

$$R^2 = r^2_{yx_1} + (r^2_{yx_2 \cdot x_1})(1 - r^2_{yx_1})$$

Adjusted R^2 (eq. 13–10):

$$R^2_{\text{Adjusted}} = R^2 - \frac{k(1 - R^2)}{n - k - 1}$$

PRACTICE PROBLEMS

1. Suppose we were interested in the extent to which rates of divorce and the mean age of the population within states affected state-level rates of violent crime. To examine these relationships, we took a random sample of 35 states and obtained the divorce rate per 100,000 population for each, the mean age in each state, and rates of violent crime per 100,000. Assume that we obtained the multiple regression output in Figure 13–4. With this output, answer the following questions.

   a. Specify the exact least-squares multiple regression equation.

   b. Interpret both partial slope coefficients and the intercept value.

   c. Using this output, how would you examine the relative importance of each independent variable?

   d. What is the total variance explained?

   e. Conduct a hypothesis test using the obtained output for both the entire regression model and the independent slope coefficients. Use an alpha level of .01 for both tests. What are your formal hypothesis statements? What do you conclude based on the F test and the two t tests?

Regression

Variables Entered/Removed[b]

Model	Variables Entered	Variables Removed	Method
1	Divorce, Age[a]		Enter

a All requested variables entered.
b Dependent variable: Violent crime.

Model Summary

Model	R	R Square	Adjusted R Square
1	.795[a]	.632	.609

a Predictors: (Constant), divorce and age.

ANOVA[b]

Model		Sum of Squares	df	Mean Square	F	Sig.
1	Regression	324.538	2	162.269	27.531	.000[a]
	Residual	188.604	20	5.893		

a Predictors: (Constant), divorce, age.
b Dependent variable: Violent crime.

Coefficients[a]

Model		Unstandardized Coefficients		Standardized Coefficients	t	Sig.
		B	Std. Error	Beta		
1	(Constant)	19.642	2.736		.600	.552
	Divorce	.871	.119	.594	4.268	.000
	Age	−.146	.158	−.133	−3.110	.001

a Dependent variable: Violent crime.

Figure 13–4   Multiple regression output for problem (1)

2. Suppose we are interested in the reasons why escapes occur in local jails. To investigate this issue, we take a random sample of 30 jails. We ask the jail managers how many escapes they have had from their facilities in the past year. This is our dependent variable. Based on our knowledge of the literature, we also know that work-related morale and the extent to which facilities are understaffed affect things like supervision and motivation to identify and solve problems. To measure the level of morale, we ask jail employees to respond to a number of questions regarding their morale (e.g., I think my supervisors appreciate my work, I feel secure in my job, I like the people I work with, etc.). With their responses we compute a morale index with high scores indicating high morale and

low scores indicating low morale. To determine the extent to which an institution is understaffed, we construct a jail staff-to-inmate ratio. Again, high scores indicate a large number of staff relative to inmates and low scores indicate a small number of jail staff relative to inmates. The data we obtain are listed below:

Jail	# of Escapes	Morale Score	Staff-to-Inmate Ratio
1	12.00	3.00	.22
2	10.00	7.00	.41
3	3.00	14.00	.66
4	7.00	8.00	.45
5	9.00	9.00	.32
6	13.00	5.00	.33
7	17.00	2.00	.10
8	12.00	5.00	.30
9	15.00	4.00	.20
10	9.00	5.00	.50
11	3.00	7.00	.60
12	5.00	3.00	.40
13	11.00	2.00	.20
14	14.00	5.00	.50
15	7.00	8.00	.40
16	10.00	5.00	.20
17	14.00	3.00	.30
18	15.00	2.00	.40
19	17.00	2.00	.10
20	6.00	8.00	.20
21	9.00	4.00	.20
22	3.00	10.00	.50
23	2.00	11.00	.60
24	4.00	7.00	.30
25	13.00	2.00	.30
26	11.00	8.00	.50
27	14.00	4.00	.30
28	9.00	4.00	.30
29	5.00	11.00	.40
30	4.00	14.00	.50

The statistics necessary to calculate the slope coefficients are as follows:

$$\sum_y = 283 \qquad \sum_{x_1} = 182 \qquad \sum_{x_2} = 10.7$$

$$s_y = 4.49 \qquad s_{x_1} = 3.47 \qquad s_{x_2} = .15$$

$$\overline{Y} = 9.43 \qquad \overline{X}_1 = 6.07 \qquad \overline{X}_2 = .36$$

$$\sum y^2 = 3,255 \quad \sum x_{x_1}^2 = 1,454 \quad \sum x_{x_1}^2 = 4.44$$

$$r_{yx_1} = -.76$$

$$r_{yx_2} = -.63$$

$$r_{yx_1 \cdot x_2} = -.59 \qquad r_{yx_2 \cdot x_1} = -.245$$

a. What would the values of b_1 and b_2 be from the above sample statistics? Interpret these coefficients.

b. From your calculated partial slope coefficients and sample means, solve for the value of the intercept (a). What is the complete multiple regression equation?

c. Using the above multiple regression equation, predict the value of y (number of escapes) from a morale score of 8 and a staff-to-inmate ratio score of .3.

d. Calculate the beta weights for each of the partial slope coefficients above. What do they tell you about the relative importance of each independent variable?

e. Calculate the multiple coefficient of determination from these sample statistics. What does this coefficient indicate?

3. In a 1994 article, Harold Grasmick and Anne McGill conducted a study on religious beliefs and attitudes toward punishing criminal offenders. They found that those people who were religiously conservative saw the character of the offender rather than environmental factors as a cause of crime and therefore were more punitive in their response to crime. You wanted to conduct a similar study. You first developed three attitude scales: one that measured Punitiveness Toward the Criminal (PUN), one that measured Religious Conservatism (REL), and one that measured a person's belief that environmental factors are responsible for crime (ENV). Those who score high on the punitiveness scale want to punish convicted criminals severely, those who score high on the religious conservatism scale take a strict interpretation of the Bible, and those who score high on the environmental factors scale think that social factors are to blame for crime rather than the evil character of the offender. Based on the Grasmick and McGill study, you expect that religious conservatism will be positively related to punitiveness and that a belief in environmental causes of crime will be negatively related to punitiveness. You take a random sample of 15 persons who respond to a questionnaire that contains your attitude scales. You conduct a multiple regression analysis on your data and present the results in Figure 13–5. With this output, answer the following questions.

Regression

Variables Entered/Removed[b]

Model	Variables Entered	Variables Removed	Method
1	ENV, REF[a]		Enter

[a] All requested variables entered.
[b] Dependent variable: Punitiveness.

Model Summary

Model	R	R Square	Adjusted R Square
1	.811[a]	.659	.602

[a] Predictors: (Constant), ENV, REL.

ANOVA[b]

Model		Sum of Squares	df	Mean Square	F	Sig.
1	Regression	481.341	2	240.670	11.595	.001[a]
	Residual	249.058	12	20.754		

[a] Predictors: (Constant), ENV, REL.
[b] Dependent variable: Punitiveness.

Coefficients[a]

Model		Unstandardized Coefficients		Standardized Coefficients	t	Sig.
		B	Std. Error	Beta		
1	(Constant)	16.245	5.514		2.946	.012
	ENV	−1.467	.443	−.608	−3.312	.006
	REL	1.075	.570	.346	1.884	.084

[a] Dependent variable: Punitiveness.

Figure 13–5 Multiple regression output for problem (3)

a. Specify the exact least-squares multiple regression equation.

b. Interpret both partial slope coefficients and the intercept value.

c. Using this output, how would you examine the relative importance of each independent variable?

d. What is the total variance explained?

e. Conduct a hypothesis test using the obtained output for both the entire regression model and the independent slope coefficients. Use an alpha level of .01 for both tests. What are your formal hypothesis statements? What do you conclude based on the F test and the two t tests?

f. Using the multiple regression equation, predict the punitiveness score for a person who has a religious conservatism score of 8 and an environmental factor score of 2.

SPSS PRACTICE PROBLEMS

We are going to continue our example from the bivariate regression and correlation exercises in the last chapter, only this time we are going to predict rates of violent crime (VIOLENT) in states using the percent of the state's population living in rural areas (PERRURAL), the infant mortality rate (INFMORT), and the percent of the state's population living below the poverty level (POVERTY). In SPSS, access the data set called STATE. Recall that the District of Columbia was an outlier in these data, so let's begin by selecting everything but DC for the subsequent analyses. You can do this by clicking on DATA, then SELECT CASES, and then IF CONDITION IS SATISFIED. In the box where it asks you specify the condition, type "STATEID NE 9"—since the value for DC in the STATEID variable is equal to 9, this will exclude DC because it is telling SPSS to select all cases that are not equal ("ne") to 9.

1. Now let's calculate the bivariate correlation coefficients for each combination of our variables. Click on ANALYZE, then CORRELATE, and then enter all of the above variables into the variables box to create a correlation matrix. Examine the correlations between each of your independent variables to make sure that multicollinearity is not going to be a problem. Comment on this now.

2. Now interpret each of the correlation coefficients for violent crime and each of the independent variables. You should see that although they vary in magnitude, each of the correlation coefficients is significant using an alpha equal to .05. Thus, at the bivariate level, we can reject the null hypotheses that each of the correlation coefficients are equal to zero in the population.

3. Let's examine what happens to the original bivariate relationship when we add two of the independent variables into a multivariate OLS regression equation. Click on ANALYZE, then REGRESSION, and then LINEAR. Let's first examine what happens when both indicators of economic deprivation are used in a model to predict violent crime. Place the appropriate variables in their respective dependent and independent variable boxes.

   a. Interpret the multiple coefficient of determination.

   b. Interpret the null hypothesis that the model does not predict a significant amount of variation in violent crime using the displayed F test.

   c. Define the multiple OLS regression equation using the output and interpret both slope coefficients.

d. Interpret both null hypotheses that state the slope coefficients for both independent variables are equal to zero.

e. What do you conclude about the relationships between violent crime, infant mortality, and percent poor?

4. Now let's examine what happens when we predict violent crime in states using percent of the state's population living below the poverty level and percent of the state's population residing in rural areas. Click on ANALYZE, then REGRESSION, and then LINEAR. Place the appropriate variables in their respective dependent and independent variable boxes.

a. Interpret the multiple coefficient of determination.

b. Interpret the null hypothesis that the model does not predict a significant amount of variation in violent crime using the displayed F test.

c. Define the multiple OLS regression equation using the output and interpret both slope coefficients.

d. Interpret both null hypotheses that state the slope coefficients for both independent variables are equal to zero.

e. What do you conclude about the relationships between violent crime, percent poor, and rural population?

Regression Analysis with a Dichotomous Dependent Variable: Logit and Probit Models

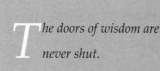

*T*he doors of wisdom are never shut.
— BENJAMIN FRANKLIN

In this chapter we learn about conducting a bivariate and multivariate regression analysis when the dependent variable is not continuous, but dichotomous. Many variables that we want to know about in criminology and criminal justice are dichotomous. A dichotomous dependent variable has only two outcomes; when these outcomes are coded "0" and "1," they are called binary dependent variables. Examples of dichotomous or binary dependent variables in criminology and criminal justice include whether or not someone has committed a crime, whether they appear for trial after posting bail, whether they test positive for drugs, or whether they are sentenced to prison or are given some nonpenal punishment. Each of these is an example of a dichotomous variable. Just as we have done with variables measured at other levels, we are still interested in explaining these dichotomous variables using explanatory or independent variables. In our last chapter we learned about ordinary least-squares (OLS) regression. OLS regression is a very powerful research tool, but it has limitations. Underlying the OLS model are important assumptions about the error term that are violated when the dependent variable is dichotomous rather than continuous. In addition, the OLS model can lead to predictions about the probability of the dichotomous dependent variable that are less than zero and greater than 1. The tools we learn in this chapter will provide us with a solution to the regression problem with dichotomous dependent variables. We will learn about logistic and probit regression models. Both the logistic and probit models allow you to estimate regression equations that can contain one or more independent variables. Unlike OLS, both models assume that the relationship between our independent variable (or variables) and the dependent variable is nonlinear. In this chapter, we will learn how to interpret logistic and probit coefficients, test for the statistical significance of the logistic and probit coefficients, and make a determination about how well our model fits the data. The logistic and probit regression models are not really different statistical tools; actually, they are very comparable approaches to the dichotomous dependent variable problem. In fact, the logistic and probit regression models will arrive at the same substantive conclusion. The selection of which model to estimate is based on things like personal preference and the availability of computer software.

INTRODUCTION

In Chapters 12 and 13 we examined the linear bivariate and multivariate regression models, respectively. In these models, one or more independent variables measured at any level were presumed to be linearly related to a dependent variable that was measured at the interval/ratio level. In those two chapters, we learned that the ordinary least-squares (OLS) regression model is a very good and general tool in analyzing the relationship between independent variables and a continuous dependent variable. While the OLS model is a very general tool, it is not so flexible that it is the only one we need to learn. The OLS model is most useful in the case of dependent variables that are continuous. Unfortunately, many of the dependent variables we would like to look at in criminology and criminal justice are not continuous but are what are often called dichotomous or binary variables. A **dichotomous variable** has only two possible outcomes, and when these two outcomes are coded "0" and "1," the variable is often referred to as a **binary variable.** Examples of dichotomous dependent variables would include whether or not a defendant shows up for trial, whether or not a victim of a crime reports the offense to the police, a life or death sentence received by a convicted murderer, whether or not someone who is arrested tests positively for drugs, and whether or not someone has committed an offense. As you can perhaps sense, there are many instances where the dependent variable we are interested in is not continuous but has only two possible outcomes. In this case, the OLS model is not generally appropriate, and we need another statistical tool.

> A **dichotomous variable** is a variable that has only two outcomes, such as "yes" or "no," or the event happened or didn't happen. When these two events or outcomes are coded "0" and "1," the variable is referred to as a **binary variable.**

In this chapter we will examine two other types of regression-based models. One is called the logistic regression model, and the second is called the probit regression model. Either one of these statistical models is appropriate to use when the dependent variable we have is a binary or dichotomous one. We will see that, like their OLS counterpart, the logistic and probit regression models allow us to estimate a coefficient that measures the effect of a given independent variable on the binary dependent variable. Also similar to the OLS model, we will be able to formally test the null hypothesis that this regression coefficient is not significantly different from zero. Before we examine the logistic and probit regression models, however, we need to understand why we might not want to estimate an OLS regression equation when we have a binary or dichotomous dependent variable.

ESTIMATING AN OLS REGRESSION MODEL WITH A DICHOTOMOUS DEPENDENT VARIABLE— THE LINEAR PROBABILITY MODEL

Case Study: Age of First Delinquent Offense and Adult Criminality

For our example, let's look at the relationship between the age at which someone begins offending (often referred to in the literature as "age of onset") and whether or not they commit a criminal offense as an adult (at age 18 or older). For a random sample of 40 adults, all of whom have admitted committing a delinquent offense before age 18, we ask whether or not they have committed an offense after age 18. In this example, the age at which one commits his first delinquent offense is our independent variable, and it is continuous. Whether or not this person has committed a crime as an adult is our dichotomous dependent variable. Rather than the frequency of adult crimes, therefore, we simply have information that indicates whether they have or have not committed an offense as an adult. These data are shown for you in Table 14–1, where a value of 0 is given for no adult offense and a value of 1 is given if the person has committed at least one offense after age 18. Coded as 0 and 1, then, this is a binary dependent variable.

In looking at Table 14–1 you get the sense that there might be a relationship between age of onset of delinquency and adult offending. You notice that more of those having younger onset ages have committed an offense as an adult compared to those who have later onset ages. We learned in Chapters 12 and 13 that you can get a good initial sense of the possible relationship between your variables by creating a scatterplot. In Figure 14–1 we provide the scatterplot for the data in Table 14–1. Notice that, unlike the case with a continuous dependent variable, there are only two points on the y axis, indicating either that there was an adult offense committed (1) or there was not (0). All of the data points in the scatterplot fall on one of two lines parallel to the x axis corresponding to one of the two possible values of the dependent variable. We can roughly see from this scatterplot that most of the "1" values

TABLE 14–1

Data on Age of Onset of Delinquency (Age of First Delinquent Offense) and the Commission of a Crime as an Adult (Age 18 and Older)

Age of First Delinquent Offense	Adult Offense	Delinquent Offense	Age of First Adult Offense
10	1	14	1
10	1	14	1
10	1	14	0
10	1	14	0
10	0	14	0
11	1	15	1
11	1	15	0
11	1	15	0
11	1	15	0
11	0	15	0
12	1	16	1
12	1	16	0
12	1	16	0
12	0	16	0
12	0	16	0
13	1	17	0
13	1	17	0
13	0	17	0
13	0	17	0
13	0	17	0

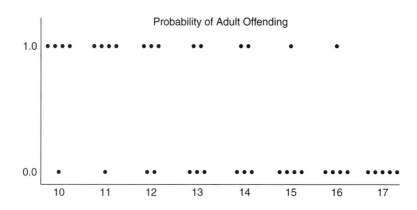

Figure 14–1 Scatterplot of age of delinquency onset and adult offending

(committed an adult offense) cluster at the younger onset ages while most of the "0" values (did not commit an adult offense) cluster at the older onset ages. It seems, therefore, that age of onset of delinquency and adult offending do covary, and that the relationship between the two variables is likely to be negative (i.e., a greater risk of adult offending as age of onset decreases).

If we wanted to, we could now presume that the relationship between onset age of delinquency and adult offending is a linear one and fit an ordinary least-squares regression line to our observed data points. This regression equation would take the form:

$$y = a + bx + \varepsilon$$

(14–1)

where

a = the y intercept or constant,

b = the OLS regression coefficient reflecting the linear relationship between onset of delinquent age and adult offending,

x = the age of onset of delinquency,

y = 0 if an adult criminal offense was not committed, 1 if there was an adult offense, and

ε = an error term.

In this OLS regression equation observed values of the dependent variable y (whether or not someone committed a criminal offense as an adult) are restricted to being either 0 or 1. Since the expected value of y is limited to 0 or 1, the regression equation models the relationship between the independent variable and the probability of the dependent variable. As such, OLS statistical models such as these, which assume a linear relationship between an independent variable and the probability of a dependent variable, are often referred to as **linear probability models.** Our regression equation in equation 14–1, then, describes the probability that someone will commit an adult offense given the age at which they first committed a delinquent offense. The regression coefficient, b, measures the linear change in the probability of committing an adult offense with each 1 year change in delinquency onset age.

Using the data in Table 14–1, we will estimate an ordinary least-squares regression equation for the probability of an adult arrest. When we do so, we observe the following regression equation:

$$\hat{y} = 2.00 - .117x$$

The y intercept is 2.00, so that when $x = 0$ the predicted probability of y is 2 adult offenses. The slope coefficient is $-.117$. The sign of this linear probability coefficient tells us that the relationship between onset age and the probability of adult offending is negative—those who commit their first delinquent act at an early age are more likely to commit an offense as an adult than those who do so at a later age. The magnitude of the coefficient tells us that a 1 year increase in delinquency onset age reduces the probability of an adult offense by .117. With this regression equation, we can determine the predicted probability of an adult offense for someone with an onset age of 12:

$$\hat{y} = 2.00 - (.117)12$$
$$\hat{y} = .596$$

The predicted probability of an adult offense for someone who committed her first delinquent act at age 13 is:

$$\hat{y} = 2.00 - (.117)13$$
$$\hat{y} = .479$$

Notice that increasing the age of one's first delinquent offense from 12 years to 13 years results in a decrease in the probability of an adult offense by .117 ($.479 - .596 = -.117$). This corresponds to the fact that the sign of the regression coefficient is negative, indicating that higher onset ages are related to a reduced probability of adult offending; in addition, the size of the decrease in the probability of an adult offense between one with an onset age of 12 compared with age 13 is .117, which is the magnitude of the OLS regression coefficient.

Let's now use the linear probability equation to estimate the probability of adult offending for someone who committed his first delinquent offense at age 8:

$$\hat{y} = 2.00 - (.117)8$$
$$\hat{y} = 1.064$$

Although it is always hazardous to estimate the probability of an event that is beyond one's data (notice that we do not have anyone in the observed data with a delinquency onset age of 8), it is especially problematic here. We have a predicted probability of 1.064 of committing an adult offense. This is impossible because, as we learned in Chapter 6, probabilities have an upper bound of 1.0. One of the problems with using an OLS regression model on binary dependent variables, then, is that it may lead to predicted probabilities of the dependent variable that lie outside the limiting values of 0 and 1.0.

The reason why predicted values of y for the dependent variable may be less than zero or greater than 1 is that the OLS model assumes that the best line that fits the data is a straight line (that is what a linear relationship means). An implication of this is that a 1 unit increase in the independent variable, x, produces the same change in the expected probability of the dependent variable, y, *at all values of* x. In other words, the linear probability model assumes that the relationship between the independent and dependent variables is linear across all values of the independent variable. In our example, this means that the probability that someone will commit an adult offense is a linear function of onset age (x) and that a 1 unit change in onset age produces a $-.117$ decrease in the probability of adult offending at all values of onset age.

The actual relationship between the independent and dependent variables, however, might not be linear. Let us illustrate. We will use the data in Table 14–1 to draw a scatterplot of the relationship between the age of onset of delinquency and whether or not someone commits an offense as an adult. We also will include in that scatterplot the linear regression line using equation 14–1 and an S-shaped curve. In looking at Figure 14–2 you can notice several things that indicate that age of delinquency onset and adult offending might not be best characterized as a linear relationship. First, it clearly appears that the straight regression line from the linear probability model does not provide a very good fit through these data points. The S-shaped curve does, however, appear to provide a better fit than the straight line. This would lead us to believe that the relationship between onset age and adult offending is nonlinear. Another indication that the relationship may be nonlinear is that it appears from examining the data points that the expected change in the dependent variable for a 1 unit change in the independent variable is not constant for each value of the independent variable (as the linear model assumes). It would appear instead that the effect of a 1 unit change in the independent variable is greater for the values in the middle of the observed distribution and the effect of onset age becomes smaller as the probability of adult offending approaches either zero or 1.

There is another problem with the linear probability model. One of the assumptions of the ordinary least-squares model is that the error term is normally distributed and independent of the x (independent) variable. In order to examine this assumption with our current problem, we will calculate a predicted value of y (the predicted probability of an adult offense, the dependent variable) at each value of x (age of onset of delinquency, the independent variable) and then determine the error term by subtracting the observed

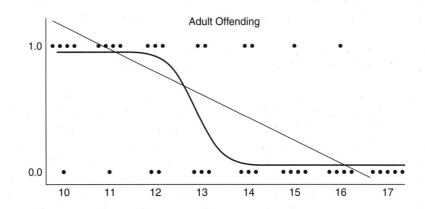

Figure 14–2   Fitting a straight line and an S-shaped curve to age of delinquency onset and adult offending data

value of y from this predicted value. We have calculated each of these predicted y values and the error term for each value of x in Table 14–2.

Notice that for each observed value of the independent variable there are only two possible values for the error term. For example, among those who committed their first delinquent offense at age 10, the predicted probability of committing an offense as an adult is .84. For those who committed an adult offense ($y = 1$), the error is .16, while for those who did not commit an adult offense ($y = 0$), the error is $-.84$. As you can see from Table 14–2, because the dependent variable takes on only two values (0 or 1), the error term in our regression equation (eq. 14–1) can assume only two values for any given value of x. This means that the error term is not normally distributed but is distributed as a binomial variable. You may remember from our earlier discussion of binomial variables that the variance is estimated as $\sqrt{\dfrac{pq}{n}}$, where $q = 1 - p$.

The variance of a binomial variable does not have constant variance, but is greatest when $p = .50$ and declines as p approaches 0 and 1. The variance of a binomially distributed error term in a linear probability model, therefore, is not constant but depends on the predicted value of y. Observations where the predicted value of y are closer to 0 and 1 will have small variances, while observations where the predicted value of y is closer to .50 will have greater variances. Because the error terms in a linear probability model do not have constant variance, the errors are said to be heteroscedastic, in violation of the OLS assumption of homoscedasticity. As a consequence of **heteroscedasticity,** hypothesis tests about estimated parameters such as the regression coefficient b may be incorrect.

When the dependent variable is binary (0, 1; a dichotomy), it is not a very good idea to use OLS and estimate a linear probability model of the type shown in equation 14–1. This is because: (1) unless restrictions are placed on the values of the independent or x variable, predicted values of the depen-

TABLE 14–2

Predicted Probability of y (ŷ) and the Value of the Error Term (y − ŷ) for Each Value of Onset Age of Delinquency (Data from Table 14–1)

Age of Onset	$\hat{y}$	$(y - \hat{y})$ for:	
		$y = 0$	$y = 1$
10	.84		
11	.74		
12	.61	−.61	.39
13	.47	−.47	.53
14	.32	−.32	.68
15	.21	−.21	.79
16	.13	−.13	.87
17	.07	−.07	.93

dent variable, the probability of y, might not be bounded by 0 and 1, and (2) the error terms will not be normally distributed nor will they have constant variance. We should not be too alarmed at the failure of our linear estimation strategy, however, because our scatterplot in Figure 14–2 clearly shows that the relationship between our two variables is in fact not linear.

What we should try, then, is a nonlinear estimation strategy that fits a smooth S-shaped curve to our data points rather than a straight line. In the sections that follow we will learn about two nonlinear regression procedures that will prove very valuable in working with dichotomous dependent variables: the logistic and probit regression models. Both the logistic and probit distributions are S-shaped probability distributions that would seem to fit the case of a dichotomous variable quite well. Examples of the cumulative normal probit and cumulative logistic distributions are shown in Figure 14–3. As you can see, both of these distributions are curves, rather than straight lines, and the logistic and probit distributions are very comparable to one another, suggesting that statistical models based on them should give similar results. We will use the logit and probit distributions to develop a regression strategy similar to the OLS method we already have in our toolbox. The difference between the logit/probit models and OLS is that the former are nonlinear models and do not require the assumption of constant variance. Both sets of regression models do, however, share some other assumptions, such as the fact that the dependent variable is a function of one or more independent variables, the observations are random and independent, and no two independent variables are highly correlated.

THE LOGIT REGRESSION MODEL WITH ONE INDEPENDENT VARIABLE

The **logistic regression model** is based upon something called the cumulative logistic probability function. In the logistic regression model we directly

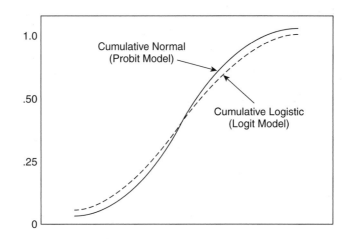

Figure 14–3   Probit and logit distributions

estimate the probability of an event occurring. In the case of one independent variable, the logistic regression model is:

$$\text{Prob (Event)} = \frac{1}{1 + e^{-(\beta_0 + \beta_1 x_1)}} \tag{14–2}$$

where

β_0 = the constant (y intercept) for the model estimated from the data,

β_1 = the regression coefficient estimated from the data,

x = the independent variable, and

e = the base of the natural logarithms, which is approximately equal to 2.718.

In the OLS linear regression model, the constant and each regression coefficient (slope) were estimated using the principle of least squares. In the least-squares method we estimated values of β_0 and β_1 that minimized the sum of the squared differences between the observed values of the dependent variable (y) and those values of y predicted from the regression equation ($\hat{y}$). In the logistic regression model, these coefficients are estimated according to the principle of maximum likelihood. In maximum likelihood estimation (MLE), the coefficients of a regression equation are estimated so as to maximize the probability or likelihood of obtaining the observed data. In other words, values for the unknown constant and regression coefficient are chosen so as to make the data "most likely." To use the MLE method, we first construct something called a *likelihood function*, which expresses the probability of the observed data as a function of the unknown regression coefficients (β_0 and β_1). The maximum likelihood estimates of these parameters (b_0 and b_1) are selected as values that maximize this likelihood function. It is in this sense that the estimated regression coefficients are those that make the observed data "most likely." The questions that we now have to address concern exactly how we estimate these regression coefficients, how we interpret them, and how we assess how well a logistic regression model fits the data.

Put your mind at rest if you are already panicking at the prospect of having to hand-calculate a logistic or probit regression model. As in the last chapter, our goal is for you to be able to understand the basics of logistic and probit regression models. To achieve this end, we use models estimated with computer programs and concentrate our efforts on interpretation rather than calculation. Although the specific output you get from logistic or probit regression procedures varies with the software program you use, most give you at a minimum the following information: (1) the constant and estimated logistic/probit regression coefficient for each independent variable in the model, (2) the estimated standard error of each coefficient, (3) a Wald or t test for the statistical significance of the estimated regression coefficient (whether it is significantly different from zero), and (4) various indicators of how well the model fits the data.

In Table 14–3, we have estimated a logistic regression model for the data found in Table 14–1, regarding the onset age of delinquency and whether or not someone commits an offense as an adult. Before we begin interpreting these results, let's reintroduce the logistic regression model with one independent variable (eq. 14–2):

$$\text{Prob (Event)} = \frac{1}{1 + e - (\beta_0 + \beta_1 x_1)}$$

This logistic regression equation does not look anything like the multivariate regression equation we learned about in the last chapter. We can, however, express the logistic regression equation a little differently so that it does look more familiar. We will let P be the probability of the dependent variable occurring. In our example this will be the probability that someone commits a criminal offense as an adult. Let's begin by multiplying both sides of the equation above by $1 + e - (\beta_0 + \beta_1 x_1)$ to get:

$$1 + e^{-(\beta_0 + \beta_1 x_1)} P = 1$$

TABLE 14–3

Results of Logistic Regression Analysis for Age of Onset of Delinquency and Adult Offending (Data in Table 14–1)

Variable	Beta	Standard Error	Wald Statistic	df	Sig.	Odds Multiplier
Constant	7.640	2.604	8.608	1		
Onset age	−.598	.197	9.214	1	.001	.550
−2 log likelihood for baseline model (constant only)					54.548	
−2 log likelihood for model with age of onset					41.553	

We then divide both sides by P and subtract 1 to get:

$$e^{-(\beta_0 + \beta_1 x_1)} = \frac{1}{P} - 1$$

or

$$e^{-(\beta_0 + \beta_1 x_1)} = \frac{1 - P}{P}$$

Since by definition $e^{-(\beta_0 + \beta_1 x_1)} = \frac{1}{e^{(\beta_0 + \beta_1 x_1)}}$, we can rewrite this expression as:

$$e^{(\beta_0 + \beta_1 x_1)} = \frac{P}{1 - P}$$

Next, by taking the natural logarithm of both sides, we obtain the following regression equation:

$$\beta_0 + \beta_1 x_1 = \ln\left(\frac{P}{1 - P}\right)$$

Moving expressions from one side of the equals sign to the other, we have:

$$\ln\left(\frac{P}{1 - P}\right) = \beta_0 + \beta_1 x_1 \tag{14–3}$$

This now looks more like our familiar regression model, with a dependent or y variable on the left-hand side and a constant and regression coefficient for the independent or x variable on the right-hand side. The dependent variable, however, looks a little unusual and deserves some comment.

The expression $\left(\frac{P}{1 - P}\right)$ is the probability of an event over its complement (the probability of the event not occurring, or 1 minus the probability). We learned earlier in this book that the ratio of a probability and its complement is the **odds** of an event occurring. The term "ln" in front of the odds is the natural logarithm. The dependent variable in a logistic regression analysis, therefore, is not the probability of an event, but the natural log of the odds of the event occurring. In the example we have been working with in this chapter, the dependent variable is the natural log of the odds that someone will commit an adult offense.

> The **odds** of an event occurring is equal to the ratio of the probability of an event to its complement: $\text{Odds} = \frac{P}{1 - P}$. The natural logarithm of the odds of an event is the dependent variable in a logistic regression analysis.

Because the dependent variable in a logistic regression analysis is the natural log of the odds of the dependent variable, the regression coefficient is interpreted as the change in the natural log of the odds that is associated with a 1 unit change in the independent variable. For example, in our delinquency onset and adult offending example, the logistic regression coefficient is equal to $-.598$. This tells us that a 1 unit (1 year) increase in the age at which someone commits their first delinquent offense decreases the log of the odds (from now on the "log of the odds" will refer to the natural log of the odds) of an adult offense by .598. Because it is sometimes easier to think of the odds of an event rather than the log of the odds, we can take the antilog of the estimated regression coefficient. This antilog is generally referred to in the literature as the "odds multiplier," and it can be obtained with most hand calculators (taking the antilog of a number is the same as exponentiating it). If the logistic regression coefficient is positive, the value of its antilog or odds multiplier will be greater than 1, indicating an increase in the odds of the dependent variable occurring. If the logistic regression coefficient is negative, the value of its antilog or odds multiplier will be less than 1, indicating a reduction in the odds of the dependent variable. When the coefficient is zero, the antilog or odds multiplier will be equal to 1.0, indicating that when the independent variable increases by 1 unit, the odds of the dependent variable are not changed. In our logistic regression example shown in Table 14–3, the antilog or odds multiplier of $-.598$ is .550 ($e^{-.598} = .550$). The first thing this tells us is that the effect of increasing the age of onset for delinquency is to lower the odds of committing an offense as an adult. In addition, the magnitude tells us that when the age at which one commits their first delinquent act increases by 1 year, the odds of them committing an offense as an adult decrease by a factor of .550. If you find that talking about the odds of an event is not much easier than talking about the log of the odds of an event occurring, we would readily agree. We would now like to show you how you can take the information from a logistic regression analysis and determine the probability of an event.

Predicted Probabilities in Logit Models

Although the logistic regression coefficient is not directly interpreted as a probability, we can use the results from our regression analysis to obtain an estimate of the probability of an event occurring. From equation 14–2 and the logistic regression results in Table 14–3, the estimated probability ($\hat{p}$) of committing an offense as an adult can be found for any given value of the independent variable x with the following formula:

$$\hat{p} = \frac{1}{1 + e^{-(\beta_0 + \beta_1 x_1)}}$$

Following Roncek (1991), we can multiply the right side of this equation by 1 in the form of $\dfrac{e^{(\beta_0 + \beta_1 x_1)}}{e^{(\beta_0 + \beta_1 x_1)}}$ so that we have a formula for the probability (P) that does not have a negative sign for e in the denominator:

$$\hat{p} = \frac{e^{(\beta_0 + \beta_1 x_1)}}{1 + e^{(\beta_0 + \beta_1 x_1)}} \tag{14–4}$$

To find the predicted probability of a given value of x, the independent variable, this formula instructs you to choose a particular value of the independent variable (x), multiply it by the obtained logistic regression coefficient (b), add the value of the constant, and then exponentiate this sum. The result is the numerator of the estimated probability, and the denominator is 1 plus the numerator. Let's go through some examples with the logistic regression equation estimated from our age of onset and adult offending data.

From the results of our logistic regression model reported in Table 14–3, we can determine that the log of the odds that one who commits his first delinquent offense at age 10 will commit an adult offense is:

$$\ln \frac{\hat{p}}{1-\hat{p}} = 7.640 - .598(10)$$

$$\ln \frac{\hat{p}}{1-\hat{p}} = 1.660$$

We can then use this log odds to plug into our estimated probability equation:

$$\hat{p} = \frac{e^{1.66}}{1+e^{1.66}}$$

$$\hat{p} = \frac{5.26}{6.26}$$

$$\hat{p} = .84$$

The predicted probability of committing an offense as an adult for someone who committed his first delinquent act at age 10, then, is .84. The corresponding probability that this person would not commit an adult offense is 1 − .84 = .16. The predicted odds of committing an adult offense for someone who first commits a delinquent act at age 10, then, is equal to .84/.16 = 5.25.

Now, let's increase the age of delinquency onset and ask what the probability is of committing an adult offense for one who commits her first delinquent offense at age 11. The log odds would be:

$$\ln \frac{\hat{p}}{1-\hat{p}} = 7.640 - .598(11)$$

$$\ln \frac{\hat{p}}{1-\hat{p}} = 1.062$$

We can then use this log odds to plug into our estimated probability equation:

$$\hat{p} = \frac{e^{1.062}}{1+e^{1.062}}$$

$$\hat{p} = \frac{2.89}{3.89}$$

$$\hat{p} = .74$$

The predicted probability of committing an offense as an adult for someone who committed her first delinquent act at age 11, then, is .74. The corresponding probability that she would not commit an adult offense is $1 - .74 = .26$. The odds of committing an adult offense for someone who first commits a delinquent offense at age 11, then, is equal to $.74 / .26 = 2.85$. Notice that by increasing the age of the first delinquent offense by 1 year (from age 10 to age 11), we have decreased the log odds of an adult offense by .598 ($1.660 - 1.062 = .598$). This value of .598 by which we have reduced the log of the odds of committing an adult offense is precisely the value of the logistic regression coefficient for age of onset of delinquency (see Table 14–3). You can now perhaps see more clearly that the logistic regression coefficient reflects the change in the natural logarithm of the odds of the dependent variable for a 1 unit (in this case, 1 year) change in the independent variable.

Notice also that by increasing the age of onset of delinquency, we have reduced the probability of an adult offense by .10 ($.84 - .74$). The probability of an adult offense for someone who committed their first delinquent offense by age 10 is .10 higher than the probability for one whose onset age of delinquency is 1 year later, at age 11. Please note that the .10 difference in the probabilities of adult offending *is not* the value of the logistic regression coefficient ($b_{\text{onset age}} = -.598$). The logistic regression coefficient, therefore, does not tell us the change in the probability of the dependent variable for a 1 unit change in the independent variable, but rather the change in the log of the odds of the dependent variable occurring. Finally, since the odds of committing an adult offense for someone who was 11 years old at the time of his first delinquent act is 2.85 ($.74 / .26$), and the odds of an adult offense for someone whose first delinquent act was at age 10 is 5.25 ($.84 / .16$), the ratio of these two odds is equal to .543, which, within rounding error, is the value of the "odds multiplier" in our logistic regression analysis in Table 14–3. The "odds multiplier," then, is actually the ratio of two ratios.

We have stressed that the logistic regression coefficient cannot be interpreted directly in probability terms, but we can use it to estimate the predicted probability of the dependent variable at different values of the independent variable. Using equation 14–4, in the second column of Table 14–4 we have calculated for you (you should do your own calculations for practice) the predicted probability of an adult offense for each age of delinquency onset from 10 years to 17 years ($\hat{p}$). We also have provided some other important information. In the third column we report the probability that there will be no adult offense committed ($1 - \hat{p}$), and in the fourth column we show the change in predicted probability with each increase of 1 year in the age of onset of delinquency. In the fifth column we report the odds of committing an adult offense for each delinquency onset age $\left(\dfrac{\hat{p}}{1 - \hat{p}}\right)$. Finally, in the last column we report the natural log of the odds that an adult offense was committed $\left[\ln\left(\dfrac{\hat{p}}{1 - \hat{p}}\right) = 7.640 - (.598)\text{onset age}\right]$.

TABLE 14–4

Predicted Probabilities, Change in Probability by Increasing Age by One Year, and Natural Log of the Odds (Log Odds) for Relationship between Age of Onset of Delinquency and Adult Crime (Data from Table 14–3)

Age of Delinquency Onset	($\hat{p}$) Predicted Probability	$(1 - \hat{p})$	Change in Predicted Probability	Odds	Log Odds
10	.84	.16	——	5.250	1.660
11	.74	.26	−.10	2.846	1.062
12	.61	.39	−.13	1.564	.464
13	.47	.53	−.14	.887	−.134
14	.32	.68	−.15	.471	−.732
15	.21	.79	−.11	.266	−1.330
16	.13	.87	−.08	.149	−1.928
17	.07	.93	−.06	.075	−2.526

There are several important things to learn about logistic regression analysis from this table. First, notice that the probability that an offense is committed as an adult decreases as the age of onset of delinquency increases. The predicted probability of an adult offense is .84 when delinquency first occurs at age 10, it decreases to .74 at age 11, .61 at age 12, .47 at age 13, .32 at age 14, .21 at age 15, .13 at age 16, and .07 at age 17. The fact that the probability of an adult offense decreases as the age of delinquency onset increases is consistent with the negative sign we obtained for our logistic regression coefficient for onset age. Second, notice that the change in the probability of an adult offense is greater when the predicted probability is near .50 than when it is higher or lower. For example, increasing the onset age of delinquency from 10 years to 11 years decreases the probability of an adult offense by .10, and increasing the onset age of delinquency from 16 to 17 years decreases the probability of an adult offense by .06. However, increasing the age of delinquency onset from 13 to 14 years decreases the probability of an adult offense by .15. In other words, unlike the case of ordinary least-squares regression, the change in the probability of the dependent variable with a 1 unit change in the independent variable is not constant at different values for a logistic regression. That is because in logistic regression we are not fitting a straight line to the data, but an S-shaped curve, and as you can see from Figure 14–3, the slope (measuring the effect of x or the independent variable) is greater in the middle of the probability distribution (when the predicted probability is near .50) than at either of the two ends. The effect of the independent variable on the probability of the dependent variable is nonlinear in a logistic regression. The effect of a given x or explanatory variable on the probability of the dependent variable y depends on the specific value of x.

Looking at the odds column in Table 14–4, we can clearly see that, consistent with the predicted probability results and the sign of the logistic regression coefficient, the odds of an adult offense decrease as the age of onset of delinquency increases. The odds that an adult offense is committed are 2.846 if the first delinquent act is committed at age 11, but these odds decrease to 1.564 if delinquency onset does not occur until age 12. Recall that the odds of each of these events is a ratio, the ratio of the probability that an adult offense is committed to the probability that an adult offense is not committed $\left[\left(\dfrac{\hat{p}}{1 - \hat{p}} \right) \right]$. Now take the ratio of the odds that an adult offense is committed for an onset age of 12 (1.564) to the odds that an adult offense is committed for an onset age of 11 (2.846). This ratio of two odds or **odds ratio** is equal to .550 (1.564/2.846 = .550), so by increasing the onset of delinquency age from 11 to 12 years old we are reducing the odds of an adult offense by a factor of .550 (i.e., we are cutting the odds by slightly over one-half). This value of .550, you will recall, is the value of the odds multiplier we found in our logistic regression analysis (see Table 14–3). This odds multiplier reflects the change in the odds of the dependent variable occurring by increasing the dependent variable by 1 unit (1 year in this case). At any value of age of delinquency onset, if you take the ratio of the odds of an adult offense to the odds of an adult offense for 1 year younger, you will find a value of .550 (within rounding error). The change in the odds of the dependent variable at different values of the independent variable, then, is constant at different values of x. In our example, increasing the age of onset of delinquency by 1 year reduces the odds of an adult offense by slightly over one-half.

Finally, look at the last column in Table 14–4, which reports the natural log of the odds of an adult offense. The log odds of an adult offense for one whose first delinquent act was at age 10 is 1.660: 7.640 − (.598)10 = 1.660. Increasing the age of onset for delinquency to age 11 decreases the log odds of an adult offense to 1.062. In other words, increasing the independent variable by 1 year (from 10 years to 11 years) results in a decline in the log odds of the dependent variable by .598 (1.660 − 1.062 = .598). This is precisely the value of the logistic regression coefficient we obtained (−.598) in Table 14–3. The difference in the log odds of the dependent variable between any two adjacent ages will be .598. Thus, increasing the age of onset of delinquency by 1 year decreases the log of the odds of an adult offense by .598.

We would like to end this section by emphasizing two important points. First, with a continuous independent variable, the logistic regression coefficient cannot be directly interpreted in probability terms. The obtained logistic regression coefficient of −.598 is not the decrease in the probability of an adult offense that occurs by increasing the age of delinquency onset by 1 year; rather, it is the change in the natural log of the odds of an adult offense. Second, because the relationship between the independent and the dependent variable in a logistic regression analysis is nonlinear (the effect of x on the probability of y depends on the value of x), the logistic regression coefficient cannot be interpreted in the same manner as an ordinary least-squares regression coefficient. When the relationship between x and y is nonlinear, there is no constant effect of x on the probability of y.

Significance Testing for Logistic Regression Coefficients

The regression coefficient from our logistic model (b) is a sample estimate of an unknown population parameter (β) that reflects the relationship between onset of delinquency age and the probability of adult offending in the population. As we did with the slope coefficient in an ordinary least-squares regression, we can conduct a statistical test that a given logistic regression coefficient is not significantly different from zero in the population. The null hypothesis of this test is that the population coefficient is equal to zero (H_0: $\beta = 0$), implying that there is no relationship between the independent and the dependent variable. The research or alternative hypothesis would be either the nondirectional alternative that the logistic regression coefficient is different from zero (H_1: $\beta \neq 0$) or one of the directional alternatives (H_1: $\beta > 0$ or $\beta < 0$).

Depending upon which statistical software package you use, the hypothesis test will be done with either a t statistic or a Wald statistic. Most of these statistical software programs routinely report the standard error of the regression coefficient along with the estimated logistic regression coefficient. We reported the standard error for our logistic coefficient in Table 14–3. If you have the standard error of the coefficient, you can conduct your own t test. The obtained t statistic is simply the ratio of the estimated regression coefficient to its standard error:

$$t_{\text{obtained}} = \frac{\text{Estimated regression coefficient}}{\text{Standard error of the regression coefficient}}$$

The t statistic is distributed as a Student's t distribution with $n - k$ degrees of freedom. In this case k refers to the number of parameters that are estimated in the model (the constant counts as an estimated parameter). Thus in our example, there are two estimated parameters—the constant (b_0) and the coefficient for the effect of delinquency onset age (b_1)—so there are $n - 2$ or 38 degrees of freedom.

With our knowledge of 38 degrees of freedom—and knowledge of our alpha level and whether or not we are conducting a one- or two-tailed hypothesis test—we could get a critical value of t from our t table (Table E–3 in Appendix E), compare the obtained t to the critical t, and make a decision about the null hypothesis.

A comparable hypothesis test that $\beta = 0$ can be conducted with the Wald statistic. The **Wald statistic** has a chi-square distribution, so observed values of the Wald are compared with critical values from a chi-square table. The critical value is based upon the alpha level selected and the number of degrees of freedom. The degrees of freedom for the Wald statistic depend upon the level of measurement for each independent variable. With continuous independent variables, there is 1 degree of freedom. In this case, the Wald statistic is simply the square of the t statistic [Wald $= t^2 = (b/\text{standard error})^2$]. With nominal or ordinal variables there are $k - 1$ degrees of freedom, where k is the number of categories or levels of the variable. For example, an ordinal-level measure of social class with three categories (lower, middle, and upper class) would have 2 degrees of freedom $(3 - 1 = 2)$.

Let's test the null hypothesis, that the logistic regression coefficient for onset age of delinquency is equal to zero, against the alternative that it is less than zero (since we can appeal to a great deal of theory and prior research that suggests that the earlier the onset of delinquency, the greater the likelihood of future crime).

H_0: $\beta_{\text{onset age}} = 0$

H_1: $\beta_{\text{onset age}} < 0$

Our research or alternative hypothesis, therefore, is that delinquency onset age and adult offending are negatively related. We will use an alpha of .05 for our hypothesis test.

We will first test this hypothesis with the t statistic. The t distribution is given in Table E–3 of Appendix E. There is no row for 38 degrees of freedom, so we will use 40 degrees of freedom. With a one-tailed alternative hypothesis and an alpha of .05, we find that the critical value of t is -1.684. The critical region is any obtained value of t less than or equal to -1.684, and our decision rule is to reject the null hypothesis if $t_{\text{obt}} \leq -1.684$. We can calculate our obtained t statistic from the information provided in Table 14–3. With an estimated logistic regression coefficient of $-.598$ and a standard error of .197,

$$t_{\text{obt}} = \frac{b}{\text{standard error of } b}$$

$$t_{\text{obt}} = \frac{-.598}{.197}$$

$$t_{\text{obt}} = -3.04$$

Since $t_{\text{obt}} < -1.684$, our decision is to reject the null hypothesis and presume that the logistic regression coefficient is significantly less than zero. We would conclude that age of onset of delinquency and the probability of adult offending are negatively related in the population; that is, youths who commit their first delinquent offense at an earlier age are at greater risk of committing a criminal offense as adults than those who commit their first delinquent offense at a later age.

Now let's conduct the identical hypothesis test with the Wald statistic. Using the chi-square table in Table E–4 of Appendix E, we can see that the critical value of Wald with an alpha of .05 and 1 degree of freedom is 3.841. Our critical region is any obtained Wald statistic that is greater than or equal to 3.841, and our decision rule is to reject the null hypothesis if our obtained

Wald statistic is greater than or equal to 3.841. From Table 14–3 we can see that the obtained Wald is 9.214. Since this is greater than our critical value of 3.841, our decision is to reject the null hypothesis that $\beta = 0$ and conclude that the onset age of delinquency and the risk of offending as an adult are significantly related in the population. If you did not want to use the Wald statistic but wanted a t test, you could simply take the square root of the Wald. The square root of 9.214 is 3.04, which is exactly the same as the value of the t statistic in the paragraph above. We would reject the null hypothesis.

Usually, statistical software programs will report the exact two-tailed probability of your obtained test statistic. If you are conducting a one-tailed hypothesis test (as we are doing in this example), you need to divide this reported two-tailed probability by 2 to get the correct one-tailed probability.

Model Goodness-of-Fit Measures

When we conducted an ordinary least-squares (OLS) regression analysis, we had a measure of how good the variable(s) was at explaining the variance in the dependent variable. This was the R^2 coefficient. Although statisticians have developed a few "pseudo-R^2" measures for logistic (and probit) regression models that are comparable to the OLS R^2 coefficient, none are exactly like it and not many have gained wide acceptance. In addition, some software packages with logistic regression capability report one or more of these pseudo-R^2 measures, while others do not. For these reasons, we will not discuss these measures in this chapter but suggest that you review the statistical literature. Nevertheless, there is some way that we can ascertain how well our logistic regression model fits the data.

A crude test of the model's fit is to test the null hypothesis that the independent variable(s) in the model is equal to zero. This is comparable to what we did with the F test in the OLS regression model. In the case of a logistic regression, we determine the *likelihood* of a given model, which is the probability of the observed results given the sign and magnitude of the estimated regression parameters. Because the likelihood is a number less than 1, it has become conventional to use -2 times the natural logarithm of the likelihood (often referred to as $-2LL$, or the **likelihood ratio statistic**) as an indicator of how well a given model fits the data. A good model, one wherein the probability of the observed results is high, is one with a small value of $-2LL$, so small values of $-2LL$ are better than larger values. If the model has a perfect fit to the data, the likelihood would equal 1.0, and $-2LL$ would equal zero.

To determine how well a statistical model (say the logistic regression model we have been examining in this chapter) fits the data, the first step is to estimate a baseline model that includes no independent variables, only the constant. From this model we can determine the value of $-2LL$, which measures how likely the observed results are with no independent variables considered. We then estimate a model that includes the constant and the independent variable(s) we are considering, and determine the $-2LL$ for this model. If the independent variable(s) is useful in explaining the dependent variable, the fit of the model that includes this variable(s) will be better than the baseline or constant-only model, and how useful the independent variable(s) is will be seen in a lower $-2LL$ value. The difference between $-2LL$ for the baseline model and $-2LL$ for the model with the independent variable(s) in it is a chi-square statistic. The number of degrees of freedom for this chi-square statistic is equal to the difference in the degrees of freedom between the two respective models (baseline and the one that includes the independent variable). We can, therefore, conduct a chi-square test that all of the logistic regression coefficients in the independent variable model are equal to zero. This is comparable to the OLS F test.

In Table 14–3 we reported the value of $-2LL$ for two models. The first is the baseline model that includes only the constant. The value of this initial log likelihood function is 54.548. The number of degrees of freedom in this logistic regression model is $n - k$, where k is the number of parameters that are being estimated. In this baseline model only the constant is being estimated, so there are $40 - 1$ or 39 degrees of freedom. The next model contains age of onset of delinquency as an additional parameter to be estimated. The value of the log likelihood function for this model is 41.553. Since we estimate one more parameter (the logistic regression coefficient for delinquency onset age), there are 38 degrees of freedom for this model.

The statistical test that all independent variables in the model are equal to zero is a chi-square test. Our obtained value of chi-square is the difference in the $-2LL$ between the model that includes the independent variable and the baseline model with only the constant. The degrees of freedom for the chi-square test is equal to the difference between the degrees of freedom for the two models. We will use an alpha level of .05 for our hypothesis test. With 1 degree of freedom and an alpha of .05, the critical value of chi-square is 3.841 (from Table E–4 of Appendix E). Therefore, our critical region is any obtained value of chi-square greater than or equal to 3.841 and our decision rule is to reject the null hypothesis if our obtained value of chi-square is greater than or equal to 3.841. The obtained chi-square from the difference between the model with independent variables and the baseline model will always be positive because the model fit will not get worse (we will not have a lower value of $-2LL$) when we estimate additional parameters. In our problem, the difference between the $-2LL$ values is 12.995. Our obtained value of chi-square of 12.995 is greater than the critical value of 3.841, and so we would reject the null hypothesis that all independent variables in the model are equal to zero. Of course, we knew this because we only have one independent variable in our model at the moment (onset of delinquency age) and we already know that this is significantly different from zero based upon our t test and

Wald test. This chi-square test for model fitness will become more useful when we discuss models with more than one independent variable.

Case Study: Race and Capital Punishment

Before we discuss the probit regression model, let's go through another example of a logistic regression with one independent variable. In this second example we will have a binary (dichotomous) independent variable as well as a binary dependent variable. The independent variable in this example is the race of the victim in a homicide where the value of 0 means the victim was African-American and 1 means the victim was white. The dependent variable is the decision of the local prosecutor to charge the defendant with a capital crime (a charge that could bring a sentence of death) where the value 0 is given if the prosecutor charges the homicide a noncapital crime and 1 is given if the prosecutor charges the homicide a capital murder. In the state where we have collected our data, the local prosecutor has a great deal of discretion as to whether or not to charge a murder as a capital crime, and we think that one of the factors that might go into this decision is the race of the victim. We take a sample of 29 murder cases in this state and record the race of the victim and what the prosecutor's charging decision was. The data for this example are shown in Table 14–5, and from these data we create a contingency table or cross-tabulation showing the joint distribution of the independent and dependent variables in Table 14–6.

From Table 14–6 you can see that there were 18 cases where the victim was African-American and 11 cases where the victim was white. In 14 of the 18 African-American victim cases, the prosecutor charged a noncapital crime and in the other 4 cases the prosecutor charged a capital murder. In 3 of the 11 cases with a white victim the prosecutor charged a noncapital crime while in the other 8 the prosecutor charged the suspect with a capital murder. From Table 14–6 one of the first things we can do with these data is calculate the probability or relative risk that a prosecutor will charge a capital offense in African-American and white victim cases. Doing this, we determine that the risk of a capital murder charge was .22 (4/18) for suspects who killed African-Americans and .73 (8/11) for those who killed whites. The odds of a capital murder charge, then, are .28 (.22/.78) for cases with an African-American victim and 2.70 (.73/.27) for cases with a white victim. There is a much greater risk of being charged with a capital crime for those who murder whites compared with those who murder African-Americans. This difference in the relative risk of a capital murder charge leads us to suspect that there is a relationship between the race of the victim in a murder case and the probability of a capital murder charge.

To further examine this relationship, we decide to do a logistic regression analysis with the prosecutor's charging decision as the dependent variable and the race of the victim as the independent variable. The results for this logistic regression analysis are shown in Table 14–7. The estimated regression model is:

TABLE 14–5

Race of Victim and the Decision of the Prosecutor to File a Capital Charge for 29 Hypothetical Cases

Case Number	Victim's Race[*]	Prosecutor's Charging Decision[**]
1	0	0
2	0	0
3	0	0
4	0	0
5	0	0
6	0	0
7	0	0
8	0	0
9	0	0
10	0	0
11	1	0
12	1	0
13	0	1
14	0	1
15	0	1
16	1	1
17	1	1
18	1	1
19	1	1
20	1	1
21	1	1
22	1	1
23	0	0
24	0	0
25	0	0
26	1	1
27	0	1
28	1	0
29	0	0

[*] Coded 0 for African-American victim and 1 for white victim.
[**] Coded 0 for charge of noncapital crime and 1 for charge of capital crime.

$$\ln\left(\frac{\text{Probability of capital charge}}{\text{Probability of noncapital charge}}\right) = -1.253 + 2.234x_1$$

The logistic regression coefficient for the relationship between the race of the victim and the log odds of a capital murder charge is 2.234. Since the

TABLE 14–6

Joint Frequency Distribution of Race of Victim in a Homicide and the Charging Decision of the Prosecutor

Prosecutor's Decision	African-American	White	Total
Noncapital charge	14	3	17
Capital charge	4	8	12
Total	18	11	29

TABLE 14–7

Results of Logistic Regression Analysis for Race of Homicide Victim and Prosecutor's Charging Decision (Data from Table 14–5)

Variable	Beta	Standard Error	Wald Statistic	df	Sig.	Exp(*b*)
Constant	−1.253	.567	4.88	1		
Victim's race	2.234	.883	6.40	1	.0114	9.34

Baseline model (constant only) −2 log likelihood: 39.336
With victim's race in model −2 log likelihood: 31.960

independent variable is coded 0 for African-American victims and 1 for white victims, the sign of this coefficient tells us that the log odds of a capital murder charge are higher for those who kill whites compared with those who kill African-Americans. The magnitude of the regression coefficient tells us that a 1 unit change in the independent variable, going from an African-American to a white victim, increases the log odds of a capital murder charge by 2.234.

To learn more about the logistic regression coefficient, we would like to show you that we could have estimated this logistic regression model by hand calculations directly from the observed joint frequency distribution of the variables in Table 14–6. We have already discovered that the odds of a capital murder charge in cases with an African-American victim are .28 and the corresponding odds for a white victim homicide are 2.70. Keeping in mind that a logistic regression coefficient is the natural log of the odds of the dependent variable occurring in white victim cases to the odds of the dependent variable occurring in African-American victim cases, we can express this relationship in the following equation:

$$b_{\text{victim's race}} = \ln\left(\frac{\text{Odds of capital charge for white victim cases}}{\text{Odds of capital charge for African-American victim cases}}\right)$$

The logistic regression coefficient, then, is the natural log of two odds or an odds ratio. From this equation and our knowledge of the odds of a capital charge for the two kinds of murder cases, we can find (within rounding error since the probabilities for both of the odds are rounded) the value of the logistic regression coefficient:

$$b_{\text{victim's race}} = \ln\left(\frac{2.70}{.28}\right)$$

$$b_{\text{victim's race}} = \ln(9.64)$$

$$b_{\text{victim's race}} = 2.267$$

As you can see from this solution, the logistic regression coefficient for the victim's race is simply the natural log of the two ratios: the odds that the prosecutor will charge a capital offense in a white victim case ($.73/.27 = 2.70$) and the odds of a capital charge when the victim is African-American ($.22/.78 = .28$). The regression coefficient tells us that when a white victim is slain the log of the odds of a capital charge is higher by a factor of approximately 2.2.

Now, if we exponentiate or take the antilog of the logistic regression coefficient for the victim's race ($e^{2.234} = 9.34$) we get what we have called the odds ratio or odds multiplier. Notice that the odds ratio is simply the ratio of two odds. One of these odds is the odds of a capital charge in a white victim case (2.70), and the other is the odds of a capital charge in an African-American victim case (.28). The ratio of these two odds (2.70/.28) is approximately equal to our odds multiplier of 9.3 (2.70/.28 is actually equal to 9.64, but we mentioned that there is rounding error in the probabilities that comprise both of these ratios). This tells us that the odds of a capital charge are over 9 times higher in white killings than in African-American killings. We would immediately remind you that this does not mean that the probability of a capital charge in white victim cases is over 9 times higher than in African-American victim cases—only that the odds are.

If we were to test the significance of the regression coefficient for victim's race, we could use the t test and take the ratio of the regression coefficient to its estimated standard error. We would then compare this obtained t with a critical t at some alpha level and with the appropriate degrees of freedom. The degrees of freedom are equal to $n - k$, where n is our sample size and k is the number of unknown population parameters we are estimating in our model (the constant counts as 1, and each independent variable counts as 1). The null hypothesis would be that the regression coefficient in the population is equal to zero ($\beta_{\text{victim's race}} = 0$), against either a one-tailed ($\beta_{\text{victim's race}} < 0$ or $\beta_{\text{victim's race}} > 0$) or two-tailed alternative ($\beta_{\text{victim's race}} \neq 0$).

Let's conduct a hypothesis test for the regression coefficient involving victim's race, and let's test the two-tailed nondirectional alternative, with an alpha of .05. To find our critical value of t we go to the t table (Table E–3 in Appendix E), with $n - 2$ or 27 degrees of freedom and our two-tailed alpha of .05. From the table we can find that our critical value of t is ± 2.052. The critical region is comprised of all obtained t coefficients that are either less than or equal to −2.052 or greater than or equal to +2.052. Our decision rule will be to reject the null hypothesis if $t_{obt} \leq -2.052$ or if $t_{obt} \geq 2.052$. Our obtained value of t is equal to 2.53 (2.234/.883). Since this obtained t falls into the critical region (2.53 > 2.052), our decision is to reject the null hypothesis. We would conclude that there is a relationship in the population between the race of the victim killed in a homicide and the prosecutor's decision to charge the murder as a capital crime.

We can assess the fit of this logistic regression model by examining the improvement in the likelihood function when we compare the baseline (constant only) model to one that includes the victim's race. From Table 14–7 we can see that with no independent variables in the model the value of −2LL is 39.336. With the race of the victim as an independent variable in the model the value of −2LL is 31.960. The difference between these two values (the improvement in the fit of the model) is 7.376. We know that this difference is distributed as a chi-square statistic with 1 degree of freedom, so we can test the null hypothesis that all independent variables in the model are equal to zero by comparing this obtained chi-square to a critical value. With an alpha of .05 and 1 degree of freedom (the difference in the degrees of freedom between the two models), the critical value of chi-square is 3.841 (See Table E–4, Appendix E). Our obtained value is greater than this, so our decision is to reject the null hypothesis.

THE PROBIT REGRESSION MODEL WITH ONE INDEPENDENT VARIABLE

Case Study: Age of First Delinquent Offense and Adult Criminality

You may have noticed in looking at the scatterplot of the raw data in our onset age of delinquency and adult offending data in Figure 14–1 that the shape of the observed distribution looks a lot like a cumulative probability distribution that we learned about in Chapter 3. The **probit regression model** that we will learn about in this section is based on the assumption that the distribution of the probabilities of a given dependent variable follows the cumulative normal probability function. This means that the predicted probabilities in a probit regression model correspond to the area under the normal curve.

The logistic regression model, you will remember, is based upon the assumption that the distribution of the probabilities of a dependent variable follows the logistic probability function. Figure 14–3 shows quite clearly that the logit and probit probability distributions are quite similar, differing only at the tails. This would lead us to suspect that the substantive conclusions we would draw from a logistic regression would be the same as those from a probit regression (although the magnitude of the estimated regression coefficients would be different). When you have a dichotomous dependent variable, then, the choice between estimating a logistic or a probit regression model is based on personal preference and the availability of computer software to do the estimation for you.

In order to understand the probit regression model, we would ask you to think about the dependent variable in your regression analysis as an unobserved—that is, latent—continuous variable. For example, in the first example we were working with in the last section, think of the probability of adult offending as an indicator of the theoretical construct "propensity to commit adult crime." Criminal propensity as an adult can be neither directly observed nor measured; the only way we know it exists is because someone has committed an offense as an adult. Let's refer to this unobserved dependent variable as z. For now, this dependent variable z is itself a function of a single independent variable, the age at which the onset of delinquency occurs. So we have a one-variable model that we can write as:

$$z = \beta_0 + \beta_1 x_1 \tag{14–5}$$

Keep in mind that we do not directly observe z, as it is an unobserved theoretical construct of criminal propensity as an adult. What we do observe is whether or not someone has committed an offense as an adult. We give this person a "score" of 0 if they have not committed an adult offense and a "score" of 1 if they have; these scores are the data in Table 14–1. If z is an indicator of the propensity or potential to commit a crime as an adult, each person has a threshold level which, once crossed, the potential to commit crime becomes the commission of a crime. As long as criminal potential is under the threshold, an adult crime has not been committed, but when that threshold has been crossed, a crime has occurred. Let's designate the threshold value as z^* and the commission of an adult offense as y, keeping in mind that $y = 0$ when there is no adult offense and $y = 1$ when there is an adult offense. We can write this as:

$$y = 0 \text{ if } z \leq z^*$$

$$y = 1 \text{ if } z > z^*$$

The first expression states that an adult criminal offense is not committed if the threshold value of z stays at or less than z^*, and the second expression states that an adult criminal offense is committed whenever z exceeds the threshold value of z^*. Further, the probit regression model assumes that z^* is a standard normal variable (a z variable that we learned about in Chapter 6) with a mean of 0 and a standard deviation of 1.

The standard normal probability function is written as:

$$P_i = F(z_i) = \frac{1}{\sqrt{2\pi}} \int_{-\infty}^{z_i} e^{\frac{-s^2}{2}} \, ds$$

where z = a random variable that is normally distributed with a mean of 0 and a standard deviation of 1.

P_i is the probability that an event will occur (in other words, that y will equal 1). The higher the value of z_i the higher the probability that the event will occur. To estimate the unobserved variable z^* (and thereby obtain our familiar-looking regression equation), we take the inverse of the standard normal cumulative distribution function:

$$z = F^{-1}(P_i) = \beta_0 + \beta_1 x_1$$

where β_0 and β_1 are estimated probit regression coefficients. As with the logistic regression coefficients, the probit coefficients are estimated by the maximum likelihood method. Also, as was true with logistic regression, there are readily available computer software programs that do the hard work of estimation for you. We will examine the results of a probit regression with the two examples we have been using thus far in this chapter.

Table 14–8 reports the results of a probit regression with the probability of adult offending as the dependent variable and the age of onset of delinquency as the independent variable. The estimated probit equation is:

$$z_i = 4.597 - .360(\text{onset age})$$

The value of the probit regression coefficient for age of onset of delinquency is $-.360$. Like the logistic regression coefficient, the probit coefficient has no intuitive interpretation. We can say that the sign of the coefficient is negative, indicating that there is an inverse relationship between the onset of delinquency and the probability of adult offending. In other words, the younger one is when he commits his first delinquent offense, the higher the probability that he will commit an offense as an adult. The magnitude of the coefficient gives us the change in standard deviation units in the unobserved standard normal variable (z^*) for a 1 unit change in the independent variable. This interpretation is not intuitively appealing, however, and it would be nice to convert this probit coefficient into something more immediately meaningful.

TABLE 14–8

Results of Probit Regression Analysis for Relationship between Age of Onset of Delinquency and the Probability of Adult Offending (Data from Table 14–1)

Variable	Beta	Standard Error	Wald Statistic	df	Sig.
Constant	4.597	1.460	9.91	1	
Onset age	−.360	.109	10.91	1	.001

Baseline model (constant only)−2 log likelihood: 54.548

With victim's race in model−2 log likelihood: 41.478

Predicted Probabilities in Probit Models

Since the dependent variable in a probit regression is a standard normal variable, we can estimate the predicted z score for the dependent variable at each age of delinquency onset and then go to the standard normal probability distribution (the z table, Table E–2 of Appendix E) and find our predicted probability. For example, let's take someone who committed their first delinquent offense at age 10. For this person, their predicted "score" on the unobserved standard normal variable is:

$$\hat{z} = 4.597 - .360(10)$$

$$\hat{z} = 4.597 - 3.60$$

$$\hat{z} = .997 \text{ (which we will round up to 1.00)}$$

The predicted value of the standard normal variable, or predicted z score, is 1.00, or 1 standard deviation unit to the right of the mean of this unobserved standard normal dependent variable. To find the predicted probability of a z score that is less than or equal to this, we simply go to our z table and find the area under the normal curve. Figure 14–4 shows that the area to the left of the mean of the standard normal distribution is .50, and the area of the curve from the mean to a point that is 1.00 standard deviation units to the right of the mean is .3413. The probability of a z score that is less than or equal to 1.00, then, is .84, and the predicted probability of an adult offense for someone who committed their first delinquent act at age 10 is .84. In our logistic regression analysis, the predicted probability of an adult offense for one who committed their first delinquent act at age 10 was also .84 (see Table 14–2), so you can see the similarity between logistic and probit regression models.

Now let's calculate the standard normal score for someone who commits their first delinquent offense at age 11:

$$\hat{z} = 4.597 - .360(11)$$

$$\hat{z} = 4.597 - 3.96$$

$$\hat{z} = .64$$

The standard normal score for this person is .64. The difference between this standard normal score and the standard normal score for the person with an onset of delinquency at age 10 is $-.360$ ($.64 - 1.00 = -.360$). This is exactly equal to the value of the probit coefficient and reveals another way that the probit coefficient indicates the amount of change in the unobserved standard normal dependent variable for a 1 unit change in the independent variable. In our case, increasing the age of onset of delinquency by 1 year reduces the standard normal dependent variable by .360 standard deviation unit. In Table 14–9 we report the predicted probability of an adult offense for each age of delinquency onset. For comparison, we also report the corresponding predicted probability from the logistic regression model. You can see that these two regression models for binary dependent variables give us very

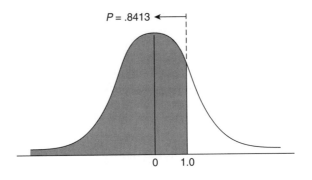

Figure 14–4 Area of the standard normal curve that corresponds to the probability of a z score of 1.00 or less

TABLE 14–9

Predicted Probability of y (ŷ) at Each Value of Onset Age from Probit and Logistic Regression Models (Data from Table 14–1)

Age of Onset	Probit ŷ	Logistic ŷ
10	.841	.840
11	.739	.743
12	.610	.606
13	.468	.467
14	.330	.325
15	.212	.209
16	.123	.127
17	.064	.074

comparable results. Both show that more than 8 out of 10 persons are predicted to commit at least one adult offense if they commit their first delinquent offense at age 10, whereas the probability of an adult offense is reduced to about .50 when onset of delinquency is delayed until age 13 and is less than .08 when onset of delinquency is delayed until age 17.

Significance Testing for Probit Coefficients

As we did for the logistic regression coefficient, we can test the null hypothesis that the probit regression coefficient is not significantly different from zero, with the implication that there is no relationship in the population between the independent and the dependent variable. The hypothesis that the probit β is equal to zero can be tested with either the t statistic or the Wald statistic, depending upon the software that you use. Remember that the relationship between the t and Wald statistics is:

$$\frac{b \text{ Coefficient}}{\text{Standard error}} = t$$

$$t^2 = \text{Wald}$$

Most software programs produce either the t or the Wald statistic and the exact two-tailed probability. If you are conducting a one-tailed hypothesis test, you need to divide the obtained probability by 2 to obtain the correct one-tailed test. We will test the following one-tailed hypothesis:

H_0: $\beta_{\text{onset age}} = 0$

H_1: $\beta_{\text{onset age}} < 0$

Our research or alternative hypothesis, therefore, is that delinquency onset age and adult offending are negatively related in the population. We will use an alpha of .05 for our hypothesis test. Looking at Table 14–8, we can see that the Wald statistic is 10.91, with a one-tailed probability of .001. Since our obtained probability is less than our critical alpha of .05, we will reject the null hypothesis. As was true for our logistic regression analysis, we would conclude that delinquency onset age and the probability of adult offending are negatively related in the population.

Model Goodness-of-Fit Measures

As with our logistic model, we can assess the overall fit of our probit regression model by comparing how well the model with one independent variable compares with a model that contains only the constant (our baseline model). We do this by taking the difference between the likelihood ratio statistics ($-2LL$) for the model with just the constant and the model with the independent variables. The difference between the two likelihood ratio statistics is a chi-square statistic with 1 degree of freedom. The hypothesis test is that all independent variables in the model are equal to zero.

We will test this hypothesis with an alpha of .05. With 1 degree of freedom and an alpha of .05, we can see from Table E–4 in Appendix E that the critical value of chi-square is 3.841. We will reject the null hypothesis, then, if our obtained chi-square statistic is greater than or equal to 3.841. From Table 14–8 we can see that the difference in $-2LL$ between the baseline and the model with the independent variable in it is 13.07. We will, therefore, reject the null hypothesis that all independent variables in the model are equal to zero.

Case Study: Race and Capital Punishment

We will now go through another example of a probit regression equation. In this example both the independent and the dependent variable are binary variables. We will use the race of victim and prosecutor's charging decision

TABLE 14–10

Results of Probit Regression Analysis for Relationship between Race of the Victim in a Homicide and the Decision of the Prosecutor to Charge a Capital Offense (Data from Table 14–5)

Variable	Beta	Standard Error	Wald Statistic	df	Sig.
Constant	−.765	.329	5.41	1	
Race of victim	1.369	.521	6.91	1	.001

Baseline model (constant only) −2 log likelihood: 39.336
With victim's race in model −2 log likelihood: 31.960

data that were reported in Table 14–5. We would like to remind you that the race of the victim was coded 0 if the murder victim was an African-American and 1 if the victim was white. For the dependent variable, the prosecutor's charging decision was coded 0 for a noncapital charge and 1 for a capital charge. In Table 14–10 we report the results of the probit regression analysis. The estimated probit equation is:

$$\hat{z} = -.765 + 1.369(\text{race of victim})$$

The probit coefficient for the race of the victim is 1.369. Since this variable was coded 0 for African-American victims and 1 for white victims, the positive sign of the coefficient tells us that the prosecutor is more likely to charge a capital than a noncapital crime when the person killed in the homicide is white rather than black. The magnitude of 1.369 tells us that a 1 unit change in the independent variable (in other words, moving from a homicide with an African-American to a white victim) increases the unobserved z score (z^*) by 1.369 standard deviation units.

To make more sense of this probit coefficient, we will convert it into a probability. To find the probit value in the case of an African-American victim ($x = 0$), we simply substitute for x in the equation above and solve:

$$\hat{z} = -.765 + 1.369(0)$$

$$\hat{z} = -.765 \text{ (which we will round down to .76)}$$

With a predicted score on a standard normal variable of $-.765$, we can go to the z table (E–2) and find our predicted probability. Figure 14–5 shows that the probability of a z score less than or equal to $-.76$ is .22. The predicted probability that a prosecutor will charge a homicide as a capital crime in cases involving an African-American victim is, then, .22. This is identical to the predicted probability for a capital charge in our logistic regression analysis.

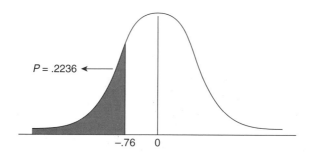

Figure 14–5 Area of the standard normal curve that corresponds to the probability of a z score of −.76 or less

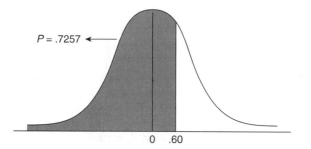

Figure 14–6 Area of the standard normal curve that corresponds to the probability of a z score of .60 or less

To find the probit value in the case of a white victim ($x = 1$), we simply substitute for x in the equation above and solve:

$$\hat{z} = -.765 + 1.369(1)$$

$$\hat{z} = -.765 + 1.369$$

$$\hat{z} = .60$$

The expected score on the unobserved standard normal variable for white victim cases, then, is .60. The difference between this and the expected z score in African-American victim cases is −1.36 ($-.76 - .60 = -1.36$), which is (within rounding error) equal to the value of our obtained probit regression coefficient. As you can see, therefore, the probit regression coefficient reflects the change in the unobserved standard normal variable (z^*) for a 1 unit change in the independent variable.

With a predicted score on a standard normal variable of .60, we can go to the z table (E-2) and find our predicted probability of a capital charge in white victim cases. Figure 14–6 shows that the probability of a z score less than or equal to .60 is .73 (.7257). The predicted probability that a prosecutor will charge a homicide as a capital crime in cases involving a white victim is, then, .73. This too is identical to the predicted probability for a capital charge in white victim cases from our logistic regression analysis.

Let's now test the null hypothesis, that the probit coefficient in the population is equal to zero, against the two-tailed alternative that it is different from zero:

H_0: $\beta_{\text{victim's race}} = 0$

H_1: $\beta_{\text{victim's race}} \neq 0$

The null hypothesis expresses the position that the race of the victim and the prosecutor's charging decision are not related to each other. We will use an alpha level of .05 for this hypothesis test. We can test the null hypothesis with either the t statistic, which is equal to the value of the coefficient divided by its standard error, or by the Wald statistic, which is equal to the square of this. In Table 14–10 we can see that the Wald statistic is 6.91 and that the probability of observing a Wald this large has a probability less than our critical value of .05. Our decision, therefore, would be to reject the null hypothesis in favor of the alternative and conclude that there is a relationship between the race of the victim in a homicide and the prosecutor's charging decision in the population. Prosecutors are more likely to charge a homicide as a capital offense if the person slain is white rather than African-American.

Finally, we can examine the fit of our model by comparing the likelihood ratio statistic ($-2LL$) for the baseline model, which contains only the constant, with our model that contains the independent variable. Recall that this is a test of the null hypothesis that all independent variables in the model are equal to zero. The likelihood ratio statistic for our baseline model is 39.336 (see Table 14–10), and for our one independent variable model it is 31.960. The difference between these values is a chi-square statistic with 1 degree of freedom. The critical value of chi-square with 1 degree of freedom and an alpha of .05 is 3.841 (see Table E–4), and our decision rule in this hypothesis test will be to reject the null hypothesis if our observed chi-square is greater than or equal to 3.841. The obtained difference between the baseline and independent variable model is equal to 7.376. Since this is greater than our critical value of 3.841, our decision will be that the one-variable model provides a significantly better fit to the data than the constant-only model, and that we cannot conclude that all independent variables are equal to zero.

LOGISTIC REGRESSION MODELS WITH TWO INDEPENDENT VARIABLES

Case Study: Age at Which Delinquency First Occurs and Gender

In the logistic regression models discussed thus far, we considered the effect of only one independent variable. While it is useful to look at only one variable when first learning about a new statistical technique because it keeps things simple, one-variable models are not very accurate depictions of the real world. This is because events are rarely well explained by considering only one factor or variable. In order to better explain and understand our dependent variable, whatever it is, we will have to make our initial regression equation more complicated and consider other variables. In this section we will discuss the case of the two-variable logistic regression model. We will learn the basics of this two-variable model with the understanding that generalizations to models with more than two variables will be straightforward.

One of the first decisions you have to make in moving from a one-variable to a two-variable regression model is which variable to add. The answer to this question is not strictly a statistical matter but is based on your substantive understanding of the issue. Your selection of each new independent variable should be based on either a sound theoretical expectation or the results of previous research. Whatever the source, you should be confident that the variable you add is capable of explaining or helping you understand the dependent variable. If you think a potential explanatory or independent variable is not related to the dependent variable, you should not include it in your model. There is a statistical component, however, in that the independent variable that you add to your one-variable model should be conceptually and empirically independent of the other independent variable(s) that is already in your model, but still related to the dependent variable. In other words, the two independent variables should not be strongly related to each other but each should be strongly related to the dependent variable. You do not want to add a second independent variable that is essentially a "carbon copy" of the first, and you want both to be able to explain or account for the dependent variable. Ideally, then, the independent variable you add should have a strong correlation with the dependent variable but a weak correlation with the other independent variable. As we learned in our chapter on multiple least-squares regression, when two independent variables are too strongly correlated they are said to be multicollinear; **multicollinearity** will create problems in our regression analysis.

> **Multicollinearity** occurs whenever the independent variables in your regression equation are too highly correlated with one another.

As our first example, let's use the onset of delinquency and adult offending data. In addition to the age at which somebody commits their first delinquent offense, another variable that may explain the probability of adult criminal offending is gender. The research literature in criminology consistently finds that males are more likely to offend, both as adolescents and as adults, than females. In our data, gender is a very good candidate as a second independent variable. Gender is strongly related to adult offending (Pearson's $r = .65$) and is only weakly related to the age of one's first delinquent offense ($r = .33$). In this new example, then, we have two independent variables, the age at which delinquency is first committed and the person's gender. The dependent variable remains whether or not an adult offense was committed, with a "no" coded as 0 and an "at least one offense" coded as 1. The raw data are displayed in Table 14–11.

TABLE 14–11

Data on Age of Onset of Delinquency (Age of First Delinquent Offense), Gender, and the Commission of a Crime as an Adult (Age 18 and Older)

Age of First Delinquent Offense	Gender	Adult Offense
10	0	1
10	0	1
10	0	1
10	1	1
10	1	0
11	0	1
11	0	1
11	0	1
11	0	1
11	1	0
12	0	1
12	0	1
12	1	1
12	1	0
12	1	0
13	0	1
13	0	1
13	0	0
13	1	0
13	1	0
14	1	1
14	0	1
14	0	0
14	1	0
14	1	0
15	0	1
15	1	0
15	1	0
15	1	0
15	0	0
16	0	1
16	1	0
16	1	0
16	1	0
16	1	0
17	0	0
17	1	0
17	1	0
17	1	0
17	1	0

TABLE 14–12

Results of Two-Variable Logistic Regression Analysis for Age of Onset of Delinquency, Gender, and Adult Offending (Data in Table 14–11)

Variable	Beta	Standard Error	Wald Statistic	df	Sig.	Exp(B)
Constant	6.582	3.237	4.134			
Onset age	−.643	.258	−6.211	1	.006	.526
Gender	3.244	1.048	9.582	1	.001	25.636

−2 Log likelihood for baseline model (constant only): 54.548
−2 Log likelihood for model with two independent variables: 27.922

Our two-variable logistic regression model looks like the following:

$$\ln\frac{p}{1-p} = \beta_0 + \beta_1 x_1 + \beta_2 x_2$$

$$\ln\frac{p}{1-p} = b_0 + b_1(\text{onset of delinquency}) + b_2(\text{gender})$$

This equation tells us that the dependent variable, the log of the odds of an adult crime, is related to both the age at which delinquency first occurs and gender. As in the one independent variable model, the unknown parameters of this two-variable model (β_0, β_1, and β_2) are all estimated according to the maximum likelihood principle. Using our computer software, the results of this two-variable logistic regression model are shown in Table 14–12. Our equation for adult offending is:

$$\ln\frac{p}{1-p} = 6.582 - .643(\text{delinquency onset age}) + 3.244(\text{gender})$$

In words, this means that the log of the odds of committing an adult offense is negatively related to the age at which delinquency first occurs and positively related to gender. We know that in a multivariate model (a regression model with more than one independent variable) the effect of one independent variable is measured while holding constant the effect of the others. Holding the gender of the person constant, then, a 1 unit (1 year) increase in the age at which delinquency is first committed lowers the log of the odds of the dependent variable by .643. Holding the age of delinquency onset constant, a 1 unit increase in gender (being male rather than female) increases the log of the odds of adult offending by 3.244. In other words, those who commit delinquent offenses at an earlier age and are male (since "male" is coded 1 and "female" is coded 0) are more likely to commit an offense as an adult. The odds multiplier tells us that the odds of an adult crime being committed are approximately cut in half for each 1 year increase in the age at which delinquency first onsets and that the odds are 25 times higher for males rather than females.

Since the log of the odds of a dependent variable is no more easily understood in a two-variable logistic regression model than in a one-variable model, we can estimate the predicted probability of the dependent variable occurring at different values of the independent variable. For example, the predicted probability of an adult offense for a male ($x_2 = 1$) who committed his first delinquent act at age 10 ($x_1 = 10$) would be:

$$\hat{p} = \frac{e^{b_0 + b_1(\text{onset age}) + b_2(\text{gender})}}{1 + e^{b_0 + b_1(\text{onset age}) + b_2(\text{gender})}}$$

$$\hat{p} = \frac{e^{6.582 - .643(10) + 3.244(1)}}{1 + e^{6.582 - .643(10) + 3.244(1)}}$$

$$\hat{p} = \frac{e^{3.396}}{1 + e^{3.396}}$$

$$\hat{p} = \frac{29.844}{30.844}$$

$$\hat{p} = .97$$

Let's now change this case to a female who commits her first delinquent offense at age 10:

$$\hat{p} = \frac{e^{b_0 + b_1(\text{onset age}) + b_2(\text{gender})}}{1 + e^{b_0 + b_1(\text{onset age}) + b_2(\text{gender})}}$$

$$\hat{p} = \frac{e^{6.582 - .643(10) + 3.244(0)}}{1 + e^{6.582 - .643(10) + 3.244(0)}}$$

$$\hat{p} = \frac{e^{.152}}{1 + e^{.152}}$$

$$\hat{p} = \frac{1.164}{2.164}$$

$$\hat{p} = .54$$

The probability of an adult offense for a female who commits her first delinquent offense at age 10 is about half of that for a male who commits his first delinquent offense at age 10. Now, let's take a male who commits his first act of delinquency at age 11 rather than age 10:

$$\hat{p} = \frac{e^{b_0 + b_1(\text{onset age}) + b_2(\text{gender})}}{1 + e^{b_0 + b_1(\text{onset age}) + b_2(\text{gender})}}$$

$$\hat{p} = \frac{e^{6.582 - .643(11) + 3.244(1)}}{1 + e^{6.582 - .643(11) + 3.244(1)}}$$

$$\hat{p} = \frac{e^{2.753}}{1 + e^{2.753}}$$

$$\hat{p} = \frac{15.690}{16.690}$$

$$\hat{p} = .94$$

When the onset age of delinquency is increased by 1 year for a 10-year-old male, the probability of adult offending barely diminishes, from .97 to .94, while the difference between a male and a female committing their first delinquent act at age 10 was dramatic. This clearly tells us that the probability of adult offending is affected more by gender than by the age at which delinquent conduct first occurs.

As we did in our one-variable logistic regression model, we can test the null hypothesis that each of the two regression coefficients is equal to zero in the population against some alternative hypothesis. This test, you will recall, is based on either the Wald statistic or the t statistic, where $t = b/$standard error of b and Wald $= t^2$. The null hypothesis we would test is that each regression slope β is equal to zero controlling for all other independent variables in the model. The null and alternative hypotheses regarding the relationship between onset of delinquency age and adult offending are:

H_0: $\beta_{\text{onset age}} = 0$; controlling for gender.

H_1: $\beta_{\text{onset age}} < 0$; controlling for gender.

We are testing the directional alternative hypothesis that there is an inverse relationship between the age of onset for delinquency and adult offending because there is a substantial amount of empirical literature that suggests that the earlier the age one gets involved in delinquency, the higher the risk of offending in the future.

The null and alternative hypotheses regarding the relationship between gender and adult offending are:

H_0: $\beta_{\text{gender}} = 0$; controlling for onset age.

H_1: $\beta_{\text{gender}} > 0$; controlling for onset age.

We are testing the directional alternative hypothesis that there is a positive relationship between gender and adult offending. Recall that the variable gender is coded 1 for males and 0 for females, and the research in our field consistently shows that males are more likely to commit criminal offenses at every age than females. Given this, the expected sign of the regression coefficient should be positive. Both hypothesis tests will be conducted with an alpha of .05, and we will do a Wald test. Recall that the Wald statistic is simply the square of the ratio of the regression coefficient to its standard error and that it has a chi-square distribution with 1 degree of freedom. With an alpha of .05 and a one-tailed hypothesis test, the critical value of chi-square that will lead us to reject the null hypothesis is 3.841 (see Table E–4 in Appendix E). Looking at the obtained Wald statistic for the coefficients in Table 14–12, we can see that both are greater than 3.841, and therefore we would reject both null hypotheses. We would conclude that in the population the age at which one first commits a delinquent offense is significantly related to the probability of adult offending when controlling for gender, and that a person's gender is significantly related to the probability of adult offending when controlling for the age of onset of delinquency.

Because both independent variables are significantly related to the dependent variable, we may want to know about the *relative importance* of each. The next question we may want to ask, then, is which independent variable is more important in explaining the dependent variable. There are a number of ways we can quickly assess the relative importance of explanatory variables in a logistic regression analysis. We've already discussed one way. We can calculate the probability of the dependent variable for different values of one of the independent variables, keeping the value of the second independent variable the same or constant, and then repeat the process for the second independent variable. For example, we looked at the change in the probability of an adult offense for both a male and a female who committed their first delinquent act at age 10 and found that the male was substantially more likely to commit an adult offense than the female (.97 vs. .54). We then compared a male who committed his first delinquent act at age 10 with another who committed his first act at age 11 and found that the predicted probability of an adult offense was lower, but not very different (.97 vs. .94). This suggests that gender has more of an impact on the probability of adult offending that does the onset age of delinquency. Another very simple way to examine the relative strength of our independent variables is to compare the t or Wald coefficients. In comparing two coefficients, the one with the larger (absolute value) t or Wald statistic has the greater explanatory "punch." For example, in the two-variable regression model for adult offending that we have just examined, the absolute value of the Wald statistic for the age of onset of delinquency was 6.211 and for gender it was 9.582. It would appear, then, that—when one of the variables is held constant—gender (controlling for delinquency onset age) is more strongly related to the probability of adult offending than delinquency onset age (controlling for gender).

Yet another way to determine the relative strength of our independent variables is to compare the likelihood ratio statistic ($-2LL$) for two models: (1) a model that includes all independent variables and the constant and (2) a model that includes all independent variables except one. The difference between the likelihood ratio statistics between the two models can then be compared with different independent variables dropped from the model. The variable that, after being removed from the model, results in a more substantial deterioration of the fit of the model has the stronger effect.

For example, our two-variable logistic regression model has a likelihood ratio statistic of 27.992 (see Table 14–12). When gender is not included in the model, the likelihood ratio statistic is 41.553 (see Table 14–3). The model that does not include gender, then, shows a worse fit to the data; the difference between the model with and the model without gender is 13.56. When age is not included in the model and gender is alone, the likelihood ratio statistic is

36.595. The difference between this model and the two-variable model is 8.60. Because the drop in the likelihood ratio statistic is greater when gender is removed (13.56) than when age is removed (8.60), gender is more strongly related to the probability of adult offending than is the age of delinquency onset (keep in mind that a lower value of the likelihood ratio statistic indicates a better-fitting model).

As we did with our one-variable logistic regression model, we can test the overall fit of our model with the likelihood ratio statistic. We will compare the likelihood ratio statistic for the model that includes only the constant (the baseline model) to the model that includes both independent variables. The difference between these two likelihood ratio statistics is a chi-square statistic with the degrees of freedom equal to the difference between the degrees of freedom for the two respective models. This hypothesis test is that the regression coefficients for all independent variables in the model are equal to zero. You will remember that this hypothesis test is equivalent to the F test in an ordinary least-squares regression analysis.

In Table 14–12 you can see that the likelihood ratio statistic for the baseline (constant only) model is 54.548. This model has only one parameter to estimate, so there are $n - k = 40 - 1$ or 39 degrees of freedom. When age of delinquency onset and gender are added to the model, the likelihood ratio statistic drops to 27.922. This model has three parameters to estimate, so there are 37 degrees of freedom ($40 - 3 = 37$). The difference in the likelihood ratio statistic between the two models, therefore, is 26.626 ($54.548 - 27.922$) with 2 degrees of freedom ($39df - 37df$). Let's test the null hypothesis that all independent variables in the model are equal to zero against the alternative that they are not equal to zero:

$$H_0: \beta_{\text{delinquency onset}} = 0, \beta_{\text{gender}} = 0$$
$$H_1: \beta_{\text{delinquency onset}} \neq 0, \beta_{\text{gender}} \neq 0$$

We will test the null hypothesis that all regression coefficients are equal to zero with an alpha of .01. From the table of chi-square values (Table E–4) you can see that the critical value of chi-square with an alpha of .01 and 2 degrees of freedom is 9.210. Since our obtained value of chi-square (26.626) is greater than the obtained value of 9.210, our decision is to reject the null hypothesis.

Case Study: Race of Victim, the Brutality of a Homicide, and Capital Punishment

Let's return to our example of the logistic regression equation involving the race of the victim and the prosecutor's decision to charge the suspect with capital or noncapital murder. In our one-variable logistic regression model we found that prosecutors were more likely to charge a case as a capital offense if the homicide involved the killing of a white victim as opposed to an African-American victim. More specifically, the odds of a capital charge were about 9 times greater for those cases that involved the killing of a white compared to those that involved the killing of an African-American.

Although this finding may suggest that the prosecutor's decision to seek a death sentence is based at least in part on the race of the victim, we cannot yet be confident in that conclusion. It may be that prosecutors are more likely to charge a homicide as a capital offense in white victim cases because on average killings of whites are conducted in a more brutal and egregious manner than are killings of African-American victims. Therefore, the brutality of the offense, rather than race, may be most important. If in fact it is the brutality of the offense that governs a prosecutor's charging decision and not the race of the victim, then once we have controlled for the brutality of the homicide the previously observed relationship between the victim's race and the charging decision should diminish and perhaps even vanish.

Let's say that in addition to the race of the victim we have other detailed information about each of the 29 homicide cases we have sampled, including information such as the number of victims killed, the type of weapon used, whether the victim pleaded for his or her life, and other indicators of how brutal the homicide was. With this information we are able to classify each of the 29 homicides as either not especially brutal (coded 0) or brutally committed (coded 1). Keep in mind that the victim's race is coded 0 for African-American and 1 for white, and the dependent variable is coded 0 for a noncapital charge and 1 for a capital charge. These data are shown in Table 14–13.

With the information in Table 14–13, we estimate a two independent variable logistic regression model, the results of which are given in Table 14–14. The regression equation is:

$$\ln \frac{\hat{p}}{1-\hat{p}} = -2.684 + 2.797(\text{victim's race}) + 3.233(\text{brutality})$$

As expected, both logistic regression equations are positive. Controlling for the brutality of the offense, the log of the odds of a capital charge are increased by 2.797 in a white victim case compared to a case with an African-American victim. Controlling for the race of the victim, the log of the odds of a capital charge are 3.233 higher for homicides that have at least one brutality factor than for those where brutality is absent. The odds multiplier tells us that the odds of a capital charge are 16 times higher in white than black victim cases, controlling for brutality, and the odds are over 25 times higher in brutal than nonbrutal cases, controlling for the race of the victim. The decision of the prosecutor to charge a homicide as a capital offense, then, is related to both the race of the victim and the presence of brutality in the case.

Since it is hard to actually get a sense as to what these effects mean for the victim's race and for the presence of brutality, let's calculate the probability of a capital charge in the following four kinds of offenses involving:

1. A white victim and no brutality.
2. A white victim and brutality.
3. An African-American victim and no brutality.
4. An African-American victim and brutality.

TABLE 14–13

Race of Victim, Presence of Brutality, and the Decision of the Prosecutor to File a Capital Charge for 29 Hypothetical Cases

Case Number	Victim's Race[*]	Brutality[**]	Prosecutor's Charging Decision[***]
1	0	0	0
2	0	0	0
3	0	0	0
4	0	0	0
5	0	0	0
6	0	0	0
7	0	0	0
8	0	0	0
9	0	1	0
10	0	0	0
11	1	0	0
12	1	0	0
13	0	0	1
14	0	1	1
15	0	1	1
16	1	0	1
17	1	1	1
18	1	1	1
19	1	1	1
20	1	1	1
21	1	0	1
22	1	0	1
23	0	1	0
24	0	0	0
25	0	0	0
26	1	1	1
27	0	1	1
28	1	0	0
29	0	0	0

[*]   Coded 0 for African-American and 1 for white.
[**]   Coded 0 for no brutality present and 1 for brutality present.
[***]   Coded 0 for a noncapital crime and 1 for a capital crime.

TABLE 14–14

Results of Two-Variable Logistic Regression Analysis for Race of Victim, Homicide Brutality, and the Prosecutor's Charging Decision (Data from Table 14–13)

Variable	Beta	Standard Error	Wald Statistic	df	Sig.	Exp(B)
Constant	−2.684	1.049	6.546			
Victim's race	2.797	1.235	5.129	1	.012	16.395
Brutality	3.233	1.277	6.410	1	.006	25.355

−2 Log likelihood for baseline model (constant only): 39.336
−2 Log likelihood for model with two independent variables: 22.523

The probability of a capital charge for a homicide with a white victim and no brutality is:

$$\hat{p} = \frac{e^{b_0 + b_1(\text{victim's race}) + b_2(\text{brutality})}}{1 + e^{b_0 + b_1(\text{victim's race}) + b_2(\text{brutality})}}$$

$$\hat{p} = \frac{e^{-2.684 + 2.797(1) + 3.233(0)}}{1 + e^{-2.684 + 2.797(1) + 3.233(0)}}$$

$$\hat{p} = \frac{e^{.113}}{1 + e^{.113}}$$

$$\hat{p} = \frac{1.12}{2.12}$$

$$\hat{p} = .53$$

The probability of a capital charge for a homicide with a white victim and brutality is:

$$\hat{p} = \frac{e^{b_0 + b_1(\text{victim's race}) + b_2(\text{brutality})}}{1 + e^{b_0 + b_1(\text{victim's race}) + b_2(\text{brutality})}}$$

$$\hat{p} = \frac{e^{-2.684 + 2.797(1) + 3.233(1)}}{1 + e^{-2.684 + 2.797(1) + 3.233(1)}}$$

$$\hat{p} = \frac{e^{3.346}}{1 + e^{3.346}}$$

$$\hat{p} = \frac{28.39}{29.39}$$

$$\hat{p} = .96$$

The probability of a capital charge for a homicide with an African-American victim and no brutality is:

$$\hat{p} = \frac{e^{b_0 + b_1(\text{victim's race}) + b_2(\text{brutality})}}{1 + e^{b_0 + b_1(\text{victim's race}) + b_2(\text{brutality})}}$$

$$\hat{p} = \frac{e^{-2.684 + 2.797(0) + 3.233(0)}}{1 + e^{-2.684 + 2.797(0) + 3.233(0)}}$$

$$\hat{p} = \frac{e^{-2.684}}{1 + e^{-2.684}}$$

$$\hat{p} = \frac{.07}{1.07}$$

$$\hat{p} = .06$$

And the probability of a capital charge for a homicide with an African-American victim and brutality is:

$$\hat{p} = \frac{e^{b_0 + b_1(\text{victim's race}) + b_2(\text{brutality})}}{1 + e^{b_0 + b_1(\text{victim's race}) + b_2(\text{brutality})}}$$

$$\hat{p} = \frac{e^{-2.684 + 2.797(0) + 3.233(1)}}{1 + e^{-2.684 + 2.797(0) + 3.233(1)}}$$

$$\hat{p} = \frac{e^{.549}}{1 + e^{.549}}$$

$$\hat{p} = \frac{1.73}{2.73}$$

$$\hat{p} = .63$$

These estimated probabilities will help us to better understand the relationship between the race of the victim, the brutality of the homicide, and the prosecutor's charging decision.

Notice that in cases where there is no brutality, the probability that the prosecutor will charge a capital murder is substantially higher in white victim cases than in black victim cases ($\hat{p} = .53$ vs. .06). This difference in predicted probabilities between homicides involving victims of different races also exists in cases where brutality is present ($\hat{p} = .96$ vs. .63). Holding constant the brutality of the crime, therefore, the race of the victim still matters for the prosecutor's charging decision: killers of whites are substantially more likely to be charged with a capital crime than are defendants who kill African-Americans. It is not true, then, that prosecutors are more likely to seek a capital charge in white victim cases because homicides involving white victims are more brutally done than those involving black victims. As you can see, the probability that the prosecutor will charge a capital offense in cases involving an African-American victim and brutality ($\hat{p}$ = .63) is not that different from those cases involving a white victim and no brutality ($\hat{p}$ = .53).

Notice also that, holding constant the race of the victim, there is a strong effect for the brutality of the crime, and this is particularly true in cases with an African-American victim. When the victim is white, the probability that the defendant will be charged with a capital crime is much higher if the homicide has been done in a brutal manner ($\hat{p}$ = .96 vs. .53). This is even more true when the victim is African-American, where the probability of a capital charge is over 10 times higher when there is brutality in the homicide than when it is absent ($\hat{p}$ = .63 vs. .06). What these predicted probabilities clearly tell us is that both the race of the victim and the presence of brutality in a homicide make a difference to the prosecutor when she decides to charge a crime as a capital or noncapital offense.

We can test the null hypothesis that the two estimated logistic regression coefficients are not significantly different from zero in the population with either the Wald test or the t statistic. The null and alternative hypotheses are:

H_0: $\beta_{\text{race of victim}}$ = 0; controlling for brutality.

H_0: $\beta_{\text{race of victim}}$ > 0; controlling for brutality.

H_0: $\beta_{\text{brutality}}$ = 0; controlling for race of victim.

H_1: $\beta_{\text{brutality}}$ > 0; controlling for race of victim.

In both cases the alternative or research hypothesis is the directional one that the coefficient in the population is significantly greater than zero. This is because homicides involving white victims and those where there is brutality are both coded as 1, and we expect these cases to have a higher probability of a capital charge.

We will test the null hypothesis with an alpha level of .05 and 1 degree of freedom. From our chi-square table (Table E–4 in Appendix E), we can see that the critical value of chi-square is 3.841. We will reject the null hypothesis if the absolute value of our obtained Wald statistic (remember, the Wald statistic follows a chi-square distribution) is greater than or equal to 3.841. Looking at Table 14–14, we can see that the Wald statistic for both the race of the victim and the presence of brutality is greater than 3.841. We therefore reject the null hypothesis that the coefficients in the population are equal to zero and conclude that both the race of the victim and the presence of brutality in the case are significantly related to the prosecutor's charging decision even when controlling for one variable.

If we wanted to examine the relative explanatory power of our two variables we could do a couple of things. One would be to compare their respective Wald statistics. Referring to Table 14–14, the Wald statistic for the race of the victim is 5.129, while for the presence of brutality it is 6.410. We would conclude from this that the presence of brutality has a more pronounced impact on the prosecutor's charging decision than does the race of the victim.

We also can compare the likelihood ratio statistic for our two-variable model with each of the one-variable models. When both race of victim and brutality are in the regression model, the value of −2LL is 22.523. When the victim's race is dropped from the model, the model fit is less satisfactory, with a −2LL value of 29.565. The difference between this and the two-variable model is 7.042. When brutality is dropped from the model, this model fit is even less satisfactory, with a −2LL value of 31.960 (see Table 14–7). The difference between this and the two-variable model is 9.437. Since the fit of the model deteriorates more when brutality is dropped than when the race of the victim is dropped, it has the stronger effect.

Finally, we can examine the overall fit of the model by examining the difference in the likelihood ratio statistic between a baseline model that includes only the constant and the two-variable model. The difference between these two likelihood ratio statistics is a chi-square statistic with 2 degrees of freedom. This test is analogous to the *F* test in an ordinary least-squares regression that all independent variables in the model are equal to zero. We will use an alpha of .05 for our hypothesis test. With an alpha of .05 and 2 degrees of freedom, the critical value of chi-square is 5.991. Our decision, then, will be to reject the null hypothesis that all independent variables in the model are equal to zero if our obtained chi-square is greater than or equal to 5.991. Our hypothesis and the alternative are:

H_0: $\beta_{\text{race of victim}} = 0$, $\beta_{\text{brutality}} = 0$

H_0: $\beta_{\text{race of victim}} \neq 0$, $\beta_{\text{brutality}} \neq 0$

Table 14–14 indicates that the likelihood ratio statistic for the baseline model (constant only) is 39.336. For the model with two independent variables, the likelihood ratio statistic is 22.523. The difference is 16.813. This obtained chi-square statistic is greater than the critical value of 5.991, so our decision is to reject the null hypothesis that all logistic regression coefficients in the model are equal to zero.

PROBIT REGRESSION MODELS WITH TWO INDEPENDENT VARIABLES

Case Study: Age at Which Delinquency First Occurs and Gender

We would like to conclude this chapter with a brief discussion of probit regression models that contain more than one independent variable. With what you have learned thus far, you should be convinced that the logit and probit models are very comparable. Just as our probit model with one independent variable led us to conclusions similar to those produced by our logisitic regression model, the same is true for the two-variable model. Thus, we repeat our observation that the choice between the two models is really a matter of personal preference and computer software availability.

TABLE 14–15

Results of Probit Regression Analysis for Relationship between Age of Onset of Delinquency, Gender, and the Probability of Adult Offending (Data from Table 14–11)

Variable	Beta	Standard Error	Wald Statistic	df	Sig.
Constant	3.887	1.868	4.33	1	
Onset age	−.377	.145	6.76	1	.001
Gender	1.884	.562	11.24	1	.001

−2 Log likelihood for baseline model (constant only): 54.548
−2 Log likelihood for model with both independent variables: 27.618

The two independent variable probit model takes the following general form:

$$z = \beta_0 + \beta_1 x_1 + \beta_2 x_2$$

where z is an unobserved, standard normal variable. Using the two examples we have discussed thus far in this chapter, in Table 14–15 we report the results of a probit regression model for the probability of adult offending, with onset age of delinquency and gender as the two independent variables. The estimated probit regression equation for these data is:

$$\hat{z} = 3.887 - .377(\text{onset age}) + 1.884(\text{gender})$$

The age at which delinquency is first committed has a negative effect on offending as an adult holding gender constant. Youths who commit their first delinquent offense at an earlier age are more likely to commit a crime as an adult than are those who are older when they commit their first delinquent act. The interpretation for the probit regression coefficient is that a 1 unit (1 year) change in the age of delinquency onset decreases the unobserved standard normal dependent variable by .377 standard deviation unit, after controlling for the effect of gender. Gender has a positive effect on adult offending holding constant the age of delinquency onset. Males are more likely to commit an offense as adults than are females. The probit regression coefficient tells us that, compared to females, being male increases the unobserved standard normal dependent variable by 1.884 standard deviation unit, after controlling for onset age of delinquency.

Since these probit coefficients are not easily interpretable, we can translate them into more easily understood probabilities. The probit prediction of an adult offense for a male who commits his first delinquent offense at age 12 is:

$$\hat{z} = 3.887 - .377(12) + 1.884(1)$$

$$\hat{z} = 3.887 - 4.524 + 1.884$$

$$\hat{z} = 1.25$$

The probit prediction, then, is a z score of 1.25, and this is the predicted value of our unobserved standard normal variable. To convert this z score into a probability we simply go to the standard normal table (Table E–2 of Appendix E) to find the probability of a z score less than or equal to 1.25. You should be fluent enough with the standard normal table to find that this probability is approximately equal to .89. Now let's determine the probability of an adult offense if we increase the age of onset for delinquency from 12 to 13 years old. The predicted z score is:

$$\hat{z} = 3.887 - .377(13) + 1.884(1)$$

$$\hat{z} = 3.887 - 4.901 + 1.884$$

$$\hat{z} = .87$$

The probability of a z score less than or equal to .87 is approximately .81. When we increase the age of onset for delinquency by 1 year, then, we reduce the probability of an adult offense by .08 (.89 vs. .81). Now let's change the hypothetical person from a 13-year-old male to a 13-year-old female. The predicted z score is:

$$\hat{z} = 3.887 - .377(13) + 1.884(0)$$

$$\hat{z} = 3.887 - 4.901$$

$$\hat{z} = -1.01$$

The predicted probability of a z score less than or equal to -1.01 is approximately .16. The change in the predicted probability of an adult offense between a male who commits his first delinquent offense at age 13 and a female is dramatic (.81 vs. .16), demonstrating the very powerful effect that gender has on the risk of committing a criminal offense as an adult.

We can test the null hypotheses that the probit regression coefficients in the population are equal to zero. Specifically, we will test the null hypothesis that the probit coefficient for onset age is equal to zero controlling for gender, and that the probit coefficient for gender is zero in the population controlling for onset age:

H_0: $\beta_{\text{onset age}} = 0$; controlling for gender.

H_1: $\beta_{\text{onset age}} < 0$; controlling for gender.

As in the logistic regression model, we are testing the directional alternative hypothesis that there is an inverse relationship between the age of onset for delinquency and adult offending because there is a substantial amount of empirical literature that suggests that the earlier the age one gets involved in delinquency, the higher the risk of offending in the future. The null and alternative hypotheses regarding the relationship between gender and adult offending are:

H_0: $\beta_{\text{gender}} = 0$; controlling for onset age.

H_1: $\beta_{\text{gender}} > 0$; controlling for onset age.

We are testing the directional alternative hypothesis that there is a positive relationship between gender and adult offending. Recall that the variable gender is coded 1 for males and 0 for females, and the research in our field consistently shows that males are more likely to commit criminal offenses at every age than females. Given this, the expected sign of the regression coefficient should be positive. Both hypothesis tests will be conducted with an alpha of .05, and we will do a Wald test. With an alpha of .05 and a one-tailed hypothesis test, the critical value of chi-square which will lead us to reject the null hypothesis is 3.841 (see Table E–4). Looking at the obtained Wald statistic for the coefficients in Table 14–15, we can see that both are greater than 3.841, and therefore we would reject both null hypotheses. We would conclude that the age at which one first commits a delinquent offense is significantly related to the probability of adult offending, controlling for gender, and that a person's gender is significantly related to the probability of adult offending, controlling for the age of onset of delinquency. These conclusions are, of course, identical to those obtained with the two-variable logistic regression model.

An examination of the change in predicted probabilities discussed above and the magnitude of the two respective Wald statistics would lead us to believe that gender has a greater impact on the probability of adult offending than does the age of delinquency onset. We would come to the same conclusion by an examination of the difference in the likelihood ratio statistics for a series of models. The likelihood ratio statistic for the model that includes both independent variables is 27.618 (see Table 14.15). When gender is dropped from the model and only delinquency onset age is included, the $-2LL$ value is 41.478 (see table 14–8), a decline in the chi-square value of 13.86. When age of delinquency onset is dropped, the $-2LL$ for this one independent variable model is 36.595 (table not shown), a difference of 8.977 with the two-variable model. Since the fit of the model deteriorates more when gender is removed, we can conclude that its impact on adult offending is greater than that for onset age.

Finally, we can get a crude sense of the overall fit of the model by examining the difference between the likelihood ratio statistics for the baseline model that contains only the constant and the two independent variables model. Recall that the difference between these two models is a chi-square statistic where the degrees of freedom are equal to the difference in the number of parameters estimated in the two models (in this case there are 2 degrees of freedom).

H_0: $\beta_{\text{delinquency onset}} = \beta_{\text{gender}} = 0$

H_1: $\beta_{\text{delinquency onset}} \neq 0, \beta_{\text{gender}} \neq 0$

We will test the null hypothesis that all independent variables in the model are equal to zero with an alpha of .05. With an alpha of .05 and 2 degrees of freedom, the critical value of chi-square is 5.991. We will reject the null hypothesis if our obtained chi-square statistic is greater than or equal to 5.991. The likelihood ratio statistic for the baseline model is 54.548, and for the two-variable model it is 27.618. The resulting chi-square statistic is 26.930, which is greater than the critical value of 5.991. We would, therefore, reject the null hypothesis that both independent variables are unrelated to the probability of adult offending.

Case Study: Race of Victim, the Brutality of a Homicide, and Capital Punishment

As a final exercise, let's estimate a probit regression model for our data on the race of the victim, the presence of brutality in a homicide, and the probability that a prosecutor will charge a capital offense. The results from that probit regression model are reported in Table 14–16. The estimated probit regression equation is:

$$\hat{z} = -1.510 + 1.591(\text{victim's race}) + 1.864(\text{brutality})$$

This model indicates that, controlling for the presence of brutality in a homicide, defendants who kill whites are more likely to be charged with a capital crime than are those who kill African-Americans. It also shows that brutality has an independent effect; that is, prosecutors are more likely to charge a defendant with a capital crime if the homicide was done particularly brutally, controlling for the race of the victim. The probit coefficient for victim's race suggests that there is an increase of 1.591 standard deviation units on the unobserved standard normal dependent variable for defendants whose victims are white rather than African-American, controlling for brutality. The coefficient for brutality indicates that there is an increase in 1.864 standard deviation units on the unobserved dependent variable when brutality is present in the crime compared to when it is absent.

Since these probit coefficients have no intuitive interpretation, we will use the probit equation to calculate the probability of a capital charge for four homicide scenarios:

1. A defendant kills a white victim with no brutality.
2. A defendant kills a white victim with brutality.

TABLE 14–16

Results of Probit Regression Analysis for Relationship between Prosecutor's Charging Decision, Race of the Victim, and Brutality of the Homicide (Data from Table 14–13)

Variable	Beta	Standard Error	Wald Statistic	df	Sig.
Constant	−1.510	.500	−9.120	1	
Race of victim	1.591	.652	5.954	1	.001
Brutality	1.864	.677	7.581	1	.001

−2 Log likelihood baseline model (constant only): 39.337

−2 Log likelihood with both independent variables in model: 22.444

3. A defendant kills an African-American victim with no brutality.

4. A defendant kills an African-American victim with brutality.

For the first case, the estimated z score would be:

$$\hat{z} = -1.510 + 1.591(1) + 1.864(0)$$

$$\hat{z} = -1.510 + 1.591$$

$$\hat{z} = .08$$

The predicted probability from the z table would be .53. For the second case, the estimated z score would be:

$$\hat{z} = -1.510 + 1.591(1) + 1.864(1)$$

$$\hat{z} = -1.510 + 1.591 + 1.864$$

$$\hat{z} = 1.94$$

The predicted probability for this second case would be .97. For the third case, the estimated z score would be:

$$\hat{z} = -1.510 + 1.591(0) + 1.864(0)$$

$$\hat{z} = -1.51$$

The predicted probability for this third case would be .06. For the fourth case, the estimated z score would be:

$$\hat{z} = -1.510 + 1.591(0) + 1.864(1)$$

$$\hat{z} = -1.51 + 1.864$$

$$\hat{z} = .35$$

The predicted probability for this fourth case would be .64.

Holding constant the race of the victim, then, in white victim cases the probability that the prosecutor will charge a capital crime increases from .53, in cases where there is no brutality, to .97, when brutality is present. In African-American victim cases, the probability of a capital charge increases from .06, in cases where there is no brutality, to .64, when there is brutality present. Clearly, the presence of brutality in a homicide is strongly related to the prosecutor's charging decision, even when controlling for the race of the victim. When there is no brutality present in the homicide, the probability that the prosecutor will charge a capital offense decreases from .53 for white victim cases to .06 when the victim is African-American. In the presence of brutality the probability of a capital charge decreases from .97 in white victims cases to .64 when an African-American is killed. When holding constant the presence of brutality, then, the race of the victim still matters: Those who kill whites are substantially more likely to be charged with a capital crime than are those who kill African-Americans.

With a Wald statistic we can test the null hypotheses that the probit regression coefficients in the population are equal to zero.

H_0: $\beta_{\text{race of victim}} = 0$; controlling for brutality.

H_1: $\beta_{\text{race of victim}} > 0$; controlling for brutality.

H_0: $\beta_{\text{brutality}} = 0$; controlling for race of victim.

H_1: $\beta_{\text{brutality}} > 0$; controlling for race of victim.

This Wald statistic has a chi-square distribution with 1 degree of freedom. We will use an alpha of .05. With an alpha of .05 and 1 degree of freedom, our critical chi-square statistic is 3.841. We will, therefore, reject the null hypothesis if the observed Wald statistic is greater than or equal to 3.841. Looking at Table 14–16, we can see that both Wald statistics are greater than 3.841, and therefore we would conclude that both the race of the victim and the presence of brutality have a significant effect on the prosecutor's charging decision. Looking at the relative magnitudes of the Wald statistics, we can conclude that brutality is a slightly more important factor in the prosecutor's charging decision than the race of the victim. This is confirmed by examining the difference in the likelihood ratio statistics for a series of models. The value of $-2LL$ for the full two-variable model is 39.337; when brutality is dropped from the model $-2LL$ is 31.960. The difference in likelihood ratio statistics, is 7.377. When the race of the victim is dropped from the model, the $-2LL$ is 29.565, and the decrease from the two-variable model is 9.772. Since the model fit is worse when brutality is dropped, we suspect that it plays a more important role in the prosecutor's charging decision than does the race of the victim.

Finally, the overall model fit for the two-variable model can be determined by taking the difference between its likelihood ratio statistic and that for the baseline model that contains only the constant. The difference between these two models is a chi-square statistic with 2 degrees of freedom (because in the two-variable model we are estimating two more parameters than in the constant-only model).

H_0: $\beta_{\text{race of victim}} = \beta_{\text{brutality}} = 0$

H_1: $\beta_{\text{race of victim}} \neq 0$, $\beta_{\text{brutality}} \neq 0$

With an alpha of .05 and 2 degrees of freedom, the critical value of chi-square is 5.991. We will reject the null hypothesis if the obtained chi-square statistic is greater than or equal to 5.991. The difference in the two likelihood ratio statistics is 16.893, which far exceeds the critical value of 5.991. We would, therefore, reject the null hypothesis and would presume that both probit coefficients in the population are significantly different from zero.

SUMMARY

In this chapter we examined both bivariate and multivariate regression models when we have a dichotomous or binary dependent variable. Although initially we might be tempted to estimate an ordinary regression model in this instance, doing so would violate key assumptions of the OLS model—that the error terms are normally distributed and homoscedastic. In addition, probability predictions from an OLS linear probability model may not be confined between 0 and 1, which would violate the bounding rule of probabilities. Because the OLS tool does not work with binary dependent variables, we investigated two other regression models, the logistic and probit models.

The logistic regression model is based upon the cumulative logistic distribution. The dependent variable in this regression model is the natural logarithm of the odds of the dependent variable occurring. The logistic regression model allows us to estimate regression coefficients that show the relationship between any independent variable and our dichotomous dependent variable. Since translating these coefficients is a bit clumsy, we learned how to convert our logistic regression information into estimated probabilities.

The probit regression model is based upon the cumulative normal distribution. The dependent variable in a probit regression is an unmeasured standard normal or z variable. It too produces regression coefficients that reflect the relationship between one or more independent variables on a dichotomous dependent variable. Like the logistic regression model, we can use the information from a probit model to calculate the expected probability of the dependent variable based on determined values of the dependent variable.

KEY TERMS

binary variable	multicollinearity
dichotomous variable	odds
heteroscedasticity	odds ratio
likelihood ratio statistic	probit regression model
linear probability model	Wald statistic
logistic regression model	

KEY FORMULAS

Linear probability model (eq. 14–1):

$$y = a + bx + \varepsilon$$

Logistic regression model (eq. 14–3):

$$\ln\left(\frac{P}{1-P}\right) = \beta_0 + \beta_{1x1}$$

Predicted probabilities from logit model (eq. 14–4):

$$\hat{p} = \frac{e^{(b_0 + b_{1x1})}}{1 + e^{(b_0 + b_{1x1})}}$$

Probit regression model (eq. 14–5):

$$z = \beta_0 + \beta_1 x_1$$

PRACTICE PROBLEMS

1. Out of a group of 700 criminal defendants:

   a. If 250 test positive for drugs, what is the probability that any one defendant randomly chosen will have tested positively? What are the odds?

   b. If 500 have at least one prior arrest, what is the probability that any one defendant chosen randomly will have a prior arrest? What are the odds?

   c. If 630 have a juvenile record, what is the probability that any one defendant chosen randomly will have a juvenile record? What are the odds?

   d. If 180 eventually get sentenced to prison, what is the probability that any one defendant chosen randomly will be sent to prison? What are the odds?

2. Presented below are the results from a hypothetical logit regression analysis using gender of the defendant (female = 0, male = 1) as the independent variable to predict guilty verdicts (not guilty = 0, guilty = 1) in 52 randomly selected cases involving homicides committed by one spouse against another.

Variable	Beta	Standard Error	Wald	df	Sig.
Gender	.3278	.1369	5.736	1	.016
Constant	.0561	.1105	.257	1	.611

   a. Interpret the regression coefficiet.

   b. Test the null hypothesis that the logistic regression coefficient for gender in the population is zero against the alternative hypothesis that it is different from zero. Use an alpha of .05.

   c. Compute the probabilities of a guilty verdict for both male and female defendants from the above equation. What are their respective odds of a guilty verdict?

3. The following table reports the results of a two independent variable logistic regression model. The dependent variable is the decision of the police to arrest a suspect (0 = no, 1 = yes). One independent variable is the expressed desire of the victim that the suspect be arrested (0 = no, 1 = yes), and the second is the age of the victim. The sample size is 50.

Variable	Beta	Standard Error	t Ratio
Desire to arrest	.8147	.9385	.868
Age	.1593	.0410	3.889
Constant	−7.246		

Initial log likelihood function (constant only model)
−2 log likelihood 66.406

With desire and age in the model
−2 log likelihood 34.586

	Chi-Square	df
Model chi-square	31.821	1

With this table, answer the following questions:

a. What is the equation for the two independent variable logistic regression model?

b. Interpret the two regression coefficients.

c. What is the predicted probability of arrest for a victim who expresses that an arrest should be made and is 50 years old?

d. Using an alpha of .05, test the null hypothesis.

e. Which variable is more important in understanding the police decision to make an arrest? What are your conclusions from this model?

4. In the table below you will find a two independent variable probit model. The dependent variable is the probability of rearrest after release from prison boot camp (0 = not arrested, 1 = rearrested). The independent variables are whether the person has a stable job on release (0 = no, 1 = yes) and the number of prior arrests the person has. The sample size is 50.

Variable	Coefficient	Standard Error	t Ratio
Job	−1.0186	.4297	−2.371
Prior arrests	.1824	.0620	3.031
Constant	−.2582		

Initial log likelihood function
(constant only model) −2 log likelihood: 69.324

With job and prior arrests in the model
−2 log likelihood: 49.044

With this table, answer the following questions:

a. What is the regression equation for this probit model?

b. Interpret the regression coefficients.

c. What is the predicted probability of rearrest for a person with no job after release and five prior arrests? For a person with a job after release and one prior arrest?

d. Using an alpha of .05, test the null hypotheses associated with this model.

SPSS PRACTICE PROBLEMS

1. In these exercises we are interested in the factors related to a homicide defendant being convicted. The data in HOMICIDE contains a sample of homicide cases by defendant from 33 counties. The variable CONVICT is a dichotomous variable coded 0 for those defendants not convicted and 1 for those defendants convicted. The first variable we will examine is the number of prior convictions each defendant had, PRCONV. This variable ranges from 0, for those defendants with no prior convictions, to 4, for those with 4 or more prior convictions. Under ANALYZE, click on RE-GRESSION, and then BINARY LOGISTIC. Place CONVICT in the dependent variable box and PRCONV in the covariate box. Interpret all results including the null hypothesis that the regression coefficient is equal to zero in the population.

2. Using the regression equation above, calculate the probability of a defendant with no prior convictions being convicted of the homicide. Now calculate the probability of a defendant with 4 or more prior convictions (coded 4) being convicted of the homicide. Interpret the differences.

3. Now let's examine a multiple logistic regression model by adding the defendant's gender to the above equation. Under ANALYZE, click on RE-GRESSION, and then BINARY LOGISTIC. Place CONVICT in the dependent variable box and PRCONV and SEX in the covariates box. Interpret all results including the null hypotheses that the regression coefficient is equal to zero in the population.

4. Now calculate the probability of a male defendant with 1 prior conviction being convicted. Next, calculate the probability of a female defendant with 1 prior conviction being convicted.

REVIEW & PRACTICE

Review of Basic Mathematical Operations

INTRODUCTION

Many of you undoubtedly have avoided taking a statistics class because you believed that the mathematics involved would be too difficult for your meager skills. After many years of teaching undergraduate statistics courses, we have probably heard all the stories. Some students protest, "I'm not very good at math, so how can I ever

> *I never did very well in math — I could never seem to persuade the teacher that I hadn't meant my answers literally.*
>
> — Calvin Trillin

hope to pass a statistics course! Statistics is nothing but math!" Others are more pessimistic, "I've *never* been good at math, I did lousy in junior high, high school, and college. I just have a mental block against doing math!" Others are only slightly more optimistic, claiming that they are simply rusty, "I haven't had a math course since high school, I've forgotten everything since then!"

This anxiety you brought with you to the course was probably only made worse when you thumbed through the chapters of this book, seeing all the equations, formulas, and strange symbols. Even letters in a different alphabet! "Boy," you thought, "I am sunk, maybe I should change my major or start planning for summer school"! Put your mind at rest, you need do none of those things. The study of statistics does require some mathematical skills, but they are no more than the ability to add, subtract, multiply, and divide. Let us assure you that, if you can do these simple mathematical operations, you can do statistics.

In this statistics text, we have emphasized the conceptual and logical dimension of statistical analyses of crime data. Most complex statistical analyses are now performed by computer programs. You will undoubtedly learn one of these programs in this or some other course. The computer application that is part of this text introduces you to one such statistical software program called SPSS. This stands for the *S*tatistical *P*ackage for the *S*ocial *S*ciences. This is only one such statistical package that will do the calculations for you for the statistics described in this book. There are many others available, and all of them perform high-speed and accurate calculations of simple and complex statistics.

Although computer software programs can perform the calculations for us much quicker than we could by hand and with far greater accuracy, we need to know some basics about statistics so that we know which statistical analyses to perform in which situations. We also need to know how to interpret and diagnose the mass of statistical information most computer programs spit out for us. In other words, no matter how fast, accurate, or sophisticated the statistical computer package you use, *you still need to know what you are doing*. Therefore, in this statistics course you need to learn how to hand-calculate the various statistical procedures.

The hand calculation of statistics is not that daunting a task. Again, all you need to know how to do mathematically is to add, subtract, multiply, and divide. The task will be made simpler by two things we have provided in each chapter of the text:

1. Clear and simplified examples.

2. A step-by-step approach in which even the most difficult statistical procedures are broken down into simple steps.

In addition, you will probably find it necessary to use a hand calculator to do the numerical operations for you. There are a great many kinds of calculators on the market now. Some of these calculators seem as complex as personal computers, with graphic screens and everything! Others, in addition to basic mathematical operations, actually calculate some of the statistics in this book for you, such as standard deviations and correlation coefficients.

We would recommend that you use a calculator for your calculations. You do not, however, need a very fancy or expensive one. All you really need is a calculator that, in addition to mathematical operations such as adding and subtracting, has a square root key ($\sqrt{}$) and a square key (x^2). The square key will enable you to square (multiply by itself) any number. A simple calculator that does these things is all you really need to work the problems described in this text.

Before we describe some simple mathematical operations, we would like to show you some common symbols used in statistics. Mathematical operations involve many symbols in their own right; as if this were not difficult enough, many statistics are symbolized by a Greek letter. To help you through the symbolism, the following are some common math symbols and Greek letters you will find in this text:

COMMON MATHEMATICAL SYMBOLS

$+$	Addition	$>$	Greater than
$-$	Subtraction	$\geq$	Greater than or equal to
$*$	Multiplication	$\approx$	Approximately equal to
/ or $\div$	Division	x^2	The number x squared
$=$	Equals	$\sqrt{x}$	The square root of the number x
$\neq$	Is not equal to	$\ln x$	The natural log of the number x
$\pm$	Plus or minus	$\log x$	The common log of the number x
$<$	Less than	$|x|$	The absolute value of the number x
$\leq$	Less than or equal to		

COMMON GREEK LETTERS USED IN STATISTICS

Uppercase	Lowercase	
A	α	alpha
B	β	beta
Γ	γ	gamma
Δ	δ	delta
E	ϵ	epsilon
Λ	λ	lambda
M	μ	mu
P	ρ	rho
Σ	σ	sigma
T	τ	tau
Φ	ϕ	phi
X	χ	chi

MATHEMATICAL OPERATIONS

Most of you are familiar with the four basic mathematical operations: addition, subtraction, multiplication, and division. In this text, the operations of addition and subtraction are shown with their common symbols, $+$ and $-$. In the text, the operations of multiplication and division are shown with several different symbols. For example, the operation of multiplying x by y may be shown as xy, $x \times y$, $x*y$, $x \cdot y$, or $(x)(y)$. The operation of dividing x by y may be shown as $x \div y$, or x/y.

In addition to the standard operations of addition, subtraction, multiplication, and division, there are three other very frequent mathematical operations in statistics. One of these is the squaring of a number. A number squared is symbolized by the number being squared shown with a superscript of 2.

For example, 4 squared is shown as 4^2, and 7 squared is shown as 7^2. When you square a number, you multiply that number by itself, so that 4 squared is equal to $4 \times 4 = 16$, and 7 squared is equal to $7 \times 7 = 49$. These expressions tell us that 4 squared is equal to 16 and 7 squared is equal to 49. One squared is equal to 1, because $1^2 = 1 \times 1 = 1$. When calculating the square of fractions, it is probably easier to first convert the fraction to a decimal and then square. For example, the square of one-half $\left(\frac{1}{2}\right)^2$ would be equal to $.50^2$, or $(.50)(.50) = .25$. The square of one-third $\left(\frac{1}{3}\right)^2$ would be equal to $.33^2$ or $(.33)(.33) = .1089$.

A second frequent mathematical operation in statistics is taking the square root of a number. This is symbolized by placing the number we want the square root of within something called a radical sign ($\sqrt{}$). For example, the square root of 2 is shown as $\sqrt{2}$, and the square root of 9 is shown as $\sqrt{9}$. The square root of a number is the value that, when squared, results in the original number. For example, the square root of 9 is 3 ($\sqrt{9} = 3$) because when 3 is squared we obtain 9 ($3^2 = 3 \times 3 = 9$). The square root of 25 is 5 ($\sqrt{25} = 5$) because when 5 is squared, we obtain 25 ($5^2 = (5)(5) = 25$). As with the squaring of fractions, it will probably be easier to convert a fraction into a decimal before taking the square root. For example, the square root of one-half ($\sqrt{1/2}$) is equal to $\sqrt{.5}$, which is equal to .707 because $.707^2 = .5$. The square root of a negative number, $\sqrt{-x}$, is not defined because there is no number x that, when squared (multiplied by itself), results in a negative number. This is because the multiplication of two negative numbers always results in a positive product.

The third other operation that you will frequently see in this text is the summation operation. This is actually an addition operation, but because it appears with its own symbol we need to call special attention to it. The operation of summation is symbolized by the uppercase Greek letter sigma (Σ). The summation sign stands for "the sum of," and the operation requires you to add a series of scores for a given variable. For example, presuming that there are five scores for the variable Age (itself symbolized as x), the ages of five persons might be as follows:

$$x_1 = 13 \qquad x_4 = 20$$
$$x_2 = 18 \qquad x_5 = 17$$
$$x_3 = 25$$

The operation Σx instructs you to sum or add each of these x scores or ages. That is, instead of stating that you should take the first person's age and add it to the second person's age, and then add this sum to the third person's age, and so on, a formula will simply state the sum of all the x scores or Σx. In this example, then, $\Sigma x = 13 + 18 + 25 + 20 + 17 = 93$. Think of the symbol Σ, then, as a mathematical operation that says "add all of the x scores up and determine the sum."

ORDER OF OPERATIONS

Many statistical formulas require you to perform several mathematical operations at once. At times these formulas may seem very complex, requiring addition, division, squaring, square roots, and summation. Your task of comprehending statistical formulas would not be so difficult if it did not matter how all the calculations were performed, so long as they were all completed. Unfortunately, however, statistical formulas require not only that all mathematical operations be conducted, but also that they be conducted in the right order, because you will get different results depending on the order in which the operations are performed!

For example, take the very simple equation below that requires you to add and divide a few numbers:

$$15 + 10 \div 5$$

Notice that you will get completely different results depending on whether you complete the addition before dividing or do the dividing first:

$$(15 + 10) \div 5 \qquad\qquad 15 + (10 \div 5)$$
$$25 \div 5 = 5 \qquad\qquad 15 + 2 = 17$$

As you can see, the order in which you perform your mathematical operations does make a substantial difference, and must, therefore, be correctly followed. Fortunately, there are some standard rules that tell you the order in which operations should be performed. In addition, we would like to emphasize that even the most complex formula or mathematical expression can be simplified by solving it in sequential steps. We now illustrate these rules of operation and our recommended step-by-step approach for solving mathematical expressions.

The first rule is that any operation that is included in parentheses should be performed before operations not included in parentheses. For example, for the following expression

$$15 + (10 \div 5) \times (7 \times 2)$$

the order of operations would be to first divide 10 by 5 and multiply 7 by 2. We now have simplified the expression

$$15 + 2 \times 14$$

How do we solve the remainder of this? Do we first add $15 + 2$ and then multiply by 14 to get 238? Or do we first multiply 2 by 14 and then add 15 to get 43?

The second rule of the order of operations is that you should first obtain all squares and square roots first, then multiplication and division, and last complete the addition and subtraction. Because in the expression just listed we have no squares or square roots to calculate, we know that we should first multiply the 2 and 14 to get 28.

$$15 + 28$$

After this we should add this to 15 to get the final sum of 43.

To summarize, the rules of operation for solving mathematical expressions are, in order:

- Solve all expressions in parentheses.

- Determine the value of all squares and square roots.

- Perform division and multiplication operations.

- Perform all addition and subtraction operations.

We will practice these rules with some exercises momentarily, but first, we need to illustrate the parentheses rule in combination with the rule of squares.

The rules are to perform all operations within parentheses first, then squares and square roots, multiplication and division, and then addition and subtraction. As an example, assume that we have the following six scores: 46, 29, 61, 14, 33, and 25. With these scores, examine the two expressions, Σx^2 and $(\Sigma x)^2$. These two expressions look virtually identical because they both require a summation of scores and that a number be squared. Notice, however, that in the first expression there are no parentheses. We know that the summation sign tells us that we have to add the six scores. Before we do this, however, following the correct order of operations, we must first square each x score, and then sum them:

$$\Sigma x^2 = 46^2 + 29^2 + 61^2 + 14^2 + 33^2 + 25^2$$

$$= 2,116 + 841 + 3,721 + 196 + 1,089 + 625$$

$$= 8,588$$

In this first expression, then, we have followed the order of operations by first squaring each x score and then taking the sum (squaring before addition).

Notice that in the second expression we have a parentheses $(\Sigma x)^2$. As the order of operations is to conduct all calculations within parentheses first, this expression tells us to first sum the six scores and then square the sum:

$$(\Sigma x)^2 = (46 + 29 + 61 + 14 + 33 + 25)^2$$

$$= 208^2$$

$$= 43,264$$

To reiterate the point made above, Σx^2, called the sum of the x squares, is obtained by first squaring each x score and then adding all squared numbers. This is different from the expression, $(\Sigma x)^2$, called the sum of the xs, squared, which is obtained by first adding up all the x scores and then squaring the sum.

OPERATIONS WITH NEGATIVE NUMBERS AND FRACTIONS IN DENOMINATORS

In many statistical calculations you have both positive and negative scores. Positive scores are shown with no sign at all, so that a positive 10 appears as 10. Negative numbers are shown with a minus sign in front of them, so that a negative 10 appears as -10. Negative numbers are less than zero, and positive numbers are greater than zero. It is important to keep track of the signs of numbers because it makes a substantial difference for the final result of a mathematical operation.

For example, when a positive number is added to a positive number, nothing special happens, and the sum of the two numbers can be obtained directly: $10 + 14 = 24$. When a negative number is added to a positive number, however, it has the same effect as subtraction. For example, adding a negative 14 to 10 is the same thing as subtracting 14 from 10: $10 + (-14) = 10 - 14 = (-4)$. When a positive number is subtracted from another positive number, nothing special happens, and the difference between the two numbers can be obtained directly: $25 - 10 = 15$. When a negative number is subtracted from either a positive or negative number, the sign changes to a positive number, so that $25 - (-10) = 25 + 10 = 35$, $(-10) - (-7) = (-10) + 7 = (-3)$. Remember, then, that the subtraction of a negative number changes the sign of the number from negative to positive.

When two positive numbers are multiplied, nothing special happens, and the product of the two numbers can be obtained directly: $6 \times 3 = 18$. When two numbers are multiplied and one is positive and the other negative, the resulting product is negative. For example: $25 \times (-3) = -75$; $(-14) \times 5 = -70$. When two negative numbers are multiplied, the resulting product is always positive: $(-23) \times (-14) = 322$. So, the rule is that the multiplication of either two positive or two negative numbers results in a positive product, whereas the multiplication of one positive and one negative number results in a negative product.

The same pattern occurs when the operation is division rather than multiplication. When two positive numbers are divided, nothing special happens, and the result (the *quotient*) is positive: $125 \div 5 = 25$; $10 \div 20 = .5$. When two numbers are divided and one is positive and the other negative, the quotient is negative: $250 \div (-25) = (-10)$; $(-33) \div 11 = -3$. When two negative numbers are divided, the quotient always is positive: $(-16) \div (-4) = 4$. So, the rule is that the division of either two positive or two negative numbers results in a positive quotient, whereas the division of one positive and one negative number has a negative quotient.

ROUNDING NUMBERS OFF

Whenever you are working with statistical formulas, you need to decide how precise you want your answer to be. For example, should your answer be correct to the tenth decimal place? the fifth? the third? It is also important to decide when to round up and when to round down. For example, having decided that we want to be accurate only to the second decimal place, should the number 28.355 be rounded up to 28.36 or rounded down to 28.35? It is important to make these decisions explicit, because two people may get different answers to the same statistical problem simply because they employed different rounding rules.

Unfortunately, any rule as to when to round off cannot always be hard and fast. When we are dealing with large numbers, we can frequently do our calculations with whole numbers (integers). In this case, we would not gain much precision by carrying out our calculations to one or two decimal places. When we are dealing with much smaller numbers, however, it may be necessary, in order to be as precise as possible, to take a number out to three or four decimal places in our calculations. With smaller numbers, there is a substantial gain in precision by including more decimal places in our calculations. Whenever possible, however, we have tried to limit our precision to two decimal places. This means that most of the time numbers will include only two decimal places. We warn you, however, that this will not always be the case.

The question as to how to round can be answered a little more definitively. When rounding, the following convention should be applied. When deciding how to round, look at the digit to the right of the last digit you want to keep. If we are rounding to the second decimal place, then, look at the third digit to the right of the decimal point. If this digit is larger than 5, you should round up. For example, 123.148 becomes 123.15, and 34.737 becomes 34.74. If this digit is less than 5, you should round down. For example, 8.923 becomes 8.92, and 53.904 becomes 53.90.

What do you do in the case where the third digit is a 5, 34.675, for example? Do you round up or round down? You cannot simply say that you should always round up or always round down because there will be systematic bias to your rounding decision. Your decision rule will be consistent to be sure, but it will be biased because numbers are always being overestimated (if rounded up) or underestimated (if rounded down). You would like your decision rule to be consistent, but consistently fair, that is, never in the same direction. This way, sometimes the 5 will be rounded up and sometimes it will be rounded down, and the number of times it is rounded up and down will be approximately the same. One way to ensure this is to adopt the following rounding rule: if the third digit is a 5, then look at the digit immediately *before* the 5; if that digit (the second decimal place) is an even number, then round up; if it is an odd number, then round down. For example, the number 34.675 should be rounded down to 34.67 because the number immediately before the 5 is an odd number. The number 164.965 should be rounded up to 164.97 because the number before the 5 is an even number. Notice that the number of occasions you will decide to round up (if the immediately preceding digit is an even number 0, 2, 4, 6, or 8) is the same as the number of occasions when you will decide to round down (if the immediately preceding digit is an odd number

1, 3, 5, 7, 9). Because even numbers should appear in our calculations as frequently as odd numbers there is no bias to our rounding decision rule.

EXAMPLES

Let's go through a few examples step by step to make sure that we understand all the rules and procedures. We will begin by solving the following problem:

$$25 + 192 - (3 + 5)^2$$

Following the rules of operation, we first solve within the parentheses:

$$25 + 192 - (8)^2$$

Then square the 8:

$$25 + 192 - 64$$

Now we can solve for the final answer either by adding 25 to 192 and then subtracting 64, or subtracting 64 from 192 and then adding 25. Either way, we get the same result:

$$217 - 64 = 153 \qquad 25 + 128 = 153$$

Now let's solve a more complicated-looking problem. Please note that this problem is only more complicated looking. When we solve it step by step, you will see that it is very manageable and that all you really need to know is addition, subtraction, multiplication, and division:

$$\left[(32 + 17)^2 / 10 \right] + \left[\sqrt{16} / (10 - 6)^2 \right]$$

First, we solve within parentheses:

$$\left[(49)^2 / 10 \right] + \left[\sqrt{16} / (4)^2 \right]$$

Then, calculate all squares and square roots:

$$(2,401/10) + (4/16)$$

Then, do the division:

$$240.1 + .25$$

Finally, do the addition:

$$240.35$$

One more problem that is probably as difficult as any you will have to face in the book:

$$\sqrt{\frac{(116 - 27)^2 + 21}{\sqrt{15} + 1}} - \frac{(212 - 188)}{2}$$

Following the rules of operations, we first want to solve within all the parentheses first:

$$\sqrt{\frac{(89)^2 + 21}{\sqrt{15 + 1}}} - \frac{24}{2}$$

Then, calculate all squares and square roots. Notice, however, that in the denominator of the first term we first have to use addition (15 + 1) before taking the square root of the sum. Notice also that we cannot take the square root of the entire first term until we solve for all that is under the square root sign:

$$\sqrt{\frac{7,921 + 21}{4}} - 12$$

Now, we will continue to solve that part of the problem within the square root by first completing the numerator (by addition) and then dividing:

$$\sqrt{\frac{7,942}{4}} - 12$$

$$\sqrt{1,985.5} - 12$$

Finally, now that we have completed all the operations within the square root sign, we can complete that:

$$44.56 - 12$$

Notice that the result for the first expression was 44.558. Because the third decimal place is greater than 5, we round the second digit up, so that 44.558 becomes 44.56. Then we complete the problem by subtracting 12:

$$32.56$$

We hope that you now feel greater confidence in solving math equations. As long as things are performed in a step-by-step manner, in accordance with the rules of operations, everything in any equation can be solved relatively easily. To make sure that you comprehend these rules, as well as to brush up on your math skills, complete the following exercises. We have provided answers for you at the end of the section. If you can do these problems, you are ready to tackle any of the statistics problems in this text. If some of the problems in the exercises below give you difficulty, simply review that section of this appendix or consult a mathematics book for some help.

Practice Problems

1. Calculate each of the following:
    a. $5^2 + 3$
    b. $(35/7) - 4$

    c. $\sqrt{64} + 7 - (4/2)$

    d. $[(35)(.3)]/10 + 15$

2. Calculate each of the following:

    a. $45 + \sqrt{\dfrac{125}{15 - (3)^2}}$

    b. $18 + \left(12^*10\right) - \sqrt{150 - 50}$

    c. $(18 + 12)^* 10 - \sqrt{150 - 50}$

    d. $[(23 + 17) - (5 * 4)]/(8 + 2)^2$

    e. $(-5) * 13$

    f. $(-5) * (-13)$

    g. $[18 + (-7)] * [(-4) - (-10)]$

    h. $125/-5$

    i. $450 - [(-125/-10)/2]$

3. With these 10 scores, 7, 18, 42, 11, 34, 65, 30, 27, 6, 29, perform the following operations:

    a. Σx

    b. $(\Sigma x)^2$

    c. Σx^2

4. Round the following numbers off to two places to the right of the decimal point:

    a. 118.954

    b. 65.186

    c. 156.145

    d. 87.915

    e. 3.212

    f. 48.565

    g. 48.535

Solutions to Problems

1. a. 28

    b. 1 (Remember to do the division before the subtraction.)

    c. 13

    d. 16.05

2. a. 49.56

    b. 128

    c. 290

    d. .20 (Remember to do all operations within parentheses first, starting with the innermost parentheses.)

    e. −65

    f. 65

    g. 66

    h. −25

    i. 443.75 (Following the rules of operation, you should have divided the two negative numbers (−125 and −10) first, then divided by 2, finally subtracted that quotient from 450.)

3. a. This expression says to sum all x scores: $7 + 18 + 42 + 11 + 34 + 65 + 30 + 27 + 6 + 29 = 269$.

    b. Notice the parentheses in this expression. It tell you to first sum all the x scores and then square the sum: $(7 + 18 + 42 + 11 + 34 + 65 + 30 + 27 + 6 + 29)^2 = (269)^2 = 72{,}361$.

    c. Following the order of operations, first square each x score, and then sum these squared scores: $7^2 + 18^2 + 42^2 + 11^2 + 34^2 + 65^2 + 30^2 + 27^2 + 6^2 + 29^2 = 49 + 324 + 1{,}764 + 121 + 1{,}156 + 4{,}225 + 900 + 729 + 36 + 841 = 10{,}145$.

4. a. 118.95

    b. 65.19

    c. 156.15 (Round up because the number to the left of the 5 is an even number.)

    d. 87.91 (Round down because the number to the left of the 5 is an odd number.)

    e. 3.21

    f. 48.57

    g. 48.53

An Introduction to SPSS 11.0

Prepared by Paige Gordier, Lake Superior State University

SPSS 11.0 for Windows is a user friendly and very powerful statistics program. This appendix provides a basic introduction to the program and procedures necessary to run the statistics discussed in this text. The standard version and the student version of SPSS do things in the same manner. The only difference is that the size of the data files can be significantly larger using the standard version of the program.

Remember: SPSS has a tutorial program available under the HELP pull-down menu. This tutorial provides step-by-step instructions on how to operate the program and provides working examples. You can access this feature at any time during the use of SPSS.

SPSS BASICS

Click with the left button of the mouse unless otherwise indicated.

Step One: Opening SPSS

Double-click the SPSS 11.0 for Windows icon or click Start in the lower left-hand corner of the screen and then click Program in the drop-down menu. Click SPSS 11.0 for Windows in the next menu.

Step Two: Getting Started

1. SPSS will now be operating and a window will appear that prompts you to indicate what type of data you will be using (see Figure B–1).
   a. Click *Type in Data* and then *OK* if you want to enter new data.
   b. Or click *Open an Existing File,* and then *OK* if the data are already saved on disk.
   c. Or click directly on the file name if it appears in the visible window.

Figure B–1 First window to appear after opening SPSS.

2. At any point, you may go to the top of the screen and click the File menu to start using a different or new data set. Before you can close the data file, the program will ask you if you want to save the data you were previously working on.

   a. Click *File, New,* and indicate Data as your choice to have a clean screen appear where you may enter data.

   b. Or click *File, Open,* and indicate Data as your choice to locate another existing file.

Step Three: Entering Data

1. Starting with an empty data file you will usually want to name your variables and set up the characteristics of the variables.

2. At the bottom of the screen are two tabs: (1) *Data View*—where you enter the data and edit the data; and (2) *Variable View*—where you name

and define the characteristics of the data. It is best to define all the variables before you start entering the data.

3. Click the *Variable View* tab

    a. Enter a name for each variable in the first column. (Note: A valid name can be only one word with a maximum of eight characters.)

    b. Once you enter the first variable name the program will fill in the remaining information (e.g., width, decimals, type, etc.). You may change any of these characteristics if you wish but the default choices usually work well for most data.

    c. For some data you will want to specify the value labels for certain variables. If so, click the value label cell and then specify in the Value Labels box what each of your values represents (see Figure B–2).

Example:

    a. Click *Name* and type in the name of the variable: Sex.

    b. Click *Label* and type in the title of the variable: Sex of Person.

    c. Click *Values*, then the button for *Values*, and then type in the following:

> Value: 1
> Value Label: Female

Click Add

> Value: 2
> Value Label: Male

Click Add

Now your labels will appear on any output with this variable.

4. Click the *Data View* tab

    a. Your data view screen will now have your variable names on the top of each column and you are ready to enter data.

    b. You may type in the data at this time.

Figure B–2   Value Labels Box

c. If a score is missing, you may just press *Enter* or *Tab* to skip that cell and a period (.) will appear. This indicates to the program that the data for that cell is missing.

d. You may move around the screen using the arrow keys or the mouse.

e. You may edit any data by using the delete button or just typing over the data. You can also use the *Cut, Copy,* and *Paste* functions to enter and edit data. You may also insert rows or columns by going to the word *Data* at the top of the screen and then clicking *Insert Case* or *Insert Variable* in the drop-down menu that appears.

Step Four: Transforming and Recoding Data

1. At times you will want to change the data that you have entered into other values to create new variables or change variable values. This may be done by transforming or recoding the data.

2. Click *Transform* at the top of the screen, as shown in Figure B–3.

3. In the drop-down menu select *Compute* if you want to create a new variable by combining or doing some mathematical calculation with the current data. In the Compute Variable dialog box, the name of the variable to be computed is typed in the Target Variable box and the numerical expression or equation for calculating the target variable is typed in the Numerical Expression box. Click *OK* when ready to do the analysis. The computed variable is displayed on the screen and saved with the original data as a new variable.

4. In the drop-down menu select *Recode* if you want to change a variable into a new variable or change the values currently recorded for a variable. Usually you will want to select *Recode into Different Variables* as that reduces the chance that you will lose your original data (that will

Figure B–3   Options under the "Transform" Dialogue Menu.

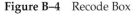

Figure B–4   Recode Box

occur if you select *Recode into Same Variables*). In the dialog box that appears you will have to indicate the old values and the new values for the target variable (see Figure B–4).

Step Five: Saving the Data

1. You can save the data at any time. Click *File* at the top of the screen, and then click the *Save* or *Save As* option.
2. You may also click the picture of the computer disk at the top of the screen to save your data.
3. Data must be saved with a *.sav* extension. Your output files need to be saved with a *.spo* extension on the file name.

Step Six: Printing Output of the Analysis

1. To print the contents of the output of your analysis, make sure the SPSS Output Navigator is the active window at the top left of the screen (see Figure B–5). If it is not the active window, click Window in the menu bar and the SPSS Output Navigator. The content of the active window is displayed on the right-hand side of the screen and the output objects on the left-hand side of the screen. Use the arrow keys to move around the screen.
2. Before printing, indicate whether the entire contents (All Visible Output) (the default) or just part of the contents (Selection) of Output Navigator are to be printed.
   a. In the left pane of the Output Navigator highlight what contents of Output Navigator are to be printed.

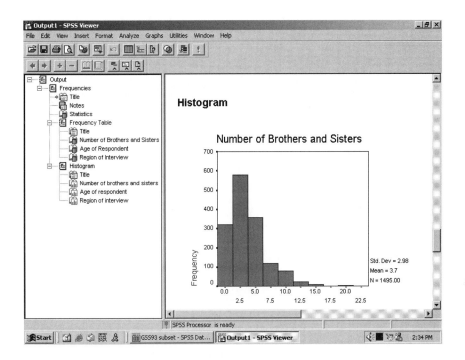

Figure B–5 SPSS Output Window

    b. From the Output Navigator click *File,* and then click *Print.*

3. You may also copy output from SPSS and move it to other programs. For example, you may copy graphs from SPSS output (use the copy objects option) and then open WORD and paste the object into that document. This allows you to put SPSS output directly into research papers. It also permits you to easily change fonts and sizes of charts and graphs to produce professional-looking statistical reports.

Step Seven: Exiting SPSS

1. To end an SPSS session, click *File* at the top of the screen and then click *Exit SPSS* in the drop-down menu. You also may click the X in the top-right corner of the screen.

2. You will be asked if you want to save any changes that you have made to your data or any output that was produced.

Step Eight: Analyzing the Data

1. After entering your data or opening an existing data file, click *Analyze* or *Graph* at the top of the screen.

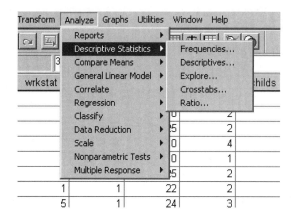

Figure B–6   Functions under analyze menu

2. The drop-down menus for Analyze and Graph provide you with a list of the available choices (see Figure B–6).
3. When you put the cursor on any of the options, more choices will appear.

SPSS STATISTICAL PROCEDURES

The following are general instructions for running a number of the statistical procedures available in SPSS. Examples specific to your text follow this section.

Frequencies

1. Click *Analyze* and then on *Descriptive Statistics* in the drop-down menu. Click *Frequencies,* which opens the Frequencies dialog box (shown in Figure B–7).
2. Click one or more variables from the left box. The variable will be highlighted and then can be moved to the variable box by clicking the arrow button.
3. To get optional descriptive and summary statistics click *Statistics* at the bottom of the dialog box and indicate which statistics you want by marking the boxes.
4. To get optional bar charts or histograms, click *Charts* in the dialog box. Click the charts or histograms desired in the dialog box. Click *Continue* when through.
5. Click *OK* when you are ready to analyze the data.

Descriptives

1. Click *Analyze, Descriptive Statistics,* and then *Descriptives.* This opens the Descriptives dialog box.

Figure B–7 Frequencies dialogue box

2. Move the variables of interest to the variable box on the right. By default, mean, standard deviation, minimum score, and maximum score will be displayed.
3. If you want additional statistics, click the *Options* button at the bottom of the dialog box and indicate the statistics you want. Click *Continue* when through.

Percentiles

1. Go to the *Frequencies* option under *Descriptive Statistics.*
2. Make sure that the scores are listed from worst to best (ascending order if large score is good).
3. Click *Statistics* and then *Percentile(s).*
4. The percentiles desired must be indicated by typing a number between 0 and 100 into the percentile box and then clicking *Add* (see Figure B–8). Do this for each percentile desired. Click *Continue* to get out of Statistics.
5. The default for Cut Points is 10 equal groups yielding the 10th, 20th, etc., percentiles.
6. Click *OK* to analyze the data.

Standard Scores (z scores)

1. A *z* score for each variable analyzed is calculated assuming a large score is good whether or not the data are listed in ascending or descending order. If a small score is good, the sign of the *z* score is reversed (e.g., –2.0 should be 2.0).
2. Click *Descriptive Statistics* and then *Descriptives.*

Figure B–8   Statistics options in frequencies command

3. Click Save standardized values as variables in the Descriptives dialog box. Highlight the variables you want z scores for and move them to the right-hand box.
4. Click *OK* to analyze the data.
5. The z scores will appear as a new variable with a Z in front of the original variable name. For example, if the analyzed variable name was "sentence" the z scores will be named "zsentence."

t Tests

Click on *Analyze* and then *Compare Means.* Indicate then which type of *t* test you want to use.

One-Sample t Test

1. Click one or more variables from the left to use in the analysis. Highlight the variables and move them into the Test Variable(s) box. Click the value in Test Value and enter the population mean.
2. By default, the confidence interval is 95%. If you want to change this value, click *Options* in the dialog box and indicate the confidence interval you want to use. Click *Continue* when through.
3. Click *OK* when ready to analyze the data.

Independent-Samples t Test (2 independent groups)

1. Click one or more variables from the left variable box to use in the analysis. Move the variable(s) into the Test Variable(s) box.

2. Click a variable to form the two groups and then click on the arrow button for Grouping Variable.

3. You must define a value of the grouping variable for each group. To define groups, click *Define Groups* and enter the value for which each group is identified (for example, males may be 1 and females 2, if sex is the grouping variable).

4. Click *OK* when ready to analyze the data.

Paired-Samples t-Test (dependent groups and repeated measures)

1. Highlight the two related variables in the left variable box and then move them to the right to the paired Variable box. Other pairs can be entered.

2. Click *OK* when ready to analyze the data.

Analysis of Variance

One-Way ANOVA

1. Click *Compare Means* and then *One-Way ANOVA* on the drop-down menu.

2. Highlight one or more variables from the left variable box to test. Click the arrow button to put the variable(s) in the Dependent List box.

3. Highlight a variable for forming groups and click the arrow button to put it in the Factor Box.

4. Click *Options, Descriptive,* and any other options desired. You must select descriptive statistics like the mean and standard deviation for each group. When through click *Continue.*

5. If you want post hoc tests, click *Post Hoc* and click one of the tests available. When through click *Continue.*

6. Click *OK* when ready to analyze the data.

Two-Way Factorial ANOVA (and other ANOVAs)

1. Click *General Linear Model* and then *Univariate.*

2. On the left side, the variables available in the data set are listed in a box, as shown in Figure B–9.

3. On the right side is Dependent Variable, Fixed Factors, Random Factors, and Covariance boxes.

4. Put the variable to be analyzed in the Dependent Variable box.

5. Put the variables for the rows and columns in the Fixed Factors box.

6. Click *Options* to get the means for rows, columns, and cells.

   a. On the left side, in the Factors box, are listed Overall, the name of the row variable, the name of the column variable, and the name of the row and column interaction.

   b. On the right side is the Display Means box.

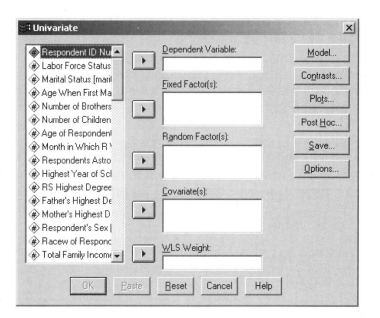

Figure B–9 ANOVA dialog box

    c. Put everything from the Factors box into the Display Means box.

    d. Click *Continue* to return to the GLM—General Factorial menu.

7. Also, post hoc tests effect size. Observed power, etc., are available in Options. If post hoc tests are selected, it must be identified whether the post hoc tests are for rows, columns, or both.

8. Click *OK* to analyze the data.

Chi-Square

One-Way Chi-Square

1. Click *Nonparametric Tests*. Click *Chi-Square*.

2. Highlight a variable from the left box and move it to the Test Variable List. Do this for each variable to be analyzed.

3. Under Expected Range, the Get from Data should already be selected by default. If not, mark it.

4. Under Expected Values, All Categories Equal will be marked. If you do not want all categories equal, click *Values* and enter an expected value for each category by typing in a value and then clicking *Add*. The expected values are used with all the variables in the Test Variable List.

5. Click *Options* and then click *Descriptives* in the dialog box.

6. Click *OK* to analyze the data.

Figure B–10 Crosstabs dialogue box

Two-Way Chi-Square

1. Click *Descriptive Statistics* and then *Crosstabs*. This opens the Crosstabs dialog box.
2. Move the variables you want to use as the row and column variables over to the right.
3. Click *Statistics* in the Crosstabs dialog box as shown in Figure B–10. Click *Chi-square, Contingency coefficient, Correlation,* and anything else you want.
4. Click *Cell* in the Crosstabs dialog box. Click *Observed, Expected,* and all three options under Percentages. When through click *Continue.*
5. Click *OK* to analyze the data.

Correlation

1. Click *Correlate* and then *Bivariate.*
2. Move two or more variables from the left variable box into the Variables box.
3. Click one or more of the correlation coefficients in the box (usually Pearson).

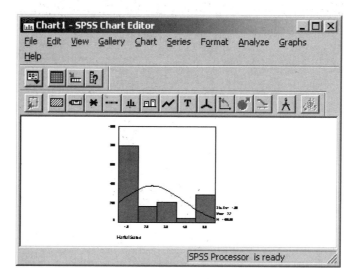

Figure B–11   Chart editor box

4. If you want a significance test, click the type of significance test: one-tailed or two-tailed.
5. Click *OK* to analyze the data.

Linear Regression

1. Click *Regression* and then *Linear.*
2. Highlight a variable from the left variable box for the dependent score and move it to the Dependent box. Highlight and move one or more variables designated as the Independent variable(s) to the Independent box.
3. Click one of the regression models.
4. Click *OK* to analyze the data.

Charts and Graphs

Histograms

1. Click *Graphs,* and then *Histogram.*
2. In the Histogram dialog box, highlight a variable from the left and move it to the Variable box on the right.
3. If the default format for histogram is acceptable, click *OK* to obtain the graph. If you want to display the normal curve with the histogram, click *Display normal curve* before clicking *OK.*
4. You can use the SPSS Chart Editor to edit any chart by double-clicking the graph itself (see Figure B–11).

Line Charts

1. Click *Graphs* and then *Line*.
2. In the Line Charts dialog box click *Simple line chart* and *Summaries for Groups of Cases*. Then click *Define*, select the variable to be put into the Category Axis box, and click N of cases.
3. Click *OK* when ready to obtain the graph.

Scatterplot

1. Click *Graphs*, then *Scatter*, and then *Simple* in the Scatterplot dialog box.
2. Now click *Define*. Move a variable from the left variable box and put it in the X Axis box. Do the same thing for a second variable to put it in the Y Axis box.
3. Click *OK* when ready to obtain the graph.

STEP-BY-STEP SPSS PROBLEMS

Interpreting Data Distributions: Graphical Techniques (Example for Chapter 3)

For the data provided in Chapter 3 end-of-chapter problem #5, construct a frequency distribution to display the data and also an appropriate graph.

Step One: Enter the Data in SPSS

1. Using two columns in the Data View Screen of a new data file, type in the 25 scores and the gender for the 25 recruits.
2. You may go to the Variable View Screen to label the columns and establish value labels for the Gender variable.

Step Two: Analyze the Data

1. Click the word Analyze to reveal the pull-down menu.
2. Click Descriptive Statistics and then click Frequencies.
3. In the new window that appears, mark the two variables and move them to the active window on the right.
4. Click the word Charts at the bottom of the window and then indicate what type of charts or graphs you would like to use to display your data.
5. Click Continue and then OK.

Step Three: Reading the Output

1. The output window will appear with all the requested frequency distributions and charts/graphs (Table B–1 below). The frequency distribution for the recruits' scores is shown and the pie chart is used to illustrate the percentage of the group of each gender.

TABLE B–1

Frequency Distribution

		Frequency	Percent	Valid Percent	Cumulative Percent
Valid	10.00	5	20.0	20.0	20.0
	11.00	3	12.0	12.0	32.0
	13.00	2	8.0	8.0	40.0
	14.00	2	8.0	8.0	48.0
	15.00	7	28.0	28.0	76.0
	16.00	3	12.0	12.0	88.0
	19.00	1	4.0	4.0	92.0
	20.00	2	8.0	8.0	100.0
	Total	25	100.0	100.0	

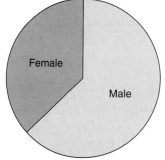

Measures of Central Tendency, Dispersion, and Variability (Example for Chapters 4 and 5)

The following scores were recorded from 20 rookie police officers on a firearms skills test:

| 25 | 21 | 17 | 18 | 16 | 24 | 24 | 20 | 19 | 17 |
| 15 | 20 | 21 | 17 | 19 | 23 | 25 | 15 | 19 | 24 |

Find the mode, median, and mean (measures of central tendency). Also find the range, variance, and standard deviation (measures of dispersion and central tendency).

Step One: Enter the Data in SPSS

1. Using only one column in the Data View Screen of a new data file, type in the 20 scores.

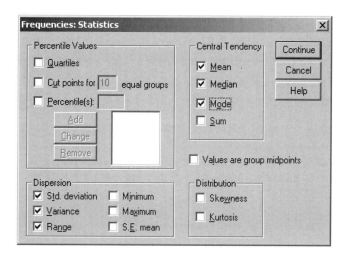

Figure B–12 Statistics options in frequencies command

2. You may go to the Variable View Screen and label the column if you wish.

Step Two: Analyze the Data

1. Click the word Analyze to reveal the pull-down menu.
2. Click Descriptive Statistics and then click Frequencies.
3. In the new window that appears, mark the variable you are studying and move it to the right-hand side by clicking the arrow between the two small windows.
4. At the bottom of the window, click the word Statistics, which will cause a window with a number of boxes to appear, as shown in Figure B–12.
5. Mark the boxes corresponding to the statistics of interest for the question (i.e., mode, median, mean, range, variance, and standard deviation).
6. Click Continue and then OK.

Step Three: Reading the Output The output window will appear with all the requested statistics presented in a chart (Table B–2).

Exploratory Data Analysis (Example for Chapter 6)

For the data provided in Chapter 5 end-of-chapter problem five, construct a boxplot display from these data.

TABLE B–2

Statistics

Scores

N	Valid	20
	Missing	0
Mean		19.9500
Median		19.5000
Mode		17.00[a]
Std. Deviation		3.31623
Variance		10.99737
Range		10.00

[a]Multiple modes exist. The smallest value is shown.

Step One: Enter the Data in SPSS   Using one column in the Data View Screen of a new data file, type in the data.

Step Two: Analyze the Data
1. Click the word Analyze to reveal the pull-down menu.
2. Click Descriptive Statistics and then click Explore.
3. In the new window that appears, mark the variable and move it to the Dependent List.
4. Click the word Plots at the bottom of the window and then indicate that you want a boxplot display to be produced (see Figure B–13).
5. Click Continue and then OK.

Step Three: Reading the Output   The output window will appear with a stem-and-leaf display (Table B–3 below).

Probability and Probability Distributions (Example for Chapter 6)

There are several functions within SPSS that relate to the material in Chapter 6. SPSS can take a variable and convert it to standard scores (z scores) and also produce a normal curve over a histogram so the researcher can compare the two distributions.

For the following data from the Chapter six problem, produce a histogram of the original data and compare to a normal distribution. Then convert the raw scores to z scores.

Step One: Enter the Data in SPSS   Using one column in the Data View Screen of a new data file, type in the data.

Figure B–13   Plots box in explore dialog box

TABLE B–3

Boxplot of Rape Rates for 18 States

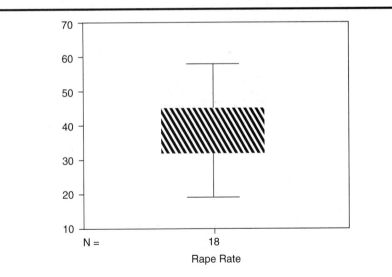

Step Two: Analyze the Data

1. Click the word Analyze to reveal the pull-down menu.
2. Click Descriptive Statistics and then click Frequencies.
3. In the new window that appears, mark the variable and move it to the right.

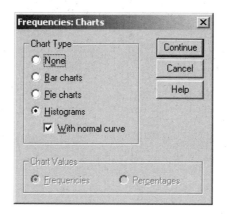

Figure B–14   Chart options in frequencies command

4. Click the word Charts at the bottom and indicate that you want a histogram with the normal curve, as in Figure B–14.
5. Click Continue and then OK to produce the histogram.
6. To transform the data to z scores, return to Analyze, then Descriptive statistics, and then Descriptives.
7. Move the variable to the right and indicate that you want to save the new scores.
8. Click OK.

Step Three: Reading the Output
1. The histogram will appear with a normal curve displayed over the top of the data. It provides an easy way to determine if the data fit a normal curve.
2. The standardized scores will appear in the data view window where a new variable will now exist with the original variable name preceded by a 'z' (Table B–4 below).

Point Estimation and Confidence Intervals (Example for Chapter 7)

Use SPSS to calculate the 95 percent and 99 percent confidence intervals for the following sample of test scores:

14 15 14 16 19 20 22 14 15 14 25 25 20 14 14 11 16 18 22 24

Step One: Enter the Data in SPSS   Using one column in the Data View Screen of a new data file, type in the data.

TABLE B-4

Offense	zOffense
18.00	−.22171
17.00	−.39794
29.00	1.71685
11.00	−1.45534
25.00	1.01192
13.00	−1.10288
27.00	1.36438
18.00	−.22171
23.00	.65945
18.00	−.22171
10.00	−1.63157
18.00	−.22171

Step Two: Analyze the Data

1. Click the word Analyze to reveal the pull-down menu.
2. Click Compare Means and then click One sample T Test.
3. In the new window that appears, mark the variable and move it to the right.
4. Click the word Options and then indicate what confidence interval you want (e.g., 95%, 99%, etc.), as shown in Figure B–15.
5. Click Continue and then OK to produce the confidence intervals.

Step Three: Reading the Output

The confidence intervals will be indicated in the chart that appears (Table B–5).

Figure B–15 Options box in *T* test dialog box

TABLE B–5

One-Sample T Test

				Test Value = 0		
					95% Confidence Interval of the Difference	
	t	df	Sig. (2-tailed)	Mean Difference	Lower	Upper
VAR00001	18.530	19	.000	17.6000	15.6121	19.5879

Hypothesis Tests with Two Categorical Variables: The Chi-Square Test (Example for Chapter 9)

Use SPSS to test the null hypothesis that the variables are independent using the data from Chapter 9 end-of-chapter problem #2.

Step One: Enter the Data in SPSS You will need to use two columns to input the data into SPSS. The first column will be for Type of Institution and you will use a 1 to indicate "Low Crime Rate" and 2 to indicate "High Crime Rate." The second variable will designate the level of Social Organization: 1 for "Socially Organized" and 2 for "Socially Disorganized."

Step Two: Analyze the Data
1. Click the word Analyze to reveal the pull-down menu.
2. Click Descriptive Statistics and then Crosstabs.
3. In the new window that appears, mark the variable Type and move it into the Row variable box. Then move the Social Organization variable to the Column variable box.
4. Click the word Statistics and then indicate that you want the program to run Chi-Square.
5. Click Continue and then OK.

Step Three: Reading the Output The output will have the contingency table for the data and then the second box will have the Chi-Square statistic and the level of significance indicated (Table B–6).

Hypothesis Tests with One Categorical and One Continuous Variable: t Test for the Difference of Means and Proportions (Example for Chapter 10)

Use SPSS to do Chapter 10 end-of-chapter problem #6.

TABLE B–6

Chi-Square Tests

	Value	df	Asymp. Sig. (2-sided)	Exact Sig. (2-sided)	Exact Sig. (1-sided)
Pearson Chi-Square	19.575[b]	1	.000		
Continuity Correction[a]	18.275	1	.000		
Likelihood Ratio	21.439	1	.000		
Fisher's Exact Test				.000	.000
Linear-by-Linear Association	19.497	1	.000		
N of Valid Cases	250				

[a] Computed only for a 2×2 table.
[b] 0 cells (.0%) have expected count of less than 5. The minimum expected count is 24.80.

Step One: Enter the Data in SPSS   As this is a one-sample t test, you will need only one column to enter the data in.

Step Two: Analyze the Data
1. Click the word Analyze to reveal the pull-down menu.
2. Click Compare Means and then One-Sample t test.
3. Move the test variable into the test variable box and then indicate the population mean, in this case 15, in the test value box.
4. Click OK.

Step Three: Reading the Output   The output will be in a box and will contain the test value at the top. The t test result and the significance level will be in the main table (Table B–7 below).

TABLE B–7

One-Sample Test

	Test Value = 15				95% Confidence Interval of the Difference	
	t	df	Sig. (2-tailed)	Mean Difference	Lower	Upper
VAR00001	1.309	14	.212	1.4000	−.8945	3.6945

Hypothesis Tests Involving Three or More Means: Analysis of Variance (Example for Chapter 11)

Use analysis of variance to determine if there is a significant difference in sentence length with respect to the race of the offender.

White	Black	Hispanic
15	10	9
14	10	10
10	15	14
9	11	10
7	9	12
14	7	8
10	12	8
12	10	10
11	15	9
8	8	7

Step One: Enter the Data in SPSS   Using two columns in the Data View Screen of a new data file, type in the sentence lengths for the three groups in one continuous list and then indicate if they are white (1), black (2), or Hispanic (3) in a Race column.

Step Two: Analyze the Data
1. Click the word Analyze to reveal the pull-down menu.
2. Click Compare Means and then One-way ANOVA.
3. Move the Sentence variable to the dependent list and the Race variable to the factor box.
4. To add a secondary test to determine where the differences between the groups actually are, click Post Hoc and indicate which test you would like to run (usually the Tukey test is used).
5. Click Continue and then OK.

Step Three: Reading the Output
1. The output window will appear with the requested ANOVA result shown (Table B–8).
2. In this example the *F* Statistic was not found to be significant, therefore there was no statistically significant difference in sentence length between the groups and no need to look at any Post Hoc tests.

TABLE B–8

Anova

Sentence					
	Sum of Squares	df	Mean Square	F	Sig.
Between Groups	9.267	2	4.633	.744	.485
Within Groups	168.200	27	6.230		
Total	177.467	29			

Hypothesis Tests for Two Continuous Variables: Correlation and Regression (Example for Chapter 12)

Using the data from Chapter 12 end-of-chapter problem #4, draw a scatterplot of the data points, calculate the regression line, and determine the correlation between the variables.

Step One: Enter the Data in SPSS   Using two columns in the Data View Screen of a new data file, type in the Self-Control data in one column and the Self-Reported Delinquency in the other column, as shown in Figure B–16.

Step Two: Analyze the Data
1. Click the word Analyze to reveal the pull-down menu.
2. Click Regression and then Linear.
3. Move the Delinquency variable to the dependent box and the Control variable to the independent variable list (you may use multiple independent variables).
4. Click Plots to add a scatterplot to the output.
5. Click Continue and then OK.

Note: You also may run the correlation separately from the regression analysis:
1. Click the word Analyze to reveal the pull-down menu.
2. Click Correlate and then Bivariate.
3. Move the variables of interest into the variables box.
4. Click OK.

Step Three: Reading the Output
1. The output window will appear with the requested regression analysis results shown. The output for this analysis is quite extensive and will result in five tables and also a scatterplot.

Figure B–16   Data editor view

TABLE B–9

Coefficients[a]

Model		Unstandardized Coefficients		Standardized Coefficients		
		B	Std. Error	Beta	t	Sig.
1	(Constant)	−12.942	5.308		−2.438	.041
	CONTROL	.428	.082	.880	5.238	.001

[a]Dependent variable: DELINQUE.

2. To determine the regression line you will need to look at the Coefficients table (Table B–9). From the table you can find the regression coefficient $b = .428$ and the y intercept $= -12.942$. The value of $r = .88$ and is also produced in the Coefficients table.

3. The output for a correlation table with the two variables is shown in Table B–10. Note that the correlation table produces the r value and also indicates the significance level for each variable pair.

TABLE B–10

Correlations

		Control	Delinque
Control	Pearson Correlation	1.000	.880**
	Sig. (2-tailed)	.	.001
	N	10	10
Delinque	Pearson Correlation	.880**	1.000
	Sig. (2-tailed)	.001	.
	N	10	10

**Correlation is significant at the 0.01 level (2-tailed).

Multiple Regression and Partial Correlation (Example for Chapter 13)

Use the following data to determine how much of the change in the dependent variable Sentence length can be predicted by the four independent variables.

Sentence Length	Age	Number of Prior Convictions	Level of Violence (Scale 1-low to 5-high)	Prior Prison Commitments
15	28	2	4	1
12	21	1	3	0
22	35	3	5	2
8	20	1	1	0
10	30	2	3	0
7	19	0	2	2
2	25	0	1	0
14	35	2	2	1
25	36	3	4	2
50	40	4	5	3

Step One: Enter the Data in SPSS   Using five columns in the Data View Screen of a new data file, type in the data just as it appears above.

Step Two: Analyze the Data
   1. Click the word Analyze to reveal the pull-down menu.
   2. Click Regression and then Linear.

3. Move the Sentence Length variable to the dependent box and the four independent variables to the independent variable list.

4. Note: There are different methods to enter the variables. If you leave the method as "Enter" all the independent variables will be put into the equation. If you prefer for the computer to design the best model by eliminating variables with weak predictive ability, change the method to "Stepwise".

5. Click Continue and then OK.

Step Three: Reading the Output

1. The output window will appear with the requested Regression analysis results shown in Table B–11.

2. The Model Summary will provide the R Square value for the regression equation and the Coefficients table provides the information for each of the independent variables in the model.

Regression Analysis with a Dichotomous Dependent Variable: Logistic Regression (Example for Chapter 14)

Within SPSS discriminant analysis can be used for situations where you want to build a predictive model to determine group membership (with two or more groupings). The procedure is based upon linear combinations of independent variables that will best discriminate between the groups.

Use SPSS to determine the best discriminators when looking at whether a convicted killer will receive the death penalty or a prison term.

Death (yes – 1)	# of Victims	Offender's Age	# of Prior Prison Sentences
1	3	42	2
0	2	32	2
1	2	39	3
0	1	25	1
0	1	21	0
1	3	26	0
1	3	41	4
1	2	20	1
0	2	25	0
1	2	41	0
1	3	31	2
0	2	27	4

TABLE B–11

Model Summary

Model	R	R Square	Adjusted R Square	Std. Error of the Estimate
1	.935[a]	.874	.774	6.4748

[a]Predictors: (Constant), PRISON, AGE, VIOLENCE, CONVICT.

Coefficients[a]

Model		Unstandardized Coefficients		Standardized Coefficients		
		B	Std. Error	Beta	t	Sig.
1	(Constant)	10.670	16.139		.661	.538
	AGE	−.483	.711	−.266	−.680	.527
	CONVICT	10.156	5.361	.982	1.894	.117
	VIOLENCE	−1.468	3.134	−.161	−.468	.659
	PRISON	5.385	2.781	.435	1.936	.111

[a]Dependent variable: SENTENCE.

Step One: Enter the Data in SPSS   Type in the data with each variable having its own column. In the Data View Screen of a new data file, type in the data.

Step Two: Analyze the Data
1. Click the word Analyze to reveal the pull-down menu.
2. Click Classify and then Discriminant.
3. In the new window that appears, mark the dependent variable and move it to the right. Indicate what are the independent variables and move them to the right, as shown in Figure B–18.
4. Click OK to produce the output.

Step Three: Reading the Output
1. The output for the discriminant analysis is very detailed and provides a tremendous amount of information. At least 11 tables will be produced during this process.

Figure B–18 Linear regression dialog box

2. The tables will provide information on the possible models, what independent variables are the best for discriminating between the dichotomous values of the dependent variable, and the Wilk's Lambda and Chi-Square values.

C

Solutions to Problems

CHAPTER 1 SOLUTIONS TO PROBLEMS

1. Since selecting a systematic random sample involves using a list that is not ordered in any way, the results should be similar to a sample selected using a simple random sample.

2. Multistage cluster sampling techniques can be used to select a random probability sample when there is no population list available. You actually work toward the sample you want by extracting a sample of groups or clusters that are available, and then sampling the elements of interest from these selected clusters.

3. The goal in obtaining or selecting a sample is to select it in a way that increases the chances of this sample being representative of the entire population. Probability sampling techniques not only serve to minimize any potential bias we may have when selecting a sample, thereby making our sample more representative of the population, but they also allow us to gain access to probability theory in our data analysis. This body of mathematical theory allows us to estimate more accurately the degree of error we have when generalizing results obtained from known sample statistics to unknown population parameters.

4. The fundamental element in probability sampling is *random selection.* When a sample is randomly selected from the population, this means every element of the population (e.g., individual, school, city) has a known and independent chance of being selected for the sample. All probability sampling methods rely on a random selection procedure.

5. We could use the probability sampling technique of selecting a weighted sample or the nonprobability sampling technique of quota sampling.

6. The danger in using nonprobability samples is that they may not be representative of the population. This means that the generalizations we make from our sample to the population may be wrong.

7. Nonprobability samples are appropriate when we want to sample a unique population, such as gang members or other deviant individuals, who are not available from some population list. Purposive/judgment samples and snowball samples are often used in these cases. In addition, if your research is exploratory in nature, it is appropriate to use a nonprobability sample.

CHAPTER 2 SOLUTIONS TO PROBLEMS

1. a. Interval/ratio.
   b. Interval/ratio.
   c. Interval/ratio.
   d. Nominal.
   e. Nominal.
   f. Interval/ratio.

2. The categories of a variable measured at the ordinal level of measurement can be ordered, but the distance between the categories is not quantifiable. Categories for interval-level variables have a known and equal distance between them. In addition to this, ratio-level variables have a true zero point.

3. Arrest is the independent variable and future drunk-driving behavior is the dependent variable.

4. Gender is the independent variable and fear is the dependent variable.

5. The numerator would be the number of victimizations against 14–18 year olds and the denominator would be the total population of 14–18 year olds.

6. Rates allow you to make comparisons across different places and times.

7.

	f	Proportion	Percent
Less than $10	16	.029	2.9
$10 – $49	39	.071	7.1
$50 – $99	48	.087	8.7
$100 – $249	86	.156	15.6
$250 – $999	102	.186	18.6
$1,000 or more	251	.458	45.8
	n = 542		

8. The units of analysis are incarcerated adolescent males. The independent variable would be previous childhood abuse and the dependent variable would be the offense they committed.

9. The units of analysis are the 50 states of the United States. The independent variable would likely be unemployment and the dependent variable would be crime.

10. The units of analysis would be the police jurisdictions.

CHAPTER 3 SOLUTIONS TO PROBLEMS

1. The first grouped frequency distribution is not a very good one for a number of reasons. First, the interval widths are not all the same size. Second, the class intervals are not mutually exclusive. A score of "10" could go into either the second or third class interval. Third, the first class interval is empty—it has a frequency of zero. Fourth, there are too few class intervals, the data are "bunched up" into only three intervals and you do not get a very good sense of the distribution of these scores. The second grouped frequency distribution avoids each of these four problems.

2. Since "number of executions" is a quantitative, continuous variable (measured at the interval/ratio level) you could use a histogram or a line chart to graph the frequencies. You could not use a pie or bar chart because they are for nominal or ordinal level data.

3. a. "Self-Reported Drug Use" is measured at the ordinal level because our values consist of rank-ordered categories. We do not have interval-/ratio-level measurement because while we can state that someone who reported using drugs "a lot" used drugs more frequently than someone who reported "never" using drugs, we do not know exactly how much more frequently.

   b. Since there were 30 students who reported "never" using, 150 − 30 or 120 must have been using drugs at some level of frequency. The ratio of users to nonusers, then, is 120/30, or 4-to-1.

   c. 35/10 or 3.5-to-1.

   d. First we would want to arrange the data in some order. Since we have ordinal-level data, we can order the categories in ascending or descending order.

Value	f	Proportion	%
Never	30	.20	20.00
A few times	75	.50	50.00
More than a few times	35	.233	23.33
A lot	10	.067	6.67

e. Since the proportion of nonusers ("never") was .20, the proportion of respondents who reported using drugs must be $1 - .20$, or .80. Another way to determine this is to determine the relative frequency of users $(75 + 35 + 10)/150 = 120/150 = .80$. The percent using drugs is, then, 80%.

f. .067 of the respondents reported using drugs "a lot."

4. a. Since these data are measured at the nominal level, there is no way to "correctly" order the values in any numerical order. For our frequency distribution, then, we can employ any ordering of the values.

Value	f	Proportion	%
Community facility	5,428	.2616	26.16
Minimum security	3,285	.1583	15.83
Medium security	1,733	.0835	8.35
Maximum security	875	.0422	4.22
Pretrial release	9,430	.4544	45.44

b. $3,285/20,751 = .1583; .1583 \times 100 = 15.83\%$.

c. $875/20,751 = .0422$.

d. $430/20,751 = .4544; .4544 \times 100 = 45.44\%$.

e. Since these data are measured at the nominal level, the correct graph to use would be either a pie chart or a bar chart. We provide several different types for you.

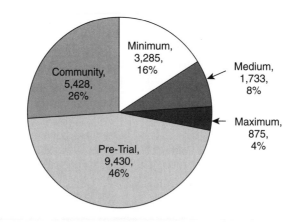

Figure 3C–1   Pie Chart of Distribution of Correctional Facilities

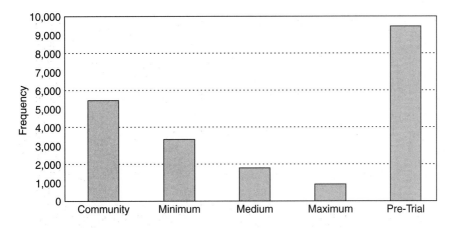

Figure 3C–2 Frequency Distribution of Inmates in Correctional Institutions

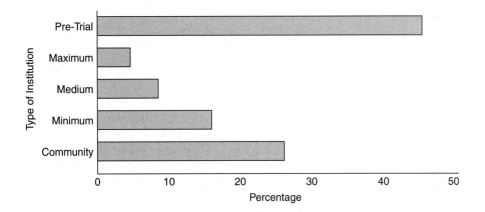

Figure 3C–3 Percent Distribution of Inmates in Correctional Institutions

5. a.

Value	f	cf	p	cp	%	c%
10	5	5	.20	.20	20	20
11	3	8	.12	.32	12	32
12	0	8	.00	.32	0	32
13	2	10	.08	.40	8	40
14	2	12	.08	.48	8	48
15	7	19	.28	.76	28	76
16	3	22	.12	.88	12	88
17	0	22	.00	.88	0	88
18	0	22	.00	.88	0	88
19	1	23	.04	.92	4	92
20	2	25	.08	1.00	8	100

b.

Value	f	p	%
Male	16	.64	64
Female	9	.36	36

c. Using the cumulative frequency column we can determine that 10 recruits scored 13 or lower on the exam. That means that 25 − 10 or 15 recruits must have scored 14 or higher, so 15 recruits passed the exam. Since 15/25 = .60, we can calculate that 60 percent of the recruits passed the test. We also could have used the cumulative percent column to find this answer. Using the cumulative percent column we can determine that 40 percent of the recruits scored 13 or lower on the exam. This means that 100 percent − 40 percent or 60 percent of the recruits must have scored 14 or higher and passed the exam.

d. Three of the 25 recruits or .12 of the total (3/25) received a score of 18 or higher on the exam and "passed with honors."

e. Using the cumulative frequency column we can easily see that 10 recruits received a score of 13 or lower on the exam.

f. In this class of recruits, .64 were male and .36 were female.

g. The test scores would have to be graphed with a histogram since the data are quantitative.

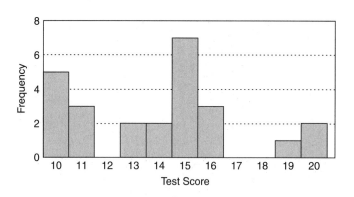

Figure 3C–4   Distribution of Test Scores for Recruit Class

A pie chart of the percents for the gender data would look like this:

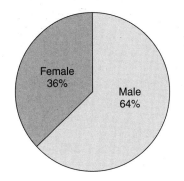

Figure 3C–5   Gender Distribution of Recruit Class

h. A cumulative frequency distribution for the test scores would look like this:

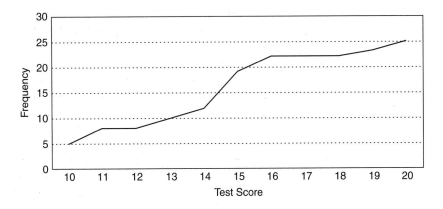

Figure 3C–6   Cumulative Frequency Line Graph for Test Score Data

6. The grouped distribution with interval width of 5 with real limits and midpoints:

Stated Limits	Real Limits	f	m	p	%	cf	cp	c%
6–10	5.5–10.5	3	8	.04	4	3	.04	4
11–15	10.5–15.5	18	13	.24	24	21	.28	28
16–20	15.5–20.5	15	18	.20	20	36	.48	48
21–25	20.5–25.5	13	23	.17	17	49	.65	65
26–30	25.5–30.5	11	28	.15	15	60	.80	80
31–35	30.5–35.5	10	33	.13	13	70	.93	93
36–40	35.5–40.5	4	38	.05	5	74	.98	98
41–45	40.5–45.5	1	43	.01	1	75	.99	99

   a. The real limits are shown.

   b. The midpoints of each class interval are shown.

   c. Looking at the cumulative frequencies we can determine that 60 of these people reported committing their first offense before age 31. The result is equal to the sum of the frequencies for the first five class intervals.

   d. .24 of these persons committed their first offense between the ages of 11 and 15. It is the proportion for the second class interval.

   e. Looking at the cumulative percent column, we can determine that 48 percent of the 75 persons committed their first offense at or before the age of 20. This means that 100 percent − 48 percent or 52 percent of them committed their first offense after age 20.

   f. Using the column of cumulative percents, we can determine that 28 percent committed their first offense before the age of 16.

  7. A time plot of the property crime victimization data from the NCVS would look like the following:

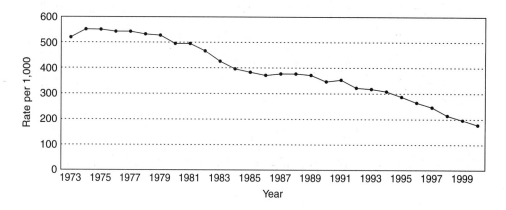

Figure 3C–7   Time Plot of NCVS Property Crime Victimization Rates per 1,000 Households

The time trend shows a fairly flat trend in the property crime victimization rate during the 1970s. Beginning in 1980 there was a consistent decline in the rate of property victimizations that lasted until the mid-1980s, after which rates leveled off until 1989. Beginning in the 1990s there has been a consistent decline in the rate of property victimizations until the end of the time series in the year 2000, at which time rates were approximately one-third of what they were in 1973.

8.

Year	Original Number of Arrests	Smoothed Number
1970	322,300	322,300
1971	383,900	371,167
1972	407,300	418,267
1973	463,600	448,600
1974	474,900	464,833
1975	456,000	465,000
1976	464,100	471,133
1977	493,300	479,133
1978	480,000	336,300
1979	435,600	462,267
1980	471,200	458,300
1981	468,100	508,067
1982	584,900	545,500
1983	583,500	597,367
1984	623,700	641,933
1985	718,600	695,000
1986	742,700	770,267
1987	849,500	880,933
1988	1,050,600	1,049,300
1989	1,247,800	1,102,233
1990	1,008,300	1,062,667
1991	931,900	973,633
1992	980,700	976,800
1993	1,017,800	1,063,767
1994	1,192,800	1,165,433
1995	1,285,700	1,258,067
1996	1,295,100	1,317,067
1997	1,370,400	1,342,033
1998	1,360,600	1,365,367
1999	1,365,100	1,367,100
2000	1,375,600	1,375,600

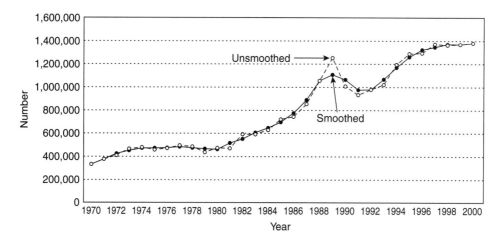

Figure 3C–8   Estimated Number of Arrests of Adults for Drug Abuse Violations

CHAPTER 4 SOLUTIONS TO PROBLEMS

1. The mode for these data is "some friends" because this value appears more often than any other value ($f = 85$). The mode tells us that in our sample more youths reported having "some" delinquent friends than any other possible response. We could not calculate a mean with these data because this variable is measured at the ordinal level, and the mean requires data measured at the interval/ratio level. For example, while we can say that someone with "some" delinquent friends has more delinquent friends than someone with "none," we do not know exactly how many more (1? 2? 10?). Without this knowledge, we cannot calculate the mean as a measure of central tendency.

2. To find the median salary, let's first rank-order the data from low to high:

Salary ($)	
$25,900	
26,100	
27,800	
28,400	the median salary
29,500	
31,000	
32,100	

With 7 scores, the median is the fourth score from the top or bottom, and the median salary for these correctional officers is $28,400. Notice that one-half of these salaries are higher than the median and one-half are lower. The mean salary is:

$$\overline{X} = \frac{\$25,900 + \$26,100 + \$27,800 + \$28,400 + \$29,500 + \$31,000 + \$32,100}{7}$$

$$\overline{X} = \$28,686$$

The median and mean salaries are very close to each other.

3. The best measure of central tendency for these data is probably the median. The mean would not be the best in this case because it would be inflated due to the presence of a positive outlier. New Orleans, Louisiana, with a homicide rate of 43.3 per 100,000, is substantially higher than the other cities. When New Orleans is included in the data, the mean is equal to 10.62 homicides per 100,000 and the median is 7.25. Without New Orleans the mean is reduced to 6.99 and the median is 6.80.

4. The mean is:

$$\overline{X} = \frac{339}{20}$$

$$\overline{X} = 16.95$$

On average these heroin addicts committed nearly 17 crimes in the past two years.

The median is the average of the 10th and 11th scores in the rank-ordered frequency distribution:

$$mdn = \frac{8+9}{2}$$

$$mdn = 8.5$$

The median number of crimes over the two years was 8.5.

The median is the preferred measure of central tendency for these data. The value of the mean is inflated by the existence of two extremely large scores (88, 112).

5. The most appropriate measure of central tendency for these data is the mode, because the data are measured at the nominal level. The modal or "most frequent" reason for requesting the police is for "other reasons."

6. The mode is the interval 30%–39% of police officers, since this interval has the highest frequency (38).

$$\text{Median} = 29.5 + \left(\frac{\frac{100+1}{2} - 44}{38} (10) \right)$$

$$\text{Median} = 31.2$$

31.2 percent of the officers in the department do narcotics investigation.

To calculate the mean with these grouped data, remember you first must determine the midpoint of each class interval. With the midpoints, you can find the mean:

$$\overline{X} = \frac{4.5(5) + 14.5(13) + 24.5(26) + 34.5(38) + 44.5(14) + 54.5(2) + 64.5(2)}{100}$$

$$\overline{X} = 30.2$$

On average, then, approximately 30 percent of the officers in these city police departments do narcotics investigation work.

7. Mean number of executions:

$$\overline{x} = \frac{11}{7}$$

$$\overline{X} = 1.57 \text{ executions per year.}$$

The median number of executions per year is equal to 1.

When executions for the year 1984 (21) are added to the data, the mean becomes:

$$\overline{X} = \frac{32}{8} = 4 \text{ executions per year.}$$

The median becomes 1.5 executions. The median is the more appropriate measure of central tendency for the 1977–1984 data distribution because it is less affected by the inclusion of the 1984 data than is the mean.

8. Again, with grouped data you need to find the midpoint of each class interval before you can calculate the mean. The mean is:

$$\overline{X} = \frac{1(36) + 4(87) + 7(45) + 10(23) + 13(9)}{200}$$

$$\overline{x} = \frac{1,046}{200}$$

$$\overline{x} = 5.23 \text{ times}$$

The median is:

$$mdn = 2.5 + \left(\frac{\frac{201}{2} - 36}{87} (3) \right)$$

$$mdn = 4.72 \text{ times}$$

The mode is equal to the interval 3–5 times because it contains the highest frequency (87).

9. The mean is equal to:

$$\overline{X} = \frac{1,386}{20}$$

$$\overline{X} = 69.3 \text{ mg of glucose per minute}$$

The median is equal to 69.5.

The mean and the median are very comparable to one another. This would suggest that there are no or few extreme or outlying scores in the data, and that the data are not skewed.

CHAPTER 5 SOLUTIONS TO PROBLEMS

1. Measures of central tendency capture the most "typical" score in a distribution of scores (the most common, the score in the middle of the ranked distribution, or the average), while measures of dispersion capture the variability in our scores or how they are different from each other or different from the central tendency. It is important to report both central tendency and dispersion measures for our variables because two groups of scores may be very similar in terms of their central tendency but very different in terms of how disperse the scores are.

2. The variation ratio for those whose current offense is a property crime is:

$$vr = 1 - \frac{75}{125}$$

$$vr = .40$$

so, .40 of the current offenses do not fall into the modal category.

The variation ratio for those whose current offense is a violent crime is:

$$vr = 1 - \frac{50}{110}$$

$$vr = .54$$

so, .54 of the current offenses do not fall into the modal category.

The variation ratio for those whose current offense is a drug crime is:

$$vr = 1 - \frac{110}{230}$$

$$vr = .52$$

so, .52 of the current offenses do not fall into the modal category.

Finally, the variation ratio for those whose current offense is a status offense is:

$$vr = 1 - \frac{320}{575}$$

$$vr = .44$$

so, .44 of the current offenses do not fall into the modal category.

The most dispersion in these nominal-level variables is for drug crimes and violent crimes. For drug crimes, .52 of the cases are in a value other than the modal value, and for violent crimes, the proportion is .54.

3. First we need to calculate the mean. This problem will give you experience in calculating a mean for grouped data. You should find the mean equal to 8.6 prior thefts. We are now ready to do the calculations necessary to find the variance and standard deviation.

m_i	$m_i\bar{x}$	$(m_i - \bar{x})^2$	f	$f(m_i - \bar{x})^2$
2	$2 - 8.6 = -6.6$	43.56	76	3,310.56
7	$7 - 8.6 = -1.6$	2.56	52	133.12
12	$12 - 8.6 = 3.4$	11.56	38	439.28
17	$17 - 8.6 = 8.4$	70.56	21	1,481.76
22	$22 - 8.6 = 13.4$	179.56	10	1,795.60
27	$27 - 8.6 = 18.4$	338.56	8	2,708.48
				$\Sigma = 9,868.80$

$$s^2 = \frac{9,868.80}{204}$$

$s^2 = 48.38$ is the variance

$$s = \sqrt{\frac{9,868.80}{204}}$$

$s = 6.95$ is the standard deviation

4. To answer these questions, let's first rank-order the data.

5	9
5	9
6	10
7	10
8	10
9	10
9	11
9	11
9	12
9	12

a. The range is $12 - 5 = 7$ years education.

b. The median position is $20/2 = 10.5$, so the truncated median position is equal to 10. The position of the quartiles, then, is $10+1/2 = 5.5$. With this, we can identify the first quartile as equal to 8.5

and the third quartile as equal to 10, so the interquartile range is IQR = 10 − 8.5 = 1.5.

c. To calculate the variance and standard deviation, we first have to determine the mean. The mean is equal to 9 years of education. Here are the calculations necessary to determine the variance and standard deviation:

x_i	$x_i - \bar{x}$	$(x_i - \bar{x})$
11	11 − 9 = 2	4
8	8 − 9 = −1	1
12	12 − 9 = 3	9
9	9 − 9 = 0	0
9	9 − 9 = 0	0
9	9 − 9 = 0	0
10	10 − 9 = 1	1
10	10 − 9 = 1	1
10	10 − 9 = 1	1
11	11 − 9 = 2	4
9	9 − 9 = 0	0
9	9 − 9 = 0	0
5	5 − 9 = −4	16
9	9 − 9 = 0	0
7	7 − 9 = −2	4
6	6 − 9 = −3	9
10	10 − 9 = 1	1
12	12 − 9 = 3	9
9	9 − 9 = 0	0
5	5 − 9 = −4	16
		$\Sigma = 76$

$$s^2 = \frac{76}{19}$$

$$s^2 = 4$$

The variance is equal to 4.

d. Using the calculations from (c):

$$s = \sqrt{\frac{76}{19}}$$

$$s = 2$$

The standard deviation is equal to 2.

5. Let's calculate the variation ratio for each of the three years:

$$vr_{1980} = 1 - \frac{852}{1,723}$$

$$vr_{1980} = .50$$

$$vr_{1990} = 1 - \frac{979}{2,161}$$

$$vr_{1990} = .55$$

$$vr_{2000} = 1 - \frac{1,211}{3,202}$$

$$vr_{2000} = .62$$

The variation ratio is consistently increasing from 1980 to 2000. This tells us that the dispersion in the nominal-level data is increasing. Practically, this says that the racial heterogeneity of the penitentiary is increasing over time.

6. Let's rank-order these data first:

18.3

25.9

28.2

28.7

34.0

34.6

35.4

40.0

40.9

42.3

42.4

44.6

45.6

45.9

47.0

53.4

54.4

58.9

a. Since the highest rape rate is for South Carolina at 58.9 and the lowest is for North Dakota at 18.3, the range is: 58.9 − 18.3 = 40.6.

b. The position of the median is (18 + 1)/2 = 9.5, so the truncated median position is 9.0. We now can determine the first and third quartile positions to be $9 + 1/2 = 5$. The third quartile score is 45.9 and the first quartile score is 34. The interquartile range, therefore, is $45.9 - 34.0 = 11.9$.

c. Here are the calculations necessary to determine the variance and standard deviation. First, practice your mean calculation skills. The mean rape rate per 100,000 for this sample of 18 states is 40 (actually, it's 40.03, but let's make our calculations easy and round it to 40 per 100,000).

x	$(x - 40)$	$(x - 40)^2$
42.40	2.40	5.76
44.60	4.60	21.16
47.00	7.00	49.00
42.30	2.30	5.29
40.00	.00	.00
35.40	− 4.60	21.16
40.90	.90	.81
45.90	5.90	34.81
34.00	− 6.00	36.00
28.20	− 11.80	139.24
34.60	− 5.40	29.16
18.30	− 21.70	470.89
53.40	13.40	179.56
28.70	− 11.30	127.69
58.90	18.90	357.21
54.40	14.40	207.36
45.60	5.60	31.36
25.90	− 14.10	198.81
		$\Sigma = 1887.47$

So the variance would be:

$$s^2 = \frac{1,915.27}{17}$$

$$s^2 = 112.66$$

d. Using the calculations in (C), the standard deviation would be:

$$s = \sqrt{\frac{1,915.27}{17}}$$

$$s = 10.61$$

7. Here are the summary statistics necessary to construct boxplots for the murder rates for states by region.

South

N	= 1.7	Higher outer fence	=	13.7
Mdn	= 6.9	High inner fence	=	10.7
Q_1	= 5.7	Low inner fence	=	2.7
Q_3	= 7.7	Lower outer fence	=	−0.3
IQR	= 2	High adjacent value	=	10.7
		Low adjacent value	=	3.2
		Extreme outlier	=	46.4

West

N	= 1.3	Higher outer fence	=	24.2
Mdn	= 3.7	High inner fence	=	16.1
Q_1	= 2.6	Low inner fence	=	−5.5
Q_3	= 8	Lower outer fence	=	−13.6
IQR	= 5.4	High adjacent value	=	9.8
		Low adjacent value	=	2.0

Midwest

N	= 1.2	Higher outer fence	=	18.45
Mdn	= 3.55	High inner fence	=	12.5
Q_1	= 2.65	Low inner fence	=	−3.3
Q_3	= 6.6	Lower outer fence	=	−9.2
IQR	= 3.95	High adjacent value	=	7.7
		Low adjacent value	=	1.5

Northeast

N	= 9	Higher outer fence	=	7.8
Mdn	= 3.3	High inner fence	=	5.7
Q_1	= 2.2	Low inner fence	=	0.1
Q_3	= 3.6	Lower outer fence	=	−2.0
IQR	= 1.4	High adjacent value	=	5.0
		Low adjacent value	=	1.5

CHAPTER 6 SOLUTIONS TO PROBLEMS

1. a. $P(x = \$30{,}000) = (16/110) = .14$.
   b. $P(x = \$35{,}000) = (7/110) = .06$.
   c. They are mutually exclusive events because a person cannot simultaneously have a starting salary of both $30,000 and $35,000. There is no joint probability of these two events.

d. $P(x \geq \$31{,}000) = (19/110) + (12/110) + (15/110) + (8/110) + (7/110) = (61/110) = .55.$

e. There are two ways to calculate this probability. First: $P(x \leq \$30{,}000) = (16/110) + (10/110) + (9/110) + (8/110) + (6/110) = (49/110) = .45.$ Or you can recognize that this event is the complement of the event in (d) above and calculate the probability as $1 - .55 = .45.$

f. $P(x = \$28{,}000 \text{ or } \$30{,}000 \text{ or } \$31{,}500 \text{ or } \$32{,}000 \text{ or } \$32{,}500) = (10/110) + (16/110) + (19/110) + (12/110) + (15/110) = (72/110) = .65.$

g. $P(x < \$25{,}000) = 0.$

h. $P(x = \$28{,}000 \text{ or } \$32{,}000 \text{ or } \$35{,}000) = (10/110) + (12/110) + (7/110) = (29/110) = .26.$

2. The probability and cumulative probability of 0–10 acquittals if the probability of an acquittal is .40 is shown below.

# of Acquittals	p	cp
0	.0060	1.0000
1	.0403	.9940
2	.1209	.9537
3	.2150	.8328
4	.2508	.6178
5	.2007	.3670
6	.1115	.1663
7	.0425	.0548
8	.0106	.0123
9	.0016	.0017
10	.0001	.0001

The probability of getting 7 or more acquittals if the true probability of an acquittal is .40, then, is .0548. To test our hypothesis, we will do the five steps:

Step 1.

H_0: P(acquittal with a public defender is .40).

H_1: P(acquittal with a public defender is $> .40$).

Step 2. The test statistic is a binomial statistic with a binomial probability distribution.

Step 3. Our alpha level is .05. We will reject the null hypothesis if the probability of observing 7 or more acquittals out of 10 cases is .05 or lower.

Step 4. We calculated the full probability distribution above. The probability of observing 7 or more acquittals out of 10 cases when the probability of an acquittal is .40 is equal to .0548.

Step 5. Since our observed probability is greater than .05, we will fail to reject the null hypothesis. Defendants with public defenders are no more likely to be acquitted than are defendants with other types of lawyers.

3. a. $z = 1.5$.

   b. $z = -1.7$.

   c. $z = -3.0$.

   d. .0668, or slightly more than 6 percent of the cases have an-IQ score above 115.

   e. .6832

   f. A raw score of 70 corresponds to a z score of -3.0. The probability of a z score less than or equal to -3.0 is .001.

   g. A raw score of 125 corresponds to a z score of 2.5. The probability of a z score greater than or equal to 2.5 is .006.

4. a. P(deterred) = (80/120) = .67.

   b. This is an unconditional probability. It is the probability that someone was deterred in the entire sample. It is not based upon a prior condition.

   c. P(not deterred) = $1 - .67 = .33$, since this is the complement of the event in (a) above, or (40/120) = .33.

   d. P(impulsive) = (30/120) = .25.

   e. These are not mutually exclusive events because it is possible to be both impulsive and not deterred. P(impulsive or not deterred) = (30/120) + (40/120) − (25/120) = /(45/120) = .38.

   f. P(deterred | not impulsive) = (75/90) = .83.

   g. P(deterred | impulsive) = (5/30) = .17.

   h. To determine if being deterred and impulsivity are independent events, let's compare the unconditional probability of being deterred against the conditional probability of being deterred given that a person was not impulsive and then given that a person was impulsive.

   $$P(\text{deterred}) = .67$$

   $$P(\text{deterred} \mid \text{not impulsive}) = (75 / 90) = .83$$

   $$P(\text{deterred} \mid \text{impulsive}) = (5 / 30) = .17$$

   The unconditional probability is not comparable to the conditional probabilities, it looks like the probability that someone would be deterred by punishment depends upon whether or not they are impulsive. They are far more likely to be deterred by punishment if they are not impulsive. They are not independent events.

   i. P(impulsive and not deterred) = P(impulsive) × P(not deterred | impulsive) = (30/120) × (25/30) = (.25) × (.83) = .21.

   j. P(not impulsive and deterred) = P(not impulsive) × P(deterred | not impulsive) = (90/120) × (75/90) = (.75) × (.83) = .62.

5. a. A raw score of 95 is better than .9332 or 93 percent of the scores. It is not in the top 5 percent, however, so this candidate would not be accepted.

   b. A raw score of 110 is better than .9986 or 99 percent of the scores. It is in the top 5 percent, and so this candidate would be accepted.

   c. A z score of 1.65 or higher is better than 95 percent of the scores. The z score of 1.65 corresponds to a raw score of 96.5, and that is the minimum score you need in order to be accepted.

6. A population is the universe of cases about which we would like to know and make inferences about. A population is generally quite large, consisting of many elements. An example would be the population of all adolescents in the United States. The population has characteristics (such as the mean or proportion of some variable) that are not usually known but are knowable. A sample is a subset of a population and consists of many fewer elements. We usually take a sample from a population, use the information from the sample, which we know, to make an inference about some unknown population characteristic or parameter. An example would be a sample of 100 adolescents that we might take from the population of all adolescents in the United States. The population would have a distribution of some characteristic, let's say the number of delinquent acts committed. This characteristic would have a population mean (μ) and a standard deviation (σ). The sample of 100 adolescents also would have a distribution with a sample mean ($\bar{x}$) and a sample standard deviation (s). A sampling distribution is a theoretical probability distribution. It is a distribution of an infinite number of samples. For example, if we were to take an infinite number of samples of size 100 from our population of adolescents, and if for each sample of size 100 we calculated a mean, we would have a distribution of an infinite number of sample means. This theoretical probability distribution of sample means also would have a mean (μ) and a standard deviation $\left(\dfrac{\sigma}{\sqrt{n}}\right)$.

7. a. The area to the right of a z score of 1.65 is equal to .0495.

   b. The area to the left of a z score of -1.65 is equal to .0495.

   c. The area either to the left of a z score of -1.65 or to the right of a z score of 1.65 is equal to .099.

   d. The area to the right of a z score of 2.33 is .0099.

   e. Yes, the probability of a z-score ≤ -2.56 is .005.

8. a. P(no violence) = (60/250) = .24.

b. P(guards only) = (55/250) = .22.

c. Since these are mutually exclusive events, P(metal detectors or guards only) = (60/250) + (55/250) = .46.

d. P(no measures) (80/250) = .32.

e. Since P(guards and metal detectors or had 1–4 violent acts) are not mutually exclusive acts, (55/250) + (75/250) − (15/250) = (115/250) = .46.

f. Since P(used metal detectors only or 5+ violent acts) are not mutually exclusive acts, (60/250) + (115/250) − (30/250) = (145/250) = .58.

g. P(no violence | no preventive measures) = (5/80) = .06.

h. P(no violence | some prevention) $= \left(\dfrac{10 + 15 + 30}{60 + 55 + 55} \right) = \left(\dfrac{55}{170} \right) = .32 \cdot$

i. P(5+ violent acts | metal detectors only) = (30/60) = .50.

j. P(5+ violent acts | guards and metal detectors) = (10/55) = .18.

k. Let's calculate the unconditional probability that the school would have 5 or more violent acts:

$$P(5 + \text{violent acts}) = (115 / 250) = .46.$$

Now let's calculate the conditional probability of 5+ violent acts at each different level of the independent variable:

P(5 + violent acts | no preventive measures)   = (50 / 80) = .62

P(5 + violent acts | metal detectors only)   = (30 / 60) = .50

P(5 + violent acts | guards only)   = (25 / 55) = .45

P(5 + violent acts | guards and metal detectors) = (10 / 55) = .18

The conditional probabilities are not comparable to the unconditional probability of five or more violent acts. In fact, it looks as if the type of preventive measure a school uses is related to the probability that five or more violent acts were committed. These events are not independent events.

l. P(no violent acts and guards only) = (60/250) × (15/60) = .06.

m. P(no preventive measures and 5+ violent acts) = (80/250) × (50/80) = .20.

n. P(guards together with metal detectors and 1–4 violent acts) = (55/250) × (15/55) = .06.

9. a. To see how unusual 9 prior arrests are in this population, let's transform the raw score into a z score: $z = \dfrac{9 - 6}{2} = 1.50$. Taking a z score

of 1.50 to the z table we can see that the area to the right of this score comprises approximately 7 percent of the area of the normal curve. Those who have 9 prior arrests then, are in the top 7 percent of this population. Since they are not in the top 5 percent we would not consider them unusual.

b. A raw score of 11 prior arrests corresponds to a z score of: $z = \dfrac{11 - 6}{2} = 2.50$. A z score of 2.50 is at the right or upper end of the distribution. Z scores of 2.50 or greater are greater than approximately 99 percent of all the other scores. Those who have 11 prior arrests then, do have an unusually large number of prior arrests since they are in the top 5 percent.

c. A raw score of 2 prior arrests corresponds to a z score of: $z = \dfrac{1 - 6}{2} = -2.0$. A z score of -2.0 falls lower than almost 98 percent of all the other scores. Those with only two prior arrests, then, do have an unusually low number for this population since they are in the bottom 5 percent.

10. The *central limit theorem* is a statistical proposition which holds that if an infinite number of random samples of size n are drawn from *any* population with mean μ and standard deviation σ, then as the sample size becomes large, the sampling distribution of sample means will become normal with mean μ and standard deviation equal to $\dfrac{\sigma}{\sqrt{n}}$.

The central limit theorem allows us to make three assumptions about sampling distributions when the sample size is large: (a) We can assume that the mean of the sampling distribution is equal to the population mean; μ (b) We can assume that the standard deviation of the sampling distribution is equal to $\dfrac{\sigma}{\sqrt{n}}$; and (c) We can assume the sampling distribution is normally distributed even if the population from which the sample was drawn is not.

CHAPTER 7 SOLUTIONS TO PROBLEMS

1. The purpose of confidence intervals is to give us a range of values for our estimated population parameter rather than a single value or a point estimate. The estimated confidence interval gives us a range of values within which we believe, with varying degrees of confidence, that the true population value falls. The advantage of providing a range of values for our estimate is that we will be more likely to include the population parameter. Think of trying to estimate your final

exam score in this class. You are more likely to be accurate if you are able to estimate an interval within which your actual score will fall (e.g., "somewhere between 85 and 95") than if you give only a single value as your estimate (e.g., "it will be an 89"). Notice that the wider you make your interval (e.g., "somewhere between 40 and 95"), the more accurate you are likely to be in that your exam score will probably fall within that very large interval. However, the price of this accuracy is precision; you are not being very precise by estimating that your final exam score will be between 40 and 95. In this case, you will be very confident, but not very precise. Notice also that the more narrow or precise your interval is, the less confident you may be about it. If you predicted that your final exam score would be between a 90 and a 95, you would be very precise. You also would probably be far less confident of this prediction than the one where you stated your score would fall between a 40 and a 95. Other things being equal (like sample size), there is a trade-off, therefore, between precision and confidence.

2. At small sample sizes, the t distribution is flatter than a z distribution and has fatter tails on both ends of the distribution. When the sample size is 100 or more, the two distributions are virtually identical. We can be confident in using the z distribution rather than the t distribution when our sample size is 50 or more. If the population does not depart dramatically from normality, we can use the z distribution with sample sizes of 30 or more.

3.

$$4.5 \pm 1.96 \left(\frac{3.2}{\sqrt{110}} \right)$$

$$4.5 \pm 1.96 \left(\frac{3.2}{10.49} \right)$$

$$4.5 \pm 1.96(.31)$$

$$4.5 \pm .61$$

$$3.89 \leq \mu \leq 5.11$$

We are 95 percent confident that the mean level of marijuana use in our population of teenagers is between 3.89 times and 5.11 times a year. This means that if we were to take an infinite number of samples of size 110 from this population and estimate a confidence interval around the mean for each sample, 95 percent of those confidence intervals would contain the true population mean.

4.

$$4.5 \pm 1.96 \left(\frac{3.2}{\sqrt{55}} \right)$$

$$4.5 \pm 1.96 \left(\frac{3.2}{7.42} \right)$$

$$4.5 \pm 1.96 \, (.43)$$

$$4.5 \pm .84$$

$$3.66 \leq \mu \leq 5.34$$

Our confidence interval is much wider when our sample size is 55 than when it was 110. This is because with a smaller sample size, our sampling error becomes greater. Because the standard deviation of the sampling distribution is a function of sample size, it increases whenever the sample size (n) decreases. When our sample size was reduced from 110 to 55, the standard deviation of the sampling distribution increased from .31 to .43. The increase in the standard deviation of the sampling distribution (standard error) increased the width of our interval. With a sample size of 55, we are 95 percent confident that the true population mean is between 3.66 and 5.34 times per year.

5. The standard deviation of the sampling distribution is the standard deviation of an infinite number of sample estimates [means ($\bar{x}$), or proportions (p)] each drawn from a sample with sample size equal to n. It also is called the standard error. The sample size affects the value of the standard error (see above). At a fixed confidence level, increasing the sample size will reduce the size of the standard error and, consequently, the width of the confidence interval.

6. Because we have a small sample, $n = 20$, we have to use the t distribution to build our 99 percent confidence interval around the sample mean. We go, therefore, to the t table (Table E–3) to find our t value, with $n - 1$ or 19 degrees of freedom. In finding the correct t value from the table, we hope you remembered that confidence interval problems are always two-tailed problems, since you cannot be certain if your point estimate over- or underestimates the true population value. The critical value with 19 degrees of freedom and an $\alpha = .01$ is equal to 2.861. The interval would be:

$$11 \pm 2.861 \left(\frac{1.7}{\sqrt{20}} \right)$$

$$11 \pm 2.861 \left(\frac{1.7}{4.47} \right)$$

$$11 \pm 2.861 \, (.38)$$

$$11 \pm 1.09$$

$$9.91 \leq \mu \leq 12.09$$

7. To find a 95 percent confidence interval around a sample mean of 560 with a standard deviation of 45 and a sample size of 15, you would have to go to the t table. With $n = 15$, there are 14 degrees of freedom. Since confidence intervals are two-tailed problems, the value of t you should obtain is 2.145. Now you can construct the confidence interval:

$$560 \pm 2.145 \left(\frac{45}{\sqrt{15}} \right)$$

$$560 \pm 2.145 \left(\frac{45}{3.87} \right)$$

$$560 \pm 2.145(11.63)$$

$$560 \pm 24.95$$

$$535.05 \leq \mu \leq 584.95$$

You can say that you are 95 percent confident that the true police response time is between 534 seconds (almost 9 minutes) and 586 seconds (almost 10 minutes).

8. Using the z distribution, the 95 percent confidence interval for the traditional treatment group is:

$$95\% \text{ c.i.} \ = \ .61 \pm 1.96 \sqrt{\frac{.61(1 - .61}{75}}$$

$$= \ .61 \pm 1.96 \sqrt{\frac{.24}{75}}$$

$$= \ .61 \pm 1.96 \sqrt{.003}$$

$$= \ .61 \pm 1.96(.055)$$

$$= \ .61 \pm .108$$

$$.502 \leq \rho \leq .718$$

$$95\% \text{ c.i.} \ = \ .50 \text{ to } .72, \text{ or } 50\% \text{ to } 72\%$$

For the Paint Creek Youth Center group it is:

$$95\% \text{ c.i.} \ = \ .51 \pm 1.96 \sqrt{\frac{.51(1 - .51)}{73}}$$

$$= \ .51 \pm 1.96 \sqrt{\frac{.25}{73}}$$

$$= \ .51 \pm 1.96 \sqrt{.003}$$

$$= .51 \pm 1.96(.055)$$

$$= .51 \pm .108$$

$$.402 \leq \rho \leq .618$$

$$95\% \text{ c.i.} = .40 \text{ to } .62, \text{ or } 40\% \text{ to } 62\%$$

9. We would see that when we increased the confidence interval from a 95 percent to a 99 percent confidence interval, the width of the confidence interval also would increase. This is because the price of wanting to be more confident (99 percent confident as opposed to 95 percent confident) that our estimated interval contains the true population parameter is a wider interval (all other things being equal). You should remember from the discussion in the chapter that you can increase the level of your confidence without expanding the width of the interval by increasing your sample size.

CHAPTER 8 SOLUTIONS TO PROBLEMS

1. The z test and z distribution may be used for making one-sample hypothesis tests involving a population mean under two conditions: (1) if the population standard deviation (σ) is known, or (2) if the sample size is large enough ($n \geq 100$), so that the sample standard deviation (s) can be used as an unbiased estimate of the population standard deviation. If either of these two conditions is not met, hypothesis tests about one population mean must be conducted with the t test and t distribution.

2. In our first hypothesis test, the null and alternative hypotheses would be:

   H_0: $\mu = \$2,222$
   H_1: $\mu \neq \$2,222$

   If we believed the dollar amount lost by burglary victims to be *higher* than \$2,222, our null hypothesis would be the same, but we would assume the following about the alternative hypothesis: H_1 $\mu > \$2,222$.

3. The null and alternative hypotheses are:

   H_0: $\mu = 4.6$
   H_1: $\mu > 4.6$

   Although we do not know the population standard deviation, our sample size is greater than 50 ($n = 64$), so we can use the z test and the z distribution. Our decision rule is to reject the null hypothesis if our obtained value of z is 2.33 or greater (reject H_0 if $z_{obt} \geq 2.33$). The value of z_{obt} is:

$$z_{obt} = \frac{6.3 - 4.6}{1.9 / \sqrt{64}} = 7.08$$

Because 7.08 is higher than the critical value of 2.33 and falls in the critical region, we will reject the null hypothesis that the population mean is equal to 4.6 times.

4. The null and alternative hypotheses are:

H_0: $\mu = 3.5$

H_1: $\mu < 3.5$

Our decision rule is to reject the null hypothesis if our obtained value of z is −1.65 or less. The value of z_{obt} is:

$$z_{obt} = \frac{2.9 - 3.5}{.7 / \sqrt{59}} = -6.67$$

Because this is lower than the critical value of −1.65 and falls in the critical region, we will reject the null hypothesis that the population mean is equal to 3.5 acts of vandalism.

5. The null and alternative hypotheses are:

H_0: $\mu = 25.9$

H_1: $\mu \neq 25.9$

Our decision rule is to reject the null hypothesis if our obtained value of z is ≥ 2.58 or ≤ −2.58. The value of z_{obt} is:

$$z_{obt} = \frac{27.3 - 25.9}{6.5 / \sqrt{75}} = 1.87$$

Because this value is not higher than the critical value of 2.58 and does not fall in the critical region, we fail to reject the null hypothesis that the population mean is equal to 25.9 months.

6. The null and alternative hypotheses are:

H_0: $\mu = 15$

H_1: $\mu \neq 15$

Because we do not know the population standard deviation and our sample size is substantially less than 50 ($n = 15$), we must use the t test and the t distribution. Our decision rule is to reject the null hypothesis if our obtained value of $t \geq 2.145$ or if $t \leq$ obtained ≤ -2.145. The value of t_{obt} is:

$$t_{obt} = \frac{16.4 - 15}{4 / \sqrt{15}} = 1.36$$

Because this value is not higher than the critical value of 2.145 and does not fall in the critical region, we fail to reject the null hypothesis that the population mean is equal to 15 hours.

7. The null and alternative hypotheses are:

H_0: $\mu = 4$

H_1: $\mu > 4$

Our decision rule is to reject the null hypothesis if our obtained value of $t \geq 2.718$. The value of t_{obt} is:

$$t_{obt} = \frac{6.3 - 4}{1.5 / \sqrt{12}} = 5.35$$

Because this is greater than the critical value of 2.718 and falls in the critical region, we decide to reject the null hypothesis that the population mean is equal to 4 arrests.

8. The null and alternative hypotheses are:

H_0: $\mu = 25$

H_1: $\mu < 25$

Our decision rule is to reject the null hypothesis if our obtained value of $t \leq -1.729$. The value of t_{obt} is:

$$t_{obt} = \frac{23 - 25}{6 / \sqrt{20}} = -1.49$$

Because this value is not less than the critical value of -1.729 and does not fall in the critical region, we fail to reject the null hypothesis that the population mean is equal to 25 minutes.

9. The null and alternative hypotheses are:

H_0: $p = .45$

H_1: $p < .45$

Because this is a problem involving a population proportion with a large sample size ($n = 200$), we can use the z test and the z distribution. Our decision rule is to reject the null hypothesis if our obtained value of z is -2.33 or less. The value of z_{obt} is:

$$z_{obt} = \frac{.23 - .45}{\sqrt{\dfrac{.45(.55)}{200}}} = -6.29$$

Because this is less than the critical value of -2.33 and falls in the critical region, we will reject the null hypothesis that the population proportion is equal to .45, or 45 percent.

10. The null and alternative hypotheses are:

H_0: $p = .20$

H_1: $p \neq .20$

Because this is a problem involving a population proportion with a large sample size ($n = 60$: $60 \times .2 > 5$), we can use the z test and the z distribution. Our decision rule is to reject the null hypothesis if our obtained value of $z_{obt} \leq -1.96$ or $z_{obt} \geq 1.96$. The value of z_{obt} is:

$$z_{obt} = \frac{.31 - .20}{\sqrt{\frac{.20(.80)}{60}}} = 2.12$$

Because this is greater than the critical value of 1.96 and falls in the critical region, we decide to reject the null hypothesis that the population proportion is equal to .20, or 20 percent, of the homes.

11. The null and alternative hypotheses are:

$H_0: p = .31$
$H_1: p > .31$

Because this is a problem involving a population proportion with a large sample size ($n = 110$), we can use the z test and the z distribution. Our decision rule is to reject the null hypothesis if our obtained value of z is 1.65 or greater. The value of z_{obt} is:

$$z_{obt} = \frac{.42 - .31}{\sqrt{\frac{.31(.69)}{110}}} = 2.50$$

Because this is greater than the critical value of 1.65 and falls in the critical region, we will reject the null hypothesis that the population proportion is equal to .31, or 31 percent.

CHAPTER 9 SOLUTIONS TO PROBLEMS

1. a. The type of institution is the independent variable and satisfaction with one's job is the dependent variable.

   b. There are a total of 185 observations.

   c. There are 115 persons who were not satisfied with their job and 70 persons who reported that they were satisfied with their job.

   d. There were 45 people working in medium security institutions and 140 employed in maximum security institutions.

   e. This is a 2×2 contingency table.

   f. 30 correctional officers are in medium security institutions and like their jobs.

   g. 100 correctional officers are in maximum security institutions and do not like their jobs.

h. There is $(2 - 1)$ or 1 degree of freedom.

i. The risk of not being satisfied with your job is .33 (15/45) in medium security institutions and .71 (100/140) in maximum security institutions. It looks as if the type of institution one works in is related to job satisfaction. Officers are far more likely to be dissatisfied with their jobs if they work in maximum security facilities, as opposed to medium security ones.

j.

Step 1.

H_0: Type of institution and level of job satisfaction are independent.

H_1: Type of institution and level of job satisfaction are not independent.

Step 2. Our test statistic is a chi-square test of independence, which has a chi-square distribution.

Step 3. With 1 degree of freedom and an alpha of .05, our $\chi^2_{crit} = 3.841$. The critical region is any obtained chi-square to the right of this. Our decision rule is to reject the null hypothesis when $\chi^2_{obt} \geq 3.841$.

Step 4. When we calculate our obtained chi-square we find that it is $\chi^2_{obt} = 21.11$.

Step 5. With a critical value of 3.841 and an obtained chi-square statistic of 21.11, our decision is to reject the null hypothesis. Our conclusion is that type of institution and job satisfaction for a correctional officer are not independent; there is a relationship between these two variables in the population.

We could use several different measures of association for a 2 × 2 contingency table. Our estimated value of Yule's Q would be −.67, which would tell us that there is a strong negative relationship between type of institution and job satisfaction. More specifically, we would conclude that those who work in maximum security facilities have less job satisfaction. Since we have a 2 × 2 table, we also could have used the phi coefficient as our measure of association. Our estimated value of phi is .34. Phi indicates that there is a moderate association or correlation between type of institution and job satisfaction (remember that the phi coefficient is always positive).

2. a. The independent variable is whether or not the neighborhood is socially disorganized and the dependent variable is the neighborhood crime rate.

b. There are a total of 250 observations.

c. There are 100 socially organized neighborhoods and 150 socially disorganized neighborhoods.

d. There are 188 low crime rate neighborhoods and 62 high crime rate neighborhoods.

e. This is a 2 × 2 contingency table.

f. There are 52 socially disorganized neighborhoods with high crime rates.

g. There are 90 socially organized neighborhoods with low crime rates.

h. There is 1 degree of freedom.

i. The risk of a high crime rate for those neighborhoods that are socially organized is .10, while for socially disorganized neighborhoods it is .35. This would suggest that social disorganization in the neighborhood is related to the crime rate.

j.

Step 1.

H_0: Social organization in the neighborhood and neighborhood crime rates are independent.

H_1: Social organization in the neighborhood and neighborhood crime rates are not independent.

Step 2. Our test statistic is a chi-square test of independence; which has a chi-square distribution.

Step 3. With 1 degree of freedom and an alpha of .01, our $\chi^2_{crit} = 6.635$. The critical region is any obtained chi-square to the right of this. Our decision rule is to reject the null hypothesis when $\chi^2_{obt} \geq 6.635$.

Step 4. When we calculate our obtained chi-square we find that it is $\chi^2_{obt} = 20.07$.

Step 5. With a critical value of 6.635 and an obtained chi-square statistic of 20.07, our decision is to reject the null hypothesis. Our conclusion is that social organization in the neighborhood and neighborhood crime rates are not independent; there is a relationship between these two variables in the population.

We could use several different measures of association for a 2 × 2 contingency table. Our estimated value of Yule's Q would be .65, which would tell us that there is a strong positive relationship between social disorganization and the neighborhood crime rate. More specifically, we would conclude that socially disorganized neighborhoods have higher rates of crime than those that are socially organized. Since we have a 2 × 2 table, we also could have used the phi coefficient as our measure of association. Our estimated value of phi is .28. Phi indicates that there is a weak association or correlation between social organization in the neighborhood and neighborhood crime rates (remember than the phi coefficient is always positive).

3. a. The independent variable is the jurisdiction where the defendant was tried, and the dependent variable is the type of sentence a defendant receives.

b. There are a total of 425 observations.

c. There are 80 defendants from rural jurisdictions, 125 from suburban courts, and 220 who were tried in urban courts.

d. There are 142 defendants who received jail time only, 95 who were fined and sent to jail, 112 who were sentenced to less than 60 days of jail time, and 76 who were sentenced to 60 or more days of jail.

e. This is a 4 × 3 contingency table.

f. There are 38 defendants from suburban courts who received less than 60 days of jail time as their sentence.

g. There are 22 defendants tried in rural courts who received a sentence of a fine and jail.

h. There are $(4 - 1) \times (3 - 1)$ or 6 degrees of freedom.

i. The risk of 60 or more days of jail time is .20 for those tried in rural courts, .16 for those tried in suburban courts, and .18 for those tried in urban courts. There seems to be a slight relationship here, with those tried in rural courts more likely to be sentenced to more than 60 days of jail time.

j.

Step 1.

H_0: Place where tried and type of sentence are independent.

H_1: Place where tried and type of sentence are not independent.

Step 2.   Our test statistic is a chi-square test of independence, which has a chi-square distribution.

Step 3.   With 6 degrees of freedom and an alpha of .01 our $\chi^2_{crit} = 16.812$. The critical region is any obtained chi-square to the right of this. Our decision rule is to reject the null hypothesis when $\chi^2_{obt} \geq 16.812$.

Step 4.   When we calculate our obtained chi-square we find that it is $\chi^2_{obt} = 21.85$.

Step 5.   With a critical value of 16.812 and an obtained chi-square statistic of 21.85, our decision is to reject the null hypothesis. Our conclusion is there is a relationship between where in the state a defendant was tried and the type of sentence they received.

Location of the trial and type of sentence are both nominal-level variables. We will use lambda as our measure of association. The value of lambda is:

$$\lambda = \frac{283 - 269}{283}$$

$$\lambda = .05$$

Our lambda coefficient tells us that there is only a very weak relationship between the location of the trial and the type of sentence received.

4. a. The independent variable is race and the dependent variable is the number of property crimes committed.

   b. There are a total of 360 cases.

   c. There are 257 persons who committed 0–4 property crimes, and 103 persons who committed 5 or more property crimes.

   d. There are 110 non-white persons and 250 whites.

   e. This is a 2 × 2 table.

   f. 33 non-white offenders committed 5 or more property offenses.

   g. 180 white offenders committed 0–4 property crimes.

   h. There is 1 degree of freedom.

   i. For non-whites, the risk of 5 or more property crimes is .30, and for whites it is .28. There does not seem to be much of a difference in the relative risks.

   j.

Step 1.

H_0: Race and the number of property crimes committed are independent.

H_1: Race and the number of property crimes are not independent.

Step 2.   Our test statistic is a chi-square test of independence, which has a chi-square distribution.

Step 3.   With 1 degree of freedom and an alpha of .05, our $\chi^2_{crit} = 3.841$. The critical region is any obtained chi-square to the right of this. Our decision rule is to reject the null hypothesis when $\chi^2_{obt} \geq 3.841$.

Step 4.   When we calculate our obtained chi-square we find that it is $\chi^2_{obt} = .25$.

Step 5.   With a critical value of 3.841 and an obtained chi-square statistic of .25, our decision is to fail to reject the null hypothesis. Our conclusion is that one's race and the number of property crimes they commit are independent. There is no relationship in the population between these two variables. Since our conclusion is that there is no relationship in the population, we do not need to calculate a measure of association.

5. a. Employment is the independent variable and the number of arrests after three years is the dependent variable.

   b. There are 115 observations or cases.

   c. There are 45 persons who reported having stable employment, 30 who reported sporadic employment, and 40 who reported being unemployed.

   d. There are 54 persons who had no arrests after three years and 61 who had one or more arrests.

   e. This is a 2 × 3 contingency table.

   f. 16 persons who were sporadically employed had one or more arrests.

   g. 10 unemployed persons had no arrests.

   h. There are $(2-1) \times (3-1) = 2$ degrees of freedom.

   i. For those with stable employment, the risk of having one or more arrests is .33, for those with sporadic employment it is .53, and for the unemployed it is .75. The relative risk of at least one arrest increases as one's employment situation becomes worse.

   j.

Step 1.

H_0: Employment status and the number of arrests after three years are independent.

H_1: Employment status and the number of arrests after three years are independent.

Step 2.   Our test statistic is a chi-square test of independence, which has a chi-square distribution.

Step 3.   With 2 degrees of freedom and an alpha of .05, our $\chi^2_{crit} = 5.991$. The critical region is any obtained chi-square to the right of this. Our decision rule is to reject the null hypothesis when $\chi^2_{obt} \geq 5.991$.

Step 4.   When we calculate our obtained chi-square we find that it is $\chi^2_{obt} = 15.33$.

Step 5.   With a critical value of 5.991 and an obtained chi-square statistic of 15.33, our decision is to reject the null hypothesis. Our conclusion is that employment status and the number of arrests upon release are not independent. There is a relationship between the two variables in the population.

Since both employment status and the number of arrests after three years are ordinal- level variables, we will use gamma as our measure of association. The value of gamma is:

$$\gamma = \frac{1,800 - 520}{1,800 + 520}$$

$$\gamma = .55$$

There is a moderately strong positive association between employment status and the number of arrests. More specifically, as one moves from stable to sporadic to nonemployed, the risk of having one or more arrests increases.

6. a. The independent variable is the type of offender one is: adolescent limited vs. life course persistent. The dependent variable is the number of adult crimes.

   b. There are 320 total observations.

   c. There are 93 persons who committed 0–4 adult offenses, 78 who committed 5–9 adult offenses, 71 who committed 10–14 adult offenses, and 78 who committed 15 or more offenses as an adult.

   d. There are 137 life course persistent offenders and 183 adolescent limited offenders.

   e. This is a 2 × 4 contingency table.

   f. 37 life course persistent offenders have 10–14 adult offenses.

   g. 15 adolescent limited offenders have 15 or more adult offenses.

   h. There are $(2-1)(4-1) = 3$ degrees of freedom.

   i. The risk of 0–4 adult offenses is .43 for the adolescent limited and .11 for the life course persistent offender. This would suggest that life course persistent offenders commit more offenses as adults.

   j.

Step 1.

H_0: Offender type (adolescent limited vs. life course persistent) and number of adult arrests are independent.
H_1: Offender type (adolescent limited vs. life course persistent) and number of adult arrests are not independent.

Step 2.   Our test statistic is a chi-square test of independence, which has a chi-square distribution.

Step 3.   With 3 degrees of freedom and an alpha of .01 our $\chi^2_{crit} = 11.345$. The critical region is any obtained chi-square to the right of this. Our decision rule is to reject the null hypothesis when $\chi^2_{obt} \geq 11.345$.

Step 4.   When we calculate our obtained chi-square we find that it is $\chi^2_{obt} = 82.27$.

Step 5.   With a critical value of 11.345 and an obtained chi-square statistic of 82.27, our decision is to reject the null hypothesis. Our conclusion is that offender type and the number of adult arrests are not independent. There is a relationship between the two variables in the population.

The correct measure of association is a bit tricky. You could say that offender type is an ordinal-level variable since the life course persistent offender is a more serious type of offender. Since the number of adult offenses is also ordinal you could use gamma. If you decide to do this, the value of gamma is:

$$\gamma = \frac{17,258 - 3,208}{17,258 + 3,208}$$

$$\gamma = .69$$

There is a strong positive association between offender type and the number of adult offenses. More specifically, life course persistent offenders have more adult offenses than adolescent limited offenders.

If you are not willing to assume that offender type is ordinal, and instead assume that it is a nominal-level variable, you could estimate a lambda coefficient. The value of lambda is:

$$\lambda = \frac{227 - 179}{227}$$

$$\lambda = .21$$

According to lambda, there is only a weak relationship between the two.

CHAPTER 10 SOLUTIONS TO PROBLEMS

1. An independent variable is the variable whose effect or influence you want to measure on the dependent variable. In causal terms, the independent variable is the cause, and the dependent variable is the effect. Low self-control is taken to affect one's involvement in crime, so self-control is the independent variable and involvement in crime is the dependent variable.

2. An independent sample t test should be used whenever the two samples have been selected independently of one another. In an independent sample t test, the sample elements are not related to one another. In a dependent sample or matched groups t test, however, the sample elements are not independent, but are instead related to one another. An example of a dependent sample would be when the same sample elements or persons are measured at two different points in time, as in a "before and after" experiment. A second common type of dependent sample is a matched-groups design.

3. The null and alternative hypotheses are:

$H_0: \mu_1 = \mu_2$
$H_1: \mu_1 < \mu_2$

The correct test is the pooled variance independent-samples t test, and our sampling distribution is the Student's t distribution. We will reject the null hypothesis if $t_{obt} \leq -2.390$. The obtained value of t is:

$$t_{obt} = \frac{5.1 - 8.2}{\sqrt{\dfrac{[(40-1)(1.8)^2] + [(25-1)(1.9)^2]}{40+25-2}}\sqrt{\dfrac{40+25}{(40)(25)}}}$$

$$= -6.74$$

Because our obtained value of t is less than the critical value and falls into the critical region, we decide to reject the null hypothesis of equal means. We conclude that those whose coworkers disapprove of stealing from their employer steal things less frequently than those whose coworkers are more tolerant of theft.

4. The null and alternative hypotheses are:

$H_0: p_1 = p_2$

$H_1: p_1 \neq p_2$

Because this problem involves two population proportions, our test statistic is the z test and our sampling distribution is the z or standard normal distribution. Our decision rule is to reject the null hypothesis if $z_{obt} \leq -1.96$ or $z_{obt} \geq 1.96$.

The value of z_{obt} is:

$$z_{obt} = \frac{.33 - .38}{\sqrt{(.35)(.65)}\sqrt{\dfrac{150+110}{(150)(110)}}}$$

$$= -.83$$

As z_{obt} is not less than -1.96 or greater than 1.96 and does not fall into the critical region, we decide not to reject the null hypothesis. We cannot, therefore, reject the notion that the proportion rearrested is not different between those given fines and those given prison sentences.

5. The null and alternative hypotheses are:

$H_0: \mu_1 = \mu_2$

$H_1: \mu_1 < \mu_2$

The problem instructs you not to presume that the population standard deviations are equal ($\sigma_1 \neq \sigma_2$), so the correct statistical test is the separate variance t test, and the sampling distribution is the Student's t distribution. With approximately 60 df and an alpha of .05 for a one-tailed test, the critical value of t is -1.671. The value for t_{obt} is:

$$t_{obt} = \frac{18.8 - 21.3}{\sqrt{\dfrac{(4.5)^2}{50-1} + \dfrac{(3.0)^2}{25-1}}}$$

$$= -2.84$$

As $t_{obt} \leq t_{crit}$, we reject the null hypothesis of equal population means. Our conclusion is that the mean score on the domestic disturbance scale is significantly lower for males than for females. In other words, males are less likely to see the fair handling of domestic disturbances as an important part of police work.

6. The null and alternative hypotheses are:

H_0: $\mu_D = 0$

H_1: $\mu_D < 0$

Our sample members (the judges) were deliberately matched in order to be comparable, so we have matched samples. The appropriate test statistic, then, is the dependent samples or matched-groups t test, and the sampling distribution is the Student's t distribution. Our decision rule is to reject the null hypothesis if $t_{obt} \leq -2.624$. The value of t_{obt} is:

$$t_{obt} = \frac{-1.4}{2.64 / \sqrt{15}}$$

$$= -2.05$$

As our t_{obt} (-2.05) is not less than or equal to -2.624, we do not reject the null hypothesis. There is no difference in the number of capital cases lost on appeal between trained and untrained judges.

7. The null and alternative hypotheses are:

H_0: $p_1 = p_2$

H_1: $p_1 > p_2$

Because this is a difference of proportions problem, the correct test statistic is the z test, and our sampling distribution is the z or standard normal distribution. Our decision rule is to reject the null hypothesis if $z_{obt} \geq 2.33$.

The value of z_{obt} is:

$$z_{obt} = \frac{.43 - .17}{\sqrt{(.32)(.68)} \sqrt{\frac{100 + 75}{(100)(75)}}}$$

$$= 3.71$$

Because our obtained z is greater than the critical value of z (2.33) and z_{obt} falls into the critical region, we reject the null hypothesis. Delinquent children have a significantly higher proportion of criminal parents than do nondelinquent children.

8. The null and alternative hypotheses are:

H_0: $\mu_D = 0$

H_1: $\mu_D \neq 0$

Because the two samples are the same youths at two points in time (before and after dropping out), we have dependent samples. The correct test statistic, then, is the dependent samples or matched-groups t test, and the sampling distribution is the Student's t distribution. Our decision rule is to reject the null hypothesis if $t_{obt} \leq -2.228$ or if $t_{obt} \geq 2.228$.

The value of t_{obt} is:

$$t_{obt} = \frac{-.27}{3.07 / \sqrt{11}}$$

$$= -.29$$

As our critical value of t is not greater or equal to 2.228 nor less than or equal to -2.228 and does not fall into the critical region, we fail to reject the null hypothesis. We cannot reject the assumption that the number of delinquent offenses committed before dropping out is the same as the number after dropping out.

CHAPTER 11 SOLUTIONS TO PROBLEMS

1. An analysis of variance can be performed whenever we have a continuous (interval- or ratio-level) dependent variable and a categorical variable with three or more levels or categories, and we are interested in testing an hypothesis about the equality of our population means.

2. If we have a continuous dependent variable and a categorical independent variable with only two categories or levels, the correct statistical test would be a two-sample t test, assuming that the hypothesis test involved the equality of two population means.

3. It is called the analysis of variance, because we make inferences about the differences among population means based upon a comparison of the *variance* that exists within each sample, relative to the variance that exists between the samples. More specifically, we examine the ratio of variance between the samples to the variance within the samples. The greater this ratio, the more between-sample variance there is relative to within-sample variance. Therefore, as this ratio becomes greater than 1, we are more inclined to believe that the samples were drawn from different populations with different population means.

4. As suggested in the answer to the last question, the two types of variance we use in the ANOVA F test are the variance between the samples and the variance within the samples:

$$F = \frac{\text{Between group variance}}{\text{Within group variance}}$$

5. The formulas for the three degrees of freedom are:

$$df_{total} = n - 1$$

$$df_{between} = k - 1$$

$$df_{within} = n - k$$

To check your arithmetic, make sure that $df_{total} = df_{between} + df_{within}$.

6. a. The independent variable is the level of stress reported by the women in the sample, and the dependent variable is the number of times they have physically punished their children in the past month.

b. The total sum of squares is:

$$SS_{total} = 343.2$$

The between-groups sum of squares is:

$$SS_{between} = 242.6$$

The within-group sum of squares can be found by subtraction:

$$SS_{between} = 100.6$$

c. The correct number of degrees of freedom are:

$$df_{between} = k - 1 = 3 - 1 = 2$$

$$df_{within} = n - k = 30 - 3 = 27$$

$$df_{total} = n - 1 = 30 - 1 = 29$$

You can see that $df_{between} + df_{within} = df_{total}$.

The ratio of sum of squares to degrees of freedom now can be determined:

$$SS_{between} / df_{between} = 242.6 / 2 = 121.30$$

$$SS_{within} / df_{within} = 100.6 / 27 = 3.73$$

The F ratio is: $F_{obt} = 121.30/3.73 = 32.52$.

d.

H_0: $\mu_{high\ stress} = \mu_{medium\ stress} = \mu_{low\ stress}$

H_1: $\mu_{high\ stress} \neq \mu_{medium\ stress} \neq \mu_{low\ stress}$

Our decision rule will be to reject the null hypothesis if $F_{obt} \geq 3.35$.

$F_{obt} = 32.52$. Since our obtained value of F is greater than the critical value, our decision is to reject the null hypothesis. We conclude that the population means are not equal, and that the frequency of using physical punishment against one's child does vary by the amount of stress the woman feels. Going to the studentized q table, you find the value of q to be equal to 3.49. To find the critical difference, you plug these values into your formula:

$$CD = 3.49\sqrt{\frac{3.73}{10}}$$

$$CD = 2.13$$

The critical difference for the mean comparisons, then, is 2.13. Find the difference between each pair of sample means in the problem to test each null hypothesis.

H_0: $\mu_{\text{high stress}} = \mu_{\text{medium stress}}$

H_1: $\mu_{\text{high stress}} \neq \mu_{\text{medium stress}}$

High stress	8.30
Medium stress	−3.30
	5.00

Since the absolute value of the difference between these sample means is greater than the critical difference score of 2.13, we would reject the null hypothesis. We would conclude that the frequency of using physical punishment for mothers experiencing high stress is greater than for those experiencing medium stress.

H_0: $\mu_{\text{high stress}} = \mu_{\text{low stress}}$

H_1: $\mu_{\text{high stress}} \neq \mu_{\text{low stress}}$

High stress	8.30
Low stress	−1.60
	6.70

The difference between the high and low stress sample means is greater than the critical difference score of 2.13. We would reject the null hypothesis and conclude that, on average, high stress mothers more frequently use physical punishment than low stress mothers.

H_0: $\mu_{\text{medium stress}} = \mu_{\text{low stress}}$

H_1: $\mu_{\text{medium stress}} \neq \mu_{\text{low stress}}$

Medium stress	3.30
Low stress	−1.60
	1.70

The difference between medium and low stress mothers is not greater than the critical difference score of 2.13. There is no significant difference between mothers experiencing medium stress and low stress in the frequency with which they resort to physical punishment.

e. Eta^2 is:

$$eta^2 = \frac{242.6}{343.2}$$

$$eta^2 = .71$$

This tells us that there is a moderately strong relationship between a woman's feelings of stress and the frequency with which she uses physical punishment against her children. Specifically, about 71 percent of the variability in the frequency of physical punishment is explained by the mother's feelings of stress.

7. a. The independent variable is the state's general policy with respect to drunk driving ("get tough," make a "moral appeal," or "not do much"), and the dependent variable is the drunk-driving rate in the state.

   b. The correct degrees of freedom for this table are:

   $$df_{between} = k - 1 = 3 - 1 = 2$$

   $$df_{within} = n - k = 45 - 3 = 42$$

   $$df_{total} = n - 1 = 45 - 1 = 44$$

   You can see that $df_{between} + df_{within} = df_{total}$.

   The ratio of sum of squares to degrees of freedom now can be determined:

   $$SS_{between} / df_{between} = 475.3 / 2 = 237.65$$

   $$SS_{within} / df_{within} = 204.5 / 42 = 4.87$$

   The F ratio is: $F_{obt} = 237.65/4.87 = 48.80$.

   c.

   $H_0: \mu_{get\ tough} = \mu_{moral\ appeal} = \mu_{control}$
   $H_1: \mu_{get\ tough} \neq \mu_{moral\ appeal} \neq \mu_{control}$

   Our decision rule will be to reject the null hypothesis if $F_{obt} \geq 5.18$. $F_{obt} = 48.80$. Since our obtained value of F is greater than the critical value, our decision is to reject the null hypothesis. We conclude that the population means are not equal.

   d. Going to the studentized table, you find the value of q to be equal to 4.37. To find the critical difference, you plug these values into your formula:

   $$CD = 4.37 \sqrt{\frac{4.87}{15}}$$

   $$CD = 2.49$$

The critical difference for the mean comparisons, then, is 2.49. Find the difference between each pair of sample means and test each null hypothesis:

H_0: $\mu_{\text{get tough}} = \mu_{\text{moral appeal}}$

H_1: $\mu_{\text{get tough}} \neq \mu_{\text{moral appeal}}$

$$
\begin{array}{lr}
\text{"Get tough"} & 125.2 \\
\text{"Moral appeal"} & -\,119.7 \\
\hline
 & 5.5
\end{array}
$$

Since the difference in sample means is greater than the critical difference score of 2.49, we would reject the null hypothesis. States that make a "moral appeal" have significantly lower levels of drunk driving on average than do states that "get tough."

H_0: $\mu_{\text{get tough}} = \mu_{\text{control}}$

H_1: $\mu_{\text{get tough}} \neq \mu_{\text{control}}$

$$
\begin{array}{lr}
\text{"Get tough"} & 125.2 \\
\text{"Control"} & -\,145.3 \\
\hline
 & 20.1
\end{array}
$$

Since the difference in sample means is greater than the critical difference score of 2.49, we would reject the null hypothesis. States that "get tough" with drunk driving by increasing the penalties have significantly lower levels of drunk driving on average than do states that do nothing.

H_0: $\mu_{\text{moral appeal}} = \mu_{\text{control}}$

H_1: $\mu_{\text{moral appeal}} \neq \mu_{\text{control}}$

$$
\begin{array}{lr}
\text{"Moral appeal"} & 119.7 \\
\text{"Control"} & -\,145.3 \\
\hline
 & 25.6
\end{array}
$$

The "moral appeal" states have significantly lower levels of drunk driving than the control states. It appears, then, that doing *something* about drunk driving is better than doing little or nothing.

e. Eta^2 is:

$$
\text{eta}^2 = \frac{475.3}{679.8}
$$

$$
\text{eta}^2 = .70
$$

This tells us that there is a strong relationship between the state's response to drunk driving and the rate of drunk driving in that state. Specifically, about 70 percent of the variability in levels of drunk driving is explained by the state's public policy.

8. a. The independent variable is the fear felt by people in a certain area of the city and the dependent variable is the number of times a person was victimized in the past five years.

b. The correct degrees of freedom for this table are:

$$df_{between} = k - 1 = 5 - 1 = 4$$
$$df_{within} = n - k = 250 - 5 = 245$$
$$df_{total} = n - 1 = 250 - 1 = 249$$

$$SS_{between}/df_{between} = 12.5/4 = 3.12$$
$$SS_{within}/df_{within} = 616.2/245 = 2.51$$

The F ratio is: $F_{obt} = 3.12/2.51 = 1.24$

c.

H_0: $\mu_{very\ high} = \mu_{high} = \mu_{medium} = \mu_{low} = \mu_{very\ low}$

H_1: $\mu_{very\ high} \neq \mu_{high} \neq \mu_{medium} \neq \mu_{low} \neq \mu_{very\ low}$

Our decision rule will be to reject the null hypothesis if $F_{obt} \geq 2.37$. $F_{obt} = 1.24$. Since our obtained value of F is not greater than or equal to the critical value, our decision is to not reject the null hypothesis. We conclude that different fear spots are not different in terms of their actual risk of victimization.

d. Since we failed to reject the null hypothesis, Tukey's HSD test is not appropriate.

e. The value of eta^2 is:

$$eta^2 = \frac{12.5}{628.7}$$
$$eta^2 = .02$$

There is no relationship between a person's fear of a given geographical area and the actual frequency of criminal victimization in that area. Only 2 percent of the variability in fear spots is explained by victimization levels.

9. a. The independent variable is the gender of the girl's friendship network, and the dependent variable is the number of delinquent acts committed.

b.   The total sum of squares = 154

The between-groups sum of squares = 98

The within-group sum of squares = 56

c. $df_{between} = k - 1 = 3 - 1 = 2$

$df_{within} = n - k = 21 - 3 = 18$

$df_{total} = n - 1 = 21 - 1 = 20$

You can see that $df_{between} + df_{within} = df_{total}$.

The ratio of sum of squares to degrees of freedom now can be determined:

$$SS_{between}/df_{between} = 98/2 = 49$$
$$SS_{within}/df_{within} = 56/3.11$$

The F ratio is: $F_{obt} = 49/3.11 = 15.75$.

d.

H_0: $\mu_{boys} = \mu_{boys \ and \ girls} = \mu_{girls}$
H_1: $\mu_{boys} \neq \mu_{boys \ and \ girls} \neq \mu_{girls}$

With an alpha of .05 and 2 between-groups and 18 within-group degrees of freedom, our critical value of F is 3.55. Our decision rule is to reject the null hypothesis when $F_{obt} \geq 3.55$. The obtained F is 15.75, $F_{obt} > F_{crit}$ so our decision is to reject the null hypothesis and conclude that some of the population means are different from each other.

e. The value of the critical difference score is:

$$CD = 3.61\sqrt{\frac{3.11}{7}}$$

$$CD = 2.41$$

A sample mean difference equal to or greater than an absolute value of 2.41 will lead us to reject the null hypothesis. We now will conduct a hypothesis test for each pair of population means.

H_0: $\mu_{mostly \ boys} = \mu_{boys \ and \ girls}$
H_1: $\mu_{mostly \ boys} \neq \mu_{mostly \ girls}$

"Mostly boys"	7
"Boys and girls"	-6
	$|1|$

Since this difference is less than the critical difference score of 2.41, we will fail to reject the null hypothesis. Girls who hang around with mostly boys are no different in the number of delinquent acts they commit than girls who hang around boys and girls.

H_0: $\mu_{mostly \ boys} = \mu_{mostly \ girls}$
H_1: $\mu_{mostly \ boys} \neq \mu_{boys \ and \ girls}$

"Mostly boys"	7
"Boys and girls"	-2
	$|5|$

Since this difference is greater than the critical difference score of 2.41, we will reject the null hypothesis. Girls who hang around with mostly boys commit significantly more delinquent acts than girls who hang around with mostly girls.

H_0: $\mu_{\text{girls and boys}} = \mu_{\text{mostly girls}}$

H_1: $\mu_{\text{girls and boys}} \neq \mu_{\text{mostly girls}}$

$$\begin{array}{r} \text{"Girls and boys"} \quad 6 \\ \text{"Mostly girls"} \quad -2 \\ \hline |4| \end{array}$$

Since this difference is greater than the critical difference score of 2.41, we will reject the null hypothesis. Girls who hang around with both girls and boys commit significantly more delinquent acts than girls who hang around with mostly girls.

It would appear that Professor Warr's hypothesis is correct. The presence of boys in a friendship network puts females at higher risk of delinquent behavior.

    f. The value of eta^2 is:

$$\text{eta}^2 = \frac{98}{154}$$

$$\text{eta}^2 = .64$$

There is a moderately strong relationship between the presence of boys in a girl's friendship group and the number of delinquent acts committed.

CHAPTER 12 SOLUTIONS TO PROBLEMS

1. a. There is a moderate negative linear relationship between the median income level in a neighborhood and its rate of crime. As the median income level in a community increases, its rate of crime decreases.

    b. There is a weak positive linear relationship between the number of hours spent working after school and self-reported delinquency. As the number of hours spent working after school increases, the number of self-reported delinquent acts increases.

    c. There is a strong positive linear relationship between the number of prior arrests and the length of current sentence. As the number of prior arrests increases, the length of the sentence received for the last offense increases.

    d. There is a weak negative linear relationship between the number of jobs held between the ages of 15–17 and the number of arrests as an adult.

e. There is no linear relationship between the divorce rate and a state's rate of violent crime.

2. a. $(-.55)^2 = .30$. Thirty percent of the variance in neighborhood crime rates is explained by the median income level of the neighborhood.

b. $(.17)^2 = .03$. Three percent of the variance in self-reported delinquency is explained by the number of hours a youth works after school.

c. $(.74)^2 = .55$. Fifty-five percent of the variance in sentence length is explained by the number of prior arrests.

d. $(-.12)^2 = .01$. One percent of the variance in the number of arrests as an adult is explained by the number of jobs held when 15–17 years of age.

e. $(-.03)^2 = .0009$. Less than 1 percent of the variance in a state's violent crime rate is explained by its divorce rate.

3. a. An increase in the fine imposed by $1 decreases the number of price-fixing citations by .017.

b. An increase of 1 percent in unemployment increases the rate of property crime by .715.

c. An increase in one year's education increases a police officer's salary by $1,444.53.

4. a. Scatterplot of data points:

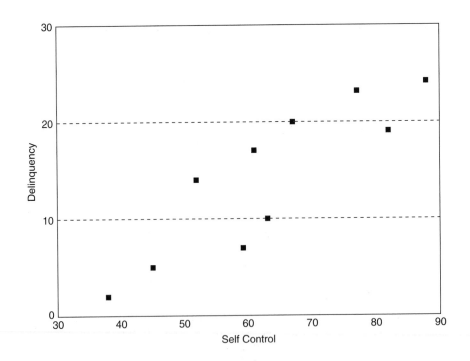

b. The value of the regression coefficient b is:

$$b = \frac{10(9890) - 632(141)}{10(42,230) - (632)^2}$$

$$= \frac{98,900 - 89,112}{422,300 - 399,424}$$

$$= .428$$

The value of the slope coefficient is .428. This tells us that a one score increase on the low self-control scale increases the number of self-reported criminal acts by .428.

c. The value of the y intercept is:

$$14.1 = a + .428(63.2)$$

$$14.1 = a + 27.05$$

$$14.1 - 27.05 = a$$

$$a = -12.95$$

The value of the y intercept or a, then, is equal to -12.95.

d. The predicted number of self-reported offenses when the self-control scale is equal to 70 can now be determined from our regression prediction equation:

$$\hat{y} = -12.95 + .428(70)$$

$$= -12.95 + 29.96$$

$$= 17.01$$

The predicted number of offenses, therefore, is 17.01.

e. We can use our computational formula to determine the value of r:

$$r = \frac{10(9,890) - 632(141)}{\sqrt{[10(42,230) - (632)^2][10(2,529) - 141]^2}}$$

$$= \frac{9,788}{11,123.68}$$

$$= .88$$

There is a strong positive correlation between low self-control and the number of self-reported criminal offenses.

We now want to conduct a hypothesis test about r. Our null hypothesis is that $r = 0$, and our alternative hypothesis is that $r > 0$. We predict direction because we have reason to believe that there is a positive correlation between low self-control and the number of self-reported crimes. To determine if this estimated r value is significantly different from zero with an alpha level of

.01, we calculate a t statistic, with $n - 2$ degrees of freedom. The critical value of t with $10 - 2 = 8$ degrees of freedom, an alpha level of .01, and a one-tailed test is 2.896. Our decision rule is to reject the null hypothesis if $t_{obt} > 2.896$. Now we calculate our t statistic:

$$t = .88\sqrt{\frac{10-2}{1-(.88)^2}}$$

$$= .88(5.90)$$

$$= 5.19$$

We have a t_{obt} of 5.19. Since $5.19 > 2.896$, we decide to reject the null hypothesis. There is a significant positive correlation between low self-control and self-reported crime in the population. As levels of self-control decrease, rates of self-reported crime increase.

f. Our r was .88, $(.88)^2 = .77$, so 77 % of the variance in self-reported crime is explained by low self-control.

g. Based on our results, we would conclude that there is a significant positive linear relationship between low self-control and self-reported offending. Our results are consistent with the earlier findings of Grasmick et al. (1993) and the theory of low self-control developed by Gottfredson and Hirschi (1990).

5. a. Scatterplot of data points:

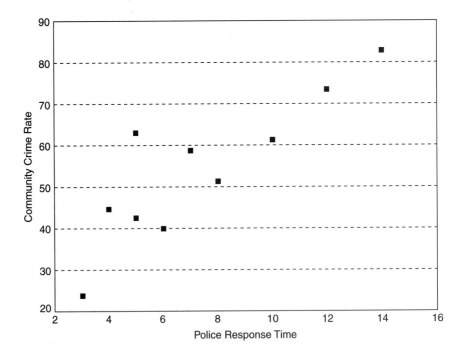

b. The value of the regression coefficient is:

$$b = \frac{10(4,491.4) - 74(541.1)}{10(664) - (74)^2}$$

$$= \frac{4,872.6}{1,164}$$

$$= 4.19$$

The value of the slope coefficient is 4.19. This tells us that a 1 minute increase in police response time increases the crime rate by 4.19 per 1,000. The longer the response time, the higher the crime rate. Stated conversely, the faster (shorter) the response time, the lower the crime rate.

c. The value of the y intercept is:

$$54.11 = a + 4.19(7.4)$$

$$54.11 = a + 31.01$$

$$54.11 - 31.01 = a$$

$$a = 23.1$$

The value of the y intercept or a, then, is equal to 23.1.

d. The predicted community rate of crime when the police response time is 11 minutes can now be determined from our regression prediction equation:

$$\hat{y} = 23.1 + 4.19(11)$$

$$= 23.1 + 46.09$$

$$= 69.19$$

The predicted crime rate, therefore, is 69.19 crimes per 1,000 population.

e. The value of r is:

$$r = \frac{10(4,491.4) - 74(541.1)}{\sqrt{[10(664) - (74)^2][10(32,011.2) - (541.1)^2]}}$$

$$= \frac{4,872.6}{5,639.5}$$

$$= .86$$

There is a strong positive correlation between low self-control and the number of self-reported criminal offenses.

We now want to conduct a hypothesis test about r. Our null hypothesis is that $r = 0$, and our alternative hypothesis is that $r > 0$. We predict direction because we have reason to believe that there is a positive correlation between the number of minutes it takes the police to respond and the community's rate of crime (the longer the response time, the higher the crime rate). To determine if this estimated r value is significantly different from zero with an alpha level of .05, we calculate a t statistic, with $n - 2$ degrees of freedom. We go to the t table to find our critical value of t with $10 - 2 = 8$ degrees of freedom, an alpha level of .05, and a one-tailed test. The critical value of t is 1.86. Our decision rule is to reject the null hypothesis if $t_{obt} > 1.86$. Now we calculate our t_{obt}.

$$t = .86\sqrt{\frac{10-2}{1-(.86)^2}}$$

$$= .86(5.50)$$

$$= 4.77$$

We have a t_{obt} of 4.77. Since $4.77 > 1.86$, we decide to reject the null hypothesis. There is a significant positive correlation between the length of police response time and community crime rates.

f. Our r was .86, $(.86)^2 = .74$, so 74 percent of the variance in community crime rates is explained by police response time.

g. Based on our results, we would conclude that there is a significant positive linear relationship between police response time and community crime rates.

6. a. Scatterplot of data points:

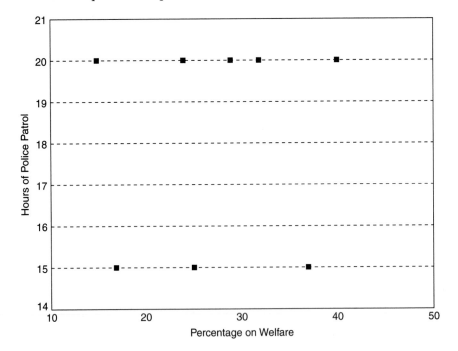

b. The value of the slope coefficient is:

$$b = \frac{12(4,525) - 245(265)}{12(6,777) - (245)^2}$$

$$= \frac{54,300 - 64,925}{81,324 - 60,025}$$

$$= -.499$$

The value of the slope coefficient is $-.499$. This tells us that a 1 percentage point increase in the percent of the population that is on welfare decreases the hours of daily police patrol by $-.499$ (about one-half hour). The greater the percent of the population receiving public assistance in a neighborhood, the fewer the number of hours of police patrol.

c. The value of the y intercept is:

$$22.1 = a + -.499(20.4)$$

$$22.1 = a + -10.18$$

$$22.1 + 10.18 = a$$

$$a = 32.28$$

The value of the y intercept or a, then, is equal to 32.28.

d. The predicted number of daily hours of police patrol when the percent receiving public assistance in the neighborhood is 30 percent can now be determined from our regression prediction equation:

$$\hat{y} = 32.28 + (-.499)(30)$$

$$= 32.28 - 14.97$$

$$= 17.31$$

The predicted number of hours of police patrol, therefore, is 17.31 hours.

e. From our calculations in part (b) above, we have all the information we need to solve for r:

$$r = \frac{12(4,525) - 245(265)}{\sqrt{[12(6,777) - (245)^2][12(7,275) - (265)^2]}}$$

$$= \frac{-10,625}{\sqrt{363,680,425}}$$

$$= -.56$$

There is a moderately strong negative correlation between the percent of the community on welfare and the number of daily hours of police patrol.

We now want to conduct a hypothesis test about r. Our null hypothesis is that $r = 0$, and our alternative hypothesis is that $r < 0$. We predict direction because we have reason to believe that there is a negative correlation between the affluence of the neighborhood and the number of hours of daily police patrol. To determine if this estimated r value is significantly different from zero with an alpha level of .05, we calculate a t statistic, with $n - 2$ degrees of freedom. We go to the t table to find our critical value of t with $12 - 2 = 10$ degrees of freedom, an alpha level of .05, and a one-tailed test. The critical value of t is -1.812. The critical value is negative because in our alternative hypothesis we predicted that the population value of r was less than zero. Our decision rule is to reject the null hypothesis if $t_{obt} \leq 1.812$. Our obtained t value is:

$$t = -.56\sqrt{\frac{12 - 2}{1 - (-.56)^2}}$$

$$= -.56(3.81)$$

$$= -2.13$$

We have a t_{obt} of -2.13. Because $-2.13 \leq -1.812$, we decide to reject the null hypothesis. There is a significant negative correlation between the percent of a neighborhood that is receiving public assistance and the number of hours of daily police patrol.

f. Our r was $-.56$, $(-.56)^2 = .31$, so 31 percent of the variance in the number of hours of police patrol is explained by the percent of the neighborhood that is on welfare.

g. Based on our results, we would conclude that there is a significant negative linear relationship between the affluence of a neighborhood and the number of hours of police patrol it receives per day.

h. The values of b and r without community numbers 11 and 12 are:

$$b = \frac{10(4,525) - 239(175)}{10(6,757) - (239)^2}$$

$$= \frac{42,650 - 41,825}{67,570 - 57,121}$$

$$= .079$$

$$r = \frac{10(4,265) - 239(175)}{\sqrt{[10(6,757) - (239)^2][10(3,175) - (175)^2}}$$

$$= \frac{825}{3,428.5}$$

$$= .24$$

We would conclude from this new data that there is not a very strong relationship between the percent of neighborhood families on welfare and the number of hours of police patrol. You can see that without the last two observations the slope of the data points changes. These last two data points are very unusual. They are unusually affluent neighborhoods, with only 4 and 2 percent of the persons receiving public assistance, respectively. Moreover, they receive an unusually high number of hours of police patrols. These two neighborhoods are, then, outliers, and as outliers they can distort the data.

CHAPTER 13 SOLUTIONS TO PROBLEMS

1. a. The least-squares regression equation for this problem is:

$$y = a + b_1 x_1 + b_2 x_2$$

$$= 19.642 + (.871) \text{divorce rate} + (-.146) \text{age}$$

   b. The partial slope coefficient for the variable DIVORCE indicates that as the divorce rate per 100.000 population increases by 1 the rate of violent crime per 100,000 increases by .871, controlling for the mean age of the state's population. The partial slope coefficient for the variable AGE indicates that as the mean age of the state's population increases by 1 year, the rate of violent crime per 100,000 decreases by .146, controlling for the divorce rate. The intercept is equal to 19.642. This tells us that when both the divorce rate and mean age are equal to zero, the rate of violent crime is 19.642 per 100,000.

   c. The standardized regression coefficient for DIVORCE is .594, while that for AGE is − .133. Based on this, then, we would conclude that the divorce rate is more influential in explaining state violent crime rates than is the mean age of the population. A second way to look at the relative strength of the independent variables is to compare the absolute value of their respective t ratios. The t ratio for DIVORCE is 4.268, while that for AGE is − 3.110. Based on this, we would conclude that the divorce rate is more influential in explaining rates of violence than the mean age of a state's population.

   d. The divorce rate and mean age together explain approximately 63 percent of the variance in rates of violent crime. The adjusted R^2 value is .61, indicating that 61 percent of the variance is explained.

   e. The null and alternative hypotheses are:

   H_0: β_1, $\beta_2 = 0$; or $R^2 = 0$

   H_1: β_1 or $\beta_2 \neq 0$; or $R^2 \neq 0$.

   $F_{\text{obt}} = 27.53$. The probability of an F of 27.53, if the null hypothesis were true, is .00001. Since this probability is less than our alpha of

.01, our decision is to reject the null hypothesis that all the slope coefficients are equal to zero.

H_0: $\beta_{divorce} = 0$

H_1: $\beta_{divorce} > 0$

$t_{obt} = 4.268$. The probability of obtaining a t this size if the null hypothesis were true is equal to .0001. Since this probability is less than our alpha level of .01, we decide to reject the null hypothesis. We conclude that the population partial slope coefficient is greater than zero.

H_0: $\beta_{age} = 0$

H_1: $\beta_{age} < 0$

$t_{obt} = -3.11$. The probability of obtaining a t statistic this low if the null hypothesis were true is equal to .0011. Since this is less than .01, we will reject the null hypothesis.

2. a.

$$b_{morale} = \left(\frac{4.49}{3.47}\right)\left(\frac{(-.76)-(-.63)(.67)}{1-(.67)^2}\right)$$

$$= 1.29\left(\frac{(-.76)-(-.42)}{1-.45}\right)$$

$$= -.800$$

$$b_{staff} = \left(\frac{4.49}{.15}\right)\left(\frac{(-.63)-(-.76)(.67)}{1-(.67)^2}\right)$$

$$= 29.93\left(\frac{(-.63)-(-.51)}{1-.45}\right)$$

$$= -6.585$$

The partial slope coefficient for employee morale is $-.800$. This tells us that as the score on our measure of employee morale increases by 1, the number of jail escapes decreases by .800, controlling for the staff/inmate ratio. The partial slope coefficient for the staff-to-inmate ratio is -6.585. This indicates that as the staff/inmate ratio increases by 1 unit, the number of jail escapes decreases by 6.585.

b.

$$\bar{y} = a + b_1\bar{x}_1 + b_2\bar{x}_2$$

$$9.43 = a + (-.800)(6.07) + (-6.585)(.36)$$

$$9.43 = a - 7.227$$

$$9.43 + 7.227 = a$$

$$16.657 = a$$

The value of the intercept is 16.657, and the full regression equation is:

$$y = 16.657 + (-.800)x_1 + (-6.585)x_2$$

c.

$$\hat{y} = 16.657 + (-.800)(8) + (-6.585)(.3)$$

$$= 16.657 + (-6.400) + (-1.975)$$

$$= 16.657 + (-8.375)$$

$$= 8.282$$

With a staff morale score of 8 and a staff-to-inmate ratio of .3, we would predict that there would be approximately 8 escapes per year.

d. The beta weights are:

$$b^{*}_{morale} = (-.800)\left(\frac{3.47}{4.49}\right)$$

$$= -.616$$

$$b^{*}_{staff} = (-6.585)\left(\frac{.15}{4.49}\right)$$

$$= -.197$$

The beta weight for staff morale is −.616, while the beta weight for staff/inmate ratio is −.197. Because the beta weight for morale is greater than that for the staff-to-inmate ratio, it has a stronger effect on the number of jail escapes.

e.

$$R^2 = (-.76)^2 + (-.245)^2[1 - (-.76)^2]$$

$$= .58 + (.06)(.42)$$

$$= .58 + .03$$

$$= .61$$

Together, staff morale and the staff-to-inmate ratio explain approximately 61 % of the variance in jail escapes.

3. a. The least-squares regression equation from the supplied output would be:

$$\hat{y} = 16.245 + (-1.467)\text{ENV} + 1.075(\text{REL})$$

b. The partial slope coefficient for the environmental factors variable is −1.467. This tells us that as a person's score on the environmental causes of crime scale increases by 1, their score on the punitiveness scale decreases by 1.467, controlling for religious conservatism. The partial slope coefficient for the religious conservatism scale is 1.075. As a person's score on religious conservatism increases by 1 unit, their score on the punitiveness scale increases by 1.075, controlling for their score on environmental factors as a cause of crime. The value of the intercept is 16.245. When both independent variables are zero, a person's score on the punitiveness scale is 16.245.

c. The beta weight for ENV is −.608. The beta weight for REL is .346. A 1 unit change in the ENV variable produces almost twice the change in the dependent variable as the REL variable. Comparing these beta weights would lead us to conclude that the environmental factors scale is more important in explaining punitiveness scores than the religious conservatism variable.

    The t ratio for ENV is −3.312, while that for REL is only 1.884. We would again conclude that ENV has the greater influence on the dependent variable.

d. The adjusted R^2 coefficient indicates that together, the environmental factors and religious conservatism scales explain approximately 60 % of the variance in the punitiveness measure.

e.

$H_0: \beta_{ENV}, \beta_{REL} = 0$; or $R^2 = 0$

$H_1: \beta_{ENV}$ or $\beta_{REL} \neq 0$; or $R^2 \neq 0$

The probability of an F of 11.59, if the null hypothesis were true, is .0016. Since this probability is less than our chosen alpha of .01, our decision is to reject the null hypothesis that all the slope coefficients are equal to zero.

$H_0: \beta_{ENV} = 0$

$H_1: \beta_{ENV} < 0$

The output gives you a t_{obt} of −3.312, and the probability of obtaining a t this size if the null hypothesis were true is equal to .0062. Since this probability is less than our chosen alpha level of .01, we decide to reject the null hypothesis. We conclude that the population partial slope coefficient is less than zero.

$H_0: \beta_{REL} = 0$

$H_1: \beta_{REL} > 0$

    The t ratio for the variable ENV is $t_{obt} = 1.884$. The probability of obtaining a t statistic of this magnitude if the null hypothesis were true is equal to .0840. Since this probability is greater than .01, our decision is to fail to reject the null hypothesis. The partial slope coefficient between religious conservatism and punitiveness toward criminal offenders is not significantly different from zero in the population, once a belief in environmental causes of crime are controlled.

f.
$$\hat{y} = 16.245 + (-1.467)\text{ENV} + (1.076)\text{REL}$$
$$= 16.245 + (-1.467)(2) + (1.076)(8)$$
$$= 16.245 + (-2.934) + 8.608$$
$$= 21.92$$

The predicted value of y is 21.92.

CHAPTER 14 SOLUTIONS TO PROBLEMS

1. a. Probability = 250/700 = .36
   Odds = .36/.64 = .56
   b. Probability = 500/700 = .71
   Odds = .71/.29 = 2.45
   c. Probability = 630/700 = .90
   Odds = .90/.10 = 9.00
   d. Probability = 180/700 = .26
   Odds = .26/.74 = .35

2. a. The regression coefficient is .3278. This tells us that the log of the odds of a guilty verdict is .3278 higher for males than for females. The antilog of .3278 is 1.39. This tells us that the odds of a guilty verdict for males is increased by a factor of 1.39 compared to females.

   b. The two-tailed significance of the regression coefficient is .016. A one-tailed significance level is .008 (.016/2). This is less than our selected alpha of .05, so we can reject the null hypothesis.

   c. The predicted log odds that a male would plead guilty is:

   $$\ln \frac{\hat{p}}{1-\hat{p}} = .0561 + (.3278)(1)$$
   $$= .0561 + .3278$$
   $$= .3839$$

   The predicted probability of a guilty plea for a male is:

$$\hat{p} = \frac{e^{.3839}}{1+e^{.3839}}$$

$$= \frac{1.468}{2.468}$$

$$= .595$$

The predicted log odds that a female would plead guilty is:

$$\ln \frac{\hat{p}}{1-\hat{p}} = .0561 + (.3278)(0)$$

$$= .0561$$

The predicted probability of a guilty plea for a female is:

$$\hat{p} = \frac{e^{.0561}}{1+e^{.0561}}$$

$$= \frac{1.058}{2.058}$$

$$= .514$$

For males the odds are .595/.405 = 1.47. The odds of a guilty plea for a female are .514/.486 = 1.06.

3. a. The equation for the model is:

$$b_0 + b_1 x_1 + b_2 x_2 = -7.2476 + (.8147)(\text{desire}) + (.1593)(\text{age})$$

  b. A 1 unit increase in the desire of the victim to have an arrest made increases the log of the odds of an arrest by .8147, when holding the age of the victim constant. The log of the odds of an arrest increase by .1593 when age increases by 1 year, holding constant the expressed desire of the victim for an arrest.

  c. The predicted probability that an arrest will be made is:

$$\hat{p} = -7.246 + .81476 + .1593\,(50)$$

$$\hat{p} = \frac{e^{1.53}}{1+e^{1.53}}$$

$$= \frac{4.618}{5.618}$$

$$= .82$$

The odds of an arrest in this case are .82/.18 = 4.55.

  d. The *t* ratio for the desire variable is .868. We cannot reject the null hypothesis that the population regression coefficient for desire is zero. The t ratio for the age variable is 3.889, and we can reject the null hypothesis that the population coefficient for age is zero.

e. The coefficient for desire is not significant once age is controlled. The coefficient for age is significant even with desire controlled. On the basis of this, we would conclude that the age of the victim has more of an effect on the log odds of an arrest than the desire of the victim that an arrest be made.

4. a. The probit equation is:

$$z = -.2582 + (-1.0186)(job) + (.1824)(priors)$$

b. The coefficient for the job variable tells us that having a stable job decreases the unmeasured variable z by 1.0186 standard deviation units, controlling for the number of prior arrests. The coefficient for the prior arrests variable tells us that a change of 1 arrest increases the unmeasured variable z by .1824 standard deviation units, controlling for the existence of a job after release.

c. To determine the predicted probability of rearrest for someone with no job after release and 5 prior arrests, first we obtain the predicted z score:

$$z = -.2582 + (-1.0186)(0) + (.1824)(5)$$

$$= -.2582 + .9120$$

$$= .6538$$

The predicted probability for this z score is .74. The predicted probability of rearrest for someone with a job on release and 1 prior arrest is approximately .14.

d. We decide to reject the null hypothesis if the t ratio for job and prior arrests is either greater than or equal to 2.021 or less than or equal to −2.021. As the t ratio for Job is −2.371 and that for prior arrests is 3.031, we can reject both null hypotheses.

Codebooks to Data Sets

CODEBOOK A

NCVS93.SAV

Codebook for NCS93.SAV SPSS/PC System File Containing Incidents of Violent Crime for Female Victims from the National Crime Victimization Survey in 1993

DAYDARK: Was it daylight or dark outside when this incident happened?
1 Light
2 Dark
3 Dawn or Dusk

HITYOU: Did the offender hit you, knock you down, or actually attack you in any way?
1 Yes
2 No

REPORTED: Were the police informed or did they find out about this incident in any way?
1 Yes
2 No
3 Don't know

WHOREP: How did the police find out about it?
1 Respondent
2 Other household member
3 Someone official called police (guard, school official, etc.)
4 Someone else
5 Police were at the scene

      6   Offender was a police officer
      7   Some other way

HOWFAST: (If the police came) How soon after the police found out did they respond?
      1   Within 5 minutes
      2   Within 10 minutes
      3   Within an hour
      4   Within a day
      5   Longer than a day
      6   Don't know how soon

MSA: Where does victim live
      1   Central city
      2   Suburban
      3   Rural

PPAGE: Victim's age—continuous ranging from 12 to 90

INCOME: Victim's family income—14 categories ranging from less than $10,000 to over $75,000

PPMAR: Victim's marital status
      1   Married
      2   Widowed
      3   Divorced
      4   Separated
      5   Never married

PPRACE: Race/ethnicity of victim
      1   White
      2   Black
      3   American Indian
      4   Asian or Pacific Islander

PRIVATE: Place of victimization
      0   Private residence
      1   Public location

SINGMUL: Single or multiple offender(s)
      1   Single offender
      2   Multiple offenders
      3   Don't know

SOSTRANG: Single offender known or stranger
      1   Knew or had seen before
      2   Stranger
      3   Don't know
      6   Not known if response was stranger or don't know

SOREL: Single offender relationship to victim if not a stranger
1   Spouse at time of incident
2   Ex-spouse at time of incident
3   Parent or step-parent
4   Own child or step-child
5   Brother/sister
6   Other relative
7   Boyfriend or girlfriend, ex-boyfriend or ex-girlfriend
8   Friend or ex-friend
9   Roommate or boarder
10 Schoolmate
11 Neighbor
12 Someone at work, customer
13 Other nonrelative

INTIMATE: Single offender victim/offender relationship—Recoded
1   Intimate (spouse, ex-spouse, boyfriend, ex-boyfriend)
2   Stranger
3   Other relative (parent, child, sibling, other)
4   Acquaintance or friend

SOSEX: Single offender sex
1   Male
2   Female

SOONLY: Single offender had victimized respondent before
0   No violent history
1   Offender had victimized respondent before—violent history

MOSTRANG: Multiple offenders known or stranger
1   All known
2   Some known
3   All strangers
4   Don't know
5   Don't know if 1 or 2

MULNUMB: Number of offenders if multiple—Continuous ranging from 2 to 30 offenders

WEAPON: Offender(s) had weapon
0   No weapon present
1   Weapon present

TOC: Type of violent crime—included completed and attempted crimes within each crime category
1   Rape and sexual assault
2   Robbery
3   Assault

Questions Concerning Injuries and Medical Expenses

INJURY: Injuries sustained by victim. To obtain information about injuries, respondents are simply asked to identify any injuries they sustained as the result of their victimization. Injuries can range in severity from gunshot or knife wounds to cuts and bruises. If a respondent said she was injured in any way, she is classified as injured.

0 No
1 Yes

MEDICAL CARE: Question: "Were you injured to the extent that you received any medical care, including self-treatment?" If victims said their injuries required medical care, no matter where that care was received (e.g., emergency room, hospital, doctor's office, or self-treated) they are coded as receiving medical care.

0 No
1 Yes

MEDEXP: Question: "What was the total amount of your medical expenses resulting from this incident, including any expenses paid by insurance? Include hospital and doctor bills, medicine, braces, and any other injury-related medical expenses."

Continuous ranging from 0 to $17,000

INSURANCE: Question: "At the time of the incident, were you covered by any medical insurance, or were you eligible for benefits from any other type of health benefits program such as Medicaid, Veterans Administration, or Public Welfare?"

0 No
1 Yes
8 Don't know

NIGHTHOS: Question: "Did you stay overnight in the hospital?"

1 Yes
2 No

NUMDAYS: Number of days in hospital. Question: "How many days did you stay in the hospital?"

Continuous ranging from 2 to 14 days

LOSEWORK: Lost work because of injuries. Question: "Did you lose time from work because of injuries?"

0 No
1 Yes

HOWMUCH: Number of work days lost because of injuries. Question: "How much time did you lose because of injuries?" Responses are continuous from less than 1 day (coded 0) to actual number of days.

Continuous ranging from 0 to 180 days

PAYLOST: Pay lost for injuries. Question: "During these days, did you lose any pay that was not covered by unemployment, sick leave, annual leave, or some other source? If yes, about how much pay did you lose?"

Continuous ranging from $30 to $1,200

TOTBUCKS: Other time lost. Question: "Did you lose time from work because of this incident for any other reason—repairing damaged property, replacing stolen items, police—related activities such as cooperating with an investigation, court-related activities such as testifying in court, or any other reason? If yes, did you lose wages because of these absences? If yes, about how much pay did you lose?"

Continuous ranging from $40 to $4,000

CODEBOOK B

HOMDEF.SAV

Codebook for HOMDEF.SAV SPSS/PC System File Containing Sample of Homicide Defendants From A Sample of 33 Counties, 1988

CASE: Case identification number

CONVICT: Verdict of trial
    0   Not convicted
    1   Convicted

DAGE: Defendant's age, continuous

DEATH: Defendant received the death penalty
    1   Yes
    2   No, other sentence

FAMCAT: Type of family category of defendant for all family-related murders
    1   Sibling
    2   Parent
    3   Child
    4   Spouse
    5   Other

FUNNEL: Outcome of trial
    1   Acquitted
    2   Convicted
    3   Insanity

INCAR: Did defendant receive an incarceration sentence?
    0   No incarceration
    1   Incarceration

INTIMATE: Did homicide involve intimates such as husbands or wives, ex-husbands or ex-wives, or boyfriends or girlfriends?
    0   Not intimate
    1   Intimately related

KNOWN: Did defendant and victim know each other?
    1   Known victim
    2   Unknown victim

LIFE: Did defendant receive a life sentence?
    1   Life sentence
    0   Other sentence

MURCON: Did defendant receive a murder conviction or conviction for some other felony?
1   Murder conviction
2   Other felony conviction
3   No conviction

NUMVICT: Number of victims in murder
1   One victim
2   Two victims
3   Three victims
4   Four victims
5   Five victims

OUTCOME: Sentence received from trial
1   Other sentence
2   Death sentence
3   Life sentence
4   Prison term
5   Jail term
7   Probation
8   Not convicted

PRCONV: Defendant's prior convictions
0   No prior convictions
1   One prior conviction
2   Two prior convictions
3   Three prior convictions
4   Four or more prior convictions

PRIARR: Defendant's prior arrests
0   No prior arrests
1   One prior arrest
2   Two prior arrests
3   Three prior arrests
4   Four or more prior arrests

PRINCR: Defendant's prior incarcerations
0   No prior incarcerations
1   One prior incarceration
2   Two prior incarcerations
3   Three prior incarcerations
4   Four or more prior incarcerations

PRITIME: Sentence length in days received by defendants—continuous

PROVOKE: Defendant said there was victim provocation involved in homicide (e.g., they were first to use violence, self-protection, etc.)
0   No victim provocation
1   Provocation involved

RACE: Race of defendant
1   White
2   Black
3   Other

SEX: Sex of defendant
0   Female
1   Male

TYPE: Type of trial: Jury or judge
1   Judge
2   Jury

VHISP: Ethnicity of victim: Hispanic or Non-Hispanic
1   Hispanic
2   Non-Hispanic

VRACE   Race of victim
1   White
2   Black
3   Other

VSEX: Sex of victim
1   Male
2   Female

CODEBOOK C

YOUTH.SAV

Codebook for Youth. SAV SPSS System File for Survey of High School Youth about Attitudes Toward Delinquency and Delinquent Behavior

V1:   Respondent's sex
1   Male
0   Female

V2:   Age of respondent
Continuous

V21:   Number of hours of week respondent watches television
Continuous

V22:   Number of hours a week respondent studies
Continuous

V63:   Does respondent's parents know where he/she is when he/she is away from home?
1   Never

2   Sometimes
3   Usually
4   Always

V77:   How wrong do respondent's best friends think it is to steal something worth less than $10?
1   Always wrong
2   Usually wrong
3   Sometimes wrong
4   Seldom wrong
5   Never wrong

V79:   How wrong do respondent's best friends think it is to drink liquor under age?
1   Always wrong
2   Usually wrong
3   Sometimes wrong
4   Seldom wrong
5   Never wrong

V109:   Suppose respondent drank liquor under age, is caught, taken to court and punished. How much of a problem would that punishment create for his life?
1   No problem at all
2   Hardly any problem
3   A little problem
4   A big problem
5   A very big problem

V119:   How much would respondent's chances of having good friends be hurt if he were arrested for damaging someone else's property?
1   Hurt very little
2   Hurt a little
3   Hurt a lot

PARNT2:   Parental index added two questions: (1) Do respondent's parents know where he is when he is away from home? (2) Do respondent's parents know who he is with when he is away from home?

Continuous—High score indicates high parental supervision

FROPINON: Friends' attitudes toward delinquent acts index: An additive index of questions which asked respondents how wrong their best friends thought it was to steal or damage property or to drink.

Continuous—High score indicates more support of delinquency

FRBEHAVE: Index of friends' engagement in delinquent acts: An additive index of questions which asked respondents how many friends they had who had ever damaged or stolen property or had drunk liquor under age.

Continuous—High score indicates higher proportion of friends who engage in delinquency

CERTAIN: Certainty of punishment index: An additive index of questions which asked respondents how likely it was that they would be caught by police for damaging property, stealing, or drinking.

Continuous—High score indicates greater perceived risk of punishment

MORAL: Morality index: An additive index of questions which asked respondents how wrong they thought it was to steal, damage property, or drink under age.

Continuous—High score indicates stronger disapproval of delinquency

DELINQ1: Delinquency index at Time 1: An additive index of questions which asked respondents how many times in the last year they had done a number of things including drink, take drugs, steal property, break into a building, destroy property, threaten to or beat somebody up, carry a weapon, or sell drugs.

Continuous—High score indicates high involvement in delinquency

DELINQ2: Delinquency index at Time 2: Same index as DELINQ1 but questions asked 1 year later.

Continuous—High score indicates high involvement in delinquency

CODEBOOK D

STATE 2000. SAV

Codebook for State 2000. SAV SPSS/PC System File Containing State-Level Crime Data and Other Demographic Variables from UCR and Statistical Abstracts: 2000

STATE:	Alphanumeric variable listing every state
STATEID:	State ID coding states alphabetically 1–51
REGION:	Four regions of the country
	1 South
	2 West
	3 Midwest
	4 Northeast
MURDER:	Rate of murder per 100,000 population
VIOLENT:	Rate of violent crime per 100,000 population
BURGLARY:	Rate of burglary per 100,000 population
INMEXP:	Expenditures per inmate per day
DEATHSEN:	Number of people sentenced to death
POPDENS:	Population per square mile of land
PERRURAL:	Percent of population living in nonmetropolitan (rural) areas
INFMORT:	Infant mortality rates per 1,000 live births
DIVORCE:	Divorce rate per 1,000 population
POVERTY:	Percent of population living below the poverty level

Statistical Tables

TABLE E–1

Table of Random Numbers

10480	15011	01536	02011	81647	77603	69179	14194	62590	36207	20969	99570	91291	90700
22368	46573	25595	85393	30995	73258	27982	53402	93965	34095	52666	19174	39615	99505
24130	48360	22527	97265	76393	03469	15179	24830	49340	32081	30680	19655	63348	58629
42167	93093	06243	61680	07856	29718	39440	53537	71341	57004	00849	74917	97758	16379
37570	39975	81837	16656	06121	45938	60468	81305	49684	60672	14110	06927	01263	54613
77921	06907	11008	42751	27756	14663	18602	70659	90655	15053	21916	81825	44394	42880
99562	72905	56420	69994	98872	53633	71194	18738	44013	48840	63213	21069	10634	12952
96301	91977	05463	07972	18876	43514	94595	56869	69014	60045	18425	84903	42508	32307
89579	14342	63661	10281	17453	38588	57740	84378	25331	12566	58678	44947	05585	56941
85475	36857	53342	53988	53060	71568	38867	62300	08158	17983	16439	11458	18593	64952
28918	69578	88231	33276	70997	79936	56865	05859	90106	31595	01547	85590	91610	78188
63553	40961	48235	03427	49626	69445	18663	72695	52180	20847	12234	90511	33703	90322
09429	93969	52636	92737	88974	33488	36320	17617	30015	08272	84115	27156	30613	74952
10365	61129	87529	85689	48237	52267	67689	93394	01511	26358	85104	20285	29975	89868
07119	97336	71048	08178	77233	13916	47564	81056	97735	85977	29372	74461	28551	90707
51085	12765	51821	51259	77452	16308	60756	92144	49442	53900	70960	63990	75601	40719
02368	21382	52404	60268	89368	19885	55322	44819	01188	65255	64835	44919	05944	55157
01011	54092	33362	94904	31273	04146	18594	29852	71585	85030	51132	01915	92747	64951
52162	53916	46369	58586	23216	14513	83149	98736	23495	64350	94738	17752	35156	35749
07056	97628	33787	09998	42698	06691	76988	13602	51851	46104	88916	19509	25625	58104
48663	91245	85828	14346	09172	30168	90229	04734	59193	22178	30421	61666	99904	32812
54164	58492	22421	74103	47070	25306	76468	26384	58151	06646	21524	15227	96909	44592
32639	32363	05597	24200	13363	38005	94342	28728	35806	06912	17012	64161	18296	72851
29334	27001	87637	87308	58731	00256	45834	15398	46557	41135	10367	07684	36188	18510
02488	33062	28834	07351	19731	92420	60952	61280	50001	67658	32586	86679	50720	94953
81525	72295	04839	96423	24878	82651	66566	14778	76797	14780	13300	87074	79666	95725
29676	20591	68086	26432	46901	20849	89768	81536	86645	12659	92259	57102	80428	25280
00742	57392	39064	66432	84673	40027	32832	61362	98947	96067	64760	64584	96096	98253
05366	04213	25669	26422	44407	44048	37937	63904	45766	66134	75470	66520	34693	90449
91921	26418	64117	94305	26766	25940	39972	22209	71500	64568	91402	42416	07844	09018
00582	04711	87917	77341	42206	35126	74087	99547	81817	42607	43808	76655	62028	76630
00725	69884	62797	56170	86324	88072	76222	36086	84637	93161	76038	65855	77919	88006
69011	65795	95876	55293	18988	27354	26575	08625	40801	59920	29841	80150	12777	48501
25976	57948	29888	88604	67917	48708	18912	82271	65424	69774	33611	54262	85963	03547
09763	83473	73577	12908	30883	18317	28290	35797	05998	41688	34952	37888	38917	88050
91567	42595	27958	30134	04024	86385	29880	99730	55536	84855	29080	09250	79656	73211
17955	56349	90999	49127	20044	59931	06115	20542	18059	02008	73708	83517	36103	42791
46503	18584	18845	49618	02304	51038	20655	58727	28168	15475	56942	53389	20562	87338
92157	89634	94824	78171	84610	82834	09922	25417	44137	48413	25555	21246	35509	20468
14577	62765	35605	81263	39667	47358	56873	56307	61607	49518	89656	20103	77490	18062
98427	07523	33362	64270	01638	92477	66969	98420	04880	45585	46565	04102	46880	45709
34914	63976	88720	82765	34476	17032	87589	40836	32427	70002	70663	88863	77775	69348
70060	28277	39475	46473	23219	53416	94970	25832	69975	94884	19661	72828	00102	66794
53976	54914	06990	67245	68350	82948	11398	42878	80287	88267	47363	46634	06541	97809
76072	29515	40980	07391	58745	25774	22987	80059	39911	96189	41151	14222	60697	59583
90725	52210	83974	29992	65831	38857	50490	83765	55657	14361	31720	57375	56228	41546
64364	67412	33339	31926	14883	24413	59744	92351	97473	89286	35931	04110	23726	51900
08062	00358	31662	25388	61642	34072	81249	35648	56891	69352	48373	45578	78547	81788
95012	68379	93526	70765	10592	04542	76463	54328	02349	17247	28865	14777	62730	92277
15664	10493	20492	38391	91132	21999	59516	81652	27195	48223	46751	22923	32261	85653

TABLE E–1

Table of Random Numbers

16408	81899	04153	53381	79401	21438	83035	92350	36693	31238	59649	91754	72772
18629	81953	05520	91962	04739	13092	97662	24822	94730	06496	35090	04822	86774
73115	35101	47498	87637	99016	71060	88824	71013	18735	20286	23153	72924	35165
57491	16703	23167	49323	45021	33132	12544	41035	80780	45393	44812	12515	98931
30405	83946	23792	14422	15059	45799	22716	19792	09983	74353	68668	30429	70735
16631	35006	85900	98275	32388	52390	16815	69298	82732	38480	73817	32523	41961
96773	20206	42559	78985	05300	22164	24369	54224	35083	19687	11052	91491	60383
38935	64202	14349	82674	66523	44133	00697	35552	35970	19124	63318	29686	03387
31624	76384	17403	53363	44167	64486	64758	75366	76554	31601	12614	33072	60332
78919	19474	23632	27889	47914	02584	37680	20801	72152	39339	34806	08930	85001
03931	33309	57047	74211	63445	17361	62825	39908	05607	91284	68833	25570	38818
74426	33278	43972	10119	89917	15665	52872	73823	73144	88662	88970	74492	51805
09066	00903	20795	95452	92648	45454	09552	88815	16553	51125	79375	97596	16296
42238	12426	87025	14267	20979	04508	64535	31355	86064	29472	47689	05974	52468
16153	08002	26504	41744	81959	65642	74240	56302	00033	67107	77510	70625	28725
21457	40742	29820	96783	29400	21840	15035	34537	33310	06116	95240	15957	16572
21581	57802	02050	89728	17937	37621	47075	42080	97403	48626	68995	43805	33386
55612	78095	83197	33732	05810	24813	86902	60397	16489	03264	88525	42786	05269
44657	66999	99324	51281	84463	60563	79312	93454	68876	25471	93911	25650	12682
91340	84979	46949	81973	37949	61023	43997	15263	80644	43942	89203	71795	99533
91227	21199	31935	27022	84067	05462	35216	14486	29891	68607	41867	14951	91696
50001	38140	66321	19924	72163	09538	12151	06878	91903	18749	34405	56087	82790
65390	05224	72958	28609	81406	39147	25549	48542	42627	45233	57202	94617	23772
27504	96131	83944	41575	10573	08619	64482	73923	36152	05184	94142	25299	84387
37169	94851	39117	89632	00959	16487	65536	19071	39782	17095	02330	74301	00275
11508	70225	51111	38351	19444	66499	71945	05422	13442	78675	84081	66938	93654
37449	30362	06694	54690	04052	53115	62757	95348	78662	11163	81651	50245	34971
46515	70331	85922	38329	57015	15765	97161	17869	45349	61796	66345	81073	49106
30986	81223	42416	58353	21532	30502	32305	86482	06174	07901	54339	58861	74818
63798	64995	46583	09785	44160	78128	83991	42865	92520	83531	80377	35909	81250
82486	84846	99254	67632	43218	50076	21361	64816	51202	88124	41870	52689	51275
21885	32906	92431	09060	64297	51674	64126	62570	26123	05155	59194	52799	28225
60336	98782	07408	53458	13564	59089	26445	29789	85205	41001	12535	12133	14645
43937	46891	24010	25560	86355	33941	25786	54990	71899	15475	95434	98227	21824
97656	63175	89303	16275	07100	92063	21942	18611	47348	20203	18534	03862	78095
03299	01221	05418	38982	55758	92237	26759	86367	21216	98442	08303	56613	91511
79626	06486	03574	17668	07785	76020	79924	25651	83325	88428	85076	72811	22717
85636	68335	47539	03129	65651	11977	02510	26113	99447	68645	34327	15152	55230
18039	14367	61337	06177	12143	46609	32989	74014	64708	00533	35398	58408	13261
08362	15656	60627	36478	65648	16764	53412	09013	07832	41574	17639	82163	60859
79556	29068	04142	16268	15387	12856	66227	38358	22478	73373	88732	09443	82558
92608	82674	27072	32534	17075	27698	98204	63863	11951	34648	88022	56148	34925
23982	25835	40055	67006	12293	02753	14827	23235	35071	99704	37543	11601	35503
09915	96306	05908	97901	28395	14186	00821	80703	70426	75647	76310	88717	37890
59037	33300	26695	62247	69927	76123	50842	43834	86654	70959	79725	93872	28117
42488	78077	69882	61657	34136	79180	97526	43092	04098	73571	80799	76536	71255
46764	86273	63003	93017	31204	36692	40202	35275	57306	55543	53203	18098	47625
03237	45430	55417	63282	90816	17349	88298	90183	36600	78406	06216	95787	42579
86591	81482	52667	61582	14972	90053	89534	76036	49199	43716	97548	04379	46370
38534	01715	94964	87288	65680	43772	39560	12918	86537	62738	19636	51132	25739

Source: Adapted with permission from Byer. W. H. (Ed.). 1991. *CRC Standard Probability and Statistics: Tables and Formulae, XII.3.* Boca Raton, Florida: CRC Press.

TABLE E–2

Area under the Standard Normal Curve (z Distribution)[*]

z	.00	.01	.02	.03	.04	.05	.06	.07	.08	.09
0.0	.0000	.0040	.0080	.0120	.0160	.0199	.0239	.0279	.0319	.0359
0.1	.0398	.0438	.0478	.0517	.0557	.0596	.0636	.0675	.0714	.0753
0.2	.0793	.0832	.0871	.0910	.0948	.0987	.1026	.1064	.1103	.1141
0.3	.1179	.1217	.1255	.1293	.1331	.1368	.1406	.1443	.1480	.1517
0.4	.1554	.1591	.1628	.1664	.1700	.1736	.1772	.1808	.1844	.1879
0.5	.1915	.1950	.1985	.2019	.2054	.2088	.2123	.2157	.2190	.2224
0.6	.2257	.2291	.2324	.2357	.2389	.2422	.2454	.2486	.2517	.2549
0.7	.2580	.2611	.2642	.2673	.2704	.2734	.2764	.2794	.2823	.2852
0.8	.2881	.2910	.2939	.2967	.2995	.3023	.3051	.3078	.3106	.3133
0.9	.3159	.3186	.3212	.3238	.3264	.3289	.3315	.3340	.3365	.3389
1.0	.3413	.3438	.3461	.3485	.3508	.3531	.3554	.3577	.3599	.3621
1.1	.3643	.3665	.3686	.3708	.3729	.3749	.3770	.3790	.3810	.3830
1.2	.3849	.3869	.3888	.3907	.3925	.3944	.3962	.3980	.3997	.4015
1.3	.4032	.4049	.4066	.4082	.4099	.4115	.4131	.4147	.4162	.4177
1.4	.4192	.4207	.4222	.4236	.4251	.4265	.4279	.4292	.4306	.4319
1.5	.4332	.4345	.4357	.4370	.4382	.4394	.4406	.4418	.4429	.4441
1.6	.4452	.4463	.4474	.4484	.4495	.4505	.4515	.4525	.4535	.4545
1.7	.4554	.4564	.4573	.4582	.4591	.4599	.4608	.4616	.4625	.4633
1.8	.4641	.4649	.4656	.4664	.4671	.4678	.4686	.4693	.4699	.4706
1.9	.4713	.4719	.4726	.4732	.4738	.4744	.4750	.4756	.4761	.4767
2.0	.4772	.4778	.4783	.4788	.4793	.4798	.4803	.4808	.4812	.4817
2.1	.4821	.4826	.4830	.4834	.4838	.4842	.4846	.4850	.4854	.4857
2.2	.4861	.4864	.4868	.4871	.4875	.4878	.4881	.4884	.4887	.4890
2.3	.4893	.4896	.4898	.4901	.4904	.4906	.4909	.4911	.4913	.4916
2.4	.4918	.4920	.4922	.4925	.4927	.4929	.4931	.4932	.4934	.4936
2.5	.4938	.4940	.4941	.4943	.4945	.4946	.4948	.4949	.4951	.4952
2.6	.4953	.4955	.4956	.4957	.4959	.4960	.4961	.4962	.4963	.4964
2.7	.4965	.4966	.4967	.4968	.4969	.4970	.4971	.4972	.4973	.4974
2.8	.4974	.4975	.4976	.4977	.4977	.4978	.4979	.4979	.4980	.4981
2.9	.4981	.4982	.4982	.4983	.4984	.4984	.4985	.4985	.4986	.4986
3.0	.4987	.4987	.4987	.4988	.4988	.4989	.4989	.4989	.4990	.4990

[*] Proportion of the area under the normal curve corresponding to the distance between the mean (0) and a point that is z standard deviation units away from the mean.

Source: Adapted with permission from Frederick Mosteller and Robert E. K. Rourke. 1973. *Sturdy Statistics.* Table A=1. Reading, MA: Addison-Wesley.

TABLE E–3

The t Distribution

df=n-1	Level of Significance for a One-Tailed Test					
	.10	.05	.025	.01	.005	.0005
	Level of Significance for Two-Tailed Test					
	.20	.10	.05	.02	.01	.001
1	3.078	6.314	12.706	31.821	63.657	636.619
2	1.886	2.920	4.303	6.965	9.925	31.598
3	1.638	2.353	3.182	4.541	5.841	12.941
4	1.533	2.132	2.776	3.747	4.604	8.610
5	1.476	2.015	2.571	3.365	4.032	6.859
6	1.440	1.943	2.447	3.143	3.707	5.959
7	1.415	1.895	2.365	2.998	3.499	5.405
8	1.397	1.860	2.306	2.896	3.355	5.041
9	1.383	1.833	2.262	2.821	3.250	4.781
10	1.372	1.812	2.228	2.764	3.169	4.587
11	1.363	1.796	2.201	2.718	3.106	4.437
12	1.356	1.782	2.179	2.681	3.055	4.318
13	1.350	1.771	2.160	2.650	3.012	4.221
14	1.345	1.761	2.145	2.624	2.977	4.140
15	1.341	1.753	2.131	2.602	2.947	4.073
16	1.337	1.746	2.120	2.583	2.921	4.015
17	1.333	1.740	2.110	2.567	2.898	3.965
18	1.330	1.734	2.101	2.552	2.878	3.922
19	1.328	1.729	2.093	2.539	2.861	3.883
20	1.325	1.725	2.086	2.528	2.845	3.850
21	1.323	1.721	2.080	2.518	2.831	3.819
22	1.321	1.717	2.074	2.508	2.819	3.792
23	1.319	1.714	2.069	2.500	2.807	3.767
24	1.318	1.711	2.064	2.492	2.797	3.745
25	1.316	1.708	2.060	2.485	2.787	3.725
26	1.315	1.706	2.056	2.479	2.779	3.707
27	1.314	1.703	2.052	2.473	2.771	3.690
28	1.313	1.701	2.048	2.467	2.763	3.674
29	1.311	1.699	2.045	2.462	2.756	3.659
30	1.310	1.697	2.042	2.457	2.750	3.646
40	1.303	1.684	2.021	2.423	2.704	3.551
60	1.206	1.671	2.000	2.390	2.660	3.460
120	1.289	1.658	1.980	2.358	2.617	3.373
∞ z-test	1.282	1.645	1.960	2.326	2.576	3.291

Source: Table E–3 is adapted with permission from Table III of Fisher and Yates, *Statistical Tables for Biological. Agricultural and Medical Research* (6th ed.). Published by Longman Group UK Ltd., 1974.

TABLE E–4

Critical Values of the Chi-Square Statistic at the .05 and .01 Significance Level

			Area to the Right of the Critical Value
	Level of significance		
df	0.5	0.1	
1	3.841	6.635	
2	5.991	9.210	
3	7.815	11.345	
4	9.488	13.277	
5	11.070	15.086	
6	12.592	16.812	
7	14.067	18.475	
8	15.507	20.090	
9	16.919	21.666	
10	18.307	23.209	
11	19.675	24.725	
12	21.026	26.217	
13	22.362	27.688	
14	23.685	29.141	
15	24.996	30.578	
16	26.296	32.000	
17	27.587	33.409	
18	28.869	34.805	
19	30.144	36.191	
20	31.410	37.566	
21	32.671	38.932	
22	33.924	40.289	
23	33.924	40.289	
24	36.415	42.980	
25	37.652	44.314	
26	38.885	45.642	
27	40.113	46.963	
28	41.337	48.278	
29	42.557	49.588	
30	43.773	50.892	
40	55.758	63.691	
50	67.505	76.154	
60	79.082	88.379	
70	90.531	100.425	
80	101.879	112.329	
90	113.145	124.116	
100	124.342	135.807	

Source: Adapted from Donald Owen, *Handbook of Statistical Tables,* © 1962 by Addison-Wesley Publishing Company. Inc. Reprinted by permission of Addison-Wesley Publishing Company. Inc.

TABLE E–5

The F Distribution

p = .05

n_2 \ n_1	1	2	3	4	5	6	8	12	24	∞
1	161	200	216	225	230	234	239	244	249	254
2	18.51	19.00	19.16	19.25	19.30	19.33	19.37	19.41	19.45	19.50
3	10.13	9.55	9.28	9.12	9.01	8.94	8.84	8.74	8.64	8.53
4	7.71	6.94	6.59	6.39	6.26	6.16	6.04	5.91	5.77	5.63
5	6.61	5.79	5.41	5.19	5.05	4.95	4.82	4.68	4.53	4.36
6	5.99	5.14	4.76	4.53	4.39	4.28	4.15	4.00	3.84	3.67
7	5.59	4.74	4.35	4.12	3.97	3.87	3.73	3.57	3.41	3.23
8	5.32	4.46	4.07	3.84	3.69	3.58	3.44	3.28	3.12	2.93
9	5.12	4.26	3.86	3.63	3.48	3.37	3.23	3.07	2.90	2.71
10	4.96	4.10	3.71	3.48	3.33	3.22	3.07	2.91	2.74	2.54
11	4.84	3.98	3.59	3.36	3.20	3.09	2.95	2.79	2.61	2.40
12	4.75	3.88	3.49	3.26	3.11	3.00	2.85	2.69	2.50	2.30
13	4.67	3.80	3.41	3.18	3.02	2.92	2.77	2.60	2.42	2.21
14	4.60	3.74	3.34	3.11	2.96	2.85	2.70	2.53	2.35	2.13
15	4.54	3.68	3.29	3.06	2.90	2.79	2.64	2.48	2.29	2.07
16	4.49	3.63	3.24	3.01	2.85	2.74	2.59	2.42	2.24	2.01
17	4.45	3.59	3.20	2.96	2.81	2.70	2.55	2.38	2.19	1.96
18	4.41	3.55	3.16	2.93	2.77	2.66	2.51	2.34	2.15	1.92
19	4.38	3.52	3.13	2.90	2.74	2.63	2.48	2.31	2.11	1.88
20	4.35	3.49	3.10	2.87	2.71	2.60	2.45	2.28	2.08	1.84
21	4.32	3.47	3.07	2.84	2.68	2.57	2.42	2.25	2.05	1.81
22	4.30	3.44	3.05	2.82	2.66	2.55	2.40	2.23	2.03	1.78
23	4.28	3.42	3.03	2.80	2.64	2.53	2.38	2.20	2.00	1.76
24	4.26	3.40	3.01	2.78	2.62	2.51	2.36	2.18	1.98	1.73
25	4.24	3.38	2.99	2.76	2.60	2.49	2.34	2.16	1.96	1.71
26	4.22	3.37	2.98	2.74	2.59	2.47	2.32	2.15	1.95	1.69
27	4.21	3.35	2.96	2.73	2.57	2.46	2.30	2.13	1.93	1.67
28	4.20	3.34	2.95	2.71	2.56	2.44	2.29	2.12	1.91	1.65
29	4.18	3.33	2.93	2.70	2.54	2.43	2.28	2.10	1.90	1.64
30	4.17	3.32	2.92	2.69	2.53	2.42	2.27	2.09	1.89	1.62
40	4.08	3.23	2.84	2.61	2.45	2.34	2.18	2.00	1.79	1.51
60	4.00	3.15	2.76	2.52	2.37	2.25	2.10	1.92	1.70	1.39
120	3.92	3.07	2.68	2.45	2.29	2.17	2.02	1.83	1.61	1.25
∞	3.84	2.99	2.60	2.37	2.21	2.09	1.94	1.75	1.52	1.00

(Continued)

TABLE E–5

The F Distribution (Continued)

p = .01

n_1 / n_2	1	2	3	4	5	6	8	12	24	∞
1	4052	4999	5403	5625	5764	5859	5981	6106	6234	6366
2	98.49	99.01	99.17	99.25	99.30	99.33	99.36	99.42	99.46	99.50
3	34.12	30.81	29.46	28.71	28.24	27.91	27.49	27.05	26.60	26.12
4	21.20	18.00	16.69	15.98	15.52	15.21	14.80	14.37	13.93	13.46
5	16.26	13.27	12.06	11.39	10.97	10.67	10.27	9.89	9.47	9.02
6	13.74	10.92	9.78	9.15	8.75	8.47	8.10	7.72	7.31	6.88
7	12.25	9.55	8.45	7.85	7.46	7.19	6.84	6.47	6.07	5.65
8	11.26	8.65	7.59	7.01	6.63	6.37	6.03	5.67	5.28	4.86
9	10.56	8.02	6.99	6.42	6.06	5.80	5.47	5.11	4.73	4.31
10	10.04	7.56	6.55	5.99	5.64	5.39	5.06	4.71	4.33	3.91
11	9.65	7.20	6.22	5.67	5.32	5.07	4.74	4.40	4.02	3.60
12	9.33	6.93	5.95	5.41	5.06	4.82	4.50	4.16	3.78	3.36
13	9.07	6.70	5.74	5.20	4.86	4.62	4.30	3.96	3.59	3.16
14	8.86	6.51	5.56	5.03	4.69	4.46	4.14	3.80	3.43	3.00
15	8.68	6.36	5.42	4.89	4.56	4.32	4.00	3.67	3.29	2.87
16	8.53	6.23	5.29	4.77	4.44	4.20	3.89	3.55	3.18	2.75
17	8.40	6.11	5.18	4.67	4.34	4.10	3.79	3.45	3.08	2.65
18	8.28	6.01	5.09	4.58	4.25	4.01	3.71	3.37	3.00	2.57
19	8.18	5.93	5.01	4.50	4.17	3.94	3.63	3.30	2.92	2.49
20	8.10	5.85	4.94	4.43	4.10	3.87	3.56	3.23	2.86	2.42
21	8.02	5.78	4.87	4.37	4.04	3.81	3.51	3.17	2.80	2.36
22	7.94	5.72	4.82	4.31	3.99	3.76	3.45	3.12	2.75	2.31
23	7.88	5.66	4.76	4.26	3.94	3.71	3.41	3.07	2.70	2.26
24	7.82	5.61	4.72	4.22	3.90	3.67	3.36	3.03	2.66	2.21
25	7.77	5.57	4.68	4.18	3.86	3.63	3.32	2.99	2.62	2.17
26	7.72	5.53	4.64	4.14	3.82	3.59	3.29	2.96	2.58	2.13
27	7.68	5.49	4.60	4.11	3.78	3.56	3.26	2.93	2.55	2.10
28	7.64	5.45	4.57	4.07	3.75	3.53	3.23	2.90	2.52	2.06
29	7.60	5.42	4.54	4.04	3.73	3.50	3.20	2.87	2.49	2.03
30	7.56	5.39	4.51	4.02	3.70	3.47	3.17	2.84	2.47	2.01
40	7.31	5.18	4.31	3.83	3.51	3.29	2.99	2.66	2.29	1.80
60	7.08	4.98	4.13	3.65	3.34	3.12	2.82	2.50	2.12	1.60
120	6.85	4.79	3.95	3.48	3.17	2.96	2.66	2.34	1.95	1.38
∞	6.64	4.60	3.78	3.32	3.02	2.80	2.51	2.18	1.79	1.00

Values of n_1 and n_2 represent the number of degrees of freedom associated with the between and within estimates of variance, respectively.
Source: R. P. Runyon and A. Haber. *Fundamentals of Behavioral Statistics,* 6th ed. New York: McGraw-Hill. Table D (pp. 463–465). 1987. Reprinted with permission from McGraw-Hill.

TABLE E-6

Studentized Range Statistic, q

q Value When Alpha = .05

k \ v	2	3	4	5	6	7	8	9	10	11	12	13	14	15	16	17	18	19	20
1	18.0	27.0	32.8	37.1	40.4	43.1	45.4	47.4	49.1	50.6	52.0	53.2	54.3	55.4	56.3	57.2	58.0	58.8	59.6
2	6.09	8.3	9.8	10.9	11.7	12.4	13.0	13.5	14.0	14.4	14.7	15.1	15.4	15.7	15.9	16.1	16.4	16.6	16.8
3	4.50	5.91	6.82	7.50	8.04	8.48	8.85	9.18	9.46	9.72	9.95	10.15	10.35	10.52	10.69	10.84	10.98	11.11	11.24
4	3.93	5.04	5.76	6.29	6.71	7.05	7.35	7.60	7.83	8.03	8.21	8.37	8.52	8.66	8.79	8.91	9.03	9.13	9.23
5	3.64	4.60	5.22	5.67	6.03	6.33	6.58	6.80	6.99	7.17	7.32	7.47	7.60	7.72	7.83	7.93	8.03	8.12	8.21
6	3.46	4.34	4.90	5.31	5.63	5.89	6.12	6.32	6.49	6.65	6.79	6.92	7.03	7.14	7.24	7.34	7.43	7.51	7.59
7	3.34	4.16	4.68	5.06	5.36	5.61	5.82	6.00	6.16	6.30	6.43	6.55	6.66	6.76	6.85	6.94	7.02	7.09	7.17
8	3.26	4.04	4.53	4.89	5.17	5.40	5.60	5.77	5.92	6.05	6.18	6.29	6.39	6.48	6.57	6.65	6.73	6.80	6.87
9	3.20	3.95	4.42	4.76	5.02	5.24	5.43	5.60	5.74	5.87	5.98	6.09	6.19	6.28	6.36	6.44	6.51	6.58	6.64
10	3.15	3.88	4.33	4.65	4.91	5.12	5.30	5.46	5.60	5.72	5.83	5.93	6.03	6.11	6.20	6.27	6.34	6.40	6.47
11	3.11	3.82	4.26	4.57	4.82	5.03	5.20	5.35	5.49	5.61	5.71	5.81	5.90	5.99	6.06	6.14	6.20	6.26	6.33
12	3.08	3.77	4.20	4.51	4.75	4.95	5.12	5.27	5.40	5.51	5.62	5.71	5.80	5.88	5.95	6.03	6.09	6.15	6.21
13	3.06	3.73	4.15	4.45	4.69	4.88	5.05	5.19	5.32	5.43	5.53	5.63	5.71	5.79	5.86	5.93	6.00	6.05	6.11
14	3.03	3.70	4.11	4.41	4.64	4.83	4.99	5.13	5.25	5.36	5.46	5.55	5.64	5.72	5.79	5.85	5.92	5.97	6.03
15	3.01	3.67	4.08	4.37	4.60	4.78	4.94	5.08	5.20	5.31	5.40	5.49	5.58	5.65	5.72	5.79	5.85	5.90	5.96
16	3.00	3.65	4.05	4.33	4.56	4.74	4.90	5.03	5.15	5.26	5.35	5.44	5.52	5.59	5.66	5.72	5.79	5.84	5.90
17	2.98	3.63	4.02	4.30	4.52	4.71	4.86	4.99	5.11	5.21	5.31	5.39	5.47	5.55	5.61	5.68	5.74	5.79	5.84
18	2.97	3.61	4.00	4.28	4.49	4.67	4.82	4.96	5.07	5.17	5.27	5.35	5.43	5.50	5.57	5.63	5.69	5.74	5.79
19	2.96	3.59	3.98	4.25	4.47	4.65	4.79	4.92	5.04	5.14	5.23	5.32	5.39	5.46	5.53	5.59	5.65	5.70	5.75
20	2.95	3.58	3.96	4.23	4.45	4.62	4.77	4.90	5.01	5.11	5.20	5.28	5.36	5.43	5.49	5.55	5.61	5.66	5.71
24	2.92	3.53	3.90	4.17	4.37	4.54	4.68	4.81	4.92	5.01	5.10	5.18	5.25	5.32	5.38	5.44	5.50	5.54	5.59
30	2.89	3.49	3.84	4.10	4.30	4.46	4.60	4.72	4.83	4.92	5.00	5.08	5.15	5.21	5.27	5.33	5.38	5.43	5.48
40	2.86	3.44	3.79	4.04	4.23	4.39	4.52	4.63	4.74	4.82	4.91	4.98	5.05	5.11	5.16	5.22	5.27	5.31	5.36
60	2.83	3.40	3.74	3.98	4.16	4.31	4.44	4.55	4.65	4.73	4.81	4.88	4.94	5.00	5.06	5.11	5.16	5.20	5.24
120	2.80	3.36	3.69	3.92	4.10	4.24	4.36	4.48	4.56	4.64	4.72	4.78	4.84	4.90	4.95	5.00	5.05	5.09	5.13
∞	2.77	3.31	3.63	3.86	4.03	4.17	4.29	4.39	4.47	4.55	4.62	4.68	4.74	4.80	4.85	4.89	4.93	4.97	5.01

(Continued)

TABLE E-6

Studentized Range Statistic, q (Continued)

q Value When Alpha = .01

k \ v	2	3	4	5	6	7	8	9	10	11	12	13	14	15	16	17	18	19	20
1	90.0	135	164	186	202	216	227	237	246	253	260	266	272	277	282	286	290	294	298
2	14.0	19.0	22.3	24.7	26.6	28.2	29.5	30.7	31.7	32.6	33.4	34.1	34.8	35.4	36.0	36.5	37.0	37.5	37.9
3	8.26	10.6	12.2	13.3	14.2	15.0	15.6	16.2	16.7	17.1	17.5	17.9	18.2	18.5	18.8	19.1	19.3	19.5	19.8
4	6.51	8.12	9.17	9.96	10.6	11.1	11.5	11.9	12.3	12.6	12.8	13.1	13.3	13.5	13.7	13.9	14.1	14.2	14.4
5	5.70	6.97	7.80	8.42	8.91	9.32	9.67	9.97	10.24	10.48	10.70	10.89	11.08	11.24	11.40	11.55	11.68	11.81	11.93
6	5.24	6.33	7.03	7.56	7.97	8.32	8.61	8.87	9.10	9.30	9.49	9.65	9.81	9.95	10.08	10.21	10.32	10.43	10.54
7	4.95	5.92	6.54	7.01	7.37	7.68	7.94	8.17	8.37	8.55	8.71	8.86	9.00	9.12	9.24	9.35	9.46	9.55	9.65
8	4.74	5.63	6.20	6.63	6.96	7.24	7.47	7.68	7.87	8.03	8.18	8.31	8.44	8.55	8.66	8.76	8.85	8.94	9.03
9	4.60	5.43	5.96	6.35	6.66	6.91	7.13	7.32	7.49	7.65	7.78	7.91	8.03	8.13	8.23	8.32	8.41	8.49	8.57
10	4.48	5.27	5.77	6.14	6.43	6.67	6.87	7.05	7.21	7.36	7.48	7.60	7.71	7.81	7.91	7.99	8.07	8.15	8.22
11	4.39	5.14	5.62	5.97	6.25	6.48	6.67	6.84	6.99	7.13	7.25	7.36	7.46	7.56	7.65	7.73	7.81	7.88	7.95
12	4.32	5.04	5.50	5.84	6.10	6.32	6.51	6.67	6.81	6.94	7.06	7.17	7.26	7.36	7.44	7.52	7.59	7.66	7.73
13	4.26	4.96	5.40	5.73	5.98	6.19	6.37	6.53	6.67	6.79	6.90	7.01	7.10	7.19	7.27	7.34	7.42	7.48	7.55
14	4.21	4.89	5.32	5.63	5.88	6.08	6.26	6.41	6.54	6.66	6.77	6.87	6.96	7.05	7.12	7.20	7.27	7.33	7.39
15	4.17	4.83	5.25	5.56	5.80	5.99	6.16	6.31	6.44	6.55	6.66	6.76	6.84	6.93	7.00	7.07	7.14	7.20	7.26
16	4.13	4.78	5.19	5.49	5.72	5.92	6.08	6.22	6.35	6.46	6.56	6.66	6.74	6.82	6.90	6.97	7.03	7.09	7.15
17	4.10	4.74	5.14	5.43	5.66	5.85	6.01	6.15	6.27	6.38	6.48	6.57	6.66	6.73	6.80	6.87	6.94	7.00	7.05
18	4.07	4.70	5.09	5.38	5.60	5.79	5.94	6.08	6.20	6.31	6.41	6.50	6.58	6.65	6.72	6.79	6.85	6.91	6.96
19	4.05	4.67	5.05	5.33	5.55	5.73	5.89	6.02	6.14	6.25	6.34	6.43	6.51	6.58	6.65	6.72	6.78	6.84	6.89
24	3.96	4.54	4.91	5.17	5.37	5.54	5.69	5.81	5.92	6.02	6.11	6.19	6.26	6.33	6.39	6.45	6.51	6.56	6.61
30	3.89	4.45	4.80	5.05	5.24	5.40	5.54	5.65	5.76	5.85	5.93	6.01	6.08	6.14	6.20	6.26	6.31	6.36	6.41
40	3.82	4.37	4.70	4.93	5.11	5.27	5.39	5.50	5.60	5.69	5.77	5.84	5.90	5.96	6.02	6.07	6.12	6.17	6.21
60	3.76	4.28	4.60	4.82	4.99	5.13	5.25	5.36	5.45	5.53	5.60	5.67	5.73	5.79	5.84	5.89	5.93	5.98	6.02
120	3.70	4.20	4.50	4.71	4.87	5.01	5.12	5.21	5.30	5.38	5.44	5.51	5.56	5.61	5.66	5.71	5.75	5.79	5.83
∞	3.64	4.12	4.40	4.60	4.76	4.88	4.99	5.08	5.16	5.23	5.29	5.35	5.40	5.45	5.49	5.54	5.57	5.61	5.65

Source: H. L. Hartner "Table of Range and Studentized Range." *The Annals of Mathematical Statistics.* Vol. 31. No. 4. 1960. Reprinted with permission from the Institute of Mathematical Statistics.

References

Abel, G. G. (1987), Self-reported sex crimes of nonincarcerated paraphiliacs, Journal of Interpersonal Violence, 2: 3–25.

Agnew, Robert. (1992). Foundation for a general strain theory of crime and delinquency. *Criminology* 30: 47–87.

Akers, Ronald (1992). *Drugs, Alcohol and Society: Social Structure, Process, and Policy.* Belmont, CA: Wadsworth Publishing.

Applegate, Brandon K., Cullen, Francis T., and Fisher, Bonnie S. (2002). Public views toward crime and correctional policies: Is there a gender gap? *Journal of Criminal Justice* 30: 89–100.

Bachman, R. (1992). *Death and Violence on the Reservation: Homicide, Suicide and Family Violence in American Indian Populations.* Westport, Conn: Auburn House of Greenwood Publishing.

Baskin, Deborah A. and Ira B. Sommers (1998). *Casualities of Community Disorder: Women's Careers in Violent Crime.* Boulder, CO: Westview Press.

Baskin, Deborah R. & Sommers, Ira B. (1998). *Casualties of Community Disorder: Women's Careers in Violent Crime,* Boulder, CO: Westview Press, p. 28.

Benoit, J. L., and Kennedy, W. A. (1992). The abuse history of male adolescent sex offenders, *Journal of Interpersonal Violence,* 7: 543–548.

Berk, R. A., Campbell, A., Klap, R., and Western, B. (1992). The deterrent effect of arrest in incidents of domestic violence: A Bayesian analysis of four field experiments. *American Sociological Review* 57: 698–708.

Blau, J. R. and Blau, P. M. (1982). The cost of inequality: Metropolitan structure and violent crime. *American Sociological Review* 47: 114–129.

Boneau, C. A. (1960). The effects of violations of assumptions underlying the *t* test. *Psychological Bulletin* 57: 49–64.

Boritch, H. (1992). Gender and criminal court outcomes: An historical analysis. *Criminology,* 30: 293–325.

Braga, A. A., Weisburd, D. L., Waring, E. J., Mazerolle, L. G., Spelman, W., and Gajewski, F. (1999). Problem-oriented policing in violent crime places: A randomized controlled experiment, Criminology, 37: 541–580.

Brame, R. and MacKenzie, D. L. (1996). Shock incarceration and positive adjustment during community supervision: A multisite evaluation. In *Correctional Boot Camps: A Tough Intermediate Sanction,* edited by D. L. MacKenzie and E. E. Herbert (NCJ 157639). Washington, D.C.: National Institute of Justice.

Brener, N. D., Simon, T. R., Krug-Etienne, G. (1999). Recent trends in violence-related behaviors among high school students in the United States, JAMA-Journal-of-the-American-Medical-Association, 282: 440–446.

Bushway, Shawn D. (1998). The impact of an arrest on the job stability of young white American men. *Journal of Research in Crime and Delinquency,* 35, 454–479.

Cameron, M. O. (1964). *The Booster and the Snitch: Department Store Shoplifting.* New York: Free Press.

Cook, Philip J. and John H. Laub. (1998). "The Epidemic in Youth Violence." In *Youth Violence: Crime and Justice* (vol. 24), edited by Michael Tonry and Mark H. Moore. Chicago: University of Chicago Press.

Corzine, Jay, Huff-Corzine, Lin, and Whitt, Hugh P. (1999). Cultural and subcultural theories of homicide. In *Homicide: A Sourcebook of Social Research,* M. Dwayne Smith & Margaret A. Zahn (eds.) Thousand Oaks, CA: Sage.

Cressey D. R. (1953). *Other People's Money: A Study in the Social Psychology of Embezzlement.* New York: Free Press.

Criminal victimization in the United States, 1991, (NCJ-139563). Bureau of Justice Statistics, U.S. Department of Justice, U.S. Washington, D.C.

Crutchfield, R. D., Geerken, M. R., and Gove, W. R. (1982). Crime rate and social integration. *Criminology* 20: 467–478.

Daly, K. (1987). Discrimination in the Criminal Courts: Family, Gender, and the Problem of Equal Treatment. *Social Forces,* 66: 152–175.

Daly, Kathleen (1994). *Gender, Crime and Punishment.* New Haven, CT: Yale University Press.

Death Row U.S.A. (2002) Fall. NAACP Legal Defense and Education Fund: New York, New York.

Decker, Scott H. and Barrik Van Winkle. (1996). *Life in the Gang: Family, Friends, and Violence.* Cambridge, England: Cambridge University Press.

DeFronzo, J. (1983). Economic assistance to impoverished Americans. Relationship to incidence of crime. *Criminology* 21: 119–136.

Doerner, W. G. (1978). The index of southerness revisited: The influence of wherefrom upon whodunnit. *Criminology* 16: 47–56.

Doerner, W. G. (1983). Why does Johnny Reb die when shot? The impact of medical resources upon lethality. *Sociological Inquiry* 53: 1–15.

Dunford, F. W., Huizinga, D., Elliot, D. (1990) The Role of Arrest in Domestic Assault: The Omaha Police Experiment, *Criminology,* 28: 183–206.

Durose, M.R. & Langan, P. A. 2001, State Court Sentencing of Convicted Felons, 1998, NCJ 190637, U.S. Department of Justice, Bureau of Justice Statistics, Table 1.3.

Elliott, D. and S. Ageton. (1980). "Reconciling Race and Class Differences in Self-Reported and Official Estimates of Delinquency." *American Sociological Review,* 45: 95–110.

Farnworth, M. and M.J. Leiber. (1989) "Strain Theory Revisited: Economic Goals, Educational Means, and Delinquency" *American Sociological Review,* 54(2): 263–274.

Felson, Richard B., Allen E. Liska, Scott J. South, and Thomas L. McNulty. (1994). "The Subculture of Violence and Delinquency: Individual versus School Context Effects." *Social Forces,* 73(1): 155–174.

Fisher, B. and Nasar, J. L. (1995). Fear spots in relation to microlevel physical cues: exploring the overlooked, Journal of Research in Crime and Delinquency, 32: 214–239.

For a wonderful review of validity issues regarding the measurement of crime, see Mosher, Clayton, J., Miethe, Terance D., and Phillips, Dretha M. (2002). *The Mismeasure of Crime.* Thousand Oaks, CA: Sage.

Fox, J. A., and Zawitz, M. W. (2001). *Homicide Trends in the United States.* Washington D. C.: Bureau of Justice Statistics, U. S. Department of Justice.

Gaes, G. G. (1985). The effects of overcrowding in prison. In Crime and Justice: an Annual Review of Research, Volume 6, Tonry, Michael; Morris, Norval (Eds.), Chicago, IL: University of Chicago Press: pp. 95–146.

Garner, J., Fagan, J., Maxwell, C. (1995) Published findings from the Spouse Assault Replication Program: A Critical Review, *Journal of Quantitative Criminology,* 11: 3–28.

Garner, Joel, Jeffrey Fagan, and Christopher Maxwell. (1995). "Published Findings from the Spousal Assault Replication Program: A Critical Review." *Journal of Quantitative Criminology,* 11: 3–28.

Gastil, R. P. (1971). Homicide and regional culture of violence. *American Sociological Review* 36: 412–427.

Gastil, R. P. (1975). *Cultural Regions of the United States.* Seattle, WA: University of Washington Press.

Gilsinan, J. F., (1989). They is clowning tough: 911 and the social construction of reality, *Criminology,* 27:329–344.

Glueck, Sheldon and Eleanor Glueck (1950). *Unraveling Juvenile Delinquency.* Cambridge, MA: Harvard University Press.

Grasmick, Harold G., Charles R. Tittle, Robert J. Bursik, Jr., and Bruce J. Arneklev (1993). Testing the core implications of Gottfredson and Hirschi's general theory of crime. *Journal of Research in Crime and Delinquency* 30: 5–29.

Grasmick, H. G. and McGill, A. L. (1994). Religion, attribution style, and punitiveness toward juvenile offenders, *Criminology,* 32: 23–46.

Greenwood, P. W. and Turner, S. (1993). Evaluation of the Paint Creek Youth Center: a residential program for serious delinquents, *Criminology,* 31: 263–279.

Grossman, David C., Jolly J. Neckerman, Thomas D. Koepsell, Ping-Yu Liu, Kenneth N. Asher, Kathy Beland, Darin Frey, and Frederick P. Rivara. (1997). "Effectiveness of a Violence Prevention Curriculum among Children in Elementary School: A Randomized Controlled Trial." *The Journal of the American Medical Association,* 277(20), 1605–1612.

Hackney, S. (1969). Southern violence. In *Violence in America,* Graham, H. D. and Gurr, T. R. (eds.). New York: Signet. pp. 479–500.

Hagan, John (1993). The social embeddedness of crime and unemployment. *Criminology* 31: 465–491.

Hate Crime Statistics—2000. Federal Bureau of Investigation, Uniform Crime Reporting Program. United States Department of Justice. Washington, D. C.

Heyl, B. S. (1979). *The Madam as Entrepreneur: Career Management in House Prostitution.* New Brunswick, NJ: Transaction Press.

Hirschel, David J. and Ira W. Hutchinson III (1992). Female spouse abuse and the police response: The Charlotte, North Carolina Experiment. *Journal of Criminal Law and Criminology* 83: 73–119.

Hirschel, J. D., Hutchison, I. W., Dean, C. W. (1992). Review essay on the law enforcement response to spouse abuse: past, present, and future. Justice Quarterly, 9: 247–283.

Hirschi, Travis (1969). *Causes of Delinquency*. Berkeley: University of California Press.

Humphries, D. and Wallace, D. (1980). Capitalist accumulation and urban crime, 1950–1971. *Social Problems* 28: 179–193.

Kaufman, P., Chen, X., Choy, S. P., Peter, K., Ruddy, S. A., Miller, A., Fleury, J. J., Chandler, K. A., Planty, M. G., & Rand, M. R. 2001. Indicators of School Crime and Safety: 2001. NCES 2002-113/NCJ-190075, Washington, D.C.: U.S. Departments of Education and Justice.

Keitner, C. I. (2002). Victim or vamp? Images of violent women in the criminal justice system, *Columbia Journal of Gender and Law*, 11: 38–72.

Kelly, K. D. and DeKeseredy, W. A. (1994). Women's fear of crime and abuse in college and university dating relationships, *Violence and Victims*, 9: 17–30.

Kleck G. and Patterson, E. B. (1993). The impact of gun control and gun ownership on violence rates. *Journal of Quantitative Criminology* 9(3): 249–287.

Kohfeld, C. W. and Sprague, J. (1990). Demography, police behavior, and deterrence, Criminology, 28: 111–136.

Loftin, C. and Hill, R. H. (1974). Regional subculture and homicide. *American Sociological Review* 39: 714–724.

Loftin, C., McDowall, D., Wiersema, B., and Cottey, T. J. (1991). Effects of restrictive licensing of handguns on homicide and suicide in the District of Columbia. *The New England Journal of Medicine* (325)23: 1615–1620.

Lundsgaurde, H. (1977). *Murder in Space City.* New York: Oxford University Press.

MacKenzie, D. L. (1994). Results of a multisite study of boot camp prisons. *Federal Probation* 58(2): 60–66.

MacKenzie, D. L. Brame, R., McDowall, D., and Souryal, C. (1995). Boot camp, prisons and recidivism in eight states. *Criminology* 33(3): 401–430.

MacKenzie, D. L. and Piquero, A. (1994). The impact of shock incarceration programs on prison crowding. *Crime and Delinquency* 40(2): 222–249.

MacKenzie, D. L. and Souryal, C. (1996). Multisite study of correctional boot camps. In *Correctional Boot Camps: A Tough Intermediate Sanction,* edited by D. L. MacKenzie and E. E. Herbert (NCJ-157639). Washington, D.C.: National Institute of Justice.

Maurer, D. W. (1964). *Whiz Mob: A Correlation of the Technical Argot of Pick-Pockets with Their Behavior.* New Haven, CT: College and University Press.

McDowall, D., Lizotte, A. J., and Wiersema, B. (1991). General deterrence through civilian gun ownership: An evaluation of the quasiexperimental evidence. *Criminology* 29(4): 541–557.

Meckler, Laura. (2002). Associated Press. Feds arrest deadbeat fathers. In *The News Journal*, Thursday, August 1, 2002, p. A3.

Megargee, E. I. (1972). Standardized reports of work performance and inmate adjustment for use in correctional settings. *Correctional Psychologist*, 5: 48–58.

Messner, S. F. (1982). Poverty, inequality, and the urban homicide rate. *Criminology* 20: 103–114.

Messner, S. F. (1983a). Regional and racial effects on the urban homicide rates: The subculture of violence revisited. *American Journal of Sociology* 88: 997–1007.

Messner, S. F. (1983b). Regional differences in the economic correlates of urban homicide rates. *Criminology* 21: 477–488.

Messner, Steven F. and Rosenfeld, Richard. (1999). Social structure and homicide: Theory and research. In *Homicide: A Sourcebook of Social Research,* M. Dwayne Smith & Margaret A. Zahn (eds.). Thousand Oaks, CA: Sage.

Miller B. A., Nochajski, T. H., Leonard, K. E., Blane, H. T., Gondoli, D. M., and Bowers, P. M. (1990). Spousal violence and alcohol/drug problems among parolees and their spouses. *Women & Criminal Justice* 1(2): 55–72.

Moffitt, Terrie E. (1997). Adolescence-limited and life-course-persistent offending: A developmental taxonomy. *Psychological Review* 100: 674–701.

Moffitt, Terrie E., Avshalom Caspi, Michael Rutter, and Phil A. Silva (2001). *Sex Differences in Antisocial Behavior*. New York: Cambridge University Press.

Nacci, P. L., (1978). The importance of recidivism research in understanding criminal behavior. *Journal of Criminal Justice*, 6: 253–260.

Novak, Kenneth J., Frank, James, Smith, Brad W., and Engel, Robin Shepard. (2002). Revisiting the decision to arrest: Comparing beat and community officers. *Crime & Delinquency* 48(1): 70–98.

Nurco, D. N., Hanlon, T. E., Kinlock, T. W. (1988). Differential criminal patterns of narcotic addicts over an addiction career, *Criminology*, 26: 407–423.

Ogle, R. S. (1999). Prison privatization: an environmental Catch-22 Justice-Quarterly, 16: 579–600.

Ogle, R. S., Maier-Katkin, D., and Bernard, T. J. (1995). A theory of homicidal behavior among women, Criminology, 33: 173–193.

Pate, A. M., and Hamilton, E. E. (1992). Formal and informal deterrents to domestic violence: The Dade County spouse assault experiment. *American Sociological Review* 57: 691–697.

Peete, Thomas, Gregory Kowalski, and Don Duffield (1994). Crime, social disorganization, and social structure: A research note on the use of interurban ecological models. *American Journal of Criminal Justice* 19: 117–132.

Pogarsky, Greg (2002). Identifying deterrable offenders: Implications for deterrence research. *Justice Quarterly* 19: 431–452.

Prus, R. C. and Sharper, C. R. D. (1977). *Road Hustler*. Lexington, MA: Lexington Books.

Raine, Adrian (1994). *The Psychopathology of Crime: Criminal Behavior as a Clinical Disorder*. New York: Academic Press.

Rapaport, E. (1991). The death penalty and gender discrimination. *Law and Society Review*, 25: 367–383.

Reed, J. S. (1971). To live and die in Dixie: A contribution to the study of southern violence. *Political Science Quarterly* 86: 429–486.

Regoli, R. M. and J. D. Hewitt. (1994). "Delinquency in Society: A Child-Centered Approach." New York: McGraw-Hill.

Rennison, C. M. and Welchans, S. (2000). Intimate partner violence. Washington, D.C.: Bureau of Justice Statistics, U.S. Department of Justice.

Rennison, Callie Marie and Welchans, Sarah. (2000). Intimate partner violence. NCJ-178247, Bureau of Justice Statistics, U.S. Department of Justice.

Sampson, Robert J. and John H. Laub (1993). *Crime in the Making: Pathways and Turning Points Through Life*. Cambridge, MA: Harvard University Press.

Sampson, Robert J. and John H. Laub (1997). A life course theory of cumulative disadvantage and the stability of delinquency. pp. 133–161 in T. P. Thornberry (ed.). *Developmental Theories of Crime and Delinquency*. New Brunswick, NJ: Transaction Books.

Scheffe, H. (1959). *The Analysis of Variance*. New York: Wiley.

Sechrest, D. K. (1991). The effects of density on jail assaults, Journal of Criminal Justice, 19: 211–223.

Sherman, L. (1974). *Police Corruption*. New York: Doubleday.

Sherman, L. W. and Berk, R. A. (1984a). The specific deterrent effects of arrest for domestic assault. *American Sociological Review* 49: 261–272.

Sherman, L. W. and Berk, R. A. (1984b). The Minneapolis domestic violence experiment. Washington, D.C.: The Police Foundation.

Sherman, L. W., Smith, D. A., Schmidt, J. D., and Rogan, D. P. (1992). Crime, punishment, and stake in conformity: Legal and informal control of domestic violence. *American Sociological Review* 57: 680–690.

Sherman, Lawrence W., Patrick Gartin, and Michael Buerger (1989). Hot spots of predatory crime: Routine activities and the criminology of place. *Criminology* 27: 27–56.

Short, J. F. and Strodtbeck, F. L. (1965). *Group Process and Gang Delinquency.* Chicago: University of Chicago Press.

Short, James F., Jr. and Ivan Nye. (1957–58). "Reported Behavior as a Criterion of Deviant Behavior." *Social Problems*, 5: 207–213.

Smith H.W. (1975) *Strategies of Social Research,* Englewood Cliffs NJ: Prentice Hall.

Smith, M. D. and Parker, R. N. (1980). Type of homicide and variation in regional rates. *Social Forces* 59: 136–147.

Spohn, C. C. and Spears, J. W. (1997). Gender and case processing decisions: A comparison of case outcomes for male and female defendants charged with violent felonies. *Women & Criminal Justice*, 8: 29–45.

Stalans, L. J. (1996). Family harmony or individual protection? *American Behavioral Scientist*, 39: 433–447.

Steffensmeier, D., Kramer, J. and Streifel, C. (1993). Gender and Punishment, Criminololgy, 31: 411–446.

Stevens, D. J. and Ward, C. S. (1997). College education and recidivism: educating criminals is meritorious, *Journal of Correctional Education*, 48: 106–111.

Stevens, Dennis, J. and Ward, Charles S. (1997). College education and recidivism: Educating criminals is meritorious. *Journal of Correctional Education* 48(3): 106–111.

Tukey, John (1977). *Exploratory Data Analysis.* Reading, MA: Addison-Wesley.

Tyler, Tom (1990). *Why People Obey the Law.* New Haven: Yale University Press.

Uniform Crime Reports: Crime in the United States: 1982. Federal Bureau of Investigation, U.S. Department of Justice, Washington, D.C.

Uniform Crime Reports: Crime in the United States: 1992. Federal Bureau of Investigation, U.S. Department of Justice, Washington, D.C.

Wallerstein, J. S. and Wyle, C. J. (1947). "Our Law-Abiding Law Breakers," *Probation*, 25: 107–112.

Warr, Mark (2002). *Companions in Crime: The Social Aspects of Criminal Conduct.* New York: Cambridge University Press.

Weisburd, David Lisa Maher, and Lawrence W. Sherman (1992). Contrasting crime general and crime specific theory: The case of hot spots of crime. *Advances in Criminological Theory* 4: 45–69.

The Washington Post. NRA money and handgun voting. Pp. A21, C4. Wednesday, December 8, 1993, early edition.

Wilkinson, K. P. (1984). A research note on homicide and rurality. *Social Forces* 63: 445–452.

Williams, K. R. (1984). Economic sources of homicide: Reestimating the effects of poverty and inequality. *American Sociological Review* 49: 283–289.

Williams, K. R. and Flewelling, R. L. (1987). Family, acquaintance, and stranger homicide: Alternative procedures for rate calculations. *Criminology* 25: 543–560.

Williams, K. R. and Flewelling, R. L. (1988). The social production of criminal homicide: A comparative study of disaggregated rates in American cities. *American Sociological Review* 53: 421–431.

Wolfgang, M. E. and Ferracuti, F. (1967). *The Subculture of Violence.* London: Tavistock.

Worden, A. P. (1993). The attitudes of women and men in policing: Testing conventional and contemporary wisdom. Criminology, 31, 203–242.

Zimring, F. E. (1991). Firearms, violence and public policy. *Scientific American,* November: 48–54.

CHAPTER 1 NOTES

[1]Kaufman, P., Chen, X., Choy, S. P., Peter, K., Ruddy, S. A., Miller, A., Fleury, J. J., Chandler, K. A., Planty, M. G., & Rand, M. R. 2001. Indicators of School Crime and Safety: 2001. NCES 2002-113/NCJ-190075, Washington, D.C.: U.S. Departments of Education and Justice.

[2]For a wonderful review of validity issues regarding the measurement of crime, see Mosher, Clayton, J., Miethe, Terance D., and Phillips, Dretha M. (2002). *The Mismeasure of Crime.* Thousand Oaks, CA: Sage.

[3]For a detailed discussion of weighted samples, see Smith H.W. (1975) *Strategies of Social Research,* Englewood Cliffs NJ: Prentice Hall. For an example of a weighted sample used in criminological research, see Farnworth, M. and M.J. Leiber. (1989) "Strain Theory Revisited: Economic Goals, Educational Means, and Delinquency" *American Sociological Review,* 54(2): 263–274. These authors collected a weighted sample of adolescents to over sample the number of youths thought to be "at risk" of delinquency.

CHAPTER 2 NOTES

[1]Durose, M.R. & Langan, P. A. 2001, State Court Sentencing of Convicted Felons, 1998, NCJ 190637, U.S. Department of Justice, Bureau of Justice Statistics, Table 1.3.

CHAPTER 7 NOTES

[1]Baskin, Deborah R. & Sommers, Ira B. (1998). *Casualties of Community Disorder: Women's Careers in Violent Crime,* Boulder, CO: Westview Press, p. 28.

[2]Rape statutes for most states are now written with gender neutral language. However, for the sake of this example, we are going to focus exclusively on male offenders. Hence, rapists here will be referred to with he and not he/she. See Abel, et al. (1987), and Rennison & Welchans (2000).

CHAPTER 8 NOTES

[1]Megargee 1972.
[2]Meckler 2001.

CHAPTER 10 NOTES

[1]See Brame & MacKenzie, 1996; MacKenzie, Brame, McDowall, & Souryal, 1996; MacKenzie & Souryal, 1995; MacKenzie, 1994; MacKenzie & Piquero, 1994.
[2]MacKenzie & Souryal, 1996: 293.

[3]Berk et al., 1990; Dunford, 1990; Hirschel, Hotchinson, & Dean, 1992; Maxwell, Garner, & Fagan, 1999; Pate & Hamilton, 1992; Sherman, Schmidt, Rogan, & Smith, 1992.

CHAPTER 13 NOTES

[1]The order of variables does not matter because in regular multiple regression models the variables are entered into the equation all at once. There is a type of multiple regression analysis, called *stepwise* regression, where the order in which variables appear in the equation does matter. In stepwise regression, variables are entered one at a time, with successive variables explaining the variance that previously entered variables left unexplained. We will not consider this more detailed regression model in this book.

[2]Excellent and detailed treatments of multiple regression analysis can be found in: Greene, 1990; Cohen and Cohen, 1983; Hanushek and Jackson, 1977; and Draper and Smith 1981.

[3]This is true only for a given regression equation. You cannot compare *t* values across different regression equations to determine the relative effects of different independent variables.

Index